JACK LONDON:
A BIBLIOGRAPHY

Courtesy of the Oakland Public Library

JACK LONDON

Jack London:
A Bibliography

Compiled by

Hensley C. Woodbridge
Carbondale, Illinois

John London
Burien, Washington

George H. Tweney
Seattle, Washington

THE TALISMAN PRESS
Georgetown, California 1966

Table of Contents

PART ONE

Writings by Jack London

Books	24-138
Collections in English	139-142
Anthologies in English	143-149
Foreign Language Collections and Anthologies	150-212
Short Stories	213-241
Contributions to Periodicals	241-249
Contributions to Newspapers	250-260
Introductions and Prefaces	261
Separately Published Ephemera	262-276
Spurious Works	277-281
Motion Pictures Based on London's Works	282-288

PART TWO

Writings About Jack London

Books and Pamphlets in English	290-297
Parts of Books about London in English	298-306
Articles about London in English	307-337
Foreign Writings about London	338-353
Theses and Dissertations	354-357
Reviews of Books in English	358-373
Reviews of Books in Foreign Languages	373-385
Title Index	386
Personal Name Index	403

JACK LONDON AT GLEN ELLEN, CALIFORNIA

Illustrations

Jack London at his writing desk   frontispiece

Jack London at Glen Ellen, California   8

Son of the Wolf   ·25

The God of His Fathers   29

Children of the Frost   32

Cruise of the Dazzler   35

Call of the Wild   41

The Iron Heel   77

Martin Eden   82

Manuscript page of *Martin Eden*   84

John Barleycorn   113

Valley of the Moon   115

Manuscript page of *"The Hussy"*   221

"Bonin Islands"   242

What Life Means to Me   265

Jack London by Himself   271

Resignation from the Socialist Party   273

Residence in Oakland, California, 1898-1900   331

Preface

It is our hope that this bibliography will prove useful to the book collector, the book dealer, the librarian and to the student of American and comparative literature.

For the collector and dealer, we have provided a full description of the first edition of each of London's separately published works. Librarians will find data on reprints, translations, reviews, as well as biographical and critical material on London. Students of American and comparative literature will find a wealth of bibliographical data concerning translations of his works. London is the most widely read and most translated of all American authors. Though our bibliography presents abundant proof on this point, the reasons for this overwhelming popularity are still not altogether apparent.

The sections that deal with London's separately published books, and his contributions to newspapers, as well as the sections on spurious works, are arranged chronologically. Otherwise the entries of the other sections are arranged alphabetically. The material concerning London is arranged by language, with material in English preceding that in other languages. The order in this section is: books devoted to London, chapters of books devoted to London, periodical and newspaper material, unpublished material concerning him. Book reviews are arranged first by language, with English preceding, then alphabetically by title of work reviewed, and finally alphabetically by the name of the periodical or newspaper in which the review appeared.

Innumerable clues were gathered concerning London's publications when Hensley C. Woodbridge was allowed to explore the Jack London correspondence in the Huntington Library in San Marino, California. It is both sad and unfortunate that it has been impossible to check all of these clues because files of many of the newspapers are non-existent; other files are either incomplete or inaccessible. Thus, the correspondence would lead one to believe that some of London's stories were reprinted in a Hokianga (New Zealand) newspaper. Mr. A. G. Bagnall of the National Library Centre of Wellington, New Zealand, has written that "There are no surviving files of Hokianga newspapers for the period in question." The correspondence contains a clipping that

10

shows that chapter 21 of *Adventure* was published in the Akron *Press*. No file of this newspaper is extant. Many of the socialist and labor papers for the pre-World War I period have not survived, or exist only in fragmentary form. As a result of World War II, many of the libraries of Europe had books and periodicals destroyed.

Ideally, every item listed should have been examined by one of the compilers. Unfortunately, such an ideal situation would have meant the everlasting postponement of the project, for the vast majority of the translations are not available in the United States, and would be available only if one had the time and means to visit the leading libraries in almost every country of any size and importance. We have depended upon data provided by national libraries, bibliographical centers and published national bibliographies. We have listed in our acknowledgments the most important organizations and individuals with whom we have corresponded. The list is not complete; some have supplied but a missing pagination or missing volume number and while our gratitude is no less great, it did not seem wise to list every single correspondent.

Wherever possible, translations have been given with the English original. Thus, at a glance the user can determine the languages into which a given London title has been translated. However, there are times when the contents of the foreign title are not in any way the same as the original English title. In many cases the translation was not made from the original American edition or an American reprint, but was made from a British edition with a different title, or is a translation. Thus, the Persian translation of *The Daughter of the Snows* was made from a Russian translation rather than from the original text. In certain cases, the titles then have been changed beyond recognition and only a comparison of the texts could determine the original.

We have attempted to identify the languages into which various works have been translated. In certain cases, especially in regard to Serbian, Croatian and Slovenian, we have found it impossible to do so in every case. These languages, especially when Serbian is transliterated, are very similar, and more is needed than the barest bibliographical details provided by some of the sources. Our identification of works in these languages has been, to a great degree, based on the place of publication. We also regret certain inconsistencies found in

the Russian transliterations. We also regret that complete consistency
has not been achieved in regard to the bibliographical data presented.
For example, the Dutch national bibliography has only in recent years
given the pagination for its entries. We have provided as complete
information as the sources used provided. In many cases we attempted
to provide additional data.

In part two we have listed both the important and the trivial. It
is our opinion that the scholarly biography of Jack London is yet to
be written and that his future biographer, so as to get a well-rounded
picture, will have to examine what his contemporaries wrote concerning him as well as what doctoral candidates have written of him. We
make these remarks even though there now exist the published biographies and studies by his wife, Charmian London; his daughter, Joan
London; Irving Stone, Philip Foner and Richard O'Connor. Yet when
these are examined, it is seen that none attempted to be definitive.
Their style and approach are sufficiently popular that it has often been
impossible to trace the bibliographical clues which these authors have
provided. Foner, for example, provides the text of the definition of
a scab, but gives no indication as to when London wrote it or where it
was first published. The bibliography of Jack London provided by
his wife must be used with the greatest caution; for newspaper
material, the subject rather than the headlines is given; volume and
pagination are completely lacking and items are listed which do not
occur in the sources given. In the past decade, London has been the
subject of a few serious articles by Baskett, Labor, Peterson, Shivers
and a few others. He has also been the subject of some almost scur-
rilous articles in the so-called men's magazines.

It is unfortunate that a greater thorough knowledge of London
studies in the Soviet Union and Eastern Europe is not readily available. It would be our opinion that one of the most thorough studies
yet written on *The Iron Heel* is the work of Miss Badanova of Tashkent. The German Jung, some two decades before Foner, published
an anthology in German translation of London's works to show his
socialist leanings. The various anniversaries of his birth and death
are appropriately noted in the Russian press and collected editions
of his works are constantly appearing over the world with the excep-
tion of the United States where his works as they enter the public
domain are appearing with greater frequency in paperback form.

Thus on May 15, 1961, Mr. Olafur F. Hjartar, Librarian of the Landsbokasafn Islands, wrote: "A publishing company in Reykjavik, Isafoldarprentsmija h.f., plans to publish all of Jack London's works in the near future, so you can see that he is very popular in Iceland." The recent ten-volume Polish set of his works is well-bound and well-printed. The latest Russian set was composed of 14 volumes and contains his most important works.

With the cooperation and assistance of librarians and scholars throughout the world, it is our hope that we have produced a bibliography that will be of service regardless of the language or country.

We are indebted to Robert Greenwood and Newton Baird of the Talisman Press for their continued interest in this project. Their interest and encouragement has meant much to the compilers.

Our interest in Jack London will continue and those who learn of additions or corrections should feel free to call them to the attention of the compilers.

Hensley C. Woodbridge,
Southern Illinois University,
Carbondale, Illinois

John London, A.B.A.A.,
JOHN LONDON RARE BOOKS,
Burien, Washington

George H. Tweney,
Seattle, Washington

Acknowledgments

Many individuals have contributed to the accuracy and completeness of this bibliography. Some, such as the three hundred librarians who checked their catalogs for theses and dissertations on London, the labor editors who provided data on London's definition of a scab, and those who provided paginations of various kinds, we hope will excuse us if we do not list all of their names. The authors owe them their thanks, and our gratitude is no less personal because they are not listed by name.

The idea for this bibliographical study originated with Clell Peterson of the Murray State University faculty. Thanks to a sabbatical leave during the summer of 1961, which was granted by President Ralph H. Woods and the Board of Regents of Murray State University, Hensley C. Woodbridge was able to use the Huntington Library. Several Murray State University faculty members and students, among them Edmond Steytler and Fred Faulkner, have called our atttention to items which might otherwise have been missed, or have helped with certain linguistic problems.

Our grateful thanks are given to the members of the Staff of the Huntington Library. The friendliness and helpfulness of this library staff are extraordinary. We were able not only to make use of the large collection of London first editions, reprints and translations, but were allowed to explore the London manuscripts and correspondence. Without the use of this collection, this bibliography might never have been completed.

We are grateful to Mr. Lloyd A. Arvidson of the University of Southern California Library. He secured the cooperation of Miss Chouming Hsia and of Tom Kaposi, who worked with the Chinese and Hebrew items. Helen W. Azhderian, head of the reference department, arranged for Glenn Bunday to provide full information concerning the movie versions of Jack London's works.

We are indebted to the Cutler Translation Bureau of Los Angeles for the transliteration of our material in Bengali, Bulgarian, Persian, and much of the Russian, as well as certain other languages.

Use has also been made, either in person, through correspondence, or photoduplication, of material in the Los Angeles Public Library, the University of California Library at Los Angeles, the Bancroft Library and the University of California Library at Berkeley.

Mrs. William Simpson checked numerous items in the California State Library at Sacramento; Mrs. Frances Buxton, California Librarian of the Oakland Public Library, allowed the Jack London scrapbooks to be microfilmed for our use; the California State Library allowed its Jack London entries in its card catalog to be photostated.

Joan London, daughter of Jack London, has provided encouragement, and numerous items, as well as a bibliographical listing of most of her sources for her *Jack London and His Times*. Her interest in our project has been heart-warming.

Significant and unremitting cooperation and assistance have been given by Mr. George H. Tweney of Seattle, Washington. Mr. Tweney has been a Jack London collector for many years, and has one of the largest private collections of London material in his library. Every book ever written by London is present in first edition form, and in every known variant of the first edition. Invaluable assistance came from this collection in being able to personally examine every first edition, in all known variants, and compare each with such of those as are present in the private collection of John London, as well as with the descriptions in the Merle Johnson and the Gaer bibliographies. Mr. Tweney's collection also includes a significant number of London pamphlets, separates, socialist publications, magazines in which London articles and short stories first appeared, and other significant ephemera. Numerous small, but at the same time annoying puzzles were solved by having this wealth of material close at hand for continuous personal examination and comparison. Finally, Mr. Tweney had given so much of his personal time in assisting the authors in many different ways, that it became obvious that he should be listed as the third author of this compilation, and upon the invitation of the two original authors, he agreed that his name should be added to the title page. We are indeed grateful for his continuing interest and assistance.

In many cases without the direct knowledge of the respective institutions, John London and George H. Tweney have made frequent use of the collections of the Seattle Public Library, the University of Washington Library, the University of British Columbia Library, the New York Public Library, the Boston Public Library, the University of Michigan Library, the Firestone Library at Princeton University, and several other university libraries in various parts of the United States. Friendly cooperation has also come at various times from numerous dealers in the rare book trade, and from members of the Antiquarian Booksellers Association of America. This has been just one more instance of the frequent and friendly relationships that exist in this old and honorable profession.

In spite of the fact that John London is in the profession of selling rare books, dealers sometimes cannot resist the temptation to collect a few choice items for their own personal collections. Accordingly, in his comparatively small, but somewhat unusual collection of Jack London ephemera and pamphlets, it has been possible to find the answer to more than one bibliographical puzzle. Also, his extensive collection of bibliographies of all kinds—which are the hidden stock in trade of every successful rare book dealer—has proved most useful in being able to check another author's description of some particular title.

We desire to thank Donald J. Gilluley for withdrawing from his own proposed London bibliography in September, 1962, after a year's work on it. He has also been kind enough to add several items to our own compilation.

We also desire to thank Prof. Hal Waters for withdrawing from the completion of his own proposed London bibliography late in 1965. He has kindly allowed an early draft of his material to be utilized and some two dozen items have been added to this bibliography from this draft.

Certain items were checked in the Harvard University Library and in the Boston Public Library by Audrey Hosford of the Harvard University Library Staff. Harold Merklen of the New York Public Library has also provided data on several entries. Various departments of the Library of Congress have also proved most helpful.

We have corresponded with King Hendricks of Utah State University, Irving Shepard of Glen Ellen, California, Archie Green of the University of Illinois, Philip Foner of the Citadel Press and Peter Tamony of San Francisco. They have all been very helpful and cooperative.

Acknowledgment to Deming Brown and Columbia University Press for permission to use the London portion of *A Guide to Soviet Russian Translations of American Literature* (New York, King's Crown Press,

Columbia University, 1954), compiled by Glendora W. Brown and Deming B. Brown. All material prior to 1948 in Russian has been taken with their consent from the above-mentioned volume, pp. 109-148, items 635-1040.

Albert Phiebig of White Plains has for five years seen to it that a steady stream of London translations has reached us. Our gratitude to him is almost unlimited. He provided London translations from some countries which did not issue national bibliographies, and he also provided the Chinese translations (now in the University of Southern California Library), the Persian translations (now in the Huntington Library), as well as translations in certain languages of India and Pakistan, along with those of better known European tongues.

Our thanks to Mr. Julius Barclay of the Stanford University Library for examining the London contributions to Oakland High School *Aegis* in the Special Collections Division of Stanford University Library where the most complete set of this periodical may be found.

Hensley C. Woodbridge desires to express his appreciation also to the Association of College and Research Libraries for a grant in 1962.

Hensley C. Woodbridge's wife, Annie, has been a source of constant understanding and encouragement over the six years that this work has been in progress.

We acknowledge also the help of Mr. Dick North, Mr. Tony Bubka, Mr. Alan M. Cohn, and Mr. Bruce Giffin.

In London, Colin Clair undertook to check the British Museum and the newspaper collection at Colindale. Almost all references to British serial publications of London's works, and reviews of his works are the work of Clair, who by using current foreign bibliographies in the British Museum has also added to the "up-to-dateness" of this compilation.

In Albania, we are indebted to Mihal Hanxhari, director of the Biblioteka Shkencore.

In Argentina, to Fernando Garcia Cambeiro.

In Australia, to G. D. Richardson, principal librarian, Public Library of New South Wales; Mrs. Marjorie Hancock, Deputy Mitchell librarian of Sydney and E. K. Sinclair, editor of *The Age* of Melbourne.

In Belgium, to J. Lambert of the Bibliotheque Royal de Belgique.

In Brazil, to Lelia C. C. da Cunha of the Instituto Brasileiro do Bibliografia e Documentacao.

In Bulgaria, to Professor T. Borov, Director of the Bulgarian Bibliographical Institute of Sofia.

In Canada, to Martha Shepard and J. P. Bourque of the National Library of Ottawa.

In Chile, to Guillermo Feliu Cruz, Biblioteca nacional.

In Czechoslovakia, to Dr. Jaroslav Kunc of the Narodni knihovna of Prague.

In Denmark, to Palle Birkelund of Det Kongelige Bibliotek, who supplied a photostat of the London section of this library's catalog, as well as certain other material.

In Estonia, to the Director of the Estonian Public Library.

In Finland, to *American Fiction in Finland* by Philip Durham and Tauno F. Mustanoja (Helsinki, 1960).

In Germany to the Deutsche Bucherei of Leipzig, and to the card service of Hans Bentz.

In Hungary, to Dr. Géza Sebestyén, acting head, National Széchényi Library.

In Iceland, to Olafur F. Hjartar of the Landsbokasafn Islands.

In India, to the deputy librarian of the National Library.

In Ireland, to R. J. Hayes, Director of the National Library of Ireland.

In Italy, to the Director of the Centro Nazionale di Informazioni bibliografiche.

In Japan to the Director of the National Diet Library.

In Latvia, to A. Deglava, Director of the State Library.

In Lithuania, to the Director of the State Library.

In the Netherlands, to the library staff of the Bibliotheek der Rijsuniversiteit of Leiden.

In New Zealand, to Herbert Roth of the National Library Service, Wellington, and to Iris Park of the Alexander Turnbull Library of Wellington. Miss Park was so kind as to provide a typed copy of all London references in the *Maoriland Worker*.

In Norway, to Erling Gronland of the Oslo Universitetsbiblioteket.

In Poland, to Dr. Bogdan Horodyski of the Biblioteka narodowa.

In Portugal, to the staff of the Biblioteca Nacional de Lisboa.

In Rumania, to the Director of the Biblioteca centrala de stat.

In Russia, the Vsesoiuznoi gosudsrstvennoi bibliotekoi inostranoi literatury supplemented the data found in *A Guide to Soviet Russian Translations of American Literature* by G. W. and D. B. Brown by (1) providing a bibliography of London in Russian from 1948 to 1960; (2) a bibliography of Russian biographical and critical studies on London; and (3) this organization provided data on translations of London's work in the Soviet Union in languages other than Russian.

Mr. Vil Bykov has not only supplied data of his own works concerning London, but has been so kind as to identify the English original of almost all the translations given by Brown, but not identified by Brown; he also provided data on the contents of the various sets of London's collected works into Russian and provided much other data of value concerning London in the U.S.S.R.

In South Africa, to Miss C. A. Hittos, copyright department for the Director of the State Library.

In Sweden, to Sven Rinman of the Kung. Biblioteket, who furnished a photostat of the London entries in this library's card catalog; Tore Nystrom of the same library checked most of the data concerning Swedish reviews and critical comments.

In Turkey, to Sami N. Ozerdim, acting Director of the National Library and Bibliographical Institute.

In Uzbekistan, to N. M. Manin, Chief of the Exchange Division, in Tashkent and to Miss I. M. Badanova, who kindly sent a list of her publications on London.

In Yugoslavia, to Janko Djonovic, Assistant Director of the Narodna Biblioteka.

The authors realize that it would be folly to claim that this London bibliography is "complete." No bibliography of any kind is ever complete in the true sense of the word. However, the search has been diligent and sincere, and if anything of significance has escaped, it has been far from intentional. Needless to say, dealers' catalogues from now on will probably be replete with descriptions of Jack London material being offered for sale, accompanied by the comment, "Not in Woodbridge, London and Tweney." With this help, perhaps the bibliography will one day be truly "complete."

ABBREVIATIONS

ACS	*Short stories* . . . 1960 (American Century Series). No. 206.
BH	*The Bodley Head Jack London* . . . 1963. No. 209.
BSS	*The best short stories* . . . c1945. No. 188.
BSS-EB	*The best short stories* . . . 1962. No. 207.
BW	*Brown Wolf and other Jack London stories* . . . 1920. No. 182.
CF	*Children of the frost* . . . 1902. No. 7.
CS	*The cruise of the Snark* . . . 1911. No. 89.
CWOS	*The call of the wild and other stories* . . . 1926. No. 183.
CWOS-1960	*The call of the wild and other stories* . . . 1960. No. 203.
CWP	*The call of the wild* . . . Platt & Munk, 1960. No. 205.
CWSS	*The call of the wild and selected stories* . . . 1960. No. 204.
DC	*Dutch courage* . . . 1922. No. 164.
DR	*Dva rasskaza* . . . 1949. No. 195.
ER	*London's Essays of revolt* . . . 1926. No. 185.
F	*Jack London: American rebel* . . . edited by P. Foner . . . 1947. No. 191.
FM	*Faith of men* . . . 1904. No. 45.
FSS	*Four short stories* . . . 1947. No. 194.
FSSt	*Four short stories* . . . [n.d.] No. 216.
GHF	*God of his fathers* . . . 1901. No. 4.
H	Hendricks, King. *Creator and Critic* . . . 1961. No. 1169.
HD	*Human drift* . . . 1917. No. 145.
HP	*House of pride* . . . 1912. No. 96.
JLSB	*Jack London's Stories for Boys* . . . 1936. No. 187.
LF	*Lost face* . . . 1910. No. 70.
LL	*Love of life* . . . 1907. No. 56.
LLOS	*Love of life and other stories* . . . 1946. No. 189.
Mex	*The Mexican* . . . 1952. No. 199.
MF	*Moonface* . . . 1906. No. 43.
NB	*The night-born* . . . 1913. No. 106.
OMM	*On the Makaloa mat* . . . 1919. No. 162.

O	Indicates material found in the Jack London scrapbooks of the Oakland Public Library, Oakland, Calif.
R	*The Road* . . . 1907. No. 59.
Re	*Revolution and other essays* . . . 1910. No. 72.
RO	*The red one* . . . 1918. No. 154.
SA	*Stories of adventure* . . . [n.d.] No. 218.
SDT	*Sun dog trail* . . 1951. No. 197.
SP-1946	*The scarlet plague* . . . *three stories* . . . 1946. No. 190.
SS	*Son of the sun* . . . 1912. No. 99.
SSM	*Short stories* . . . Moscow, 1950. No. 196.
SSMo	*Short stories* . . . Moscow, 1962. No. 208.
SSS	*Selected stories of Jack London* . . . 1930. No. 186.
SSTa	*South Sea tales* . . . 1911. No. 93.
ST	*Selected tales* . . . [n.d.] No. 217.
St-K	*Stories* . . . Kaunas, 1958. No. 202.
St-T	*Stories* . . . Tallinn, 1958. No. 201.
StSt	*Strength of the strong* . . . 1914. No. 121.
SW	*Son of the wolf* . . . 1900. No. 1.
TA	*Tales of adventure* . . . 1956. No. 200.
TFN	*Tales of the far north* . . . [n.d.] No. 220.
TFP	*Tales of the fish patrol* . . . 1905. No. 40.
TWS	*Tales of the white silence* . . . [n.d.] No. 221.
TT	*Turtles of Tasman* . . . 1916. No. 142.
WC	*War of the classes* . . . 1905. No. 33.
WFOS	*White Fang and other stories* . . . c1963. No. 210.
WGL	*When God laughs* . . . 1911. No. 82.

PART ONE
WRITINGS BY JACK LONDON

THE SON OF THE WOLF. 1900

1. THE SON OF THE WOLF | Tales of the Far North | BY |
JACK LONDON | [publisher's device]| BOSTON AND NEW YORK |
HOUGHTON, MIFFLIN AND COMPANY | The Riverside Press,
Cambridge | 1900
[viii] [1] 2-251p. 19.5 x 12.5 cm. Slate gray cloth
stamped in silver on cover and spine. Frontis. with tissue
guard.
On verso of title-page (p.[iv]): COPYRIGHT, 1900, BY
JACK LONDON | ALL RIGHTS RESERVED
Contents: The White Silence; The Son of the Wolf; The
Men of Forty-Mile; In a Far Country; To the Man on Trail;
The Priestly Prerogative; The Wisdom of the Trail; The
Wife of a King; An Odyssey of the North.
State 1: Publisher's imprint at bottom of spine reads:
Houghton | Mifflin & Co.
State 2: Publisher's imprint at bottom of spine reads:
Houghton | Mifflin ·&· Co
The imprint in each case is from a slightly different
font of type, state 1 being slightly heavier and darker
than state 2 [not attributable to wear in the type face,
etc., as they are decidedly different fonts of type].
In addition, there is the distinct "dot" separating the
"&" as indicated above. London has examined both states in
the collection of George H. Tweney of Seattle, Washington,
This variant was first brought to Mr. Tweney's attention
by the late Mr. Ben Abramson, rare book dealer of Chicago,
Illinois.
State 3: Bound in green cloth, with overall square
white panel on front cover delineating title in green,
with profile design of trapper and dog. Back of spine also
has overall white panel delineating title, head of
trapper, author's name and publisher's imprint in green.
State 4: Bound in green cloth, with overall square
white panel on front cover delineating trapper and dog in
green, but title is stamped in red. Backstrip is original green cloth, with title, author's name and publisher's imprint in red, and trapper's head profile in
embossed green.
As is shown above there exist two states of the slate-
colored binding, and there is no known priority for the
first edition. The *bona fide* collector would require all
four states in his collection in order to be able to state
with confidence that he possessed the "first edition".

[24]

THE SON OF THE WOLF

Tales of the Far North

BY

JACK LONDON

BOSTON AND NEW YORK
HOUGHTON, MIFFLIN AND COMPANY
The Riverside Press, Cambridge
1900

[Item 1]

In addition, Mr. Tweney engaged in correspondence with
Charmian Kittredge London some years before her death,
and had her word that Jack London himself did not know
which issue came first. One of the green binding copies
in Mr. Tweney's collection also has an autograph of the
author's inserted, which attests that it is the "first
edition".

The authors would like to emphasize again that no known
priority can be established for any of the four states
mentioned above. This was Jack London's first published book and one of his most important. All four states
would appear to be significant.

The first dust wrapper has the belt design as on the
slate binding in black.

2. Reprints:
____, New York, Grosset & Dunlap [c1907] 251pp.
____, Boston and New York, Houghton Mifflin Co., 1930,
also [c1928, published in 195?] 251pp. (The Riverside
Library).
____, Stuttgart, Tauchnitz, 1958, 135pp.
____, London, A. P. Watt & Son [1900] 251pp.
____, London, Isbister & Co., 1902.
____, London, Pitman, 1910, 252pp. (cheap edition).
____, London, Everett & Co. [1913] 256pp. (Everett's
Library).
____, London, Newnes, 1920, 256pp.
____, published as *An odyssey of the north,* London, Mills
& Boon [1915] 284pp. (Mills & Boon's Shilling Cloth
Library).

3. Translations:
Sinut na vulka, tr.: Boris Tabakov, Sofia, M. G. Smrikarov,
1942, 167pp. (Khudozhestvena bibl. Tzvetove, II:8).
Contents: Bialoto mulchanie. Sinut na vulka. Muzhete ot
chetiridesetata milia. V dalechna strana. Chovekut na put.
Pravoto na sveshchenika. Zakona na putuvaneto. Suprugata
na edin tzar. Odiseia na severnata zemia. [The order of
the stories is the same as that of the original].
                                    (Bulgarian)
Pei Fang Ti Ao Te Sai, tr.: Ch'en Fu-an, Shanghai, Shang
tsa ch'u pan she, 1953, 221pp. Contents: Pai Se Ti Ching
Chi. Lang Te Ern Tzu. Ssu Shih Li Ho Pan Ti Jen Men. Tsai
Yao Yüan Ti Ti Fang. Wei Liao Lu Shang Ti Hsing Jen Kan
Pei. Chiao Shih Ti T'e Ch'uan. Lü T'u Hsueh Shih. I Ko
Huang Ti Ti Ch'i Tzu. [*Pei Fang Ti Ao Te Sai* is the same
order as the original].   (Chinese)

Syn vlkuv, tr.: J. Staněk, Přerov, Prerovsky obzor, 1918, 125pp.
_____, tr.: I. Schulz, Prague, Srdoe, 1918, 146pp.; Srdce, 1922, 138pp.; Srdce, 1922, 140pp.
_____, tr.: B. Šimková, Prague, Kočí, 1923, 160pp.
(Czech/Slovak)
Ulvedhundedn, authorized translation, Copenhagen, Hagerup, 1914, 240pp.; 1917, 1923, 216pp.
_____, Copenhagen, Martin, 1929, 304pp.
_____, tr.: Tom Smidth, Copenhagen, Martin, 1934, 320pp.; 1947, 256pp.
_____, Copenhagen, Grafisk Forlag, 1952, 250pp.
(Danish)
Zwerftochten in het Noorden, tr.: J. P. Wesselink-van Rossum, Amsterdam, Boekh. en Uitg. Mij Joh. Müller, 1923.
(Dutch)
Suden poika, tr.: A. I. R[elander] Helsinki, Kustannusoy. Suomi, 1925, 155pp. (Finnish)
Le fils du loup, tr.: S. Joubert, Paris, L'Edition française illustrée, 1920, 270pp.
_____, tr.: S. Joubert, Paris, Hachette, 1931, 237pp. (Les meilleurs romans étrangers); Paris, Hachette, 1940, 186pp. (Bibliotheque verte). Contents: Jack London. Le fils du loup. La prérogative du prêtre. L'homme à la balafre. La grande interrogation. Le grand silence blanc. Au bout de l'arc-en-ciel. Une odyssée at Klondike. [Four of the stories are from *The son of the wolf;* the others are from *The God of his fathers.*] (French)
Der Sohn des Wolfs, tr.: Erwin Magnus, Berlin, Universitas, 1927, 277pp.; 1955, 245pp.; Berlin, Buchergilde Gutenberg, 1927, 276pp.; Frankfurt-am-Main, Buchergilde Gutenberg, 1955, 245pp. (German)
Északi Odisszea, tr.: Ákos Farkas, Budapest, Légrády, 1924, 210pp. 1924, 2nd printing (Hungarian)
Il paese lontano. Racconti del Nord, tr.: Gastone Rossi, Milan, Sonzogno, 1939, 313pp. (Translation of *The son of the wolf. Faith of men. Lost face).*
(Italian)
Den hvite stilhet og andre fortællinger fra det høie nord, tr.: Holger Sinding, Kristiania, Narvesen, 1911, 109pp.
(Norwegian)
Odyssea Północy, tr.: Stanisława Kuszelewska, Warsaw, Ignis, 1922, 252pp. Also editions of Warsaw, E. Wende, 1925; Warsaw, Kurier Polski, 1939, Warsaw, E. Kuthan, 1947. The contents of the 1922 edition do not match the original: Historia Keesha (The story of Keesh). Napój Hyperborejów (A hyperborean brew). Bury Wilk (Brown Wolf). Przygoda Markusa O'Briena (The passing of Marcus O'Brien).

Batard. Syn Wilka (The son of the wolf). Prawo zycia
The law of life).   (Polish)
Syn volka, tr.: M. M. Birinski, Leningrad, Mysl, 1924,
160pp. Contents: Syn volka (The son of the wolf). Beloie
bezmolvie (The white silence). Obitateli "Forty Mail"
(The men of Forty Mile). V daliokoi strane (In a far
country). Putniku na bolshoi doroge (To the man on the
trail). Sviashchennye prerogativy (The priestly prerogative). Zavety mudrosti Bolshoi dorogi (The wisdom of the
trail). Zhena korolya (The wife of a king). Severnaga
odisseya (An odyssey of the north).
_____, tr.: E. K. Pimenova, Leningrad, Seyatel, 1926, 96pp.
Contents: Syn volka (The son of the wolf). Balaya tishina
(The white silence). Zhiteli Forty Mail (The men of Forty
Mile). V dalekoi strane (In a far country). Prava
svyashchennica (The priestly prerogative).
                                      (Russian)
Bele samote, tr.: Olga Graher, Maribor, Obzorja, 1955,
148pp.
Vargens son: Skildringar fran Polartrakterna, tr.:
M. Drangel, Stockholm, Bohlin, 1908, 251pp.; 1909, 255pp.;
1912, 252pp.; 1918, 207pp.; 1923, 201pp.; 1926, 207pp.
Contents: Pa de tysta hvita vidderna. Vargens son. Männen
vid Forty-Mile. I fjärran land. Pa sparjakt. Pa ämbetets
vägnar. Vad vandringslagen bjuder. Matadorens hustru.
En my Odyssevs.
Vargens son. Skildringar fran Nordlandet, tr.: Ernst
Grafstrom, Stockholm, B. Wahlstroms, 1912, 144pp. Contents:
Den vita Stillheten. Vargens son. Mannen i Forty-Mile. Vad
som händer i fjärran land. "För Mannen pa Langfärd!"
Pa ämbetets vägnar. Hon som var gift med en Kung. En
Nordlandets Odyssevs. Vandringslagens Bud.
Vargens son, Stockholm, Lindquist, 1958, 162pp. (Tiger-
bockerna 10).
En nordens odysse, tr.: A. P. B--m, Stockholm, Holmquist,
186pp.   (Swedish)
Syn volka, tr.: O. Krivinok, Kharkov, 1929, 176pp.
                                      (Ukranian)

                THE GOD OF HIS FATHERS. 1901

4.   The | God of His Fathers | & Other Stories | *By* | JACK
LONDON | [ornament]| [publisher's device] | New York |
McCLURE, PHILLIPS | & COMPANY | Mcmi
     [x] 1-299p. 19 x 13 cm. Dark blue cloth with gilt de-
sign and lettering on front cover and spine.
     On verso of title-page (p.[iv]): *Copyright, 1901, by* |
McCLURE, PHILLIPS & CO. | [rule] | [Two lines of press

The

God of His Fathers

& Other Stories

By

JACK LONDON

New York
McCLURE, PHILLIPS
& COMPANY
Mcmi

[Item 4]

signature]
    Contents: The God of His Fathers; The Great Interrogation; Which Make Men Remember; Siwash; The Man with the Gash; Jan, the Unrepentant; Grit of Women; Where the Trail Forks; A Daughter of the Aurora; At the Rainbow's End; The Scorn of Women.

5. Reprints:
    ____, New York, Doubleday, Page & Co., 1909; Garden City, Doubleday, Page & Co., 1914; Garden City, Garden City Publishing Co., 1925 each with 299pp.
    The God of his fathers: tales of the Klondyke, London, Isbister, 1902, 308pp., London, Pitman, 1907.
    The God of his fathers..., London, McClure, Phillips & Co., 1901, 299pp.
    ____, London, Everett,[n.d.] [1913] 255pp.
    ____, London, Mills & Boon, 1915, 286pp. (cheap edition), 1915, 158pp.

6. Translations:
    Buh jeho otcu, tr.: Ivan Schulz, Prague Ustř. tiskové družstvo, 1921, 197pp.
    Buh jeho octu. Velká otázka. Nac co se zapomíná. Siwoška. Muž s s jizvou. Zatvrzely Jan. Síla ženy. Na rozcestí. Dcera severní záře. Na konci duhy, tr.: I. Schulz, Prague, Koči, 1924, 157pp.   (Czech/Slovak)
    Hans fædres gud, tr.: A. Mikkelsen, Copenhagen, Martin, 1918, 136pp.; Martin, 1928, 272pp.   (Danish)
    De God zijner vaderen, Amsterdam, Gebr. E. & M. Cohen, 1922   (Dutch)
    Hänen isäiensä jumala ynna muita kertomuksia, tr.: T. Tainio, Tampere, Matti Vuolukka, 1914, 277pp.
    ____, tr.: Aito Kare, Turku and Helsinki, Kustannusliike Minerva oy, 1921, 141pp.
    ____, Helsinki, Carl Geislerin, 1927, 88pp.
                    (Finnish)
    Siwash, tr.: Erwin Magnus, Berlin, Universitas, 1929, 291pp.; Berlin, Büchergilde Gutenberg, 1929, 291pp.
    Contents: Die grosse Frage. Was sie nie vergessen. Siwash. Der Mann mit der Schmarre. Jan, der Unverbesserliche. Frauenmut. Wo die Wege sich trennen. Eine Tochter des Nordlichts. Am Ende des Regenbogens. Krieg der Frauen. Der Gott seiner Väter.
    Goldsucher, tr.: Rudolf Neubert, Linz, Vienna, Ibis-Verlag 1950, 268pp.   (German)
    As ösök istene, tr.: Zoltán Bartos, Budapest, Népszava, 1924, 146pp.   (Hungarian)
    Jo tevu dievas, tr.: K. Puida, Kaunas, Tulpe, 1929, 146pp.

Contents: Jo tevu dievas (The God of his fathers). Nakties
stovykla (Night camp?). Tai, kas nepamirstama (Which makes
men remember) Kur skiriasi keliai (Where the trail forks).
Sivašaite (Siwash). Moteriškes galia (The grit of women).
(Lithuanian)
Hans fedres gud, tr.: A. Eskeland, Oslo, Gyldendal, 1940,
1941, 159pp.   (Norwegian)
Bóg ojców jego, tr.: Stanisława Kuszelewska, Warsaw, Ignis,
1924, 196pp.; also editions of Warsaw, Biblioteka Groszowa,
1925 and Warsaw, E. Kuthan, 1949. Contents of 1924 ed.:
Mieszkańcy Czterdziestej mili (Men of forty mile).
Zhańbione czoło (Lost face). Obyczaj białych ludzi (The
white man's way). U Krańca Teczy (At the rainbow's end).
Nieoczekiwane (The unexpected). Zaufanie (Trust). Bóg
ojców jego (The God of his fathers).
(Polish)
Bog yevo ottsov, Moscow, Universalnaya Biblioteka, 1917,
94pp.
____, Moscow and Petrograd, Gosizdat, 1923, 92pp.
____, tr.: N. M. Tsymovich, Leningrad, Mysl, 1924, 184pp.
(Russian)
Hans fäders gud och andra berättelser fran Klondyke, tr.:
M. Drangel, Stockholm, Bohlin, 1911, 280pp.; 1916, 254pp.;
1917, 190pp.; 1918, 222pp.; 1923, 1926, 220pp.
____, Stockholm, Dahlberg, 1919, 222pp.
____, Stockholm, Romanbibl., 1922, 216pp.
____, tr.: A. Berg, Stockholm, Holmquist, 1911, 152pp.;
1913, 173pp.; 1918, 192pp.   (Swedish)
Bog ego ottzov, tr.: L. Vsevolozhskoi and P. Burgardta,
Kiev, 1927, 194pp.   (Ukranian)

CHILDREN OF THE FROST. *1902*

7. CHILDREN OF THE | FROST | BY | JACK LONDON | AUTHOR OF
"THE SON OF THE WOLF," "THE GOD OF | HIS FATHERS," ETC. |
WITH ILLUSTRATIONS BY RAPHAEL M. REAY | New York | THE
MACMILLAN COMPANY | LONDON: MACMILLAN & CO., LTD. | 1902 |
All rights reserved
    [iv]v [vi] vii [viii] [1-2] 3-261p. 19 x 13 cm. Green
cloth decorated in red, black, and white. Lettering on
front cover and spine white. Frontis. Three pages of publisher's advertisements at back.
    On verso of title-page (p.[iv]): COPYRIGHT, 1902 | BY
THE MACMILLAN COMPANY. | [rule] | Set up and electrotyped
September, 1902. | [Three lines of press signature]
    Contents: In the Forests of the North; The Law of Life;
Nem-Bok the Unveracious; The Master of Mystery; The
Sunlanders; The Sickness of Lone Chief; Keesh, the Son of

CHILDREN OF THE FROST

BY

JACK LONDON

AUTHOR OF "THE SON OF THE WOLF," "THE GOD OF
HIS FATHERS," ETC.

WITH ILLUSTRATIONS BY RAPHAEL M. REAY

New York
THE MACMILLAN COMPANY
LONDON: MACMILLAN & CO., LTD.
1902

All rights reserved

Keesh; The Death of Ligoun; Li Wan, the Fair; The League
of the Old Men.

8. Reprints:
____, London, Macmillan, 270pp.
____, Chicago, M. A. Donohue [1913] 261pp.
____, London, George Newnes [1913] 253pp.
____, New York, Regent Press [1913] 261pp.
____, London, Mills & Boon [1915] 290pp.

9. Translations:
Detzata na snegovete, tr.: M. Vecherov, Sofia, Argus,
1922, 87pp. Contents: V gorite na Severa. Nam-Bok
luzhliviia. Charodeistvo. Kish, sin na Kisha.
(Bulgarian)
Děti severu, tr.: I. Schulz, Prague, Kraft, 1921, 164pp.
____, tr.: I. Schulz, Prague, Kočí, 1924, 158pp.
(Czech/Slovak)
Pohjolan metsissä, Oulu, Kust. Sanomalehtiosuuskunta
Kansas tahto, 1914, 176pp. (9 stories plus two from
The God of his fathers) [Partially reprinted in 1923 as
Pakkasen lapsia, Helsinki, Kustannusoy, 114pp.]
Pakkasen lapsia, tr.: Ilmari Uotila, Helsinki, Kustannus-
liike Minerva oy, 1920, 105pp.   (Finnish)
Les enfants du froid, tr.: Louis Postif, Paris, Hachette,
1932, 237pp. (Les meilleurs romans étrangers); Hachette,
1939, 252pp. (Bibliothèque verte).   (French)
In den Wäldern des Nordens. Aus d. Goldgräberzeit in
Klondike, tr.: Erwin Magnus, Berlin, Gyldendalscher
Verlag, [1925] 268pp. Berlin, Universitas, 1949, 259pp.;
1959, 316pp.; Vienna, Wiener Volksbücherverlag, 1950,
220pp.; Gütersloh, Bertelsmann Lesering, 1959, 316pp.;
Gütersloh, Mohn, 1961, 187pp. (SM-Bücher 57).
(German)
I figli del gelo, tr.: Ida Lori, Milan, Bietti, 1929,
274 pp.   (Italian)
Sala bērni, tr.: M. Paulockis, Riga, Laikmets, 1936,
129pp.   (Latvian)
Deti snegov, tr.: A. Tarasova, Moscow, Universalnaya
Biblioteka, 1917, 170pp.
____, Moscow and Petrograd, Gosizdat, 1923, 168pp.
(Russian)
Otroci mraza, tr.: Pavel Holeček, Ljubljani, Mladinska
knjiga, 1951, 189pp. (Pionirska knjižnica)
(Slovenian)
Deti moroza, Kiev, Goslitizdat Ukrainy, 1957, 137pp.
(Ukranian)

THE CRUISE OF THE DAZZLER.   1902

10. ST. NICHOLAS BOOKS [printed in green in upper rectangle]
| THE CRUISE | [ornament] OF THE [ornament] | DAZZLER |
BY JACK LONDON [in black enclosed within green rec-
tangle] | [zodiac vignette in green filling largest rec-
tangle] | NEW YORK [dot] THE CENTURY CO [dot] MCMII [in
black enclosed within green rectangle]
   [iv] v-vii [viii] [1-2] 3-250p. 19 x 12.5 cm. Cream-
colored cloth. "ST. NICHOLAS BOOKS" in black at top of
spine and front cover. Balance of lettering orange. Decorations on spine and front cover in green, orange, and
black. Cream-colored dust wrapper printed in green, with
design repeated from the binding. Frontis.
   On verso of title-page (p.[iv]): Copyright, 1902 by
| THE CENTURY CO. ⌋ [rule] | *Published October, 1902* |
THE DEVINNE PRESS
   The true first issue was bound in cream cloth with
"Published October, 1902" on copyright page as noted
above. "St. Nicholas Books" in black on spine and front
cover, balance of lettering red. Decorations on spine and
front cover green, orange, and black. The first dust
wrapper is cream; the printing is green. The design is
repeated from the binding. Previously published in *St.
Nicholas*, 29:784-912 (July 1902).
   [Listed as no. 77 of "Eighty-eight fabulous American
books" in Van Allen Bradley, *More gold in your attic*,
New York, Fleet Publishing Corp., 1962, p.201].

11. Reprints:
   _____, New York, Grosset & Dunlap, c1902 vii, 250pp.
(Every boy's library - Boy Scout edition).
   _____, New York, Century, 1910, 1916, vii, 250pp. (St.
Nicholas books).
   _____, New York, Grosset, 1930, [?]pp. (Juveniles of
distinction).
   _____, London, Hodder and Stoughton, 1906, 272pp.
   _____, London, Collins, 1917, 188pp.
   _____, London, Mills & Boon, 1915, 288pp. (cheap edition);
Mills & Boon, 1923, 185 pp.; Mills & Boon, 1928, 186pp.
(Library edition).
   _____, Edited and introduced by I. O. Evans, New York,
Archer House, 1963, 158pp.

12. Translations:
   I ikuni, tr.: Esad Mekuli, Prishtinë, Mustafa Bakija,
   1956, 132pp.   (Albanian)
   Joe mesi piráty, tr.: Z. Burian, Prague, Toužimský a

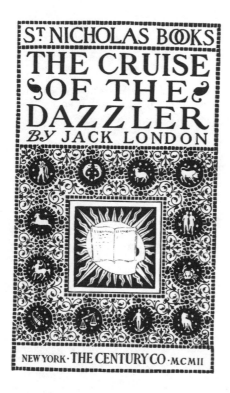

[Item 10]

Moravec, 1938, 133pp.
Na palubě "Dazzlera", tr.: J. Vorel, Prague, Zenit, 1922,
124pp.
Křižování Dazzlera, tr.: L. F., Prague, Koči, 1925, 123pp.
(Czech/Slovak)
De Kruistocht van de Meteor, Utrecht, A. W. Bruna
& Zoon Uitgevers, [n.d.,] 240pp.   (Dutch)
Aavoilla ulapoilla, tr.: Toivo Wallenius, Porvoo, Werner
Söderström, 1915, 112pp.; Werner Söderström, 1921, 1934,
167pp.   (Finnish)
La croisière du 'Dazzler', tr.: L. Postif, Paris,
Hachette, 1948, 192pp.   (French)
Joe unter Piraten, tr.: Erwin Magnus, Berlin,
Universitas, 1930, 191pp.; Universitas, 1959, 157pp.;
Universitas, 1960, 158pp.; Karlsruhe, Kindt, 1947, 175pp.
(Pony-Ausgaben Bdch.3); Gütersloh, Bertelsmann-Lesering,
1959, 157pp.   (German)
Ee prausini korvetta, tr.: Lilian Kalamaro, Athens,
Alikiotis, 1950, 112pp.   (Greek)
A Dazzler-cirkálón, tr.: Zoltán Bartos, Budapest,
Légrády, 1923, 126pp.; 2nd ed., [192?].
(Hungarian)
Á Blossa, tr.: Halldór Stefánsson, Reykjavik, Steindór
Gunnarsson, 1921, 115pp.   (Icelandic)
La crociera del Risplendente, tr.: Adele Levi, Milan,
Bietti, 1930, 253pp.   (Italian)
Jon rømmer hjemmefra, Oslo, Gyldendal, 1938, 126pp.
(Norwegian)
Wyprawa na "Błysku", tr.: Natalia Łosiowa, Warsaw, Rój,
174 pp.   (Polish)
Puteshestviya na "Oslepitelmom", tr.: V. Romanov,
Leningrad and Moscow, Knizhny Ugol, 1924, 162pp.
(Russian)
Pustolovine mladog džoa, tr.: Djordje Milakić, Belgrade,
Rad, 1956, 203pp.   (Serbian?)
La expedición del pirata, tr.: Adela Grego, Valencia,
Prometeo, 1927, 237pp.; Buenos Aires, Editorial Futuro,
1953, 186pp. [Also contains "Páginas de mi vida",
pp.9-14]; Barcelona, Ediciones G. P., 1957, 160pp.
[This edition of the translation claims to be a trans-
lation of *The filibuster's trail*, no work by this title
exists in the London canon. Also contains "Una reliquia
del Plioceno" and "Batard."]
_____, Mexico, Novarro, 1956, 192pp.
*La expedición del pirata, Revista literaria: novelas y
cuentos*, no. 1,690 (Sept. 29, 1963), 40pp.
(Spanish)
En Kryssning med Blixten, tr.: Ernest Grafström,

Stockholm, Holmquists, 1913, 128pp. [A note in Huntington 338313 states that this is a pirated edition]; another Holmquist ed., 1913, 131pp.; Stockholm, Wahlstrom, 1920, 48pp.
Pa kryss med Blixten, tr.: E. Lundquist, Uppsala, Lindblad, 1961, 140pp.
Pa kryssning med Blixten, tr.: Axel Bergström, Stockholm, W. Bille, 1910, 202pp.
Pa kryss med Blixten, Stockholm, Alb. Bonnier, 1917, 159pp.
_____, tr.: Ernst Lundquist, Stockholm, Bohlin, 1917, 1921, 149pp.; 1924, 146pp.

(Swedish)

A DAUGHTER OF THE SNOWS. 1902

13. A DAUGHTER | OF THE SNOWS | [rule] | BY | Jack London | AUTHOR OF "THE SON OF THE WOLF" AND "THE GOD OF | HIS FATHERS" | *With Illustrations in Color by* | FREDERICK C. YOHN | [rule] | [publisher's device] | [rule] | PHILADELPHIA | J. B. LIPPINCOTT COMPANY | MCMII [Title within double-rule border]
    [6] 7-334p. 19 x 12.5 cm. Red cloth with white, green, and gilt decorations. Lettering on front cover and spine white. Frontis. in color with tissue guard. Two pages of publisher's advertisements at back.
    On verso of title-page (p.[4]): COPYRIGHT, 1902 | BY | JACK LONDON | Published October, 1902 | [Two lines of press signature]

14. Reprints:
    _____, New York, Grosset & Dunlap [1902?] 334pp.
    _____, London, Isbister, 1904, 334pp.
    _____, London, Nelson, 1907, 1913, 376pp.
    _____, London, Mills & Boon [1920] 1921, 1923, 1925, 286pp.

15. Translations:
    Na vialata granitza, tr.: St. Stoianov and V. Popov, Sofia, Khudozhnik, 1934, 156pp. (Bibl. Kultura 3).
    Dushcheria na snegovete, tr.: D. Podvurzachov, Sofia, Knizhna tzentrale, 1938, 264pp.; Sofia, Kultura, 1946, 320pp.   (Bulgarian)
    Dcera sněhu, tr.: S. Krotký, Prague, Nozarová, 1919, 158pp.
    _____, tr.: A. Jeřábek, Prague, Procházka, 1920, 278pp.; Prague, Koči, 1924, 2 vols. (128, 128pp.).
    _____, tr.: B. Z. Nekovařík, Zlín, Tisk, 1938, 292pp.; Tisk, 1947, 276pp.   (Czech/Slovak)

Sneens datter, tr.: Aslaug Mikkelsen, Copenhagen, Martin,
1911, 282pp.; 1917, 288pp.; 1921, 256pp.; 1928, 2 vols.
264, 264pp.).   (Danish)
Een dochter van de sneeuwvelden, tr.: J. P. Wesselink-van
Rossum, Amsterdam, Boekh. en Uitg. Mij. Joh. Müller,
1923, [?]pp.   (Dutch)
Lumikenttien tytär, tr.: Aune Tudur, Helsinki, Otava,
1917, 1921, 360pp.; 1937, 342pp.   (Finnish)
Fille des neiges, tr.: Fanny Guillermet, Paris &
Neuchâtel, Attinger Frères, 1918, 235pp.; 1919
____, tr.: Louis Postif, Paris, Hachette, 1933, 256pp.
(Les meilleurs romans étrangers).   (French)
An der weissen Grenze, tr.: Erwin Magnus, Berlin,
Universitas, 1933, 257pp.; Berlin, Büchergilde Gutenberg,
1934, 257pp.; Berlin, Universitas, 1952, 223pp.; Vienna,
Büchergilde Gutenberg, 1952, 227pp.; Hamburg, Rowohlt,
1960, 1962, 235pp. (rororo-Taschenbuch-Ausgabe 342).
                                    (German)
A havasok lánya, Budapest, Tolnai, 1924, 3 vols.
Az alaszkai Diana, tr.: Zoltán Bartos, Budapest, Népszava,
1924, 217pp. [Also published in the Az angol amerikai
irodalom remekei series, Budapest, Anonymus, 217pp.]
                                    (Hungarian)
La figlia delle nevi, tr.; Giovanni Marcellini, Milan,
Modernissima, 1926; Modernissima, 1928, 264pp.; Milan,
Cavallotti, 1948, 192pp.
____, tr.: Mario Benzi, Sesto S. Giovanni-Milano, Barion,
1929, 366pp.; 1938, 335pp.
____, tr.: Adele Levi, Milan, Bietti, 1931, 287pp.
____, tr.: Tullo Tulli, Milan, Sonzogno, 1932, 380pp.
                                    (Italian)
Sneens datter, tr.: Ben Horne, Oslo, Gyldendal, 1935,
1943, 1947, 2 vols. (152, 150pp.)   (Norwegian)
Córka śniegów, tr.: St. Kuszelewska, Warsaw, Rój, 1928,
330pp.; also Warsaw, 1929; Warsaw, Wydawnictwa Ludowe,
1948.   (Polish)
Kći snega, tr.: R. Jovčic and K. Mihailović, Belgrade,
Sportska kniga, 1954, 250pp.; 1955, 237pp.
K'erketa na snegot, tr.: Meto Jovanovski, Skopje, Kultura,
1955, 232pp.   (Serbian?)
En Nordlandets dotter, tr.: M. Drangel, Stockholm, Bohlin,
1911, 426pp.; 1916, 336pp.; 1918, 344pp.; 1924, 349pp.;
1926, 343pp.
Nordlandets dotter, Stockholm, Dahlberg, 1919, 317pp.;
Stockholm, Romanbiblioteket, 1923, 267pp.
Snövilddernas dotter, tr.: Ernst Grafstrom, Stockholm,
Holmquist, 1913, 192pp.; 1913, 199pp.; 1917, 256pp.;
1919, 264pp.   (Swedish)

Doch' snegov, Kiev, Goslitizdat Ukrainy, 1957, 247pp.
[Title in Russian]   (Ukranian)

THE KEMPTON-WACE LETTERS. 1903

16. The | Kempton-Wace Letters | *"And of naught else than*
Love would we | discourse." --DANTE, Sonnet II. | New
York | THE MACMILLAN COMPANY | LONDON: MACMILLAN & CO.,
LTD. | 1903 | *All rights reserved*
    [vi] 1-256p. 19 x 13 cm. Green decorated cloth stamped
in black. Top edges gilt. Lettering on spine gilt. Lettering on front cover white. Three pages of publisher's
advertisements at back.
    On verso of title-page (p.[iv]): COPYRIGHT, 1903, |
By THE MACMILLAN COMPANY. | [rule] | Set up and electro-
typed May, 1903. | [Three lines of press signature]

17. Reprints:
The foregoing first edition was reprinted in September,
1903, in exactly the format and binding as described
above, except that the title page reads as follows:

The | Kempton-Wace Letters | BY | JACK LONDON | AUTHOR OF
"THE CALL OF THE WILD," ETC. | AND | ANNA STRUNSKY |
"And of naught else than Love would we | discourse." --
DANTE, Sonnet II. | New York | THE MACMILLAN COMPANY |
LONDON: MACMILLAN & CO., LTD. | 1903 | *All rights*
reserved

    There is also a slight variation in the second of the
three pages of publisher's advertisements at the back, in
that both *The Virginian* and *Dorothy Vernon of Haddon Hall*
are listed in this reprinting, whereas just *The Virginian*
appears on this page of the first edition. In all other
respects, the two editions are the same. This first reprinted edition is significant in the fact that the
authors' names appear on the title page for the first
time.
    _____, London, Mills & Boon [1903?] 244pp.
    _____, London, Isbister, 1903, 285pp.

18. Translations:
Dopisy Kemptona a Wace o podstatě lidské lásky, tr.:
K. Vít, Prague, Kočí, 1925, 172pp.
                            (Czech/Slovak)
Listy Kemptona do Wacé a, Warsaw, Tania Ksiazka, 1926,
2 vols. (128, 126pp.).   (Polish)
Pisma o lyubvi, tr.: D. P. Nosovich, Leningrad, Mysl,

1924, 176pp.   (Russian)
Kärlekens väsen, tr.: Ernst Lundquist, Stockholm, Bohlin,
1922, 197pp.; 1926, 200pp.   (Swedish)

THE CALL OF THE WILD. *1903*

19. Illustrated by PHILIP R. GOODWIN | and CHARLES LIVINGSTON
BULL | THE CALL | OF THE WILD | *By* | *JACK LONDON* |
[vignette] | New York | THE MACMILLAN COMPANY | LONDON:
MACMILLAN & CO., Ltd. | 1903 | *All rights reserved* |
Decorated by CHAS. EDW. HOOPER [Title within double-rule
border on decorative background of glacier scene in blue-
gray, lettering in black]
    [8] 9 [10] 11-12 [13-14] 15-231p. 19 x 13 cm. First
edition bound in vertically ribbed green cloth decorated
in white, dark orange, and dark green. Lettering on front
cover and spine gilt. Top edges gilt. Frontis. in color
with tissue guard, included in pagination. Two pages of
publisher's advertisements at back. Dust wrapper stiff
gray paper printed in green, with design repeated from
the binding. Second edition binding horizontally ribbed
green cloth, third edition standard grade cloth with design embossed.
    On verso of title-page (p.[8]): [vignette] | COPYRIGHT,
1903, | BY JACK LONDON. | [rule] | Set up, electrotyped,
and published July, 1903. | [Three lines of press signa-
ture]
    Frontispiece tipped-in, with protective sheet attached.
Illustrations on pages (29), (35), (127), (155), (215),
(228) tipped-in. The following pages, on glazed paper,
are tipped-in: 43, 67, 203. Pages 141 and 143 on glazed
paper.

20. Serializations:
Reprinted from the *Saturday Evening Post*, 175:1-3, 30-31
(June 20, 1903); 175:9-11, 19-20 (June 27, 1903); 176:
9-11, 24 (July 4, 1903); 176:10-11 (July 11, 1903); 176:
12-13, 24 (July 18, 1903).

21. Reprints:
    _____, Toronto, George N. Morang & Company Limited, c1903.
This first Canadian edition collates exactly to the first
American edition described above, except Morang imprint
appears at foot of title page, and Canadian copyright appears on verso. Binding appears to be slightly lighter-
colored vertically ribbed green cloth decorated in white,
blue, and dark green. Top edges are gilt.
    _____, New York, Grosset & Dunlap, c1903; [1915] (Every

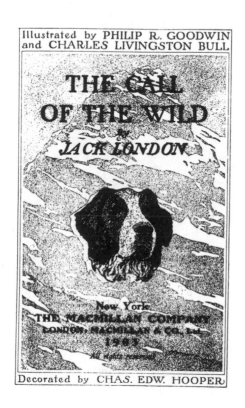

[Item 19]

boy's library. Boy Scout edition); [1931] (Famous dog
stories); [1935]; Grosset, 1946 (Children's favorite
series) and Toronto, McLeod, 1946 (Companion Library);
Grosset, 1950 (Famous dog stories); Toronto, McLeod, 1950
each with 211pp.
_____, New York, Grosset & Dunlap [1913] 231pp.
_____, New York, Macmillan, 1904, 1905, 1910, 1908, 231pp.
_____, illustrations by Paul Bransom, New York, Macmillan,
1912, 1916, 1953, 254pp.
_____, edited with an introduction and notes by Theodore C.
Mitchell, New York, Macmillan, 1917, 1936, 1947, 1955,
xxxi, 132pp. (Macmillan's Pocket American and English
classics).
_____, New York, The Regent Press [c1903] 231pp.
_____, Philadelphia, David McKay, 1914, 211pp. (The Golden
Book series).
_____, Chicago, M. A. Donohue, [1912], [?]pp.
_____, con notas y vocabularie; edited by Oreste Vera
Pérez, Padre Las Casas, Chile, Imprenta "San Francisco",
1939, 75pp. [English text for Chilean students.]
*Ivanhoe... including also passages from ... The call of
the wild ...,* Syracuse, New York, L. W. Singer Co., 1942
(The prose and poetry individualized program. [The
novel]).
The call of the wild, White Fang and The scarlet plague,
with an introduction by Bernard Fergusson, London,
Collins, 1953, 3 vols. in 1, 384pp. (Collins New Classics
series).
The Call of the wild, ed. by Mary Yost Sandrus, New York,
Scott, 1959, 189pp.
_____, ed. by Helen J. Harlow, New York, Globe, 1959,
132pp.
_____, with an introduction by Pierre Berton, New York,
Heritage Press, 1961, 158pp.
_____, London, Methuen [1954] 106pp.
_____, Hamilton & Co., 1962, 112pp. (Panther Books).
_____, school edition, New York, Macmillan, 1960, xiv,
103pp. [Literary heritage. A Macmillan paperback series.
Volume contains an introduction as well as questions and
projects].
_____ and *White fang,* introduction by Frank Luther Mott,
New York, Washington Square Press, 1962, pp. 1-102.
Introduction, pp. vi-xxiii.
_____, Adapted with notes and exercises by Winifred W.
Jones, 3,000 word level. Engelwood Cliffs, Prentice-Hall
International, 1962, 128pp.
_____, illustrated by Karel Kozer, New York, Macmillan,
1963, [?]pp.

____, illustrated by Robert Todd, with an afterword by Clifton Fadiman, New York, Macmillan, 1963, 142pp.
____, Braille editions (U.S.): Grade 1 1/2, 3 vols. Hand-copied. Also: English Braille, [n.d.] 1 vol. Press-Braille, American Printing House for the Blind, Louisville, Kentucky, 1955, 1 vol. Braille edition (transcribed for the National Library for the Blind, London, England): 1 vol. (1920). Talking books: read by Jim Denver and William Lazar. 12 records. 1952.
____, on 4 ultra microgrove 16 rpm talking book phonograph records. Reader: Jeff Chandler. St. Joseph, Michigan, Audio Book Co. 1961.
Five great dog novels edited by Blanche Cirker, New York, Dover, [n.d.,]pp.1-70.
Text editions: *The call of the wild*, abbreviated and simplified for use in schools (Easy readers no. 1), Copenhagen, Grafisk Forlag, 1944, 56pp. A second edition, though printed in Copenhagen, bears an Oslo, Gyldendal imprint, 1954.
____ ... adapted and abridged by Olive Price, New York, Grosset & Dunlap, 1961, 61pp.
____ ... Classics illustrated: featuring stories by the world's greatest authors published by Gilberton Co., New York, no. 91, Jan. 1952, no pagination. Illustrated by Maurice del Bourge. Translated into Norwegian as *Nar villdyret vakner*... Illustrerte klassikere, Fredrikstad, Illustrerte Klassikere A/S, [n.d., no pagination]. Each has a one-page biography of Jack London.
____, New York, Watts, 1966, 158pp. (Large type ed. Keith Jennison book).
Selections: "Buck, the dog that loved his master," *Child Library Readers. Book Five*, edited by William H. Elson and Mary H. Burris, Chicago, Scott, Foresman, 1923, pp.27-32.
"Buck, the lead dog," Miriam Blanton Huber, *Story and verse for children*, New York, Macmillan, 1965, pp.775-778.
"Buck wins a wager," *High School prize speaker*, edited by William Leonard Snow, Boston, Houghton Mifflin, 1916, pp.106-110; also published as "The wager on Buck," California Writers' Club. *Bulletin*, 4:1-3 (Dec. 1916).
"The call of the wild," in Thomas B. Costain and John Beecroft, *More stories to remember*, N. Y., Popular Library, 1958, 3:219-291.
"The call of the wild," in William J. Iverson and Agnes L. McCarthy, *Prose and poetry journeys*: sixth edition, Syracuse, Chicago, L. W. Singer, c1963, pp.2-14.
Leland B. Jacobs and Shelton L. Rort, *Ideas in literature*, *book 1*, Columbus, Ohio, Merrill Books, c1966. [pp.515-528

reproduce the first two chapters of this novel.]
"For the love of a man," Beth Brown, *All dogs go to heaven:
an anthology of stories about dogs*, New York, Grosset &
Dunlap, 1961, pp.144-155; *Children's Digest*, 8,74:101-119
(Jan. 1958); *The book of friendship*, with introduction by
Samuel McChord Crothers, New York, Macmillan, 1922,
pp.39-46; P. R. Fenner, *Dogs, dogs, dogs*, New York, Watts,
1951, pp.35-78; J. A. Goodman, ed., *Fireside book of dog
stories*, New York, Simon and Schuster, [c1943]pp.3-14; J.
W. McSpadden, ed., *Famous dogs in fiction*, New York,
Crowell, 1930, pp.288-305; E. L. Mally, ed., *Treasury of
animal stories*, New York, Citadel, 1946, pp.465-476; J. C.
Minot, *Best animal stories I know*, Boston, Wilde, 1929,
pp.237-256; F. Salten, *Felix Salten's favorite animal
stories*, New York, Messner, 1948, pp.229-243; E. T. Seton,
ed., *Famous animal stories*, New York, Coward-McCann, 1932,
pp.256-260; *Wide horizons*, New York, Holt, 1958,
pp.523-532.
____, New York, Washington Square Press, 1963, 102pp.
plus "Reader's supplement for greater understanding and
appreciation of *The Call of the wild* by Jack London,"
36pp. [Reader's enrichment series RE 103.]

22. Translations:
Kushtrimi i të parëre, tr.: Zef Simoni, Tirana, Naim
Frasheri, 1963, 16pp.   (Albanian)
Oplos krobi, Baku, Azernashr, 1927, 83pp.
                                   (Azerbaidzhanian)
Aranyer dak, tr.: Abul Hussain Choudhuri; ed. by Abdul
Jabbar Choudhuri, Dacca, East Pakistan, Great Bengal
Library, 1959, 116pp.   (Bengali)
Diboto zove, tr.: G. Efremov, Sofia, Al. Paskalev, 1921,
116pp. (Vsemirna bibl.).
Kogato gorata zove, tr.: Georgi Zhechev, Sofia, D.
Madzharov, 1935, 107pp. (Bibl. Zlatni stranitzi)
Zovut na divoto, tr.: G. Efremov, Sofia, Gladston, 1935,
96pp. (Bibl. Sviat i nauka).   (Bulgarian)
La crida del bosc,tr.: A. Rovira Virgili, Barcelona, Ed.
La Rosa dels Vents (Coleccion Alló que perdura, no. 3)
                                   (Catalan)
Volání divočiny, tr.: B. Lážňovský, Prague, Topič, 1918,
120pp.
____, tr.: Lážňovský, Prague, Kočí, 1922, 128pp.; 1930,
126pp.
____, tr.: B. Z. Nekovařík, Zlín, Tisk, 1937, 117pp.;
Prague, Práce, 1949, 1951, 98pp.
Volání divočiny a jiné povídky, tr.: A. J. Stastný,
Prague, Naše vojsko, 1956, 318pp.

Volanie divočiny, Bratislava, Bibliotheka, 1943, 104pp.
____, tr.: Pavol Branko, Bratislava, B. Buocik, 1948, 111pp.
____, tr.: E. V. Tvarožek, Bratislava, Slov. vyd. detskej knihy, 1955, 98pp.   (Czech/Slovak)
Naar naturen kalder, tr.: Aslaug Mikkelsen, Copenhagen, Peter Hansen, 1907, 264pp.; 1912, 190pp.
____, tr.: Aslaug Mikkelsen, Copenhagen, Hagerup, 1917, 1923, 160pp.
____, tr.: Aslaug Mikkelsen, Copenhagen, Martin, 1930, 352pp.; 1935, 256pp.
____, tr.: E. Schack Steenberg, Copenhagen, 1947, 222pp.
____, Copenhagen, Grafisk Förlag, 1956, 207pp.
                                                           (Danish)
Als de natuur roept, tr.: S. J. Barentz-Schönberg, Amsterdam, H. J. W. Becht, 1911; Amsterdam, De Arbeiderspers, 1956, 160pp.
Als de Natuur roept and *Pit-tah, de grijze wolf*, Amsterdam, De Arbeiderspers, 1939, 556pp.
De roep der Wildernis, tr.: Martin Deelen, Bussum, Classics Nederland, 1958, 48pp.   (Dutch)
"Vabadus kutsub," *Vikerkaar*, nos. 1-20 (1924).
Kui loodus kutsub, tr.: L. Rebane, Tartu, Noor-Eesti, 1932, 148pp.   (Estonian)
Golos krovi [Title in Russian] (The call of the wild), tr.: Der Nister, Kiev, 1935, 207pp.

                                                    (Evreiskian)
Erämaan ääni, tr.: F. Davidson, Tampere, E. Kaatra, 1907, 139pp.; Tampere, Isak Julin, 1912, 139pp.
Kun erämaa kutsuu, Turku, Sosialistin kirjapaino-osuuskunta, 1922, 163pp.   (Finnish)
L'appel de la forêt, tr.: Mme. la comtesse de Galard, Paris, F. Juven, 1908; Paris, Nelson, 1934, 176pp.; Nelson, 1939, 181pp. (Bibliothèque Nelson illustrée); ... with Bourget preface, Paris, Renaissance du livre, 1948, 192pp.; Club de lectures des jeunes, Paris, Le Club, 1960, vol. 2 contains an abridged translation of this volume.
____, honoré d'une médaille d'argent de la société protectrice des animaux, tr.: Galard, Paris, F. Juven, [n.d.,]282pp. This edition contains the Bourget preface and the same four stories which apparently appeared serially in *Le tempa*(Paris). Huntington 338234 contains a typed translation of the Bourget preface.
____. *Buck, histoire d'un chien de l'Alaska*, tr.: Galard, Paris, F. Juven, 1909, 155pp. Contains letter-preface by Paul Bourget as well as Batard, Une relique préhistorique, La foi des hommes and Les mille douzaines d'oeufs.
Buck: histoire d'un chien de l'Alaska L'appel de la forêt,

Paris, Boivin, 1925, 91pp.
Buck, Saumur, L'école émancipée, 1927, 32pp.
____, tr.: la comtesse Maurice de Bacque, Paris, Maurice
de Bacque, 1931, 173pp.
____, tr.: Galard, Lausanne, Guide du livre, 1963, 184pp.
(French)
Der Ruf der Wildnis, tr.: Fritz Born, Konstanz, See-
Verlag, 1923, 163pp.
____, tr.: Augusta Bronner, Vienna, Amandus- Ed., 1947,
43pp. (Orion-Roman, Serie C).
____, tr.: Franz Mairhofer, Linz, Vienna, Ibis-Verlag,
1947, 204pp.; Linz, Trauner, 1956, 172pp.
____, tr.: Paola Meister-Calvino, Zurich, Schweizer
Spiegel-Verlag, 1947, 168pp. (Spiegel Bibliothek der
Jungen).
Wenn die Natur ruft, tr.: Lisa Löns, Hannover, Sponholtz,
1907, v, 202pp.; other Löns translations published by
Sponholtz are: 1916, 114pp.; 1925, 147pp. (Sponholtz'
Jugend-bücherei); 1927, 190pp.; 1934, 154pp. (Sponholtz'
Jugend-bücher); 1947, 133pp.; 150, 135pp.; 1956, 152pp.
(Grüne Reihe 14) [This translation was also published in
Berlin, Tribüne, 1954, 127pp.]
____, no tr. given, Berlin, Sieben Stäbe, 1927, 190pp.;
Sieben Stäbe, 1930, 189pp.; Berlin, Deutsche Buchgemein-
schaft, 1928, 229pp.; Berlin, Volksverband der Bücher-
freunde, Wegweiser-Verlag, 1929, 96pp.; Aarau, Sauer-
länder, 1949, 92pp. (Salamander-Bücher 1); Aarau, Frank-
furt/Main, Sauerländer, 1959, 88pp. (Juventus-Bücherei
Reihe 1, Drachenbücher 1). Selection: *Der Ruf (Wenn die
Natur ruft)*, Stuttgart, Waldorf-Astoria Zigarettenfabrik,
1926, 16pp. (Waldorf-Bücherei. Reihe 5: Tiergeschich-
ten 8). (German)
Book-O. Skýlos Tis Aláskas, tr.: Yiánnis B. Eoaunídis,
Athens, G. S. Vlessa,[n.d.,]86pp.
(Greek)
Kol kedumin, tr.: R. Algad, Tel-Aviv, Y. Chechik, 1962,
108pp. [Juvenile].   (Hebrew)
A vadon szava, tr.: Zoltán Bartos, Budapest, Athenaeum,
1921, 155pp. (Olcsó regény 58); other editions published
in 1929, 1942, 168pp.; 1949, 168pp. (Népkönyvtár 4).
____, tr.: Réz Ádám, Budapest, Szépirod, Kiadó, 1954,
175pp. (Olcsó könyvtár).   (Hungarian)
Obyggoirnar kalla, tr.: Olafur Friðriksson, Reykjavik,
Isafoldarprentsmioja, 1951, 149pp.; Isafoldarprentsmioja,
1959, 149pp.   (Icelandic)
Kembali ke alam bebas, tr.: M. D. Aliff, Djarkarta,
P. T. Pembangunan, 1958, 161pp.   (Indonesian)
Scairt an duchais, tr.: Niall o Dombnaill, Baile Átha

Cliath, Oifig Díolta Foillseascháin Rialtais, 1932,
229pp.   (Irish)
Il richiamo della foresta, preface and tr.: Dàuli, Milan,
Modernissima, 1924, [?]pp.: 1928, 219pp.; Milan, Delta,
1929, 190pp.
____, tr.: Quirino Maffi, Milan, Bietti, 1928, 204pp.;
1936, 224pp.
____, tr.: Gastone Rossi, Milan, Sonzogno, 1928, [?]pp.;
1930, [?]pp.
____, tr.: D. Carter, Milan, Corbaccio, 1936, [?]pp.;
Milan, Corticelli, 1940, 180pp.; 1944, [?]pp.
____, Milan, Corticelli, 1940, 180pp.; Corticelli, 1940,
180pp.; Corticelli, 1944, [?]pp.; Milan, Lombarda, 1946,
127pp.
____, tr.: Berto Minozzi, Milan, Cavallotti, 1951, 147pp.
____, tr.: G. Toschi, Milan, La Sorgente, 1953, [?]pp.
____, tr.: Bruno Paltrinieri, Milan, Fabbri, 1955, 151pp.
____, tr.: Laura Ferajorni Guicciardi, Torin, S. A. I. E.,
1955, 300pp.
____, tr.: G. Falzone Fontanelli, Bologna, C. E. L. I.,
1958, 178pp.
____, tr.: Silvana Gottardi, Florence, Bemporad-Marzocco,
1958, 103pp.
____, Milan, La Sorgente, 1959, 147pp.
La storia di un cane, tr.: A. Calitri, preface by G.
Prezzolini, Milan, Morreale, 1926, xiv, 174pp.
                                         (Italian)
Yasei no yobi goe, tr.: Toshihiko Sakai, Tokyo,
Sobunkaku, 1928, 176pp.
____, tr.: Sakai, Tokyo, Shun'yodo, 1932, 124pp. (Sekai
meisaku bunko).
____, tr.: Kanesada Hanazono, Tokyo, Kaizosha, 1936, 177pp.
(Kaizo bunko).
____, tr.: Seiki Yamamoto, Tokyo, Ban'yusha, 1950, 206pp.
____, tr.: Shin'ichi Miura, Tokyo, Kawade Shobo, 1955,
120pp. (Kawade bunko).
Areno no yobi goe, tr.: Yamamoto, Tokyo, Kadokawa Shoten,
1953, 163pp. (Kadokawa bunko).
____, tr.: Kinzo Iwata, Tokyo, Iwanami Shoten, 1954, 133pp.
(Iwanami bunko).
Umi no okami. Areno youyobi goe, tr.: Yamamoto, Tokyo,
Mikasa Shobo, 1955, 330pp. (Hyakumannin no sekai bungaku.
Translation of The seawolf. The call of the wild).
                                         (Japanese)
Dongseong eui sarang, tr.: Sung-in Lee, Seoul, Chungmunsa,
1961, 228pp.; Seoul, Baeginsa, 1963, 216pp.
                                         (Korean)
Naar vilddyret kalder, tr.: Holger Sinding, Kristiania,

J. Dybwad, 1907, 173pp.
Vilddyret vaagner, tr.: Sigmun Rein, Kristiania, H.
Erichsen, 1914, 125pp.
Naar vilddyret lokkar, tr.: Jon Bakke, Kristiania, O.
Norli, 1921, 136pp.; 1935, 128pp.
Naar vilddyret vakner, tr.: Ben Horne, Oslo, Gyldendal,
1934, 1941, 156pp.   (Norwegian)
Avayé vahshat, tr.: Parviz Daryoush, Teheran, Safi Ali
Shah Publishing Institution, 1957, 148pp.
                                             (Persian)
Przygody psa w Klondyke, tr.: Wacława Sieroszewskiego,
Kracow, Z. Klemensiewicz, 1909, ix, 84pp.
Zew krwi, tr.: Stanisława Kuszelewska, Warsaw, E. Wende i
Ska, 1924, 135pp.; other editions, all Warsaw are: Bib-
lioteka Groszowa, 1933; E. Kuthan, 1945, 1946, 1949.
_____, Lwów, no publisher, 1925, 128pp.
_____, tr.: Stanisława Kuszelewska, Rzym, Polski Dom
Wydawniczy, 1947, 115pp.
_____, tr.: Eleanora Romanowicz in *Zew krwi i inne
opowiadania*, Warsaw, Iskry, 1955, pp.9-82; also separately
published, Warsaw, Iskry, 114pp.; Iskry, 1958.
                                             (Polish)
Chamado selvagem: romance, tr.: Sylvio Monteiro,[São
Paulo] Livraria exposição do livro, 1964 108pp.
O grito da selva, tr.: Monteiro Lobata, São Paulo, Comp.
ed. nacional, 1935, 218pp. (Coleção para todos 1).
O apelo da selva, tr.: Rui Guedes da Silva, Lisbon,
Portugalia, [n.d.,](Coleção juvenil 3).
                                             (Portuguese)
Chemaerea strabunilor, tr.: A. Ghitulescu, Bucharest,
Editura tineretului, 1957, 143pp.
                                             (Rumanian)
Dikava sila, tr.: R. Rubinova, Moscow, Gosizdat., 1922,
122pp.

Zov predkov, tr.: M. Likiardopulo and V. Koshevich,
Moscow, Universalnaya Biblioteka, 1918, 198pp. Also contains: Ublyudok (The story of Jees Uck). Tysyacha
dyuzhin (The one thousand dozen). Reprinted in 1923,
193pp.
Zov pustyni, tr.: Zin. Lvovski, Leningrad, Mysl, 1925,
1926, 160pp.   (Russian)
Glas divljine, tr.: Mihailo Djordjevic, Belgrade, Biblioteka Narodna knjiznica osmo kolo 34, 1929, 123pp.
_____, tr.: Borivoje Nedić, Belgrade, 1946, 254pp.;
Belgrade, Prosveta, 1954, 161pp.   (Serbian)
La llamada de la selva, tr.: Salvador y Fernando Valera,
Valencia, Prometeo, 1926, 250pp. Also contains: La casa

del orgullo (The house of pride) and Koolau el leproso
(Koolau, the leper).

____, Santiago, Zig-Zig, 1930, 130pp.; 1945, 156pp. (Co-
lección la linterna, serie ultramar 4).

____, tr.: Francisco R. Vadillo, Madrid, Marisal, 1939,
68pp.

____, *Excelsior*, no. 154:3-96 (April 18, 1940).[The sub-
title of this serial published in Santiago de Chile is:
Revista quincenal de literature. It also contains La casa
del orgullo, pp.97-114.]

____, Madrid, Diana, 1951, 61pp.

____, tr.: Jaime Puig Moltó, México, Novarro, 1956, 182pp.
[Pp.161-182, "El silencio blanco" is a translation of
"The white silence"].

El llamado de la selva, tr.: M. Fernández, Buenos Aires,
Semca, 1946, 238pp.

____, tr.: Ricardo Debenetti, Buenos Aires, Siglo Veinte,
1951, 155pp.; Buenos Aires, Cauce, 1956, 138pp.

____, tr.: Elsa Oesterheld, Buenos Aires, Edit. Codex,
1951, 383pp.

____, Santiago, Edit. American Playbook, 1955, 209pp.

____, tr.: Cora Bosch, Atlántida, 1958, 122pp. (Biblio-
teca Billiken).

El llamado de la selva y otros cuentos, tr.: Julio
Vacarezza, Buenos Aires, Acme, 1951, 1954, 275pp.; Acme,
1952, 278pp. Contents: El llamado de la selva, tr.:
Vacarezza; El silencio blanco (The white silence), La
liga de los ancianos (The league of old men) and El
hereje (The apostate) translated by M. Barbera.

                              (Spanish)

Skriet fran vildmarken, tr.: M. Drangel, Stockholm,
Bohlin, 1907, 1909, 1910, 1911, 195pp.; 1913, 1916, 156pp.;
1920, 1925, 157pp.; 1924, 141pp. (Pojkböcker, Bohlins 1);
1917, 191pp. (Världsberömda böcker. Nordiska förlagets
nya eliterserie 7); Stockholm, Nordiska Forlag, 1913,
158pp.

När vildmarken kallar, tr.: Ernst Grafström, Stockholm,
Holmquist, 1914, 127pp.; also published in 1914, 147pp.
(Holmquists bokförlags 1-kr. böcker); 1919, 155pp.

____, tr.: Anders Saxon, Stockholm, Bokforl. Nutiden,
1919, 104pp.

Skriet fran vildmarken, tr.: Hans G. Westerland, Stockholm, Bonniers, 1952, 143pp.

____, tr.: Tom Wilson, Uppsala, Lindblads, 1953, 112pp.

____, tr.: Ernst Ekwall, Stockholm, Lindqvists, 1955,
182pp.

____ and *Varghunden*, tr.: Laveringar and Bertil Lybeck,
Stockholm, Saxon & Lindström, 1935, 288pp.

Skriet fran vildmarken samt novellerna Den odödliga hunden, Drama till sjöss, Livets lag, Stockholm, Folket i bild, 1959, 221pp.[*Skriet* ... translated by Olov Jonason; other items translated by Marten Edlund].
(Swedish)
Vahşetin çağirişi, Istanbul, Selamet Basimevi, 1935, 184pp. Also contains translation of six stories
____, tr.: Sofi Huri, Istanbul, Amerikan Bord Neşriyat Dairesi,[n.d.,]128pp.   (Turkish)
Golos krovi, tr.: Der Nister, Kiev, 1935, 207pp.
(Ukranian)
Tieng goi cua ru'ng tham, tr.: Cãn-Huy-Tǎng, Saigon, Song mo'i, 1961, 70pp.   (Vietnamese)
Zov divljine, tr.: Mihailo Djordjević, Sarajevo, Mladost, 1954, 116pp.
Di shtime fun blut, New York, 1919, ix, vi, 180pp.
(Yiddish)

THE PEOPLE OF THE ABYSS. 1903

23. THE PEOPLE OF | THE ABYSS | BY | JACK LONDON | AUTHOR OF "THE CALL OF THE WILD," "CHILDREN | OF THE FROST," ETC., ETC. | *WITH MANY ILLUSTRATIONS* | *FROM PHOTOGRAPHS* | New York | THE MACMILLAN COMPANY | LONDON: MACMILLAN & CO., LTD. | 1903 | *All rights reserved*
    [vi] vii-xiii [xiv] 1-319p. 21 x 14.5 cm. Dark blue cloth decorated in gilt and black. Top edges gilt, all other edges uncut. Lettering on spine gilt. Lettering on front cover black outlined in gilt. Frontis. Three pages of publisher's advertisements at back.
    On verso of title-page (p.[iv]): COPYRIGHT, 1903, | BY THE MACMILLAN COMPANY. | [rule] | Set up, electrotyped, and published October, 1903. | [Three lines of press signature]
    In the George H. Tweney collection, there is a copy of this title that agrees with the first edition collation in every detail, except the original covers are in plain slate gray cloth with no decorations at all. The front cover is lettered in black: The People | of The Abyss | [rule] | Jack London. The spine has no decoration either, but is lettered the same as the first edition. This copy may be an earlier variant of the first edition. In rebinding, the copy has been trimmed to 18.5 x 12.5 cm.

24. Reprints:
    ____, London, Isbister, 1903, xiv, 322pp. This edition does not contain chapter headings. It contains a "Publisher's Note" in which there is quoted "Jack London in

London" as it appeared in the second number of *T. P.'s Weekly* (published on Nov. 14, 1902), pp.vii-viii. This note does not appear in the American edition.

____, New York, Macmillan, 1904, 1906, xiii, 319pp.

____, a study of the social and economic conditions of life in the East End of London with 24 illustrations from actual photographs, 1909, xiv, 322pp. Pp.vii-viii contain the same "Publisher's note" as that found in the Isbister edition.

____, London, Pitman, 1910, 336pp. (cheap edition).

____, London, T. Nelson and sons, [1914] ix, [11]-366 (Nelson's library); Nelson, 1917, 1919, 366pp.

____, New York, Grosset & Dunlap,[n.d.][1907,c1903], xiii, 319pp.

Selections: "A London sweating den," pp.62-66; "The carter and the carpenter," pp.125-128; "Night in the slums," pp.139-141; "Coronation day," pp.609-613; "In the slums of London," pp.649-650 in *The cry for justice* ... edited by Upton Sinclair, Philadelphia, Winston, 1915. See also contents of Foner and Sheperd anthologies.

25. Translations:
Chovekut na bezdnata, tr.: Liudmil Stoianov, Sofia, Georgi D. Iurukov, 1932, 208pp. (Bibl. Vsemirni romani. 4).
                       (Bulgarian)
Afgrundens Folk, tr.: E. S. Steenberg, Copenhagen, Martin, 1913, 264pp.; 1919, 1924, 192pp.; 1929, 286pp.
                       (Danish)
Kurjalistoa, tr.: Kaapo Murros, Hancock, Michigan, Työmichen Kustannusyhtiö, 1911, 277pp.
Kadotuksen kansa, tr.: Kaapo Murros, Helsinki, Otava, 1922, 261pp.
                       (Finnish)
Le peuple de l'abîme, tr.: Paul Gruyer and Louis Postif, Paris, Crès, 1926, 249pp.; Paris, Hachette, 1931, 248pp.
                       (French)
Menschen der Tiefe, tr.: Erwin Magnus, Berlin, Universitas, 1928, 270pp.
____, tr.: E. Magnus, Berlin, Gutenberg, 1929, 275pp.
Volk am Abgrund, introduction by Max Barthel, Berlin, Universitas, 1941, 259pp.
In den Slums, introduction by Max Barthel, Berlin, Universitas, 1942, 235pp.; Berlin, Tribüne, 1960, 278pp.
                       (German)
A mélység, tr.: Soma Braun, Budapest, Athenaeum, 197pp. 1928 (Korunk mesterei). (Összes munkái 12).
A mélység lakói, Budapest, 1948, 155pp. (Nagy elbeszélok. Nyugati irodalom).
                       (Hungarian)
Il popolo dell'abisso, tr.: Gianni d'Arezzo, Milan,

Corticelli, 1928, 239pp.
_____, tr.: Arturo Salucci, Milan, Bietti, 1930, 1933,
249pp.   (Italian)
Naraku no hitobito, tr.: Ritsujiro Wake, Tokyo, Osaka
Mainichi Shinbunsha, 1922.
_____, tr.: Seiki Yamamoto, Tokyo, Ban'yusha, 1950, 311pp.
                                   (Japanese)
Avgrunnens folk, tr.: Inge Debes, Oslo, Gyldendal, 1935,
1947, 208pp.   (Norwegian)
Mieszkańcy otchłani, K. Tarnowska; introduction by
B. Dudziński, Warsaw, Ksiazka i Wiedza, 1950, 231pp.
                                   (Polish)
Avgrundens folk, tr.: M. Drangel, Stockholm, Alb.
Bonnier, 1945, 257pp.   (Swedish)
Na dne Londona [Title in Russian], tr.: A. Ceifi, Kazan,
Tatizdat, 1932, 188pp.   (Tatar)

THE FAITH OF MEN. 1904

26. The Faith of Men | AND OTHER STORIES | BY | JACK LONDON |
AUTHOR OF "THE CALL OF THE WILD," "PEOPLE | OF THE ABYSS,"
ETC., ETC. | New York | THE MACMILLAN COMPANY | LONDON:
MACMILLAN & CO., LTD. | 1904 | *All rights reserved*
    [iv] v [vi][1-2] 3-286p. 19 x 13 cm. Light blue cloth
decorated in white, green, and black. Top edges gilt, all
other edges uncut. Lettering on spine gilt. Lettering on
front cover black. Two pages of publisher's advertisements at back.
    On verso of title-page (p.[iv]): COPYRIGHT, 1904, |
BY THE MACMILLAN COMPANY. | [rule] | Set up, electro-
typed, and published April, 1904. | [Three lines of
press signature]
    Contents: A Relic of the Pliocene; A Hyperborean Brew;
The Faith of Men; Too Much Gold; The One Thousand Dozen;
The Marriage of Lit-Lit; Batard; The Story of Jees Uck.

27. Reprints:
_____, London, Heinemann, 1904, 252pp.; Heinemann, 1914;
Heinemann, 1916, 1931, 189pp.
_____, Chicago, Donohue [1904] 286pp.
_____, New York, Regent Press [1904] [286?]pp.
_____, New York, Leslie-Judge Co., 1925, 286pp.
_____, Macmillan, 1925, New York, 286pp.

28. Translations:
Lüan paljon kultaa ynnä muita kertomuksia Klondykesta,
Dulu, Sanomalehti-osuuskunta Kansas tahta, 1911, 167pp.
                                   (Finnish)

La fede degli uomini, tr.: Maria Carlesimo Pasquali,
Milan, Bietti, 1931, 234pp.   (Italian)

THE SEA-WOLF. 1904

29. THE SEA-WOLF | BY | JACK LONDON | AUTHOR OF "THE CALL OF
THE WILD," "PEOPLE OF THE ABYSS," | "CHILDREN OF THE
FROST," ETC. | *WITH ILLUSTRATIONS BY W. J. AYLWARD* |
New York | THE MACMILLAN COMPANY | LONDON: MACMILLAN & CO.,
LTD. | 1904 | *All rights reserved*
    [vi] vii [viii] 1-366p. 19 x 12.5 cm. Light blue cloth
decorated in white, orange, and dark blue. Top edges
gilt. Lettering on spine gilt. Lettering on front cover
white. Frontis. with tissue guard. Three pages of publisher's advertisements at back.
    On verso of title-page (p.[vi]): COPYRIGHT, 1904 |
BY JACK LONDON. | COPYRIGHT, 1903, 1904, | BY THE
CENTURY COMPANY. | COPYRIGHT, 1904, | BY THE MACMILLAN
COMPANY. | [rule] | Set up and electrotyped. Published
October, 1904. | [Three lines of press signature]
    Spine may be lettered either in gilt or white. Merle
Johnson's *American first editions* says "former probably
first." Many collectors ascribe no priority to either.

30. Serializations:
The Sea-wolf was reprinted from *Century Magazine,*
67:400-413, 584-598, 693-708, 875-887 (Jan.-April 1904);
68:39-53, 290-299, 352-364, 512-524, 770-780, 851-863
(May-Oct. 1904), 69:27-40 (Nov. 1904)

31. Reprints:
____, London, Heinemann, 1904, 324pp.; 1910 (Popular
edition), 320pp.; 1933, 1949, 317pp.; 1905, 182pp.;
1931, 315pp.; 1951, 314pp.
____, London, Newnes, 1913.
____, New York, Grosset & Dunlap,[c1904,][c1916,][1922]
321pp.
____, New York, Grosset & Dunlap, c1904, c1931, 368pp.
____, New York, Regent Press,[c1904,][1912] 366pp.
____, New York, McClure Book Co. [1916][?]pp.
____, New York, Macmillan, 1916, vii, 366pp.; 1926,
c1931, 1939, 1945, 1948, 366pp.
____, New York, Arcadia House, 1950,[c1931] 366pp.
____, Chicago, Donohue, 19[?][?]pp.
____, New York, Grosset, 1941, 321pp. (Madison Square
Books); Grosset, 19[?] 321pp. (Books of distinction);
Grosset and Toronto, McLeod, 1955, 366pp.
____, New York, Pocket Books, 1945, 292pp. (Pocket Books

No. 325).
_____, with an introduction by Lewis Gannett, New York,
Bantam Books, published as a Bantam Classic, Nov. 1960,
Dec. 1960, Dec. 1961, xvii, 252pp. (FC74). This edition
with the Gannett introduction, also published in Feb.
1963 as A Bantam Pathfinder ed., xvii, 252pp. (FP22).
Braille edition (U. S.): Grade 1 1/2. 4 vols.
Braille edition (transcribed for the National Library for
the Blind, London, England): 5 vols. 1934.
Talking books: read by William Lazar. American Foundation
for the Blind. New York. 13 records (re-recorded).
Selection: "Fog," in N. C. Wyeth, ed., *Great stories of
the sea and ships*, Philadelphia, David McKay,[c1940]
pp.212-219.
"Jack London's sketch of 'Wolf Larsen'," San Francisco
Examiner, June 15, 1905, p.2. [Brief selection].

32. Translations:
Morskilat vulk, tr.: Bogdana Radina and Boris Svetlinov;
introduction by Liudmil Stioanov, Sofia, G. Ignatov,
1927, 271pp. (Biseri ot zenameniti romani na vsemirnata
literatura).
Morski vulk, tr.: G. Zhechev and B. Svetlinov, Sofia,
D. Madzharov, 1935, 234pp. (Bibl. Zlanti stranitzi 4).
                              (Bulgarian)
Hai Lang, tr.: Ch'iu Chu-ch'ang, Shanghai, Hsin Wen
i Ch'u Pan She, 1954, 348pp.   (Chinese)
Mořský vlk, tr.: J. Novák, Prague, Vilímek, 1918, 1920,
363pp.
_____, tr.: J. Novák, Prague, Kočí, 1922, 2 vols. (188,
182pp.).
_____, tr.: M. Nekvindová-Nešporová, Zlín, Tisk, 1938,
1948, 383pp.
Morský vlk, tr.: P. Branko, Bratislava, Pravada, 1949,
364pp.   (Czech/Slovak)
Ulf Larsen, tr.: M. C. Jensen, Copenhagen, Peter Hansen,
1910, 344pp.
_____, authorized translation, Aarhus, Hagerup, 1918,
280pp.
_____, Copenhagen, Martin, 1929, 2 vols. (280, 336pp.)
                              (Danish)
De zeewolf, tr.: S. J. Barentz-Schönberg, Amsterdam,
H. J. W. Becht, 1915.
_____, tr.: Martin Deelen, Bussum, Classics Nederland,
1958, 48pp.   (Dutch)
Mere hunt, tr.: J. Parktal, Tallinn, Tallinna Eesti
Kirjastus Ühisus, 1913, 240pp.
_____, tr.: J. Parktal, Tallinn, Ploompuu, 1914, 240pp.

_____, tr.: J. Variste, Tartu, Eesti Kirjastuse Kooper-
atiiv, 1936, 320pp.   (Estonian)
Merisusi, tr.: Helmi Krohn, Helsinki, Otava, 1915, 355pp.;
Otava, 1923, 435pp.; Otava, 1938, 411pp.; Otava, 1953,
327pp.
Susi-Larsen, Turku, Sosialistin kirjapaino osuuskunta,
1915, 455pp.   (Finnish)
Le loup des mers, tr.: Paul Gruyer and Louis Postif,
Paris, Hachette, 1947, 253pp. (Collection Les meilleurs
romans étrangers) [This book was filmed in France as
Le vaisseau fantome].   (French)
Der Seewolf, tr.: Erwin Magnus, Berlin, Universitas, 1926,
325pp.; Universitas, 1927, 337pp.; Berlin, Büchergilde
Gutenberg, 1927, 1934, [?]pp.; bearbeitet von Max Barthel,
Berlin, Dt. Buch-Gemeinschaft, 1939, 315pp.; bearbeitet
von Max Barthel und Helmut Giese, Berlin, Universitas,
1940, 355pp.; bearbeitet von Helmut Giese, Berlin, Universitas, 1947, 335pp.; Zürich, Büchergilde Gutenberg,
1947, 316pp.; Berlin, Universitas, 1949, 335pp.
_____, tr.: Silvia Gartner, Vienna, Ibis, 1949, 410pp.
_____, tr.: Eduard Thorsch, Zürich, Schweizer Druck-
und Verlagshaus, 1950, [?]pp.; Vienna, Wiener Volksbuchverlag, 1950, 304pp.
Die Robbeninsel, tr.: Robert Peterka, Vienna, Österreich,
Rota-Verlag Ges., 1952, 192pp. (Bären-Reihe 61); bearbeitet von Max Barthel, Berlin, Darmstadt, Dt. Buch-
Gemeinschaft, 1954, 355pp.; bearbeitet von Helmut Giese
und Thomas Bünger, Frankfurt am Main, Büchergilde
Gutenberg, 1954, 251pp.; Gütersloh, Bertelsmann-Lesering,
1961, 316pp.   (German)
O phalassolikos, Athens, P. Dimitrakos, 1951, 166pp.
                                       (Greek)
Z'ev ha-yam, tr.: Shimeon Halkin, Tel-Aviv, Idit, 1954,
278pp.   (Hebrew)

A tengeri farkas, tr.: Zsigmond Fulop, Budapest, Athenaeum, 1923, 334pp.; also 1927, Összes munkai 8.
_____, tr.: Zoltán Bartos, Szántó Istvan, Kossuth Kiadó,
two editions published in 1957 by this same firm, 272pp.,
295pp.   (Hungarian)
"Slagsmal um borö", tr.: Bárdur Jakobsson in *Fyrir
Kalrmenn*, Akureyri [1946], pp. 7-22 [A chapter from The
sea-wolf].   (Icelandic)
Il lupo di mare, tr.: G. Prezzolini, Milan, Morreale,
1923, 1924, 316pp.
_____, tr.: Mario Benzi, Sesto S. Giovanni-Milano, Barion,
1929, 399pp.; Barion, 1937, 367pp.
Il lupo dei mari, tr.: G. Sesostra, Milan, Sonzogno, 1927,

313pp.
_____, tr.: Gastone Rossi, Milan, Sonzogno, 1928, [1931],
316pp.
_____, tr.: Aldo Ciatti, Milan, Bietti, 1930, 1935, 1941,
355pp.
_____, Milan, Sonzogno, 1940, 315pp.
                                                        (Italian)
"Júrås Vilkas", tr.: V. Kaija, Liepåjas Atbalss, nos.
109-166 (March 1-Aug. 5, 1912); separately published
Liepåja, Liepåjas Atbalss, 1912, 283pp.
                                                        (Latvian)
Júros vilkas, tr.: Pr. Morkûnas, Kaunas, 1930, 2 vols.
(148, 192pp.)
Júru vilkas, tr.: E. Kuosaite, Vilnius, Valst. grož. lit.
1-kla, 1956, 363pp.   (Lithuanian)
Ulf Larsen, tr.: Nils Lie, Oslo, Gyldendal, 1935, 1943,
1947, 360pp.   (Norwegian)
Gorgue daria, tr.: Djavad Peyman, Teheran, 1960, 324pp.
                                                        (Persian)
Wilk morski, tr.: J. B. Rychliński, Warsaw, Ignis, 1922,
2 vols.; other 2-vol. Ignis editions are those of 1923
(270, 244pp.) and 1924 (259, 243pp.); Warsaw, E. Wende,
1925, 3 vols. (167, 168, 167pp.); Warsaw, E. Kuthan, 1947,
428pp.; Warsaw, Iskry, 1955, 315pp.; Iskry, 1956, 309pp.
_____, tr.: S. Kuszelewska, Rome, War Relief Services,
National Catholic Welfare Conference, 1946, 254pp.
                                                        (Polish)
O lôbo do mar, tr.: Monteiro Lobato, São Paulo, Comp. ed.
nacional, 1934, 322pp. (Obras primas universais 1); 2nd
ed., 1941, 320pp. (Biblioteca do espirito moderno.
Série 4a: Literatura 8); 1954, 306pp. (Colecão "Para
todos" 40; reprinted in 1957, 305pp.)
                                                        (Portuguese)
Lup Larsen, tr.: Dan Dutescu. Cuvînt înainte de Petre
Solomon. Coperta de A. Stoicescu, Bucharest, Editura
tineretului, 1958, 327pp. (Cutezătorii).
                                                        (Rumanian)
Morskoi volk, tr.: D. M. Gorfinkel, Leningrad and Moscow,
Novella, 1924, 272pp.
_____, tr.: Zin. Lvovski and Ye. A. Barot, Leningrad and
Moscow, Mysl, 1925, 1927, 293pp.
_____, tr.: and abridged by E. K. Pimenova, Moscow and
Leningrad, Gosizdat, 1926, 96pp.   (Russian)
Morski vuk, tr.: Branko Kojic, Zagreb, Glas rada, 1953,
274pp.   (Serbian)
"El lobo de mar", *Por esos mundos*, 10:271-280, 366-373,
457-464, 512-519, 11:67-75, 111-120, 251-259, 367-374,
422-429, 497-507, 12:78-85, 138-144, 258-266, 331-338,

567-576, 13:74-81, 109-113 (1905-1906).
El lobo de mar, tr.: Adela Grego, Valencia, Prometeo,
1927, 277pp.
____, supervisión de Hector F. Engel, Buenos Aires,
Editorial Acme, 1955, 224pp. (Colección centauro no. 16).
(Spanish)
Varg-Larsen, tr.: M. Drangel, Stockholm, Bohlin, 1909,
411pp.; 1910, 400pp.; 1914, 349pp., 1926, 432pp.
____, Stockholm, B. Wahlstrom, 1914, 256pp.
____, Stockholm, Bjorck & Borjesson, 1916, 318pp.
(Berömda böcker 62-63).
____, Stockholm, Dahlberg, 1919, 336pp.
____, Stockholm, Romanbibliotek, 1922, 2 vols.
____, tr.: Lisbeth & Louis Renner, Stockholm, Forum,
1953, 291pp.
____, tr.: Hans G. Westerlund, Stockholm, Folket, 1958,
303pp.
Haavargen, tr.: A. Berg, Stockholm, Holmquist, 1917,
2 vols. (Swedish)
Morskoi volk [Title in Russian] Kiev, Goslitizdat
Ukrainy, 1958, 278pp. (Ukranian)

WAR OF THE CLASSES. 1905

33. War of the Classes | BY | JACK LONDON | AUTHOR OF "THE
SEA-WOLF," "THE CALL OF | THE WILD," ETC. | New York |
THE MACMILLAN COMPANY | LONDON: MACMILLAN & CO., LTD. |
1905 | *All rights reserved*
[iv] v-xvii [xviii] xix [xx][1-2] 3-278p. 19 x 12.5 cm.
Dark red cloth. Lettering on spine gilt. Three pages of
publisher's advertisements at back. Also noted in gray
paper wrappers, lettered in black on front cover.
On verso of title-page (p.[iv]): COPYRIGHT, 1905 |
BY THE MACMILLAN COMPANY. | [rule] | Set up and electro-
typed. Published April, 1905. | [Three lines of press
signature]
Contents: The Class Struggle; The Tramp; The Scab; The
Question of the Maximum; A Review; Wanted: A New Law of
Development; How I Became a Socialist.
The paper wrappers copy in the George H. Tweney collection is dated 1906 at the bottom of the title page,
otherwise collates internally exactly as the first
edition. It is not known if there was a paper wrappers
edition dated the same year as the red cloth first edition, 1905. The paper wrappers are slate gray color.

34. Reprints:
____, London, Heinemann, 1905, xix, 278pp.

_____, London, Mills & Boon, 1920, 217pp.
_____, New York, Regent Press, 1905, xix, 278pp.
_____, New York, Grosset & Dunlap [c1905, 1908] 278pp.
_____, New York, Macmillan, 1910, 1912, xviii, 278pp.
_____, Chicago, M. A. Donohue [1912] 278pp.
Selections appear in Foner. "Stolen thunder," in H. R.
Warfel and Stanley Williams, eds., *American mind,* New
York, American Book Co., 1947, pp.1005-1007.

35. Translations:
Klassernes kamp, tr.: Knud Poulsen, Copenhagen, Martin,
1926, 160pp.   (Danish)
Luokkien sota, Kustantaja, Amerikan Suom. Sosialististen
Kustannusliikkeiden, 1923, 149pp.   (Finnish)
Borba klassov, Petrograd, Nevskaya Tipografiya, 1918, 77pp.
_____, tr.: D. Ye. Deikhtenberg, edited and with an intro-
duction by D. O. Zaslovski, Leningrad, Mysl, 1924, 152pp.
                        (Russian)

THE GAME. 1905

36. THE GAME | BY JACK LONDON | AUTHOR OF "PEOPLE OF THE
ABYSS," "THE CALL | OF THE WILD," "THE SEA-WOLF," ETC. |
[vignette] | *WITH ILLUSTRATIONS AND DECORATIONS BY* |
HENRY HUTT AND T. C. LAWRENCE | New York | THE MACMILLAN
COMPANY | LONDON: MACMILLAN & CO., LTD. | 1905 | *All
rights reserved*
    [14] 15-182p. 19 x 13 cm. Green cloth decorated in
white and brown. Top edges gilt. Lettering on spine gilt.
Lettering on front cover red. Frontis. in color with
tissue guard, included in pagination. Six pages of publisher's advertisements at back.
    On verso of title-page (p.[6]): [vignette] | COPYRIGHT,
1905, | BY THE MACMILLAN COMPANY. | [rule] | Set up and
electrotyped. Published June, 1905. | [vignette]
[Three lines of press signature]
    The dust wrapper is of stiff powder-blue paper lettered
in deep red. The binding and wrapper are identical in
type; the latter does not have the white and brown decoration of the cover of the binding.
    The second issue is rubber stamped on the copyright
page; Copyright 1905, | By the Metropolitan Magazine Co.
    In the George H. Tweney collection there is a rare
advance issue of *The game*. It is bound in light tan paper
wrappers, with both the front wrapper and the title page
as follows:
    The Game | by | Jack London | Author of "People of the
Abyss," "The Call | of the Wild," "The Sea-Wolf," etc. |

New York | The Macmillan Company | London: Macmillan
& Co., Ltd. | 1905 | *All rights reserved*
    19 x 12 cm. Front wrapper lettered as above, half-
title, publisher's mark, title-page lettered as above,
copyright page (Published May, 1905), text, pp. 1-102,
blank leaf, back wrapper.
    This may have been a pre-publication pamphlet for re-
view purposes, or it may have been privately distributed
for other reasons. It appears to include all of the textual material as in the first edition, but without any of
the illustrative material.
    In the John London collection there is a copy of both
the first issue without the *Metropolitan Magazine* rubber
stamp on the copyright page, and there is also a copy of
the second issue with the rubber stamp. Collectors should
be warned to examine this page carefully when evaluating
a first edition, as there are known copies in which the
rubber stamp has been erased to make a spurious first
issue out of a bona-fide second issue.

37. Serializations:
The Game was published serially in the *Metropolitan Magazine*, 22:1-8, (April 1905), 22:181-193 (May 1905). It
was published serially in *The Tatler*, 16:12, 14, viii
(April 5, 1905), 52, 54 (April 12, 1905), 92, 94 (April
19, 1905), 132, 134 (April 26, 1905).

38. Reprints:
____, London, Heinemann, 1905, 184pp.; 1913, 93pp.
(Heinemann's seven-penny net novels); 1930, 214pp.; 1932,
254pp.
____, New York, Macmillan, 1910, 182pp.
____, New York, Grosset & Dunlap, 1913, 182pp.
____, New York, Regent Press, 1913, 182pp.
____, Chicago, Donohue, 19[?]pp.

39. Translations:
Berbata na ringa, tr.: G. Zhechev, Sofia, D. Madzharov,
1936, 58pp. [This translation was made from the Russian
rather than from the English.]   (Bulgarian)
Sport, tr.: J. P. Wesselink-van Rossum, Utrecht, A. W.
Bruna & Zoon Uitgevers,[n.d.,]192pp. (Bruna's
Bibliotheek).   (Dutch)
Viimeinen ottelu, tr.: Einari Merikallio, Helsinki,
Urheilijain kustannus oy, 1917, 105pp.
                                       (Finnish)
"Le jeu du ring," tr.: Paul Gruyer and Louis Postif, *Les
oeuvres libres*, no. 71:109-158 (1927); Paris, Crès,

1928, 231pp.   (French)
A játék, tr.: Zoltán Bartos, Budapest, Pantheon, 1922,
100pp.; reprinted under the title of *Játék az élettel,*
Budapest, Légrády, 1925, 139pp.   (Hungarian)
Il romanzo di un boxeur, tr.: G. Rossi, Milan, Sonzogno,
1928, 96pp.   (Italian)
"Lošimas," tr.: Keidošius, *Sportas,* Dec. 28, 1956, Jan. 4,
15, 18, 1957, Feb. 1, 19, 1957, March 15, 19, 20, 1957.
                                      (Lithuanian)

TALES OF THE FISH PATROL. 1905

40. TALES OF THE FISH | PATROL | BY | JACK LONDON | AUTHOR OF
"THE SEA-WOLF," "PEOPLE OF THE | ABYSS," "THE CALL OF THE
WILD," ETC. | *WITH ILLUSTRATIONS BY* | *GEORGE VARIAN* |
New York | THE MACMILLAN COMPANY | LONDON: MACMILLAN & CO.,
LTD. | 1905 | *All rights reserved*
   [10] 11-243p. 19 x 12.5 cm. Dark blue cloth decorated
in yellow, green, and blue. Lettering on spine gilt.
Lettering on front cover pale green. Top edges gilt.
Frontis. Three pages of publisher's advertisements at
back.
   On verso of title-page (p.[4]): COPYRIGHT, 1905, |
BY PERRY MASON COMPANY. | COPYRIGHT, 1905, | BY THE MAC-
MILLAN COMPANY. | [rule] | Set up and electrotyped. Pub-
lished September, 1905. | [Three lines of press signa-
ture]
   Contents: White and Yellow; The King of the Greeks;
A Raid on the Oyster Pirates; The Siege of the "Lanca-
shire Queen"; Charley's Coup; Demetrios Contos; Yellow
Handkerchief. Merle Johnson's *American First Editions*
states, "Two states of binding; no established priority."

41. Reprints:
   ____, Chicago, Donohue,[n.d.,][?]pp.
   ____, London, Heinemann, 1906, 243pp.; 1914, 158pp.
(Heinemann's seven-penny net novels); 1916, 158pp.
   ____, abbreviated and simplified for use in schools
(Easy readers), Copenhagen, Grafisk Forlag, 1952, 60pp.

42. Translations:
   Zukles sargybinio pasakojimai, tr.: D. Judelevičius,
Kaunas, Valst. grož. lit. 1-kla, 1947, 154pp. Contents:
Baltieji ir geltonieji. Žygis prieš austriu piratus.
"Lankaširo karalienes" apgula. Čarlio "Coup". Demetrijus
Kontas. Geltonoji Skara. [The order is the same as the
original.]   (Lithuanian)
   Patruilbaten, tr.: Ernst Grafstrom, Stockholm, Holmquist,

1913, 1917, 1918, 156pp.
Fiskepatrullens berättelser, tr.: Ernst Lundquist, bound
with *Pa kryss med Blixten,* Stockholm, Bohlin, 1917, 1921,
1924, [?]pp. (Swedish)

MOON-FACE. *1906*

43. MOON-FACE | AND OTHER STORIES | BY | JACK LONDON | AUTHOR
OF "THE CALL OF THE WILD," "PEOPLE | OF THE ABYSS," ETC.,
ETC. | New York | THE MACMILLAN COMPANY | LONDON: MAC-
MILLAN & CO., LTD. | 1906 | *All rights reserved*
[iv] v [vi][1-2] 3-273p. 19 x 13 cm. Dark blue cloth
decorated in gilt and green. Top edges gilt, other edges
uncut. Spine and front cover lettered in light green.
Four pages of publisher's advertisements at back.
On verso of title-page (p.[iv]): COPYRIGHT, 1906, |
BY THE MACMILLAN COMPANY. | [rule] | Set up and electro-
typed. Published September, 1906. | [Three lines of press
signature]
Contents: Moon-Face; The Leopard Man's Story; Local
Color; Amateur Night; The Minions of Midas; The Shadow
and the Flash; All Gold Canyon; Planchette.
Merle Johnson's *American First Editions* states, "An advance copy at the Library of Congress has no month of
publication on the copyright page."

44. Reprints:
_____, New York, Grosset & Dunlap, [c1906]273pp.
_____, Chicago, New York, M. A. Donohue, [c1906]273pp.
_____, Regent Press, New York, [c1906]273pp.
_____, London, Heinemann, 1906, 280pp.; Heinemann, 1914;
Heinemann, 1916, 1931, 159pp.
_____, New York, Grosset & Dunlap, 191[?]273pp.

45. Translations:
Uplněk, tr.: J. Bartos, Prague, Koci, 1925, 156pp. Contents: Uplněk. Povídka krotitele leopardu. Místní
zabarveni. Ochotnicky vecer. Stin a blesk. Zlata souteska.
Trinozka. (Czech/Slovak)
Maaneansigt, tr.: Knud Poulsen, Copenhagen, Martin, 1921,
171pp. (Danish)
Mondgesicht, tr.: Erwin Magnus, Berlin, Universitas, 1928,
254pp. Contents: Lokalkolorit. Mondgesischt. Die
geschichte vom Leopardenmann. Amateurabend. Die lieblinge
des Midas. Der Schatten und das Funkeln. Die Goldschlucht.
Die Planchette. (German)
Leopardmannen, tr.: C. Helander, Oslo, Gyldendal, 1941,
159pp. (Norwegian)

Månansiktet och andra historier, tr.: Ernst Lundquist, Stockholm, Bohlin, 1925, 1927, 188pp.
Månansiktet och andra berattelser, tr.: Oscar Nachman, Stockholm, Holmquist, 1914, 115pp.; 1914, 208pp.; 1918, 170pp.
Månansiktet, Stockholm, Dahlberg, 1919, 215pp.; Roman-biblioteket, 1922, 223pp.

(Swedish)

WHITE FANG. 1906

46. WHITE FANG | BY | JACK LONDON | AUTHOR OF "THE CALL OF THE WILD," "THE | SEA WOLF," ETC., ETC. | New York | THE MACMILLAN COMPANY | LONDON: MACMILLAN & CO., LTD. | 1906 | *All rights reserved*
     [iv] v-vii [viii-x][1-2] 3-327p. 19 x 13 cm. Gray cloth decorated in white and black. Lettering on spine gilt. Lettering on front cover white. Frontis. in color with tissue guard. Four pages of publisher's advertisements at back.
     On verso of title-page (p.[iv]): COPYRIGHT, 1905 | BY JACK LONDON. | COPYRIGHT, 1906, | BY THE OUTING PUB-LISHING COMPANY. | COPYRIGHT, 1906, | BY THE MACMILLAN COMPANY. | [rule] | Set up and electrotyped. Published October, 1906. | [Three lines of press signature]
     The illustrations, frontispiece, and those illustrations opposite pp.72, 128, 152, 190, 228, 276, 314 are often missing.
     The first issue does not have a tipped-in title-page; copies are fairly uncommon with the title-page as a part of the signature.

47. Serializations:
     The novel originally ran serially in *Outing Magazine,* 48:129-141, 395-423, 449-470, 589-604, 708-716 (May-Sept. 1906), 49:65-81 (Oct. 1906).
     In Great Britain it ran serially in *T. P.'s Weekly,* 8:429-432, 463-465, 495-497, 527-528, 559-561, 595-597, 627-629, 663-664, 695-697, 727-729, 767-768, 811-812, 845-847 (Oct. 5-Dec. 28, 1906), 9:7-8, 39-41, 71-72, 103-104, 136-137, 167-169 (Jan. 4-Feb. 8, 1907).

48. Reprints:
     ____, New York, Grosset & Dunlap [1906] [?]pp.; [1914] vi, 327pp.; [c1933] 276pp.; [1939?] 276pp. [A Thrushwood book]; 194[?] vi, 329pp.; 19[?] 330pp. [Favorite book of younger generation]; 1937, 330pp. [Juveniles of distinction]; 1950, 276pp. [Famous dog stories].

____, New York, Washington Square Press, 1965, 233pp.
plus "Reader's supplement for greater understanding and
appreciation of *White Fang* by Jack London," 39pp. [Read-
er's enrichment series RE 119].
No Jack London title has had a longer printing history in
Great Britain than *White Fang*. Methuen & Co. of London,
while seriously misusing the term edition, has produced
the following editions and printings:
Modern classics (abridged) edition: 1st, 1925; 2nd, 1927;
3rd, 1928; 4th, 1929; 5th, 1932; 6th, 1933; 7th, 1934;
8th, 1935; 9th, 1936; 10th, 1937; 11th, 1938.
The copyright page of the so-called 32nd edition gives
the following printing history; material in brackets has
been supplied from other sources:
First published (Crown 8vo), Feb. 1907; 2nd-5th ed., 1907
[4th, Colonial Library, 310pp.]; 6th, 1908 [Colonial
Library, 310pp. plus firm's March 1909 catalogue]; 7th,
1909; 8th, 1911; 9th, 1913.
10th, 1914 (Fcap, 8vo, cheap form) [248pp.]; 11th, 1915;
12-14th, 1916; 15th, 1918; 16th-17th ed., 1919; 18th,
1920; 19th, 1922 (Crown 8vo).
20th, 1922 (Fcap, 8vo, cheap form); 21st, 1923 (Crown 8vo,
cheap form); 22nd, 1924; 23rd-24th, 1925; 25th, 1926
(Fcap, 8vo); 26th, 1927 (Crown 8vo, cheap form); 27th,
1929; 28th, 1929 [290pp. with frontispiece in color and
12 other illustrations by D. C. Eyles]; 29th, 1932 (Crown
8vo, cheap form).
30th, 1932 (Fcap, 8vo, cheap form); 31st, 1932 (Fcap,
8vo); 32nd, 1933 (Fcap, 8vo, cheap form); 33rd, 1934
(Crown 8vo, cheap form); 34th, 1935 (Fcap, 8vo, cheap
form); 35th ed., 1937 (Crown, 8vo, cheap form).
____, London, Nelson & Sons [1908] 284pp. (Nelson's
Library).
____, New York, Macmillan, 1914, vii, 327pp.; [c1934]
1946, 329pp.
____, New York, Regent Press [1914, c1906] vii, 327pp.
____, London, George Newnes [1914] 124pp. (Newnes' 6d
Copyright Novels).
____, Chicago, M. A. Donohue [1914] [?]pp.
Braille editions (U.S.): Grade 2, 4 vols. Grade 1 1/2,
handcopied. Press-Braille, Braille Institute of America,
Los Angeles, California, 1948, 2 vols. English Braille,
[n.d.] 1 vol.
Braille edition (transcribed for the National Library for
the Blind, London, England): 3 vols., 1922.
Talking books: read by Jim Sickle. American Printing
House for the Blind, 8 records. 1957 (re-recorded).

49. Translations:
_____ ... Adapted for the 7th and 8th classes of the secondary school. Tallinn, Pedagoogiline Kirjandus, 1940, 72pp.
_____, Georg Schnöckelborg ed., Paderborn, Schöningh, 1954, 95pp. (Schöninghs engl. Schulausgaben 118).
Dhëmbi i bardhë, tr.: Bujar Doko, Tirana, Ndermarrja Shteterore e Botimeve, 1958, 160pp.
                                                    (Albanian)
Belyi klyk [title given in Russian translation] tr.: V. Mikaelian, Erevan, Armgiz, 1946, 256pp.
                                                    (Armenian)
Belyi klyk [Title in Russian], Minsk, Gizbel., 1939, 204pp.   (Belorussian)
Beliiat zub, tr.: M. Seizova-Iurukova, Sofia, Suglasie, 194pp. (Mozaika ot znameniti cuvremenni romani XXIII. Bezp. premiia).
_____, tr.: G. Mikhăilov, Sofia, Sluntze, 1946, 222pp.
_____, tr.: Asen G. Khristoforov, Sofia, Nar. mladezh, 1956, 220pp. (B-ka Prikliucheniia i nauchna fantastika. Za sredna i gorna uchilishchna vuzrast).
                                                    (Bulgarian)
Hsüeh Hu, tr.: Chiang T'ien-tso, Peking, Jen Min Wen Hsüeh Ch'u Pan She, 1955, 257pp.   (Chinese)
Bijeli ocnjak, tr.: Mihailo Djordjevic, Sarajevo, Svjetlost, 1957, 240pp.   (Croatian)
Bílý tesák, tr. H. Jost, Prague, Neumannová, 1913, 229pp.; 1920, 382pp.; Prague, Koči, 1924, 1928, 126pp.
_____, tr.: B. Z. Nekovařík, Zlin, Tisk, 1936, 246pp.; 1948, 239pp.; tr.: Nekovařík, introduction by D. Šajner, Prague, ELK, 1947, 275pp.; tr.: Nekovařík, Prague, Práce, 1949, 98pp.; tr.: Nekovařík, introduction by J. Langer, Prague, Stát. nakl.; dětské knihy, 1950, 333pp.
_____, Prague, Melentrich, 1939, 166pp.
_____, tr.: V. Svoboda, Prague, Stát. nakl. dětské knihy, 1957, 225pp.
Biely tesák, tr.: P. Branko; Bratislava, Smena, 1952, 205pp.; tr.: Branko, introduction by Z. Klátik, Bratislava, Šlov. wyd. detskej knihy, 1955, 190pp.
                                                    (Czech/Slovak)
Pit-tah, de grijze wolf, tr.: S. J. Barentz-Schönberg, Amsterdam, H. J. W. Becht, 1910.
Wittand, de wolfshond, Bussum, Het Goede Boek [1948] 220pp.
Wittand, tr.: Martin Deelen, Bussum, Classics Nederland, 1957, 47pp.   (Dutch)
Valgekihv, Tallinn, Ploompuu, 1913, 195pp.; Tallinn, Tallinna Eesti Kirjastus ühisus, 1913, 195pp.; Tallinn,

Kirjastus-Osasühisus "Kaja", 1923, 160pp.
____, tr.: M. Sillaots, Tallinn, Eesti Riiklik Kirjastus, 1956, 212pp. (Series: Seiklusjutte maalt ja merelt).
(Estonian)
Belyi klyk [Title in Russian] tr.: D. Vengerov, Moscow, 1957, 311pp. (Evreiskian)
Valkohammas, tr.: Kaapo Murros, Turku, Socialistin kirja-posuuskunta, 1910, 211pp.
____, tr.: Toivo Wallenius, Helsinki, Helsingin Kaiku, 1911, 272pp.
Susikoira, tr.: Antii Rykkonen, Helsinki, Helsingin kustannusoy, 1911, 350pp.
____, tr.: Toivo Wallenius, Helsinki, Otava, 1918, 260pp.; Otava, 1937, 310pp.
____, [in Cyrillic character] Petrozavodsk, Valtion kustannusliike Kirja, 1935, 177pp.
Susien saaliina, Helsinki, Otava, 1913, 32pp. (first 3 chapters). (Finnish)
Croc-blanc, tr.: Paul Gruyer and Louis Postif, Paris, Crès, 1922, 280pp.; Paris, Plon, 1927, 207pp.; (Nouvelle bibliothèque Plon); Paris, Hachette, 1932, 264pp; Paris, Plon, 1938, 253pp.; Paris, Hachette, 1945, 256pp. (Bibliothèque verte). (French)
Wolfsblut, tr.: Marie Laue, Freiburg i. Br., F. E. Fehsenfeld, 1912, 419pp. (included in *Die Welt der Fahrten und Abenteuer*, vols. 8-9); Freiburg i. Br., Fehsenfeld, 1926, 294pp.; Berlin, Universitas, 1928, 285pp.; Freiburg i. Br., Fehsenfeld, 1931, 282pp.; Hamburg, Dt. Buch-Gemeinschaft, 1948, 269pp.; Freiburg, Die Brücke, 1949, 79pp.; Hamburg, Rowohlt, 1951, 195pp. (Rororo Taschenbuch 19); reprinted in 1952, 149pp. Leipzig, List, 1953, 1954, 1955, 1959, 233pp.; Munich, List, 1955, 184pp. (List Bücher 52); Berlin, Kultur und Fortschritt, 1958, 228pp.; Frankfurt, Büchergilde Guten-berg, 1959, 227pp.
____, tr.: Fritz Benke, Linz & Vienna, Ibis, 1948, 257pp.; Munich & Leipzig, List, 1947, 213pp.; Vienna, Dt. Buch-Gemeinschaft, 1945, 245pp.
____, tr.: Erika Ziha, Vienna, Buchgemeinschaft Donauland, 1958, 299pp.
Eine Beute der Wölfe, Berlin, Leipzig, Hillger, 1912, 32pp. (Deutsche Jugendbücherei 78); Stuttgart, Reclam, 1949, 1960, 80pp. (Reclams Universal-Bibliothek 7615); Deutsche Jugendbücherei reprinted in Berlin, Dt. Jugend-bücherei, 1953, 32pp. [Selections from novel with no tr. given].
Wolfszahn, tr.: Eduard Thorsch, Zurich, Schweizer Druck-und Verlagshaus, 1947, 279pp.

Weisszahn, der Wolfssohn, tr.: Romana Segantini, Zurich, Rascher, 1948, 296pp. (Abenteurerbücher für die Jugend).
(German)
Fsrkasvér, tr.: Pécsi Mária Dobosi, Budapest, Singer-Wolfner, 1922, 232pp.; other editions of this translation are those of 1922, 1924, 1925, 214pp.; 1930 (Rózsaszin regények 12); 1943, Budapest, Forrás ny., 189pp. (A kalandregény mestere); Budapest, Uj idők, 1949, 208pp.
(Hungarian)
Mac an mhac tíre, tr.: An t-Athair Tadhg Ó Cúrnáin, Baile Átha Cliath [Dublin] Oifig Díolta Foillseacháin Rialtais, 1936, 6 + 296pp.   (Irish)
Zanna bianca, Milan, Modernissima, 1925, 299pp.
____, tr.: Gian Dàuli, Milan, Modernissima, 1928, 222pp.; Milan, Cavallotti, 1948, [?]pp.
____, tr.: Gastone Rossi, Milan, Sonzogno, 1928, 315pp.; Sonzogno, 1941, [?]pp.
____, tr.: Quirino Maffi, Milan, Bietti, 1930, 350pp.; 1933, 347pp.
____, tr.: Elsa Cugini, Sesto S. Giovanni-Milano, Barion, 1937, 335pp.; 1941, [?]pp.
____, tr.: Dora Mangold Favilli, Milan, Corticelli, 1946, [?]pp.
____, tr.: Aurelia Nutini, Florence, Berporad-Marzocco, 1949, 205pp.; 4th ed., 1957, 184pp.; 5th ed., 1959, 204pp.
____, tr.: A. Locatelli, Turin-Milan-Genoa, S. E. I., 1953, 267pp.
____, tr.: Laura Ferajorni Guicciardi, Turin, S. A. S., 1953, 332pp.; Turin, S. A. I. E., 1955, 328pp.; 1958, 224pp.
____, tr.: Beatrice Boffito, Milan Rizzoli, 1953, 280pp.
____, tr.: Bruno Paltrinieri, Milan, Fabbri, 1955, 152pp.
____, tr.: Maria Antonietta Canda, Milan, Vallardi, 1956, 184pp.
____, tr.: A. Locatelli, Turin, Società editrice internazionale, 1965, 267pp.
"Amore fra i lupi," in *Le più belle storie della foresta,* tr.: Elena Spagnol, [Milan] Bompiani, c1964, pp.131-135 [Brief selection from *Zanna bianca*].
____, Milan, Cino del Duca, 1965, 245pp.
(Italian)
Shiroi kiba, tr.: Kihachi Kitamura, Tokyo, Shinchosa, 1940, 306pp. (Shincho bunko); in *Sekai bungaku zenshu,* 2nd series, vol. 9, Tokyo, Shinchosha, 1931.
____, tr.: Kensho Honda, Tokyo, Iwanami Shoten, 1957, 303pp.
____, Tokyo, Shincho-sha, 304pp., 1958.
Areno ni umarete, Tokyo, Iwanami Shoten, 1936, 303pp.

(Iwanami bunko).
White Fang, tr.: Toshihiko Sakai, Tokyo, Kaizosha, 1929, 313pp. (Kaizo bunko); Tokyo Sobunkaku, 1925, 349pp.
____, Huntington 338265 is a Japanese translation. [Originally copyrighted by Jack London in U. S. A., copyrighted in Japan by George Thomas Folster. This book is published in Japan by arrangement with Mr. George Thomas Folster. 317pp.]   (Japanese)
Belyi klyk [Title in Russian] tr. from the Russian by N. Volzhinoĭ and G. Sebepov, Alma-Ata, Kazakh. gos. izd., 1948, 204pp.   (Kazakh)
Baltoji iltis, tr.: K. Riška, Kaunas, "Iliustruoto Pasaulio" biblioteka no. 6, 1938, 224pp.
____, tr.: St. Navickas, Vilnius, Valst. grož. lit. 1-kla, 1949, 207pp.
Kolo alb, tr.: Mircja Aleksandresku and Marius Mejurjanu, Kisinev, Skoala sovetike, 1958, 221pp. Translated from the Rumanian.   (Moldavian)
Ulvehunden, tr.: Alf Harbitz, Oslo, Gyldendal, 1952, 176pp.   (Norwegian)
Biały Kieł, tr.: S. Luszelewska, Warsaw, Rój, 3 vols. in 2 (127, 128, 261pp.); other editions of this translation are: Warsaw, Rój, 1928, 1937; Łódź, Ksiazka, 1947; Kraków, Ksiazka, 1948; Warsaw, Ksiazka i Wiedza, 1949.
____, tr.: A. Przedpełska-Trzeciakowska, Warsaw, Iskry, 1955, 1956, 233pp.   (Polish)
Caninos brancos, tr.: Monteiro Lobato, São Paulo, Comp. ed. nacional, 1933, 189pp. (Coleçãu Terramear 12); 1954, 227pp.   (Portuguese)
Colt alb, tr.: G. M. Amza, Bucharest, G. M. Amza, 1941, 239pp.

____, tr.: Mircea Alexandrescu and Marius Măgureanu, Bucharest, Editura tineretului, 1955, 184 + 6; 1959, 1961, 223pp.
Supusul zeilor, tr.: C. Sp. Popescu, Bucharest, Casa Scoalelor, 1928, 336pp.   (Rumanian)
Bely klyk, tr.: A. Kutukova, Moscow, Universalnaya Biblioteka, 1917, 320pp.
____, tr.: Rubinova, Moscow, Yunaya Rossiya, 1918, 192pp.
____, tr.: Ye. A. Barot and Zin. Lvovski, Leningrad, Mysl, 1925, 1926, 193pp.
____, tr.: Z. Lvovski, Leningrad, Seyatel, 1926, 292pp.
____, Moscow, Tsentralny Komitet Soyuza Tekstilshchikov, 1927, 1928, 119pp.
____, tr.: N. Volzhina, Moscow and Leningrad, Izdatelstvo Datskoi Literatury, 1936, 286pp.; 1937, 276pp.; 1937, 207pp. [A juvenile publication].
____, tr.: N. Volzhinoi, Moscow, Goslitizdat, 1954, 184pp.;

Kaliningrad, 1959, 185pp.; Tambov, 1960, 184pp.
(Russian)
Beli očnjak, tr.: Mihailo Djordjević, Belgrade, Izdanje
Novo pokolenje, 1946, 282 + 6pp.; Sarajevo, Svjetlost,
1957, 254pp.
_____, tr.: Andreja Miličević and *Glas divljine,* tr.:
Borivoje Nedić, Belgrade, Rad, 1961, 320pp.
(Serbian)
_____, tr.: Pavel Holeček, Ljubljana, Mladinska knjiga,
1957, 280pp. (Slovanian)
Colmillo blanco, tr.: Ramón D. Perés, Barcelona, Gili,
1925, 252pp.; (Colección selecta internacional). [Con-
tains a "Próloge del traductor," pp.1-4] Barcelona, Molino,
1954; 254pp.; Buenos Aires, Siglo XX, 1945, 250pp.; also
in Biblioteca Billiken No. 39.
_____, tr.: José Novo Cerro, Buenos Aires, México, Espasa
Calpe, 1947, 209pp. (Colección Austral no. 766).
_____, tr.: Elena Dukelsky, Buenos Aires, Biblioteca
nueva, 1948, 256pp.
_____, Madrid. Imprenta Diana, 1950, 95pp.
_____, tr.: Manuel Barbera, Buenos Aires, Acme, 1951,
286pp.; Acme, 1954, 284pp. (3rd ed.) (Colección Robin
Hood).
_____, tr.: Arturo Avellano, Barcelona, Aymá, 1955, 229pp.
_____, tr.: Maria Angelica Lamas de Corboda, Buenos Aires,
Editorial Sopena Argentina, 1955, 173pp. (Biblioteca
Mundial Sopena).
_____, no tr. given, Santiago de Chile, Editorial Zig-Zag,
1960, 178pp. (Biblioteca juvenil. Serie amarilla no. 17).
El lobo durmiente, Santiago, Imprenta Selecta, 1933,
111pp. [This is the title of the second volume of the
translation of White fang; *Colmillo blanco* is the title
of vol. 1]. (Spanish)
Varghunden, tr.: M. Drangel, Stockholm, Bohlin, 1908,
1910, 1912, 336pp.; 1916, 222pp.; 1920, 1925, 297pp.
_____, tr.: E. Grafström, Stockholm, Wahlstrom, 1917,
192pp.
_____, tr.: Tom Wilson, Uppsala, Lindblads, 1954, 207pp.
_____, tr.: Gemma Funtek-Snellman, Stockholm, Lindqvist,
1957, 192pp. (Enkronasböckerna 1).
(Swedish)
Kurt hücumu, tr.: Hayrullah Örs-Mustafa Nihat Özön, Istanbul, Cumhuriyet Basimevi, 1944, 30pp.; 2nd ed. of same
publisher, 1944, 31pp.
Kurt kani, tr.: Behçet Cemal, Istanbul, Doğan Kardeş
Yayinlari A. Ş. Basimevi, 1955, 143pp.
(Turkish)
Bilyj zub, tr.: M. Riabovoi, Kiev, Detizdat, 1939, 216pp.

____, tr.: O. Syncenko, Kiev, Goslitizdat Ukrainy, 1957, 190pp. (Ukranian)

SCORN OF WOMEN. 1906

50. SCORN OF WOMEN | *IN THREE ACTS* | BY | JACK LONDON | AUTHOR OF "THE CALL OF THE WILD," | "WHITE FANG," ETC., ETC. | New York | THE MACMILLAN COMPANY | LONDON: MACMILLAN & CO., LTD. | 1906 | *All rights reserved*
   [iv] v [vi] vii [viii] ix-x [1-2] 3-256p. 17.5 x 12 cm. Red cloth with white spine. Top edges gilt. Lettering on spine black. Lettering on front cover white. Three pages of publisher's advertisements at back.
   On verso of title-page (p.[iv]): COPYRIGHT, 1906, | BY THE MACMILLAN COMPANY. | [rule] | Set up and electrotyped. Published November, 1906. | [Three lines of press signature]

51. Reprints:
   ____, New York, Macmillan, 1907, x, 256pp.
   ____, London, Macmillan, 1907, 266pp.

BEFORE ADAM. 1907

52. BEFORE ADAM | BY | JACK LONDON | AUTHOR OF | "THE CALL OF THE WILD," "THE SEA | WOLF," "PEOPLE OF THE ABYSS," | "WHITE FANG," ETC., ETC. | WITH NUMEROUS ILLUSTRATIONS BY | CHARLES LIVINGSTON BULL | New York | THE MACMILLAN COMPANY | LONDON: MACMILLAN & CO., LTD. | 1907 | *All rights reserved*
   [vi] vii [viii-ix][x-xi map][xii] 1-242p. 19 x 13 cm. Tan pebble-grain cloth. Red lettering outlined in white on cover and spine. Six animal footprints in brown diagonally across binding, from lower spine to upper right corner of front cover. Frontis. in colors. Four pages of publisher's advertisements at back. Pages uncut.
   On verso of title-page (p.[iv]): COPYRIGHT, 1906, | BY JACK LONDON. | COPYRIGHT, 1906, 1907, | BY THE RIDGEWAY COMPANY. | COPYRIGHT, 1907, | BY THE MACMILLAN COMPANY | [rule] | Set up and electrotyped. Published February, 1907. | [Three lines of press signature]
   The dust wrapper is of the same design, printed in dark red. The George H. Tweney Collection contains two copies of the first edition. One of these is described above; the other has the title on the spine, also the publisher's name, both printed in red, and not outlined in white. Both copies are almost mint condition so it

cannot be caused by the white outline wearing away in the
one copy. No priority of issue can be established. Another explanation is that there was an omission in the
stamping process on the copy lacking the white outline.

53. Serializations:
    Before Adam was serialized in *Everybody's Magazine*, 15:445-
    455, 614-623, 844-852 (Oct.-Dec. 1906); 16:107-115, 251-
    257 (Jan.-Feb. 1907).

54. Reprints:
    ____, London, T. W. Laurie, 1908, 1910 (popular ed.),
    308pp.; 1911, [?]pp.; 1916, 96pp.; 1929, 192pp. (Eclectic
    Library), 1933, 191pp.
    ____, Chicago, M. A. Donohue, [1912] [?]pp.
    ____, London, W. Collins, 1913, 1925, 250pp.
    ____, London, Mills & Boon, 1916, 192pp.; 1922, 188pp.
    ____, Chicago, M. A. Donohue, [1917] 228pp.
    ____, London, London Book Co., [1928] 250pp. (Novel
    library).
    ____, biographical introduction by Willy Ley; epilogue
    by Loren Eiseley, illustrated by Leonard Everett Fisher,
    Macmillan, New York, London, 1962, 172pp.

55. Translations:
    Do Adama, tr.: S. Gjulikehvjan, Erevan, Ajpetrat, 1962,
    202pp.   (Armenian)
    Do Adama, Baku, 1926, 84pp.   (Azerbaidjani)
    Predi Adama, tr.: Petko Stoianov, Sofia, Iv.Koiumdzhiev,
    1933, 128pp.   (Bulgarian)
    Prije Adama, tr.: Viatko Saric, Zagreb, Mladost, 1952,
    104pp.   (Croatian)
    Før Adam, tr.: J. Frost, Copenhagen, Hagerup, 1911, 1918,
    144pp.   (Danish)
    Vóór Adam's tijd, tr.: S. J. Barentz-Schönberg, Amster-
    dam, H. J. W. Becht, 1920.   (Dutch)
    Ennen Aatamia, tr.: Kaapo Murros, Helsinki, Vihtori
    Kosonen, 1907 (on title page) (1908 on back of title
    page) 171pp. [With Huntington 338232 is *Jack London*, 13pp.
    This sketch is apparently intended for publicity pur-
    poses.] Ibid., Helsinki, Kustannusoy Alfa, 1920, 151pp.
                                              (Finnish)
    Avant Adam, tr.: Paul Dehesdin, Paris, F. Juven, 1912,
    260pp. [Pp.1-9 are entitled: "Extrait de: Jack London.
    Sa vie et son oeuvre littéraire ce qu'il est et ce qu'il
    a fait."]
    Les demi-hommes, tr: Louis Postif, Paris, Editions de
    France, 1936, 209pp.   (French)

Vor Adam, tr.: Ernst Untermann, Stuttgart, Franckh, 1915, 160pp. Franckh. 1921, 144pp. (Bücher der Zeit 2); Franckh. 1927-1930 (Franck's Bücher f. jung und alt).
(German)
Beyn okhley Adam, tr.: H. Ben-Dov, Tel Aviv, J. Shimeoni, 1961, 128pp. (Hebrew)
Ádám elött, tr.: Dezsö Schöner, Budapest, Népszava, 1918, 179pp. (Világosság-könyvtär 26-33); other editions of 1919, 1928.
____, Novi Sad, Testvériség-Egység, 1954, 181pp.
____, tr.: Imre Szász, Határ Gyozö, Victor János, Budapest-Bucarest, Szépirodalmi Könyvkiadó-Allámi Irodalmi ds Müvészeti Kiadó, 1956, 212pp.
(Hungarian)
Prima di Adamo, tr.: Giovanni Marcellini, Milan, Modernissima, 1928, 223pp.; ... with preface by Cesare Musatti, Milan, Coop. libro popolare, 1952, 131pp.
____, tr.: A. Lami, Sesto S. Giovanni-Milano, Barion, 1929, 190pp.
____, tr.: Giuseppina Taddei, Milan, Bietti, 1930, 218pp.
____, tr.: Milan, Sonzogno, 1939, 248pp.
(Italian)
Adam izen, tr.: Hikosaburo Shinozaki, Tokyo, Rakuyodo, 1916, 266pp.
____, tr.: Sen Shimizu, Tokyo, Shun'yodo, 1932, 174pp. (Sekai meisaku bunko). (Japanese)
Pirms Ādama, tr.: K. Vilde, Riga, Valters un Rapa, 1923, 95pp. (Latvian)
Pred Adama, tr.: Ruža Panova and Golapka Ugrinova, Skoje, Detsha radost, 1958, 143pp. (Macedonian)
Przed Adamem, tr.: S. M., Warsaw, Tania Ksiazka, 1926, 160pp.; also Warsaw, 1939; Warsaw, Wiedza Powszechna, 1957, 149pp. (Polish)
Inainte de Adam, Bucharest, Editoura, I. Brănisteanu, 1926, 136pp. (Rumanian)
Do Adama, tr.: E. Pimenova, Moscow, Universalnaya Biblioteka, 1917, 184pp.; Moscow and Petrograd, Gosizdat., 1923, 186pp.
____ tr.: Zin. Lvovski, Leningrad, Mysl, 1925, 1926, 164pp. (Russian)
Pre Adama, tr.: Dusan Jankovic, Belgrade, Izdanje knjizare "Avala", 1946, 148pp. (Serbian)
Antes de Adán, tr.: Fernando Valera, Valencia, Prometeo, 1925, 240pp. Pp.7-21 is entitled: "La vida del novelista. Jack London por si mismo"; Buenos Aires, Argonauta, 1946, 158pp. (Biblioteca moderna) [pp.7-15 are entitled "Vida de Jack London por si mismo."]
____, tr.: Fernando Valera, Valencia, Prometeo, [n.d.,]

214pp. Also contains "El csamiento de Lit-Lit,"
pp.195-214.   (Spanish)
Före Adam, tr.: M. Drangel, Stockholm, Bohlin, 1909, 235,
212pp; (2 vols.); 1915, 184pp.; 1916, 1917, 192pp.; 1924,
154pp.
____, tr.: A. Berg, Stockholm, Holmquist, 1918, 186pp.
____, tr.: Eva Håkanson, Stockholm, Natur och Kultur,
1959, 159pp. (Skattkammarbiblioteket).
____, Stockholm, Dahlberg, 1919, 221pp.
____, Stockholm, Romanbiblioteket, 1922, 204pp.
____, Stockholm, Åhlen & Åkerlund, 1921, 190pp.
                                         (Swedish)

LOVE OF LIFE. 1907

56. LOVE OF LIFE | AND OTHER STORIES | BY | JACK LONDON |
AUTHOR OF "THE CALL OF THE WILD," "PEOPLE | OF THE ABYSS,"
ETC., ETC. | New York | THE MACMILLAN COMPANY | LONDON:
MACMILLAN & CO., LTD. | 1907 | *All rights reserved*
[iv] v [vi] [1-2] 3-265p. 19 x 13 cm. Blue cloth
stamped in gilt on front cover and spine. Front cover enclosed in narrow white border. Four pages of publisher's
advertisements at back.
    On verso of title-page (p.[iv]): COPYRIGHT, 1906, |
BY THE MACMILLAN COMPANY. | [rule] | Set up and electro-
typed. Published September, 1907. | [Three lines of press
signature]
    Contents: Love of Life; A Day's Lodging; The White
Man's Way; The Story of Keesh; The Unexpected; Brown Wolf;
The Sun-Dog Trail; Negore, the Coward.

57. Reprints:
____, London, Everett, 1908, 292pp.; Everett, 1912, [?]pp.
____, London, Mills & Boon, 1916, 290pp.; 1924, 289pp.
____, Chicago, M. A. Donohue, 19[?] [?]pp.

58. Translations:
Liubev k zhizni, tr.: Zh. Tutunchan, Erevan, Aĭpetrat,
1952, 164pp. [Title in Russian]   (Armenian)
Je Ai Sheng Ming, tr.: Yin Fu, Shanghai, Hsin Wen i Ch'u
Pan She, 1954, 279pp. Contents do not match: Je Ai Sheng
Ming (Love of life). Pei Feng ti Ao Te Sai (Odyssey of
the north). Lao T'ou Tzu T'ung Meng (League of the old
men), Tiu Lien (Lost face). Chi Hsi ti Ku Shih (The story
of Keesh). Po Po T'u K'o ti Chi Chih (The wit of Porportuk).   (Chinese)
Láska k životu a jiné povídky, tr.: Mašek, Prague, Graf-
ikona, 1919, 69pp.

____, tr.: L. F. and K. Vít, Prague, Kočí, 1925, 142pp.
Contents: Hnědý vlk (Brown wolf). Zpusob bílého muže
(White man's way). Negore zbalělec (Negore, the coward).
Pěstitel žaludu. Kalifornská lesní hra...
Láska k životu, tr.: M. Beck, Prague, Svoboda, 1949,
106pp.
____, tr.: S. Kýška, Bratislava, Mladá letá, 1958, 127pp.
(Czech/Slovak)
Armastus elu vastu, tr.: L. Anvelt and A. Hint, Tallinn,
Eesti Riiklik Kirjastus, 1950, 201pp. Contents do not
match: Armastus elu vastu (Love of life). Lugu Kiisist
(The story of Keesh). Naiste visadus (Grit of women).
Teadmamees (The master of mystery). Hiinlane (The
Chinago). Mapuhi maja (The house of Mapuhi). Usutaganeja
(The apostate). Mehhiklane (The Mexican).
Da liefde voor het leven, tr.: J. P. Wesselink-van-
Rossum, Amsterdam, Boekh, en Uitg. Mij Joh. Müller, 1923.
(Dutch)
L'amore della vita, tr.: Maria Carlesimo Pasquali, Milan,
Bietti, 1931, 227pp. (Italian)
Liubov' k zhizni, tr.: S. Ermatov, Frunze, Kirgizgosizdat,
1960, 220pp. [Title in Russian]. (Kirghiz)
____, tr.: E. Mullokandov, Stalinabad, Tadzhikgosizdat,
1958, 109pp. [Title in Russian]. (Tadzhik)
Liubov' k zhizni i drugiye rasskazy, tr.: Ye. Broido,
edited by Yev. Zamyatim, Petrograd, Vsemir. Lit., 1922,
124pp.Contents: Liubov' k zhikni (Love of life). Neo-
zhidannoe (The unexpected). Negor-trus (Negore, the
coward.) Puti belogo cheloveka (The white man's way).
Liubov' k zhizni, Kn; izd., Gorkii, 1955, 188pp.
(Russian)
Yasamak hirsi, tr.: Mahemet Harmanci, Ankara, Varlik
Yayinevi, 1961, 94pp. (Varlik Büyük cep Kitaplari: 193).
Contents do not match: Yasamak hirsi (Love of life).
Beyaz issizlik (White silence). Meksikali (The Mexican).
Ates yakmak (To build a fire). Altin damari (All gold
canyon). Yüz karasi (Lost face).
Karlek till livet, tr.: M. Drangel, Stockholm, Bohlin,
1913, 287pp.; 1916, 1917, 176pp.; 1922, 191pp.; 1925,
192pp.; Stockholm, B. Wahlström, 1944, 236pp. (Gyllene
serien 13).
____, tr.: A. Berg, Stockholm, Holmquist, 1918, 240pp.;
1920, 201pp.
____, Stockholm, Dahlberg, 1919, 224pp.
____, Stockholm, Romanbiblioteket, 1922, 232pp.
(Swedish)

THE ROAD. 1907

59. THE ROAD | BY | JACK LONDON | AUTHOR OF "THE CALL OF THE WILD," | "WHITE FANG," ETC. | *ILLUSTRATED* | New York | THE MACMILLAN COMPANY | 1907 | *All rights reserved* [viii] ix [x] xi [xiv] 1-224p 20.5 x 14 cm. Gray cloth stamped in black, and lettered in gilt on front cover and spine. Top edges gilt. Frontis. Four pages of publisher's advertisements at back.

    On verso of title-page (p.[iv]): COPYRIGHT, 1907, | BY INTERNATIONAL MAGAZINE COMPANY. | COPYRIGHT, 1907, | BY THE MACMILLAN COMPANY. | [rule] | Set up and electrotyped. Published November, 1907. | [Three lines of press signature]

    Contents: Confession; Holding Her Down; Pictures; "Pinched"; The Pen; Hoboes That Pass in the Night; Road-Kids and Gay-Cats; Two Thousand Stiffs; Bulls.

60. Reprints:
    _____, London, Mills & Boon, 1914, 302pp. (Popular ed.), 1923, 184pp.; London, Pendulum, 1946, 118pp.
    _____, with an introduction by Glen Mullin, New York, Greenberg [1926] ix-xviii, 224pp. (The rogues' bookshelf).

61. Translations:
Skitnitzi, tr.: Georgi Zhechev, Sofia, D. Madzharov, 1936, 75pp. (Contents: Priznanie. Putni stzenki. Dve khiliado "stifove". Skitnitzi, koito putuvat noshchi).
                                  (Bulgarian)
Cesta, tr.: J. Vorel, Prague, Procházka, 1922, 169pp.
    _____, tr.: M. Mašková, Prague, Kočí, 1923, 187pp.
                           (Czech/Slovak)
Vagabondliv, tr.; A. Mikkelsen, Copenhagen, Martin, 1919, 192pp.; 1928, 1931, 256pp.   (Danish)
Tusschen de wielen, tr.: W. L. Leclerq, Amsterdam, Maatsch. voor goede en goedkoope lectuur, 1922 (Wereldbibliotheek No. 427) [3rd edition appeared in 1932 as *Tussen de wielen,* Amsterdam, Wereldbibliotheek.]
                                    (Dutch)
Doroga, tr.: Der. Nister, Kiev, 1935, 141pp. [Title in Russian].   (Everskian)
Kulkurielämää. Nuorunden muistelmia, Helsinki, Otava, 1919, 106pp.   (Finnish)
Abenteurer des Schienenstranges. Trampfahrten durch Nordamerika, tr.: Erwin Magnus, Berlin, Gyldendalscher Verlag, 1924, 269pp.; Berlin, Universitas, 1926, 261pp.; Berlin, Dt. Buch-Gemeinschaft, 1939, 285pp.; Berlin, Universitas, 1946, 260pp.; Zürich, Büchergilde Gutenberg, 1947, 258pp.;

another ed., 259pp.; Berlin, Universitas, 1949, 260pp.;
Frankfurt/M., Mainz, Bielefeld, Büchergilde Gutenberg,
1949, 260pp.; Vienna, Büchergilde Gutenberg, 1951, 222pp.;
Vienna, Volksbuchverlag, 1951, 222pp.
____, tr.: Rud. Lampert, Linz, Vienna, Ibis-Verlag, 1947,
256pp.
____, source gives no tr. Berlin, Aufbau, 1952, 1953,
1954, 221pp.; Aufbau, 1961, 174pp. (bb-Taschenbuch des
Aufbau-Verlages 98).
Begegnung mit der Unterwelt [Selection] Vienna, Globus,
1947, 29pp. (Das neue Abenteuer No. 1).
____, in Kurzschrift. Abenteurer des Schienenstranges. In
verkürzter Verkehrsschrift. Wolfenbüttel, Heckner, 1939,
23pp. (Heckners bunte Reihe 51/52). [Other shorthand
editions were published by Ebenda in 1947 and 1948.]
                                        (German)
Az országúton, tr.: Ákos Farkas, Budapest, Légrády, 1924,
198pp.; 2nd ed., 1925; ibid., tr.: Imré Szász, Szepirod,
Kiadó, 1957, 206pp. (Olcsó könyvtár 1957:22).
                                        (Hungarian)
Flækingar, tr.: Steindór Sigursson, Reykjavík, Heimil-
isritiŏ, 1947, 222pp. (Reyfarinn 4)   (Icelandic)
La strada, tr.: L. Viscardini, Milan, Modernissima, 1929,
257pp.
____, Milan, Bietti, 1930, 244pp.
____, tr.: Maria Carlesimo Pasquali, Milan, Sonzogno,
1934, 244pp.   (Italian)
Klaidona piedzevojumi, tr.: J. Dandens, Riga, 1926, 188pp.
                                        (Latvian)
Landstrykerliv, tr.: Ben Horne, Oslo, Gyldendal, 1934,
1941, 141pp.   (Norwegian)
Na szlaku. Szkice autobiograficzne, tr.: S. Kuszelewskiej,
1923, Warsaw, Ignis, 1923, 236pp.   (Polish)
Doroga, tr.: S. A. Adrianov, Leningrad, Mysl, 1924, 160pp.
Dorozhnyie parni i vesyolyie koty, Leningrad, Priboi,
1926, 74pp. [Excerpts].
Kogda ya byl brodyagoi, tr.: D. Ye. Deikhtenberg, Leningrad and Moscow, Kniga, 1924, 140pp.
Moi skitaniya, Moscow, Gosizdat., 1922, 204pp.; Moscow
and Petrograd, Gosizdat., 1923, 180pp.; Leningrad, Priboi,
1926, 64pp. [Excerpts or abridgement](Russian)
Skitnice i probisveti, tr.: Jovan Popovic, Belgrade,
Izdanje Nolit, 1937, 212pp. Contents: Kako sam postao
skitnica. Jedna ispovest. Mufte putnici. Ukeban. U
prugastoj nosnji. Armija generala Kelija. Cigani. Nocna
putovanja. Gonilac skitnica.   (Serbian)
Cesta, tr.: Milka Mirtio, Ljubljana, Prešernova druzba,

1962, 132pp. (Tiskarna Ljudska pravica).
                          (Slovenian)
Vagabondlif, tr.: M. Drangel, Stockholm, Bohlin, 1916,
164pp.; other editions 1917, 1925.
_____, tr.: E. Swanberg, Stockholm, Holmquist, 1918, 188pp.;
1919, 221pp.
_____, Stockholm, Dahlberg, 1919, 220pp.; Stockholm,
Romanbiblioteket, 1922, 220pp.   (Swedish)

THE IRON HEEL. 1908

62. THE IRON HEEL | BY | JACK LONDON | AUTHOR OF "THE CALL OF
THE WILD," | "WHITE FANG," ETC. | New York | THE MAC-
MILLAN COMPANY | LONDON: MACMILLAN & CO., LTD. | 1908 |
All rights reserved
     [iv] v [vi] vii [viii] ix-xiv [xv-xvi] 1-354p. 19 x 13
cm. Dark blue cloth stamped in gilt and light blue. Four
pages of publisher's advertisements at back.
     On verso of title-page (p.[iv]): COPYRIGHT, 1907, |
BY JACK LONDON. | [rule] | Set up and electrotyped. Pub-
lished February, 1908. | [Three lines of press signature]
     A number of copies were issued by Appeal to Reason,
Girard, Kansas. These constitute a later issue.
     Merle Johnson's *American First Editions* states, "An
advance copy has been noted in printed wrappers, dated
1907, no month of publication on the copyright page."
     Huntington 337696 is of interest for several reasons.
Pasted in this copy of the first edition are: 1) Letter
to London dated March 10, 1911 from W. G. Henry concerning the dramatization of the Iron Heel into three acts
for the socialists of Oakland on March 19. The dramatization was the work of Henry who also played the part of
Ernest Everhard. 2) A clipping from the Oakland *World*,
March 11, 1911, announces performances, gives cast and
summarizes drama act by act. 3) Carbon of letter by
Jack London to Comrade Harris dated Oct. 26, 1914 concerning this book.

63. Dramatizations:
Dramatized in *Socialistic dialogues and recitations* com-
piled by Josephine R. Cole and Grace Silver, Chicago,
Charles H. Kerr & Company, 1913, 59pp.
"The machine breaks," condensed from Act II, Scene II of
the Iron Heel. Dramatized by W. G. Henry.

64. Reprints:
_____, New York, Macmillan, 1908, 1909, xiv, 354pp.; 1934,
1937, xix, 354pp.

THE IRON HEEL

BY

JACK LONDON

AUTHOR OF "THE CALL OF THE WILD,"
"WHITE FANG," ETC.

New York
THE MACMILLAN COMPANY
LONDON: MACMILLAN & CO., LTD.
1908

[Item 62]

_____, New York, Grosset & Dunlap, c1907, [1910][1911]
[1917], xiv, 354pp.
_____, New York, Regent Press [c1907][1913] xiv, 354pp.
_____, London, Everett, [1908] 374pp.; 1912, 287pp.
(Everett's Library).
_____, Toronto, Macmillan Co. of Canada, 1910 [c1907] xiv,
354pp.
_____, London, Mills & Boon, [1916] 292pp. (Mills & Boon's
Shilling Cloth Library); 1923, 292pp.; 10th ed. with
Anatole France preface, 1928, 292pp., reissued by London,
T. Werner Laurie, 1936, 1939, 1948, 292pp.
_____, Moscow, Co-operative publishing society of foreign
workers in the U. S. S. R., 1934, 307pp.
_____, London, Werner Laurie, 1936, 1948, 292pp.
_____, Toronto, McCleod, 1948, 354pp.
_____, New York, Grayson Publishing Corp., 1948, xvii,
354pp.
_____, with a preface by Anatole France, Harmondsworth and
New York, Penguin Books [1944] v-viii, 219pp.
_____, New York, Arcadia House, 1950, xvii, 354pp.
_____, introduction by Max Lerner, New York, Sagamore,
1958, 303pp. (American century series: S-23); also Mac-
millan, 1958, 303pp.
_____, London, Mayflower Publishers, 1959, 316pp.
_____, Chicago, Donahue, 19[?][?]pp.
_____, London, Unwin,[n.d.,]374pp. (Colonial ed.).
Portions of this book were published in the Oakland *World*
on April 4, April 11, May 2, May 9, 1908, p.4 of each
issue. The *World* also published a letter on this novel by
George Geddes, April 25, 1908, p.2.
Partially reprinted in *Shingle Weaver*, 9, 7-52 (April 22,
1911 - March 16, 1912).
CHAPTER V. OF | THE IRON HEEL | (A WARNING RE SPAIN,
AND -) | BY JACK LONDON | PUBLISHED BY THE SOCIALIST
LABOR PARTY OF AUSTRALIA ... DECEMBER, 1936. (The Worker
Newspaper and Printery, St. Andrew's Place, Sydney) 31pp.
Selections appear in Foner and Sheperd.

65. Translations:
Zheleznaya pyata, Moscow, 1923, 147pp. [Title in
Russian].   (Armenian)
Zheliaznata peta, tr.: Pelin Velkov, Sofia, Knigo-Lotos,
1945, 272pp.; 1946, 288pp.
_____, tr.: G. Chakalov, Sofia, Nar. kultura, 1954, 232pp.;
1956, 249pp.
_____, Sofia, Obshcho rab. koop. d-vo Osvobozhdenie, 1921,
189pp. (Khudozhestvena bibl. Osvobozhdenie 8); Sofia,
Antikvar, 1932, 216pp.; Sofia, D. Madzharov, 1936, 175pp.,

Sofia, D. Gologanov, 1941, 218pp.; Sofia, Doverie, 1932, 224pp.   (Bulgarian)
Chicagská Komuna, tr.: J. Čermák, Prague, Komunistické kninkup, a nakl., 1921, 248pp.
Železná Pata, tr.: J. Vorel, Prague, Procházka, 1921, 344pp.
____, tr.: Z. Pohorecká, Prague, Kočí, 1924, 2 vols. (157, 134pp.)
____, tr.: J. Bílý, Prague, Svoboma, 1949, 338pp.; with Anatole France preface, Prague, Mladá fronta, 1951, 247pp.
... Povídky vybral a přel. A. J. Stastný. Doslov B. Fedrman, Prague, Stat. nakl. dětské knihy, 1953, 427pp.
____, tr.: Š. Kýška. Štúdiu a doslov npl. Ján Boor, Bratislava, Slov. vyd. krásnej literatury, 1953, 283pp.
                     (Czech/Slovak)
Jernhælen, tr.: Olav Kringen, Copenhagen, Martin, 1918, 2 vols. (160, 144pp.); Martin, 1941, 270pp.
                     (Danish)
La fera kalkanumo, tr.: George Saville, Leipzig, Sennacieca asocio tutmonda eldona fako kooperativa, 1930, 362pp. ["Enkonduko de la tradukinto al la esperantlingva eldono," pp.9-12. Pp.11-12 give the text in Esperanto of London's resignation from the socialist party].
                     (Esperanto)
Raudne kand, tr.: A. Aava, Tallinn, Eesti Riiklik Kirjastus, 1955, 271pp.   (Estonian)
Rautakorko, tr.: Elof Kristianson, Fitchburg, Mass., Suom. Sos, Kustannusyhtiö, 1910, 328pp.
____, Helsinki, Otava, 1921, 331pp.; Otava, 1924, 352pp.
                     (Finnish)
Le talon de fer, roman d'anticipation sociale, tr.: Louis Postif, preface by Anatole France, Paris, Crès, 1923, v, 315pp.; tr.: Postif, preface by France, introduction by P. Vaillant-Courturier, Paris, Edit. Sociales internationales, 1933, 358pp. (Collection horizons); tr.: Postif, avant-propos by Francis Jourdain, preface by France, introduction by Vaillant-Courturier, Paris, Editions hier et aujourd'hui, 1946, 287pp.   (French)
Zhelznaya pyata, Tiflis, 1923, 293pp. [Title in Russian translation]   (Georgian)
Die eiserne Ferse, tr.: Fritz Born, Konstanz, See-Verlag, 1922, 271pp.; Berlin, Universitas, 1927, 294pp.; Moscow and Leningrad, Verlagsgenossenschaft ausl. Arbeiter in der UdSSR., 1935, 331pp.; Potsdam, Märkische Druck- und Verlags GmbH., 1948, 286pp.; Vienna, Globus-Verlag, 1948, 318pp.
____, tr.: Eduard Thorsch, Zürich, Büchergilde Gutenberg, 1948, 295pp.   (German)

A vas-pata, tr.: Mészáros Zoltán, Budapest, Népszava, 1923, 264pp.
_____, tr.: Szinnai Tivadar, Budapest, Szikra, 1949, 308pp.
(Hungarian)
Il tallone di ferro, preface and tr.: G. Dàuli, Milano, Modernissima, 1928, 342pp.
_____, a cura di G. Delaudi, Milan, Monanni, 1928, 296pp.
_____, with preface by Anatole France, tr.: A. Ambrosini, Milan, Barion, 1945, [?]pp.
Il tallone di fer, Florence Nerbini, 1945, [?]pp.
_____, preface and translation by Aldo Palumbo, Florence, Parenti, 1955, xxvi, 274pp.   (Italian)
Dzelzs papēdis, tr.: A. Bauga, Riga, LVI, 1950, 228pp.
(Latvian)
Jernhælen, tr.: O. Kringen, Kristiania, J. Aass, 1910, 392pp.   (Norwegian)
Zelazna stopa, Warsaw, Stow. Pracown. Ksieg, 1923, 344pp.
_____, tr.: Josef Nondschein, Warsaw, Ludowa Spoldz. Wydawnicza, 1951, 322pp.   (Polish)
Otacao de ferro, tr.: Silvia Leon Chalreu, Rio de Janeiro. Ed. do povo ltda., 1947, 286pp. [Also contains preface by Anatole France; introduction by P. Vaillant-Courturier.]
(Portuguese)
Călciul de fier, tr.: and preface by D. Mazilu, Bucharest, Biblioteca pentru toti, 1960, xxii, 448pp. [Chief authorities cited in the preface are Russak, Foner and Lenin.]
Sub călcâiul de fier, tr.: Ana Canarache, Bucharest, Tempo, 1945, 246pp.   (Rumanian)
Zhelznaya pyata, tr.: Ye. Broido, Moscow, Universalnaya Biblioteka, 1917, 398pp.; Moscow, Gosizdat.; 1922, 1927, 372pp.
_____, tr.: I. A. Mayevski, Moscow, I. A. Mayevski, 1922, 372pp.
_____, tr.: V. P. V., edited by E. G. Lundberg, Petrograd, Gosizdat, 1922, 260pp.
_____, tr.: P. G. Guber, Moscow, Krasnaya Nov. 1923, 112pp. (abridged).
_____, tr.: Zin. Lvovski, Leningrad and Moscow, Novella, 1924, 230pp.; Leningrad, Mysl, 1924, 230pp.; Mysl, 1927, 232pp.
_____, tr.: Ye. G. Guro, edited by Z. A. Vershinina; introduction by Karl Radek, Moscow and Leningrad, ZIF, 1930, 300pp.   (Russian)
Gvozdena peta, tr.: Ognjan Radovic, Belgrade, Zagreb, Izdanje, Kultura, 1946, 271 5pp.; Izdanje Kultura, 1946, 211 3pp.; Belgrade, Ljub. Ristovic, 1950, 250 2pp.; Belgrade, Rad, 1952, 322pp.   (Serbian)
Železna peta, tr.: Ivan Buk, Ljubljana, Zadružna založba,

1926-1927, 2 vols. (145, 158pp.)
____, tr.: Janez Gradisnik, Ljubljani, Slovenski
Knjitžni Zavod, 1950, 229pp.   (Slovenian)
El talón de hierro, tr.: Antonio Guardiola, Valencia,
Prometeo, 1927, 312pp.
____, novela de anticipación social, tr.: Silvestre Otazú,
prólogo de Anatole France, Buenos Aires, Editorial
Futuro, 1944, 262pp.; Buenos Aires, Ediciones Siglo
Veinte, 1956, 278pp.; Buenos Aires, Ediciones Siglo
Veinte, [n.d.,] 240pp. (Grandes novelistas contemporaneos)
[n.d. edition contains no France preface].
____, Mexico, Editorial Diana, 1950, 262pp.
                                       (Spanish)
Järnhälen, tr.: M. Drangel, Stockholm, Bohlin, 1912,
367pp.; Skandia, 1916, 319pp.; Stockholm, Bohlin, 1926,
349pp. [A translation was also published in 1920, 349pp.]
____, tr.: A. Berg, Stockholm, Holmquist, 1919, 314pp.
____, tr.: Olle Moberg, Stockholm, Arbetarkultur, 1954,
278pp.
____, tr.: J. H. Landén, Stockholm, Folket i Bilds Förlag,
1958, 275pp. ["Slutord", p.[276] by Marten Edlund.]
                                       (Swedish)
Zheleznai piata, tr.: V. Trotzini, Kiev, 1928, 238pp.
[Title in Russian].
____, tr.: V. Koval', Kiev, Goslitizdat Ukrainy, 1959,
238pp.   (Ukranian)
Der ayzerner knafl, tr.: M. Weinberg, New York, Nay-Tsayt,
1919, 380pp.   (Yiddish)

MARTIN EDEN. 1909

66. MARTIN EDEN | BY | JACK LONDON | AUTHOR OF "THE CALL OF
THE WILD," ETC., ETC. | *WITH FRONTISPIECE BY THE KINNEYS* |
New York | THE MACMILLAN COMPANY | 1909 | *All rights
reserved*
    [vi] 1-411p. 19 x 13 cm. Dark blue cloth stamped in
light green. Lettering on spine and front cover gilt.
Frontis. in sepia tone. Ten pages of publisher's advertisements at back.
    On verso of title-page (p.[iv]): COPYRIGHT, 1908, |
BY JACK LONDON.   [rule]   Set up and electrotyped. Published September, 1909.   [Three lines of press signa-
ture]

67. Serializations:
This autobiographical novel of the greatest importance
for the study of London's life was first published serially in the *Pacific Monthly*, 20:235-254, 402-418,

MARTIN EDEN

BY

JACK LONDON

AUTHOR OF "THE CALL OF THE WILD," ETC., ETC.

WITH FRONTISPIECE BY THE KINNEYS

New York

THE MACMILLAN COMPANY

1909

[Item 66]

485-504, 621-640 (Sept.-Dec. 1908); 21:33-46, 166-175,
258-272, 420-429, 530-544, 637-652 (Jan.-June 1909),
22:85-95, 190-206, 300-316 (July-Sept. 1909). It also ran
in *Uncle Remus's, the home magazine*, 24, 6:5-8, 40-41
(Feb. 1909), 25,1:10-12, 34-36, 25,2:20, 22, 24, 36, 39;
25,3:18-21, 41-42; 25,4:19-20, 39-41; 25,5:18-21; 25,
6:16-17, 30-31 (March-August 1909); 26,1:18-23; 26,2:24-
27; 26,3:16-17, 46-47; 26,4:24-26; 26,5:14-15, 30; 26,
6:26-27, 34-35 (Sept. 1909-Feb. 1910); 27,1:28-29, 41;
27,2:24-29; 27,3:24-27, 36-37; 27,4:22-27 (March-
June 1910).

68. Reprints:
_____, London, Heinemann, 1910, 1921, 413pp.; 1915, 416pp.
_____, New York, Macmillan, 1910, 1913, 1938, 411pp.
_____, New York, Grosset & Dunlap, 1911, 1913, 411pp.
_____, Chicago, Donohue, 19[?][?]pp.
_____, New York, Books of distinction, 1942, 411pp.
_____, New York, Penguin Books, 1946, 346pp. (Penguin
books 587).
_____, New York, Signet Books, 1946, 346pp. (Signet Book
587); Toronto, Sinnott, 1946, 346pp.
_____, New York, Arcadia House, 1950, 411pp.
_____, introduction and notes by Sam S. Baskett, New York,
Rinehart, 1956, xxvi, 384pp.
Braille edition (transcribed for the National Library for
the Blind, London, England): 7 vols. 1921.
"To the valley of death," Oakland *Enquirer*, Nov. 24, 1916,
p.3 [Chapter 15 of this novel].

69. Translations:
Martin Iden, tr.: Shaban Demiraj, Tirana, N. SH. Botimeve
"Naim Frashëri", 1959, 439pp.   (Albanian)
Martin Iden, tr.: A. Varsamian, Erevan, Aïpetrat, 1951,
500pp.   (Armenian)
Martin Idn, tr.: Pacho Stoianov, Sofia, Mozaïka ot
znameniti suvremenni romani, 1930, 468pp. (Mozaïke ot
znameniti suvremenni romani, 21:6-7); Mozaïka ...,
1945, 319pp.
_____, tr.: Orlin Vasilev, Sofia, D. Madzharov, 1935,
340pp.
_____, tr.: Angel Georgiev, Sofia, Luch, 1947, 400pp.
                               (Bulgarian)
Martin Eden, tr.: I. Schulz, Prague, Tisk. družstvo soc.
str. čal. lidu prac., 1921, 467pp.; Prague, Ûstř. tisk
družstvo čsl. strany čsl. lidu pracujícího, 1929, 467pp.
_____, tr.: M. Reisingrová, Prague, Kočí, 1924, 4 vols.
(128, 128, 127, 100pp.); Prague, Zlín, Tisk, 1937, 2 vols.

37

"Now Longfellow——" she was saying.

"Yes, I've —————— read 'im," he broke in impulsively. " 'The Psalm of Life,' 'Excelsior,' an' . . . . I guess that's all."

She nodded her head and —————— smiled, and he felt, somehow, that her smile was tolerant, pitifully tolerant. ————————————— He was a fool to attempt to make a sentence that way. That Longfellow chap most likely had written countless books of poetry.

"Excuse me, miss.

Manuscript page of *Martin Eden*

(243, 218pp.).

____, tr.: Reisingrová and B. Šimáčková, Prague, Svoboda, 1948, 381pp.

____, tr.: A. J. Štastný, Prague, Stát. nakl. krás. lit. hudby a umění, 1953, 389pp.; Prague, Naše vojsko, 1956, 333pp.; with an introduction by Z. Stolba, Prague, Stát. nakl. lrás. lit. hudby a umění, 1955, 421pp.

____, tr.: Š. Kýška, introduction by J. Boor, Bratislava, Slov. vyd. krásnej literatury, 1955, 417pp.

(Czech/Slovak)

Martin Eden, tr.: Aslaug Mikkelsen, Copenhagen, Martin, 1913, 408pp.; Martin, 1919, 2 vols. (240, 238pp.); 1928, 2 vols. (256, 256pp.); 1932, 2 vols. (320, 318pp.); 1947, 2 vols. (Danish)

Martin Eden, tr.: M. Reiman, Tartu, Noor-Eesti, 1928, 445pp. (Estonian)

Martin Eden, tr.: Ville Hynynen, Helsinki, Otava, 1920, 572pp.; Otava, 1960, 360pp. (Finnish)

Martin Eden, tr.: C. Cendrée, Paris, L'édition française illustrée, 1920, [?]pp.; Paris, Crès, 1929, 369pp.

____, tr.: Madeleine Follain, Lausanne, La guide du livre, 1948, 399pp. (Collection La guide du livre 114).

____, tr.: Claude Sirven, Genève, Les amis du livre, 1956, 439pp. (French)

Martin Iden, Tbilisi,[no pub.,]1934, 553pp.

(Georgian)

Martin Eden, tr.: Erwin Magnus, Berlin, Universitas, 1927, 2 vols. (270, 273pp.); Berlin, Büchergilde Gutenberg, 1927, 2 vols. (269, 271pp.).

____, tr.: Richard C. Seiler, Zürich, Schweizer Druck-und Verlagshaus, 1950, 375pp.

____, tr.: Eduard Thorsch, Zürich, Büchergilde Gutenberg, 1950, 450pp.

____, Berlin, Aufbau-Verlag, 1955, 1956, 467pp.; 1957, 466pp. (German)

Martin Eden, tr.: Yaskov Kopelevic, Tel-Aviv, Idit, 1954, 399pp. (Hebrew)

Martin Eden, tr.: Bartos Zoltán, Budapest, Athenaeum, 1924, 2 vols; 1927, Összes munkai 9-10; 1943, 378pp.

____, tr.: Bernát Pál revised by Görgey Gábor, Budapest, Európa, 1958, 468pp. (Hungarian)

"Martin Eden," tr.: Jon Björnsson, *Morgunblaðið*,8:101-305 (1921), 9:1-83 (1922). (Icelandic)

Martin Eden, tr.: Gian Dàuli, Milan, Modernissima, 1925, [?]pp.; Modernissima, 1928, 406pp.; Milan, Cavallotti, 1948, 300pp.

____, tr.: Mario Benzi, Milan, Bietti, 1928, 1934, 1936, 404pp.

_____, tr.: Gastone Rossi, Milan, Sonzogno, 1928, 1933, 378pp.
_____, tr. : A. Lami, Sesto S. Giovanni-Milano, Barion, 1929, 1933, 414pp.
_____, tr.: Oriana Previtali, Milan, Rizzoli [1952][?]pp.
_____, Milan, Corbaccio, [n.d.,][?]pp.
_____, Milan, Carroccio, 1953, 96pp. (Italian)
Zetsubo no seishua, tr.: Kazue Saito and Nobutaka Kiuchi, Tokyo, Shinsetususha, 1956, 338pp. (Japanese)
"Mártinš Idens," *Jaunâ Dienas Lapa,* nos. 5-83 (Jan. 20-April 23, 1913).
_____, tr.: E. Kauliņa, Riga, LVI, 1958, 334pp., 1959, 393pp.
_____, tr.: E. Kauliņa, Riga, Latgosizdat, 1959, 393pp.
                                                (Latvian)
Martynas Idnas, tr.: Pr. Šileika, Kaunas-Marijampolé, Dirva, 1930, 2 vols. (233, 254pp.).
_____, Kaunas, Valst. grož. lit. 1-kla, 1949, 406pp.
                                                (Lithuanian)
Martin Eden, tr.: Nordahl Grieg, Oslo, Gyldendal, 1934, 1941, 2 vols. (216, 191pp.).   (Norwegian)
Martin Eden, tr.: A. Doustdar, Teheran, Ali Akbar Elmi Publishing Institute, 1956, 292pp. (Persian)
Martin Eden, tr.: S. Kuszelewska, Warsaw, Ignis, 1923, 2 vols. (327, 289pp.)[Later editions of this translation appeared in Warsaw, 1926, 1932, 1937.]
_____, tr.: J. M., Chicago, Ksiegarnia Ludowa, 1936, 288pp. (vol. 2 only).
_____, Warsaw, Ksiazka, 1948, 387pp.; Warsaw, Iskry, 1953, 237pp.; 1954, 402pp.; Warsaw, Ksiazka i Wiedza, 1949.
_____, tr.: Z. Glinka, Warsaw, Iskry, 1956, 426pp.; 1957, 475pp.; 1958, 451pp.   (Polish)
Martin Eden, tr.: Al. Iacobescu, Bucharest, Nationala-S. Ciornei, 1931, 2 vols. (240, 248pp.) (Colectinnea autorilor celebri contemporani).
_____, tr. with introduction and notes: D. Mazilu, Bucharest, Editura Pentru Literatura universala, 1959, xix, 492pp.; 1961, 488pp. [Pp. i-xx are entitled "Cuvînt înainte"; both translations are part of the Clasicii literaturii universale collection; a note in the 1961 translation states that the translator used the 2-vol. ed., Leipzig, Bernhard Tauchnitz, 1913 rather than earlier texts published in the United States or Great Britain].
                                                (Rumanian)
Martin Eden, tr.: E. Pimenova, Moscow, Universalnaya Biblioteka, 1917, 273pp.; 1918, 2 vols. (279, 273pp.); Leningrad and Moscow, Kniga, 1924, 1925, 373pp.; Leningrad, Priboi, 1927, 2 vols. (306, 312pp.)

_____, tr.: A. P. Kolmonoveki, Moscow, Trud i Kniga, 1925, 293pp.; Leningrad, Mysl, 1925, 299pp.

_____, tr.: E. K. Pimenova, with an introduction by B. Gimelfarb, Moscow and Leningrad, Gosizdat, 1929, 445pp.

_____, tr.: V. A. Aleksandrov, ed. by D. M. Gorfinkel, Leningrad, Molodaya Gvardiya, 1935, 418pp.; Magadan, Obl. Kn; izd., 1955, 476pp.

_____, tr.: S. Zaiaitzkogo, Moscow, Goslitizdat, 1948, 378pp.; Riga Latgosizdat, 1949, 352pp.; Kishinev, Gosizdat Moldavii, 1956, 355pp.

_____, Leningrad, Lenizdat, 1949, 372pp.; Chcliakinsk, Kn; izd., 1955, 348pp.; Petrozavodsk, Gos. izd. Karelo-finsk, SSR, 1950, 347pp.; Fruntze, Kirgizgosizdat, 1960, 352pp.

_____, tr.: E. Kalashnikovoi, Moscow, Goslitizdat, 1958, 359pp.; Ivanovo, Kn. izd., 1959, 366pp.

(Russian)

Martin Iden, tr.: M. M. Pesic, Belgrade, Izdanje i stampa Graficki institut Narodna misao A. D., 1928, 2 vols. (vii, 191, 194pp.).

_____, tr.: Živojin V. Simić, Redaktor Krsta Radovic, Nacrt korica A. Spiridonovic. O djelu i piscu od Dusana Puhala, Belgrade, Novo pokolenje. Svetski pisci, 1950, 375pp.

Martin Idn, tr.: Živojin Simić, Belgrade, Rad, 1960, 438pp.   (Serbian)

Martin Eden, tr.: Herbert Grün, Ljubljana, Slovenski knjižni zavod, 1956, 294pp.

Martin Idn, tr.: Živojin Simić, Bratstvo-Jedinstvo, Novi Sad, 1954, 340pp.; 1956, 353pp.

_____, tr.: Panca Mihailov & Mato Jovanovski, Skopje, Koco Racin, 1953, 671pp.   (Slovenian)

Martin Eden, tr.: Manuel Vallvé, Buenos Aires, Edición Molino, 1949, 252pp.

_____, tr.: Joaquin R. Castro, Madrid, Ed. Siglo XX, 1949, 289pp.

_____, tr.: José Clementi, Buenos Aires, Ediciones Siglo XX, 438pp.; 1950, 336pp. (Grandes novelistas contemporaneos).   (Spanish)

Martin Eden, tr.: Algot Sandberg, Stockholm, Bohlin, 1912, 1915, 432pp.; 1920, 463pp.; Stockholm, Tiden, 1952, 287pp.   (Swedish)

Martin Eden, tr.: Mete Ergin, Istanbul, Varlik Yayinevi, 1963, 390pp. (Büyük esereler Kitapliği: 50).

(Turkish)

Martin Iden, Kiev, Molodoi bol'shevik, 1936, 446pp.

_____, tr.: M. Riabovoi, Kiev, Goslitizdat Ukrainy, 1954, 328pp.; 1959, 334pp.   (Ukranian)

LOST FACE. 1910

70. LOST FACE | BY | JACK LONDON | AUTHOR OF "MARTIN EDEN,"
"THE CALL | OF THE WILD," ETC. | *ILLUSTRATED* | New York |
THE MACMILLAN COMPANY | 1910 | *All rights reserved*
    [iv] v [vi] vii [viii][1-2] 3-240p. 19 x 13 cm. Dark
blue cloth decorated in orange, white, and green. Lettering on spine and front cover white. Frontis. Four pages
of publisher's advertisements at back.
    On verso of title-page (p.[iv]): COPYRIGHT, 1910, | By
THE MACMILLAN COMPANY. | [rule] | Set up and electrotyped.
Published March, 1910.   [Three lines of press signature]
    Contents: Lost Face; Trust; To Build a Fire; That Spot;
Flush of Gold; The Passing of Marcus O'Brien; The Wit of
Porportuk.

71. Reprints:
    ____, Chicago, M. A. Donohue, [1913] 240pp.
    ____, London, Mills & Boon, 1915, 286pp.; 1916, 1919,
280pp.

REVOLUTION AND OTHER ESSAYS. 1910

72. REVOLUTION | AND OTHER ESSAYS | BY | JACK LONDON | AUTHOR
OF "MARTIN EDEN," "THE CALL OF THE WILD," | "WHITE FANG,"
ETC., ETC. | New York | THE MACMILLAN COMPANY | 1910 |
All rights reserved
    [iv] v [vi] vii [viii] ix [x][1-2] 3-309p. 19 x 12.5
cm. Dark red cloth stamped in gilt. Title "Revolution"
only appears on front cover and spine. Four pages of pub-
lisher's advertisements at back.
    On verso of title-page (p.[iv]): COPYRIGHT, 1910, | BY
THE MACMILLAN COMPANY. | [rule] | Set up and electrotyped.
Published March, 1910.   [Three lines of press signature]
    Contents: Revolution; The Somnambulists; The Dignity
of Dollars; Goliah; The Golden Poppy; The Shrinkage of the
Planet; The House Beautiful; The Gold Hunters of the North;
Foma Gordyeeff; These Bones Shall Rise Again; The Other
Animals; The Yellow Peril; What Life Means to Me.
    There is a variant of the first edition of this book
in the George H. Tweney collection. The collation is exactly as described above, with the following differences:
1. Binding is light tan cloth with lettering same as described, but in black, not gilt. 2. There are no publisher's advertisements at the end. Text ends with p. 309,
verso blank. 3. Bottom of spine has Macmillan only, with
black rule above and below, whereas copy described above
has The Macmillan | Company, with gilt rule above and

below. There is no known priority.

73. Reprints:
    ____, London, Mills & Boon, 1920, 251pp.
    "The impending revolution," *Appeal to reason,* Dec. 30,
    1916, p.3 [Passage from volume].

74. Translations:
    Revoluce ..., tr.: L. F., Prague, Kočí, 1926, 187pp.
    (Czech/Slovak)
    Revolyutsiya, tr.: A. V. Luchinskya, Leningrad, Mysl,
    1924, 153pp.   (Russian)

BURNING DAYLIGHT. *1910*

75. BURNING DAYLIGHT | BY | JACK LONDON | AUTHOR OF "THE CALL
    OF THE WILD," "WHITE FANG," | "MARTIN EDEN," ETC.| New
    York | THE MACMILLAN COMPANY | 1910 | *All rights reserved*
        [iv] v [vi-viii] 1-361p. 19 x 13 cm. Light blue cloth
    stamped in light blue and yellow. Lettering on spine and
    front cover white. Frontis. Eleven pages of publisher's
    advertisements at back.
        On verso of title-page (p.[iv]): COPYRIGHT, 1910 | BY
    THE NEW YORK HERALD COMPANY. | COPYRIGHT, 1910, | BY THE
    MACMILLAN COMPANY. | [rule] | Set up and electrotyped.
    Published October, 1910. | [Three lines of press signature]
        Merle Johnson's *American First Editions* states, "Two
    states of binding are noted; (a) with *MacMillan* at foot
    of spine; (b) with *The* | *MacMillan* | *Company.* Earliest
    known presentation copies are of the latter state."

76. Serializations:
    Before publication this novel ran serially in the New
    York *Herald,* special fiction section, pp. 1-8 of June 19,
    26, July 3, 10, 17, 24, 31, Aug. 7, 14, 21, 28, 1910.
    After publication the Washington *Herald* serialized it in
    section 3 from Sept. 4, 1910-Jan. 15, 1911 and in its
    Literary Supplement or Magazine section from Jan. 22-March
    19, 1911. The installments appeared on p.3 of the issues
    of Sept. 4, 11, 18, 25, Oct. 2, 9, 16, 23, 30, Nov. 6, 13,
    20; p.4 of Nov. 27, Dec. 4, 11; p.2 of Dec. 18, 25, Jan. 1,
    8, 15; Jan. 22, p.3; Jan. 29, p.5; Feb. 5, p.5; Feb. 12,
    p.4, Feb. 19, p.6; Feb. 26, p.7; p.8, March 5, 12, 19.
    It was serialized in the New Zealand *Herald,* April 4-25,
    1911.

77. Dramatizations:
    Burning Daylight was dramatized by Douglas William
    Hamilton of Cleveland, Ohio; it is unpublished. A copy of

the script is in the collection of Dr. C. J. Cresmer of
Los Angeles, California.

78. Reprints:
An excerpt was separately published:
BURNING   DAYLIGHT | [heavy rule] | [light rule] | BY |
JACK LONDON | [short rule] | Copyright, 1910, by the New
York Herald | Co. All rights reserved | [short rule] |
Reprinted by | Land's End Eucalyptus | Forest Site |
By Express Permission of the Author |
Title inclosed within single line border. 15.5 x 9 cm.
Front cover used as title; text including synopsis of
preceding chapters and Chapter XXVIII, and portions of
Chapter XXIX, p.[1]-[13]; advertisement on inside rear
cover, rear cover with a letter from London to a Mr.
Buck, giving permission to use the material, etc. The
letter is dated May 31, 1911. This pamphlet was issued
to promote the planting of eucalyptus trees in California.
_____, New York, Macmillan, 1911, 1913, 1914, 1915, 1934,
v, 361pp.
_____, London, Heinemann, 1911, 344pp.; 1913, 1916, 270pp.;
1937, 344pp. (Heinemann adventure books).
_____, London, Reader's Library, [1928] 252pp. (Illustra-
tions from photoplay).
_____, New York, Grosset & Dunlap, c1910, [1928?] 361pp.
_____, Chicago, Donohue, [1913][?]pp.
_____, New York, Madison Square Books, 1940, 368pp.
_____, New York, Arcadia House, 1950, 361pp.

79. Translations:
Siiaina zora, tr.: Iordan Machkarov, Sofia, Iv. G. Ignatov,
1929, 245pp. (Bibl. Liubimi romani 12); Sofia, Prometeĭ,
1947, 344pp.   (Bulgarian)
Zářící den, tr.: P. Moudrá, Prague, Kočí, 1924, 2 vols.
160, 192pp.).
_____, tr.: Z. B. Nekovařík, Zlín, Tisk, 1936, 367pp.,
1947, 359pp.
Muž vysoké hrv, tr.: G. Zdárský, Prague, Souček, 1920,
352pp.   (Czech/Slovak)
En Klondike helt, tr.: Aslaug Mikkelsen, Copenhagen,
Martin, 1913, 1915, 336pp.; 1917, 2 vols.(224, 240pp.);
1920, 2 vols. (176, 190pp.); 1928, 2 vols. (264, 284pp.);
1958, 382pp.   (Danish)
Elam Harnish, tr.: S. J. Barentz-Schönberg, Amsterdam,
H. J. W. Becht, 1914.
De goudzoekers van Aljaska, Amsterdam, Boekh. en Uitg.
Mij Joh. Müller, 1923.   (Dutch)
"Loitev Koit," Päevaleht, Jan. 2-March 13, 1923 [A trans-

lation by H. Mändmets appeared in 1923, Tallinn, Tallinna
Eesti Kirjastus-Ühisus, 405pp.]   (Estonian)
Onnen suosikki, tr.: Kerttu Tuura, Helsinki, Lindstadt in
antikvaarinen kirjakauppa, 1912, 351pp.
Klondyken kuningas, tr.: K. Tuura, Helsinki,. Otava, 1919,
430pp.; 1937, 1955, 360pp.   (Finnish)
Radieuse aurore, tr.: Alice Bossuet, Paris, La Renaissance
du livre, 1921, 300pp.; Paris, Plon, 1932, 252pp.
                              (French)
Lockruf des Goldes, tr.: Erwin Magnus, Leipzig, Grethlein
& Co., 1926, 373pp.; Berlin, Universitas, 1946, 1949,
307pp.; Universitas, 1950, 1952, 268pp.; Zurich, Bücher-
gilde Gutenberg, 1946, 292pp.; Frankfurt/M., Mainz,
Bielefeld, Büchergilde Gutenberg, 1949, 307pp., 1950,
268pp.; Hamburg, Rowohlt, 1960, 1962, 235pp. (Rororo-
Taschenbuch-Ausgabe 342).
Goldrausch, r.: Eduard Thorsch, Zürich, Schweizer Druck-
und Verlagshaus, 1947, 318pp.; Vienna, Wiener Volksbuch-
Verlag, 1948, 278pp.   (German)
Ha-behala le-zahav, tr.: Shoshana Nedava, Tel-Aviv, Ha-dov,
1950, 136pp.   (Hebrew)
Hetjan í Klondyke, Reykjavík, Isafoldarprentsmiöja, 1960,
384pp.; reprinted from *Nyjar Kvöldvökur*, 12-13 (1918-
1919).   (Icelandic)
Radiosa aurora, tr.: G. Dàuli, Milan, Modernissima, 1928,
367pp.; Milan, Cavallotti, 1948, 241pp.
____, tr.: Ida Lori, Milan, Bietti, 1928, 367pp.; Bietti,
1933; Bietti, 1935, 397pp.
____, tr.: Gastone Rossi, Milan, Sonzogno, 1928, 316pp.
____, tr.: M. Parisi, Milan, Barion, 1933; 1936, 413pp.
                              (Italian)
Rytas aušta, tr.: T. Krompolcieni, Vilna, Valst. Grož.
lit. 1-kla, 1958, 370pp.   (Lithuanian)
En Klondykehelt, tr.: Nordahl Grieg, Oslo, Gyldendal,
1934, 1941, 1954, 302pp.; 1950, 232pp.
                              (Norwegian)
Płonace światło, tr.: Adam Wydzga, Katowice, Sp. Wyd.
"Polonia", 382pp.
Złoty dzień, tr.: Adam Wydzga, Warsaw, E. Kuthan, 1949,
386pp.
Elam Harnish, tr.: Tadeusz Evert, Warsaw, Iskry, 1960,
315pp.   (Polish)
Aur si iubire, tr.: Mircea A. Dumitrescu, Bucharest,
Fortuna, [n.d.]491 + 4pp.   (Rumanian)
Byvaly and *Zolotaya zorka*, tr.: S. Tsederbaum and B.
Tsemlin, Moscow and Petrograd, 1923, 230pp. [Translation
of ... and *Burning daylight*].
Krasnoye solnyshko, tr.: Zin. Lvovski, Leningrad, Mysl,

1925, 325pp.   (Russian)
Sunce Jarko, tr.: N[ikola] B. Jovanovic, Belgrade, Bib-
lioteka Narodna knijiznica, 1929, 143 + 1pp. (No. 51)
[Part 1]. [Part 2] published under the title *Ilem Harnis*,
tr.: N. B. Jovanovic, Belgrade, Biblioteka Narodna knjiznica, 1930 (No. 59).
Beli dan, tr.: S. Luka Semenovíc, Belgrade, Rad, 1961,
344pp.   (Serbian)
Aurora espléndida, tr.: Antonio Guardiola, Valencia,
Prometeo, 1928, 224pp.; Buenos Aires, Editorial Futuro,
1943, 253pp.; Buenos Aires, Siglo XX, 1940, 1949, 196pp.
[Unnumbered final page is a glossary of English terms
left in the text of the translation.] Buenos Aires, Ediciones Siglo XX, 1952, 236pp. (Colección La Rosa de los
Vientos); Barcelona, Edición G. P., 1957, 160pp.
_____, tr.: H. C. Granch, Buenos Aires, Ed. Molino, 1947,
222pp.
_____, Santiago de Chile, Editora Interamericana, 1955,
220pp. (Colección ciencia y literatura).
Aurora esplendida, *Revista literaria: novelas y cuentos*,
no. 1,810 (Jan. 16, 1966), 64pp.   (Spanish)
Kungen af Klondyke, tr.: Algot Sandberg, Stockholm, Bohlin,
1913, 400pp.; 1920, 1925, 366pp.; Stockholm, Bonnier,
1953, 311pp.
_____, tr.: Jan Myrdal, Stockholm, Folket; Bild, 1958,
323pp.   (Swedish)

THEFT. 1910

80. THEFT | *A PLAY* | *IN FOUR ACTS* | BY | JACK LONDON | Author
of "Burning Daylight," etc. | New York | THE MACMILLAN
COMPANY | LONDON: MACMILLAN & CO. LTD. | 1910 | *All
rights reserved*
     [iv] v [vi] vii [viii] ix - xii [xiii - xiv] [1-2]
3-272p. 17.5 x 12 cm. Red cloth with white spine. Top
edges gilt. Lettering on spine black. Lettering on front
cover white.
     On verso of title-page (p.[iv]): COPYRIGHT, 1910 |
By THE MACMILLAN COMPANY | [rule] | Set up and electro-
typed. Published November, 1910 | [Two lines of press
signature]
     Often title-pages have been removed from poor copies
of the first edition and inserted in later printings.
Textual differences may be noted by the split letters "a"
and "t" in "that", page 47, line 1, and in the mutilation
of the "d" in "perplexed" page 65, line 1.
     This play was written for Olga Nethersole, the popular
actress, but it was never produced. It went the rounds of

the play agencies, but no production resulted.

81. Translations:
Krazha, tr.: E. Golyshevoi and B. Kbakova, Moscow, Iskusstvo, 1955, 108pp.
Volchi dushi, tr.: Zin. Lvovski and N. V. Lapina, Petrograd, Mysl, 1922, 103pp.   (Russian)

WHEN GOD LAUGHS. 1911

82. WHEN GOD LAUGHS | AND OTHER STORIES | BY | JACK LONDON | AUTHOR OF "MARTIN EDEN," "CALL OF THE WILD," | "WHITE FANG," ETC., ETC. | New York | THE MACMILLAN COMPANY | 1911 | *All rights reserved*
[vi] vii [viii] ix [x][1-2]3-319p. 18.5 x 12 cm. Dark olive green cloth decorated in red and light green. Lettering on spine and front cover gilt. Frontis. Four pages of publisher's advertisements at back.
On verso of title-page (p. [iv]):[Nine lines of previous magazine publishing copyright notices] | [rule] | COPYRIGHT, 1911, | BY THE MACMILLAN COMPANY. | [rule] | Set up and electrotyped. Published January, 1911. | [Three lines of press signature]
Contents: When God Laughs; The Apostate; A Wicked Woman; Just Meat; Created He Them; The Chinago; Make Westing; Semper Idem; A Nose for the King; The "Francis Spaight"; A Curious Fragment; A Piece of Steak.

83. Reprints:
____, New York, The Regent Press [c1911] [?]pp.
____, London, Mills & Boon, 1912, 320pp.; 1913, 314pp.; 1914, 298pp.
____, New York, McKinlay, Stone & Mackenzie [1911] 319pp.
____, Cleveland, International fiction library [c1911] 319pp.
____, New York, etc., M. A. Donohue & Co. [1911] [?]pp.
____, New York, Macmillan, 1919, 319pp.

84. Translations:
Koga bogovete se smeiat, tr.: Ant. Bezhanovski, Sofia, Zhivot, 1920, 96pp. Contents: Koga botovete se smeiat. Stachka. Parche meso.
____, tr.: B. Israki, Sofia, Vsemirna Bibl., 1939, 108pp. (Vsemirna bibl., no. 2).   (Bulgarian)
Als de goden lachen, tr.: J. P. Wesselink-van Rossum, Amsterdam, Boekh. en Uitg. Mij. Joh. Müller, 1923
                                        (Dutch)
Ottelukehässä, tr.: Toivo Nelimies [Yrjö Gustafsson,

Toivo Hammas, Uuno Mattila, Toivo Mähönen] Turku, Helsinki,
Kustannusoy. Kansanvalta, 1925, 117pp. [2 stories].
(Finnish)
Az istenek kacagnak. Mikor az Isten kacag, tr.: J. Jenő,
Tersánzky Budapest, Athenaeum, 1926, 186pp.
(Hungarian)
Quando Dio ride, tr.: G. Dàuli, Milan, Modernissima,
[1926?] 327pp.; 2nd ed., 1928, 238pp. [Selected stories
from *When God laughs, The night born and South Sea tales.*]
Contents of ed. of 327pp.; Quando Dio ride (When God
laughs). Uccidere un uomo (To kill a man). La razzi di
MacCoy (The seed of McCoy). Il beneficio del dubbio (The
benefit of the doubt). La casa di Mapuhi (The house of
Mapuhi). La pazzia di John Harned (The madness of John
Harned). Guerra (War). Una bistecca (A piece of steak).
Il pagano (The heathen). La terribili isole Solomone (The
terrible Solomons). Il Messicano (The Mexican).
_____, tr.: Maria Carlesimo Pasquali, Milan, Bietti, 1930
269pp.
_____. *Storie di guardie del pese,* tr.: Mario Benzi, Sesto
S. Giovanni-Milano, Barion, 1938, 397pp.
(Italian)
Kai dievai juikiasi, tr.: R. Stropus, Kaunas, Valst. grož.
lit. 1-kla, 1947, 196pp. Contents: Kai dievai juikiasi.
Atskalunas. Nedora moteris. Mesos gabalas. Negi jis juos
sutvere. Čainagas. Plauk i vakarus. Semper idem. Nosis
karaliui. "Francis Spaitas". Idomus fragmentas. Kepsnio
kasnis. [The order is the same as the English original.]
(Lithuanian)

ADVENTURE. 1911

85. ADVENTURE | BY | JACK LONDON | AUTHOR OF "THE CALL OF THE
WILD," "BURNING DAYLIGHT," | ETC., ETC. | New York | THE
MACMILLAN COMPANY | 1911 | *All rights reserved*
   [vi] vii-viii [ix-x] 1-405p. 19 x 12.5 cm. Dark blue
cloth stamped in light blue and white on cover and spine.
Six pages of publisher's advertisements at back.
   On verso of title-page (p. [iv]): COPYRIGHT, 1910, |
BY STREET AND SMITH. | COPYRIGHT, 1911, | BY THE MAC-
MILLAN COMPANY. | [rule] | Set up and electrotyped. Pub-
lished March, 1911. | [Three lines of press signature]
   From a copy in the George H. Tweney collection, this
book was also issued in red cloth, with front cover and
backstrip lettering and decorations in white, internal
collation and pagination exactly as described above. No
priority of issue has thus far been established.

86. Serializations:
First published serially in *Popular Magazine*, 18,2:129-
147 (Nov. 1, 1910), 18,3:70-91 (Nov. 15, 1910), 18,4:101-
118 (Dec. 1, 1910), 18,5:134-149 (Dec. 15, 1910), 18,
6:123-137 (Jan. 1, 1911), 19,1:170-184 (Jan. 15, 1911);
also serialized in *Grand Magazine*, 13:72-94, 172-196,
349-373, 556-571, 706-719 (March-July 1911).
It was serialized without permission in at least one newspaper; on July 3, 1911 the Akron (Ohio) *Press* printed
chapter 20 of this novel. A clipping containing this chapter is in the London correspondence in the Huntington
Library along with a London letter which denies that this
newspaper was given permission to serialize this novel.

87. Reprints:
_____, New York, Regent Press [1911] viii, 405pp.
_____, Chicago, Donohue, [1913] [?]pp.
_____, London, Nelson, 1907, 373pp.; 1911, 1915, 376pp.;
1913.

_____, London, Mills & Boon, 1916, 1924, 1928, 316pp.
_____, New York, Macmillan, 1934, 405pp.
_____, New York, Arcadia House, 1950, 405pp.

88. Translations:
Prikliucheniiata na dzhoanna, tr.: D. Podvurzachov, Sofia,
Br. Miladinovi, 1933, 228pp. (Sp. Stranitzi za vsichki
III); Sofia, Chetivo, 1946, 215pp.
Avantiuristkata dzhoana, tr.: Georgi Savchev, Sofia, D.
Madzharov, 1936, 168pp.   (Bulgarian)
Olok beranda, tr.: Josefina Fajmer, Rijeka, Otokar
Kersovani, 1956, 181pp.   (Croatian?)
Paa eventyr, tr.: E. S. Steenberg, Copenhagen, Martin,
1914, 272pp.; 1917, 240pp.; 1920, 214pp.; 1928, 320pp.;
Copenhagen, Samleren, 1951, 212pp.
_____, Copenhagen, Politiken, 1944, 64pp.
                                        (Danish)
Ihmissyöjäin Saarilla, tr.: Aune Tudeer, Helsinki, Kustan-
nusoy, 1920, 151pp.; Helsinki, Otava, 1937, 295pp.
                                        (Finnish)
L'aventure de Jean Lackland, tr.: Fanny Guillermet, Paris
& Neuchâtel, Attinger, 1917, iv, 232pp.; Attinger, 1919,
[?]pp.
L'aventureuse, tr.: Paul Gruyer and Louis Postif, Paris,
Crès, 1927, iii, 263pp. Pp. i-iii, "Préface des traduct-
eurs"; Paris, Hachette, 1938, 254pp. (Bibliothèque verte
152); with a preface by J. B. Podevigne, Paris, Compagnie
des libraires et des éditeurs associés, 1956, 347pp.
                                        (French)

Abenteurer auf Berande, Zürich, Buch-Gemeinschaft Ex
Libris, 1951, 344pp.
Die Herrin auf Berande, tr.: Richard C. Seiler, Zürich,
Schweizer Druck- und Verlagshaus, 1952, 323pp.
Die Insel Berande, tr.: Erwin Magnus, Berlin, Universitas,
1927, 274pp.; 1953, 260pp.; Berlin, Dt. Buch-Gemeinschaft,
1940, 302pp.; Frankfurt/M., Büchergilde Gutenberg, 1953,
260pp.
_____, tr.: Max Barthel, Berlin, Hamburg, Dt. Buch-Gemein-
schaft, 1950, 1951, 306pp.
_____, Hamburg, Dt. Hausbücherei, 1961, 239pp.
                                        (German)
Aefintýri, tr.: Ingólfur Jónsson, Reykjavik, Prentsmiðjan
Gutenburg, 1921, 213pp.   (Icelandic)
L'avventura, tr.: Gino Sesostra, Milan, Sonzogno, 1927,
237pp.; 1942, 241pp.
_____, tr.: Rosalia Gwis-Adami, Milan, Bietti, 1933, 317pp.
L'avventura di Giovanna Lackland, tr.: Gianni d'Arezzo,
Milan, Modernissima, 1928, 287pp.
Avventura, tr.: Annie and Adriano Lami, Milan, Treves,
1933, 1938, 303pp.
*Avventura. Racconti del mare del Sud,*Sesto S. Giovanni-
Milano. Barion, 1943.   (Italian)
*Dāvida Šeldona un Dženas Lakland piedzīvojumi starp Sal-
amona salu mežoniem cilvēkēdējiem*, tr.: J. Vanags, Riga,
J. Vanags, 1923, 24pp.
Brīniskie piedzīvojumi, Riga, Laiks, 1924, 264pp.
"Piedzivojums," *Jauno Straume*, nos. 11-46 (March 22-Dec.
22, 1930).
Piedzīvojums, tr.: Z. Krodere, Riga, Grāmatu Draugs, 1933,
224pp.   (Latvian)
Pa eventyr, tr.: J. Grieg-Müller, Oslo, Gyldendal, 1943,
1947, 268pp.   (Norwegian)
Przygoda, tr.: Stanisława Kuszelewska, Warsaw, E. Wende,
1925, 303pp.; Warsaw, 1926, 2 vols.; Warsaw, Rój, 1929,
1935, 1938.   (Polish)
Priklyucheniye, tr.: M. Rosenfeld, Moscow, Universalnaya
Biblioteka, 1917, 337pp.; Moscow and Petrograd, Gosizdat.,
1923, 326pp.
_____, tr.: A. N. Kudrysvtseva and A. G. Movshenson, Lenin-
grad and Moscow, Novella, 1924, 237pp.
_____, tr.: A. G. Movshenson, Leningrad, Mysl, 1925, 200pp.
                                        (Russian)
Pustolovka, tr.: Jozefina Fajmer, Rijeka, O. Keršovani,
1954, 181pp.
_____, tr.: Nevana Čičanović-Stefoanović, Belgrade, Stožer,
1957, 201pp.   (Serbian)
Aventura, tr.: A. Nadal, Valencia, Prometeo, 1926, 223pp.;

Barcelona, Edic. G. P., 1958, 159pp. (Alcotan 82).
Aventura en las Islas Salomon, tr.: A. Nadal, Buenos Aires,
Ediciones Siglo Veinte, 1952, 212pp.
Aventura, Revista literaria: novelas y cuentos, no. 1,
587 (Oct. 1, 1961), 72pp.   (Spanish)
*Afventyr,*tr.: M. Drangel, Stockholm, Bohlin, 1916, 298pp.;
other editions 1918, 1925.   (Swedish)
Macera arayan kadin, tr.: Celal Ekrem, Istanbul, A. Halit
Kitabevi, 1941, 264pp.; 1944, 192pp. (Turkish)

THE CRUISE OF THE SNARK. 1911

89. THE CRUISE OF THE | SNARK | BY | JACK LONDON | AUTHOR OF
"BURNING DAYLIGHT," "MARTIN EDEN," | "THE CALL OF THE
WILD," ETC. | *ILLUSTRATED* | New York | THE MACMILLAN
COMPANY | 1911 | *All rights reserved*
     [vi] vii [viii] ix - xiv 1-340p. 20 x 13.5 cm. Light
blue cloth lettered in gilt on spine and front cover.
Colored print of the Snark inlaid on front cover, identical with frontispiece. Top edges gilt. Frontis. print of
the Snark in color. Four pages of publisher's advertisements at back.
     On verso of title-page (p.[iv]): COPYRIGHT, 1906, |
BY HARPER & BROTHERS. | COPYRIGHT, 1906, | BY THE INTER-
NATIONAL MAGAZINE CO. | COPYRIGHT, 1907, 1908, and 1909,
BY THE CROWELL PUBLISHING COMPANY. | COPYRIGHT, 1911, |
BY THE MACMILLAN COMPANY. | [rule] | Set up and electro-
typed. Published June, 1911. | [Three lines of press
signature]
     Contents: Foreword. The inconceivable and monstrous.
Adventure. Finding one's way about. The first landfall.
A royal sport. The lepers of Molokai. The house of the
sun. A Pacific traverse. Typee. The nature of man. The
high seat of abundance. Stone-fishing of Bora Bora. The
amateur navigator. Cruising in the Solomons. Beche de mer
English. The amateur M. D.. Backword.
     Merle Johnson's *American First Editions* states, "All
examined copies of the first edition have the title page
tipped in."
     Huntington 337699 contains the following additional
material inserted in the 1st ed.:
1. "News concerning the 'Snark'," July 7, 1910 signed
George Darbishire, 2 leaves, holograph; 2. penciled nav-
igation data signed Jack London "On board the Snark" and
dated Dec. 2, 1907; 3. The story of Captain Weaver's gold,
14 leaves, typescript; 4. "On board the Snark," Dec. 2,
1907 signed Jack London, Chronometer method; 5. "Dying
out. New Hebrides natives. Fighting to the last. Steamers

from the islands"; 6. description of Yacht Snark, 2 leaves,
typewritten description written in an attempt to sell the
yacht; 7. carbon of letter of May 2, 1909 and 2 leaves entitled "A brief explanation"; 8. "A chant of the wander-
ers," 3 leaves, 48 lines of verse, typed, holograph signature of Elwyn Hoffman.

90. Serializations:
Chapters appeared in periodicals as follows: "Lepers of
Molokai," *Woman's Home Companion*, 35:7-8,45 (Jan. 1908);
reprinted in *Contemporary Review*, 95:288-297 (March 1909);
"Adventures in dream harbor," *Harper's Weekly*, 52:22
(Aug. 8, 1908); "Finding one's way on the sea," *Harper's
Weekly*, 52:9-10 (Aug. 1, 1908); "The nature man," *Woman's
Home Companion*, 35:21-22 (Sept. 1908); *Cassell's Magazine*,
42:51-58 (Dec. 1908); "The high seat of abundance,"
Woman's Home Companion, 35:12-14, 70 (Nov. 1908); "Bêche
de mer English," *Woman's Home Companion*, 36:4 (April 1909);
Contemporary Review, 96:359-364 (Sept. 1909); "House of
the sun," *Pacific Monthly*, 23:1-11 (Jan. 1910); *Mid-
Pacific Magazine,* 9:591-596 (June 1915); "A Pacific tra-
verse," *Pacific Monthly*, 23:163-174 (Feb. 1910); "Typee,"
Pacific Monthly, 23:267-281 (March 1910); *Uncle Remus'
Home Magazine*, 27:10-12 (April 1910); "Stone-fishing of
Bora Bora," *Pacific Monthly*, 23:335-346 (April 1910);
Badminton Magazine, 32:421-425 (1911); "An amateur naviga-
tor," *Pacific Monthly*, 23:493-508 (May 1910); "Cruising
in the Solomons," *Pacific Monthly*, 23:589-602 (June 1910),
23:35-43 (July 1910); *Uncle Remus's Home Magazine*, 28:9-12
(Nov. 1910); "Amateur M.D.," *Pacific Monthly*, 24:187-203
(Aug. 1910).
"The Cruise of the Snark," *Outwest*, 36:359-369 (Dec. 1912).
Selections appeared in the *Pacific Commercial Advertiser*
(Honolulu) "Newspaper Day" section, Nov. 28, 1914:
"Haleakala," p.2; "Surfing at Waikiki," p.4 and "The
'Ditch country'," p.6.

91. Reprints:
The cruise of the "Snark", London, Mills & Boon, 1913,
354pp.; 1915, 308pp.; 1923, 1926, 307pp.
_____, Chicago, Donohue [c1911] 283pp.
_____, New York, Macmillan, 1913, 1938, 1943, xiv, 340pp.

92. Translations:
Potulky po ostrovech jižního moře, tr.: M. Reisnigrova,
Prague, Kočí, 1925, 2 vols. (131, 142pp.).
Poltulky po Južnom Tichomorí, tr.: E. V. Tvarožek, Martin,
Osveta, 1955, 208pp.   (Czech/Slovak)

Paa langfart med snarken, tr.: Aslaug Mikkelsen and Einar Mikkelsen, Copenhagen, Martin, 1916, 256pp.; 1921, 240pp.; 1929, 344pp. (Danish)
De kruistocht van de Snark, tr.: Leo Leclercq, Amsterdam, Joh. Müller, 1924. (Dutch)
"Looduslaps," tr.: R. Kullerkupp, *Kodu*, No. 2:28-31 (1922) [Selection] (Estonian)
Etelämeren auringon alla, Helsinki, Otava, 1924, 267pp. (Finnish)
La croisière du Snark, tr.: Louis Postif, Paris, Hachette, ⌊c1936⌋ 254pp. (Les meilleurs romans ètrangers); Hachette, 1953, 189pp. (Idéal-Bibliothèque). (French)
Die Fahrt der Snark, tr.: Erwin Magnus, Berlin, Universitas, 1930, 278pp.; Universitas, 1959, 261pp.; Berlin-Schöneberg, Oestergaard, 1935, 277pp. (German)
Snark. Kirándulás a föld körül, tr.: Vécsey Leó, Budapest, Légrády, 1924, 272pp. (Hungarian)
La crociera dello Snark, tr.: L. Giartosio de Courten, Rome, Sampietro, 1958, 288pp. (Italian)
Pa langfart med Snarken, tr.: Nordahl Grieg, Oslo, Gyldendal, 1934, 1941, 219pp.; 1961, 195pp. (Norwegian)
Zegluga na jachcie "Snark", tr.: Jerzy B. Rychlinski, Warsaw, Tania Ksiazka, 1927, 1939, 2 vols.; Warsaw, E. Kuthan, 1949, 262pp. (Polish)
Snark, tr.: A. G. Moveshenson, Leningrad, Mysl, 1925, 239pp.
Puteshestivie na "Snarke", Moscow, Geografgiz, 1958, 207pp. (Russian)

SOUTH SEA TALES. *1911*

93. SOUTH SEA TALES | BY | JACK LONDON | AUTHOR OF "ADVENTURE," "BURNING DAYLIGHT," | "THE CALL OF THE WILD," ETC. | *WITH FRONTISPIECE* | New York | THE MACMILLAN COMPANY | 1911 | *All rights reserved*
   [iv] v [vi][1-2] 3-327p. 19.5 x 13 cm. Light blue cloth decorated in olive green, white, and black. Lettering on front cover and spine white. Frontis. in color. Six pages of publisher's advertisements at back.
   On verso of title-page (p. [iv]): [Seven lines of previous magazine publishing copyright notices]   COPYRIGHT, 1911, | BY THE MACMILLAN COMPANY. | [rule] |Set up and electrotyped. Published October, 1911. | [Three lines of press signature]
   Contents: The House of Mapuhi; The Whale Tooth; Mauki; "Yah! Yah! Yah!"; The Heathen; The Terrible Solomons; The Inevitable White Man; The Seed of McCoy.

94. Reprints:
____, Chicago, New York, M. A. Donohue, 1911, 327pp.
____, New York, McKinlay, Stone and Mackenzie [c1911]
327pp.
____, New York, P. F. Collier [c1911] 327pp. (Seven Seas
ed.).
____, Cleveland, International fiction library [c1911]
327pp.
____, London, Mills & Boon, 1912, 314pp.; 1914, 286pp.;
1923, 1928, 186pp.
____, London, Hutchinson, 1915, 256pp.
____, London, Newnes, 1921, 128pp.
____, London, Methuen, 1939.
____, New York, Cleveland, World Publishing Co., 1946,
327pp. (Tower Books Edition; also published in Toronto,
McClelland, 1946, 327pp.). [First printing in March 1946,
12mo., green cloth binding, dust wrapper with design from
a painting by Paul Gauguin, brief biographical sketch
"About the Author" on back flap of wrapper.]
____, New York, Arcadia House, 1950, 327pp.
____, New York, Lion Books, 1952, 158pp. (No. 92).

95. Translations:
Iz iuzhnite moreta, tr.: G. Efremov, Sofia, Gladston,
1933, 100pp. (Bibl. Svetut na chudesata) Contents:
Uraganut. Ia-a! Ia-a! Ia-a! Kitoviiat zub. Iazichnikut.
Mauki.
Strashnite Solomonovi ostrovi, tr.: R. Stoianov, Sofia, Al
Paskalev, 1932, 84pp. (Vsemirna bibl; 794). Contents:
Strashnite Solomonovi estrovi. Kushchata na Mauki. Kitovi
baleni. Mauki.   (Bulgarian)
Povídky jižních moří, tr.: I. Schulz, Prague, Springer,
1917, 194pp.
____, tr.: I. Schulz, Prague, Kočí, 1924, 126pp. Contents:
Dum Mapuhiho. Vorvaní zub. Mauki. Yah! Yah! Yah! Pohan.
Strašné Šalamounovy ostrovy.   (Czech/Slovak)
Verhalen van de Zuidzee, tr.: Leo Leclercq, Amsterdam,
Boekh. en Uitg. Mij Joh. Müller, 1923, [?]pp.
                            (Dutch)
Contes des mers du Sud, tr.: Paul Gruyer and Louis Postif,
Paris, Hachette, 1931, 254pp. (Les meilleurs romans
étrangers); [Hachette, 1948, 256pp. (Bibliothèque verte);
Hachette, 1952, 190pp. (Idéal-bibliothèque). Contents:
La graine de MacCoy. Le paien. L'inevitable blanc. Les
terribilissimes iles Salomon. Maouki. Yah! Yah! Yah! La
maison de Mapouhi. Le dent de cachalot.
                            (French)
Südseegeschichten, tr.: E. Magnus, Berlin, Gyldendalscher

Verlag, 1924, 265pp.; Berlin, Universitas, 1926, 255pp.;
1927, 259pp.; 1949, 254pp.; Berlin, Tribüne, 1956, 268pp.
Contents: Die Perle, Der Walzahn. Mauki. Der blasse
Schrecken. Otto, der Heide. Die furchtbaren Salomoninseln.
Der unvermeidliche weisse Mann. Feuer auf See.
____, tr.: Eduard Thorsch, Zürich, Schweizer Druck- und
Verlagshaus, 1947, 285pp. Contents: Das Haus Mapuhis.
Der Walfischzahn. Der Heide. Mit Feuer an Bord. Die weis-
sen Teufel. "Federn der Sonne". Die furchterregenden Salomonen. "Pau." Joe Garland. Der Sheriff von Kona. [These
stories have been translated from *South Sea tales, The
house of pride* and *On the Makaloa mat.*]
____, Vienna, Wiener Volksbuchverlag, 1949, 236pp.
____, Berlin, Darmstadt: Deutsche Buchgemeinschaft, 1951,
285pp.   (German)
Racconti del mare del Sud, tr.: Teresa Novi, Venice, La
Nuova Italia, 1928, 162pp.
____, tr.: Adele Levi, Milan, Bietti, 1931, [?]pp.; 1933,
301pp.
____, tr.: Beatrice Boffito, Milan, Rizzoli, 1955, 175pp.
                                                 (Italian)
Minami no umi [South Sea tales?] tr.: Sangoro Shima,
Tokyo, Cosmos Shoin, 1925, 206pp.   (Japanese)
Opowiesci morz poludniowych, tr.: J. B. Rychlinski, Warsaw, Ignis, 1923, 1924, 1925, 244pp.; Warsaw, Biblioteka
Groszowa, 1927, 191pp.; Warsaw, Wyd. Dziennik Ludowy,
1939, 180pp.; Warsaw, E. Kuthan, 1947, 212pp. Contents:
All four contain: Poganin (The heathen). Dom czarnego
Mapuhi (The house of Mapuhi). Mauki. Straszliwy archi-
pelag (The terrible Solomons). Zab wielorybi (The whale
tooth) and "Yah! Yah! Yah!." [Wiezwyciezony bialy czlowiek
(The inevitable white man) appears in each of the above
except that of 1939. Pracownik McCoy'a (The seed of McCoy)
appears only in those published in 1923-5, 1947.]
                                                  (Polish)
Sandvichevy ostrova, tr.: A. V. Aleksandrov, O. I. Zolkind,
B. K. Ryndy-Alekseyev, Moscow and Leningrad, Gosizdat,
1927, 343pp.   (Russian)
Cuentos de los mares del Sur, tr.: A. Guardiola, Valencia,
Prometeo, 1927, 235pp.
____, tr.: Irene Munte, Barcelona, Mateu, 1958, 256pp.
(Col. Juvenil Cadete 132).   (Spanish)
I Söderhavet, tr.: Torsten and Maria Söderling, Stockholm,
Folket, 1958, 250pp.   (Swedish)
Skazi iuzhnyek morei, tr.: I. Ryl'skikh, Kiev, 1927, 88pp.
                                              (Ukranian)

THE HOUSE OF PRIDE. 1912

96. THE HOUSE OF PRIDE | AND OTHER TALES OF HAWAII | BY
    JACK LONDON | AUTHOR OF "THE SEA WOLF," "WHITE | FANG,"
    "SOUTH SEA TALES," ETC. | New York | THE MACMILLAN
    COMPANY | 1912 | *All rights reserved*
    [iv] v [vi][1-2] 3-232p. 19.5 x 13 cm. Light green
    cloth decorated in blue, black, and white. Lettering on
    front cover and spine white. Six pages of publisher's ad-
    vertisements at back.
    On verso of title-page (p.[iv]): [Six lines of previous
    magazine publishing copyright notices] | COPYRIGHT, 1912,|
    BY THE MACMILLAN COMPANY. | [rule] | Set up and electro-
    typed. Published March, 1912. | [Three lines of press
    signature]
    Contents: The House of Pride; Koolau the Leper; Good-
    by, Jack; Aloha Oe; Chun Ah Chun; The Sheriff of Kona.

97. Reprints:
    ____, Chicago, Donohue, 19[12?], [?]pp.
    ____, New York, Macmillan, 1914, 232pp.
    ____, London, Mills & Boon, 1914, 288pp.
    ____, New York, Grosset & Dunlap, 1928, 232pp.

98. Translations:
    Dum pychy. tr.: I. Schulz, Prague, Vyd. Dobrých autoru,
    1920, 117pp.
    ____, tr.: V. Smetánka, Prague, Koči, 1923, 117pp.
                              (Czech/Slovak)
    Suvun kunnia ja muita kertomuksia Hawaii-saarilta, tr.:
    Vilho Oksanen, Helsinki, Otava, 1917, 83pp. [4 stories]
                              (Finnish)
    Chun-Ah-Chun, tr.: Louis Postif, Paris, Hachette [c1940]
    [?]pp. (Les meilleurs romans étrangers). Contents: Jack
    London, par lui-même. Chun-Ah-Chun. L'orgueil de sa race.
    Aloha oe. Adieu, Jack! Koolau le lépreux. Le shérif de
    Kona. Chargement d'opium.   (French)
    A büszkeség háza, tr.: Zoltán Bartos, Budapest, Táltos,
    1923, 137pp.; Tolnai, 1924, 157pp. (Tolnai regénytára).
                              (Hungarian)
    La casa dell'orgoglio: racconti delle isole Hawai, tr.:
    Adele Levi, Milan, Bietti, 1931, 202pp.
                              (Italian)
    Sandwichøyene, tr.: Ben Horne, Oslo, Gyldendal, 1941,
    159pp.   (Norwegian)
    Dom pychy, tr.: St. Kuszelewska-Rajska, Warsaw, E. Kuthan,
    1949, 176pp. Contents: Dom pychy. Koolau Tredowaty. Zegnaj
    Jack. Aloha oe. Chun Ah Chun. Szeryf Miasta Kony. [These

are the same stories and the same order as in the American
edition. In addition, pp.163-176 are entitled "Jack London
o sobie".]   (Polish)
Dom gordosti, tr.: D. Ye Deikhtenberg, Leningrad, Mysl,
1924, 136pp.   (Russian)

A SON OF THE SUN. 1912

99. A SON | OF THE SUN | BY | JACK LONDON | AUTHOR OF | "THE
CALL OF THE WILD," "THE SEA WOLF," "MARTIN EDEN," | "THE
GOD OF HIS FATHERS," ETC. | ILLUSTRATED BY | A. O. FISCHER
AND C. W. ASHLEY | [publisher's device] | GARDEN CITY NEW
YORK | DOUBLEDAY, PAGE & COMPANY | 1912
[viii] [1-2] 3-333p. 19 x 12.5 cm. Light blue cloth
with embossed ship decoration on front cover in gray,
white, and orange. Lettering on front cover and spine gray.
Frontis.
On verso of title-page (p.[iv]): ALL RIGHTS RESERVED,
INCLUDING THAT OF TRANSLATION | INTO FOREIGN LANGUAGES,
INCLUDING THE SCANDINAVIAN | COPYRIGHT, 1911, BY THE
CURTIS PUBLISHING COMPANY | COPYRIGHT, 1912, BY DOUBLE-
DAY, PAGE & COMPANY
Contents: A Son of the Sun; The Proud Goat of Aloysius
Pankburn; The Devils of Fuatino; The Jokers of New Gibbon;
A Little Account With Swithin Hall; A Goboto Night; The
Feathers of the Sun; The Pearls of Parlay.

100. Reprints:
____, New York, Grosset & Dunlap [c1912][1916] 333pp.
____, London, Curtis, Brown & Co., 1912, 333pp.
____, London, Mills & Boon [1913] 301pp.; 1914, 284pp.
____, London, Newnes, 1915, 258pp.
____, Boston, Houghton, 1930, 251pp.
____, Toronto, The Musson Book Co.,[n.d.,] 333pp.
Reprinted as *Adventures of Captain Grief*, Cleveland,
World Publishing Co., 1954, 191pp.

101. Translations:
Sin na sluntzeto, tr.: Leonid Paspaleev, Sofia, Prometeĭ,
1947, 200pp.   (Bulgarian)
Syn slunce, tr.: I. Schulz, Prague, Neumannová, 1918,
182pp.; Neumannová, 1920, 181pp.
____, tr.: Ž. Pohorecká, Prague, Kočí, 1922, 2 vols. (106,
106pp.); tr.: Ž. Pohorecká, Zlín, Tisk, 1938, 206pp.
                                   (Czech/Slovak)
En solens søn, tr.: E. S. Steenberg, Copenhagen, Martin,
1919, 192pp.; 1927, 208pp.; 1929, 284pp.
                                   (Danish)

Auringon poika, Helsinki, Otava, 1919, 202pp.; 1924, 216pp.
(Finnish)
Ein Sohn der Sonne, tr.: Erwin Magnus, Berlin, Universitas, 1926, 301; Universitas, 1946, 1949, 299pp.; Berlin,
Deutsche Buch-Gemeinschaft, 1946, 299pp.; Zürich, Bücher-
gilde Gutenberg, 1948, 262pp.; Frankfurt/M., Mainz, Biel-
efeld, Büchergilde Gutenberg, 1949, 299pp.
(German)
A nap fia, tr.: Sándor Adorján, Budapest, Athenaeum, 1922,
232pp.
Tüzes napsugár, tr.: Ferenc Kelen, Budapest, Athenaeum,
1922, 304pp.; 1928, Összes munkái 13.(Hungarian)
Il figlio del sole, tr.: Gian Dàuli, Milan, Modernissima,
1925, 1928, 286pp.
_____, tr.: G. Rossi, Milan, Sonzogno, 1927, 238pp.
Un figlio del sole, Milan, Bietti, 1929, 316pp.; 1933,
301pp.
_____, *Quando Dio ride. Storie di guardia del pesce,* tr.:
Mario Benzi, Sesto S. Giovanni-Milano, Barion, 1938,
[?]pp.   (Italian)
Saules dēls, Riga, B. Dīrika un b-dra druk., 1913, 132pp.
_____, tr.: K. Dzintars, Jelgava, Brāli Hāni, 1925, 219pp.
(Latvian)
Saules sunūs, tr.: M. Kalpoki, Kaunas, Tulpė, 1926, 120pp.
(Lithuanian)
En solens sønn, tr.: Nordahl Grieg, Oslo, Gyldendal, 1934,
1941, 205pp.   (Norwegian)
Syn słonca, tr.: J. B. Rychliński, Warsaw, E. Wende, 1923,
1925; Ignis, 1924, each 216pp.; Warsaw, Biblioteka Groszowa, 1931, 2 vols. (163, 157pp.); Warsaw, E. Kuthan,
1945, 1947
_____, tr.: T. J. Dehnel, Warsaw, Iskry, 1957, 224pp.
(Polish)
Fiul scarelui, tr.: O. Iacint, Bucharest, Podeanu, 1943,
256pp.   (Rumanian)
Syn solntsa, tr.: V. Koshchevich, Moscow, Gosizdat., 1922,
273pp.; 1927, 274pp.
_____, tr.: Z. Lvovski, Leningrad and Moscow, Novella,
1924, 350pp.
Zhemchug Parleya, tr.: Ye. Patterson, Leningrad, Mysl,
1925, 1926, 246pp.   (Russian)
Sin sunca, tr.: Nikola B. Jovanovic, Belgrade, Biblioteka
Narodna, 1930, 68 + 2pp. Contents: Sin sunca (Son of the
sun). Ponos Alojzija Pankerna (The proud goat of Aloysius
Pankburn). (Biblioteka Narodna no. 92).
_____, tr.: Slavka Petrović, Belgrade, Izdanje knjizare
Svetlost, 1931, 227, 1pp. Contents: Sin sunca. Osetljivost
Alusijusa Pankburna. Djvavoli na Fuatinu. Osveta prevar-

enog Indijanca. Obracum sa Svitin Halom. Vece u Gobotu.
Parje sunca. Parlauovi biseri. [The order is the same as
the original English.]
____, tr.: Slavka Petrović, Sarajevo, Seljačka knjiga,
1952, 153+4pp. Contents: Sin sunca. Osjetlivost Alojzija
Penkberna. Davoli na Fuatinu. Osveta prevarenog Indijanca.
Obračun sa Svitin Holom. Veče u Gobotu. Parje sunca. Perle-
jevi biseri. Sa beleskom o piscu. [The order is the same
as the original English.]   (Serbian)
En solens son, tr.: Ernst Lundquist, Stockholm, Bohlin,
1918, 1926, 254pp.; Stockholm, B. Wahlstrom, 1936, 253pp.
(Groma biblioteket).   (Swedish)
Günes cocuğu, tr.: Ahmet Cemil, Istanbul, Remzi Kitabevi,
1938, 216pp.   (Turkish)
Syn solntza, tr.: Dzhun'kovskoĭ, Kiev, 1927, 214pp.
                                             (Ukranian)

SMOKE BELLEW. *1912*

102. SMOKE BELLEW | BY | JACK LONDON | AUTHOR OF "THE CALL OF
THE WILD," | "THE SEA WOLF," ETC. | ILLUSTRATED BY |
P. J. MONAHAN | [publisher's device] | NEW YORK | THE CEN-
TURY CO | 1912
     [viii] [1-3] 4-385p. 19.5 x 13 cm. Blue-gray cloth,
decorated in cream, white, and black. Lettering in black.
Frontis.
     On verso of title-page (p. [iv]): Copyright, 1912, by |
THE CENTURY CO. | [rule] | Copyright, 1911, 1912, by |
INTERNATIONAL MAGAZINE COMPANY | [rule] | *Published,*
October, 1912
     Merle Johnson's *American First Editions* states, "A copy
has been noted in plain grey-blue cloth; status unknown."

103. Serializations:
     "Tale one, the taste of the meat," *Cosmopolitan*, 51:16-28
(June 1911); *Nash's Magazine* 4:511-521 (Aug. 1911). "Tale
two, the meat," *Cosmopolitan*, 51:209-222 (July 1911);
Nash's Magazine, 4:657-670 (Sept. 1911). "Tale three, the
stampede to Squaw Creek," *Cosmopolitan*, 51:356-368 (Aug.
1911); *Nash's Magazine* 5:33-45 (Oct. 1911)."Tale four,
Shorty dreams," *Cosmopolitan*, 51:437-446 (Sept. 1911);
"Shorty has a dream," *Nash's Magazine*, 5:143-152 (Nov.
1911). "Tale five, The man on the bank," *Cosmopolitan*,
51:677-688 (Oct. 1911); "The man on the other bank,"
Nash's Magazine, 5:307-318 (Dec. 1911). "The race for
number three," *Cosmopolitan*, 51:823-835 (Nov. 1911);
"Tale six: ...," *Nash's Magazine*, 5:429-441 (Jan. 1912).
"The little man," *Cosmopolitan*, 52:15-25 (Dec. 1911);

"The story of the little man," *Nash's Magazine*, 5:586-596 (Feb. 1912). "The hanging of Cultus George," *Cosmopolitan*, 52:200-210 (Jan. 1912); *Nash's Magazine* 6:47-59 (April 1912). "The mistake of creation," *Cosmopolitan*, 52:335-347 (Feb. 1912); *Nash's Magazine*, 6:47-59 (April 1912). "A flutter in eggs," *Cosmopolitan*, 52:545-558 (March 1912); *Nash's Magazine*, 6:165-177 (May 1912). "The town-site of Tra-Lee," *Cosmopolitan*, 52:700-714 (April 1912); *Nash's Magazine*, 6:323-337 (June 1912). "Wonder of woman," *Cosmopolitan*, 52:761-773 (May 1912); *Nash's Magazine*, 6:463-474 (July 1912). "Wonder of woman, part two," *Cosmopolitan*, 53:107-120 (June 1912); "The wonder of woman" (concluded), *Nash's Magazine*, 5:663-676 (Aug. 1912).

104. Reprints:

_____, New York, Grosset & Dunlap, [c1912] 385pp.

_____, London, Mills & Boon, 1913, 296pp.; 1914, 292pp.

_____, London, Newnes, 1916, 253pp.; 1920, 128pp.

_____, London, Readers' Library, 1929, 250pp.

_____, Cleveland, World Publishing Co. [c1940] 269pp. (World junior library).

_____, New York, New American Library, 1954, 175pp. (Signet book 1120).

Smoke and Shorty, London, Mills & Boon, 1920, 1921, 1923, 248pp.

Braille edition (transcribed for the National Library for the Blind, London, England): 2 vols. 1938 (copy).

105. Translations:

Smok Bel'iu [Title in Russian] tr.: M. Lupsiakova, Minsk, Gos. izd. BSSR. 1947, 71pp.   (Belorussian)

Zlatotursachi v Aliaska, tr.: T. Koiudzhieva, Sofia, Iv. Koiumdzhiev, 1933, 124pp. Contents: Vkusut na mesoto. Mesoto. Zlatonosnite piasutzi na reka Skvau. Ogunut na Kusius. Chovekut na druggiia briag. Nadbiagvane za nomer treti.

Prikliucheniiata na zlototursachite, tr.: G'oncho Belev, Sofia, T. F. Chipev, 1934, 272pp. Contents: I chast Smok Beliu. Mirizmata na mesoto. Meso. Ha zhenskiia rucheĭ-za zlato. Gudzho sunuva. Cholvekut na drugiia briag. Hadprepuskane. Smok i Gudzho - Munuchkiiak. Kak besikha Kultus Czhordzh. Greshki pri sutvorenieto na zhenata. Spekulatziiata siaitzata. Kradut Tra-Li. Podvigut na zhenata.

Za slato v Aliaska, tr.: G. Belev, Sofia, Gladston, 1934, 271pp.

Smok Beliu, tr.: Nadia Popova, Sofia, Knigopechat, 1945, 103pp. Contents: Vkusut na mesoto. Na "Zhenskiia rucheĭ"

za zlato. Sustezanie za purvenstvo.
Diviiat sever, tr.: Rosina Boheva, Sofia, Chitkop, 1945,
104pp. Contents: Vkusut na mesoto. Na zhenskiia potok za
zlato. Sustezanie za purvenstvo.   (Bulgarian)
Pomama za zlatom, Franjo Brössler, Zagreb, Seljacka sloga,
1953, 1957, 255pp.   (Croatian)
Smoke a Shorty, tr.: I. Schulz, Prague, Tiskové družstvo
soc; strany čsl. lidu prac., 1922, 192pp.; Prague, Koči,
1924, 176pp.
Smoke Bellow, tr.: L. F., Prague, Koči, 1925, 158pp.
Záležitost mužu, tr.: M. Ludvová, Prague, Mladá fronta,
1947, 231pp.   (Czech/Slovak)
Det store vidunder, tr.: A. Mikkelsen, Copenhagen, Martin,
1919, 1924, 208pp.; 1929, 370pp.   (Danish)
Tusschen twee rassen, tr.: J. W. Boissevain, Haarlem,
J. W. Boissevain, 1922.
Alaska Kid, tr.: Felix van Zijl, Baarn, De Nederlandsche
Uitgoverij, 1948, 239pp.   (Dutch)
Kultas ja kuntoa, tr.: J. Saastamoinen, Helsinki, Otava,
1921, 173pp.; 1933, 386pp.; 1950, 310pp.
*Kultaa ja kuntoa ... Juttu jatkuu ... Smoke Bellew ya
Shorty uusissa seikkailuissa*, Helsinki, Otava, 1921,
208pp. [Smoky and Shorty]   (Finnish)
Belliou-La-Fumée, tr.: L. Postif, Paris, Crès, 1929, 231pp.;
Hachette, 1941, 190pp.; Hachette, 1939, 110pp. (Collection
des grands romanciers Series VI.).
Belliou et Le Courtaud, tr.: L. Postif, Paris, Crès, 1929,
250pp.
La fièvre de l'or, tr.: Louis Postif, Paris, Hachette,
1940, 192pp. (Bibliothèque verte).   (French)
Alaska-Kid, tr.: Erwin Magnus, Berlin, Universitas, 1931,
1946, 274pp.; Universitas, 1950, 1953, 258pp.; Vienna,
Vorwärts. Bücherreihe "Stimme der Jugend", 1946, 31pp.
[1. Bärenfleisch schmeckt gut]; Frankfurt/M., Büchergilde
Gutenberg, 1950, 258pp.; Vienna, Büchergilde Gutenberg,
1951, 219pp.; Berlin, Tribüne, 1955, 234pp.; Zürich,
Büchergilde Gutenberg, 1955, 213pp.; Hamburg, Deutsche
Hausbücherei, 1960, 241pp.
Kid & Co., tr.: Erwin Magnus, Berlin, Universitas, 1931,
1946, 282pp.   (German)
"Smoke Bellew. I-II," tr.: Magnus J. Skaptason, *Fröói*
(Winnipeg), 1:23-34, 67-75, 115-125, 164-185 (1912).
Gullæöiö Saga frá Klondyke, Reykjavik, St. Gunnarson,
1917, 243pp.   (Icelandic)
La febbre dell'oro, tr,: A. Salucci, Milan, Bietti, 1930,
238pp.
Smoke Bellew, tr.: Gastone Rossi, Milan, Sonzogno, 1930,
315pp.

Gli avventurieri, tr.: A. Salucci, Milan, Bietti, 1930-
1931, 2 vols., [?]pp.
Belliew detto Fumo, preface and tr.: S. Roaati, Aquila,
Vecchioni, 1930, 259pp.
Fumo Bellew, tr.: Mario Benzi, Sesto S. Giovanni, Barion,
1934, 1936, 349pp.; 1941, 320pp.   (Italian)
Smokas Belju, Vilnius, Valst. grož. lit. 1-kla, 1957,
343pp. (Nuotykiu b-ka).   (Lithuanian)
Smok Bel'iu, tr.: M. Polybok, Kishinev, Shkosla sovetika,
1957, 134pp.   (Moldavian)
Hvor gullfeberen raser, tr.: G. Reiss-Andersen, Oslo,
Gyldendal, 1935, 1943, 186pp.
Det store vidunden, tr.: Gunnar Reiss-Andersen, Oslo,
Gyldendal, 1953, 170pp.   (Norwegian)
Wyga, Gdansk, Polski Instytut Wydawniczy "Sfinks", 1925,
238pp.
_____, tr.: Jerzy Bandrowski, Warsaw, E. Wende, 1925,
193pp.; Warsaw, B. Matuszewski, 1946, 206pp.; also Warsaw,
E. Kuthan, 1948; Warsaw, Iskry, 1954, 164pp.
Bellew Zawieruchaz, tr.: K. Piotrowski, Warsaw, Iskry,
1959, 314pp.   (Polish)
In goană după aur, tr.: G. M. Amza, Bucharest, G. M. Amza,
1942, 256pp.   (Rumanian)
Smok Bellyu, tr.: Zin Lvovski, Leningrad, Mysl, 1924,
168pp.; also an edition of 177pp.
_____, Gosizdat BSSR, 1955, 140pp.
Smok i malenki, tr.: V. I. Smetanich, Leningrad, Mysl,
1924, 190pp.
Khvat Bellyu: Khvat i malysh, tr.: N. and L. Chukovski,
Moscow, Goslitizdat., 1937, 294pp.
Smok Bellyu, Moscow, Uchpedgiz, 1957, 2 vol. edition for
the blind, [?]pp.   (Russian)
Smouk Belju, tr.: Zora Knostantinović, Belgrade, Sportska
knjiga, 1957, 240pp.   (Serbian)
Smoke Bellew, tr.: H. C. Granch, Buenos Aires, Ed. Molino,
1947, 190pp.   (Spanish)
Nigger Bellew, tr.: Ernst Lundquist, Stockholm, Bohlin,
1919, 381pp.   (Swedish)
Ali teri, tr.: Selma Koray, Istanbul, Ataç Kitabevi, 1960,
88pp.   (Turkish)
Smok Bell'iu, tr.: M. Lisichenko, 1927, [?]pp.
Smok Bel'iu, tr.: M. Lupsiakova, Minsk, Goz. izd. BSSR.
Red. det. lit-ry, 1947, 71pp.   (Ukrainian)

THE NIGHT-BORN. 1913

106. THE NIGHT-BORN | AND ALSO | THE MADNESS OF JOHN HARNED,
WHEN THE | WORLD WAS YOUNG, THE BENEFIT OF | THE DOUBT,

WINGED BLACKMAIL, | BUNCHES OF KNUCKLES, WAR, | UNDER THE
DECK AWNINGS, | TO KILL A MAN, THE | MEXICAN | BY | JACK
LONDON | Author of "The Call of the Wild," "The Sea |
Wolf," "Smoke Bellew," etc | [publisher's device] | NEW
YORK | THE CENTURY CO. | 1913
    [vi] [1-2] 3-290p. 19 x 13 cm. Blue-gray cloth, dec-
orated in black. Lettering in gilt on front cover and
spine. Frontis. in colors with tissue guard. One page of
publisher's advertisements at back.
    On verso of title-page (p.[iv]): Copyright, 1913, by |
THE CENTURY CO. | [rule] | Copyright, 1910, 1911, by THE
RIDGEWAY COMPANY | Copyright, 1910, by the NEW YORK
HERALD COMPANY | Copyright, 1910, 1911, by THE CURTIS
PUBLISHING COMPANY | [rule] | *Published, February, 1913*

107. Reprints:
    ____, New York, Grosset & Dunlap [1913] 290pp.
    ____, London, Mills & Boon, 1916, v, 290pp.; 1917, 1919,
270pp.
    ____, Paris, Nelson,[n.d.,] 281pp. (Nelson's continental
library 35).

108. Translations:
Meksykanin, tr.: Jerzy Mariusz Taylor, Warsaw, Biblioteka
Romansów i Powieści, 1926, 141pp.; also Warsaw, 1930,
1931, 1934. Contents: Meksykanin (The Mexican). Wojna
(War). Na pokladzie (Under the deck awnings). Wymiar Spra-
wiedliwosci (Bunches of knuckles). Zemata (The benefit of
the doubt).
Córa nocy, tr.: Jerzy Mariusz Taylor, Warsaw, Biblioteka
Romansów i Powieści, 1927, 128pp.; other editions of 1928,
1929, 1930, 1931, 1934. Contents: Córa nocy (The night-
born). Szaleństwo Johna Harned (The madness of John Harned).
Przygoda w Mill Valley. Loo-Loo (Winged blackmail). Odwaga
Pani Setliffe (To kill a man).   (Polish)
Nattens barn.och andra berättelser, tr.: Ernst Lundquist,
Stockholm, B. Wahlstrom, 1956, 252pp. (Wahlstroms roman-
bibliotek. Röda elitserien. 13).   (Swedish)

THE ABYSMAL BRUTE. 1913

109. THE | ABYSMAL BRUTE | BY | JACK LONDON | Author of "The
Call of the Wild," "The Sea | Wolf," "Smoke Bellew," "The |
Night Born," etc. | [publisher's device] | NEW YORK | THE
CENTURY CO. | 1913
    [iv] [1-2] 3-169p. 17 x 11.5 cm. Olive cloth stamped
in yellow and black on cover and spine. Frontis. with
tissue guard. One page of publisher's advertisements at

back.
    On verso of title-page (p.[iv]): Copyright, 1913, by |
THE CENTURY CO. | [rule] | Copyright, 1911, by | STREET &
SMITH. NEW YORK | [rule] | *Published, May, 1913*
    The second binding is similar, but with the design on
front cover in green and black.
    A third issue is 16.5 x 11 cm. It is in cheap light
green cloth with the conventional oak-leaf and corn decoration in dark green and black respectively.
    The dust wrapper on the first edition is dark brown
paper, overprinted in black and light green on the front
with design of a man carrying a buck deer over his shoul-
ders and a gun in his right hand. Inside front flap a
publisher's "plug" for the book, and inside rear flap excerpts from reviewers' praises of Jack London as an author.

110. Serializations:
    Partially serialized in *Popular Magazine*, 21,4:1-35 (Sept.
    1, 1911) and in *Red Magazine*, no. 67:3-35 (Jan. 15, 1912).

111. Reprints:
    "The abysmal brute," Marysville (Cal.) *Evening Democrat*,
    March 11-16, 18-23, 1914.
    Reprinted in Stix, T. L., ed., *Sporting gesture*, N. Y.
    and London, D. Appleton-Century Co., 1934, XV, 348pp.;
    1940, XIX, 375pp.
    _____, London, G. Newnes [1914](Newnes Sevenpenny Series)
    [1917][1920] 158pp.

112. Translations:
    Purvebiten zviar, tr.: M. Nenova, Sofia, Iv. Koiumdzhiev,
    1934, 64pp.   (Bulgarian)
    Necita, tr.: L. F., Prague, Kočí, 1925, 2 vols. (86, 54pp.)
                                       (Czech/Slovak)
    Bokseren, tr.: E. S. Steenberg, Copenhagen, Martin, 1919,
    124pp.; 1925, 126pp.
    Bokseren og Ved Tasmans skildpadder, tr.: E. S. Steenberg,
    Copenhagen, Martin, 1930, 332pp.   (Danish)
    Villipeto, tr.: Maunu Korpela, Helsinki, Urheilijain Kus-
    tannusoy Suomi, 1920, 102pp.   (Finnish)
    La brute des cavernes, tr.: Paul Gruyer and Louis Postif,
    Paris, Hachette, 1934, 222pp. (Les meilleurs romans
    étrangers).   (French)
    *Der Ruhm des Kämpfers. Von Boxern, Stierkämpfern und
    aufrechten Männern*, tr.: Erwin Magnus, Berlin, Universi-
    tas, 1936, 1947, 255pp. Universitas, 1954, 257pp.; Berlin,
    Tribüne, 1957, 290pp.; Frankfurt am Main, Büchergilde
    Gutenberg, 1954, 257pp. (The abysmal brute. The faith of

men. The night born).   (German)
Hnefaleikarinn, tr.: Ragnar portsteinsson, Akureyri,
Hjartaásútgáfan, 1948, 100pp.   (Icelandic)
"Bezdibena zvērs," *Sports,* no. 11:15-16, no. 12-13:23-24,
no. 15:15-16 (1925); *Sporta žurnals,* no. 3:11, no. 4:11,
no. 5:11, no. 6:11-12, no. 7:11-12, no. 8:11-12 (1925).
                                         (Latvian)
Bokseren, tr.: John Grieg-Müller, Oslo, Gyldendal, 1954,
1956, 152pp.   (Norwegian)
*Arecybestia,*tr.: M. K., Warsaw, Rój, 1926, 1928, 117pp.;
Kościana, Drukarnia Polska, 1946, 70pp.
                                         (Polish)
Zver iz bezdny, tr.: Zin. Lvovski, Leningrad and Moscow,
Mysl, 1924, 175pp.; Leningrad, Mysl, 1925, 160pp.
____, tr.: N. Gorvits, Leningrad, Seyatel, 1925, 96pp.
                                         (Russian)
La estupenda bestia, tr.: Guillermo Labarca H., Santiago,
Letras, 1936; Buenos Aires, Anaconda, 1943; both 116pp.
                                         (Spanish)
Afgrundsdjuret, tr.: Ernst Lundquist, Stockholm, Bohlin,
1917, 168pp.; 1926, 119pp.   (Swedish)
Dağdan inme, tr.: Selçuk M. Kaskan, Istanbul [no publish-
er given on title page; outside paper cover gives
Universum Matbaasi] 1944, 120pp.   (Turkish)

JOHN BARLEYCORN. 1913

113. JOHN | BARLEYCORN | BY | JACK LONDON | Author of "The Call
of the Wild," "The | Abysmal Brute," "Smoke Bellew," |
"The Night-Born," etc. | Illustrated by | H. T. DUNN |
[publisher's device] | NEW YORK | THE CENTURY CO. | 1913
   [viii][1-2] 3-343p. 19 x 13 cm. Deep green cloth
stamped in gold on cover and spine. Frontis.
   On verso of title-page (p.[vi]): Copyright, 1913, by |
THE CENTURY CO. | [rule] | Copyright, 1913, by | THE
CURTIS PUBLISHING COMPANY | [rule] | *Published, August,*
1913

114. Serializations:
Serialized in the *Saturday Evening Post,* 185:3, 5, 50-53
(March 15, 1913), 185:18-20, 44-46 (March 22, 1913),
185:21-23, 56-58 (March 29, 1913), 185:23-25, 54 (April 5,
1913), 185:22-24, 48-49 (April 12, 1913), 185:25-27,
65-66 (April 19, 1913), 185:23-25, 42-43 (April 26, 1913),
185: 24-25, 78-79 (May 3, 1913).

115. Reprints:
John Barleycorn; or *Alcoholic memoirs,* London, Mills &

Boon, 1914, 1915, 1925, 310pp.; 1923, 306pp.
John Barleycorn, New York, D. Appleton-Century, 1938,
343pp.
____, Toronto, Morang, 1913, iv, 343pp.
Selections: "Jack London gets next to John D. Barleycorn,"
San Francisco *Bulletin*, March 14, 1913, Part II, P.13;
"My early reading," pp.206-207; "My first efforts to
write," pp.292-294; "My definite beginnings as a writer,"
pp.294-295 and "My belated education," pp.315-317 of
Century book of selections, ed.: Garland Greever and
Joseph M. Bachelor, New York, Century, 1923.

116. Translations:
Tzar Alkohol, tr.: D. Podvurzachov, Sofia, Vestnik na
zhenata, 1932, 176pp.; Sofia, Nar. prosveta, 1948, 203pp.
                          (Bulgarian)
Uspemene pijanca, tr.: Branko Kojic, Zagreb, Nakl.
poduzece "Glas Rada," 1951, 168pp.   (Croatian)
Majster Alkohol alebo Pijanské zápisky, tr.: A. Bednár,
Turč, Sv. Martin, 1948, 209pp. (Matica slovenská).
Pan Ječmínek, tr.: I. Schulz, Prague, Kraft, 1921, 212pp.;
Prague, Kočí, 1924, 2 vols. (127, 102, 26pp.).
                          (Czech/Slovak)
Kong Alkohol, tr.: L. Kohl, Copenhagen, Martin, 1914,
256pp.
____, tr.: L. Kohl and J. Ewald, Copenhagen, Martin, 1918,
208pp.; 1923, 192pp.; 1928, 304pp.   (Danish)
Koning Alcohol, tr.: Jac. v. d. Ster, Amsterdam, Republiek
der letteren, 1948, 268pp.   (Dutch)
"Kuidas ma sain lahti John Claverhousest" [How I got rid
of John Barleycorn], *Päevaleht*, July 14, 1928; "Kuningas
alkohol," *Eesti Naine*, no. 11:324-326 (1933); *Edasi*,
Nov. 28, 1954.   (Estonian)
Tuliliemen tuttavana Alkoholimuistelmia, tr.: Toivo
Wallenius, Helsinki, Otava, 1914, 246pp.; Otava, 1925,
256pp.   (Finnish)
Le cabaret de la dernière chance, tr.: Louis Postif, Paris,
Hachette, 1931, iv, 263pp. (Les meilleurs romans étrangers).
Mémoires d'un buveur, tr.: F. Guillermet, Paris, Attinger,
1918, iv, 187pp.   (French)
König Alkohol, tr.: Erwin Magnus, Berlin, Büchergilde Gut-
enberg, 1926, 243pp.; Zürich, Büchergilde Gutenberg, 1947,
239pp.; Berlin, Universitas, 1948, 242pp.
                                     (German)
Bakkus konungur, tr.: Knút Arngrímsson, Reykjavik, Felix
Gumundsson, 1933, 234pp.; Reykjavik, Ísafoldarprentsmiöja,
1960, 276pp.   (Icelandic)
Sárga sátán, Budapest, Nepszava, 1922, 174pp.; Budapest,

JOHN BARLEYCORN

BY

JACK LONDON
Author of "The Call of the Wild," "The
Abysmal Brute," "Smoke Bellew,"
"The Night-Born," etc.

Illustrated by

H. T. DUNN

NEW YORK
THE CENTURY CO.
1913

Kossuth, Kiado, 1958, 239pp. (Tarka kőnyvek)
                                (Hungarian)
All'osteria dell'ultima fortuna, tr.: Lucia Krasnik,
Milan, Modernissima, 1929, 271pp.
Il bevitore, tr.: Lucia Krasnik and *L'amore della vita,*
tr.: L. Viscardini, Sesto S. Giovanni-Milano, Barion,
1938, 367pp.
Memorie, tr.: G. Delchiaro, Milan, Monanni, 1929, 302pp.
Memorie di un bevitore, tr.: A. Salucci, Milan, Bietti,
1932, 328pp.
Ricordi di un bevitore, tr.: D. Carter and G. Dàuli,
Milan, Delta, 1928, [?]pp.; 1929, 283pp.
                                (Italian)
Kong Alkohol, tr.: Odd Hølaas, Oslo, Gyldendal, 1935,
1943, 224pp.   (Norwegian)
John Barleycorn, tr.: Antonina Sokolicz, Warsaw, E. Wende,
1926, 2 vols. (158, 125pp.); Poznán, Wielkopolska Ksie-
garnia Wydawnicza, 1949, 225pp.; Warsaw, Panstwowy in-
stytut wydawniczy, 1950, 228pp.
_____, tr.: A. Sokolicz, K. Piotrowski et al., Warsaw,
Iskry, 1957, 348pp.   (Polish)
Alcool, tr.: Paul C. Teodorescu, Bucharest, Gorjan, 1943,
350pp.   (Rumanian)
Dzhon Yachmennoye zerno ili alkogolnyie vospominaniya, ed.
of tr.: V. Onegin; forword by D. Nezhdanov, Leningrad and
Moscow, Petrograd., 1925, 198pp.
Zelyony zmi, tr.: N. M. Tsymovich, Leningrad, Mysl, 1925,
232pp.   (Russian)
Kralj Alkohol, tr.: A. Smaus, Belgrade, Izdanje Nolit,
1930, 209 + 5pp. (Biblioteka Nolit no. 15).
                                (Serbian)
Memorias de un alcoholista, tr.: Saúl Selles, Buenos Aires,
Ediciones Siglo XX, 1952, 219pp.
John Barleycorn, tr.: Sául Selles, Buenos Aires, Ediciones
Siglo XX, 1946, 319pp.   (Spanish)
John Finkelman, tr.: Algot Sandberg, Stockholm, Bohlin,
1914, 352pp.; 1915, 310pp.; 1923, [?]pp.
_____, tr.: Marten Edlund, Stockholm, Folket i bild, 1958,
277pp.
Kung Alkohol, tr.: Hanna Bergman, Stockholm, Nutiden,
1917, 150pp.   (Swedish)

THE VALLEY OF THE MOON. 1913

117. THE VALLEY OF | THE MOON | BY | JACK LONDON | AUTHOR OF
    "MARTIN EDEN," "BURNING DAYLIGHT," | "SEA WOLF," ETC., ETC.
    | WITH FRONTISPIECE IN COLORS | BY GEORGE HARPER | New
    York | THE MACMILLAN COMPANY | 1913

THE VALLEY OF
THE MOON

BY

JACK LONDON

AUTHOR OF "MARTIN EDEN," "BURNING DAYLIGHT,"
"SEA WOLF," ETC., ETC.

WITH FRONTISPIECE IN COLORS
BY GEORGE HARPER

New York
THE MACMILLAN COMPANY
1913

[Item 117]

[vi][1-2] 3-530p. 19 x 13 cm. Orange cloth decorated
in yellow and light and dark blue. Lettering on spine
gilt. Lettering on front cover white. Four pages of publisher's advertisements at back.
   On verso of title-page (p.[iv]): COPYRIGHT, 1913 | BY
COSMOPOLITAN MAGAZINE | [rule] | COPYRIGHT, 1913 | BY THE
MACMILLAN COMPANY | [rule] | Set up and electrotyped. Pub-
lished October, 1913

118. Serializations:
Serialized as "Valley of the moon, the story of a fight
against odds for love and a home," *Cosmopolitan*, 54:580-
600 (April 1913), 54:750-769 (May 1913), 55:47-65 (June
1913), 55:239-259 (July 1913), 55:352-370 (Aug. 1913),
55: 464-485 (Sept. 1913), 55:623-641 (Oct. 1913), 55:800-
819 (Nov. 1913), 56:98-116 (Dec. 1913).
Excerpt published as "Gamblers," San Francisco *Examiner*,
Sept. 27, 1913, p.20.

119. Reprints:
_____, London, Mills & Boon [1912?] 1913, 1915, 1925,
536pp.; 1917, 565pp.; 1919, 1923, 1927, 1930, 530pp.
_____, New York, Grosset & Dunlap, 1913, 1928, 530pp.
_____, Macmillan, New York, Macmillan, 1915, 530pp.
_____, London, Nelson & Sons [1917] 565pp. (Nelson's
Library).
Braille editions (U.S.): Grade 1 1/2. 9 vols. Hand-copied.
Press-braille. Clovernook Printing House for the Blind,
Mt. Healthy, Ohio. 1946. 6 vols.
Braille edition (transcribed for the National Library for
the Blind, London, England): 8 vols. 1939 (copy).

120. Translations:
Lunnata dolina, tr.: Racho Stoianov, Sofia, Suglacie, 1931,
242pp. (Bibl. Vcemirni romani 3:1). (Bulgarian)
Dolina mjeseca, tr.: G. Zlatkovic, Zagreb, Prosvjeta,
1947, 522pp.   (Croatian)
Měsíční údolí, tr.: Ž. Poherecká, Prague, Kočí, 1922,
3 vols. (128, 200, 128pp.); Zlín, Tisk, 1936-1937, 2 vols.
(337, 263pp.).
Mesačné údolie, tr.: V. Szanthmáry-Vlčková, Bratislava,
Tatran, 1949, 522pp.   (Czech/Slovak)
Maanedalen, tr.: Aslaug Mikkelsen, Copenhagen, Martin,
1914, 1917, 2 vols. (304, 372pp.); 1924, 2 vols. (288,
224pp.); 1927, 3 vols. (272, 270, 280pp.); 1959, 500pp.
                                      (Danish)
De vallei van de maan, Amsterdam, Boekh. en Uitg. Mij.
Joh. Miller, 1924, 2 vols.   (Dutch)

Kuunlaakso, tr.: Helmi Krohn, Helsinki, Otava, 1924,
2 vols. (404, 312pp.); 1938, 2 vols. (405, 306pp.).
(Finnish)
Le tourbillon, tr.: Louis Postif, Paris, Crès, 1926,
267pp.   (French)
Das Mondtal, tr.: Erwin Magnus, Berlin, Universitas, 1929,
2 vols. (300, 275pp.); Berlin, Büchergilde Gutenberg,
1929, 2 vols. (300, 275pp.); abridged version, tr.: E.
Magnus, Berlin, Universitas, also Hamburg, Berlin, Deutsche
Hausbücherei, each 1957 with 271pp.; Vienna, Volksbuch-
verlag, 1962, 271pp.
_____, tr.: Edward Thorsch, Zürich, Schweizer Druck-und
Verlagshaus, 1948, 390pp.; 1952, 382pp.
(German)
Bik at ha-yareah, tr.: Reuben Grossman (Avinoam), Tel-
Aviv, Mizpeh, 1930, 2 vols., [?]pp.   (Hebrew)
A Hold völgyében, tr.: Maria Ruzitska, Budapest, Légrády,
1924, 410pp.   (Hungarian)
[La valle della luna] I. *Nella tempesta*. II. *In serenità*,
tr.: Dienne Carter and Gian Dàuli, Milan, Modernissima,
1928, 2 vols., [?]pp.
La valle della luna, tr.: Mario Benzi, Sesto S. Giovanni-
Milano, Barion, 1929, 1933, 447pp.
_____, tr.: G. Delchiaro, Milan, Monanni, 1929, 2 vols.,
[?]pp.
_____, tr.: Gastone Rossi, Milan, Sonzogno, 1929, 2 vols.,
[?]pp.   (Italian)
Meness ieleja, tr.: J. Cīrulis, Riga, A. Freinats, 1927,
229pp.   (Latvian)
Ménulio slénys, tr.: T. Krompolc, Vilnius, Valst.
grož. lit. 1-kla, 1959, 563pp.   (Lithuanian)
Manedalen, tr.: Nordahl Grieg, Oslo, Gyldendal, 1934,1941,
2 vols. (295, 257pp.).   (Norwegian)
Dolina Ksiezyca, tr.: S. Kuszelewska, Warsaw, Rój, 1929
[Vol. 1 Kleska] 267pp.; Rój, 1930, Vol. 1, Kleska.
Vol. 2, Szczescie.
Ksiezycowa dolina, tr.: K. Tarnowska, poetry tr.:
Włodzimierz Lewik, Warsaw, Iskry, 1959, 419pp.
(Polish)
Lunnaya dolina, tr.: Z. A. Rogozina, Leningrad and Moscow,
Knizhny Ugol, 1924, 319pp.
Zemlya obetovannaya, tr.: E. K. Brodersen, Leningrad, Mysl,
1924, 262pp.
Stachka, Moscow, V. Ts. S. P. S., 1926, 48pp. [Excerpts].
(Russian)
El valle de la luna, tr.: Saúl Selles, Buenos Aires, Siglo
Veinte, 1946, 537pp. (Colección La rosa de los vientos).
_____, tr.: Valentin Fernando, Buenos Aires, Edición Siglo

Veinte, 1953, 534pp.   (Spanish)
Mandalen, tr.: M. Drangel, Stockholm, Bohlin, 1914, 2 vols.
(373, 280pp.); Bohlin, 1919, 2 vols. (432, 325); 1924,
2 vols.; 1926, 2 vols. (432, 320pp.).(Swedish)

THE STRENGTH OF THE STRONG. 1914

121. THE STRENGTH | OF THE STRONG | BY | JACK LONDON | AUTHOR
OF "THE SEA WOLF," "THE CALL OF THE WILD," | "THE VALLEY
OF THE MOON," ETC. | WITH FRONTISPIECE | New York | THE
MACMILLAN COMPANY | 1914
[iv] v [vi-viii] 1-257p. 19 x 12.5 cm. Light blue cloth
decorated in black and gold. Lettering on spine and front
cover white. Frontis. Six pages of publisher's advertisements at back.
On verso of title-page (p.[iv]): [Seven lines of pre-
vious magazine publishing copyright notices] | [rule] |
COPYRIGHT, 1914, | BY THE MACMILLAN COMPANY | Set up and
electrotyped. Published May, 1914.
Contents: The Strength of the Strong; South of the
Slot; The Unparalleled Invasion; The Enemy of All the
World; The Dream of Debs; The Sea-Farmer; Samuel.
The copy of this book in the George H. Tweney collection is in dust wrapper: white, calendared paper, very
fragile and brittle, lettered in blue on the front and
spine, and flaps and back are blank. Twelve lines of text
on front of dust wrapper extolling Jack London's ability
to tell a good story.

122. Reprints:
_____, New York, Leslie-Judge, 1914, v, 257pp.
_____, New York, Grosset & Dunlap [1914] v, 257pp.
_____, New York, Macmillan, 1919, v, 257pp.
_____, London, Mills & Boon, 1917, 298pp.; 1919, 189pp.;
1923, 289pp.

123. Translations:
Síla silných, tr.: J. Vorel, Prague, Procházka, 1921,
150pp.
Síla silného a jiné povídky, tr.: K. Vít, Prague, Kočí,
1925, 143pp.   (Czech/Slovak)
De kracht van den sterke, tr.: J. P. Wesselink-van Rossum,
Amsterdam, Boekh. en Uitg. Mij Joh. Müller, 1923.
                               (Dutch)
A méhek dala, tr.: Zoltán Bartos, Budapest, Népazava,
1923, 120pp.; Budapest, Parnasszus, 1947, 67pp. (Par-
nasszus könyvtár 4)   (Hungarian)
Wróg świata, tr.: Roman Celiński, Warsaw, Druk. Spółki

Wydaw. Powsz., 1925, 167pp.; Warsaw, 1927, 1929, 1930,
1931 are published by the Biblioteka Romansów i Powieści.
(Polish)
Sila silnykh, tr.: F. Nyuton, edited with a preface by
A. N. Gorlin, Moscow and Leningrad, Gosizdat., 1923, 94pp.
(Russian)
La fuerza de los fuertes, Santiago, Letras, 1942, 130pp.
(Spanish)
Svla dužogo, tr.: G. Kas'ianenko, Kiev, Goslitizdat
Ukrainy, 1957, 109pp.   (Ukranian)

THE MUTINY OF THE ELSINORE. 1914

124. THE MUTINY OF | THE ELSINORE | BY | JACK LONDON | AUTHOR
OF "THE CALL OF THE WILD," "THE SEA WOLF," | "THE VALLEY
OF THE MOON," ETC. | WITH FRONTISPIECE | New York | THE
MACMILLAN COMPANY | 1914
[vi] 1-378p. 19 x 12.5 cm. Yellow cloth decorated in
gray and blue. Lettering on spine gilt. Title on front
cover white, author's name in gilt. Frontis. in color.
Six pages of publisher's advertisements at back.
On verso of title-page (p.[iv]): COPYRIGHT, 1913 AND
1914 | BY JACK LONDON AND BY HEARST'S MAGAZINE | [rule] |
COPYRIGHT, 1914 | BY THE MACMILLAN COMPANY | [rule] |
Set up and electrotyped. Published September, 1914 |
[rule] | COPYRIGHT IN GREAT BRITAIN | [Three lines of
press signature]
The George H. Tweney copy of this book is also in dust
wrapper, the same fragile, calendared white paper as was
used on the wrapper of *The strength of the strong*. It is
printed in black, with a color reproduction of the frontispiece on the front, flaps and back are blank.

125. Serializations:
Reprinted from *Hearst's Magazine* where it was entitled
"The sea gangsters": 24:669-686, 846-866 (Nov.-Dec. 1913),
25:29-46, 242-259, 389-397, 505-516, 673-684, 823-836
(Jan.-June 1914), 26:102-242-259 (July-August 1914).
Excerpts from *The sea gangsters* were published in the San
Francisco *Examiner*, Nov. 23, 1913, p.18 and March 1, 1914,
p.16.
In 1914 it was serialized as "The sea gangsters" in *Vanity
Fair* (English ed.): March 26, pp.7-10, 43; April 2, pp.22-
25; April 9, pp.22-24, 44-45; April 16, pp.24-26, 46;
April 23, pp.24-26, 46-48; April 30, pp.36, 72; May 7,
pp.35, 43, 45, 47; May 14, pp.26, 43, 45, 47-48; May 21,
pp.38, 65-66; May 28, pp.28-29, 42-44; June 4, pp.30,40;
June 11, p.42; June 18, pp.62-64; June 25, p.70; July 2,

pp.44-45; July 9, p.43; June 16, p.44; June 23, p.44;
July 30, pp.44-45; Aug. 6, pp.42-43; Aug. 13, pp.35-36.

126. Reprints:
_____, New York, Grosset & Dunlap [1914] 378pp.
_____, New York, Macmillan, 1937, 378pp. (reissue of the
1914 ed.).
_____, New York, Arcadia House, 1950 [c1942] 378pp.
_____, London, Mills & Boon, 1915, 396pp.; 1916, 366pp.;
1920, 365pp.; London, Penguin, 1943, 254pp.; London, Nil-
son, 1916, 474pp.

127. Translations:
Buntovnitzite na Elsenor, tr.: M. Seizova-Turukove, Sofia,
Gladston, 1934, 266pp. (Mozaĭke ot znameniti suvremenni
romani. 25:8-9).   (Bulgarian)
Vspoura na lodi Elsinore, tr.: K. Vít, Prague, Ustř. tisk.
družstvo soc. strany čs. lidu pracujícího, 1921, 269pp.
Vzbouření na Elsinoře, tr.: M. Mašková, Prague, Koči,
1923, 3 vols. (142, 144, 157pp.).
Vzbura na Elsinore, tr.: Fero Kalina, Bratislava, Pravda,
1948, 500pp.   (Czech/Slovak)
Rundt Kap Horn, tr.: A. Mikkelsen, Copenhagen, Martin,
1929, 2 vols. (286, 288pp.); 1958, 384pp.
                                (Danish)
De muiterij op de Elsinore, Utrecht, A. W. Bruna & Zoon's
Uitg. Mij., 1921. (Bruna's bibl.).   (Dutch)
Elsinoren kapina, tr.: Tauno Nuotio, Helsinki, Otava,
1926, 476pp.; 1938, 1950, 1959, 339pp.(Finnish)
Les mutinés de 'l'Elseneur', tr.: Paul Gruyer and Louis
Postif, Paris, Crès, 1930, 297pp.; Paris, Kieffer, 1935,
269pp.; Paris, Hachette, 1936, 252pp. (Bibliothèque de la
jeunesse).   (French)
Meuterei auf der Elsinore, tr.: Erwin Magnus, Berlin,
Universitas, 1932, 261pp.; Universitas, 1946, 266pp.;
Berlin, Dt. Buch-Gemeinschaft, 1947, 266pp.; Universitas,
1959, 246pp.; Hamburg, Berlin, Dt. Hausbücherei 1959,
246pp.; Frankfurt/M., Büchergilde Gutenberg, 1960, 243pp.;
Vienna, Volcksbuchverlag, 1960; Frankfurt, Fischer, 1963,
179pp. (Fischer Bücherei 577.)   (German)
ha-Mered... tr.: Dan Son, Tel-Aviv, Karmi, 1951, 275pp.
[Juvenile]   (Hebrew)
A lázadék, Budapest, Légrády, 1924, 179pp.
                                (Hungarian)
Uppreisnin á Elsinóru, tr.: Ingólfur Jónsson ýddi, Reykjavik, Ísafoldarprentsmi ja, 1960, 379pp.
                                (Icelandic)
La rivolta dell'Elsinore, tr.: Mario Benzi, Milan, Modern-

issima, 1928, 323pp.
____, tr.: Giuseppina Taddei, Milan, Bietti, 1934, 348pp.
L'ammutinamento della "Elsinore", tr.: Mario Maltesta,
Milan, Sonzogno, 1931, 377pp.
____, tr.: Mario Losannese, Sesto S. Giovanni-Milano,
Barion, 1937, 366pp.   (Italian)
Dumpis uz Elsinoras, tr.: V. Zĭbelis, Riga, Grāmatu
Draugs, [n.d.,] 200pp.   (Latvian)
Rundt Kap Horn, tr.: Ben Horne, Oslo, Gyldendal, 1934,
1941, 271pp.   (Norwegian)
Bunt na "Elsynorze", tr.: S. Kuszelewska, Warsaw, W.
Jakowicki, 1929, 3 vols. (144, 143, 179pp.).
____, tr.: J. B. Rychliński, Warsaw, Rój, 1939, 404pp.
                                              (Polish)
Rebeliune pe Atlantic, tr.: Petru Manoliu, Bucharest,
Cultura Romaneasca, 1941, 420pp.
Răzvrătitii de pe nava Elseneur, tr.: G. M. Amza, Buchar-
est, G. M. Amza, 1942, 359pp.   (Rumanian)
Motín en alta mar, no tr. given, Santiago de Chile,
Zig-Zag, 1960, 204pp. (Biblioteca juvenil. Serie amarilla
no. 3).   (Spanish)

THE SCARLET PLAGUE. *1915*

128. The Scarlet Plague | BY | JACK LONDON | AUTHOR OF "THE
SEA WOLF," "THE CALL OF | THE WILD," "THE MUTINY OF |
THE ELSINORE," ETC. | ILLUSTRATED BY | GORDON GRANT |
New York | THE MACMILLAN COMPANY | 1915 | *All rights re-
served*
[8] 9 [10] 11-181p. 19.5 x 13 cm. Dark red cloth decorated in yellow and light red. Lettering on spine gilt.
Lettering on front cover light red. Frontis. included in
pagination. Four pages of publisher's advertisements at
back.
On verso of title-page (p.[6]): COPYRIGHT, 1912, |BY
JACK LONDON. | [rule] COPYRIGHT, 1913, | BY THE STAR CO.
| [rule] | COPYRIGHT, 1915, | BY JACK LONDON. | [rule] |
Set up and electrotyped. Published May, 1915. | [Three
lines of press signature]

129. Serializations:
First serialized in *London Magazine*, 28:513-540 (June
1912); portions of this novel appeared in 1914 in the
Hartford (Conn.) *Times* under the general title: "Wonder
tales of fact and fancy by Jack London, The Scarlet
Plague, in four parts." Part I: "Granser and the boys,"
April 18, p.25; "The beginning of the end," April 25,
p.26; "The survival of the fittest," May 2, p.14; "Begin-

ning life anew," May 9, p.22.
It was serialized in 1913 in the *American Sunday monthly
Magazine* (published on the first Sunday of each month as
a section of the New York *American*, Boston *American*,
Chicago *Examiner*, Hearst's *American*, and the second Sunday of each month in the San Francisco *Examiner* and Los
Angeles *Examiner*), June 1, pp.3-4, 18 (chapter 1); July 6,
pp. 3-5, 12-13 (chapter 2); Aug. 3, pp.3-5, 16 (chapters
3-4); Sept. 7, pp.3-5 (chapters 5-6).

130. Reprints:
_____, London, Mills & Boon, 1915, 154pp.
_____, New York, Leslie-Judge Co., 1925 (reprint of the
Sonoma ed.).
_____ [bound with *The call of the wild*], New York, Collier,
[c1931](Seven seas ed.).
_____, New York, Collier [c1915] 161pp. (Seven seas ed.).
_____, London, Staples Press, 1946, 100pp.
Famous Fantastic Mysteries, 10,3:93-118 (Feb. 1949).
The call of the wild, White fang and The scarlet plague,
with introduction by Bernard Fergusson, London, Collins,
1953, 3 vols. in 1, 384pp. (Collins New Classics series).

131. Translations:
Bagarianata chuma, tr.: V. Iurdanov, Sofia, Tzviat, 1921,
67pp. (B-ka Tzviat za iunoshi 16).   (Bulgarian)
Červená smrt, tr.: J. Valentini, Bratislava, Pravda, 1947,
158pp.   (Czech/Slovak)
De scharlaken pest, Amsterdam, Boekh. en Uitg. Mij Joh.
Müller, 1923, [?]pp.   (Dutch)
Punainen rutto, tr.: Ilmari Lehto, Helsinki, Kustannus-
liike Minerva, 1922, 114pp.   (Finnish)
La peste écarlate, tr.: Louis Gruyer and Paul Postif,
Paris, Crès, 1924, 224pp.   (French)
La peste scarlatta, tr.: Dienne Carter and Gian Dáuli,
Milan, Modernissima, 1928, 187pp.; Sesti S. Giovanni-
Milano, Barion, 1936, 1942, 1944.
_____, tr.: Gastone Rossi, Milan, Sonzogno, 1939, 250pp.
                                      (Italian)
"Purpura nāve," *Jaunās Dienas Lapas Pielikums*, nos. 130,
136, 147, 153 (June 21-July 19, 1913).
                                      (Latvian)
Raudonasis maras, tr.: K. Kezinaitis, Kaunas, 1938, 64pp.
                                      (Lithuanian)
Szkarłatna dzuma, tr.: S. Kuszelewska, Warsaw, Rój, 1927,
121pp.   (Polish)
Alaya chuma, tr.: M. Likiardopulo, Moscow, Universalnaya
Biblioteka, 1917, 1918, 96pp.; Moscow, Gosizdat., 1922,

90pp.
____, tr.: A. S. Urvich, Leningrad, Mysl, 1925, 80pp.
                                             (Russian)
Crvena kuga, tr.: Pavle Jevtic, Belgrade, Izdanje knjizarnice "Svetlost," 1931, 76 + 4pp.   (Serbian)
La peste escarlata, tr.: A. Grego, Valencia, Prometeo,
1927, 229pp.; 1947, 205pp.
La peste escarlata; El idolo rojo, Madrid, Imprenta Diana,
1954, 40pp.   (Spanish)
Roda pesten, tr.: M. Drangel, Stockholm, Bohlin, 1918,
1927, 148pp.   (Swedish)

THE STAR ROVER. 1915

132. THE | STAR ROVER | BY | JACK LONDON | AUTHOR OF "THE
VALLEY OF THE MOON," "THE | CALL OF THE WILD," "MARTIN
EDEN," ETC. | New York | THE MACMILLAN COMPANY | 1915
     [vi] 1-329p. 19 x 12.5 cm. Light blue cloth decorated
in light blue, dark blue, and white. Lettering on spine
and front cover gilt. Frontis. in color. Eight pages of
publisher's advertisements at back.
     On verso of title-page (p.[iv]): COPYRIGHT 1914, 1915
| BY THE STAR CO. | [rule] | COPYRIGHT 1915 | BY JACK
LONDON | Set up and electrotyped. Published October, 1915

133. Serializations:
This novel ran serially in 1915 in the Los Angeles
Examiner, American Sunday Monthly Magazine: Feb. 14,
pp.9-12; March 14, pp.7-8, 15-22; April 11, pp.8-9, 15-16;
May 9, pp.7-8, 17-19; June 13, pp.7-8, 17; July 11, pp.
7-8, 19; Aug. 8, pp.7-8, 18-19; Sept. 12, pp.7-8, 18-19;
Oct. 10, pp.7, 17-18.

134. Reprints:
____, New York, Grosset & Dunlap, 1917, 329pp.
____, New York, Macmillan, 1944, 329pp.
____, New York, Arcadia House, 1950, 329pp.
____, autobiographical introduction [i.e. "Jack London by
himself" reprinted from *Mainly about people*], epilogue by
Gardner Murphy, illustrated by Leonard Everett Fisher,
New York, Macmillan, 1963, 336pp.
It was published in Great Britain as *The jacket,* London,
Mills & Boon, 1915, 334pp.; 1916, 1923, 320pp.

135. Translations:
Skitnika po zvezdite, tr.: Iv. St. Andreïchin, Sofia, D.
Madzharov, 1932, 192pp. (Bibl. Zlatni stranitzi 5).
____, tr.: St. E. Rusev, Sofia, D. Madzharov, 1936, 152pp.

Skitnik mezhdu svezdite, tr.: D. Podvurzachev, Sofia,
Radikal, 1934, 280pp.; Sofia, Chetivo, 1947, 280pp.
                                    (Bulgarian)
Stopami minulých životu, tr.: M. Maskova, Prague, Koči,
1922, 3 vols. (126, 126, 126pp.).
Tulák po hvězdách, tr.: K. Vít, Prague, Ustř. družstvo
soc. strany čsl. lidu prac., 1921, 448pp.
                                    (Czech/Slovak)
Spændetrøjen, tr.: L. von Kohn and J. Ewald, Copenhagen,
Martin, 1918, 2 vols. (192, 192pp.); 1926, 320pp.; 1930,
414pp.   (Danish)
Pakkopaita, Helsinki, Otava, 1923, 412pp.; 1923, [?]pp.
                                    (Finnish)
Le vagabond des étoiles, tr.: Paul Gruyer and Louis Pos-
tif, Paris, Crès, 1925, xi, 288pp.   (French)
Die Zwangsjacke, tr.: Erwin Magnus, Berlin, Universitas,
1930, 266pp.   (German)
A kóbor csillag, tr.: Leó Vécsey, Budapest, Légrády,
1924, 1925, 479pp. (Külföldi irók régénytára. B7).
A hatalmas egy, tr.: Történet Korea, Novi Sad, Testvéri-
ség-Egyseg, 1953, 77pp.   (Hungarian)
Spennitreyjan, tr.: Sverrir Kristjánsson, Reykjavik, Isa-
foldarpremtsmiðja, 1959, 309pp.   (Icelandic)
Il vagabondo delle stelle, tr.: Dienne Carter and Gian
Dàuli, Milan, Modernissima, 1928, 255pp.; Sesto S.
Giovanni-Milano, Barion, 1941, 318pp.
_____, tr.: Tullio Tulli, Milan, Sonzogno, 1931, 315pp.
_____, tr.: Art. Salucci, Milan, Bietti, 1936, 311pp.
_____, Sesto S. Giovanni-Milano, Barion, 1937, [?]pp.
Vagabondo delle stelle, Milan, Bietti, 1932, 312pp.
                                    (Italian)
Tvangstrøien, tr.: Nordahl Grieg, Oslo, Gyldendal, 1941,
320pp.   (Norwegian)
Kaftan bezpieczeństwa, tr,: M. Andrzeykowicz, Warsaw, Rój,
1927, 1929, 3 vols. (1-125, 129-248, 249-388).
                                    (Polish)
Twangstrojan, tr.: Ernst Lundquist, Stockholm, Bohlin,
1916, 370pp.; later ed. of 1926.   (Swedish)
Mezhzvezdyni skitaletz, [Title in Russian] Kiev, Goslitizdat Ukrainy, 1957, 254pp.   (Ukranian)

                    THE ACORN-PLANTER. 1916

136. THE | ACORN-PLANTER | *A CALIFORNIA FOREST PLAY* | PLANNED
TO BE SUNG BY EFFICIENT SINGERS | ACCOMPANIED BY A CAPABLE
| ORCHESTRA | BY | JACK LONDON | NEW YORK | THE MACMILLAN
COMPANY | 1916 | *All rights reserved*
    [iv] v-vi [1-2] 3-84p. 17.5 x 12 cm. Red cloth with

white spine. Top edges gilt. Lettering on spine black.
Lettering on front cover white. Four pages of publisher's
advertisements at back.
  On verso of title-page (p.[iv]): COPYRIGHT, 1916, BY
JACK LONDON. | [rule] | Set up and electrotyped. Publish-
ed February, 1916. | [Three lines of press signature]
  The dust wrapper is white, printed in black and red.
There is no printing on back wrapper, or inside ends.

137. Reprints:
  ____, London, Mills & Boon, 1916, vi, 84pp.
  ____, translated by Fong T'u Jen, Shanghai, Commercial
Press, 1934, 136pp. [Text in Chinese and English].

THE LITTLE LADY OF THE BIG HOUSE. 1916

138. THE LITTLE LADY OF | THE BIG HOUSE | BY | JACK LONDON |
Author of "The Valley of the Moon," "The Star | Rover,"
"The Sea Wolf," Etc. | New York | THE MACMILLAN COMPANY |
1916 | *All rights reserved*
  [vi] 1-392p. 19 x 13 cm.   Blue cloth decorated in dark
blue, orange, and white. Spine lettered in gilt. Lettering on front cover white. Frontis. in color. Four pages
of publisher's advertisements at back.
  On verso of title-page (p.[iv]): Copyright, 1915 |
By JACK LONDON | [rule] | Copyright, 1916 | By JACK
LONDON | Set up and electrotyped. Published April, 1916 |
[rule] | Copyrighted in Great Britain

139. Serializations:
This novel first appeared in *Cosmopolitan Magazine,* 58:
482-486, 488-491, 494-497, 499 (April 1915); 58:627-630,
632-636, 638-641, 644-646 (May 1915); 59:38-54 (June
1915); 59:169-187 (July 1915); 59:321-338 (Aug. 1915);
59:520-536 (Sept. 1915); 59:672-688 (Oct. 1915); 59:806-
822 (Nov. 1915); 60:121-123, 126-127, 130-132, 134-135;
(Dec. 1915); 60:285-289, 291-295, 298-300; (Jan. 1916).

140. Reprints:
  ____, New York, Grosset & Dunlap, 1916, 1918, 392pp.
  ____, London, Mills & Boon, 1916, 334pp.; 1917, 1921,
332pp.
  ____, London, Nelson, 1917, 383pp.
  ____, London, Cassell, 1933, 315pp.

141. Translations:
Maklata stopanska na goliamata kushcha, tr.: D. Podvurzachov, Sofia, Suglasie, 1930, 352pp. (Mozaǐka ot

znameniti suvremenni romani 22).
_____, Sofia, D. Madzharov, 1935, 226pp. (Bibl. Zlatni stranitzi).
Malkata stopanka na golemiia dom, tr.: Orlin Vasilev, Sofia, Sluntze, 1945, 296pp.   (Bulgarian)
Malá dáma z velikého domu, tr.: B. Z. Nekovařík, Prague, Kočí, 1922, 2 vols (164, 158pp.); Zlín, Tisk, 1936, 325pp.
Malá paní z velkého domu, tr.: J. Vorel, Prague, Procházka, 1922, 393pp.   (Czech/Slovak)
"Suure maja väike kashijanna," *Postimees,* Feb. 19-April 9, 1930.   (Estonian)
Suuren talon pikkurouva, tr.: Aito Kare, Helsinki, Minerva, 1923, 219pp.; Porvoo, Werner Soderstrom, 1937, 215pp.   (Finnish)
La petite dame de la grande maison, tr.: L. Postif, Paris, Hachette, 1936, 255pp. (Les meilleurs romans étrangers).
        (French)
Die Herrin des grossen Hauses, tr.: Erwin Magnus, Berlin, Universitas, 1929, 311pp.; Berlin, Volksverb. d. Bücherfreunde. Wegweiser Verlag, 1931, 280pp.
        (German)
ha-Geveret ha-katana shel ha-bet ha-gadol, tr.: Yitshak Hirshberg, Tel-Aviv, Tevel, 1952, 247pp.
        (Hebrew)
A nagy ház kis asszonykája, tr.: Zsolt Harsányi, Budapest, Athenaeum, 1923, 255pp.; other editions were published in 1926, 361pp.; 1944, 246pp.   (Hungarian)
La piccola signora della grande casa, tr.: Aldo Traverso and Gian Dàuli, Milan, Modernissima, 1928, 470pp.; Milan, Barion, 1933, [?]pp.; Sesto S. Giovanni, Barion, 1936, 382pp.; Barion, 1945, [?]pp.   (Italian)
Lielās mājas mazā saimniece, tr.: Z. Krodere, Riga, Zalktis, 1927, 224pp. (Zelta sērija 10). (Latvian)
Maleńska pani dużego domu, tr.: Wanda Borudzka, Warsaw, Roj, 1928, 1933, 417pp.   (Polish)
Doamna mică din casa mare, tr.: Mircea A. Dumitrescu, Bucharest, Fortuna, 1942, 375pp.   (Rumanian)
Malenkaya khozyaika iz bolshovo doma, tr.: Ye. Shteinberg, Moscow, Sovremennyie Problemy, 1917, 408pp.
Malenkaya khozyaika bolshovo doma, tr.: Z. A. Ragozina, Petrograd, 1923, 1924, 333pp.; this tr. edited by M. Kuzmin, Leningrad, Seyatel, 1926, 266pp.
_____, tr.: M. K. Grinvald, Leningrad, Mysl, 1925, 328pp.
_____, Leningrad, Knizhniye Novinki, 1926, 298pp.
_____, tr.: V. O. Stanevich, Alma-Ata, Kazgoslitizdat, 1957, 284pp.
_____, tr.: V. O. Stanevich, Petrozavodsk, Gozizdat Karel, 1958, 230pp.   (Russian)

Mala ledi, tr.: Zarija D. Vukićević, Belgrade, Rad, 1957, 443pp.   (Serbian)
La muchacha de la casa grande, tr.: Adela Grego, Buenos Aires, Ediciones Siglo XX, 1952, 319pp.; Barcelona, Ediciones G. P., 1957, 223pp.   (Spanish)

THE TURTLES OF TASMAN. *1916*

142. THE | TURTLES OF TASMAN | BY | JACK LONDON | Author of "The Call of the Wild," "The Strength | of the Strong," "The Valley of the Moon" | New York | THE MACMILLAN COMPANY | 1916 | *All rights reserved*
[vi] 1-268p. 19 x 13 cm. Chocolate brown cloth decorated in blue and orange. Lettering on spine gilt. Lettering on front cover cream. Five pages of publisher's advertisements at back.
On verso of title-page (p.[iv]): [Six lines of previous magazine publishing copyright notices] | [rule] | COPYRIGHT, 1912 | BY THE CURRIER PUBLISHING COMPANY | [rule] | COPYRIGHT, 1914 | BY DODD, MEAD AND COMPANY | [rule] | COPYRIGHT, 1916 | BY JACK LONDON | [rule] | Set up and electrotyped. Published, September, 1916.
Contents: By the Turtles of Tasman; The Eternity of Forms; Told in the Drooling Ward; The Hobo and the Fairy; The Prodigal Father; The First Poet; Finis; The End of the Story.

143. Reprints:
Turtles of Tasman, and other stories, London, Mills & Boon, 1917, 307pp.
____, London, Newnes, 1921, 158pp.

144. Translations:
Dat was nog eens een kerel, tr.: J. P. Wesselink-van Rossum, Amsterdam, Boekh. en Uitg. Mij Joh. Müller, 1923, [?]pp.   (Dutch)
Kulkuri ja keijukainen, tr.: Ilmari Lehto, Helsinki, Kustannusliike Minerva, 1923, 120pp. [Contains four stories.]
____, Y. M. Kertomuksia, Porvoo, Kust. Werner Söderström, 1938, 190pp. [Includes four stories and a translation of The scarlet plague.]   (Finnish)
La tartarughe di Tasman, tr.: Olga Carbone, Milan, Modernissima, 1930, 233pp.   (Italian)

THE HUMAN DRIFT. *1917*

145. THE HUMAN DRIFT | BY | JACK LONDON | Author of "The Call of the Wild," etc. | New York | THE MACMILLAN COMPANY |

1917
  [viii] 1-184p. 19 x 13 cm. Brown cloth. Spine and
front cover lettered in gilt. Frontis. portrait of the
author. Six pages of publisher's advertisements at back.
  On verso of title-page (p.[iv]): [Eight lines of pre-
vious magazine publishing copyright notices] | [rule] |
COPYRIGHT, 1917 | BY THE MACMILLAN COMPANY | [rule] |
Set up and electrotyped. Published, February, 1917.
  Contents: The Human Drift; Nothing that Ever Came to
Anything; That Dead Men Rise Up Never; Small-Boat Sailing;
Four Horses and a Sailor; A Classic of the Sea; A Wicked
Woman; The Birth Mark.
  This was the first of Jack London's books to be pub-
lished after his death.

146. Reprints:
  ____, London, Mills & Boon, 1919, 1920, 1925, 190pp.

JERRY OF THE ISLANDS. 1917

147. JERRY | OF THE ISLANDS | BY | JACK LONDON | Author of
"The Call of the Wild," | "The Valley of the Moon," |
Etc. | New York | THE MACMILLAN COMPANY | 1917 | *All
rights reserved*
  [iv] v-ix [x] 1-337p. 19 x 13 cm. Red cloth decorated
in black. Spine lettered in gilt. Title on front cover
gilt, author's name in black. Frontis. in color. Six pages
of publisher's advertisements at back.
  On verso of title-page (p.[iv]): COPYRIGHT, 1916 AND
1917 | BY ELIZA SHEPARD AND | WILLARD L. GROWALL, | Ex-
ecutors for the Estate of Jack London | [rule] | Set up
and electrotyped. Published, April, 1917.

148. Serializations:
Published serially in *Cosmopolitan*, 62:16-22, 150, 152,
154, 156 (Jan. 1917); 62:53-60, 164-166, 168, 170 (Feb.
1917); 62:70-77, 154, 157, 159, 161-162, 164-168, 170-171,
173-174 (March 1917); 62:80-87, 122-131 (April 1917).

149. Reprints:
  ____, New York, *Daily worker*, c1916-1917
  ____, New York, Grosset [1917] 337pp.
  ____, London, Mills & Boon, 1917, 1925, 1928, 283pp.;
  1921, 275pp.
  ____, London, Leisure Library, 1930, 224pp.
  ____, London, W. Laurie, 1937, 1949, 275pp.

150. Translations:
Dzheri ostrovitianinut, tr.: D. Podvurzachov, Sofia,
Chetivo, [1946] 184pp. (Bulgarian)
Jerry z ostrovu, tr.: I. Schulz, Prague, Topič, 1919,
278pp.; Prague, Kočí, 1923, 2 vols. (126, 128pp.).
____, Pro mládež upravil, tr.: F. Š., Plzeň, Cesky deník,
1921, 16pp.
____, *Dobrodužství ze světa kanibalu*, tr.: S. Klima,
Prague, Toužimský a Moravec, 1938, 226pp.
____, tr.: F. Swidzinski, Prague, Práce, 1949, 98pp.
(Czech/Slovak)
Jerry, tr.: A. Mikkelsen, Copenhagen, Martin, 1918, 2 vols.
(160, 142pp.): 1928, 2 vols. (256, 256pp.).
(Danish)
Jerry, tr.: S. J. Barentz-Schönberg, Amsterdam, H. J. W.
Becht, 1919. (Dutch)
Jerry, tr.: A. Herms, Talinn, Elu, 1928, 206pp. (Elu
lugemisvara nos. 28-29). (Estonian)
Jeri, Helsinki, Otava, 1922, 275pp.; Otava, 1958, 266pp.
(Finnish)
Jerry dans l'île, tr.: Maurice Dekobra, Paris, Crès,
1922, viii, 309pp.; Paris, Hachette, 1933, 250pp. (Bib-
liothèque verte); Hachette, 1952, 188pp. (Ideal biblio-
thèque); Hachette, 1960, 251pp. (Bibliothèque verte 165);
Brussels, Vanderschueren, [n.d.][1946?] 252pp.
(French)
Jerry der Insulaner, tr.: Erwin Magnus, Berlin, Universi-
tas, 1927, 1946, 311pp.; Zürich, Büchergilde Gutenberg,
1947, 275pp.; Stuttgart, Hamburg, Baden-Baden, Berlin,
Rowohlt, 1949, 37pp. (Rowohlt-Rotations-Romane); Vienna,
Wiener Volksbuchverlag, 1949, 239pp. (Jack London-Reihe);
Frankfurt/M., Büchergilde Gutenberg, 1951, 252pp.;
Berlin, Universitas, 1952, 252pp.; Berlin, Darmstadt,
Vienna, Dt. Buch-Gemeinschaft, 1961, 216pp.
(German)
A beszélő kutya, tr.: Harsányi Zsolt, Budapest, Athen-
aeum, 1923, 218pp.; 1926 (Jack London Összes munkái 1);
1936, 259pp.; 1940, 255pp. (Hungarian)
Jerri delle isole, tr.: Adele Levi, Milan, Bietti, 1930,
1936, 270pp.
Jerry delle isole, tr.: Francesco de Rosa, Milan, Corti-
celli, 1954, 280pp.
____, tr.: Gian Dàuli, Milan, Modernissima, 1928, 286pp.
(Italian)
Jerry, tr.: Ben Horne, Oslo, Gyldendal, 1934, 1941,
227pp. (Norwegian)
Jerry z wysp, tr.: W. Borudzka and M. de Kleist, Warsaw,
Rój, 1928, 250pp. (Polish)

Jerryin Insula Canibalilor, tr.: G. M. Amza, Bucharest,
G. M. Amza, 1942, 256pp.   (Rumanian)
Dzherri, tr.: Ya. I. Yasinski, Leningrad, Nauchnoye
Knigoizdatelstvo, 1924, 127pp.
Dzherri s Solomonovykh Ostrovov, tr.: V. Onegin, Petro-
grad, Leningrad and Moscow, 1924, 224pp.
Ostrovityanin, tr.: D. M. Gorfinkel, Leningrad and Mos-
cow, Novella, 1924, 197pp.
Dzherri-Ostrovityanin, Krasnoiarsk, 1958, 170pp.; Kha-
barovsk, 1960, 175pp.   (Russian)
Džeri sa ostrava, tr.: Mihailo Djordjević, Belgrade,
Izdanje Izdavacke knjizarnice Radomira D. Cukovica, 1927,
300pp. (Klasicna dela omladinske knjizevnosti 14); Novi
Sad, Bratstvo-Jedinstvo, 1953, 181pp.
                              (Serbian)
Jerry, el de las islas,tr.: Fernando Valera, Valencia,
Prometeo, 1926, 246pp.
_____, Madrid, Diana, 1955, 95pp.
_____, Buenos Aires, Ed. Futuro, 1946, 249pp.
Jerry de las islas, tr.: P. Ortiz Barili, Buenos Aires,
Ed. Acmé, 1947, 290pp.
_____, under the supervision of M. E. Antonini, Buenos
Aires, Ed. Acmé, 1952, 304pp.
_____, Santiago de Chile, Zig-Zag, 1961, 168pp. (Biblio-
teca juvenil. Serie Amarilla no. 20).
Jerry, el de las islas, no tr. given, Buenos Aires,
Futuro, 1946, 249pp.   (Spanish)
Jerry, tr.: Ernst Lundquist, Stockholm, Bohlin, 1917,
296pp.; Stockholm, Ahlén & Holm, 1926, 208pp.
                              (Swedish)

MICHAEL BROTHER OF JERRY. 1917

151. MICHAEL | BROTHER OF JERRY | BY | JACK LONDON | Author of
"Jerry of the Islands," "The Call | of the Wild," "The
Sea Wolf," etc. | New York | THE MACMILLAN COMPANY |
1917 | *All rights reserved*
     [iv] v-viii [ix-x] 1-344p. 19 x 13 cm. Red cloth dec-
orated in black. Spine lettered in gilt. Title on front
cover gilt, author's name in black. Frontis. in color.
Eight pages of publisher's advertisements at back.
     On verso of title-page (p.[iv]): COPYRIGHT, 1917 |
BY ELIZA SHEPARD | AND | WILLARD L. GROWALL, | EXECUTORS
| [rule] | Set up and electrotyped. Published, November,
1917.

152. Reprints:
     _____, New York, Grosset & Dunlap, 19[?] viii. 344pp.

____, London, Mills & Boon, 1918, 1923, 1928, 332pp.
____, London, T. W. Laurie, 1950, 287pp.

153. Translations:
Maĭkel, tr.: M. Seuzova-Iurukova, Sofia, Gladston, 1932,
227pp. (Mozaĭka ot znameniti suvremenni romani 24).
(Bulgarian)
Michal, bratr Jerryho, tr.: Ivan Schulz, Prague, Pražská
akciová tiskárna, 1921, 344pp.
____, tr.: J. Hruša, Prague, Kočí, 1925, 2 vols. (160,
173pp.).
____, tr.: S. Klíma, Prague, Toužimský a Moravec, 1939,
295pp.
____, tr.: J. Hruša, Zlín, Tisk, 1939, 328pp.
(Czech/Slovak)
Michael, Jerrys broder, tr.: Knud Poulsen, Copenhagen,
Martin, 1928, 2 vols. (288, 296pp.); 1919, 2 vols. (158,
158pp.).   (Danish)
Terry de broeder van Jerry, tr.: S. J. Barentz-Schönberg,
Amsterdam, H. J. W. Becht, 1923.   (Dutch)
Jerin veli, tr.: Aune Tolvanen, Helsinki, Otava, 1922,
274pp.   (Finnish)
Michaël, chien de cirque, tr.: Louis Postif and Paul
Gruyer, Paris, Crès, 1925, 280pp.; 1926, 175pp.; Hachette,
1938, 132pp. (Collection des grands romanciers); Hachette,
1953, 188pp. (Ideal bibliothèque).   (French)
Michael, der Bruder Jerrys, tr.: Erwin Magnus, Berlin,
Universitas, 1928, 286pp.
Der Schiffshund der Makambo, Berlin, Universitas, 1931,
175pp., 1950, 303pp.; 1953, 283pp.; Frankfurt/M., Bücher-
gilde Gutenberg, 1953, 1957, 283pp.   (German)
Maĭkel, tò skulì tou tsírkou, tr.: H. Samiou, Athens, I
Phli tou Vivliou, 1947, 236pp.   (Greek)
As éneklő kutya, tr.: Harsányi Zsolt, Budapest, Athen-
aeum, vii. 371pp.; 1926, 332pp.; 1950, 231pp.; 1928,
281pp.
____, tr.: Imre Szász, Budapest, Ifj. Kiadó, 1955, 251pp.;
Budapest, Szépirod. Kiadó, 1955, 2 vols. (Olcsó könyvtár
41-42)   (Hungarian)
Micaele, fratello di Jerry, cane da circo, tr.: Gian Dàuli,
Milan, Modernissima, 1928, 312pp.
Michael cane de circo, tr.: Adele Levi, Milan, Bietti,
1930, 274pp.; 1936, 275pp.
Michael fratello di Jerry, tr.: Adele Levi, Milan,
Mursia, 1959, 278pp.   (Italian)
Michael, tr.: Ben Horne, Oslo, Gyldendal, 1935, 1943,
1947, 288pp.   (Norwegian)
Mik brat Jerzego, Warsaw, Rój, 1927, 3 vols. (123, 125-

248, 249-355pp).   (Polish)
Michaël, tr.: G. M. Amza, Bucharest, G. M. Amza, 1942,
292pp.
Mihail cîine de circ, tr.: Mircea Alexandrescu, Buchar-
est, Editura tineretului, 1959, 335pp.
_____, tr.: A. M. Amza, Bucharest, G. M. Amza, 1943,
304pp.
_____, tr.: Mircea Alexandrescu and Marius Măgureanu,
Bucharest, Editura tineretului, 1957, 342pp.
                                    (Rumanian)
Mikael, brat Dzherii, tr.: A. I. Yasinski, Leningrad,
Nauchnoye Knigoizdatelstvo, 1924, 126pp.
Maikl, brat Dzherri, tr.: M. Matveyev and T. Bogdanovich,
Leningrad, and Moscow, Petrograd, 1925, 283pp.
                                    (Russian)
Majkel brat dzerijev, tr.: Zivojin Vukadinovic, Belgrade,
Izdanje Geca Kon A;D;. 1939, 345 + 7pp. (Biblioteka
Plava Ptica 18).
Michael, Jerryjev brat, tr.: Otilija Snajder, Zagreb,
Mladost, 1951, 246pp.   (Serbian)
Miguel, hermano de Jerry, tr.: Fernando Valera, Valencia,
Prometeo, 1927, 318pp.
_____, tr.: César Horacio Silvera, Buenos Aires, Renaci-
miento, c1951 [page at end gives publication date of
1952] 308pp.
_____, tr.: Isidro Gelstein, Buenos Aires, Acme, 1958,
294pp.; 1952, 334pp.
_____, Buenos Aires, Futuro, 1947, 286pp.
Miguel, perro de circo, tr. from the French by Svea Edith,
Buenos Aires, Biblioteca nueva, 1952, 248pp. (Colección
Dick Turpin).
_____, [no tr. given,] Santiago de Chile, Zig-Zag, [n.d.,]
198pp. (Biblioteca juvenil. Serie Amarilla no. 28).
*Miguel, hermano de Jerry, Revista literaria: novelas y
cuentos,* no. 1, 482 (Oct. 4, 1959), 108pp.
Un perro de circo, tr.: Fernando de la Milla, Barcelona,
Lux, [n.d.,] 175pp. (La novela mensual).
Una vida aventurera con 250 ilustraciones, tr.: Fernando
Valera, Barcelona, Editorial Bruguera, 1958; 2nd ed.,
1963, 255pp.   (Spanish)
Michael, Jerrys bror, tr.: Ernst Lundquist, Stockholm,
Bohlin, 1919, 396pp.   (Swedish)
Majki, brat Džerijev, tr.: Smiljana and Nikola Kršić,
Sarajevo, Svjetlost, 1960, 272pp.   (Yugoslav)

THE RED ONE. 1918

154. THE RED ONE | BY | JACK LONDON | Author of "The Call of
the Wild," "Jerry | of the Island," "Adventure," etc. |
New York | THE MACMILLAN COMPANY | 1918 | *All rights
reserved*
[vi] 1-193p. 19 x 12.5 cm. Brown paper over boards
decorated in blue, orange, and black. Lettering on spine
black. Lettering on front cover black except for "Red
One" which is in orange outlined in black. Frontis. portrait of author. Four pages of publisher's advertisements
at back.
On verso of title-page (p.[iv]): COPYRIGHT, 1916, BY
JACK LONDON | COPYRIGHT, 1917, BY THE INTERNATIONAL MAG-
AZINE COMPANY | COPYRIGHT, 1918, BY ELIZA SHEPARD AND
WILLARD L. | GROWALL, EXECUTORS | [rule] | Set up and
electrotyped. Published, October, 1918
Contents: The Red One; The Hussy; Like Argus of the
Ancient Times; The Princess.
The copy in the George H. Tweney collection is mint
in dust jacket. The jacket is white calendared paper,
printed in black, reproduction of the frontispiece por-
trait of London on the front, lettered THE | RED ONE
at the top, and JACK LONDON below. Inside front flap
an advertisement for the book, back flap and back of
wrapper are blank.

155. Reprints:
____, New York, Grosset & Dunlap, 1918, 193pp.
____, London, Mills & Boon, 1919, 248pp.; 1920, 187pp.

156. Translations:
Der Rote, tr.: Erwin Magnus, Berlin, Universitas, c1928,
261pp. Contents: Der Rote. Wie vor alters zog die Argo.
Das Frauenzimmer. Die Prinzessin. Der Feind der ganzen
Welt. Samuel.   (German)
Il Dio rosso, tr.: Tullio Silvestri, Milan, Modernissima,
1929, 188pp.
____, and *Il pianto di Ah Kim,* tr.: T. Silvestri, Milano,
Sesto S. Giovanni, Barion, 1935, 379pp.; 1942, 301pp.
                              (Italian)

HEARTS OF THREE. 1918
English edition

157. HEARTS OF THREE | BY | JACK LONDON | AUTHOR OF "THE
VALLEY OF THE MOON", | "JERRY OF THE ISLANDS," | "MICHAEL,
BROTHER OF JERRY," &c., &c. | MILLS & BOON, LIMITED |

49 RUPERT STREET | LONDON, W.
18.5 x 12 cm. p.[i-ii],blank leaf, p.[iii], half-title,
p.[iv], Books by Jack London, p.[v], title page as above,
p.[vi], "Copyright in the U. S. A. by Jack London;"
Foreword [vii]-x, dated Waikiki, Hawaii, March 23, 1916,
pp.[xi]-xii, Poem, "Back to Back against the mainmast"
by George Sterling, text pp.1-292. Cahill & Co. Ltd.
Printers, London and Dublin.
Blue cloth. Black lettering on spine only. This edition has no date, but according to the catalog of the
British Museum it was published in England in 1918.
Checked by Colin Clair against the copy in the British
Museum.

HEARTS OF THREE. 1920
American edition

158. HEARTS OF THREE | BY | JACK LONDON | New York | THE MAC-
MILLAN COMPANY | 1920 | *All rights reserved*
[iv] v-ix [x] 1-373p. 19 x 12.5 cm. Red cloth. Spine
lettered in gilt.
On verso of title-page (p.[iv]): COPYRIGHT, 1920, |
BY CHARMIAN K. LONDON | [rule] | Set up and electrotyped.
Published, September, 1920

159. Serializations:
The New York *Evening Journal* serialized this volume in
1919; May 12, p.18; May 13, p.18; May 14, p.20; May 15,
p.22; May 16, p.28; May 17, p.10; May 19, p.16; May 20,
p.18; May 21, p.20; May 22, p.20; May 23, p.28; May 24,
p.9; May 26, p.16; May 27, p.22; May 28, p.20; May 29,
p.12; May 30, p.14; May 31, p.10; June 2, p.18; June 3,
p.18; June 4, p.20; June 5, p.20; June 6, p.28; June 7,
p.10; June 9, p.16; June 10, p.20; June 11, p.22; June
12, p.20; June 13, p.24; June 14, p.10; June 16, p.16;
June 17, p.18; June 18, p.20; June 19, p.20; June 20,
p.26.
The Oakland *Tribune*, magazine section, also serialized
it in 1919; Aug. 31, pp.2, 11; Sept. 7, pp.3, 10; Sept.
14, pp.2, 11; Sept. 21, pp.2, 9; Sept. 28, p.2; Oct. 5,
pp.2, 9; Oct. 12, p.2; Oct. 19, p.2; Oct. 26, p.2; Nov.
2, p.4; Nov. 9, p.10; Nov. 16, p.2; Nov. 23, p.11; Nov.
30, p.11; Dec. 7, p.11.

160. Reprints:
_____, London, Mills & Boon, 1921, xii, 292pp.

161. Translations:
Romanut na tri surtza, Sofia, Iv. Koiumdzhiev, 1929,
272pp. (Bibl. Chuden sviat).
____, tr.: D. Podvurzachov, Sofia, Iv. G. Ignatov, 1930,
294pp. (Bibl. Liubimi roman 23); Sofia, Prosveta, 1945,
400pp.   (Bulgarian)
Láska ve třech osobách, tr.: K. Koschin, Prague, Politika,
1920, 404pp.
____, tr.: K. Vít, Prague, Nakl. Dobrých autoru, 1920,
1921, 426pp.   (Czech/Slovak)
Tre hjerter, P. Jerndorff-Jensen, Copenhagen, Martin,
1922, 304pp.; 1929, 1931, 2 vols. (256, 272pp.).
                                     (Danish)
Drie harten, Amsterdam, Boekh. en Uitg. Mij Joh. Müller,
1923, [?]pp.   (Dutch)
Lugu kolmest südamest, tr.: G. Siefers, Riga, Interna-
tionale "Union", [n.d.,] 332pp. ("U" ilukirjandus.
Vol. 1).   (Estonian)
Morganin miljoonat, tr.: Aito Kare, Tampere, Helsinki,
Kustannusliike Minerva, 1923, 230pp. (Finnish)
Trois coeurs, tr.: Louis Postif, Paris, Hachette, 1938,
iv, 244pp. (Collection des grands romanciers).
                                     (French)
Prjú hjơrtu, Reykjavík, Framtí arútgáfan, 1931, 462pp.
                                     (Icelandic)
Tre cuori in lizza, tr.: Mario Benzi, Milan, Modernis-
sima, 1928, 383pp.
Il cuore dei tre, tr.: Adele Levi, Milan, Bietti, 1931,
301pp.   (Italian)
Trŕs sirdis, tr.: R. Kroders, *Latvijas Vestnesis,* nos.
225-289 (Oct. 9-Dec. 23, 1923; tr.: R. Kroders, Riga,
J. Roze, 1924, 383pp.   (Latvian)
Trys širdys, tr.: Pranas Šileika, Kaunas, Dirva, 1929,
2 vols. (194, 199pp.).   (Lithuanian)
Tre hjerter, tr.: Theodor Berge, Oslo, Gyldendal, 1935,
1943, 1947, 2 vols. (204, 190pp.)   (Norwegian)
Trzy serca, tr.: J. P. Zajaczkowski, Warsaw, Rój, 1923,
1923, 257pp.   (Polish)
Serdtza trekh, Lvov, Kn.-zhurn. izd., 1955, 324pp.
____, Alma-Ata, Kazgoslitizdat, 1957, 327pp.
                                     (Russian)
Trik žene, tr.: Ivan Petrovic, Zagreb, Knjižara Fred.
Neufeld, 1930, 48pp.
Roman Treh src, Ljubljana, Intro, 1926, 433pp.
                                     (Slovenian?)
Tres corazones, tr.: A. Guardiola, Valencia, Prometeo,
1927, 320pp.
____, tr.: Antonio Guardiola, Buenos Aires, Renacimiento,
1951, 271pp.   (Spanish)

ON THE MAKALOA MAT. 1919

162. ON THE | MAKALOA MAT | BY | JACK LONDON | Author of "The
Call of the Wild," "The | Sea Wolf," "Adventure," etc. |
New York | THE MACMILLAN COMPANY | 1919 | *All rights
reserved*
[vi] 1-229p. 19 x 12.5 cm. Light blue cloth decorated
in yellow and dark blue. Spine and front cover lettered
in yellow.
On verso of title-page (p. [iv]): COPYRIGHT, 1918 AND
1919 | BY ELIZA SHEPARD AND WILLARD L. GROWALL, EXECUTORS
| [rule] | COPYRIGHT, 1919 | BY CHARMIAN K. LONDON |
[rule] | Set up and electrotyped. Published, September,
1919
Contents: On the Makaloa Mat; The Bones of Kahelili;
When Alice Told Her Soul; Shin-Bones; The Water Baby;
The Tears of Ah Kim; The Kanaka Surf.

163. Reprints:
_____, New York, Macmillan, 1920, 229pp.
Printed in Great Britain as *Island tales*, London, Mills
& Boon, 1920, 248pp.; 1923, 254pp.

DUTCH COURAGE. 1922

164. DUTCH COURAGE | AND OTHER STORIES | BY | JACK LONDON |
New York | THE MACMILLAN COMPANY | 1922 | *All rights
reserved*
[iv] v-xii [xiii-xvi] 1-180p. 19 x 12.5 cm. Red cloth
decorated in black. Lettering on spine gilt. Lettering
on front cover black. Frontis. portrait of author.
On verso of title-page (p. [iv]): PRINTED IN THE
UNITED STATES OF AMERICA | COPYRIGHT, 1922, | BY
CHARMIAN LONDON. | [rule] | Set up and electrotyped.
Published September, 1922. | [Two lines of press signa-
ture]
Contents: Dutch Courage; Typhoon Off the Coast of
Japan; The Lost Poacher; The Banks of the Sacramento;
Chris Farrington, Able Seaman; To Repel Boarders; An
Adventure in the Upper Sea; Bald-Face; In Yeddo Bay;
Whose Business Is To Live.

165. Reprints:
_____, London, Mills & Boon, 1923, 1924, 191pp.
_____, New York, Macmillan, 1924, xii, 180pp.

166. Translations:
Il diritto alla vita, tr.: Alberto Tedeschi, Sesto S.

Giovanni-Milano, Barion, 1937, 221pp. (Italian)
Valor holandés, tr.: A. Grego, Valencia, Prometeo, 1927,
234pp.; Buenos Aires, Continental, 1945, 153pp.
(Spanish)

THE ASSASSINATION BUREAU, LTD. 1963

167. JACK | LONDON | *Completed by Robert L. Fish from notes
by Jack London* | THE | ASSASSINATION | BUREAU, | Ltd. |
McGraw-Hill Book Company, Inc. | New York Toronto
London
[vi] 1-184p. 20 x 13 cm. Mottled brown paper over
boards. Gilt lettering on spine running from top to
bottom, with small ornament in red separating author's
name from title. Text ends on p.179, with note at bottom
of page as follows: *"Jack London stops and Mr. Fish
begins on page 122".* Page [180] blank, pp.181-183: "Jack
London's Notes for the Completion of the Book", p.184:
"Ending as Outlined by Charmian London". Pictorial paper
dust wrapper in brown, decorated in red, black and white.
Brief biographical sketch of Jack London on back wrapper.
On verso of title-page (p.[iv]): THE ASSASSINATION
BUREAU, Ltd. | [Five lines of copyright notice] | Library
of Congress Catalog Card Number: 63-20448 | First Edition
| 38655
This book was issued simultaneously by the same publisher in a paperback edition. No priority of issue has
been established. The internal collation is exactly the
same as described above. The wrappers are glossy coated
paper, front wrapper in mauve with black and orange decorations, lettering in white and black. Spine and back
wrapper white, with lettering in black, mauve and orange.

168. Translations:
Moord op bestelling, tr.: Johan de Molenaar, Amsterdam,
Elsevier, 1965, 159pp. (Elsevier paperback)
(Dutch)
"Assassini S.P.A.," tr.: Maria Gallone, Milan, Rizzoli,
1965, 198pp. (Italian)

LETTERS FROM JACK LONDON. 1965

169. *Letters from* Jack London | [printer's device] *Containing
an Unpublished Correspondence* | *Between* London *and* Sin-
clair Lewis | *Edited by King Hendricks and Irving Shepard*
| Published by The Odyssey Press, New York [publisher's
device]

[iv] v [vi] vii-ix [x][1]-502p. 23.5 x 15 cm. Gray
paper over boards, green buckram backstrip. Gilt lettering on spine. Large embossed script letters "JL" on front
cover. Light rust-colored endpapers. Top edges of pages
tinted orange. Thirty-one photographic illustrations on
sixteen unnumbered pages between text pages 246-247.
Pictorial glossy paper dust wrapper in white, lettered
and decorated in green, orange, brown and black. Brief
biography of London and the editors on the wrapper ends.

On verso of title-page (p.[iv]): TO THE MEMORY OF |
ELIZA LONDON SHEPARD | Library of Congress catalog card
number: 65-22039 | C 1965 by King Hendricks and Irving
Shepard. | All rights reserved. | Printed in the U. S. A.

Contents: Foreword; 1876-1899--The Early Years;
Chronology; 1900-1905--Rise to Fame; Chronology; 1906-
1909--The Years of the *Snark;* Chronology; 1910-1916--The
Years of The Beauty Ranch; Chronology; London-Lewis
Letters; Index.

This recent publication is included here because the
bulk of the textual material has been written by Jack
London.

170. Translations:
The following Russian translations of various letters
taken from *LETTERS from Jack London* are the work of Vil
Bykov:
"Neizvestnoe pismo Dzheka Londona," *Literaturnaya gazeta,*
Jan. 11, 1966 [London to Anna Strunsky, letter date
Oct. 13, 1904].
"Muzhchyna sredi muzhchyn k 90-letiiu so dnia rozhdeniia
Dzheka Londona," *Literaturnaya rossya,* no. 3(159):16
(Jan. 1, 1966) [London to Houghton Mifflin, Jan. 31,
1900].
[Letter to George Brett, March 7, 1907] *Ogonek,* no. 2
Jan. 1966.

COLLECTIONS IN ENGLISH

171. *The works of Jack London,* New York, McKinlay, Stone &
      Mackenzie, 1906-190[?] 12 vols.
      1. Adventure.
      2. Before Adam. The game.
      3. Burning daylight.
      4. The call of the wild. The scarlet plague.
      5. The mutiny of the Elsinore.
      6. The iron heel.
      7. Martin Eden.
      8. The sea-wolf.
      9. South Sea tales.
      10. The valley of the moon.
      11. [Title not located.]
      12. White fang.

172. Collection of British [sic] authors. Tauchnitz edition,
      Leipzig, Bernhard Tauchnitz, [1911-1913] [4 vols.]
      Vol. 4273. Burning daylight, 1911, 384pp.
      Vol. 4323. The call of the wild, 1912, 262pp.
      Vol. 4352. When God laughs and other stories, 1912,
          277pp.
      Vol. 4426. A son of the sun, 1913, 270pp.

173. *The works of Jack London,* New York, The Review of
      Reviews Co., 1917:
      Adventure, 405pp.
      **Before Adam,* 228pp.
      Burning daylight, 360pp.
      **The call of the wild,* 211pp.
      The cruise of the Snark, 340pp.
      The iron heel, 354pp.
      **Martin Eden,* 411pp.
      **The sea-wolf,* 366pp.
      South Sea tales, 327pp.
      When God laughs, 319pp.
      **White Fang,* 321pp.
      The valley of the moon, 530pp.
      The starred items were part of the Authorized edition
      published for the Review of Reviews Co. by the Macmil-
      lan Co., 1911. The pagination of both sets is the same.
      The 1911 ed. included *Love of life,* which did not appear
      in the 1917 set.

174. Sonoma edition, New York, Macmillan, 1919, 27 vols. in
      21: The volumes are unnumbered and each volume has an

individual title-page. The data given are taken from the set in the Huntington Library; the set was reprinted in 1925-1930. The arbitrary arrangement that follows is alphabetical by title:

Adventure, 405pp.

Before Adam, 228pp. and *The game,* 182pp.

Burning daylight, 361pp.

The call of the wild, 211pp. and *The scarlet plague,* 181pp.

The faith of men, 286pp. and *Tales of the fish patrol,* 243pp.

The house of pride and other tales of Hawaii, 232pp. and *The turtles of Tasman,* 268pp.

The iron heel, 354pp.; this edition was reprinted in 1924 by Macmillan and the covers bear the words: "Sonoma edition". It differs from the 1919 ed. The pagination of the 1924 ed. is xix. 354pp.; pp.vii-xii are "Foreword" signed Anthony Meredith; pp.xiii-xvii comprise an introduction by Anatole France. None of the prefatory matter appears in the 1919 ed.

Jerry of the islands, 337pp.

The little lady of the big house, 392pp.

Lost face, 240pp. and *Children of the frost,* 261pp.

Martin Eden, 411pp.

Love of life and other stories, 265pp. and *The red one,* 193pp.

Michael, brother of Jerry, 344pp.

Moon-face and other stories, 273pp. and *The strength of the strong,* 257pp.

The mutiny of the Elsinore, 378pp.

The sea-wolf, 366pp.

South Sea tales, 327pp.

The star rover, 329pp.

The valley of the moon, 530pp.

When God laughs and other stories, 319pp.

White Fang, 327pp.

The following sets are undated:

175.   Everett's Library, London, Everett & Co.,[n.d.]
    The God of his fathers, 255pp.
    The iron heel, 287pp.
    Love of life, 252pp.
    The son of the wolf, 256pp.

176.   Macmillan's Standard Library was published in New York, Grosset & Dunlap,[n.d.]
    The call of the wild, 238pp.

    A daughter of the snows, 334pp.
    The people of the abyss, xiii, 319pp.
    The sea-wolf, 366pp.
    The son of the wolf, 251pp.
    War of the classes, xvii, 278pp.

177. Mills & Boon's Shilling Cloth Library, London, Mills & Boon, [n.d.]
    Adventure, 316pp.
    Children of the frost, 290pp.
    The cruise of the Dazzler, 288pp.
    The cruise of the Snark, 307pp.
    The God of his fathers, 285pp.
    John Barleycorn, 306pp.
    The house of pride, 287pp.
    The iron heel, 292pp.
    The jacket, 1915, 320pp.
    Lost face, 280pp.
    An odyssey of the north, 283pp.
    The road, 302pp.
    The scarlet plague, 153pp.
    Smoke Bellew, 292pp.
    A son of the sun, 301pp.
    South Sea tales, 285pp.
    The valley of the moon, 536pp.
    When God laughs and other stories, 298pp.

178. Nelson's Continental Library of the Best British and American Literature, Paris, Thomas Nelson and Sons: [n.d.]
    Vol. 22. The mutiny of the Elsinore, 474pp.
    Vol. 29. The little lady of the big house, 383pp.
    Vol. 35. The night born, 281pp.
    Vol. 46. White Fang, 288pp.
    Vol. 49. A daughter of the snows, 380pp.
    Vol. 53. Jerry of the islands, 254pp.
    Vol. 55. Strength of the strong, 254pp.
    Vol. 64. Michael, brother of Jerry, [?]pp.

179. Regent Press, New York, [n.d.]
    The call of the wild, 231pp.
    Burning daylight, 361pp.
    Before Adam, 242pp.
    The faith of men, 286pp.
    Martin Eden, 411pp.
    White Fang, 327pp.

180. The Fitzroy edition of the works of Jack London are
     edited and introduced by I. O. Evans. They are published
     in Great Britain by Arco Publications in London. In New
     York, they were published by Archer House; later they
     were available from H. Moorepack, 440 E. 79th St., New
     York. The arrangement is alphabetical by title.
     The Call of the wild, Arco, 1963, 127pp.
     Children of the frost, Arco and Archer House, 1963,
       160pp.
     The Cruise of the Dazzler, Arco, 1962; Archer House
       [1963] 158pp.
     A daughter of the snows, Arco, 1962; Archer House,
       [1963] 255pp.
     The people of the abyss, Arco, 1962; Archer, 1963,
       187pp.
     The son of the wolf, Arco, 1962; Archer House, 1963,
       190pp.

ANTHOLOGIES IN ENGLISH

181. *The Chinago and other stories,* New York, Leslie-Judge
Co., c1911, pp.155-319. [Copies examined in the Hunt-
ington Library and the North Texas State University
Library have this pagination.] Contents: The Chinago.
Make westing. Semper Idem. A nose for the king. The
"Francis Spaight". A curious fragment. A piece of steak.

182. *Brown wolf, and other Jack London stories,* as chosen by
Franklin K. Mathiews, New York, Macmillan, 1920, 312pp.;
New York, Macmillan, 1963, 187pp. (Acorn books 21).
Contents: Brown Wolf. That spot. Trust. All gold canyon.
The story of Keesh. Nam-Bok, the unveracious. Yellow
handkerchief. Make westing. The heathen. The hobo and
the fairy. Just meat. A nose for the king.

183. *The call of the wild and other stories* with an introduction by Frank Luther Mott, New York, Macmillan, 1926;
reissued with new illustrations, 1927 (Modern Reader's
Series) xxxv, 268pp.

184. ____, New York, Macmillan, 1936, 1949 and 1951, both
[c1931], xxxv, 268.; New York, Arcadia House, 1950, xxxi,
268pp. Contents: The call of the wild. To build a fire.
The heathen. The strength of the strong.

185. *London's essays of revolt,* edited and introduction by
Leonard D. Abbott, New York, Vanguard Press, 1926, 115pp.
Contents: Foreword. The apostate. The dream of Debs.
How I became a socialist. The scab. What life means to
me. Revolution.

186. *Selected stories of Jack London* published for Three Pay
Sales Corporation ... by The World Syndicate Publishing
Company, Cleveland, New York, 1930, 319pp. Contents:
The house of Mapuhi. The whale tooth. Mauki. "Yah! Yah!
Yah!" The heathen. The terrible Solomons. The inevitable
white man. The seed of McCoy. When God laughs. The apos-
tate. A wicked woman. "Just meat". Created he them. The
Chinago. Make westing. Semper idem. A nose for the king.
The "Francis Spaight". A curious fragment. A piece of
steak.

187. *Jack London's stories for boys.* Illustrated by C. Richard
Schaare, New York, Cupples & Leon, [c1936] 121pp. Contents: *Love of Life, Moon Face, Lost Face.*

188. *The best short stories of Jack London,* Garden City, New
York, The Sun Dial Press, [c1945], 311pp. Contents: The
White silence. To build a fire. An odyssey of the north.
The league of the old men. Lost face. A piece of steak.
The heathen. Samuel. On the Makaloa mat. A daughter of
the aurora. The law of life. The story of Jees Uck.

To the man on trail. The story of Keesh. The wit of Porportuk. Love of life. The Mexican. All gold canyon. The
wisdom of the trail. The house of Mapuhi. The pearls of
Parlay.

189. *Love of life and other stories,* introduction by George
Orwell, London, P. Elek [1946] 290pp. Contents: Love of
life. Chun Ah Chun. The Mexican. The house of Mapuhi.
Mauki. The seed of McCoy. The apostate. Just meat. The
Chinago. Make westing. Semper idem. A nose for the king.
The "Francis Spaight". A piece of steak. The feathers
of the sun.

190. *The scarlet plague. Love of life. The unexpected: three
stories* ..., London, Staples Press, Ltd., 1946, 100pp.

191. Foner, Philip S., *Jack London: American rebel. A collection of his social writings together with an extensive study of the man and his time,* New York, Citadel
Press, 1947, ix, 533pp. Contents: Preface. Jack London:
American rebel. Fiction: *The iron heel* [selections entitled The philomtahs. The vortex. The general strike.
The beginning of the end. Last days. The end. The scarlet livery. In the shadow of Sonoma. The rearing abysmal
beast. The Chicago commune]. *The people of the abyss*
[selections: Nightmare. The terrorists]. The apostate.
The dream of Debs. South of the slot. The strength of
the strong. In the laundry [selection from *Martin Eden*].
Autobiographical writings: In the powerhouse [a selection
from *John Barleycorn*]. Tramp days [selections from *The
road:* My life in the underworld: a reminiscence and a
confession. "Holding her down". "Pinched". The pen].
How I became a socialist. In the London slums [selections
from *The people of the abyss:* The descent. Preface.
Those on the edge. The carter and the carpenter. Carrying the banner. The management]. What life means to me.
Newspaper articles: Explanation of the great socialist
vote of 1904. Something rotten in Idaho. Strike methods:
American and Australian. Essays: What communities lose
by the competitive system. Wanted: a new law of development. The class struggle. The scab. The tramp. Revolution. Reviews and comments: "The octopus". "Foma
Gordyeeff". "The jungle". Introduction to "The cry for
justice". Sources. Bibliography. In 1958 this volume
was printed in Berlin by the Seven Seas Publishers,
503pp. It is part of Seven Seas Books: a collection of
works by writers in the English language. It contains
a page entitled: "Briefly, About the book" and following
p.503 there is a page: "Briefly, About the author."
This edition omits several selections that appear in the
1947 edition. The introduction to this volume has been

reprinted as: Foner, Philip S., *Jack London: American rebel*, New York, Citadel Press, c1964, iv, 155pp. (C143). This introduction differs in several respects from that of 1947. The preface and bibliography have been slightly changed, while pp.130-151 are "Supplementary material," which Foner describes (p.iv) as follows: "This section consists mainly of additional material from letters of London or interviews with him in the contemporary press for which there was no room in the original edition. There are also some extracts from London's writings which were not included in that edition. Finally, there are a few comments by other students of Jack London and some additional information which has come to light since 1947."

192. _____, *Jack London, Amerikansk rebell: En biografi*, tr.: Olle Moberg, Stockholm, Arbetarkulturs Förlag, 1951, 240pp. [This is a translation of Foner's introduction. Pp.229-240, "Vad livet betyder for mig" is a translation of London's "What life means to me".]

193. _____, *Jack London, americký rebel*, tr.: K. Bém, Prague, Mladá fronta, 1951, 147pp. [Translation of introduction.]

194. *Four short stories*, edited, with an introduction, by K. R. H. Ewing, London, Longmans [1949] x, 86pp. (Essential English library). Contents: Love of life. Demetrios Contos. In a far country. The house of Mapuhi.

195. *Dva rasskaza*, obrakatka y slovar C. A. Kreines and C. C. Tolstogo, Moscow, Izdatelstvo na inostrannyh yazykah, 1949, 1950, 1951, 1960, 30pp. [Pagination given for 1960 ed.] This text contains "That spot" and "For the love of man" from *The call of the wild* simplified for easy reading in English.

196. *Short stories*, Moscow, Foreign Language Publishing House, 1950, 400pp. Contents: Predislovie [Preface] by E. Merkel. Love of life. The white silence. To build a fire. The man with the gash. A day's lodging. The one thousand dozen. Finis: a tragedy of the far northwest. The story of Keesh. Grit of women. The wisdom of the trail. The white man's way. All gold canyon. Mauki. "Yah! Yah! Yah!" The house of pride. Koolau, the leper. The Chinago. A piece of steak. The apostate. Bulls. The Mexican. "Pinched". The people of the abyss [excerpts].

197. *Sun-dog trail, and other stories*, Cleveland, World Publishing Co., 1951, 251pp. Contents: The sun-dog trail. Brown wolf. The strength of the strong. The shadow and the flash. Moon-face. At the rainbow's end. To build a fire. Make westing. Too much gold. A son of the sun. A raid on the oyster pirates. Love of life.

198. *The Call of the Wild. White Fang. The Scarlet Plague*

with an introduction by Bernard Fergusson, London and
Glasgow, Collins, 1952 [1953] 381pp.
199. *The Mexican*. "Pinched", Tallinn, Eesti Riiklik Kirjastus,
1952, 80pp.
200. *Jack London's Tales of adventure* edited by Irving
Shepard, Garden City, New York, Hanover House, [c1956],
531pp. Contents: Introduction. The young man: The child.
The oyster pirate [from *John Barleycorn*]. The "Sophie
Sutherland" [from *John Barleycorn*]. That dead men rise
up never. The electrician. Two thousand stiffs. The
brain merchant. Through the rapids on the way to Klondike. From Dawson to the sea. The adventurer: Story of
a typhoon off the coast of Japan. The run across.
Bonin Islands: an incident of the sealing fleet of '93.
Holding her own. The inconceivable and monstrous. A
Pacific traverse. Cruising in the Solomons. The reporter:
Selections from *The people of the abyss:* Preface. The
descent. The carter and the carpenter. Carrying the
banner. The management. The Russo-Japanese war. Selected
dispatches. The trip to Ping Yang. Cossacks fight then
retreat. Over the Pekin road on the way to the Yalu.
Beware the monkey cage. The story of an eye-witness [The
San Francisco earthquake, 1906]. The Jeffries-Johnson
fight. Selected articles. Never a man so fit. The
"abysmal brute". The ape and the tiger. Johnson whips
Jeffries. The novelist: Selections from *The sea wolf*,
The iron heel, Martin Eden; The poker game from *Burning
daylight*. The strike from *The valley of the moon*. Round-
ing the cape from *The mutiny of the Elsinore*. The mountain meadow massacre from *The star rover*. The short
story writer: To the man on trail. The white silence.
An odyssey of the north. Jan, the unrepentant. The man
with the gash. The law of life. The one thousand dozen.
Bâtard. All gold canyon. The apostate. Love of life.
The passing of Marcus O'Brien. Flush of gold. Lost face.
A piece of steak. The seed of McCoy. The Mexican. The
strength of the strong. War. The pearls of Parlay. The
race for number three. Samuel. Told in the drooling
ward. The princess.
201. *Stories*, Tallinn, Eesti Riiklik Kirjastus, 1958, 64pp.
Contents: Love of life. A piece of steak. Under the
deck awnings. To kill a man.
202. *Stories* ... ed.: V. Rachmanovas, Kaunas, Valst. ped. lit.
1-kla, 1958, 112pp. [An English language reader for the
10th grade, intermediate school]. Contents: Pronuncia-
tion table. A piece of steak. The Chinago. Under the
deck awnings. The Mexican. To kill a man. Love of life.
Vocabulary.

203. *The call of the wild and other stories* ... with biographical illustrations and pictures of contemporary scenes
together with an introduction and captions by Louis B.
Salomon, New York, Dodd, Mead & Co., 1960, viii, 142pp.
(Great illustrated classics). Contents: The call of the ·
wild. The man with the gash. Jan, the unrepentant. The
white silence. To the man on trail. The wisdom of the
trail. An odyssey of the north. The law of life. A
daughter of the Aurora.

204. *The call of the wild and selected stories* with a foreword by Franklin Walker, New York, New American Library,
1960, 176pp. (Signet Classic CD20). Contents: The call
of the wild. Diable--a dog. An odyssey of the north.
To the man on trail. To build a fire. Love of life.

205. *The call of the wild. The Cruise of the Dazzler and
other stories of adventure with the author's special
report,* New York, Platt & Munk, 1960, 528pp. (Platt &
Munk Great writers collection). Contents of part three:
Selected short stories. In Yeddo Bay. Chris Farrington,
able seaman. The "fuzziness" of Hoockla-Heen. Dutch
Courage. The lost poacher. An adventure in the upper
sea. Nam-Bok, the liar. Jan, the unrepentant. Diable,
a dog. The law of life. Siwash. The man with the gash.
Too much gold. Keesh, the son of Keesh. In a far country.
The men of forty mile. The marriage of Lit-Lit. The leopard man's story. An impression: London's special
report on the gold strike in Alaska: Gold hunters of the
north. About Jack London: Biographical notes.

206. *Short stories* edited with an introduction by Maxwell
Geismar, New York, Hill and Wang, 1960, xx, 228pp.
(American Century Series AC33). Contents: Introduction.
Love of life. To build a fire. The apostate. The Chinago.
Make westing. Semper idem. A curious fragment. The whale
tooth. Mauki. Yah! Yah! Yah! Good-by, Jack. Aloha oe.
The eternity of forms. Told in the drooling ward. The
strength of the strong. South of the slot. The unparal-
leled invasion. The sea farmer.

207. *The best short stories of Jack London* with an introduction by Eugene Burdick, New York, Fawcett, 1962, viii,
190pp. (Premier D180). Contents: To build a fire. An
odyssey of the north. Lost face. A piece of steak. The
heathen. The law of life. To the man on trail. The wit
of Porportuk. Love of life. The pearls of Parlay.

208. *Short stories,* compiled by B. Baratov-Umanskiy, Moscow,
Foreign Languages Publishing House, 1962, 330pp. Contents: Ot izdatelstva ["Preface" from the Publishing
House.] To the man on trail. In a far country. An odyssey of the north. Which make men remember. Grit of

women. The great interrogation. Where the trail forks.
At the rainbow's end. Batard. Brown wolf. That spot.
The house of Mapuhi. The Mexican. The end of the story.
By the turtles of Tasman. Kommentariy (Commentary by
M. V. Lagunova).

209. *The Bodley Head Jack London*, edited by Arthur Calder-
Marshall, London, John Lane, The Bodley Head, 1963,
377pp. Contents: The apostate. The white silence. To
build a fire. The league of the old men. Batard. The
call of the wild. A nose for the king. South of the
slot. The unparalleled invasion. The dream of Debs. The
heathen. Yah! Yah! Yah! The madness of John Harned. The
Mexican. A piece of steak. Make westing. Told in the
drooling ward. The shadow and the flash.

210. *White fang and other stories* with illustrations of the
author, his environment and from early editions of the
book; introduction by A. K. Adams, New York, Dodd, Mead
& Co., [c1963], 308pp. (Great illustrated classics).
Stories are: The one thousand dozen. All gold canyon.
The sun of the wolf. In a far country.

211. *The Bodley Head Jack London*, edited and introduced by
Arthur Calder-Marshall, London, Bodley Head, 1964, vol.
2, 454pp. Contents: *John Barleycorn. The cruise of the
Dazzler. The road.*

212. *The sea-wolf, and selected stories*. Afterword by Franklin Walker, New York, New American Library [1964]
(Signet Classic CP217). Contents: The sea-wolf. The law
of life. The one thousand dozen. All gold canyon. Moon-
face.

213. *Great short works of Jack London*. Edited and with an
introduction by Earle Labor, Harper & Row, New York,
1965, xx, 379pp. (A perennial classic). Contents: Introduction. Bibliography. Bâtard. The Call of the wild.
White Fang. To build a fire. In a far country. The law
of life. Love of life. An odyssey of the North.

214. *Stories of Hawaii* edited by A. Grove Day, New York,
Appleton-Century, 1965, 282pp. Contents: Introduction.
The house of pride. The house of pride. Koolau the
leper. Good-by, Jack. Aloha oe. Chun Ah Chun. The
sheriff of Kona. On the Makaloa Mat. The bones of Kahekili. When Alice told her soul. Shin bones. The water
baby. The tears of Ah Kim. The Kanaka surf. Other
writings: A royal sport: Surfing at Waikiki. From "My
Hawaiian aloha."

215. *Jack London's Stories of the North* selected by Betty M.
Owen; introduction by Charles Rathbone, New York, Scholastic Book Services, 1966, viii, 248pp. Contents: A
word to the reader. The white man's way. The story of

Keesh. The sundog trail. Nam-Bok, the unveracious. To build a fire. The unexpected. The wife of a king. The son of the wolf. Love of life.

* * *

The following collections are undated. The Little blue books were published in the 1920's, while the other items probably appeared early in the 1950's.

216.   *Four short stories* edited by Dr. Walter Fischer, Paderborn, Verlag Ferdinand Schöningh, [n.d.] 80pp. (Best.-Nr. EL 110). Contents: Some remarks about the author and his works. An odyssey of the north. A piece of steak. The heathen. The pearls of Parlay. Annotations.

217.   *Selected tales,* Bielefeld, Berlin, Hannover, Velhagen & Klasing, [n.d.] 75pp. (Englische und amerikanische Lesebogen 28; berechtigte Ausgabe). [The textbook material contains a brief biography of London, and English-German glossary and linguistic notes.] Contents: White and yellow. Charley's coup. A relic of the Pliocene. The faith of men.

218.   *Stories of adventure,* Girard, Kansas, Haldeman-Julius Publications, [n.d.] 64pp. (Little blue book no. 1168). Contents: A Goboto night. Dutch courage. To repel boarders. An adventure in the Upper Sea. Bald-face.

219.   *Stories of ships and the sea,* Girard, Kansas, Haldeman-Julius Co., 64pp. (Little blue book no. 1169). Contents: Chris Farrington: able seaman. Typhoon off the coast of Japan. The lost poacher. The banks of the Sacramento. In Yeddo Bay.

220.   *Tales of the far north,* Girard, Kansas, Haldeman-Julius Co., [n.d.] 63pp. Contents: The men of forty-mile. The wisdom of the trail. In a far country. (Little blue book no. 288).

221.   *Tales of the white silence,* Girard, Kansas, Haldeman-Julius Co., [n.d] 64pp. Contents: To the man on trail. The white silence. The priestly prerogative. (Little blue book no. 1024).

FOREIGN LANGUAGE COLLECTIONS AND ANTHOLOGIES

ADYGHE
222. *Izbrannye rasskazy*, tr.: Iu. Namitokova, Maĭkop, Adygnatzizdat, 1939, 130pp. [Title given in Russian.]

ALBANIAN
223. *Balua*, tr.: Gjergj Zheji, Tirana, NSHF, 1956, 31pp.

AZERBAIDJANI
224. *Iakh! Iakh! Iakh!* Rasskazy, Baku, Azerneshp, 1927, 115pp.
225. *Rasskazy*, tr.: M. Rzakulizade, Baku, Detiunizdat, 1957, 114pp. [Both titles given in Russian.]

BASHKIR
226. *Rasskazy*, tr.: from the Russian, Ufa, Bashknigosizdat, 1955, 175pp. [Title in Russian.]

BULGARIAN
227. Between 1934 and 1938 several Bulgarian publishers, all in Sofia, published Jack London's *Suchineniia*.
   1. Sin na sluntzeto, tr.: G. Dinolov, Br. Miladinovi, 1934, 182pp. *(A son of the sun)*.
   2. Dushcheria na snegovete, D. Podvurzachov, Napred, 1934, 264pp. *(A daughter of the snows)*.
   3. Puteshestvie na oslepitelniĭ, tr.: G. Mikhailov, B. A. Kozhukharov, 1934, 176pp. Contents: Puteshestvie na "Oslepitelnii" *(The cruise of the Dazzler)*. Bogut na negovite pradedi. Tova, koeto ne se zabravia nikoga. Silnoto sredstvo. Chovekut s Belega. Semper idem.
   4.-5. Buntut b Ilsen'or, tr.: Dimitur Simidov and Liuben Velchev, Br. Miladinovi, 1934, 326pp. *(Mutiny of the Elsinore)*. [Vol. 4 contains 164pp.; vol. 5, pp.165-326 in addition to being the conclusion to the translation of the Mutiny of the Elsinore contains Malkata feia, Rodenata v moschchta and Kosternurkite na Tesman.]
   6. Pokvarena zhena, tr.: G. Mikhaĭlov, Gladston, 1934, 179pp. Contents: Pokvarena zhena. Prezpenieto na zhenata. Bushcheriata na Aurora. Sivachka. Sresha v khizhata. Liubovta na zhenata. Na kraia na dugata. Tam, deto putischata se razdeliat. Strakhlivetzut Negor. Liubov kum zhivota.
   7. Dzheri ostrovitianinut, tr.: D. Podvurzachov, Stranitza va vsichki, 1935, 102pp. *(Jerry of the islands)*.

8. *Beliiat zub,* tr.: G. Mikhailov, Stranitza za vsichki, 1935, 231pp.; 1938, 226pp. *(White Fang).*
9. *Martin Eden,* tr.: Pacho Stoianov, B. A. Kozhukharov, 1935-1936, 412pp.
10.-11. *Lunnata dolina,* tr.: Orlin Vasilve, Br. Miladinovi, 1936, 252pp., 204pp.
12. *Divoto zove,* tr.: D. Danov, Br. Miladinovi, 1936, 82pp. *(The call of the wild).*
13. *Prikliucheniiata na dzhoanna,* D. Podvurzachev, Radikal, 1937, 212pp. *(Adventure).*
14. *Za clato y Aliaska,* Al. Paskalev, [1937?] 271pp. *(Smoke Bellew).*
15. *Malkata stopanka na Golemiia dom,* tr.: Orlin Vasilev, 1937, 301pp. *(The little lady of the big house).*
16. *Morski vulk,* tr.: G. Zhechev, Radikal, 1937, 288pp. *(Sea wolf).*
17. *Skitnik mezhdu zvezdite,* tr.: D. Podvurzachov, Radikal, 1937, 279pp. *(The star rover).*
18. *Romanut na tri surtza,* tr.: D. Podvurzachov, Knizhna tzentrala, 1937, 307pp. *(Hearts of three).*
19. *Pomore sus "Chark",* tr.: K. Ia. Buzharova; introduction by Svetoslav Kamburov-Furen, Radikal, 1937, 162pp. *(Cruise of the Snark).*
20. *Gonitba na pirati,* tr.: G. Zhechev, Radikal, 1937, 94pp. *(Tales of the fish patrol).* Contents: Belite i Zhultite. Kralat na gurtzite. Gonitba na pirati na stridi. Obsadata na "Lankashirska kralitza". Khitrata izmislitza na Charli. Dimitri Kontos. Zhultata kurna.
21. *Siiaina zora,* tr.: Iordan Machkarov, Iv. G. Ignatov, 1938, 260pp. *(Burning daylight).*
22. *Khorota na bezdnata,* tr.: Liudmil Stoianov, Georgi D. Iurukov, 1937, 176pp. *(The people of the abyss).*
23. *Zheliaznata peta,* tr.: G. Karaslavov, Knizhna tzentrala, 1937, 206pp. *(The iron heel).*
24. *Sport.* 1. Purvobiten zviar. 2. Igrata. 3. Posledna borba, tr.: Todor Genov and Orlin Vasilev, Radikal, 1937, 136pp. *(The abysmal brute. The game. The red one).*
25. *Do Adama. Alenata Chuma,* tr.: Todor Genov, Radikal, 1937, 160pp. *(Before Adam).*
26. *Tzar Alkokhol,* tr.: D. Podvurzachov, Radikal, 1937, 189pp. *(John Barleycorn).*
27. *Kogato svetut beshe mlad. Razkazi,* tr.: Orlin Vasilev, Radikal, 1938, 146pp. Contents: Kogato svetut beshe mlad. Zlato, mnogo zlato. "Ia-a! Ia-a!" Zhenata na kralia. Parche meso. Ia-cho. Obichaiat na beliia chovek. Zhitelite na forta

Mail. Begletzut Dzhoni.
28. *Izpoved. Razkazi*, tr.: Orlin Vasilev, G. Milkhailov
and others, Knizhna tzentrala, 1938, 154pp. Contents: Kak lugakh edna zhena. "Muftadzhii" i
"koftadzhii". Zhelezoputni zaitzi. "Bikove".
Putnik. Muzhka viarnost. Bolestta na bezmulvniia
vozhd. Zakonut na zhivota. "Petnoto". Zlatnata
zora. Bialata tishina.
29. *Bludniiat bashcha*. Razkazi, tr.: S. Andreev, L.
Stoianov and others, Knizhna tzentrala, 1938,
204pp. Contents: Bludniiat bashcha. Nam-Bok
luzhliviia. Predanie za Kisha. Velikiiat vupros.
Sgovorut na startzite. Magesnichestvo. Sinut na
vulka. Severano Odiseia. Kish, sinut na Kisha.
Kraia na prilaz kata. Otmushchenieto na Porportuk.

228. *Razkazi*, tr.: Bl. Arabov, Plovdiv, Otetz Paisiĭ, 1917,
48pp. (Nova khudozh. bibl., nos. 18-19). Contents: Nos
za kralia. Silno sredstvo. Semper idem. Iz raskazite
na edin ukrotitel na leopardi.
229. *Zhelezoputni zaĭtzi*, Sofia, Gutenberg, 1917, 32pp. (Bibl.
Zabavno chetivo). Contents: Zhelezoputni zaĭtzi. Da
ubiesh chovek! Dvoĭstvena lichnost.
230. *Na sever. Razkazi*, tr.: Liudmil Stoianov, Sofia, Al.
Paskalev, 1919, 131pp. (Vsemirna bibl., nos. 237-244).
Contents: Velikiiat vupros. Prikazka za gordiia Agei.
Kurvavo otmuschchenie. Na Sever. Predanie za Kisha.
Putiat na luzhlivite sluntza.
231. *Iazichnika. Pazkaz iz shivota na moriatzite*, tr.: by
Krum Cholakov from the Russian, Sofia, Khemus, 1922,
31pp. (Iliustrovano Malka biblioteka za uchenitzite ot
progimmaziite, no. 79) [One of the South Sea tales.]
232. *Sivoto vulche. Razkaz*, tr.: S. Andreev, Sofia, Khemus,
1924, 16pp. (Malka bibl., no. 98); reprinted in 1927,
16pp. (V tzarstvoto na zhivotnite i rasteniiata, no. 26).
233. *Prikliucheniia. Zlato, Mnogo zlato i drugu razkazi*, tr.:
S. M. A., Sofia, St. Atanasov, 1929, 114pp. (Bibl. za
samoobrazovanie, 14:6). Contents: Zlato, mnogo zlato.
Kurvavo otmushchenie. Druzhte zapadna posoka. Na sever.
Suiuz na startzite. A-cho. Obitchaiat na beliia chovek.
Borba za shivot. Drugar.
234. *Kraiat na prikazkata*, Sofia, Nova literatura, 1931, 47pp.
(Bibl. Dzhek London, 1:3). Contents: Kraiat na prikazkata. Semper idem.
235. *Liubovta na zhenata*. Razkazi, tr.: G'oncho Belev, Sofia,
Azubka, 1931, 56pp. (Evtina bibl. za zheni, no. 4).
Contents: Liubovta na zhenata. Sinut na vulka. Muzhka
viarnost. Bialata tishina.

236. *Neochakvanoto,* Sofia, Nova literatura, 1931, 60pp. Bibl. Dzhek London, 1:6-7). Contents: Neochakvanoto and Murgaviiat vulk.
237. *Posledna borba,* Sofia, Angel Georgiev, 1931, 32pp. (Bibl. Dzhek London, 1:5).
238. *Strakhlivetzut,* Sofia, Angel Georgiev, 1931, 44pp. (Bibl. Dzhek London, 1:8).
239. *Khavaiski surtza,* tr.: Dim Stoevski, Sofia, A. Paskalev, 1932, 62pp. (Vsemirna bibl., no. 799). Contents: Khavaĭski surtza. Zlatniiat dol. Posleslovie.
240. *Putiat na luzhlivite sluntza. Razkasi,* tr.: Iv. Georgiev, Sofia, Nova literatura, 1932, 183pp.
241. *V zlatna Kalifomiia. Razkazi za iunoshi,* tr.: Racho Stoniov, Sofia, Khemus, 1932, 64pp. Contents: Bregovete na Sakramento. Kris Farington, moriak purvoklasen. Brezoglava. Sever i iug (Kafiaviiat vulk). Taĭnata na malkiia Kish.
242. *Velikoto chudo,* tr.: Simeon Andreev, Sofia, Al. Packlev, 1932, 82pp. (Vsemirna bibl., no. 797.) Contents: Velikoto chudo. Ezichnik. Na predela.
243. *Malkata feia,* tr.: Liuben Velchev, Sofia, Br. Miladinovi, 1933, 64pp. (Bibl. Moderna domakinia). Contents: Malkata feia. Rodenata noshchno vreme. Kostenurkite na Tesman.
244. *Zhenata na kralia,* tr.: M. Nenova, Sofia, Iv. Koiumdzhiev, 1933, 47pp. Contents: Zhenata na kralia. Rodena v noshta. Kogato svetut beshe mlad.
245. *Chudoto na zhanata,* tr.: L. Stoianov, Sofia, Iv. Koiumdzhiev, 1934, 44pp. (Bibl. Domakinia i maĭka, no. 8) [Selection from *Smoke Bellew*].
246. *Zakonut na veliiachovek. Razkazi,* tr.: Angel Georgiev, Sofia, Akademiia, 1934, 55pp. (Evtina bibl.). Contents: Zakonut na beliia chovek. Interesen otkuslek. Legendata za Kish. Kuli.
247. *Igra,* tr.: I. Kalchev, Sofia, Nov zhivot, 1935, 80pp. (Bibl. Chetivo za vsichki, no. 17). Contents: Igra. Krilatiiat shantazh. Predanie za Kisha.
248. *Zlatnoto ezero. Povest.* Ch. 1-2, Sofia, Bibl. Domakinia i maĭka, 1934, 96pp. (Bibl. Domakinia i maika, no. 7).
249. *Kafiaviiat vulk,* tr.: G'oncho Belev, Sofĭa, D. Madzharov, 1935, 80pp. (Bibl. Zlatni stranitzi). Contents: Kafiaviiat vulk. Dzhoni. Ukrotiteliat na leopardi. Liubovta na zhenata.
250. *Prisutstvie na dukha i Kish zhestokiiat,* Sofia, Doverie, 1935, 16pp.
251. *Taĭnstvenata torba ili Podvigug na Churchil,* Sofia, Doverie, 1935, 16pp. (Bibl. Vesela druzhina, no. 45).
252. *Khubavitzata Li-Van,* tr.: Liuben Velchev, Sofia, D. Madzharov, 1936, 74pp. Contents: Khubavitzata Li-Van.

Sinut na Vulka. Muzhka viarnost. Zhivotut na poeta.
253. *Liubovta kum zhivota,* tr.: Ivan Georgiev, Sofia, D.
Rusinov, 1937, 64pp. Contents: Liubovta kum zhivota
(Love of life). Severna Odiseia (An odyssey of the north).
254. *Putiat na ledenite slunzta,* Razkazi, tr.: Pelin Velkov,
Sofia, Betegraf, 1938, 77pp. (Bibl. Izbrani stranitzi
iz sevetovnata literatura). Contents: Putiat na ledenite
sluntza. Sianka i bliasuk. Zlatnata klisura.
255. *Tol stachkuva,* Sofia, Liuben Velchev, 1945, 32pp.
(Zlatni romani, no. 4) [Selection from *When God laughs*].
256. *Pobediteliat na ringa,* tr.: Leonid Paspaleev, Sofia,
Chitkoop, 1946, 29pp.
257. *Liubovta kum zhivota,* tr.: Liuben Velechev, Sofia, Nar.
mladezh, 1949, 80pp. Contents: Istoriiata na Kish (The
story of Keesh). Liubov kum zhivota (The love of life).
Tol stachkuva.
258. *Razkazi,* tr.: Liudmil Stoianov, Sofia, Nar. mladezh,
1957, 68pp. Contents: Zhazhda za zhivot. Begletz. Mauki.
259. *Zhazhda za shivot,* tr. from the English and Russian,
Sofia, Durzh. voen. izd., 1958, 236pp. Contents:
Zhazhda za zhivot. Muzhestvoto na zhenata. Pod palubniia
brizent. Kulau Prokazheniia (Koolau, the leper).
Kuschata na Mapui (The house of Mapuhi). Kus meso.
Meksikanetzut (The Mexican).
260. *Čakalov Belijat zăb - Željeznata-peta,* tr.: G. Asen and
G. Christoforov, Sofia, Nar. Kultura, 1961, 497pp.
[Translation of *White Fang* and *Iron Heel*.]

261. *Izbrani Provizvedenija,* Sofia, Nar. kultura, vols. 1-3,
1961; vols. 4-6, 1962; vols. 7-10, 1963.
    1. *Beliiat zub,* tr.: Asen G. Kristoforov and *Zheliaz-
       nata peta* tr.: G. Chakalov, 497pp. [Translation
       of *White fang* and *The iron heel*. Pp.5-39 are a
       biographical sketch of London.]
    2. *Martin Idun,* tr.: Rico Stojanov, 391pp.
    3. *Morski vulk,* tr.: Mikala Milev and *Divoto zove,*
       tr.: Sider Florin, 394pp. *(The sea wolf. The
       call of the wild).*
    4. *Siiaina zora,* tr.: Cvetan Stojanov and *Maĭkel,* tr.:
       Cvetan Stojanov, 578pp. *(Burning daylight.
       Michael, brother of Jerry).*
    5. *Lunnata dolina,* tr.: Irina Kalojanova-Vasilieva,
       495pp. *(The valley of the moon).*
    6. *Malkata stopanka na goljamata kăšta,* tr.: Neli
       Dospevska and *Părvobitnija zvjar,* tr.: Dimităr
       Lambrinov, 374pp. *(The little lady of the big
       house. The abysmal brute).*
    7. *Beliu Pushilkata,* tr.: Sider Florin and *Hora ot*

Bezdnata, tr.: Todor Vulchev, 468pp. (*Smoke Bellew. The people of the abyss*).

8. *Surtzata na trimata*, tr.: Sider Florin and *Igrata*, tr.: Irina Kaloianova Vasilieva, 375pp. (*Hearts of three. The game*).

9. *Razkazi*, 375pp. Contents: Bialoto mulchanie (The white silence). Sinut na vulka (The son of the wolf). Muzhete ot Chetirideseta milia (The men of forty mile). V dalechna strana (In a far country). Za zdraveto na putnika (For the health of the traveller [?]). Pravoto na sveshtenika (The priestly prerogative). Mudrostta na par-tinanta (The wisdom of the picture [?]). Zhena na kral (Wife of a king). Severna odiseia (Odyssey of the north). All translated by Sider Florin. Choveka s belega (The man with a gash). Dushteria na severnoto sianie (Daughter of the snows). Zakonut na zhivota (The law of life). Da nakladesh ogun (To build a fire). Ham-Bok luzhetzut (Nam-Bok the liar). Istoriata na Dzhiis Uk (The story of Jees Uk). Suiuzut na Startzite (The league of old men). Predanieto za Kish (The story of Keesh). All translated by Boris Damianov. Zhazhda za zhivot, tr.: Sider Florin (Love of life). Zlatniat prolom (Flush of gold). Kafiaviat vulk (Brown wolf). Beliazania (The marked [?]). Doverie (Trust). Otstupnika (The apostate). Kogato bog se smee (When God laughs). All translated by Boris Damianov. Samiuel (Samuel). Moriakut selianin (The sea farmer). Both translated by Todor Vulchev.

10. *Razkazi*, 432pp. Contents: "Aloha oe", tr.: Todor Vulchev. Kushtata na Mapui (The house of Mapuhi). Kulau Prokazhaniat (Koolau, the leper). Kus meso (Just meat). All translated by Sider Florin. Strashnite Solomonovi ostrovi (The terrible Sol-omons). Hramut na chestoliubieto (The house of pride). Ua! Ua! Ua! (Yah! Yah! Yah!). Kitoviat zub (The whale's tooth). All translated by Todor Vulchev. Mauki. Ezichnikut (The heathen). Semeto na Mak Koi (The seed of McCoy). Skitnikut i feiata (The hobo and the fairy). Biserite na Parle (The pearls of Parlay). All translated by Todor Vulchev. Perata na sluntzeto (The feathers of the son), tr.: Boris Damianov. Meksikanetzut (The Mexican). tr.: Sider Florin. Pogoskata na Makaloa (The Makaloa mat). I sutvori gi Bog (When God created them). Shinago (The chinago).

Na iug ot proreza (South of the slot). All translated by Todor Vulchev.

11. *Statii* (Articles). Contents: Revoliutziata (Revolution) tr.: Todor Vulchev. Kak stanah sotzia-
list (How I became a socialist). Kakov oznachava
na mane zhivotut (What life means to me). Both
translated by Boris Damianov. Toma Gordeev
(Tom Gordeff). Dzhunglata (The jungle [review]).
Both translated by Todor Vulchev. Suschineniata
nz Dzhek London v Bulgaria (Jack London's works
in Bulgaria) by Sider Florin. Azbuchen ukazatel
na Izbrani Proizvedenia v 10 toma [Alphabetical
order of selected works in ten volumes].

CHINESE

262. *Chieh K'o Lun Tun Tuan P'ien Hsiao Shuo hsüan Chi*, tr.:
Hsu T'ien-hung, Shanghai, Hsin Wen i ch'u pan she, 1957,
183pp. [Selected short stories.] Contents: Ch iang che
ti li liang (Strength of the strong). Pei Chi Chüan
Nei ti Chiu Niang (A hyperborean brew). Mao P'u Hsi ti
Fang Tzu (The house of Mapuhi). Tan Po ssu Chih Meng
(The dream of Debs). Pien Chieh che (The apostate).
I K'uai P'ai Ku (A piece of steak). Sha Jen (To kill a
man). Shih Chieh Kung ti (The enemy of all the world).
I ch' ien Ta (One thousand dozen). I Ko Chen Ch'i ti
Tuan P'ien (A curious fragment).

CROATIAN

263. *Demoni s Fuatina*, tr.: Vlatko Sarić, Zagreb, Prosvjeta,
1952, 348pp. Contents: Demoni s Fautina (The devils of
Fautino). Samo meso (Just meat). Bolna točka Alojzija-
Pankburna (The Proud Goat of Aloysius Pankburn).
Neizbježivi bijelac (The inevitable white man). Meksi-
kanac (The Mexican). Mapuhijeva kuča (The house of
Mapuhi). Šaljivci s Novog Gibbona (The jokers of New
Gibbon). Ljubav prema životu (Love of life). Mc Coyer
potomak (The seed of McCoy). Chinago. Otpadnik (The
apostate). Yah! Yah! Yah! Mauki. Istinita pripovijest
(Francis Spaight).

264. *Smeđi vuk i druge pripovijesti*, tr.: Otijija Šnajder-
Ruszkowsky, Zagreb, Matica hrvatska, 1961, 201pp.

265. *Veeren van de zon*, Utrecht, A. W. Bruna & Zoon's Uitg.
Mij., 1919, [?]pp. (Bruna's reisbibliotheek) [perhaps
a translation of The sun-dog trail].

266. *In tweestrijd*, tr.: W. J. A. Roldanus, Jr., Utrecht,
A. W. Bruna & Zoon's Uitg. Mij., 1921, [?]pp. (Bruna's
bibliotheek) [perhaps a translation of Brown wolf].

DANISH

267. *Jack Londons Bedste historier,* tr.: Mogens Knudsen,
[Copenhagen] Carit Andersens Forlag, [n.d.] 319pp.
Contents: Kærlighed til livet. Marcus O'Briens fors-
vinden. Et møde. Diable - en hund. Livets lov. Rejsen
under bisolene. Om at tænde bal. Syd for Revnen.
Meksikaneren. Kunsten at hænge pa. To tusind vagabonder.
Semper Idem. Mapuhis hus. Under dækkets solsejl. Mauki.
Farvel Jack. Farmer til søs.

DUTCH

268. *Chechaquo onder de goudzoekers,* no translator given,
Amsterdam, L. J. Veen's Uitgeversmaatschappij N. V.,
[n.d.] 185pp. Contents: De smaak van het vlees (The
taste of the meat). Het vlees (The meat). De dolle
jacht naar Vrouwenkreek (The stampede to Squaw Creek).
Shorty droomt (Shorty dreams). De man op de andere
oever (The man on the other bank). De wedren om
Nummer Eén (The race for number three). [This is a
translation of the first six chapters of *Smoke Bellew*.]

ESTONIAN

269. *Maailma veerel. (Hukatuse ootel.),* Tallinn, "Uhiselu",
1917, 24pp. (Reprinted from *Tallinna Teataja*) (On the
verge of the world. Waiting the wreck).

270. *Kahe näoga mees,* Tartu, "Odamees", 1923, 21pp.
("Odamehe" rahvaraamat, no. 8) (The double-faced man).

271. *Aljaska tütar,* Tallinn, 1925, 283pp. (The daughter of
the snows).

272. *Elu seadus,* tr.: A. Känd, Tartu, "Loodus", 1928, 62pp.
("Looduse" universaal-biblioteek, no. 39). Contents:
Elu seadus (The law of life). Nam-Bok valelik (Nam-Bok,
the liar). Üksildase pealiku haigus (The sickness of
Lone Chief).

273. *Lôunamere jutud,* tr.: A. Känd, Tartu, "Loodus", 1928,
61pp. ("Looduse" universaal-biblioteek, no. 43). Contents: Mapuhi maja (The house of Mapuhi). Mauki (Mauki).

274. *Poksija Tom King,* tr.: L. Luiga, Tartu, "Loodus", 1929,
63pp. ("Looduse" universaal-biblioteek, no. 87). Contents: Poksija Tom King (A piece of steak). Taanduja
(The apostate). Semper Idem.

275. *Fuatino kuradid.* Seiklusi Lôunamerelt, tr.: V. Pedajas,
Tallinn, "Elu", 1930, 102pp. ("Elu" lugemisvara, no.
41). Contents: Päikese poeg (A son of the sun). Aloysius Pankburni vôidetud uhkus (The proud goat of Aloysius Pankburn). Fuatino kuradid (The devils of Fuatino).
Uus-Gibboni maljahambad (The jokers of New Gibbon).

276. *Valge vaikus,* tr.: A. Känd, Tartu, "Loodus", 1930, 63pp.

("Looduse" universaal-biblioteek, no. 110). Contents: Valge vaikus (The white silence). Hingerkarjase (The priestly prerogative). Ühe kuninga naine (The wife of a king).
277. *Elu seadus*, tr.: A. Känd, Tartu-Tallinn, "Loodus", 1939, 336pp. (Kirjasôna suurmeistrid, no. 8). Contents: Elu seadus (The law of life). Nam-Bok valelik (Nam-Bok, the liar). Üksildase pealiku haigus (The sickness of Lone Chief). Mapuhi maja (The house of Mapuhi). Mauki (Mauki). McCoy (The seed of McCoy). Yah! Yah! Yah! Hundipoeg (The son of the wolf). Kaugel maal (In a far away country). Mehed Forty Mile'st (Men of forty mile). Valge vaikus (The white silence). Hingekarjase prerogatiiv (The prerogative of the priest). Kuninga naine (The wife of a king). Pôhjala Odysseia (The odyssey of the north). Poksija Tom King (A piece of steak). Taanduja (The apostate).
278. *Armastus elu vastu*, tr.: L. Anvelt and A. Hint, Tallinn, Eesti Riiklik Kirjastus, 1950, 201pp. Contents: Armastus elu vastu (Love of life). Lugu Kiišist (The story of Keesh). Naiste visadus (Grit of women). Teadmamees (The master of mystery). Hiinlane (The Chinago). Mapuhi maja (The house of Mapuhi. Usutaganeja (The apostate). Mehhiklane (The Mexican).
279. *McCoy. Yah! Yah! Yah!* tr.: A. Känd, Tartu, "Loodus", [n.d.] 64pp. ("Looduse" universaal-biblioteek no. 98). Contents: The seed of McCoy. Yah! Yah! Yah!
280. "Hukatuse ootel," Tallinna Teataja, Dec. 7-9, 1916 (Waiting the wreck).
281. "Hirmus Savoyard," tr.: J. W. Lebedev,. *Vaba Maa kirjandus ja teadus*, no. 50:389-393 (1921) (The terrible Savoyard).
282. "Piletita soitjad," *Päeveleht*, Dec. 29-31, 1925 (The hoboes). [Probably a selection from *The road*.]
283. "Hundiveri," *Romaan*, no. 9:265-270; no. 10:297-303 (1926) (Wolves).
284. "Tulised süed," *Päevaleht*, July 23-27, 1927 (Coals of fire).
285. "Tööotsija," *Esmaspäev*, Oct. 7, 1929 (The unemployed).
286. "Kuldvirveng," *Nool*, July 26, 1930 (The golden gleam).
287. "Kadunud isa," *Kodu*, no. 6:183-186, no. 7:218-221 (1931)(The lost father).
288. "Snooky," *Romaan*, no. 11:338-340 (1931)
289. "Üldstreik San-Franciscos," *Nool*, Jan. 3, 1931 (Strike in San Francisco).
290. "Rusikame ed." *Postimees*, Jan. 4-16, 1937 (The boxers). [Probably either *The game* or *The abysmal brute*.]

FINNISH

291. *Hänen isäinsä Jumala ynnä muita kertomuksia*, tr.:
T. Tainio, Tampere, Matti Vuolukka, 1914, 102pp.
[4 stories].

292. *Yllätys ynnä muita kertomuksia Alaskasta*, tr.: Vilho
Oksanen, Helsinki, 1917, 96pp. [4 stories].

293. *Kultamaan seikkailijoita*, Helsinki, Otava, 1921, 184pp.
[8 stories].

294. *Marcus O'Brienin kohtalo*, tr.: Alpo Kupiainen, Helsinki,
Kustannusliike Minerva, 1922, 110pp. [4 stories].

295. *Yön lapsi*, tr.: Aito Kare, Helsinki, Kustannusliike
Minerva, 1924, 155pp. [10 stories].

296. *Ikuinen salaisuus*, Helsinki, Otava, 1924, 184pp.
[8 stories].

297. *Meidän Herramme pettäjä*, tr.: Tauno Kopra, Helsinki,
Kustannusoy 1924, 120pp. [4 stories].

298. *Pohjolan harharetkeläisiä*, tr.: Tauno Kopra, Helsinki,
Kustannusoy, 1924, 152pp. [2 stories].

299. *Väkevän voima...*, tr.: Yrjö Talma, Helsinki, Kustannusoy,
1924, 156pp. (5 stories, adapted].

300. *Vallankumouksellinen*, tr.: Aito Kare, Helsinki, Kustannusliike Minerva, 1924, 178pp. [8 stories].

301. *Vastustamaton valkoinen mies*, tr.: Tauno Kopra, Helsinki,
Kustannusoy, 1924, 135pp. [6 stories].

302. *Erään kultalöydön salaisuus*, tr.: Toivo Nelimies,
Helsinki, Kustannusoy, 1925, 142pp. [6 stories].

303. *Kultamaan rakkautta: kertomuksia Klondykesta*, Helsinki,
Otava, 1925, 182pp. [6 stories].

304. *Kultarotko*, tr.: A. Lehto, Helsinki, Kustannusliike
Minerva, 1925, 134pp. [6 stories].

305. *Naisen ylpeys*, Helsinki, Kustannusliike Minerva, 1925,
210pp.; Porvoo, Werner Söderstrom, 1936, 210pp.
[9 stories].

306. *Suuri arvoitus*, tr.: A. I. Relander, Helsinki, Kust.
Suomi, 1927, 113pp. [4 stories].

FRENCH

307. *En pays lontain*, tr.: Louis Postif, Paris, Crès, 1926,
259pp. Paris, Hachette, c1930, 185pp. (Bibliothèque
verte); Paris, Hachette, 1931, 256pp. Contents of the
c1930 ed.: En pays lontain (In a far country). Yan,
l'irréductible (Jan, the unrepentant). Quand un homme
se souvient (Which make men remember). Où bifurque la
piste (Where the trail ends). Siwash (Siwash). Une
fille de l'aurore (A daughter of the Aurora). À l'homme
sur la piste (To the man on trail). L'abnégation des
femmes (The scorn of women).

308. *Civilisations*, tr.: Suzanne Engelson, Geneva, Connaître,

[1950] 239pp. Contents: Avant-propos. Le renégat (The apostate). À l'homme sur la piste (To the man on trail). La loi de la piste (The wisdom of the trail). L'histoire de Keesh (The story of Keesh). La loi de la vie (The law of life). L'histoire de Jees Uck (The story of Jees Uck). L'amour de la vie (The love of life.) Une tranche de bifteck (A piece of steak). Le chinago (The chinago). Ce que la vie signifie pour moi (What life means to me).

309.   *La femme d'un roi;* illustrations de Cattaneo, Paris, O. D. E. J., 1960, 187pp. (Junior de poche). Contents: Madeline: la femme d'un roi (The wife of a king). Où bifurque la piste (Where the trail forks). Yan l'impénitent (Jan, the unrepentant). Siwash (Siwash). Quand un homme se souvient (Which makes men remember). La dévouement de Passuk (Grit of women). A l'homme sur la piste (To the man on the trail). Une fille de l'aurore (A daughter of the Aurora).

310.   *Oeuvres* de Jack London, Paris, Gallimard/Hachette.
      I. *Histoires des bêtes.* 1965, 566pp. Contents: *Croc blanc (White fang)* tr.: Paul Gruyer and Louis Postif. *L'appel de la forêt (The call of the wild)* tr.: Mme. de Galard. *Michaël, chien de cirque (Michael, brother of Jerry)* tr.: Paul Gruyer and Louis Postif. [This volume contains a preface by Jean Dutourd entitled "Du chien littérature" After *Michaël,* there is published "La vie et l'oeuvre de Jack London" by Armand Himy.]
      II. *Romans du grand nord.* 1965, xvi, 593pp. Contents: *Fille des neiges (A daughter of the snows).* Bellew-la-Fumée. Bellew et Le Courtaud (*Smoke Bellew).* [All translations by Louis Postif. The prefatory matter is by Jacques Perret.]
      III. *Romans autobiographiques,* tr.: Louis Postif, préface de Roger Grenier, Paris, Gallimard/Hachette, 1965, 693pp. *Martin Eden. Le cabaret de la dernièrechance (John Barleycorn).*

GEORGIAN
311.   *Rasskazy,* tr.: Mamulashvili, Tbilisi, Gosizdat Grunzinski, SSR, 1937, 67pp. [Title in Russian].
312.   *Konetz. Skazki. Rasskazy,* tr.: B. Nanitashvili, Tbilisi, 1957, 69pp. [Title in Russian].
313.   *Zolotoe uschel'e (Rasskazy),* Tbilisi, Detiunizdat, 1960, 260pp. [Title in Russian].

GERMAN

314. *Werke*, Berlin, Büchergilde Gutenberg, 1926-1932. Unless otherwise stated all the translations are the work of Erwin Magnus. The volumes in this series are unnumbered and are arranged below in alphabetical order.

Alaska Kid, 1931, 274pp. *(Smoke Bellew)*.

Abenteurer des Schienenstranges, 1927, 259pp. *(The road)*.

Die eiserne Ferse, 1927, [?]pp. *(The iron heel)*.

Die glücklichen Inseln, 1930, 272pp.

In den Wäldern des Nordens, 1927, 259pp. *(The children of the frost)*.

Die Insel Berande, 1926, 273pp. *(Adventure)*.

Jerry der Insulaner, 1927, 311pp. *(Jerry of the islands)*.

König Alkohol, 1927, 243pp. *(John Barleycorn)*.

Lockruf des Goldes, 1929, 308pp. *(Burning daylight)*.

Martin Eden, 1927, 2 vols., 269, 271pp.

Menschen der Tiefe, 1929, 275pp. *(People of the abyss)*.

Michael der Bruder Jerry, 1928, 286pp. *(Michael, brother of Jerry)*.

Mondgesicht, 1928, 256pp. *(Moon-face)*.

Das Mondtal, 1929, 2 vols., 300, 275pp. *(The valley of the moon)*.

Meuterei auf der Elsinore, 1932, 261pp. *(Mutiny of the Elsinore)*.

Nur Fleisch, 1929, 272pp.

Der Rote, 1928, 262pp.

Der Seewolf, 1927, 337pp. *(The seawolf)*.

Der Sohn des Wolfs, 1927, 276pp. *(The son of the wolf)*.

Ein Sohn der Sonne, 1927, 300pp. *(A son of the sun)*.

Siwash, 1929, 291pp. *(God of his fathers)*.

Südsee-Geschichten, 1927, 255pp. *(South Sea tales)*.

315. London, Jack. Ein Sohn des Volkes. 12 bändige Aus-wahlreihe hrsg. von Max Barthel, Berlin, Büchergilde Gutenberg, 1934. All translations by Erwin Magnus.

1. *An der weissen Grenze*, 257pp.

2. *Südseegeschichten*, 255pp. *(South Sea tales)*.

3. *Der Seewolf*, 337pp. *(The sea wolf)*.

4. *Lockruf des Goldes*, 307pp. *(Burning daylight)*.

5. *Abenteurer des Schienenstranges*, 259pp. *(The road)*.

6. *In den Wäldern des Nordens*, 258pp. *(The children of the frost)*.

7. *Tal des Mondes*.

8. *Ein Sohn der Sonne*, 300pp. *(A son of the sun)*.

9. *Jerry, der Insulaner*, 310pp. *(Jerry of the islands)*.

10. *Drei Sonnen am Himmel*, 253pp.

11. *Die Insel Berande,* 273pp. *(Adventure).*
12. *Meuterei auf der Elsinore,* 261pp. *(Mutiny of the
    Elsinore).*

316. *Gesammelte Werke,* Berlin, Universitas [1940]. All
     translations by Erwin Magnus.
     1. *Jerry von den Inseln,* 293pp. *(Jerry of the islands).*
     2. *Ein Sohn der Sonne,* 301pp. *(A son of the sun).*
     3. *Abenteurer des Schienenstranges,* 260pp. *(The road).*
     4. *Der Seewolf,* 335pp. *(The seawolf).*
     5. *Alaska-Kid,* 274pp. *(Smoke Bellew).*
     6. *Meuterei auf der Elsinore,* 266pp. *(Mutiny of the
        Elsinore).*
     7. *Lockruf des Goldes,* 306pp. *(Burning daylight).*
     8. *Der Ruhm des Kampfers,* 255pp.
     9. *Kid & Co.,* 255pp. *(Smoke Bellew).*
     10. *Südgeegeschichten,* 254pp. *(South Sea tales).*

317. Jack London | Taschenbuchausgabe, Berlin, Universitas,
     c1963, vols. 1-6; c1964, vols. 7-10; c1965, vols. 11-12.
     All volumes translated by Erwin Magnus.
     1. *Abenteurer des Schienenstranges (The road).* 153pp.
        Ein Behenntis (Confession). Blinde Passagiere
        (Holding her down). Zigeuner (Pictures).
        Geschnappt ("Pinched"). In gestreifter Tracht
        (The pen). Nächtliche Fahrten (Hoboes that pass
        in the night). Wie ich Landstreicher wurde
        (Road-kids and gay-cats). General Kellys Armee
        (Two thousand stiffs). Der Polizist (Bulls).
     2. *Jerry der Insulaner (Jerry of the islands).* 192pp.
     3. *Siwash.* 158pp. Die Heirat der Lit-Lit (The
        marriage of Lit-Lit). Negore, der Feigling
        (Negore, the vile). Die König und sein Schmane
        (A hyperborean brew). Die grosse Frage (The
        great interrogation). Siwash (Siwash). Am Ende
        des Regenbogens (At the rainbow's end). Krieg der
        Frauen (The scorn of women). Ein Tragödie aus
        dem wilden Westen (Finis). Die Liebe zum Leben
        (Love of life).
     4. *Die Herrin des Grossen Hauses (The little lady of
        the Big House).* 192pp.
     5. *Kid & Co. (Smoke Bellew).* 155pp.
     6. *Die Geschichte vom Leopardenmann.* 159pp. Die
        Geschichte vom Leopardenmann (The leopardman's
        story). Die Lieblinge des Midas (The minions
        of Midas). Der Schatten und das Funkeln (The
        shadow and the flash). Der Einbruch (To kill a
        man). Bastard (Bâtard). Der Feind der ganzen

Welt (The enemy of all the world). Der Chinago
(The Chinago). Südlich von Slot (South of the
slot). Der Rote (The red one).
7. *Der Seewolf (The sea wolf).* 221pp.
8. *Das Mondtal (The valley of the moon).* 222pp.
9. *Ein Sohn der Sonne (A son of the sun).* 156pp.
Ein Sohn der Sonne (A son of the sun). Aloysius
Pankburns wunder Punkt (The proud goat of
Aloysius Pankburn). Die Teufel von Fuatino
(The devils of Fuatino). Die Witzbolde von Neu-
Gibbon (The jokers of New Gibbon). Eine kleine
Abrechnung mit Swithin Hall (Little account
with Swithin Hall). Ein Abend in Goboto (A
Goboto night). Federn der Sonne (The feathers of
the sun). Parlays Perlen (The pearls of Parlay).
10. *König Alkohol (John Barleycorn).* 156pp.
11. *Südseegeschichten (South Sea tales),* 154pp.
12. *Alaska-Kid (Smoke Bellew),* 156pp.

318. *Feuer auf See. Geschichten aus d. Südsee und aus d.
Wäldern d. Nordens,* tr.: Erwin Magnus, Leipzig, Insel
[1927] 74pp. (Insel-Bücherei no. 297); Leipzig, Insel,
1947, 73pp. Contents: Feuer auf See (The seed of McCoy).
Der Bund der Alten (The league of the old men). Das
Gesetz des Lebens (The law of life).
319. *Der Herr des Geheimnisses. Nam-Bok, der Lügner. Zwei
Eskimo-erzählungen,* Berlin, Hillger [1929]; Berlin-
Grunewald, Deutsche Jugend-bücherei, 1953; both 32pp.
(Deutsche Jugendbücherei No. 341). Translation of
"Master of mystery" and "Nam-Bok, the liar."
320. *Nur Fleisch,* tr.: Erwin Magnus, Berlin-Schöneberg,
Oestergaard, 1929, 271pp.; Berlin, Universitas, 1929,
272pp.; Berlin, Dt. Buchgemeinde, 1934, 271pp. Con-
tents: Westwärts (Make westing). Der Abtrünige (The
apostate). Nur Fleisch (Just meat). Der Chinago (The
chinago). Südlich vom Slot (South of the slot). Das
Feuer im Schnee (To build a fire). Die "Francis
Spaight" (The "Francis Spaight"). Eine Nase für den
König (A nose for the king). Debs' Traum (The dream of
Debs). Ein Taifun vor der japanischen küste (Typhoon
off the coast of Japan).
321. *Zwischen Yukon und Mackenzie,* Reutingen, Enzzlin Laib-
lin, 1929; 2nd ed., Ebenda, 1943; both 31pp. (Both
Bunte Bücher, vol. 198).
322. *Die glücklichen Inseln,* tr.: Erwin Magnus, Berlin,
Universitas, 1930, 274pp.; Berlin, Universitas, 1948,
272pp.; Berlin, Universitas, 1954, 247pp. Contents:
Auf der Makaloa-matte (On the Makaloa mat). Die gebeine

Kahekilis (The bones of Kahekili). Koolau, der
Aussätzige (Koolau, the leper). Le wohl, Jack (Good-by,
Jack). Aloha oe (Aloha oe). Der Sheriff von Kona (The
Sheriff of Kona). Da Haus des Stolzes (The house of
pride). Die Tränen Ah Kima (The tears of Ah Kim).
Chun Ah Chun.

323. *Das Wort der Männer*, tr.: Erwin Magnus, Berlin, Univer-
sitas, 1932, 264pp. Contents: Das Wort der Männer
(The faith of men). Fleck (That spot). Goldschimmer
(Flush of gold). Das Witz Porportuks (The wit of Por-
portuk). Die Leibe zum Leben (The love of life). Eine
Tragödie aus dem wilden Westen (Finis). Das End vom
Lied (The end of the story).

324. *Zwischen Südsee und Eismeer*, tr.: Erwin Magnus, Leipzig,
Hesse & Becker, 1932, 285pp.

325. *Die alte Argonaute. Zwei exotische Erzahlungen*, Leipzig,
Insel [1933] 71pp.; (Insel-Bücherei No. 317); Leipzig,
Insel, 1949, 54pp.; Leipzig, Insel, 1954, 56pp. Contents: Die alte Argonaute (Like Argus of the ancient
times). Koolau, der Ausfätzige (Koolau, the leper).

326. *Drei Sonnen-am Himmel*, Berlin, tr.: Erwin Magnus,
Universitas, 1934, 253pp.; München, List, 1959, 132pp.
(List-Bücher 139). Contents of the 1959 ed.: Drei
Sonnen am Himmel (The sun-dog trail). Batard (Batard).
Das Unbegreifliche. Wo die Wege sich trennen (Where the
trail forks). Der Mann mit der Schmarre (The man with
the gash).

327. *Frauenmut und andere Erzählungen*, tr.: Willi Wenk,
Basel, Verein "Gute Schriften", 1935, 80pp. (Gute
Schriften Basel No. 187).

328. *Der Ruhm des Kampfers. Von Boxern, Stierkämpfern und
aufrechten Männern*, tr.: Erwin Magnus, Berlin, Univer-
sitas, 1936, 1947, c1963, 255pp.; Frankfurt am Main,
Büchergilde Gutenberg, 1954, 257pp.; Berlin, Univer-
sitas, 1954, 257pp.; Berlin, Tribüne, 1957, 290pp.;
Berlin, Universitas, [n.d.,] 258pp. Contents: Der Ruhm
des Kampfers (The abysmal brute). Die Jagd nach dem
Mammut (A relic of the Pliocene). Der Schrei des
Pferdes (The madness of John Harned). Der Mexikaner
Felipe Rivera (The Mexican). Der Mann ohne Gewissen
(Bunches of knuckles). Wer schlug zuerst? (The benefit
of the doubt).

329. *Aloysius Pankburns wunder Punkt und andere heitere
Erzählungen*, Zürich, Schweizer Bücherfreunde, 1939,
131pp.

330. *Nächtliche Fahrten. General Kellys Armee*, tr.: Erwin
Magnus, Stuttgart, Reclam, 1940, 63pp. (Reclams Universal-Bibliothek no. 7614). [Translation of Hoboes

that pass in the night and Two thousand stiffs.]

331. *Die Goldschlucht. Zwei exotische Erzählungen,* tr.: Erwin Magnus, Leipzig, Reclam, 1930, 73pp. (Reclams Universal-Bibliothek No. 7070); Stuttgart, Reclam, 1947, 71pp.; Leipzig, Reclam, 1948, 69pp.; Leipzig, Reclam, 1955, 1957, 1959, 1961, 70pp. Contents: Die Goldschlucht (All gold canyon). Auf der Makaloa-Matte (On the Makaloa mat). Nachwort.

332. *Unter dem Sonnenzelt,* tr.: Max Barthel, Berlin, Universitas, 1938, 234pp.

333. *Eine Tochter des Nordlichts,* tr.: Fritz Benke, Linz, Pittsburgh, Vienna, Ibis, 1947, 335pp.

334. *Südsee-Geschichten,* tr.: Eduard Thorsch, Zürich, Schweizer Druck-und Verlagshaus. 1947, 285pp. Contents: Das Haus Mapuhis (The house of Mapuhi). Das Walfisch-zahn (The whale tooth). Der Heide (The heathen). Mit Feuer an Bord. Die weissen Teufel. "Federn der Sonne" (Feathers of the sun). Die furchterregenden Salomonen (The terrible Solomons). "Pau". Joe Garland. Der Sheriff von Kona (The sheriff of Kona).

335. *Der Mexikaner Felipe Rivera. Der Schrei des Pferdes: zwei Erzählungen,* tr.: Erwin Magnus, Leipzig, Insel, 1951, 1960, 69pp. (Insel-Bücherei 163). Translation of The Mexican and The madness of John Harned.

336. *Die Liebe zum Leben. Drei Erzählungen,* Leipzig, Reclam, [1953] 1956, 1957, 1960, 1961, 82pp. (Reclams Universal-Bibliothek No. 7938).

337. *Zuviel Gold: Abenteuer in Alaska,* Munich, Opacher, [n.d.,] 247pp. (Kid Weltliteratur: eine Sammlung für die Jugend, vol. 30); Opacher, 1958, 247pp. Contents: Negore, der Feigling (Negore, the vile). Die Heirat der Lit-Lit (The marriage of Lit-Lit). Ligouns Tod (The death of Ligoun). Zuviel Gold (Too much gold). Die gros grosse Frage (The great interrogation). Jan, der Unverbesserliche (Jan, the unrepentant). Infernem Lande. Auf der Rast. Die Männer von Forty-Mile (The men of Forty Mile). Eine Tochter des Nordlichts (A daughter of the aurora).

338. *Geschichten aus Alaska,* no tr. given, Frankfort, Insel, 1957, 86pp. (Insel-Bücherei Nr. 645). Contents: Das weisse Schweigen (The white silence). Das Feuer im Schnee (To build a fire). Das End vom Lied (The end of the story). Frauenmut (Grit of women).

339. *Was sie nie vergessen,* tr.: Erwin Magnus, Frankfurt, Fischer, 1959, 1962, 173pp. (Fischer-Bücherei Nr. 291). Contents: Die Männer des Sonnenlandes (The sunlanders). Die Krankheit des Einsamen Hauptlings (The sickness of Lone Chief). Negore, der Feigling (Negore, the vile).

Quartier für einen Tag (A day's lodging). Was sie nie
vergessen (Which makes men remember). Das Frau-
enzimmer (The hussy). In der Brandung (The Kanaka surf).
Der Sheriff von Kona (The sheriff of Kona). Der Chinago
(The Chinago). Die "Francis Spaight" (The Francis
Spaight).

340. *In den Wäldern des Nordens: Goldrausch in Alaska*, tr.:
Erwin Magnus, Gütersloh, Signum Taschenbucher, [n.d.,]
188pp. (SM 57). Contents: Odyssee des Nordens (Odyssey
of the North). In den Wäldern des Nordens (In the
forests of the north). Das Gesetz des Lebens (Love of
life). Nam-Bok, der Lügner (Nam-Bock, the liar). Der
Herr des Geheimnisses (The master of mystery). Die
Männer des Sonnenlandes (The sunlanders). Li Wan, die
schöne (Li Wan, the fair). Der Bund der Alten (The
league of the old men). Wie vor alters zog die Argo
(Like Argus of the ancient times). Die Goldschlucht
(All gold canyon).

341. *Westwärts und andere Erzählungen* ...tr.: Erwin Magnus,
Vorwart von Herbert Eisenreich, Zürich, Diogenes, 1965,
492pp. Contents: Die Perle (The pearls of Parlay). Chun
Ah Chun. Koolau, der Aussätzige (Koolau, the leper).
Westwärts (Make westing). Der Mexikaner (The Mexican).
Wie vor alters zog die Argo... (Like Argus of the
ancient times). Das Gesetz des Lebens (The law of life).
Die Goldschlucht (All gold canyon). Das Feuer im Schnee
(To build a fire). Jan, der Unverbesserliche (Jan, the
unrepentant). Der Sohn des Wolfs (The son of the wolf).
Das weisse Schweigen (The white silence). Eine Tochter
des Nordlichts (A daughter of the aurora). Am Ende des
Regenbogens (At the end of the rainbow). Der Abtrünnige
(The apostate). Die Liebe zum Leben (The love of life).

HEBREW

342. *Darko shel haadan halavan*, tr.: Itshak Avnon, Tel-Aviv,
Amichai, [n.d.,] 196pp. Contents: Darko shel haadan
halavan (The road of the white man). Habilti tsafui
(Unexpected). Saavyhum (Brown wolf). Parashat Kish
(The story of Keesh). Derekh Hambshemesh Hamdumah (The
way of the sun shadows). Lehavyr madurah (To build a
fire). Oto katem (That spot).

343. *Ha-mered*, tr.: Dan Soen, Tel-Aviv, Karmi and Naor,
1953, 275pp.

344. *Ketavim*, tr.: A. Halevi, Tel-Aviv, Karmi and Naor, 1954,
287pp.

345. *Sipure harpatka'ot*, tr.: Y. Likhtenbom, Tel-Aviv,
Yavneh, 1956, 133pp. *(Adventure stories)*.Contents: Al
sipun ha-a'aniyah (Under the deck awnings). Zekhut

ha-adam ha-lavon (The wisdom of the trail). Netiv ha-
shemashot ha-mat'ot (The sun dog trail). Ha-Sakanah ha-
tshubad (The yellow peril). Melekh ha-yevanim. (The
king of the Greeks). Demetrios Kontos. Le-Haye ha'rose'a
(To the man on trail). Helkat ha-shlagim (The white
silence).

HUNGARIAN

346. *A hitehagyott*, tr.: Dezső Schöner, Budapest, Népszava,
1921, 40pp. (Világosság-könyvtár 235-236).
347. *A vadallat*, tr.: Viktor Körmendy, Budapest, Légrády,
16pp. (A Pesti Hirlap regenytara 10).
348. *Fehérek és szinesek*, Budapest, Légrády, 1924, 275pp.
349. *Kalandok világa*, tr.: Ákos Farkas, Budapest, Légrády,
1924, 1925, 170pp.
350. *A korhely és a tündér*, tr.: J. Jenő Tersánszky, Budapest, Athenaeum, 1927, 172pp. (Jack London Összes
munkái 11).
351. *A magas Pszakon*, tr.: Zoltán Bartos, Budapest, Nova,
1924, 143pp. (Jack London Válogatott művei. 1).
352. *A vén kalóz kincse*, tr.: Mária Ruzitska, Budapest, Légrády, 1924 [2 printings] 303pp. (Külföldi irók
regénytára. A sor. 6); 2nd ed., 1925.
353. *A mayák kincse*, tr.: J. Jenő Tersánszky, Budapest,
Athenaeum, 1930, 410pp. (Jack London Összes munkái 15).
354. *Találkozáz az alvilággal*, tr.: Anna Garras, Budapest,
Izikra, 1947, 62pp.
355. *A bajnok és a halál*, tr.: Zoltán Bartos, Budapest,
Hungaria, 1948, 61pp.
356. *Életre-halálra*, tr.: J. Jenő Tersánszky, Budapest,
Hungária, 1948, 62pp. (Forintos regények 72).
357. *Gyémántrablók*, tr.: J. Jenő Tersánszky, Budapest,
Hungária, 1948, 62pp.
358. *A titkok ura*, tr.: Ákos Farkas, Budapest, Hungária,
1948, 61pp. (Forintos regény 67).
359. *A vérszövetség*, tr.: Erhő Ahdai, Budapest, Hungária,
1948, 63pp. (Forintos regény 64).
360. *Elbeszélesek*, Budapest, Szépirod. Kiadó, 1951, 116pp.
(Szépirodalmi kishönyvtár 33-34).
361. *Az utolsó mérközés*, tr.: Ferenc Piroska, Bucarest,
Testnevelési es sportkiadó, 1954, 144pp.
362. *Válogatott elbeszélésk*, tr.: Zoltán Bartos, Győző
Határ, Imre Szász, J. Jenő Tersánszky, Miklos Vajda,
János Viktor, Bucharest, Állami Irodalmi és Miiveszeti
Kiadó, 1955, 2 vols.; also Budapest, Kiadó, 1955,
2 vols.
Includes translations of Férfibizalom (Faith of men).
Debs alma (Dream of Debs). A szökevény (The apostate).

Az állhatatos asszony (Grit of woman). Egy király felesége (Wife of a king). A feher csend (White silence). Tüzet rakni (To build a fire). A farkas fia (Son of the wolf). Eszaki Odiszea (Odyssey of the North). Méxikan (The Mexican). Az élet törvénye - Az élet szerelme (Love of life). Mapuhi háza (House of Mapuhi). A pogány (The heathen). A büszkeség háza (House of pride). Messze földön (In a far country). Vének szövetsege (League of the old men). Egy szelet sült (Piece of steak). Dzsisz Uk története (The story of Jees Uck). Az erösek ereje (The strength of the strong).

363. *A kalózhajó. A mexikói. A szökevény*, tr.: Zoltán Bartos, Miklos Vajda, J. Jenő Tersańszky, Budapest, Ifjusági Kiadó, 1956, 255pp. Contents: A kalózhajó (The cruise of the Dazzler). A mexikói (The Mexican). A szökevény (The apostate).

364. *Három Kisregény*, Budapest, Európa Könyvkiadó, 1963, 437pp. Contents: *A vadon szava* (The call of the wild) tr.: Réz Ádám; *A beszélő kutya* (Jerry of the islands) tr.: Szász Imre; *Országuton* (The road) tr.: Szász Imre; biographical sketch by Szász Imre on Jack London, pp. 433-437.

IAKUTSK
365. *Rasskazy*, tr.: I. Egorova, Iakutsk, Iakgiz., 1950, 49pp. [Title in Russian].

ICELANDIC
366. *Sloasta ráoio*, Reykjavik, Gutenberg, 1919, 82pp. Contents: Sloasta ráoio. Halda vestur (Make westing). Gulljúfrin (All gold canyon).
367. "Gooadrykkurinn," in H. G. Wells, *Land blindingjanna*, Reykjavik, 1918, pp.85-125.
368. "Sögulok", tr.: Axel Thorsteinson, *Sunnudagsblaoio*, 1:1-6 (1923) (The end of the story [?]).
369. "Sögur Tómasar," *Morgunblaoio*, 11:167-204 (1924).
370. "Afturhvarfio til eolisins," tr.: Axel Thorsteinson, *Sunnudagablao Visis*, Sept. 6, 1936, pp.3-6.
371. *Beztu smásogur eftir...* tr.: Jón. Árnason, Reykjavik, Söguútgáfan Útsýn, 1951, 192, [8]pp. Contents: Sagan af Jees Uck (The story of Jees Uck). Sonur Mexico (The Mexican). Álitshnekkir (Lost face). Heioinginn (The heathen). Sagan af Keesh (The story of Keesh). Speki Porportuks (The wit of Porportuk).

INGUSH
372. *Rasskazy*, tr.: A. Pluev, Groznyĭ, Checkinggosizdat, 1941, 104pp. [Title in Russian].

ITALIAN
373. *Raggio d'oro*. Pagine di vita, tr.: G. Dauli, Milan, Modernissima, 1924, [?]pp.
374. *Occhio rosso*, Milan, Sonzogno, 1925, 58pp.
375. *Un dramma sulla via del Polo*, tr.: Giovanni Marcellini, Aquila, Vecchioni, 1926, 191pp. Contents: Jack London. La lega dei vecchi. Un dramma sulla via del Polo. La storia di Keesh (The story of Keesh). La figlia dell' aurora (The daughter of the aurora). Un noso per il Re (The nose for the king). Mauki (Mauki). Uno reliquia preistorica. Fare un fucco (To build a fire).
376. *I cercatori d'oro*, G. Delaudi, Milan, Monanni, 1928, 238pp.
377. *Il pianto di Ah Kim*, tr.: Tullio Silvestri, Milan, Modernissima, 1929, 264pp.
378. *Bagliore dell'oro*, tr.: Maria Carlesimo Pasquali, Milan, Bietti, 1930, 226pp.
379. *Mistero*, tr.: Adele Levi, Milan, Bietti, 1930, 263pp.
380. *La ronda*, tr.: Maria Carlesimo Pasquali, Milan, Bietti, 1930, 228pp.
381. *Donne, uomini*, bestie, Perugia, Nuovissima, 1931, 300pp.
382. *La crociera della Saetta. La strada. Il Dio dei suoi padri*, tr.: Mario Benzi and G. Levi, Milan-Sesto S. Giovanni, Barion, 1934, 381pp.; Barion, 1936. *(The cruise of the Dazzler. The road. The God of his fathers)*.
383. *Ragazzi avventurosi*. Riduzione di un racconto di J. London a cura di A. Fabietti, Milan, Nuova Italia, 1936, 62pp.
384. *Il figlio del lupo. Il gioco. La fiducia degli uomini*, tr.: Mario Benzi, Sesto S. Giovanni-Milano, Barion, 1937, 319pp. *(The son of the wolf. The game. The human drift.*
385. *Un figlio del sole. Quando Dio ride. Storie di guardie del pesce*, tr.: Mario Benzi, Sesto S. Giovanni-Milano, Barion, 1938. *(The son of the sun. When God laughs. Tales of the fish patrol)*.
386. *La legge della vita*, Milan, Sonzogno, 1939, 252pp. [Contains *The god of his fathers* and *Children of the frost*.]
387. *Il paese lontano. Racconti del Nord*, tr.: Gastone Rossi, Milan, Sonzogno, 1939, 313pp. [Contents: *The son of the wolf. Faith of men. Lost face*.]
388. *Sui mari del Sud*, tr.: Gastone Rossi, Milan, Sonzogno, 1939, 314pp. [Stories from *South sea tales, The house of pride* and *When God laughs*.]
389. *L'uomo sulla pista*, tr.: Gastone Rossi, Milan, Sonzogno, 1940, 252pp. [Stories from *The son of the wolf* and *Love of life*.]

390. *Il meglio di Jack London,* tr.: Amy Coopmans de Yoldi, Milan, Longanesi, 1954, 1030pp. Contents: Il messicano (The Mexican). L'amore alla vita (Love of life). La pista del sole (The sundog trail). Il sistema dell' uomo bianco (White man's way). *Il lupo del mare (The sea wolf).* Martin Eden *(Martin Eden).*

KAZAKH
391. *Dva rasskaza.* ("*Priznanie*" i "*Derzhis*"), tr.: M. Davlet'aev, Kazidat, Kzyl-Orda, 1930, 36pp. [Title in Russian]. [Translation of "Confession" and "Holding her down".]
392. *Rasskazy,* tr.: S. Ospanov, Alma-Ata, Kazgoslitizdat, 1951, 152pp. [Title in Russian.]

KOMI
393. *Rasskazy,* tr.: I. V. Iz'iurova, Syktyvkar, 1958, 134pp. [Title in Russian].

LATVIAN
394. London, Dž., *Raksti,* Rĩga, A. Freinats, 1922-1932, 14 vols. Illustrated. Vols. 2-13 translated by J. Cĩrulis; vol. 1 by J. Cĩrulis and P. Pečaks; vol. 14 by E. Skujina and E. Skujenieks.
    1. *Degošā Dienasgaisma,* 1922, 239pp. *(Burning daylight).*
    2. *Kad senču asinis runā,* 1922, 79pp. *(The call of the wild).*
    3. *Mārtiņš Idens,* 1923, 355pp. *(Martin Eden).*
    4. *Zēgēlejums ar Apžilbinošo,* 1923, 102pp. *(The cruise of the Dazzler).*
    5. *Pirms Ādama laikiem,* 1923, 136pp. *(Before Adam).*
    6. *Baltais Ilknis,* 1923, 188pp. *(White fang).*
    7. "*Jānis Miežagrauds,* 1924, 152pp. *(John Barleycorn).*
    8. *Dienvidjūras stasti,* 1924, 149pp. *(South sea tales).*
    9. *Spēle,* 1925, 31pp. *(The game).*
    10. *Jūras vilks,* 1925, 236pp. *(The sea wolf).*
    11. *Zēgēlejums ar Snarku,* 1926, 85pp. *(The cruise of the Snark).*
    12. *Mēness ieleja,* 1927, 116pp. *(The valley of the moon).*
    13. *Zvejnieku pārlūku piedzīvojumi,* 1929, 112pp. *(Tales of the fish patrol).*
    14. *Aļaska,* 1932, 210pp.

395. Londons, Dž., *Kopoti raksti*, Rīga, "Kaija," 30 vols.
1936-1939. Introduction by V. Lāča. V. Šūmanis translated vol. 1; A. Grēviņa translated vol. 2; J. Zariņš,
vols. 3, 9, 13, 18, 20; S. Melnalksnis, vols. 4-5,
7-8, 17, 24; E. Kauliņa, vols. 6, 11, 15-16, 21-22, 28;
R. Kroders, vol. 12; Z. Krodere, vol. 27; K. Zariņš,
vols. 26, 30; V. Ozola, vol. 14; no translator given
for vol. 10.
   1. *Salinieks Džerijs*, 1936, 221pp. *(Jerry of the
      islands)*.
   2. *Sniega meita*, 1939, 264pp. *(A daughter of the
      snows)*.
   3. *Taifuns Japānas piekrastē*, 1936, 205pp. (Trans-
      lation of Typhoon off the coast of Japan. The
      Chinago. Make westing. Just meat. The Francis
      Spaight. The apostate. South of the slot. The
      dream of Debs. A nose for the king. To build
      a fire. Finis. Flush of gold. The leopard man's
      story).
   4. *Maikls, Džerija brālis*, 1936, 271pp. *(Michael,
      brother of Jerry)*.
   5. *Stāsti*, [n.d.,] 190pp. (Translations of A hyper-
      borean brew. Nam-Bok, the liar. The marriage of
      Lit-Lit. The story of Jees-Uck. Batard. Brown
      wolf. Negore, the coward. A day's lodging. The
      sun-dog trail).
   6. *Jūras vilks*, 1936, 292pp. *(The sea wolf)*.
   7. *Smōks Biljū*, 1936, 172pp. *(Smoke Bellew)*.
   8. *Smoks un Šortijs*, [n.d.,] 199pp. *(Smoke and Shorty)*.
   9. *Stāsti*, [n.d.,] 215pp. (Translation of The end of
      the story. The wit of Porportuk. The great inter-
      rogation. The passing of Marcus O'Brien. Love of
      life. Trust. The faith of men. That spot. Which
      make men remember. The man with the gash. Lost
      face).
   10. *Lielās mājas mazā saimniece*, 1937, 304pp. *(The
      little lady of the big house)*.
   11. *Saules dēls*, [n.d.,] 323pp. *(A son of the sun)*.
   12. *Trīs sirdis*, [n.d.,] 320pp. *(Hearts of three)*.
   13. *Dziļuma cilvēki*, [n.d.,] 215pp. *(The people of the
      abyss)*.
   14. *Dabas aicinājums*, [n.d.,] 188pp. *(The call of the
      wild)*.
   15. *Martiņš Idens*, [n.d.,] 243pp. *(Martin Eden)*.
   16. *Martiņš Idens*, [n.d.,] 241pp. *(Martin Eden)*.
   17. *Stāsti*, 1937, 192pp. (Translations of A relic of
      the Pliocene. The benefit of the doubt. The
      abysmal brute. The dress suit pugilist. The

Mexican).
18. *Drausmīgās Zalamana salas,* [n.d.,] 191pp. (The terrible Solomons. The house of Mapuhi. The whale tooth. Mauki. Yah! Yah! Yah! The heathen The inevitable white man. The seed of McCoy).
19. *Baltais Ilknis,* [n.d.,] 223pp. *(White fang).*
20. *Klaidoņi,* 1937, 152pp. *(The road).*
21. *Mēness ieleja,* [n.d.,] 286pp. Poems translated by E. Ādamsons. *(The valley of the moon).*
22. *Mēness ieleja,* [n.d.,] 248pp. Poems translated by E. Ādamsons. *(The valley of the moon).*
23. *Zvejnieku pārlūku dēkas,* [n.d.,] 192pp. *(Tales of the fish patrol).*
24. *Burājums ar Snarku,* 1937, 216pp. *(The cruise of the Snark).*
25. *Stāsti,* 1937, 192pp. (Translations of Good-bye, Jack! On the Makaloa Mat. Aloha oe. The bones of Kahekili. Koolau, the leper. The sheriff of Kona. The house of pride. The tears of Ah Kim. Chun Ah Chun).
26. *Degoša Dienas gaisma,* 1937, 326pp. *(Burning daylight).*
27. *Piedzīvojums,* [n.d.,] 243pp. *(Adventure).*
28. *Vēstules par mīlu,* [n.d.,] 167pp. *(Kempton-Wace letters).*
29. *Džons Miežagrauds,* 1937, 206pp. *(John Barleycorn).*
30. *Stāsti,* 1937, 168pp. (Translations of Too much gold. The son of the wolf. The men of forty mile. An odyssey of the north. The white silence. In a far country. To the man on trail. The priestly prerogative).

396. *Cīņa dēl dzīvības. Negaidītais,* tr.: T. Reinfelde, Rīga, Darbs, 1922, 64pp. (Love of life. The unexpected).
397. *Stāsti,* Riga, A. Jessens, 1924, 36pp. Contents: Melnais pagāns (The heathen). Melis (Nam-Bok, the liar). Mapuji māja (The house of Mapuhi).
398. "Stūrītis ellē," *Sociāldemokrāts,* nos. 93-94 (April 26-27, 1929) (Frying-pan alley. A glimpse of inferno).
399. "Alaska," *Sociāldemokrāts,* nos. 169-282 (July 20-Dec. 13, 1932).
400. *Sievietes spēks. Stāsti,* tr.: J. Rūsa, Rūjiena, J. Miķelsons, 1934, 79pp. Contents: Ziemlu Odiseja (An odyssey of the north). Sievietes spēks (Grit of women). Sivašiete (Siwash). Kur ceļi šķiras (Where the trail forks).
401. *Stāsti,* tr.: E. Plandere and V. Brutāne, Rīga, LVI, 1948, 392pp. Contents: Baltais klusums (The white

silence). Ziemeļu Odiseja (An odyssey of the north).
Cilvēks ar rētu sejā (The man with the gash). Stūrgal-
vīgais Jans (Jan, the unrepentant). Kur varavīksne
beidzas (At the rainbow's end). Tūkstoš duči (The one
thousand dozen). Batars (Batard). Zīmogotais (That spot).
Ugunskurs (To build a fire). Dzīvotgriba (Love of life).
Īsā atpūta (A day's lodging). Negaidītais (The unex-
pected). Finis (Finis). Dzīves likums (The law of life).
Dižais burvis (The mastery of mystery). Kīša dels Kišs
(Keesh, the son of Keesh). Līguna nāve (The death of
Ligoun). Zelta grava (All gold canyon). Ķīnietis (The
chinago). A Kīma asaras (The tears of Ah Kim). Mek-
sikānietis (The Mexican). Atkritējs (The apostate).
Semjuels (Samuel). Mapuhi māja (The house of Mapuhi).
Kašalota zobs (The whale tooth). Mauki (Mauki). Kulaus -
spitālīgais (Koolau, the leper).

402. *Stāsti*, tr.: Ezeriņa, Rīga, LVI, 1958, 358pp. Contents:
Stāsts par Kišu (The story of Keesh). Baltā cilvēka
ceļš (The white man's way). Sniega ceļa gudrība (The
wisdom of the trail). Sievietes spēks (Grit of woman).
Baīsmīgās Zalamana salas (The terrible Solomons).
"Ek jūs! Ek jūs! Ek jūs!" ("Yah! Yah! Yah!"). Velni
Fuatino salā (The devils of Fuatino). Neliels rēķins
Svizinam Holam (A little account with Swithin Hall).
Saules Spalvas (The fathers of the sun[?]). Lepnība
nams (The house of pride). Kanaku bangotne (The Kanaka
surf). Uz makaloa paklāja (On the Makaloa mat).
Kahekili kauli (The bone of Kahekili). Kā Alīse grēkus
sūdzēja (When Alice told her soul). Kad dievi smejas
(When God laughs). Gabals gaļas (A piece of steak).
"Kruki" (Bulls). "Nokniebts" (Pinched). Stipro spēks
(The strength of the strong). Dīvains starpgadījums
(A curious fragment).

LITHUANIAN

403. *Stabmeldis. Jack Londono apysaka*, Philadelphia, Pa.,
Kovos leid, 1914. [Probably a translation of either
The apostate or The heathen.]

404. *Pagonis*, tr.: K. Puida, Kaunas, Krivule, 1925, 96pp.
[Probably a translation of The heathen.]

405. *Pasakos galas*, tr.: K. P. Kaunas, Krivule, 1926, 48pp.
Contents: Pasakos galas (The end of the story).
Padavimas apie Kiša (The story of Keesh).

406. *Zukles sargybinio paskojimai*, tr.: D. Judelevičius,
Kaunas, Valst. groz. lit. 1-kla, 1947, 134pp. Contents:
Baltieji ir geltonieji (The white and the yellow).
Graiku karalius (The king of the Greeks). Žygis prieš
austriu piratus (The raid on the oyster pirates).

"Lankaširo karalienes" apgula (The siege of the "Lancashire Queen"). Carlio "Coup" (Charley's coup). Demetrijus Kontas (Demetrius Contos). Geltonoji Skara (Yellow handkerchief).

407. *Apsakymai*, tr.: E. Kuosaite, Vilna, Valst. groš. lit. 1-kla, 1952, 131pp. Contents: Gyvenimo meile (Love of life). Pasakojimas apie Kiša (The story of Keesh). Atskalunas (The outcast[?]). Ant Sakramento krantu (The banks of the Sacramento). Rudasis vilkas (Brown wolf). Meksikietis (The Mexican).

408. *Baltoji tyla*, tr.: T. Zaleckis, Vilna, Valst. groš, lit. 1-kla, 1961, 383pp. Contents: Baltoji tyla (White silence). Vilko sunus (The son of the wolf). Keturiasdešimtojoje mylioje (The men of forty mile). Tolimoje šalyje (In a far country). Už tuos, kurie keliauja (In behalf of those who travel). Kunigo žodžio galia (The priestly prerogative). Žygio istatymas (Journey's rule[?]). Sukurti lauža (Lit fires[?]-probably To build a fire). Žmogus su randu (Man with the gash). Moters ryžtas (A woman's dedication[?]). Melagis Nam-Bokas (Nam-Bok, the liar). Kišo sunus Kisas (Keesh, son of Keesh). Didžioji misle (The great interrogation). Kai Išsiskiria keliai (Where the trail forks). Šiaures pašvaistes dukte (Daughter of the Aurora). Moteru panieka (The scorn of women). Šiaures namine (Home of the north[?]).Gyvenimo desnis (Life's course[?]).

409. "Revoliucija yra geras dalykas, kuriam ir verta pasišvesti," *Kova*, no. 27:213-214 (1905) [Probably a translation of a passage from *Revolution*].

410. "Baltojo žmogaus viršenybe," tr.: Vandraunikas, *Laisve*, nos. 205-206 (1922) (White man's superiority[?]).

411. "Kruvinas kerstas," tr.: P.M. B., *Laisve*, nos. 61-63, (1922). (Bloody revenge[?]).

412. "Jokahamos uoste," tr.: S. M., *Skautu aidas*, nos. 1-2: 10-12 (1927).

413. "'Monachiki' paslaptis," tr.: St. B., *Trimitas*, no. 4:110-116 (1927) (The secret of Manachiki[?]).

414. "Paskutine kova," tr.: A. Kalesnykietis, *Rytas*, May 28, 30, June 1-4, 7, 1927 (The last battle[?]).

415. "Tai, kas nepamirštama," *Rytas*, Sept. 12-15, 1927, (That is what is unforgettable[?].

416. "Maika. (Passakojimas apie viena eskimu šuni), tr.: Pr. Mašiotas, in Pr. Mašiotas, *Žverys ir žmones*, Kaunas, 1929, pp.63-75. (Mike, a tale about an Eskimo dog[?]).

417. "Nakties stovykla," *Lietuvos aidas*, April 16, 29, 1929 (Night camp[?]).

418. "Nosos," tr.: Kamauskas, *Rytas*, May 11, 1929 (The nose;-perhaps Nose for the king).

419. "Nakties dukra," *Rytas*, Jan. 21. 1930 (Daughter of the night;-perhaps Daughter of the aurora).
420. "Styga," tr.: V. Petr, *Lietuvos žinios*, March 15, 1930 (String[?]).
421. "Baltojo žmogaus keliai," *Naujas žodis*, no. 18:442-444, no. 19:462-465 (1931) (White man's way[?]).
422. "Vienybeje-galybe," tr.: A. Valinčius, *Socialdemokratas*, July 16. 23. 30, Aug. 13, 27, 1932 (In unity there is strength[?]).
423. "Sučiupo," *Valstiečiu laikraštis*, Dec. 5, 8, 11, 1957 (Caught;-perhaps Pinches).

PERSIAN

424. *Bot parast*, tr.: Mohammad Jaafar Mahjoub, Tehran, Amir Kabir Publishing Institute, 1951, 25pp. (The idolater[?]-perhaps a translation of The heathen).
425. *Khamooshié sepid*, tr.: Nozar, Tehran, Ranguin Press, 1951, 15pp. (Silence of dawn).
426. *Ateshpareyé zarrin*, tr.: Saeed Salem, Tehran, Mir Sadeghi Bookstore, 1955, 27pp. (The golden spark[?]).
427. *Bargasht*, tr.: Saeed Salem, Tehran, Mir Sadeghi Bookstore, 1955, 31pp. (Return).
428. *Jozaim*, tr.: Saeed Salem, Tehran, Mir Sadeghi Bookstore, 1955, 22pp. (Koolau, the leper[?]).
429. *Azkhod gozashitequié zana*, tr.: Mohammad Jaafar Mahjoub, Tehran, Sepehr Publications, 1957, 28pp. (Women's sacrifice[?]).
430. *Mossabegheh*, tr.: Alek, Tehran, Danesh Press & Bookstore, [n.d.,] 76pp. (The race[?]).
431. *Morted*, tr.: Massoud Farzan, Tehran, Afshari Publishing Institute, [n.d.,] 49pp.

POLISH

432. London, Jack, *Dzieła wybrane*, edited by Kazimierza Piotrowski-ego, Warsaw, Iskry, 1957, 10 vols.
    1. *Nowele*. Kazimierz Piotrowski, "Jack London" (1876-1916), pp.5-46. Za azdrowie wedrowca na szlaku (To the man on trail) tr.: Z. Glinka; Biała cisza (The white silence) tr.: Tadeusz Jan Dehnel; Syn wilka (The son of the wolf) tr.: T. J. Dehnel; Ludzie z Czierdziestej mili (The men of forty-mile) tr.: Z. Glinka; Małzonka króla (The wife of the king) tr.: K. Piotrowski; Prawo szlaku (The wisdom of the trail) tr.: B. Zielinski; Odyseja Północy (An odyssey of the north) tr.: A. Glinczanka; Serce kobiety (Grit of women) tr.: Z. Glinka; Wielka niewiadoma (The great interrogation) tr.: T. J. Dehnel; Rozstajne

drogi (Where the trail forks) tr.: T. J. Dehnel;
Prawo zycia (Law of life) tr.: Tadeusz Evert;
Kobieta z plemienia Siwasz (Siwash) tr.: T.
Evert; Napoj hyperboreajow (A hyperborean brew)
tr.: K. Piotrowski; Nam-Bok klamca (Nam-Bok,
the unveracious) tr.: K. Piotrowski; Li-Wan o
jasnej skórze (Li Wan, the fair) tr.: T. J.
Dehnel; Mistra tajemnicy (The master of mystery)
tr.: T. Evert; W lasach Północy (In the forests
of the north) tr.: B. Zieliński; Historia Jees
Uck (The story of Jees Uck) tr.: Krystyna
Tarnowska; Sprzysiężenie starców (The league of
old men) tr.: T. J. Dehnel; Choroba Samotenego
Wodza (The sickness of Lone Chief) tr.: K.
Piotrowski; Tysiąc tuzinow (The one thousand
dozen) tr.: Z. Glinka; Wiara w człowieka (Faith
of men) tr.: T. Evert; Zamązpójście Lit-Lit
(The marriage of Lit-Lit) tr.: K. Piotrowski;
Skarby sezamu (Too much gold) tr.: K. Piotrowski;
Historia Keesha (The story of Keesh) tr.: Z.
Glinka; Złoty mak (The golden poppy) tr.: K.
Piotrowski.
2. *Nowele*. Wyczyn Charleys (Charley's coup) tr.: B.
Zielinski; Demetrios Contos (Demetrios Contos)
tr.: B. Zielinski; Szcerozłoty Kanion (All gold
canyon) tr.: T. J. Dehnel; Miłość zycia (Love
of life) tr.: Z. Glinka; Nieoczekiwane (The
unexpected) tr.: T. J. Dehnel; Bury wilk (Brown
Wolf) tr.: K. Piotrowski; Odszczepiensiec
(The apostate) tr.: Gabriel Karski; Gdy Bogwie
sie smieja (When God laughs) tr.: T. J. Dehnel;
Jednodniowy popas (A day's lodging) tr.: T. J.
Dehnel; Powierzony skarb (Trust) tr.: Z. Glinka;
Przygoda Marcusa O'Briena (The passing of Marcus
O'Brien) tr.: B. Zielinski; Kochany kluks (That
spot) tr.: K. Piotrowski; Dom Mapuhiego (The
house of Mapuhi) tr.: B. Zielinski; Marzenie
Debsa (The dream of Debs) tr.: T. J. Dehnel;
Prawomik McCoyá (The seed of McCoy) tr.: B.
Zielinski; Aloha oe (Aloha oe) tr.: K. Tarnowska;
Na południe od toru (South of the slot) tr.: K.
Piotrowski; "Zegnaj Jack" (Good-by Jack!") tr.:
K. Tarnowska; Chinczak (The Chinago) tr.: G.
Karski; Szeryf Kony (The sheriff of Kona) tr.:
T. J. Dehnel; Befsztyk (A piece of steak) tr.:
T. Evert; Trędowaty Koolau (Koolau, the leper)
tr.: B. Zielinski.
3. *Nowele*. Straszliwy archipelago (The terrible Sol-

omons) tr.: T. J. Dehnel; Czun Ah Czun (Chun
Ah Chun) tr.: T. Evert; Poganin (The heathen)
tr.: Z. Glinka; Dobrodziejstwo wątpliwósci (The
benefit of the doubt) tr.: T. Evert; Na pokładzie
(Under the deck awnings) tr.: G. Karski; Zabic
czlowieka (To kill a man) tr.: G. Karski; Dom
Pychy (The house of pride) tr.: K. Piotrowski;
"Yah! Yah! Yah!" tr.: B. Zielinski; Zrodzona z
nocy (The night born) tr.: T. Evert; Meksykanin
(The Mexican) tr.: K. Piotrowski; Na kobiercu
Makaloa (On the Makaloa mat) tr.: K. Tarnowska;
Zew krwi (The call of the wild) tr.: Eleanora
Romanowicz.
4. *Bialy kiel (White Fang)* tr.: Anna Przedpelska-
   Trzeciakowska; *Bellew Zawierucha (Smoke Bellew)*
   tr.: K. Piotrowski.
5. *Martin Eden,* tr.: Z. Glinka.
6. *Zelazna stopa (The iron heel)* tr.: Julian Stawinski; *Mieskancy otchlani (The people of the
   abyss)* tr.: K. Tarnowska.
7. *Wilk morski (The sea wolf)* tr.: Jerzy Bogdan
   Rychlinski.
8. *Syn slonca (The son of the sun)* tr.: T. J. Dehnel;
   Jerry z wysp (Jerry of the islands) tr.: B.
   Zielinski; *Z "Podrozy Snarka" (The cruise of the
   Snark)* tr.: Jan Meysztowicz.
9. *Ksiezycowa dolina (Valley of the moon)* tr.: Krystyna Tarnowska.
10. *John Barleycorn czyli wspomnienia alkoholika (John
    Barleycorn).* tr.: Antonina Sokolicz and Szkice
    autobiograficzne: Wyznanie (Confession) tr.:
    K. Piotrowski; Trzyman sie pociagu (Holding her
    down) tr.: T. J. Dehnel; Obrazy (Pictures) tr.:
    T. J. Dehnel; Jak mnie przymknęli (Pinched) tr.:
    tr.: Z. Glinka; Nocne spotkania z trampami (Hoboes
    that pass in the night) tr.: T. J. Dehnel; "Lapsy"
    ("Bulls") tr.: B. Zielinski; Jak zostalem soc-
    jalista (How I became a socialist) tr.: K.
    Piotrowski; Czym die mnie jest zycie (What life
    means to me) tr.: K. Piotrowski; W stanie Idaho
    coś psuć się zaczyna (Something rotten in Idaho)
    tr. K. Piotrowski; Przedmowa do antologii *W imie
    sprawiedliwości* (Introduction to The cry for
    justice) tr.: K. Piotrowski.

433. *Biala cisza,* Wilno, Kurier Wileńska, 1910, 106pp.
434. *Wierność mezczyny,* tr.: St. Kuszelewska, Tow, Księgarni
     Polskich na Kresach, 1920, 138pp.; also Warsaw, Rój,

1926. Contents: Wierność mezczyzny (Faith of men) U tostaju dróg (Where the trail forks). Przyilej sutanny (The priestly prerogative). Co kaze pamietać (Which makes men remember). Rozpalać ogień (To build a fire). W dalekim kraju (In a far country).

435. *Prawo białego człowieka*, tr.: Stanisława Kuszelewska, Warsaw, Ignis, 1921, 152pp.; also Warsaw, 1925. Contents: Małzonka króla (Wife of a king). Prawo białego człowieka (Either The white man's way or The wisdom of the trail). Pytanie (The great interrogation). Zdrowie podroznego (The man on trail). Śniezna martwica (The white silence) Na postoju (A day's lodging). Córka zozy (A daughter of the Aurora). Szlak złudnych słonć (The sun-dog trail).

436. *Odyssea Północy*, tr.: Stanisława Kuszelewska, Warsaw, Ignis, 1922, 252pp.; Warsaw, E. Wende, 1925, 218pp.; Warsaw, Kurier Polski, 1939, [?]pp.; E. Kuthan, 1947, 168pp. Contents of the 1922 ed.: Historia Keesha (The story of Keesh). Napój Hyperborejów (A hyperborean brew). Bury Wilk (Brown wolf). Przygoda Markusa O'Briena (The passing of Marcus O'Brien). Batard. Syn wilka (The son of the wolf). Prawo życia (The law of life). Odyssea Północy (An odyssey of the north).

437. *Bóg ojców jego*, tr.: Stanisława Kuszelewska, Warsaw, Ignis, 1924, 196pp.; Warsaw, Biblioteka Groszowa, 1925, 191pp.; Warsaw, E. Kuthan, 1949, 132pp. Contents of the 1924 ed.: Mieszkańcy Czterdziestej mili (The men of forty mile). Zhańbine czoto (Lost face). Obyczaj białych ludzi (White man's way). U Krańca Teczy (At the rainbow's end). Nieoczekiwane (The unexpected). Zaufanie (Trust). Zwiazek starców (The league of old men). Bóg ojców jego (God of his fathers).

438. *Odszczepieniec i inne nowele*, tr.: Gabriel Karski, Warsaw, Ignis, 1924, 156pp. Other editions, all Warsaw, Biblioteka Groszowa, 1925, 156pp.; Kurier Polski, 1934 and E. Kuthan, 1948, 147pp. Contents: Odszczepieniec (The apostate). Kawał Pieczeni (A piece of steak). Na pokładzie (Under the deck awnings). Samo mięso (Just meat). Zabić (To kill a man). Chińczak (The Chinago).

439. *Miłość życia*, tr.: S. Kuszelewska, Warsaw, Biblioteka Dziet Wyborowych, 1925, 2 vols., 127pp., 131pp.; 1st volume reprinted in Warsaw, Rój, 1926, 1930, 127pp. Contents of Volume 1: Jasnoskóra Li Wan (Li wan, the fair). Kochany Kleks (That spot). Skarby Sezamu (Too much gold). Nam Bok kłamca (Nam-Bok, the unveracious). Milość życia (Love of life). Contents of Volume 2: Śmierć Ligou na (The death of Ligoun). Jutrzenka. Władca tajemnic (Master of mystery). Tysiąc tuzinow

(The one thousand dozen). Pogarda kobiet (Scorn of woman).

440. *Serce kobiety*, tr.: Stanisława Kuszelewska, Warsaw, Wende, 1925, 229pp.; Warsaw, E. Kuthan, 1946, 1948. Contents of the 1925 ed.: Serce kobiety (Grit of woman). Keesh syn Kessha (Keesh, son of Keesh). Żona z plemienia Siwash (Siwash). Zamązpojście Lit-Lit (The marriage of Lit-Lit). Śród lasów Północy (In the forests of the North). Historia Jess Uck (The story of Jess Uck). Przemyślny Porportuk (The wit of Porportuk). Negore-Tchorz (Negore, the coward).

441. *Wróg świata*, tr.: Roman Celeinski, Warsaw, Spolki Wydaw. Powsz, 1925, 167pp.; other editions, all Warsaw published by Biblioteka Romansow i Powiesci, appeared in 1927 (166pp), 1929, 1930, 1931. Contents of the 1925 ed.: Wróg świata (The enemy of all the world). Sila silnego (The strength of the strong). Na południe od rubieży (South of the slot). Niestchany majazd (The unparalleled invasion). Marzenie Debsa (The dream of Debs). Pan tajemnicy (The master of mystery).

442. *Pogarda kobiet*, tr.: S. Kuszelewska, Warsaw, Roj, 1926, 131pp.; ibid., 1928. Contents: Śmierć Ligouna (The death of Ligoun). Jutrzenka. Władca tajemnic (Master of mystery). Tysiąc tuzinów (The one thousand dozen). Pogarda kobiet (The scorn of woman).

443. *Szczerozłoty wawóz*, tr.: S. T., Warsaw, Drukarnia Polska, 1926, 1927, 135pp. Contents: Szczerozłoty wawóz (All gold canyon). Koloryt miejscowy (Local color). Przedstawienie amatorskie (Amateur night). Ekierka (Planchette).

444. *Meksykanin*, tr.: Jerzy Mariusz Taylor, Warsaw, Biblioteka Romansow i Powiesci, 1926, 141pp.; other editions all Warsaw, 1930, 1931, 1934. Contents: Meksykanin (The Mexican). Wojna (War). Na pokładzie (Under the deck awnings). Wymiar Sprawiedliowości (Bunches of knuckles). Zemsta (The benefit of the doubt).

445. *Córa nocy*, tr.: Jerzy Mariusz Taylor, Warsaw, Biblioteka Romansow i Powiesci, 1927, 128pp. Other editions of this translation, all published in Warsaw, appeared in 1928 and 1930, both 128pp.; publisher and pagination not known for those issued in 1929, 1931, 1934. Contents of the 1927 ed.: Córa nocy (The night born). Szaleństwo Johna Harned (The madness of John Harned). Przygoda w Mill Valley. Loo-Loo (Winged blackmail). Odwaga Pani Setliffe (To kill a man).

446. *Czerwony Bóg*, tr.: M. Andrzeykowicz, Warsaw, Rój, 1927, 125pp. Contents: Czerwony Bóg (The red one). Ladacznica (The hussy). Jak Argus z dawnych dni (Like Argus of the

ancient times).
447. *Gra,* tr.: Marja Kuncewiczowa, Warsaw, Roj, 1927, 127pp.;
also Warsaw, Biblioteka Echa Polskiego, 1931. Contents
of the 1927 edition: Gra (The game). Gdy bogowię sie
śmieją (When God laughs). Trędowaty Koolau (Koolau, the
leper). Aloha oe.
448. *Opowiadanie pogromcy,* tr.: S. M. Warsaw, Roj, 1927,
130pp. Contents: Koniec bajki (The end of the story).
Opowiadanie pogramcy (The leopard man's story).
Księzniczka (The princess). Pawilon kretynow. Tragedia
dalekiego pólnocozachodu.
449. *Żółwie Tasmana,* Warsaw, Roj, 1927, 139pp. Tr.: S.
Kuszelweska. Contents: Zołwie Tasmana (By the turtles
of Tasman). Nieśmiertelność kształtów (The eternity of
forms). Włóczęga i dobra wróżska (The hobo and the
fairy). Marnotrawny ojciec (The prodigal father). Cień
i błysk (The shadow and the flash).
450. *Djabli na Fuatino,* tr.: J. B. Rychińskiego, Rzym, Polski
Dom Wydawniczy, 1947, 62pp. [Besides the title story,
The goat man of Fautino; this volume contains Figle na
New Gibbon (The˜jokers of New Gibbon).]
451. *Miłość życia,* tr.: St. Kuszelewska, Warsaw, Ksiazka,
1947, 108pp. Contents: Jasnoskora Li Wan (Li Wan the
fair). Kochany Kleks (That spot). Skarby Sezamu (Too
much gold). Nam-Bok kłamca (Nam-Bok, the unveracious).
Milość życia (Love of life).
452. *Perły Parlay'a,* tr.: J. B. Rychińskiego, Rzym, Polski
Dom Wydawniczy, 1947, 66pp. [Besides the title story,
The pearls of Parlay, this volume contains Rackunki
ze Swithin Hallem (A little account with Swithin Hall).]
453. *Syn Słońca,* tr.: J. B. Rychinskiego, Rzym, Polski Dom
Wydawniczy, 1947, 61pp. [Besides the title story, *The
son of the sun,* this volume contains O honor Alojzego
Pankburna, (The proud goat of Aloysius Pankburn).]
454. *Bóg ojców jego,* tr.: Stanisława Kuszelewska, Warsaw,
Ignis, 1924, 196pp.; also editions of Warsaw, Biblioteka Groszowa, 1925, and Warsaw, E. Kuthan, 1949. Contents of 1924 ed.: Mieszkańcy Czterdziestej mili (Men
of forty mile). Zhańbione czoło (Lost face). Obyczaj
białych ludzi (The white man's way). U Krańca Teczy
(At the rainbow's end). Nieoczekiwane (The unexpected).
Zaufanie (Trust). Bóg ojców jego (The God of his
fathers).
455. *Opowieści z Połnocy i Poludnia,*tr.: Zygmunt Glinka i
Gabriel Karski, Warsaw, Nasza Księgarnia, 1953, 1955,
269pp. Contents: Historia Keesha (The story of Keesh).
Odszczepieniec (The apostate). Miłość zycia (Love of
life). Miezkańcy Czterdziestej mili (The men of forty

mile). Zaufanie (Trust). Serce kobiety (The grit of
women). Tysiąc tuzinow (The one thousand dozen).
Dziecię wody (The water baby). Nad brzegami Sacramento
(The banks of the Sacramento). Poganin (The heathen).
Kawał pieczeni (A piece of steak). Chińczak (The
Chinago).

456. *Nowele*, tr.: Kazinicrz Piotrowski, Warsaw, Iskry, 1954,
345pp. Contents: Odszczepieniec (The apostate) tr.:
Gabriel Karski. Wyczyn Charley a (Charley's coup) tr.:
Bronislaw Zielinski. Demetrios Contos tr.: B. Zielinski.
Scrcc kobicty (Grit of woman) tr.: Jak mnie przymkneli
(Pinched) tr.: Zygmunt Glinka. Zdarzenie (To kill a
man) tr.: Gabriel Karski. Bury Wilk (Brown wolf) tr.:
Stanislawa Kuszelweska. Kochany Kleks (That Spot) tr.:
S. Kuszelweska. Dom Uapuhiego (The house of Mapuhi) tr.:
B. Zielinski. Prawnuk McCoyá (The seed of McCoy) tr.:
B. Zielinski. Poganin (The heathen) tr.: Z. Glinka.
Nad brzegami Sacramento (The banks of the Sacramento)
tr.: Z. Glinka. Historia Keesha (The story of Keesh)
tr.: Z. Glinka. Serce kobiety (Grit of woman) tr.:
Z. Glinka. Miłość życia (Love of life) tr.: Z. Glinka.
Skarby Sezamu (Too much gold) tr.: S. Kuszelewska. Za
zdrowie wędrowca na szlaku (To the man on trail) tr.:
Z. Glinka. Przygoda Marcusa O'Brien (The passing of
Marcus O'Brien) tr.: S. Kuszelewska. Odyseja Północy
(Odyssey of the north) tr.: A. Glinczonka. Meksykanin
(The Mexican) tr.: K. Piotrowski.

457. *Wyga i inne opowiadania*, Warsaw, Iskry, 1955, 227pp.
Contents: Wyga (Smoke Bellew) tr.: Jerzy Bandrowski.
Kochany kleks (That spot). Skarby sezamu (Too much
gold). Przygoda Marcusa O'Briena (The passing of Marcus
O'Brien) all translated by S. Kuszelewska.

458. *Zew krwi i inne opowiadania*, Warsaw, Iskry, 1955, 146pp.
Contents: Zew krwi (The call of the wild) tr.: Eleanora
Romanowicz. Serce kobiety (Grit of woman) tr.: Zygmunt
Glinka. Miłość życia (Love of life) tr.: Zygmunt Glinka.
Odyseja Północy (Odyssey of the north) tr.: A. Glin-
czanka.

459. *Kawał pieczeni i inne opowaidania*, tr.: Gabriel Karski
and Kazimierz Piotrowski, Warsaw, Czytelnik, 1955, 169pp.
Contents: Kawał pieczeni (Piece of steak). Kochany
Kleks (That spot). Miłość życia (Love of life). Odszczepieniec (The apostate). Meksykanin (The Mexican).

460. *Nowele*, selected and edited by Kazimierz Piotrowski,
Warsaw, Iskry, 1956, 2 vols., 19[?] 214pp. 1. Odszc-
zepieniec (The apostate) tr.: Gabriel Karski; Wyczyn
Charleya (Charley's coup) tr.: Bronisława Zieliński;
Demetrios Contos tr.: Bronisława Zieliński; Jak mnie

przymkneli (Pinched) tr.: Z. Glinka; Zdarzenie (To kill
a man) tr.: G. Karski, Bury wilk (Brown wolf) tr.: Stanisława Kuszelewska; Kochany Kleks (That spot) tr.: S.
Kuszelewska; Dom Mapuhiego (The house of Mapuhi) tr.:
Bronisław Zieliński; Prawnuk McCoyá (The seed of McCoy)
tr.: B. Zieliński. 2. Poganin (The heathen) tr.: Zygmunt Glinka; Nad brzegami Sacramento (The banks of the
Sacramento) tr.: Z. Glinka; Historia Keesha (The story
of Keesh) tr.: Z. Glinka; Serce Kobiety (Grit of women)
tr.: Z. Glinka; Miłość życia (Love of life) tr.: Z.
Glinka; Skarby sezamu (Too much gold) tr.: S. Kuszelewska; Za zdrowie wędrowca na szlaku (To the man on
trail) tr.: Z. Glinka; Przygoda Marcusa O'Briena (The
passing of Marcus O'Brien) tr.: S. Kuszelewska; Odyseja
Północy (Odyssey of the north) tr.: A. Glinczanka;
Meksykanin (The Mexican) tr.: K. Piotrowski.

461. *Trzydzieści nowel*, Warsaw, Iskry, 1958, 542pp. Contents:
Biala cisza (The white silence); Małżonka króla (The
wife of a king); Wiara w człowieka (Faith of men);
Wielka niewiadoma (The great interrogation); Rozstajne
drogi (Where the trail forks); Kobieta z plemienia
Siwash (Siwash); Napój hyperborejew (A hyperborean brew);
Li-Wan o jasnej skorze (Li-Wan the fair); Mistrz taj-
emmiey (Master of mystery); Historia Jees-Uck (The story
of Jees-Uck); Sprzysiężenie starców (The league of old
men); Choroba samotnego wodza (The sickness of Lone
Chief); Zamązpójście Lit-Lit (The marriage of Lit-Lit);
Złoty mak (The golden poppy); Szczerozłoty kanion (All
gold canyon); Nieoczekiwane (The unexpected); Marzenie
Debsa (The dream of Debs); Na południe od Toru (South
of the slot); Szeryf Kony (The sheriff of Kona); Trędo-
waty Koolau (Koolau, the leper); Straszliwy archipelag
(The terrible Solomons); Czun Ah Czun (Chun Ah Chun);
Dobrodziejstwo wątpliwości (The benefit of the doubt);
Dom pychy (The house of pride); Na kobiercu Makaloa
(On the Makaloa mat); Wyznanie (Confession); Trzyman
sie pociagu (Holding her down); Nocne spotkania z
trampami (Hoboes that pass in the night); "Lapsy"
("Bulls"); Czym dla mnie jest życie (What life means
to me). [All of the translators are the same as in
Dziela wybrane.]

PORTUGUESE
462. *Obras completas de Jack London*, Lisbon, Inquérito.
    1. *Memórias de um bebedor*, tr.: Campos Lima,
        [n.d.,] 294pp. *(John Barleycorn)*. Pages 1-27
        are entitled "Nota sobre Jack London".
    2. *História de um cão de circo*, tr.: Telo de Mascar-

enhas, [n.d.,] 264pp. *(Michael, brother of Jerry).*
3. *O amor à vida,* tr.: Domingos Monteiro, [n.d.,]
241pp. *(Love of life).*
4. *A voz da selva,* tr.: Luisa Maria de Eça Leal,
1944, 190pp. *(The call of the wild).*
5. *Os milhões de Chun Ah Chun,* tr.: Adriano Marinho
and José Marinho, [n.d.,] 243pp. *(The house of
pride).* Also contains "London visto por êle
prôpio," pp.7-21.
6. *O lôbo dos mares,* tr.: Luísa Maria de Eça Leal
and José Parreira Alves, [n.d.,] 270pp.
(The sea wolf).
7. *Jerry na ilha,* tr.: Maria Isabel Espinosa, 1946,
255pp. *(Jerry of the islands).*
8. *Nas florestas do norte,* tr.: Carlos Lança, 1947,
206pp.

463. *As melhores histórias de Jack London,* tr.: Lygia Autran
Rodrigues Pereira, Rio de Janeiro, Revista branca,
1953, 225pp.
464. *Histórias de Jack London,* seleção, tradução e prefácio
de Olívia Krähenbühl, São Paulo, Cultrix, 1964, 200pp.
Contents: Notícia sôbre Jack London. O silêncio branco
(The white silence). Cara no Chão (Lost face). A liga
dos velhos (The league of old men). A casa de Mapuhi
(The house of Mapuhi). A história de Keesh (The story
of Keesh). A inteligência de Porportuk (The wit of
Porportuk). O mexicano (The Mexican). As pérolas de
Parlay (The pearls of Parlay). Para o homem na trilha
(The man on the trail). O pagão (The heathen).

RUMANIAN

The following Rumanian items appeared as part of the
Lectura, floarea literaturilor străine published in
Bucharest by Adevěrul:
465. *No. 17. Neprevăzutul,* 1925, 31pp.
466. *No. 81. Dezertorul,* tr.: Eliza Noian, 192[?] 31pp.
467. *No. 122. O grevă în America,* tr.: C. Sp. Popescu, 1927,
32pp.
468. *No. 154. Devotament de femeie,* tr.: Anna Radulescu-
Tilly, 1928, 31pp.
469. *No. 253. Intrebarea cea mare,* tr.: C. Lesanu, 1929,
31pp.
470. *No. 285. Prinţul Lilolila,* tr.: Filip Frateş, 1930, 31pp.
471. *No. 312. O aventură în Alaska,* tr.: I. Iesanu, 1931,
31pp.
472. *No. 391. Li-Wan cea frumoasă,* tr.: M. Dimitriu, 193[?]
31pp. (Li-Wan, the fair).

473. *No. 408. Acum, o, regele meu!* tr.: Em Stravi, 193[?]
     31pp.
474. *No. 486. Faţa pierdută,* tr.: Lia Frates, 1934, 32pp.
475. *No. 508. Mă vînd! ... Cine mă vrea?* tr.: Pavel Mandrea,
     1934, 32pp.
476. *No. 551. Văpaie de aur,* tr.: Ernest Minou, 1936, 32pp.
477. *Omul cu obrazu'ncrustat,* tr.: Eug. Boureanul, Bucharest,
     Advĕrul, 1925, 63pp. (Biblioteca Dimineata nr. 23).
478. *Pui de lup. Romanul unui cîine lup,* Bucharest, Ateil-
     ierele Adeverul, 1933, 79pp.
479. *Viaţa mea,* tr.: I. Plugaru; introduction by Ion Pas,
     Bucharest, Santier, 1935, 32pp.
480. *Aventura cea mare,* tr.: Ioan Rovenţa, Bucharest, Ed.
     Contemporană, 1942, 304 + 2pp.
481. *Bal mascat,* tr.: Marin Dumitrescu-Berecht, Bucharest,
     G. M. Amza, 1942, 264pp.
482. *Foamete la Londra,* tr.: Josephina Schiefer, Bucharest,
     Contemporana, 1942, 256pp.
483. *Neînvinsul,* tr.: Ioan Rovenţa, Bucharest, Cultura
     Românească, 1942, 228pp.
484. *Ultimul match,* tr.: I. St. Popescu, Bucharest, Prometau,
     1942, 152pp.
485. *Temnita profesorului,* tr.: Vlad Muşatescu, Craiova,
     ABC, 1943, 325pp.
486. *Chinezul,* tr.: A. Ghiţulescu, Bucharest, Editura
     tineretului, 1949, 32pp.
487. *Hoinarii,* tr.: Paul Lupaşcu, Bucharest, Editura de
     stat, 1949, 88pp.
488. *Indiana Pasuk,* tr.: I. J. Bănăţeanu, Bucharest, E.P.L.A.,
     1949, 24pp. Cartea poporului, 23).
489. *Oameni în bezna,* tr.: Madeleine Samitca, Bucharest,
     Editura de stat, 1949, 94pp. (Romanul popular).
490. *Povestiri din mările Sudului,* tr.: Altbuch Leonhard,
     Bucharest, Editura de stat, 1949, 96pp (Romanul popular).
491. *Sete de viaţă,* Bucharest, Editura tineretului, 1949,
     40pp. (Mica bibliotecă literară 3).
492. *Ultimul match,* tr.: Emil Fulda; introduction by Mircea
     Slavu, Bucharest, Editura tineretului, 1951, 80pp.
493. *Pagini alese,* translation with preface by Petre
     Solomon, Bucharest, E.S.P.L.A., 1953, 196pp (Biblioteca
     pentru toţi).
494. *Nuvele sportive,* Bucharest, Cultură fizică şi sport,
     1954, 132pp.
495. *Fecior de lup,* tr.: Ion Constantinescu, Bucharest, Edi-
     tura Librăriei "Universala" Alcalay & Co., [n.d.] 93pp.
     (Biblioteca pentru toţi, no. 1333. Literatura americană).

RUSSIAN
496. *Polnoye sobraniye sochineni.* S literaturnoistorisheskim
ocherkom prof. P. S. Kogana, Moscow and Leningrad, ZIF,
1924-1927, twenty-two volumes in forty-one books.
> *Vol. 1.* P. S. Kogan, O Dzheke Londone (On Jack London).
> Charmian London, Zhizn Dzheka Londona (Selections
> from *The book of Jack London). Doroga (The road)*
> translated by S. G. Zaimobski. *Rasskazy (Stories).*
> 376pp.
> *Vol. 2. Book 1. Den plameneyet (Burning daylight)* tr.:
> A.V. Krivtsova and V. Zhitomirski; ed. by Yev. Lann.
> 301pp.
> *Vol. 2. Book 2. Printsessa (The red one)* tr.: Z. A.
> Vershinina. 104pp.
> *Vol. 3. Martin Eden* tr.: S. S. Zayaitski; ed. by Ye.
> Kavaleria. 365pp.
> *Vol. 4. Morskoi volk (The sea wolf)* tr.: Z. A. Ver-
> shinina. 280pp.
> *Vol. 5. Lunnaya dolina (The valley of the moon)* tr.:
> V. Stanevich and L. Brodskaya; ed. by Yev. Lann.
> 482pp.
> *Vol. 6. Malenkaya khozyaika bolshovo doma (The little
> lady of the big house)* tr.: V. O. Stanevich; ed.
> by Z. A. Vershinina. 288pp.
> *Vol. 7. Book 1. Priklyucheniye (Adventure)* tr.: N. M.
> Klechkovski. 236pp.
> *Vol. 7. Book 2. Doch snegov (A daughter of the snows)*
> tr.: V. I. Smetanich. 248pp.
> *Vol. 8. Book 1. Severnaya odisseya (The son of the
> wolf)* tr.: Ye. G. Guro and B. Ya; ed. by Yev Lann.
> 145pp.
> *Vol. 8. Book 2. Deti moroza (Children of the frost)*
> tr.: L. Brodskaya. 144pp.
> *Vol. 8. Book 3. Poteryanny lik (Lost face)* ed. of tr.:
> Yev. Lann. 115pp.
> *Vol. 9. Book 1. Smok Bellyu (Smoke Bellew)* tr.: N. F.
> Davydova, 144pp.
> *Vol. 9. Book 2. Smok i malysh (Smoke and Shorty)* tr.:
> V. N. Orechkina, 157pp.
> *Vol. 9. Book 3. Lunny lik (Moon face)* tr.: Z. A. Ver-
> shinina, 151pp.
> *Vol. 10. Book 1. Lyubov k zhizni,* ed. of translation:
> Ye. Lann, *(Love of life)* 127pp.
> *Vol. 10. Book 2. Rozhdennaya v nochi (The night born)*
> tr.: A. M. Abramova; edited by S. G. Zaimovski,
> 157pp.
> *Vol. 10. Book 3. Sila silnykh (The strength of the
> strong)* tr.: S. S. Zayaitski, 128pp.

Vol. 11. Book 1. Gollandskaya doblest (Dutch courage)
and other stories with an introduction by Charmian
London; tr.: A. V. Krivtsova and V. Zhitomirski;
edited by Yev. Lann, 108pp.
*Vol. 11. Book 2. Rasskazy rybachyevo patrulya (Tales
of the fish patrol); Pisma Kempton-Uesa (The
Kempton Wace letters). Cherri (Cherry)* ed. of tr.:
Z. Vershinina, 267pp.
*Vol. 11. Book 3. Puteshestviye na "Oslepitelnom"
(The cruise of Dazzler)* tr.: M. M. Klechkovski,
119pp.
*Vol. 12. Book 1. Kogda bogi smeyutsya (When God
laughs)* ed. of tr.: Yev. Lann, 155pp.
*Vol. 12. Book 2. Bog yego ottsov (The God of his
fathers)* tr.: Zin. Lvovski, 188pp.
Vol. 13. Book 1. Igra (The game) and *Pervobytny zver
(The abysmal brute)* tr.: N. Utkina and L. Brod-
skaya; ed. by Yev. Lann, 115pp.
Vol. 13. Book 2. Vera v cheloveka (The faith of men)
tr.: M. P. Chekhov; edited by Z. A. Vershinina,184pp.
*Vol. 13. Book 3. Cherepakhi Tasmana (The turtles of
Tasman)* tr.: Ye. G. Guro; edited by Yev. Lann, 138pp.
*Vol. 14. Book 1. Skazki yuzhnykh morei (South Sea
tales)* tr.: Ye. Utkina; edited by Yev. Lann, 141pp.
Vol. 14. Book 2. Khram gordyni (The house of pride)
tr.: A.F.V. Krivtsova; edited by Yev. Lann, 91pp.
*Vol. 14. Book 3. Na tsynovke Makaloa (On the Makaloa
mat)* tr.: S. G. Zaimovski, 148pp.
*Vol. 15. Book 1. Puteshestviye na "Snarke" (The cruise
of the Snark)* tr.: Ye. G. Guro; edited by Z. A.
Vershinina, 196pp.
Vol. 15. Book 2. Syn solntsa (A son of the sun) tr.:
M. V. Kovolenskaya, 181pp.
*Vol. 16. Myatezh na "Elsinore" (The mutiny of the
Elsinore)* tr.: M. A. Shishmareva, 328pp.
Vol. 17. Serdtsa treh (Hearts of three) tr.: N. F.
Davydova; edited by V. A. Azov, 344pp.
Vol. 18. Book 1. Do Adama (Before Adam) and *Alaya
chuma (The scarlet plague)* tr.: L. Lanskaya; edited
by Yev. Lann, 149pp.
*Vol. 18. Book 2. Mezhzvyozdny skitalets (The star
rover)* tr.: S. Zaimovski, 283pp.
Vol 19. Zov predkov (The call of the wild) tr.: M. P.
Chekhov; edited by Z. Vershinina; *Bely klyk (White
fang)* tr.: I. G. Bakhmetyev; edited by Z. Vershin-
ina, 291pp.
*Vol. 20. Book 1. Dzherri ostrovityanin (Jerry of the
islands)* tr.: A. V. Krivtsova; edited by Yev. Lann,

186pp.

Vol. 20. Book 2. Maikel brat Dzherri (Michael, brother of Jerry) tr.: L. Brodskaya; edited by Yev. Lann, 269pp.

Vol. 21. Zheleznaya pyata (The iron heel) tr.: Ye. G. Guro; edited by Z. A. Vershinina, 262pp.

Vol. 22. Book 1. Dzhon Yachmennoye zerno (John Barleycorn) tr.: V. Azov, 192pp.

Vol. 22. Book 2. Lyudi bezdny (People of the abyss) ed. of tr.: V. Azov, 183pp. [Vol. 22's subtitle in English translation reads: "with biographical sketch and critical notes by Eugeniy Kavalery."]

497. *Polnoie sobranie sochineniy* (complete collected works). Moscow, Leningrad, Zemlya y fabrica, 1929-1930, 24 vols.

    1. O Dzheke Londone (On Jack London) by P. S. Kogan. Zhizn Dzheka Londona (fragments from *The book of Jack London*) by Charmian London. *Doroga (The road),* tr.: S. G. Zaimovski, published in two parts; pt. 1, pp.1-128; pt. 2, pp.129-256.

    2. Morskoi volk (The sea wolf) and *Rasskazy rybach-yevo patrulya (Tales of the fish patrol),* ed. of tr.: Z. A. Vershinina, 1928. Published in two parts. Pt. 1, pp.1-160; pt. 2, pp.161-309. Pt. 1 reprinted in 1929.

    3. Priklyucheniye (Adventure), tr.: M. M. Klechkov-ski, 1928, 1929 published in two parts. Pt. 1, pp.1-128; pt. 2, pp.129-200.

    4. Doch snegov (A daughter of the snows), tr.: V. I. Smetanich; *Severnaya odisseya (Son of the wolf),* tr.: Ye. G. Guro and B. Ya, 1928, 1929, publish-ed in three separate parts. Pt. 1, pp.1-56, pt. 2, pp.57-184; pt. 3, pp.185-335.

    5. Smok Bellew and *Smok y malysh (Smok Bellew and Smoke and Shorty),* tr.: N. F. Davydova and V. N. Orechkina, 1928, 1929 published in two parts. Pt. 1, pp.1-160; pt. 2, pp.161-239.

    6. Igra (The game), tr.: N. Utkina and L. Brodskaya; *Pervobytny zver (The abysmal brute),* tr.: N. Utkina and L. Brodskaya; *Sila silnykh (The strength of the strong),* 1928, 1929 published in two parts. Pt. 1, pp.1-64; pt. 2, pp.65-191.

    7. Puteshestviye na "Snarke" (The cruise of the Snark), tr.: Z. A. Vershinina; *Na tsynovke Makaloa (On the Makaloa mat),* tr.: S. G. Zaimovski, 1928 1929 published in two parts. Pt. 1, pp.1-159; pt. 2, pp.161-280.

8. *Serdtsa treh (Hearts of three)*, tr.: N. F. Davydova, 1929 published in three parts. Pt. 1,
   pp.1-32; pt. 2, pp.33-160; pt. 3, pp.161-287.
9. *Dzherri ostrovityanin (Jerry of the islands)*, tr.:
   A. V. Krivtsova; *Maikel brat Dzherri (Michael,
   brother of Jerry)*, tr.: L. Brodskaya, 1928,
   1929 published in three parts. Pt. 1, pp.1-128;
   pt. 2, pp.129-288; pt. 3, pp.289-368.
10. *Syn solntsa (A son of the sun)*, tr.: M. V. Kova-
    levskaya; *Printsessa (The princess)*, tr.: Z.
    A. Vershinina, 1928, 1929 published in two parts.
    Pt. 1, pp.1-80; pt. 2, pp.81-232.
11. *Zov predkov (The call of the wild)*, tr.: Z. Ver-
    shinina; *Bely klyk (White Fang)*, tr.: Z. Vershin-
    ina; *Do Adama (Before Adam)*, tr.: L. Lanskaya,
    1928, 1929 published in three parts. Pt. 1,
    pp.1-128; pt. 2, pp.129-256; pt. 3, pp.257-320.
12. *Mezhzvyozdny skitaelts (The star rover)*, tr.: S.
    Zaimovski; *Alaya chuma (The scarlet plague)*,
    tr.: Yev. Lann; *Vechnyie formy i drugiye rass-
    kazy (On the eternity of forms and other
    stories)*, tr.: Z. Vershinina and Yev. Lann, 1928,
    1929 published in three parts. Pt. 1, pp.1-64;
    pt. 2, pp.65-192; pt. 3, pp.193-320.
13. *Martin Iden (Martin Eden)*, tr.: S. S. Zayaitski,
    1929 published in two parts. Pt. 1, pp.1-160;
    pt. 2, pp.161-311.
14. *Deti moroza (Children of the frost)*, tr.: L.
    Brodskaya; *Bog yego ottsov (The God of his fa-
    thers)*, tr.: Z. Lvovski, 1929 published in two
    parts. Pt. 1, pp.1-128; pt. 2, pp.129-272.
15. *Myatezh na "Elsinore" (The mutiny of the Elsinore)*,
    [tr. not established] 1929 published in two
    parts. Pt. 1, pp.1-128; pt. 2, pp.129-279.
16. *Puteshestviye na "Oslepitelnom" (The cruise of
    the Dazzler)*, tr.: M. M. Klechkovski; *Gol-
    landskaya doblest (Dutch courage and other
    stories)*, tr.: A. V. Krivtsova and V. Zhitomir-
    ski; *Skazki yuzhnykh morei (South Sea tales)*,
    tr.: Ye. Utkina, 1929 published in two parts.
    Pt. 1, pp.1-160; pt. 2, pp.161-296.
17. *Vera y cheloveka (The faith of men)*, tr.: M. P.
    Chekhov; *Lunny lik (Moon-face)*, tr.: Z. A.
    Vershinina, 1929 published in two parts. Pt. 1,
    pp.1-160; pt. 2, pp.161-248.
18. *Lunnaya dolina (The valley of the moon)*, tr.: V.
    Stanevich and L. Brodskaya; introduction by A.
    Belayev, 1929 published in four parts. Pt. 1,

pp.1-64; pt. 2, pp.63-224; pt. 3, pp.225-368; pt. 4, pp.369-381.

19. *Poteryanny lik (Lost face), (Lyubov k zhizni (Love of life and other stories), Khram gordyni (The house of pride),* ed. of tr.: Yev. Lann, 1929 published in two parts. Pt. 1, pp.1-128; pt. 2, pp.129-276.

20. *Den plameneyet (Burning daylight),* tr.: A. V. Krivtsova, 1929 published in two parts. Pt. 1, pp.1-128; pt. 2, pp.129-250.

21. *Rozhdennaya v nochi (The night born)* tr.: A. M. Abramova; *Kogda bogi smeyutsya (When God laughs and other stories),* tr.: Yev. Lann, 1929 published in two parts. Pt. 1, pp.1-128; pt. 2, pp.129-156.

22. *Malenkaya khozyaika bolshovo dama (The little lady of the big house),* tr.: V. O. Stanevich, ed.: Z. A. Vershinina; *Cherepakhi Tesmana (The turtles of Tasman),* tr.: Yev. Lann, 1929 published in two parts. Pt. 1, pp.1-176; pt. 2, pp.177-336. Also contains: Gobo y feya (The hobo and the fairy). Bludnyi otets (The prodigal father). Tragediya delekogo severo-zapada (Finis). Konets skazky (The end of the story).

23. *Zheleznaya pyata (The iron heel),* tr.: Z. A. Vershinina; *Lyudi bezdny (The people of the abyss),* tr.: V. A. Azov, 1929 published in three parts. Pt. 1, pp.1-144; pt. 2, pp.145-288; pt. 3, pp.289-368.

24. *Dzhon Yachmennoye zerno (John Barleycorn), Pisma Kempton-Uesu (The Kempton-Wace letters), Cheri (Cherry), Dzhek London o sebe (Jack London about himself),* no tr. given, 1930 published in two parts. Pt. 1, pp.1-112; pt. 2, pp.113-312.

498. *Sochineniia.* Per. s angl. pod. red. E. D. Kalashnikoboi. Vstupit. stat'ia F. G. Fedunova, Moscow, Goslitizdat, 1954-1956, 8 vols.

    1. *Rasskazy, 1899-1903 (Stories). Zov predkov (The call of the wild),* 1954, 638pp.

    2, *Rasskazy, 1904-1909 (Stories) Igra (The game). Lyudi bezdny (The people of the abyss)* tr.: V. Limanovskoi; ed. by T. A. Ozerskoi, 1954, 594pp.

    3. *Rasskazy, 1910-1916 (Stories). Smok Bell'iu (Smoke Bellew),* tr.: R. M. Gal'perinoi and M. E. Abkinoi, 1955, 685pp.

    4. *Morskoi volk (The sea wolf). Belyi klyk (White fang),* tr.: T. Ozerskoi, 1955, 494pp.

5. *Zheleznaya pyata (The iron heel). Martin Iden (Martin Eden)* tr.: N. V. Bannikova, 1955, 694pp.
6. *Lunnaya dolina (The valley of the moon). Liutyi zver' (The abysmal brute)*, tr.: R. M. Gal'perinoi, 1956, 567pp.
7. *Vremia ne zhdet (Burning daylight). Maikl, brat Dzherri (Michael, brother of Jerry)*, tr.: M. F. Lorie, 1956, 590pp.
8. *Malenkaya khozyaika bolshovo doma (The little lady of the big house). Serdsa treh (Hearts of three)*, 1956, 654pp.

499. *Sobranie sochineniy v chetyrnadsati tomakh (Collected works)* edited by R. M. Samarin, Moscow, Pravda, Bibl. Ogonek, 1961

1. Samarin, R. M., Dzhek London (1876-1916). *Syn Volka (The son of the wolf). Bog ego ottsov (The God of his fathers). Deti moroza (Children of the frost).* Primechaniya (Notes).
2. *Puteshestvie na "Oslepitelnom" (The cruise of the Dazzler). Doch snegov (A daughter of the snows). Zov predkov (The call of the wild).* Kratkiy slovar morskih terminov y vyrzheniy (Short vocabulary of maritime terms). Primechaniya (Notes).
3. *Lyudi bezdny (The people of the abyss). Muzhskaya vernost (The faith of men). Rasskazy rybachego patrulya (Tales of the fish patrol).*
4. *Morskoi volk (The sea-wolf). Belyi Klyk (White fang).* Kratkiy slovar morskih terminov (Short vocabulary of maritime terms). Primechaniya (Notes).
5. *Lunnolitsyi (Moon-face and other stories). Lyubov k zhizni (Love of life and other stories). Doroga (The road).* Primechaniya (Notes).
6. *Stati (Articles). Zheleznaya pyata (The iron heel). Puteshestvie na "Snarke" (The cruise of the Snark). Krazha (Theft).* Articles included are: O pisatelskoy filosofiy zhizni (On the writer's philosophy of life). Cherty literaturnogo razvitiya (The phenomena of literary evolution). "Sprut" (review of The octopus by Norris). "Foma Gordyeev" (review of Foma Gordyieff by Gorky). O sebe (Jack London about himself). Kak ya stal sotsialistom (How I became a socialist). Zolotoi mak (The golden poppy). Predislovie k sborniku "Voina klassov" (Preface to War of the classes). Chto znachit dlya menya zhizn (What life means to me). Gnil zavelas v shtate Aidaho (Something

rotten in Idaho). Revolyutsiya (Revolution).
Kratkiy slovar morskih terminov y vyrazheniy
(Short vocabulary of maritime terms). Primechaniya (Notes).
7. *Martin Eden (Martin Eden). Poteryavshiy litso
(Lost face).* Primechaniya (Notes).
8. *Vremya-ne-zhdet (Burning daylight). Kogda bogi
smeyutsa (When God laughs).* Primechaniya (Notes).
9. *Rasskazy. Yuzhnogo morya (South Sea tales). Syn
solntsa (A son of the sun). Khram gordyni (The
house of pride). Lyutyi zver (The abysmal brute).*
Kratkiy slovar morskih terminov y vyrazheniy
(Short vocabulary of maritime terms).
10. *Smok Belyu (Smoke Bellew tales). Rozhdennaya v
nochi (The night born). Sila silnyh (The strength
of the strong).*
11. *Dzhon Yachemennoe Zerno (John Barleycorn). Smiritelnaya rubashka (The star rover). Alaya chuma
(The scarlet plague).* Primechaniya (Notes).
12. *Malenkaya khozyaika bolshovo doma (The little lady
of the big house). Cherepahi Tesmana (The turtles of Tasman). Gollandskaya doblest (Dutch
courage).* Primechaniya (Notes).
13. *Dzherry - ostrovityanin (Jerry of the islands).
Maikl, brat Dzherry (Michael, brother of Jerry).
Krasnoye bozhestvo (The red one).* Primechaniya
(Notes).
14. *Na tsynovke Makaloa (On the Makaloa mat). Serdtsa
treh (Hearts of three).* Kratkaya letopis zhizni
y tvorchestva Dzheka Londona (Dates of Jack
London's life and creative activity). Primechaniya (Notes). Alfavitnyi ukazatel proizved-
eniy D. Londona | vklyuchennyh v 1-14 toma
sobraniya sochineniy [Indeses of Jack London's
works published in fourteen volumes of the Collected works].

500. *Sobraniye sochineni,* ed. by V. A. Azov and A. N. Gorlin,
Leningrad, Gosudarstvennoe Izdatelstvo, 1925-1926,
12 vols.
1. *Lunnaya dolina (The valley of the moon). S crod-
yagami (The road).* 368pp.
2. *Smiritelnaya kurtka (The star rover).* 299pp.
3. *Krasnoe solnystko (Burning daylight).* 346pp.
4. *Morskoi volk (The sea wolf).* 277pp.
5. *Martin Iden (Martin Eden).* 413pp.
6. *Zheleznaya pyata (Iron heel).* Pervyi poet (First
poet). Voina (War). Chelovek on byl (By the

turtles of Tasman). Kak argonavty v starinu (Like
Argus of the ancient times). Sumashestvie Dzhona
Harneda (The madness of John Harned). Smert
(Finis). Konets romana (The end of the story).
Mekicanets (The Mexican). 401pp.
7. *Syn solntsa (Son of the sun). Rasskazy ob okeanii
(South Sea Tales).* 336pp.
8. *Rasskazy o dalnem severe,* tr.: Ye. N. Blagobeshchenskaya, L. M. Vaisenberg, N. S. Kaufman, Yu.
A. Nelidov and B. K. Ryndy-Alekseyev. Contents:
Belaya tishina (The white silence). Syn volka
(The son of the wolf).Zhizn na postu (The men
of Forty Mile). V daliokoi strane (In a far
country). Putnik (To the man on trail). Mudrost
tropy (The wisdom of the trail). Severnaya
Odisseya (An odyssey of the north). Lyubov k
zhizni (Love of life). Nochnaya stoyanka (A
day's lodging). Puti belogo cheloveka (The white
man's way). Skazanie o Kishe (The story of
Keesh). Neozhidannoie (The unexpected). Put
lozhnykh solnts (The sun dog trail). Zakon zhizni
(The law of life). Kranitel tainy (The master of
mystery). Bolezn bezmolvnogo vozhdya (The sickness of Lone Chief). Kish syn Kisha (Keesh, the
son of Keesh). Smert' Ligeuna (The death of
Ligoun). Liga starikov (The league of the old
men). Muzhskaia vernost' (The faith of men).
Chereschur mnogo zolota (Too much gold). Tysia-
cha dyuzhin (The one thousand dozen). Batar
(Batard). V strane kontsa radugi (At the rainbow's end). Doch Avory (A daughter of the Aurora).
Gde rashodyatsya dorogi (Where the trail forks).
Zhenskoye muzhestvo (Grit of women). Jan-neras-
kayannyi (Jan, the unrepentant). Chelovek so
shramom (The man with the gash). Neizgladimoye
(Which makes men remember).
9. *Belyi klyk (White Fang). Do Adama (Before Adam).
Alaya chuma (The scarlet plague).* 346pp.
10. *Smok Bellyu. Smona y kutsyi (Smoke Bellew tales).
Golos krovi (Call of the wild).* 352pp.
11. *Rasskazy o Sandvichevykh ostrovah (On the Makaloa
mat). Kogda bogi smeyutsya (When God laughs).
Igra (The game).* 343pp.
12. *Doch snegov (Daughter of the snows). Priklyucheniya
rybachyevo patrulya (Tales of the fish patrol).*
407pp. Volume 12 also contains P. Guber, "Dzhek
London. Biograficheskii ocherk" (Jack London.
Biographical essay).

501. *Strashnyie Solomonovy ostrova*, tr.: Zin. Lvovski,
      Moscow, Univ. Bib., 1913, 196pp. Contents: Strashnyie
      Solomonvy ostrova (The terrible Solomons). Dom Mapuhi
      (The house of Mapuhi). Kitovyi us (The whale tooth).
      Mauki (Mauki).
502. *Bog yego ottsov*, tr.: Zin. Lvovski, Moscow, Univ. Bib.,
      1914, 94pp. Contents: Bog yego ottsov (The God of his
      fathers). Na severe (A daughter of the Aurora). Velikiy
      vopros (The great interrogation). Tam, gde raskhod-
      yatsya dorogi (Where the trail forks).
503. *Kak ya stal sotsialistom*, tr.: R. V. Musselyuss, Petro-
      grad, Nevskaya Tipografiya, 1918, 80pp. Contents: Kak
      ya stal sotsialistom (How I became a socialist). [Also
      translations of The question of the maximum. Wanted:
      a new law of development. A review (Contradictory
      teachers).]
504. *Na kontse radugi*, tr.: R. Tyutryumova, Moscow, Univ.
      Bib., 1918, 91pp. Contents: Na kontse radugi (At the
      rainbow's end). Krovavaya mest (Which makes men remem-
      ber). Chelovek so shramon (The man with the gash).
      Sivashka (Siwash).
505. *Povesti i rasskazy*, tr.: B. Pegelau and F. D. Putevodny,
      Moscow, Ogonyok, 1918, 32pp. Contents: Taina (The
      story of Keesh). Uschchelye zolota (All gold canyon).
506. *Put lozhnykh solnts*, tr.: N. Pusheshnikov, Moscow,
      Univ. Bib., 1918, 92pp. Contents: Put lozhnykh solnts
      (The sun-dog trail). Na stoyanke (A day's lodging).
      Buryi volk (Brown wolf). Skazaniye o Kishe (The story
      of Keesh).
507. *Rasskazy*, tr.: Zin. Lvovski, Moscow, Univ. Bib., 1918,
      98pp. Contents: Velikoye chudo (Wonder of woman).
      Yazychnik (The heathen). U cherty (Finis).
508. *Lyubov k zhizni*, tr.: N. A. Almedingen, Petrograd,
      Nachatki Znanii, 1919, 142pp. Contents: Lyubov k zhizni
      (Love of life). Potomok Mak-koya (The seed of McCoy).
      Yazychnik (The heathen). Ryshi volk (Brown wolf).
      [Dzhek London: biograficheski ocherk (Jack London: a
      biographical sketch)precedes the stories.]
509. *Poslednyaya borba*, tr.: L. Kutukova, Univ. Bib., 1919,
      96pp. Contents: Poslednyaya borba (A piece of steak).
      Derzhite kurs na zapad (Make westing), tr.: L. Kutu-
      kova; A-cho (The Chinago), tr.: M. Likiardopulo; Negore
      trus (Negore, the coward), tr.: E. Pimenova.
510. *Povesti i rasskazy*, tr.: B. Pegelau and F. D. Putevodny,
      Moscow, Ogonyok, 1919, 64pp. Contents: Na abordash (To
      repel boarders). Sever i yug (Brown wolf). Malenkaya
      samarityanka (The hobo and the fairy).
511. *Put moroznykh solnts*, tr.: N. Pusheshnikov, edited by

Ye. Zamyatin, Petrograd, Gosizdat., 1920, 102pp. Contents: Put moroznykh solnts (The sun dog trail). Na stoyanke (A day's lodging). Buryi volk (Brown wolf). Skazaniye o Kishe (The story of Keesh). [This volume contains the same bibliography as that found in *Lyubov k zhizni i drugiye rasskazy (1922)*.]

512. *Golos krovi i drugiye rasskazy*, tr.: Zin. Lvovski et al., Moscow, Gosizdat., 1922, 222pp. Part of his *Sobraniye sochineni*. Contents: Golos krovi (The call of the wild). Konets rasskaza (The end of the story). Dvoistvennaya lichnost (When the world was young). Obychai belogo cheloveka (The white man's way). Mest (Which makes men remember). Zhan neraskayavshisya (Jan, the unrepentant).

513. *Kak ya stal sotsialistom*, tr.: P. Okhrimenko, Moscow and Leningrad, Gosizdat, 1922, 84pp. [Translations of How I became a socialist. Goliah. The Golden poppy. The shrinkage of the planet. The house beautiful. Foma Gordyeeff. What life means to me.]

514. *Lyubov k zhizni i drugiye rasskazy*, tr.: Ye. Broido, edited by Yev. Zamyatim, Petrograd, Vsemir. Lit., 1922, 124pp. Contents: Lyubov k zhizni (Love of life). Neozhidannoe (The unexpected). Negor-trus (Negore, the coward). Puti belogo cheloveka (The white man's way). Bibliography of London's works in Russian translation.

515. *Byvalyi* and *Zolotaya zorka*, tr.: S. Tsederbaum and B. Tsetlin, Moscow and Petrograd, Gosizdat., 1923, 230pp. Contents: Smoke Bellew tales. Flush of gold.

516. *Lunny lik*, tr.: Ye. Broido, Moscow and Petrograd, Gosizdat., 1923, 96pp. Contents: Lunny lik (Moon-face). Iz rasskazov ukrotitelya leopardov (The leopard man's story). Bytovyie shtrihi (Local color). Liubitelskiy vecher (Amateur night). Nos dlya korolya (A nose for the king). Interesnyi otryvok (A curious fragment).

517. *Muzhskaya vernost*, tr.: V. Koshevich, Moscow and Petrograd, Gosizdat., 1923, 96pp. Contents: Muzhskaya vernost (The faith of men). Guiperboreiskoie poilo (A hyperborean brew). Istoriya Dzhysy Uk (The story of Jees-Uck).

518. *Put lozhnykh solnts*, Moscow and Petrograd, Gosizdat., 1923, 88pp. Contents: Put lozhnykh solnts (The sun-dog trail). Na stoyanke (A day's lodging). Buryi volk (Brown wolf). Skazaniye o Kishe (The story of Keesh).

519. *Sila silnykh*, tr.: F. Nyuton, edited with a preface by A. N. Gorlin, Moscow and Leningrad, Gosizdat., 1923, 96pp. Contents: Sila silnykh (The strength of the strong). Mechta Debsa (The dream of Debs). Dzhonni zabastoval (The apostate).

520. *Strashnyie Solomonovy ostrova*, tr.: Zin Lvovski, Moscow and Petrograd, Gosizdat., 1923, 104pp. Contents are the

same as the same title published in 1913.

521. *Velikoye chudo,* tr.: Zin Lvovski, Moscow and Petrograd, Gosizdat., 1923, 97pp. Contents: Velikoye chudo (Wonder of woman). Yazychnik (The heathen). U cherty (Finis).

522. *Chelovek on byl,* tr.: V. Aleksandrov, edited by V. A. Azov, Moscow and Leningrad, Kniga, 1924, 230pp. Contents: Chelovek by byl (By the turtles of Tasman). Krasnyi bog (The red one). Bludnyi otets (The prodigal father). Brodyaga i feya (The hobo and the fairy). Nakhalka (The hussy). Kak argonavty v starinu (Like Argus of the ancient times). Vechnost form (The eternity of forms). Rasskaz slaboumnogo (Told in the drooling ward). Printesessa (The princess). Smert (Finis).

523. *Ischeznoveniye Markusa O'Braiyena,* tr.: Gart. Mezhrabpom, Moscow and Berlin, 1924, 63pp. Contents: Ischeznoveniye Markusa O'Braiyena (The passing of Marcus O'Brien). Mudrost Porporteka (The wit of Porportuk).

524. *Kulo-prokazhonnyi,* tr.: F. D. Gardt, Moscow, Gosudarstvennaya Tipografiya v Ryazani, 1924, 159pp. Contents: Kulo-prokazhonnyi (Koolau, the leper). Proshekai Dzhek! (Good-by, Jack!). Sudya iz Kona (The sheriff of Kona). Aloha oe (Aloha oe). Dom gordosti (The house of pride).

525. *Meksikanets,* V. A. Azov, ed. of translation, Leningrad, Atenei, 1924, 213pp. Contents: Meksikanets (The Mexican). Privilegiya somneniya (The benefit of the doubt). Voina (War). Puchki muskulov (Bunches of knuckles). Na palube (Under the deck awnings). Kogda mir byl eshche molod (When the world was young). Pervyi poet (The first poet). Konets romana (The end of the story).

526. *Neozhidannoye,* tr.: A. M. Karnaukhova, Leningrad, Mysl, 1924, 165pp. Contents: Neozhidannoye (The unexpected). Cherepahi Tasmana (By the turtles of Tasman). Sluchainyi priyut (A day's lodging). Ryzhiy volk (Brown wolf). Roshdennaya nochyu (The night born). Formy vechny (The eternity of forms). Brodyaga i feya (The hobo and the fairy). V dome dla slaboumnyh (Told in the drooling ward).

527. *Pakhar morya,* tr.: S. Zaimovski, Petrograd and Moscow, Mol. Gvard., 1924, 144pp. Contents: Pakhar morya (The sea-farmer). Po tu storonu vyemki (South of the slot). Sila silnykh (The strength of the strong). Vrag chelovechestva (The enemy of all the world). Besprimernoe nashestvie (The unparalleled invasion). Semuel (Samuel).

528. *Porucheniye,* tr.: N. M. Tsymovich, Leningrad and Moscow, Mysl, 1924, 178pp; ibid., Mysl, 1926, 183pp. Contents: Porucheniye (Trust). Shutka Porportuka (The wit of Porportuk). Poteryannoe litso (Lost face). Zolotaya

Zorka (Flush of gold). Ischeznovenie Matkusa O'Braiena
(The passing of Marcus O'Brien). Koster (To build a
fire). Spot (That spot). Kulaki (Bunches of knuckles).
Pod palubnym tentom (Under the deck awnings).
Krylatyi shantash (Winged blackmail).

529. *Rasskazy o smelchakakha,* tr.: V. A. Azov and A. N. Gorlin, Leningrad, Gosizdat., 1924, 116pp. Contents: "Dlya
khrabrosti" (Dutch courage). Podvig Buba (The lost
poacher). Bérega Sakramento (The banks of the Sacramento).
V Iokagamskoi buhte (In Yeddo Bay). Kris Farrington,
matros pervoy staty (Chris Farrington, able seaman).
Priklyuchenie v vozdushnom more (Adventure in the upper
sea).Priklyuchenie (To repel boarders). Lysogolovyi
(Bald face). Te, chye remeslozhit (Whose business is to
live.

530. *Revolyutsiya,* Leningrad, Mysl, 1924, 1925, 155pp. Contents: Revolyutsiya (Revolution). Goliaf (Goliah).
Znachenie dollarov (The dignity of dollars). Zolotye
maki (The golden poppy). Zemnoy shar umenshayetsa (The
shrinkage of the planet). Ohotniki za zolotom na Severe
(The gold hunters of the North). Kak ya smotryu na
zhizn (What life means to me).

531. *Sovremennyi Argonavt,* Moscow and Berlin, Mezhrabpom and
Mospoligraf, 1924, 52pp. Contents: Sovremennyi Argo-
navt (Like Argus of the ancient times). Bolezn vozhdyz
Lon (The sickness of Lone Chief).

532. *Torzhestvo pravosudiya,* tr.: S. G. Zaimovski; introduction by P. S. Kogan, Moscow and Leningrad, Mol. Gvard.,
1924, 155pp. Contents: Torzhestvo pravosudiya (The
benefit of the doubt). Pomeshatelstvo Dzhona Harneda
(The madness of John Harned). Rozhdennaia nochyu (The
night born). Peshchernyi yanki (When the world was
young). Krylatyi shantazh (Winged blackmail). Voina
(War). Pod palubnym tentom (Under the deck awnings).
M-ss Setlif (To kill a man).

533. *Yukonskiye rasskazy,* tr.: M. Matveyeva, Moscow, Prometei,
1924, 119pp. Contents: Puteshestvie po Dalnemu Severu
(Trust). Ischeznovenie Markusa O'Braien (The passing of
Marcus O'Brien). Spot (That spot). Odurachennyi (Lost
face). "Frensis Speit" (The Francis Spaight). Kitaets
(The Chinago). "Ruca Toma Diksena" (A curious fragment).

534. *Ischeznoveniye Markusa O'Braiyena,* Leningrad, Seyatel,
1925, 96pp. Contents: Ischeznoveniye Markusa O'Braiyena
(The passing of Marcu O'Brien). Kulaki (Bunches of
knuckles). Zagadka (The great interrogation). Doch
polyarnoi strany (A daughter of the Aurora). Rozhdennaya nochyu (The night born).

535. *Kusok myasa,* tr.: Zin. Lvovski, Leningrad, Seyatel,

1925, 48pp. Contents: Kusok myasa (A piece of steak). Mudrost In-Chin-Go (A nose for the king). Semper idem.

536. *Neozhidannoye*, Leningrad, Seyatel, 1925, 48pp. Contents: Neozhidannoye (The unexpected). Na perekrestke (Where the trail forks).

537. *Podvig lyubvi*, tr.: V. I. Smetanich, Leningrad, Seyatel, 1925, 93pp. Contents: Podvig lyubvi (Wonder of woman). Oshibka mirozdaniya (The mistake of creation).

538. *Proshchai, Dzhek*, tr.: M. Matveyeva et al., Leningrad, Seyatel, 1925, 48pp. Contents: Proshchai, Dzhek (Good-by, Jack). Sherif Kony (The sheriff of Kona). Frensis Speit (The Francis Spaight).

539. *Proshchai, Dzhek*, no. tr. given, Moscow, Novaya Moskva, 1925, 89pp. Contents: Proshchai, Dzhek (Good-by, Jack). Dom gordosty (The house of pride). Kulau prokazhenyi (Koolau, the leper).

540. *Rasskazy ob Amerikanskoi rabochei molodyozhi*, Moscow, Gudok, 1925, 31pp. Contents: Podrostok (The apostate). Kris Farrington, matros pervoy staty (Chris Farrington, able seaman).

541. *Shutka Porportuka*, tr.: N. M. Tsymovich, Leningrad, Seyatel, 1925, 96pp. Contents: Shutka Porportuka (The wit of Porportuk). Zolotaya Zorba (Flush of gold). Giperboreyski napitok (A hyperborean brew). Svadba Lit-Lit (The marriage of Lit-Lit).

542. *Sluchainy priyut*, tr.: A. M. Karnaukhova, Leningrad, Seyatel, 1925, 47pp. Contents: Sluchainy priyut (A day's lodging). Ryzhyi volk (Brown wolf).

543. *Soperniki*, tr.: Zin. Lvovski, Leningrad, Seyatel, 1925, 48pp. Contents: Soperniki (The shadow and the flash). Bludyni otets (The prodigal father).

544. *Vlastelin juzhnykh morei*, tr.: A. Movshenson, Leningrad and Moscow, Novella, 1925, 218pp. Contents: Vlastelin yuzhnykh morei (A son of the sun). Velichaishaya pobeda nad Alaziem Pankbernom (The proud goat of Aloysius Pankburn). Cherti na Fuatino (The devils of Fuatino). Shutniki na Novom Gibbone (The jokers of New Gibbon). Nebolshie schety s Svizinom Hollom (A little account with Swithin Hall). Noch v Goboto (A Goboto night). "Perya solntsa" (The feathers of the sun). Zhemchug Parleya (The pearls of Parlay).

545. *Zakon belovo cheloveka*, Moscow, Gosudarstvenny Institut Zhurnalistiki, 1925, 84pp. Contents: Zakon belovo cheloveka (The white man's way). Zhena korolya (The wife of a king). Severnaya Odisseya (An odyssey of the north).

546. *Dom Mapui*, tr.: Zin. Lvovski, Leningrad, Seyatel, 1926, 48pp. Contents: Dom Mapui (The house of Mapuhi). Jah! Jah! Jah! (Yah! Yah! Yah!).

547. *Dvoistvennaya lichnost y dr. rasskazy*, tr.: Zin. Lvov-ski, Leningrad, Seyatel, 1926, 48pp. Contents: Dvois-tvennaya lichnost (When the world was young). Vo imya idei (The Mexican). Na Zapad (Make westing).
548. *Malenkaya oshibka*, tr.: Zin. Lvovski, Leningrad, Sey-atel, 1926, 75pp. Contents: Malenkaya oshibka (The Chinago). Mauki (Mauki). Izmennik (The apostate).
549. *Nakazanny sudya*, Moscow and Leningrad, ZIF, 1926, 32pp. Contents: Nakazanny sudya (The benefit of the doubt). Krylatyi shantazh (Winged blackmail).
550. *Po tu storonu cherty*, Moscow and Leningrad, Kras. Prolet., 1926, 59pp.; ibid., 1927, 60pp. Contents: Po tu storonu cherty (South of the slot). Poslednyaya borba (A piece of steak).
551. *Priboi Kanaka*, tr.: A. V. Luchinskaya and M. L. Kutu-kova, Moscow and Leningrad, Gosizdat., 1926, 60pp. Contents: Priboi Kanaka (The Kanaka surf). Derzhite kurs na zapad (Make westing).
552. *Rasskazy*, no tr. given, foreword by A. Ts., Moscow, Gudok, 1962, 61pp. Contents: Kitaets A-Cho (The Chinago). Meksikanets (The Mexican).
553. *Rasskazy o dalnem severe*, tr.: Ye. N. Blagobeshchens-kaya, L. M. Vaisenberg, N. S. Kaufman, Yu. A. Nelidov and B. K. Ryndy-Alekseyev, Moscow and Leningrad, Gosizdat., 1926, 420pp.
554. *Syn volka*, tr.: E. K. Pimenova, Leningrad, Seyatel, 1926, 96pp. Contents: Syn volka (The son of the wolf). Balaya tishina (The white silence). Zhiteli Forty mail (The men of Forty Mile). V dalekoi strane (In a far country). Prava svyashchennika (The priestly preroga-tive).
555. *Vstrecha*, Moscow, Biblioteka Zhurnala Ogonyok, 1926, 48pp. Contents: Vstrecha (A day's lodging). Rasskaz o Kishe (The story of Keesh). Vse tot zhe (Semper idem).
556. *Berega Sakramento*, Moscow and Leningrad, Gosizdat., 1927, 77pp. Contents: Berega Sakramento (The banks of the Sacramento). Cris Farrington, matros (Chris Farring-ton, able seaman). Lysologovyi (Bald face). Sever i yug (Brown wolf). Tayna Malenkogo Kisha (The story of Keesh).
557. *Goliaf, rasskazy*, Moscow and Leningrad, Gosizdat., 1927, 64pp. Contents: Goliaf (Goliath). Zolotyie maki (The golden poppy).
558. *Severnaya Odisseya*, tr.: Ye. N. Blagoveshchenskaya, L. M. Vaisenberg and N. S. Kaufman, Moscow and Lenin-grad, Gosizdat., 1927, 420pp. Contents: Belaya tishina (The white silence). Syn volka (The son of the wolf). Zhizn na postu (The men of Forty Mile). V dalekoi strane

(In a far country). Putnik (To the man on trail).
Mudrost tropy (The wisdom of the trail). Severnaya
odisseya (An odyssey of the north). Lyubov k zhizni
(Love of life). Nochnaya stoyanka (A day's lodging).
Puti belogo cheloveka (The white man's way). Skazanie
o Kishe (The story of Keesh). Neozhidannoye (The unexpected). Put lozhnyk solnts (The sun-dog trail).
Zakon zhizni (The law of life). Kranitel tainy (The
master of mystery). Bolezn bezmolvnogo vozhdya (The
sickness of Lone Chief). Kish, syn Kisha (Keesh, the
son of Keesh). Smert Ligeuna (The death of Ligoun).
Liga starikov (The league of the old men). Muzhskaya
vernost (The faith of men). Chereschur mnogo zolota
(Too much gold). Tysyacha dyuzhyn (The one thousand
dozen). Batar (Batard). V kontse radugi (At the rainbow's end). Doch Avrory (A daughter of the Aurora).
Gde raskhodyatsa dorogi (Where the trail forks). Zhenskoye muzhestvo (The scorn of women). Jan-neraska-
yanni (Jan, the unrepentant). Chelovek so shramom (The
man with the gash). Neizgladimoe (Which makes men remember).

559. *Sila zhenshchiny,* tr.: Z. Lvovski, Moscow and Leningrad, Gosizdat., 1927, 94pp. Contents: Sila zhenshchiny (Grit of women). Perezhitok pliotsenovoi epohi
(A relic of the Pliocene). Semper idem. Silnoie sredstvo (Created he them). Skvernaya zhenshchina (A
wicked woman).

560. *Chelovek so shramom,* Moscow, Ts. K. S. T., 1928, 112pp.
Contents: Chelovek so shramom (The man with the gash).
Veliki vopros (The great interrogation). Sila Zhenshchiny (The scorn of women). Zaklinanie duhov (The
master of mystery). Zhitely solnechnoi strany (The sunlanders). Nam Bok Lzhets (Nam Bok, the unveracious).
Zamuzhestvo Lit-Lit (The marriage of Lit-Lit)·

561. *Rasskazy,* ed. of translation, V. Stenich; foreword by
N. Rykova, Moscow and Leningrad, Mol. Gvard., 1932,
202pp. Contents: Meksikanets (The Mexican). Izmennik
(The apostate). Chinago (The Chinago). Lyubov k zhizni
(Love of life). Poruchenie (Trust). Skazanie o Kishe
(The story of Keesh). Spot (That spot). Volk (Brown
wolf). Yazychnik (The heathen). Perezhitok doistori-
cheskoy epohi (A relic of the Pliocene).

562. *Rasskazy,* Moscow, Goslitizdat., 1935, 60pp. Contents:
Buntar (The apostate). Lyubov k zhizni (Love of life).

563. *Rasskazy,* ed. of translation, D. M. Gorfinkel, Lenin-
grad, Mol. Gvard., 1935, 288pp. Contents: Zaitsy
(Holding her down). Za reshotkoy (The pen). Meksikanets
(The Mexican). Kusok myasa (A piece of steak). Izmennik

(The apostate). Dlya khrabrosty (Dutch courage). Na
beregah Sakramento (The banks of the Sacramento). Priklyuchenie v vozdushnom more (An adventure on the upper
sea). Kris Farrington, matros pervoi stati (Chris Farrington, able seaman). Lyubov k zhizni (Love of life).
Zhenskoe muzhestvo (Wonder of woman). Gde raskhodyatsa
dorogi (Where the trail forks). Khranitel tayny (The
master of mystery). Skazanie o Kishe (The story of
Keesh). Severnaya Odisseya (An odyssey of the north).
Kulau-prokazhennyi (Koolau, the leper). Shinago (The
Chinago). Dom Mapui (The house of Mapuhi).

564. *Severnyie povesti*, Moscow, Goslitizdat., 1935, 358pp.
Contents: Bely klyk (White fang). Lyubov k zhizni
(Love of life). Severnaya odisseya (An odyssey of the
north). Odnodnewnaya stoyanka (A day's lodging). Doch
Avrory (A daughter of the Aurora). Beloye bezmolvie
(The white silence). Za zdorovie togo, kto v puti (To
the man on trail). U kontsa radugi (At the rainbow's
end). Rasskaz pro Kisha (The story of Keesh). Kish, syn
Kisha (Keesh, the son of Keesh). Zakon zhizni (The law
of life). Stroptivyi Yan (Jan, the unrepentant).

565. *Rasskazy*, ed. of translation, D. M. Gorfinkel, Leningrad, Mol. Gvard., 1936, 228pp.

566. *Rasskazy*, selected and adapted by O. Reznik, with a
foreword by the translator, Moscow, Goslitizdat., 1937,
64pp. Contents: Lyubov k zhirni (Love of life). Rasskaz
pro Kisha (The story of Keesh). Shinago (The Chinago).

567. *Rasskazy*, ed. of translation, D. M. Gorfinkel, Moscow,
Goslitizdat., 1937, 422pp. Contents: Zaitsy (Holding
her down). Za reshotkoy (The pen). Druzheskiy zavtrak
(Just meat). Kusok myasa (A piece of steak). Meksikanets
(The Mexican). Izmennik (The apostate). Priklyuchenie
v vozdushnom more (An adventure in the upper sea). Na
beregah Sakramento (The banks of the Sacramento). "Dlya
khrabrosty" (Dutch courage). Kris Farrington, matros
pervoi stati (Chris Farrington, able seaman). Lyubov
k zhizni (Love of life). Tysyacha dyuzhyn (The one
thousand dozen). Doch Avrory (A daughter of the Aurora).
Gde raskhodyatsya dorogi (Where the trail forks). Severnaya Odisseya (An odyssey of the north). Zhenskoye
muzhestvo (The scorn of women). Skazanie o Kishe (The
story of Keesh). Khranitel tayny (The master of mystery).
Puti belogo cheloveka (The white man's way). Shinago
(The Chinago). Slezy A-Kima (The tears of Ah Kim). Chun-
Ah-Chun (Chun Ah Chun). Kulau-prokazhennyi (Koolau, the
leper). Ditya morya (The water baby). Dom Mapui (The
house of Mapuhi).

568. *Rasskazy*, Moscow and Leningrad, Detizdat., 1938, 88pp.

Contents: Predanie o Kishe (The story of Keesh). Volk
Brown wolf). Kris Farrington, matros pervoi stati (Chris
Farrington, able seaman). Na beregah Sakramento (The
banks of the Sacramento). Dzhonni zabastoval (The
apostate.

569. *Rasskazy*, tr.: D. M. Gorfinkel, Moscow and Leningrad,
Detizdat., 1939, 296pp. Contents: Zaitsy (Holding her
down). Kusok myasa (A piece of steak). Mexsikanets
(The Mexican). Izmennik (The apostate). Na beregah
Sakramento (The banks of the Sacramento). "Dlya khrabrosty" (Dutch courage). Kris Farrington, matros pervoi
stati (Chris Farrington, able seaman). Volk (Brown
wolf). Lyubov k zhizni (Love of life). Doch Avrory (A
daughter of the Aurora). Severnaya Odisseya (An odyssey
of the north). Zhenskoye muzhestvo (The scorn of women).
Predanie o Kishe (The story of Keesh). Khranitel tayny
(The master of mystery). Puti belogo cheloveka (The
white man's way). Shinago (Chinago). Dom Mapui (The
house of Mapuhi).

570. *Rasskazy*, ed. by V. S. Valdman, Leningrad, Leningrad-
snaye gazetnozhurnalnoye izdatelstvo, 1948, 520pp.
Contents: Meksikanets (The Mexican). "Kitaeza" (The
Chinago). Kulau-prokazhenni (Koolau the leper). Polza
somneniy (The benefit of the doubt). Uleit cheloveka
(To kill a man). Mauki. Severnaya Odisseya (An odyssey
of the north). Chelovek so shramom (The man with the
gash). Tysyacha dyuzhyn (The one thousand dozen). Lyubov
k zhizni (Love of life). Beloye bezmolvie (The white
silence). Zolotoy kenon (All gold canyon). Dom Mapui
(The house of Mapuhi). Skazanie o Kishe (The story of
Keesh). Zakon zhizni (The law of life). Veliki kudesnik
(The master of mystery). Morskoi fermer (The sea farmer).
Volk (Brown wolf). "Gollandskaya doblest" (Dutch cour-
age). Na beregah Sakramento (The banks of the Sacram-
mento). Kris Ferrington, matros pervoi stati (Chris
Farrington, able seaman). Otbityi abordazh (To repel
boarders). Zapah myasa (The taste of the meat). Myaso
(The meat). Malenki chelovechek (The little man).
Sostyazanie (The race for number three). Oshilka miroz-
daniya (The mistake of creation). Podvig zhenshchiny
(Wonder of woman).

571. *Rasskazy*, Moscow and Leningrad, Detgiz, 1948, 148pp.
Contents: Jack London (Foreword) by M. Lorie. Lyubov k
zhizni (Love of life) tr.: L. Kislova. Skazanie o Kishe
(The story of Keesh) tr.: M. Bogoslovskaya. Otstupnik
(The apostate) tr.: Z. Gan. Na beregah Sakramento (The
banks of the Sacramento) tr.: M. Bogoslovskaya. Buryi
volk (Brown wolf) tr.: M. Bogoslovskaya. Meksikanets

(The Mexican) tr.: N. Man.
572. *Rasskazy*, Riga, Latgosizdat, 1950, 488pp. Contents:
Beloye bezmolvie (The white silence). Severnaya Odisseya
(An odyssey of the north). Chelovek so shramom (The man
with the gash). Stroptivyi Yan (Jan, the unrepentant).
"Stsapali" (Pinched). U kontsa radugi (At the rainbow's
end). Tysyacha dyuzhyn (The one thousand dozen). Batar
(Batard). Mechenyi (That spot). Koster (To build a
fire). Lyubov k zhizni (Love of life). Odnodnevnaya stoyanka (A day's lodging). Neozhidannoye (The unexpected).
Finis. Zakan zhizni (The law of life). Veliki kudesnik
(The master of mystery). Kish, syn Kisha (Keesh, the son
of Keesh). Smert Liguna (The death of Ligoun). Zolotoy
kenon (All gold canyon). "Kitaeza" (The Chinago). Slezy
a Kima (The tears of Ah Kim). Meksikanets (The Mexican).
Otstupnik (The apostate). Polza somneniy (The benefit
of the doubt). Semuel (Samuel). Morskoy fermer (The sea
farmer). Dom Mapui (The house of Mapuhi). Zub cashalota
(The whale tooth). Mauki. Kulau-prokazhennyi (Koolau,
the leper). Dzhek London (1876-1916) (On Jack London).
573. *Rasskazy*, Petrozavodsk, Gos. izd. Karelo-fin. SSR, 1950,
368pp. (Cyrillic rather than Latin alphabet used). Contents: Meksikanets (The Mexican). Kitaeza (The Chinago).
Mauki. Polza somneni (The benefit of the doubt). Ubit
cheloveka (To kill a man). Odnodnevnaya stoyanka (A
day's lodging). Neozhidannoe (The unexpected). Stroptivyi Yan (Jan, the unrepentant). Zakon zhizni (The law
of life). Veliki kudesnik (The master of mystery).
Skazanie o Kishe (The story of Keesh). Lyubov k zhizni
(Love of life). Beloye bezmolvie (The white silence).
Severnaya Odisseya (An odyssey of the north). Zolotoy
kenon (All gold canyon). Dom Mapui (The house of Mapuhi).
Volk (Brown wolf). Na beregah Sakramento (On the banks
of the Sacramento). Zapah myasa (The taste of the meat).
Myaso (The meat). Malenkiy chelovechek (The little man).
Sostyazanie (The race for number three).
574. *Rasskazy y ocherki*, Moscow, Goslitizdat, 1950, 176pp.
Contents: Dzhek London by A. Mironova. Lyubov k zhizni
(Love of life) tr.: K. Kislovay. Meksikanets (The Mex-
ican) tr.: N. Man. A-Cho (The Chinago) tr.: V. Kurella.
Otstupnik (The apostate) tr.: N. Gan. "Stsapali"
("Pinched") tr.: S. G. Zaimovski. Polza somneniya (The
benefit of the doubt) tr.: S. G. Zaimovski. Iz knigi
ocherkov "Lyudi bezdny" (Selection from *The people of
the abyss*) tr.: V. Limanovskaya.
575. *Rasskazy*, Moscow, Goslitizdat, 1952, 108pp. Contents:
Dzhek London (On Jack London) by N. Khutsishvili.
Lyubov k zhizni (Love of life). Beloye bezmolvie (The

white silence). Za teh, kto v puti! (To the man on
trail). Muzhestvo zhenshchiny (Grit of woman). Konets
skazki (The end of the story). Buryi volk (Brown wolf).
Kusok myasa (A piece of steak). Ubit cheloveka (To kill
a man). Meksikanets (The Mexican).

576. *Rasskazy*, Moscow, Mosc. rabochiy, 1953, 200pp. Con-
tents: Za tek, kto v puti! (To the man on trail).
Beloye bezmolvie (The white silence). Muzhestvo zhen-
shchiny (Grit of woman). Kusok myasa (A piece of steak).
Mechenyi (That spot). Tysyacha dyuzhin (The one thou-
sand dozen). Na beregah Sakremento (The banks of the
Sacramento). Lyubov k zhizni (Love of life). Buryi volk
(Brown wolf). Otstupnik (The apostate). Veliki kudesnik
(The master of mystery). Meksikanets (The Mexican).
Dzhek London (On Jack London) by A. Mironova.

577. *Povesti i rasskazy*, Sverdlovsk, Kn. izd., 1955, 464pp.
Contents: Povesti. Zov predkov (The call of the wild).
Igra (The game). Rasskazy. Lyubov k zhizni (Love of
life). Beloye bezmolvie (The white silence). Na Sors-
kovay Mile (The men of Forty Mile). Severnaya Odisseya
(An odyssey of the north). Muzhestvo zhenshchiny (Grit
of woman). Tysyacha dyuzhin (The one thousand dozen).
Zolotoye dno (All gold canyon). Mestuyi colorit (Local
color). Na beregah Sakramento (The banks of the Sac-
ramento). Buryi volk (Brown wolf). Mechenyi (That spot).
Skazanie o Kishe (The story of Keesh). Odnodnevnaya
stoyanka (A day's lodging). Giperboreiskiy napitok (A
hyperborean brew). Nam-Bok-lzhets (Nam-Bok the unveracious). Dom Mapui (The house of Mapuhi). Liga starikov
(The league of the old men). Otstupnik (The apostate).
Kusok myasa (A piece of steak). "Stsapali" ("Pinched").
"Bysci" ("Bulls"). "Priznanie" (Confession). Kartinki
(Pictures).

578. *Rasskazy*, Minsk, Uchpedgiz, BSSR, 1955, 397pp. Contents:
Beloye bezmolvie (The white silence). Severnaya Odis-
seya (An odyssey of the north). Muzhestvo zhenshchiny
(Grit of woman). Chelovek so shramom (The man with the
gash). Stropbivyi Ian (Jan, the unrepentant). "Stsapali"
("Pinched"). Tysyacha dyuzhyn (The one thousand dozen).
Batar (Batard). Koster (To build a fire). Lyubov k
zhizni (Love of life). Odnodnevnaya stoyanka (A day's
lodging). Neozhidannoe (The unexpected). Finis. Mestnyi
kolorit (Local color). Zolotoi kanon (All gold canyon).
"Kitaeza" (The Chinago). Slezy A Kima (The tears of Ah
Kim). Otstupnik (The apostate). Polza somneniy (The
benefit of the doubt). Semuel (Samuel). Morskoy fermer
(The sea farmer). Dom Mapui (The house of Mapuhi).
Mechenyi (That spot). Zakon zhizni (The law of life).

Veliki kudesnik (The master of mystery). Kish, syn Kisha
(Keesh, the son of Keesh). Meksikanets (The Mexican).
Kusok myasa (A piece of steak). Mauki. Kulau-prokazhennyi (Koolau, the leper). Pod palulnym tentom (Under
the deck awnings). Lyulapytnyi otryvok (A curious
fragment). Dzhek London (On Jack London).
579. *Rasskazy*, Moscow, Goslitizdat, 1956, 527pp. Reprinted
in 1957. Contents: Za teh, kto v puti! (To the man on
trail). Beloye bezmolvie (The white silence). Syn volka
(The son of the wolf). Na Sorokovoy Mile (The men of
Forty Mile). V dalekom krayu (In a far country). Zhena
korolya (The wife of a king). Muzhestvo zhenshchiny
(Grit of woman). Doch severnogo siyaniya (A daughter of
the Aurora). Zhenskoye prezrenie (The scorn of women).
Koster (To build a fire). Nam-Bok-lzhets (Nam-Bok, the
unveracious). Veliki kudesnik (The master of mystery).
Liga starikov (The league of old men). Tysyacha dyuzhyn
(The one thousand dozen). Skazanie o Kishe (The story
of Keesh). Na beregah Sakramento (The banks of the
Sacramento). Lyubov k zhizni (Love of life). Tropoy
lozhnyh solnts (The sun-dog trail). Buryi volk (Brown
wolf). Otstupnik (The apostate). Odnodnevnaya stoyanka
(A day's lodging). Dom Mapui (The house of Mapuhi). Pod
palulnym tentom (Under the deck awnings). Ubit cheloveka
(To kill a man). Syn solntsa (A son of the sun). Buynyi
harakter Aloiziya Penkberna (The proud goat of Aloysius
Pankburn). Rozhdennaya v nochi (The night born). Meksikanets (The Mexican). Dyavoly na Fuatino (The devils of
Fuatino). Malenkiy schet Suizinu Hollu (A little
account with Swithin Hall). Zhemchug Parleya (The pearls
of Parlay). Konets skazki (The end of the story). Bes-
styzhaya (The hussy). Priboi Kanaka (The Kanaka surf).
Kak argonavty v starinu (Like Argus of the ancient
times). Posleslovie (Postscript) by P. Omilyanchuk.

SPANISH
580. *El mexicano*, tr.: Armando Bazán, Buenos Aires, Ediciones
Siglo Veinte, 1946, 187pp. (Colección La rosa de los
vientos). Contents: El mexicano (The Mexican). El
poderio de los fuertes (The strength of the strong).
Samuel (Samuel). El ídolo rojo (The red one).
581. *Renunciación! Revista literaria: novelas y cuentos*, no.
1, 640 (Oct. 14, 1962), 39pp. Contents: Renunciación,
(The story of Jees Uck). La fe de los hombres (Faith
of men). La tunanta (The hussy). La fuerza de los
fuertes (The strength of the strong).

SWEDISH

582. The *Samlade skrifter av Jack London* was published in
Stockholm by Bohlin. Volumes 1-7 appeared in 1917; volumes 8-15 in 1918; volumes 16-23 in 1919; volumes 24-
30 in 1920.

1. *Vargens son. Skildringar fran Polartrakterna*, tr.:
M. Drangel, 215pp. *(The son of the wolf)*. Also
contains: "Jack London av honom själv," pp.3-13.

2. *Hans fäders gud och andra berättelser fran Klondyke*, tr.: M. Drangel, 220pp. *(God of his
fathers)*.

3. *Snölandets dotter*, tr.: M. Drangel, 349pp. *(Daughter of the snows)*.

4. *Pa kryss med "Blixten"*, tr.: Ernst Lundquist,
149pp. and *Fiskepatrullens* berättelser, tr.:
E. Lundquist, 117pp. *(Cruise of Dazzler. Tales
of the fish patrol)*.

5. *Skriet fran vildmarken*, tr.: M. Drangel, 133pp.
and *Varghunden*, tr.: M. Drangel, 297pp. *(The
call of the wild. White Fang)*.

6. *Avgrundens folk*, tr.: M. Drangel, 260pp. Reproduces
"Förord av de Engelska utgivarna," pp.5-6.
(People of the abyss. Review from T.P.'s weekly,
November 14, 1902.)

7. *Kungen av Klondyke*, tr.: Algot Sandberg, 366pp.
(Burning daylight).

8. *Järnhälen*, tr.: M. Drangel, 349 pp. *(The iron heel)*.

9. *Martin Eden*, tr.: A. Sandberg, 460pp. *(Martin
Eden)*.

10. *Köldens barn*, tr.: E. Lundquist, 190pp. and
Kärlek till livet, tr.: M. Drangel, 192pp.
(Children of the frost. Love of life).

11. *Varg-Larsen*, tr.: M. Drangel, 549pp. *(The sea-wolf)*.

12. *Kärlekens väsen*, tr.: E. Lundquist, 198pp. and
Solguld och andra berättelser, tr.: E. Lundquist,
155pp. *(Kempton-Wace letters; Flush of gold and
other stories)*.

13. *Manasiktet och andra historier*, tr.: E. Lundquist,
190pp. and *För mycket guld och andra berättelser
fran Klondyke*, tr.: M. Drangel, 194pp. *(Moonface
and [?])*.

14. *Före Adam*, tr.: M. Drangel, 158pp. and *All världens
fiende, med flere berättelser*, tr.: M. Drangel,
187pp. *(Before Adam. The strength of the strong)*.

15. *Vagabondliv*, tr.: M. Drangel, 186pp and *Aventyr*,
tr.: M. Drangel, 303pp. *(The road. Adventure)*.

16. *John Finkelman*, tr.: A. Sandberg, 244pp. *(John
Barleycorn)*.

17. *Klasskamp*, tr.: E. Lundquist, 128pp. and
    Revolution och andra essayer, tr.: E. Lundquist,
    215pp. *(War of the classes. Revolution)*.
18. *Pa langfärd med Snark*, tr.: M. Drangel, 383pp.
    (The cruise of the Snark).
19-20. *Mandalen*, tr.: M. Drangel, 432pp. *(The valley
    of the moon)*.
21. *Hedningen och andra berättelser fran Söderhaf-
    söarna*, tr.: A. Sandberg, 198pp. and *Söder-
    havsberättelser*, tr.: Birger Mörner, 115pp.
    (South Sea tales. House of pride).
22 *Nigger Bellew*, tr.: E. Lundquist, 381pp. *(Smoke
    Bellew)*.
23. *Myteriet pa "Helsingör"*, tr.: E. Lundquist, 477pp.
    (The mutiny of the Elsinore).
24. *Tvangströjan*, tr.: E. Lundquist, 414pp. *(The star
    rover)*.
25. *Nar gudarna skratta och andra historier*, tr.: E.
    Lundquist, 212pp. and *Nattens barn och andra
    berättelser*, tr.: E. Lundquist, 207pp.
26. *Jerry*, tr.: E. Lundquist, 280pp. and *Röda pesten*,
    tr.: M. Drangel, 82pp. *(Jerry of the islands.
    The scarlet plague)*.
27. *En solens son*, tr.: E. Lundquist, 240pp. and *Den
    röde guden*, tr.: E. Lundquist, 147pp. *(Son of
    the sun. The red one)*.
28. *Kvinnofijd*, tr.: E. Lundquist, 115pp.; *Ollond-
    laren*, tr.: E. Lundquist, 50pp.; *Stöld*, tr.:
    E. Lundquist, 131pp.; *Spelet*, 62pp. *(Scorn of
    woman. The acorn-planter. Theft. The game)*.
29. *Michael jerry bror*, tr.: E. Lundquist, 1920, 396pp.
    (Michael, brother of Jerry).
30. *Den lilla damen i det stora huset*, tr.: E. Lund-
    quist, 384pp. *(The little lady of the big house)*.

583. *Valda skrifter*, Malmö, Världslitteraturens Förlag, 21
    vols. Vols. 1-6, 1926; vols. 7-21, 1927. No translators
    are given for any of the material translated. The same
    volume may contain several different items with sepa-
    rate paginations.
    1. *Vargens Son (The son of the wolf)*, 232pp. Con-
       tents: Den vita tystnaden (The white silence).
       Vargens son (The son of the wolf). Männen vid
       Forty Mile (The men of forty mile). I fjärren
       land (In a far country). En skál för dem, som
       äro ute på långfärd (To the man on trail).
       Prästens kall (The priestly prerogative). Ty
       så bjuder vandringslagen (The wisdom of the

trail. Kungens gemål (The wife of a king). En
odyssé i höga norden (An odyssey of the North).
Före Adam (Before Adam), pp.1-23.
2. *Före Adam*, pp.26-188. *För mycket guld (The faith
of men)*, pp.5-88. Contents: En lämning fran
tertiärtiden (A relic of the Pliocene). En halig
dryck (A hyperborean brew). Ödets lek (The faith
of men). För mycket guld (Too much gold).
3. *För mycket guld*, pp.95-229. Contents: De tusen
dussinen (The one thousand dozen). Lit-Lits
giftermål (The marriage of Lit-Lit). Bastard
(Batard). Jees Ucks historia (The story of Jees-
Uck). *Kärlek till livet (Love of life)*, pp.5-114.
Contents: Kärlek till livet (Love of life).
Varg (A day's lodging). En dags inkvartering
(The white man's way). Den vite mannens metod
(The white man's way).
4. *Kärlek till livet*, pp.121-235. Contents: Historien
om Keesh (The story of Keesh). Det oväntade
(The unexpected). Solgårdarnas väg (The sun-dog
trail). Negore, den fege (Negore, the coward).
Varg-Larsen (The sea wolf), pp.5-134.
5. *Varg-Larsen*, pp.131-390.
6. *Varg-Larsen*, pp.397-555. *Hans fäders gud (God of
his fathers)*, pp.5-31. *Den stora fragen (The
great interrogation)*, pp.5-31. *Vad man måste
minnas (Which makes men remember)*, pp.5-25.
7. *Kvinnor (Siwash)*, pp.7-31. *Mannen med ärret (The
man with the gash)*, pp.5-26. *Nordlandets dotter
(Daughter of the snows)*, pp.5-198.
8. *Nordlandets dotter*, pp.205-433. *Hardnackade Jan
(Jan, the unrepentant)*, pp.5-18.
9. *Månansiktet och andra berättelser (Moonface)*,
pp.7-244. Contents: Manansiktet (Moonface).
Leopard-mannens historia (The leopard man's story).
Lokalfärg (Local color). En amatörafton (Amateur
night). Kung Midas' svenner (The minions of Midas).
Skuggan och blixten (The shadow and the flash).
Gulddalen (All gold canyon). Psykografen (Planchette). *Kvinnomod (Grit of women)*, pp.5-12.
10. *Kvinnomod*, pp.19-35. *Där vägen delarsig (Where the
trail forks)*, pp.5-25. *Norrskenets Dotter (A
daughter of the Aurora)*, pp.5-21. *Vid regnbågens
fot (At the rainbow's end)*, pp.5-46. *En strid
mellan kvinnor (The scorn of women)*, pp.5-46.
Avrgundens folk (People of the abyss), pp.5-112.
11. *Avgrundens folk*, pp.119-312. *Skriet från Vildmarken
(The call of the wild)*, pp.7-54.

12. *Skriet från Vildmarken (The call of the wild)*,
    pp.61-191. *Historier om fishepatrullen (Tales
    of the fish patrol)*, pp.7-118. Contents: Vita
    och gula (White and yellow). "Grekernas kung"
    (A king of the Greeks). En razzia bland ostron-
    piraterna (A raid on oyster pirates). "Lanca-
    shiredrottningens" belägring (The siege of the
    Lancashire Queen). Charleys kupp (Charley's
    coup).
13. *Historier om fishepatrullen*, pp.125-194. Contents:
    Charleys kupp. Demetrios Contos (Demetrios
    Contos). Gula Näsduken (Yellow handkerchief).
    Köldens barn (Children of the frost), pp.7-180.
    Contents: I de nordliga skogarna (In the forests
    of the north). Livets lag (Law of life). Den
    lögnaktige Nam-Bok (Nam-Bok, the unveracious).
    Hemligheternas herre (The master of mystery).
    Sol-ländarna (The sunlanders). Ensamme hövdingens
    sjukdom (The sickness of Lone Chief).
14. *Köldens barn*, pp.187-312. Contents: Keesh, son av
    Keesh (Keesh, son of Keesh). Ligouns död (The
    death of Ligoun). Li Wan, den fagra (Li Wan, the
    fair). De gamla männens förbund (The league of
    old men). *Varghunden (White Fang)*, pp.7-122.
15. *Varghunden*, pp.129-378.
16. *Varghunden*, pp.385-437. *Kempton-Wace-breven (Kemp-
    ton-Wace letters)*, pp.5-196.
17. *Kempton-Wace breven*, pp.203-286. *På kryss med
    Blixten (The cruise of the Dazzler)*, pp.5-166.
18. *Spelet (The game)*, pp.7-93. *Järnhälen (The iron
    heel)*, pp.3-162.
19. *Järnhälen*, pp.169-418.
20. *Järnhälen*, pp.425-501. *Vagabondliv (The road)*,
    pp.3-172.
21. *Vagabondliv*, pp.179-276. *Jack London, liv och werk*
    by Einar Nylen, pp.3-129.

584. *Valda arbeten*, Stockholm, B. Wahlstrom, 1929, 1945:
    1. *Kungen av Klondyke*, tr.: Algot Sandberg, 368pp.
       (Burning daylight).
    2. *Jerry*, tr.: Ernst Lundquist, 318pp.
    3. *Den lilla damen i det stora huset*, tr.: Ernst Lund-
       quist, 368pp. *(The little lady of the big house)*.
    4. *Myteriet pa "Helsingör"*, tr.: Ernst Lundquist,
       400pp. *(Mutiny of the Elsinore)*.
    5. *Michael, Jerrys bror*, tr.: Ernst Lundquist, 367pp.
       (Michael, brother of Jerry).
    6. *Mandalen*, tr.: M. Drangel, 368pp. *(Valley of the*

> *moon).*
>
> 7. *Mandalen*, tr.: M. Drangel, 368pp. *(Valley of the moon).*
> 8. *Nigger Bellew*, tr.: Ernst Lundquist, 365pp. *(Smoke Bellew).*
> 9. *Aventyr*, tr.: M. Drangel, 319pp. *(Aventure).*
> 10. *John Finkelman*, tr.: Algot Sandberg, 320pp. *(John Barleycorn).*
> 11. *Martin Eden*, tr.: Algot Sandberg, 400pp.
> 12. *Nordlandetsdotter*, tr.: M. Drangel, 320pp. *(Daughter of the snows).*
> 13. *Varg-Larsen*, tr.: M. Drangel, 400pp. *(The sea-wolf).*
> 14. *Varghunden*, tr.: M. Drangel, 317pp. *(White fang).*
> 15. *Vargens son & Skriet fran vildmarken*, both translated by M. Drangel, 214pp., 135pp. *(The son of the wolf. The call of the wild).*

585. *Jack Londons Bästa*, Stockholm, B. Wahlström, 1963, 15 vols.

> 1. *Vargens son. Skriet fran vildmarken* tr.: Brita and Alf Agdler, 255pp. 1963. *(Son of the wolf. The call of the wild).*
> 2. *Den lilla damen i det stora huset*, tr.: Gudrun Ullman, 253pp., 1964. *(The little lady of the big house).*
> 3. *Varghunden*, tr.: Barbro Johansson, 1964, 255pp. *(White Fang).*
> 4. *Varg-Larsen*, tr.: Alf Agdler, 1964, 255pp. *(The sea wolf).*
> 5. *Nordlandets dotter*, tr.: Barbro Johansson, 1964, 255pp. *(The daughter of the snows).*
> 6. *Mysteriet pa "Helsingör"*, tr.: Emil Beurin, 1964, 253pp. *(Mutiny of the Elsinore).*
> 7. *Nigger Bellew*, tr.: Ragnhild Hallén-Frish, 1964, 252pp. *(Smoke Bellew).*
> 8. *Aventyr*, tr.: Barbro Johansson, 1964, 253pp. *(Adventure).*
> 9. *John Finkelman*, tr.: Brita and Alf Agdler, 1964, 254pp. *(John Barleycorn).*
> 10. *Michael*, tr.: Gudrun Ullman, 1964, 255pp. *(Michael, brother of Jerry).*
> 11. *Jerry*, tr.: Emil Bourin, 1964, 254pp. *(Jerry of the islands).*
> 12-13. *Martin Eden*, tr.: Gudrun Ullman, 1964, 255pp.
> 14-15. *Kungen av Klondike*, tr.: Emil Bourin, 1964, 254, 255pp. *(Burning daylight).*

TATAR
586. *Taina,* tr.: Khakimdzhanov, Moscow, 1925, 24pp. [Title in Russian].
587. *Rasskazy,* tr.: G. Lufzhi, Kazan', Tatgosizdat, Sektor iunosh. det. knigi, 1951, 120pp. [Title in Russian].
588. *Dva rasskaza,* tr.: G. Lufti, Kazan', Tatgosizdat, Red. iunosh. detsk. lit., 1952, 32pp. [Title in Russian].

TURKISH
589. *Vahsetin caǧirisi,* Istanbul, Selamet Basimevi, 1935, 184pp. (*The call of the wild* and six short stories).
590. *Altin arayicilar,* Istanbul, Asri Basimevi, 1937, 16pp.
591. *Şimal hikâyeleri,* tr.: Efdal Nogan, Istanbul, Tan Evi, 1939, Contents: Kayip belikçi gemisi (The lost poacher). Francis Speyt (The Francis Spaight). Cinago (The Chinago).
592. *Ates yakmak,* tr.: Memet Fuat, Ankara, Yeditepe yayinlari, 1953, 87pp. (Yeditepe Yayinlari: 22). Contents: Onsöz. Ates yakmak (To build a fire). Bir Kalem Pirzola (A piece of steak). Porportuk'un Akli (The wit of Porportuk).
593. *Yaşamak hirsi,* tr.: Mehemet Harmanci, Istanbul, Varlik Yayinevi, 1953, 120pp. (Varlik Yayinlari, Sayi: 190. Varlik Cep Kitaplari: 75). [Probably same six stories as *Yaşamak hirsi,* 1961.]
594. *Dönek,* tr.: Fikret Uray, Istanbul, Varlik Yayinevi, 1955, 124pp.
595. *Yaşamak hirsi,* tr.: Mehmet Harmanci, Istanbul, Varlik Yayinevi, 1957, 94pp. (Varlik Yayinlari, Sayi: 491. Varlik Cep Kitaplari: 75). [Probably same six stories as in *Yaşamak hirsi,* 1961.]
596. *Yaşamak hirsi,* tr.: Mehmet Harmanci, Ankara, Varlik Yayinlari, 1961, 94pp. (Varlik Buyuk Cep Kitaplari: 193). Contents: Yaşamak hirsi (Love of life). Beyaz issizlik (The white silence). Meksikali (The Mexican). Ateş yakmak (To build a fire). Altin damari (All gold canyon). Yüz karasi (Lost face).
597. *Dönek,* tr.: Fikret Uray, Istanbul, Varlik Yayinevi, 1963, 96pp. Contents: Dönek (The apostate). Et (Just meat). Allaha ismarladik Jack (Good-by, Jack). Gurur (House of pride). Cüzamli Koolau (Koolau, the leper). Kona şerifi (The sheriff of Kona). Chun Ah Chun (Chun Ah Chun).

TURKOMAN
598. *Meksikanetz,* tr.: A. Kurbanov, Ashkhabad, Turmengosizdat, 1958, 102pp. [Title in Russian] (The Mexican and other stories).

UZBEK

599. *Khikoislar,* tr.: F. Abdullaev, Tashkent, Uzlitizdat, 1958, 174pp. Contents: Shimol Odisseiasi (The odyssey of the North). Ayd kishining mardlighi (The grit of women). Khaiotga mukhabbat (Love of life). Isionchi (The apostate). Buiuk sekhrgar. Kish ugli Kish (Keesh, son of Keesh). Meksikalik (The Mexican). Mokhov Kulau Koolau, the leper).

VIETNAMESE

600. *Mot thien tink han,* tr.: Ank Lien, Saigon, Chime-Dan, 1956, 168pp. [Translation of An odyssey of the North. Mauki. A piece of steak. Lost face. To build a fire].

UNIDENTIFIED TRANSLATIONS

601. "Alaska," *Socialdemokrats,* nos. 169-282 (July 20-Dec. 13, 1932).

602. "Baltojo žmogaus keliai," *Naujas žodis,* no. 18:442-444, no. 19:462-465 (1931) (Translation of White man's way[?]).

603. "Baltojo žmogaus virsěnybe," tr.: Vandraunikas, *Laisve,* nos. 205-206 (1922) (White man's superiority[?]).

604. "Jokahamos uoste," tr.: S. M., *Skautu aidas,* nos. 1-2: 10-12 (1927).

605. "Kruvinas kerštas," tr.: P. M. B., *Laisve,* nos. 61-63 (1922). (Bloody revenge[?]).

606. "Maika. (Pasakojimas apie viena eskimu šuni)," tr.: Pr. Masiotas, in Pr. Masiotas, *Žverys ir žmones,* Kaunas, 1929, pp.63-75. (Mike, a tale about an Eskimo dog[?]).

607. "'Monachiki" paslaptis," tr.: St. B., *Trimitas,* no. 4:110-116 (1927) (The secret of Manachiki[?]).

608. "Nakties dukra," *Rytas,* Jan. 21, 1930 (Daughter of the night - perhaps Daughter of the aurora).

609. "Nakties stovykla," *Lietuvos aidas,* April 16, 29, 1929 (Night camp[?]).

610. "Nosos," tr.: Kamauskas, *Rytas,* May 11, 1929 (The nose- perhaps Nose for the king].

611. "Paskutine kova," tr.: A. Kalesnykietis, *Rytas,* May 28, 30, June 1-4, 7, 1927 (The last battle[?]).

612. "Revoliucija yra geras dalykas, kuriam ir verta pasiš- vesti," *Kova,* no. 27:213-214 (1905) [Probably a trans- lation of a passage from Revolution].

613. "Sturitis elle," *Socialdemokrats,* nos. 93-94 (April 26- 27, 1929) (Frying-pan alley. A glimpse of inferno).

614. "Styga," tr.: V. Petr, *Lietuvos žinios,* March 15, 1930 (String[?]).

615. "Sučiupo," *Valstiečiu laikraštis,* Dec. 5, 8, 11, 1957

(Caught - perhaps Pinched).
616. '·Tai, kas nepamirštama," *Rytas,* Sept. 12-15, 1927 (That is what is unforgetable[?]).

SHORT STORIES

617. "Account with Swithan Hall," in SS. *See* also item 706.
618. "Adventure in the upper sea," *Independent*, 54:1290-1292 (May 29, 1902); *Children's Digest*, 14:135:78-86 (Feb. 1964) [cover title given as "Adventure in the clouds"]; CWP, DC, JLS, SA.
619. "All gold canyon," *Century*, 71:117-126 (Nov. 1905); BSS, BW, JLSB, MF, SSM, TA, WFOS; *Golden Book*, 19:471-484 (April 1934); O. Cargill, ed., *Social revolt*, New York, Macmillan, 1933, pp.391-405; T. P. Cross, et al., eds., *American writers*, New York, Ginn, c1939, pp.389-402; N. Foerster, ed., *American poetry and prose*, Boston, Houghton, 1934, pp.1232-1242; Gunnar Horn, *A cavalcade of world writing*, Boston, Allyn & Bacon, 1963, pp.181-200; Charles Laughton, ed., *The fabulous country*, New York, McGraw-Hill, 1962, pp.170-189; J. W. Schaefer, ed., *Out West*, Boston, Houghton, 1955, pp. 196-214; S. L. Schramm, ed., *Great short stories*, New York, Harcourt, 1950, pp.135-156; F. B. and E. D. Snyder, *A book of American literature*, New York, Macmillan, 1927, pp.894-905; Harold H. Wagenheim, *This is America*, New York, Holt, 1956, pp.392-405. Translations: "Puhta kulla org," *Peterburi Teataja Kirjandusline-teadusline lisa*, no. 27:217-221 (1912), no. 28:225-230 (1912); also translated as "Kullakuristik," *Romaan*, no. 22:684-688 (1931), no. 23:709-712 (1931) (Estonian); "Zelta grava," *Liepājas Atbalss*, nos. 284-300 (Dec. 11-31, 1911) (Latvian).
620. "Aloha oe," *Smart Set*, 28:51-54 (May 1909); *Lady's Realm*, 25:170-175 (Dec. 1908); HP, ACS. Translations: "Aloha oe," in Rafael Sabatini, *"L'estate di S. Martino*, Milan, Sonzogno, 1933, pp.306-315 (Italian); "Un cuento sentimental: la canción de Hawaii," *Semana gráfica*, no. 391:8, 22 (Jan. 7, 1939)(Spanish).
621. "Amateur night," *Pilgrim*, 7:5-6, 37 (Dec. 1903); JLSB, MF.
622. "An old soldier's story," *American Agriculturist*, 63, 20:659 (May 20, 1899); *Orange Judd Farmer*, 23:659 (May 20, 1899); *New England Homestead*, 38:659 (May 20, 1899).
623. "And Frisco Kid comes back," Oakland High School *Aegis*, 15, 4:2-4 (Nov. 4, 1895).
624. "The apostate," *Woman's Home Companion*, 33:5-7, 49 (Sept. 1906); *International Socialist Review*, 17:523-528, 558-561 (March 1917); ACS, BH, ER, F, LLOS, SS, SSM, SST, TA, WGL; J. Gaer, ed., *Our lives*, New York, Boni & Gaer, 1948, pp.173-192. Also separately printed as *The*

apostate: a parable of child labor, Girard, Kansas, [n.d.][1906?] 32pp.; *Apostate: a curious fragment,* Moscow, State Publishing House, 1929, 68pp. Braille edition (transcribed for The National Library for the Blind, London, England): 1 vol. (Grade 1). March 1949. Translations: "Tôrkumas," *Tallinna Teataja,* Aug. 23-24, 26-27, Aug. 30-Sept. 2, 1916 (Estonian); "Le renégat," tr.: Louis Postif, *Les oeuvres libres,* no. 115:5-28 (Jan. 1931) (French); "Streikotājs," tr.: G. Mīlbergs, *Jaunās Dienas Lapas Pielikums,* no. 207 (Sept. 20, 1913), no. 213 (Sept. 27, 1913), no. 219 (Oct. 4, 1913); "Pamodās," tr.: A. Laiviņš, *Dzimetenes Vēstnesis,* nos. 44-46 (Feb. 15-17, 1915); "Sāka steikot," *Sarkanais Karogs,* nos. 9-16 (Dec. 20-30, 1918) (Latvian); "Darba," tr.: J. Bite, *Dzīve,* nos. 182-186 (Aug. 13-17, 1913) (Lithuanian); *Izmennik,* Moscow, Ts. K. S. T., 1926, 16pp., ibid., tr.: D. Gorfinkel, introduction by M. Gershenzon, Moscow and Leningrad, Detizdat., 1938, 32pp.; *Na svobodu,* Moscow and Leningrad, Gosizdat., 1962, 32pp.; ibid., Moscow and Leningrad, Gosizdat., 1929, 28pp.; *Shabash,* tr.: S. G. Zaimovski, Moscow, G. F. Mirimanov, 1926, 22pp.; *Zabastoval,* tr. and adapted by M. Pollat, Moscow and Leningrad, Gosizdat., 1928, 35pp.; also appears in *Zabastoval i drugiye rasskazy iz shizni rabochei molodyozhi,* ed., Yu. Danilin, Moscow, Znaniye, 1924 (Russian) *Otpadnik,* tr.: Mihailo S. Djordjevic, Belgrade, Izdanje Novo pokolenje, 1950, 28pp. (Serbian); *Farshtraykt,* Wilmo, 1930, 13pp. (Yiddish).

625.   "At the rainbow's end," Pittsburgh *Leader,* March 24, 1901, p.31; San Francisco *Call,* June 14, 1903, p.7; Los Angeles *Tribune,* May 5, 1912, [6] of Sunday magazine section; GHF, SDT. Translations: *Sui margini dell'arcobaleno,* Milan, Sonzogno, 1937, 1941, 32pp. (Italian).

626.   "Bald face," Oakland High School *Aegis,* 22,2:[1]-2 (Sept. 6, 1901); *Satyr,* 1,6:87-88 (Dec. 1909); DC, SA.

627.   "The banks of the Sacramento," *Youth's Companion,* 78:129-130 (March 17, 1904); *C. B. Fry's Magazine,* 4:215-220 (Dec. 1905); DC, SSS. Separately published for the purpose of securing copyright in Great Britain by "Daily Mail" Publishing Office, 1904, 12 leaves printed on recto only. Translations: *Berega Sakramento,* tr.: B. Stepanian, Erevan, 1954, 28pp. (Armenian); "Sacramento kaldad," tr. O. Jôgi, *Pioneer,* no. 5:4-5 (1957) (Estonian); "'Al gedot ha-Sakramento," in *'Azim veno' azim,* ed. and tr. by Sh. Yoram, Tel-Aviv, Yavneh [1959] pp.159-178 (Hebrew); "Uz Sakramento upes," *Jaunības Tekas,* no. 1:79-88 (1925) (Latvian); *Berega Sakramento,* Moscow and Leningrad, Gosizdat, 1929, 23pp.; *"Na*

beregakh Sakramento," *Pioneer*, no. 1:27-32 (1956)
(Russian).
628. "Batard," BH, FM, TA; *Famous Story Magazine*, 3,3:362-
369 (Oct. 1926); *Sunday Illustrated Magazine of the
Commercial Appeal* (Memphis, Tenn.), Sept. 28, 1913,
pp.7-11. Translations: "Zwei Teufel," in *Unsere treuen
Freunde: die schönsten Hundegeschichten* ausgewählt von
Curt Bloch, Hamburg, Mosaik Verlag, 1963, pp.225-239
(German); "Bastardo," tr.: G. Marcellini, *Nuova antologia*, 266:320-331 (Aug. 1, 1929) (Italian); "Batars,"
Dzīve, nos. 81-85 (April 11-16, 1912); "Bastards," tr.:
Ž. Brīvlauks, *Ventas Balss*, nos. 27-32 (July 3-Aug. 7,
1925) (Latvian).
629. "The benefit of the doubt," *Saturday Evening Post*, 183:
9-11, 69-70 (Nov. 12, 1910); Birmingham *Weekly Post*,
Jan. 17, 1914, pp.17-18; NB.
630. "The bones of Kahekili," *Cosmopolitan*, 67:95-100, 102,
104 (July 1919); OMM.
631. "Born of the wild," in WF.
632. "Brown Wolf," *Everybody's Magazine*, 15:147-156 (Aug.
1906); *Windsor Magazine*, 25:531-540 (March 1907); BW,
JLSB, LL, SDT; N.V.S. Gaines, *Pathway to western literature*, Stockton, Gaines, 1910, pp.9-16; R. Blankenship, et al., eds., *Literature we appreciate*, New York,
Scribner, c1940, pp.614-627; D. E. Watkins and C. H.
Raymond, eds., *Best dog stories*, Chicago, Rand McNally,
1925, pp.103-115; *Junior classics*, New York, Collier,
1938, 7:306-321; *Animals in action: fact and fiction*,
ed. by George S. Amsbary, Chicago, Spencer Press, c1958,
pp.298-308; Zistel, E., ed. *Golden book of dog stories*,
Chicago, Ziff-Davis, 1947, 318pp. Braille edition (tran-
scribed for The National Library for the Blind, London,
England): 1 vol. (Grade 1). May 1950. Translations:
Mezi vlky. Prague, Svěcený, 1917, 32pp. (Czech/Slovak);
"Ziemeli um dienvidi," *Jaunības Tekas*, no. 2:40-50
(1924) (Latvian); *Volk* [title given in Russian], tr.:
M. Abdullin, Ufa, Bashgosizdat., 1939, 32pp. (Bashkir);
Volk [title given in Russian], tr.: Karachev S. Frunze-
Kazan', Kirgiz. gos. izd., 1937, 30pp. (Kirghiz); *Volk*
[title given in Russian], Syktyvkar, Kom. giz., 1937,
32pp. (Komi); *Volk*, tr.: V. Stenich, Moscow and Lenin-
grad, Detizdat., 1936, 32pp.; *Volk*, Moscow, Uchpedgiz.,
1938, 28pp.; *Bury volk*, tr.: S. G. Zaimovski, Moscow,
G. F. Mirimanov, 1926, 20pp.; ibid., 1927, 23pp.
(Russian); *Volk* [title in Russian], tr.: Dzh. Bakozade,
Stalinabad-Leningrad, Tadzh. gos. izd., 1940, 32pp.;
another ed., 1947, 40pp. (Tadzhik); *Volk* [title in Rus-
sian], tr.: G. Muslimov, Kasan', Tatgosizdat, 1938,

24pp. (Tatar); *Volk* [title in Russian]; tr.: S. B.
Esenova, Ashkhabad, Turkmengosizdat., 1938, 34pp.
(Turkoman); *Volk* [title in Russian], translated from
the Russian by I. Muslim, Tashkent, Uzdetizdat, 1938,
32pp. (Uzbek).

633. "Building of the boat," *Harper's Weekly*, 52:11-12
(July 18, 1908); TA; reprinted as "The inconceivable
and monstrous" in CS.

634. "Bunches of knuckles," New York *Herald*, art section,
Dec. 18, 1910, pp.2-3; NB. Translations: *Drama na more*,
Petrograd, Nevskoye Izdatelstvo, 1922, 16pp.(Russian).

635. "By the turtles of Tasman," San Francisco *Call*, monthly
magazine section, Nov. 19, 1911, pp.8-10, 17-19; TT.

636. "Charley's 'coup'," *Youth's Companion*, 79:173-174
(April 13, 1905); *Pall Mall Magazine*, 36:29-35 (July
1905); ST, TFP.

637. "Chased by the trail," *Youth's Companion*, 81:445-446
(Sept. 26, 1907); *Pall Mall Magazine*, 40:478-483 (Oct.
1907); *Junior classics*, ed. by Mabel Williams and Maria
Dalphin, New York, Collier, c1938, 9:110-119.

638. "The Chinago," *Illustrated London News*, 134:928-931
(June 26, 1909); *Harper's Magazine*, 119:233-240 (July
1909), ACS, LLOS, SSM, SST, St-K, WGL. Braille edition
(transcribed for The National Library for the Blind,
London, England): 1 vol. (Grade 1) Dec. 1948. Translations: "La hinago," tr.: Philip Kalisky, *British
Esperantist*, 6,63:41-47 (1910) (Esperanto); "A-Tsho,"
*Tallinna Teataja ja Tallinna Uudiste kirjandusline-
teadusline lisa Külaline*, no. 48:377-379, no. 49:385-
387, no. 50:394-395 (1913); also translated as "Kuli,"
Rahvaleht, May 20, 23, 1925 and in *Ajakiri Kõkgile*, no.
3:70-75 (1936) (Estonian); "A-Čo," tr.: Sudrabu Edžus,
Jaunās Dienas Lapas Pielikums, no. 209 (Sept. 21, 1912),
no. 215 (Sept. 28, 1912) (Latvian); *A-cho*, tr.: M. Likiardopulo, introduction by L. Nedal, Moscow and Leningrad, Gosizdat, 1927, 32pp.; *Khodya*, tr.: S. G. Zaimovski, Moscow, G. F. Mirimanov, 1926, 20pp.; ibid., 1928,
24pp.; *Oshibka*, tr.: V. Minina, ed. I. V. Zhilkin,
Moscow and Leningrad, Gosizdat., 1930, 32pp. (Russian);
"Chinago," *Leoplán* (Buenos Aires), no. 496:66-75 (Feb.
16, 1955); "El chinago," *Elcuento*, 1,8:73-82 (Dec.
1964) (Spanish); [The following data concerning the
Hebrew translation of this short story has been supplied
by Myron M. Weinstein, senior reference librarian,
Hebraic section, Library of Congress. Deborah Baron
translated it as "Ah Cho" and it appeared in *Ha-po'el
Ha-tsa'ir*, nos. 15-17 (1919-1920). She translated it
from a Russian abridgement. Later her *Agav-orha*,

Merhavya, Sifriyat Poalim, 1960, pp.41-55 printed a
complete translation based on the English original.]

639. "Chris Farrington: able seaman," *Youth's Companion*,
75:265-266 (May 23, 1901); *Pall Mall Magazine*, 38:289-
294 (March 1906); CWP, DC, JLS, SSS; John E. Brewton,
et al., *New horizons through reading and literature*,
book 3, River Forest, Ill., Laidlaw Brothers, c1962,
pp.219-225. Translations: "Krizas Faringtonas - pirmos
rūšies jūrininkas," tr.: Akela, *Skautu aidas*, no. 2:
4-6 (1928) (Lithuanian); *Kris Farrington, matros pervoi
stati*, D. Gorfinkel, ed. of translation, Moscow and
Leningrad, Detizdat, 1930, 32pp.; *Matros pervoi stati*,
Moscow and Leningrad, Gosizdat, 1930, 24pp. (Russian).

640. "Chun Ah Chun," *Woman's Magazine*, 21:5-6, 38-40 (Spring
1910); HP, LLOS; A. Grove Day and Carl Stroven, *A
Hawaiian reader*, New York, Appleton, 1959, pp.177-191;
ibid., New York, Popular Library, 1961, pp.183-195.
Braille edition (transcribed for The National Library
for the Blind, London, England): 1 vol. (1/2 size).
Grade 1. July 1948. Translations: *Chun Ah Chun*, Santiago, La Novela Corta, 1933, 29pp. (Spanish).

641. "Created he them," *Pacific Monthly*, 17: 393-397 (April
1907); SST, WGL; reprinted as "The turning point,"
Windsor Magazine, 26:394-400 (Sept. 1907).

642. "A curious fragment," *Town Topics*, Dec. 10, 1908, pp.
45-47; ACS, SST, WGL, Oscar Cargill, ed., *Social revolt*,
New York, Macmillan, 1933, pp.415-421. Translations:
"Fragment i çudiçëm," in *Tregime bashkëkohore amerikane*,
Prishtinë, Rilindja, 1958, pp.13-22 (Albanian) [p.12
is a biography of London] (translated by Masar Murtezai
and Ramiz Kelmendi); "Interesanta atrauta lapa," *Sarkanais Karogs*, nos. 63-65 (April 12-15, 1919); "Norauta
roka zemenēs," *Sociāldemokrāts*, nos. 269-273 (Nov. 28-
Dec. 3, 1926); *Darbs*, nos. 48-51 (June 30-July 3, 1927)
(Latvian); "Idomus fragmentas," tr.: L. Vd., *Laisvoji
mintis*, no. 7 (1916) (Lithuanian); *Legenda o ruke tkacha*.
Moscow, Tsentrainy Komitet Soyuza Tekstilshchikov, 1926,
14pp. (Russian).

643. "A daughter of the Aurora," San Francisco *Wave*, Dec. 24,
1899, pp.9-10, 16; San Francisco *Call*, Oct. 25, 1903,
p.8; Los Angeles *Tribune*, Sunday magazine section,
May 12, 1912 [6]; *National Magazine* (Boston), 13:223-
229 (Jan. 1901); *Novel Magazine*, 16:569-572 (Feb. 1913);
BSS, CWOS-1960, GF. Translations: "Une fille de
l'aurore," tr.: Louis Postif, *Annales politiques et
littéraires*, 84:339-341 (March 29, 1925) (French);
"Auroros duktė," tr.: A. M., *Akademikas*, no. 19:385-388
(1936) (Lithuanian).

644. "A day's lodging," *Collier's*, 39:18-21 (May 25, 1907);
      London Magazine, 19:264-273 (Nov. 1907); *LaFollette's
      Weekly*, Feb. 21, 1914, pp.14-15; JLSB, LL, SSM.
645. "Death of Ligoun," in CF.
646. "Demetrios Contos," *Youth's Companion*, 79:201-202
      (April 27, 1905); *Pall Mall Magazine*, 36:218-224 (Aug.
      1905); FSS, TFP; John and Laree Caughey, eds., *California
      heritage*, Los Angeles, Ward Ritchie Press, 1962,
      pp.386-398.
647. "Devils of Fuatino," in SS.
648. "Diable--a dog," *Cosmopolitan*, 33:218-226 (June 1902);
      CWP, CWSS, JLS.
649. "The dream of Debs," *International Socialist Review*,
      17:389-395, 432-434 (Jan. 1917); BH, ER, F, StSt; sep-
      arately printed in Chicago, Kerr, [n.d.,] 31pp. Trans-
      lations: "Debsa sapnis," *Strādnieks*, nos. 69-73 (June
      29-July 13, 1917) (Latvian).
650. "Dutch courage," *Youth's Companion*, 74:622-623 (Nov.
      29, 1900); CWP, DC, JLS, SA.
651. "The end of the chapter," San Francisco *News Letter*,
      June 9, 1900, pp.22-23.
652. "The end of the story," *Woman's World*, 27,11:8-9, 29-32
      (Nov. 1911); *Red Magazine*, no. 66:713-724 (Jan. 1, 1912);
      TT; reprinted as "The fearless one," *Jack London's ad-
      venture magazine*, 1,1:5-20 (Oct. 1958). Translations:
      "Sogulok," tr.: Axel Thorsteinson, *Sunnudags-blaoio*,
      1:1-6 (1923) (Icelandic); "Dziesmas izskaņa," *Madonas
      Ziņas*, no. 11-21 (March 13-May 22, 1931); "Dziesmas
      beigas ...," *Pasaules Pasts*, no. 21 (May 21, 1933);
      "Kad likteņi krustojas," *Zemes Spēks*, nos. 23-24:1-8
      (Latvian).
653. "The enemy of all the world," *Red Book*, 11:817-827 (Oct.
      1908); *International Socialist Review*, 15:167-175 (Sept.
      1914); StSt.
654. "Engaging a crew," *Harper's Weekly*, 5:14 (July 25, 1908);
      reprinted as "Adventure" in CS.
655. "Engraved oarblade," in Herzberg, M. J., comp., *Treasure
      chest of sea stories*, N.Y., J. Mesner, 1948, 349pp.
656. "The eternity of forms," *Red Book*, 16:866-873 (March
      1911); ACS, TT.
657. "Even unto death," San Francisco *Evening Post*, July 28,
      1900, pp.4-5.
658. "Eyes of Asia: the story Jack London was writing when
      he died, of a beautiful castaway who drifted into love
      and riches," *Cosmopolitan*, 77:24-31, 148-156 (Sept.
      1924).
659. "Faith of men," *Sunset*, 11:114-121 (June 1903); *Illus-
      trated News* (London), 113:31-34, 37 (Christmas no. 1903);

Sunday Illustrated Magazine of the Commercial Appeal
(Memphis, Tenn.), Nov. 9, 1913, pp.7-8, 14-15; ACS, FM,
ST. Translations: "La foi des hommes," tr.: Georges
Dupuy, *L'Illustration*, Supplément, 10-24 février, 1912,
pp. 19-30 (French); "Uzticība," *Mūsu Domas*, nos. 46-49
(April 25-May 2, 1912); *Dzīve*, nos. 93-96 (April 25-28,
1912); *Jaunās Dienas Lapas Pielikums*, no. 143 (July 6,
1912), no. 149 (July 14, 1912); ibid., tr.: Z. Brīvlauks,
Ventas Balss, nos. 17-22 (1925); "Vīriešu uztīciba,"
Ventspils Apskata Svētdienas Pielikums, nos. 8-9 (1914)
(Latvian).
"The fearless one," *see* "The end of the story."

660. "Feathers of the sun," *Saturday Evening Post*, 184:609,
72-74 (March 9, 1912); LLOS, SS.

661. "Finis (Morganson's finish)," *Success*, 10:311-314, 376
(March 1907); *Pearson's Magazine*, 33:581-592 (1912);
SSM, TT. Translations: "Beigas," tr.: Sudrabu Edžus,
Jaunā Dienas Lapa, nos. 296-301 (Jan. 2-10, 1913); "Uz
sliekšņa," tr.: K. Zariņš, *Latvija*, nos. 190-193 (Sept.
3-5, 1913) (Latvian).

662. "Flush of gold," *Hampton's Broadway Magazine*, 21:420-
426 (Oct. 1908); *Grand Magazine*, 4:400-408 (April 1908);
Golden Book, 14:303-312 (Nov. 1931); LF, TA.

663. "The Francis Spaight," in LLOS, SST, WGL. Translations:
"Šausmu brīdī," *Pūcesspieguelis*, no. 11:2-3, no. 12:4-5
(1924) (Latvian).

664. "Frisco Kid's story," Oakland High School *Aegis*, 10,
3:2-3 (Feb. 15, 1895) [Signed John London]; San Francisco *Examiner*, Dec. 3, 1916, p.2E.

665. "The 'fuzziness' of Hoockla Heen," *Youth's Companion*,
76:333-334 (July 3, 1902); *Cassell's Magazine*, June
1906, pp.25-30, CWP, JLS.

666. "The goat man of Fautino," *Saturday Evening Post*, 184:
12-15, 35-38 (July 29, 1911).

667. "A Gobotu night," *Saturday Evening Post*, 184:20-21,
65-66 (Sept. 30, 1911); *Grand Magazine*, 16:575-584
(Oct. 1912); SA, SS.

668. "God of his fathers," *McClure*, 17:44-53 (May 1901); Los
Angeles *Tribune*, May 26, 1912, Sunday magazine section,
[6]; *Golden Book*, 5:54-60 (Jan. 1927); GF; J. Cournos,
ed., *American short stories of the nineteenth century*,
New York, Dutton, 1930, pp.349-364. Translations: "Viņa
tēvu Dievs," tr.: L. Tirzmalietis, *Jaunās Avīzes Pielikums*, nos. 2-4 (Jan. 11, 18, 25, 1914) (Latvian); "Jo
tēvu dievas," *Lietuvos aidas*, July 12-13, 1928 (Lithuanian); "O Deus dos seus pais," tr.: Gustavo de
Mendonça, *Contos americanos*, Lisbon, Gleba, 1944,
pp.371-395 (Portuguese).

669. "Gods of the wild," in WF.
670. "Goliah," *Red Magazine*, 2:115-129 (1908); *Bookman*, 30: 620-632 (Feb. 1910); R.
671. "Goodby, Jack," *Red Book*,13:225-240 (June 1909); *The Weekly Tale-Teller* Christmas issue of 1912, pp.1-6; ACS, HP.
672. "The great interrogation," *Ainslee's Magazine*, 6:394-402 (1900); San Francisco *Call*, March 13, 1904, p.7; GF; reprinted as "Worlds Apart," *Top Notch*, July 30, 1914, pp.63-71. Translations: "Romantika Aļaskā," *Pēdējā Brīdī*, nos. 158-161 (July 17-20, 1935) (Latvian).
673. "The grilling of Loren Ellery," *Northern Weekly Gazette* Middlesborough), March 30, 1912, p.9.
674. "Grit of women *McClure*, 15:324-330 (Aug. 1900); San Francisco *Call*, Feb. 7, 1904, p.8; *Story-teller*, Oct. 1912, pp.113-119; GF, SSM, E. Markham, comp., *Songs and stories*, San Francisco, Powell Publishing Co., 1931, pp.185-202. Translations: "Sieviešu izturība," *Dzīve*, nos. 242-245 (Oct. 19-23, 1912); "Sieviete," tr.: Em Grants, *Latvija*, nos. 158-160 (July 27-29, 1915); "Sievietes spēks," *Atvase*, nos. 3-13 (May 9-June 1, 1918); "Sievietes varonība," tr.: Silenieks, *Siguldas Vēstnesis*, nos. 2-8 (Jan. 19-April 27, 1929) (Latvian). "Fuerzas de mujeres," *Atenea*, 4:46-56 (1927) (Spanish).
675. "The handsome cabin boy," *Owl*, 7:45-50 (July 1899).
676. "Heathen" *Everybody's Magazine*, 23:193-204 (Aug. 1910); *London Magazine*, 23:33-42 (Sept. 1909); BH, BSS, BSS-EB, CWOS, SST; B. A. Cerf, ed., *Modern American short stories*, Cleveland, World, 1945, pp.51-68; A. Hogeboom, *Tales from the high seas*, [n.p.,] Lothrop, 1948, pp.162-174; Walter Loban and Rosalind A. Olmsted, *Adventures in appreciation*, New York, Harcourt, Brace & World, c1963, pp.62-74; F. M. Mathiews, ed., *Boy Scouts' Book of good turn stories*, New York, Scribners, 1931, pp.180-213. Text edition: *The heathen: a South Sea tale*, ed. by Dr. Friedrich Behrens, Munich, Hueber, [n.d.,] 28pp. (Huebers Fremdsprachliche Texte No. 52). [This edition contains "Anmerkungen zu Jack London (1876-1916)".] Translations: "Pagan Otoo," tr.: L. Varing, *Noorusmaa*, no. 13-14:300-305, no. 15:322-326 (1927); "Pagan," tr.: J. Seilental in *Merejutte*, Tallinn, 1959, pp.18-31 (Loomingu raamatukogu no. 2) (Estonian); "Le païen," tr.: Paul Gruyer and Louis Postif, in *Les vingt meilleures* nouvelles americaines: textes choisis et présentés par Alain Bosquet, Paris, Editions Seghers, 1957, pp.223-246 [translation preceded by short biographical note, p.222]; *Otto, der Heide* ... Mit eingedr. Federzeichn. von Hans Anton Aschenborn. Auswahl und Durch-

1.

The Hussy

~~His wife, was Elizabeth West~~

There are some stories that leave to be true —— the sort that cannot be fabricated by a ready fiction-reckoner. ~~If the same~~ And there are ~~some~~ men ~~with a tale~~ with ~~the~~ stories to tell ~~who cannot~~ be doubted. Such a man was Julian Jones, though I doubt ~~that~~ the average reader of this will believe the story Julian Jones told me. ~~I the I believe~~ Nevertheless I believe it. So thoroughly am I convinced of its verity that I am willing, nay, eager, to invest capital in the enterprise and embark personally on the adventure to a far land.

It was in the Australian Building at the Panama Pacific ~~E~~ Exposition that I

Manuscript page of "The Hussy"

sicht bes. Karl Boss. Frankfurt a. M., M. Diesterweg,
1929, 30pp. (Best. Nr. 146, Kranz-Bücherei. H. 146;
2nd ed., 1933); ibid., Berlin, Leipzig, Volk und Wissen,
1946 31pp. (Volk und Wissen Sammelbücherei Gr. 1, Serie
C3); 2nd ed., Berlin, Dresden, Kinderbuchverlag, 1950,
24pp. (Unsere Welt. Gr. 1). *Otto, der Heide*. Hrsg.:
Otto Schmidt. Lesebuch. d. Dt. Stenografie. Bearb. vom
Arbeitsausschuss für Volksbildg in d. Swojet. Besat-
zungszone. Berlin, Leipzig, Volk und Wissen, 1948,
34 pp. (Best. Nr. 9085, Grundwissen, Allgemeinbildg,
[4] Bd. 11) (German); "Pagāns," tr.: Vācietis, *Svētdie-*
nas Rīts, nos. 15-19 (1922); "Melnais pagans," *Jaunības*
Tekas, no. 12:877-884 (1913); "Pagāns," tr.: A. Erss,
Līdums, nos. 311-328 (Dec. 9-30, 1915) (Latvian); "El
pagano," in *Cuentos y novelas cortas de Norteamerica*,
tr.: Francisco Pérez, Mexico, Compañía general de
ediciones, [n.d.,] pp.169-190 (Spanish).
677.   "The hobo and the fairy," *Saturday Evening Post*, 183:
12-13, 41-42 (Feb. 11, 1911); *Cassell's Magazine*, 53:
219-226 (Nov. 1911); BW, TT. Translations: "Klaidonis
un Laumiņa," *Jaunības Tekas*, no. 8:40-52 (1925)
(Latvian); "Brodiaga i feia," *Sem'ia i shkola*, no. 12:
22-25 (1956) (Russian).
678.   "House of Mapuhi," *McClure*, 32:247-260 (Jan. 1909);
Windsor Magazine, 30:17-30 (June 1909); *Golden Book*,
5:832-842 (June 1925); BSS, FSS, LLOS, SST, Carl
Stroven and A. Grove Day, *The spell of the Pacific:*
an anthology of its literature, New York, Macmillan,
1949, pp.249-269; E. C. Parnwell, *Stories of the South*
Seas, New York, Oxford University Press, 1928, pp.302-
329; Glenn McCracken and Charles C. Walcutt, *Basic*
reading, book 8, Philadelphia and New York, c1965, pp.
312-334. Translations: "Mapuhis Hus," tr.: H. Buhl,
Hjemmets Noveller, 8:397-410 (June 1, 1910) (Danish);
"Mapuhi maja," *Romaan*, no. 23:717-720, no. 24:744-750
(1925) (Estonian); *Die Perle*, Berlin, Büchergilde Gutenberg, 1928, 50pp. (German); "Mapuhi māja," *Jaunības*
Tekas, no. 10:18-32 (1922) (Latvian).
679.   "House of pride," *Pacific Monthly*, 24:599-607 (Dec.
1910); HP, SSM.
680.   "House of the sun," *Pacific Monthly*, 23:1-11 (Jan. 1910);
Mid-Pacific Magazine, 9:591-596 (June 1915).
681.   "Husky--the wolf-dog of the north," *Harper's Weekly*,
44:611-612 (June 30, 1900).
682.   "The hussy," *Cosmopolitan*, 62:18-23, 94-99 (Dec. 1916);
RO.
683.   "A hyperborean brew," *Metropolitan Magazine*, 14:85-96
(July 1901); reprinted in FM as "Hyperborean brew: the

story of the scheming white man among the strange people who live on the rim of the Arctic Sea."
684. "In a far country," *Overland Monthly*, 33:540-549 (June
1899); *Overland Monthly*, n.s. 51:270-278 (March 1908);
Los Angeles *Times*, Jan. 14, 1917, iv:12; CWP, FSS, JLS,
SW, TFN, WFOS.
685. "In the cave of the dead (Shin bones)," *Cosmopolitan*,
65:74-81, 119-121 (Nov. 1918); reprinted as "Shin-Bones,"
in OMM.
686. "In the forests of the north," *Pearson's Magazine*, 14:
875-884 (Sept. 1902); CF.
687. "In the time of Prince Charley," *Conkey's Magazine*, 5:
1-3 (Sept. 1899).
688. "In Yeddo Bay," *St. Nicholas*, 30:292-296 (Feb. 1903);
CWP, DC, JLS, SSS.
689. "The inevitable white man," *Black Cat Magazine*, 16,2:
1-10 (Nov. 1910); *Canadian Monthly*, 42:605-610 (April
1914); *Golden Book*, 17:124-130 (Feb. 1933); Oakland
Tribune, magazine section, Dec. 31, 1916, pp.2-3;
Bristol *Observer*, May 14, 1910, pp.1-2, SST. Translations: "Saatuslik valge," *Odamees*, no. 2:50-52, no.
3:79-81 (1925) (Estonian); "Neišvengiamas baltasis
žmogus," tr.: V. K., *Lietuva*, no. 234 (1923) (Lithuanian); *Majera*, tr.: Mohammad Jaafar Mahjoub, Tehran,
Amir Kabir Publishing Institute, 1951, 14pp. (Persian).
690. "Jan, the unrepentant," *Outing*, 36:474-477 (July 1900);
San Francisco *Call*, April 5, 1903, p.7; CWOS-1960, CWP,
GF, JLS, TA. Translations: *Jan l'indomabile*, Milan,
Sonzogno, 1937, 32pp. (Italian).
691. "The jokers of New Gibbon," *Saturday Evening Post*, 184:
18-19, 65-66 (Nov. 11, 1911); *Grand Magazine*, 16:283-
291 (Aug. 1912), SS. Translations: "Jaunās Gibbonas
jokupēteri," *Jaunās Dienas Lapas Pielikums*, nos. 280,
288 (Dec. 14, 21, 1912) (Latvian).
692. "Just meat," *Cosmopolitan*, 42:535-542 (March 1907);
Golden Book, 20:577-587 (Nov. 1934); BW, LLOS, SST,
WGL; reprinted as "Pals," *London Magazine*, 20:184-193
(April 1908; *Ellery Queen's Mystery Magazine*, 45,2:35-
48 (Feb. 1965). Braille edition (transcribed for The
National Library for the Blind, London, England); 1 vol.
(Grade I). Sept. 1948. Translations: "Nur Fleisch," tr.:
Erwin Magnus, in *Im Reich des Grauens: die besten un-
heimlichen Geschichten*, ausgewählt von Eileen Margo,
Hamburg, Mosaik Verlag, 1962, pp.108-129 (German);
"Gaļas gabals," tr.: G. Milbcrgs, *Jaunās Dienas Lapas
Pielikums*, no. 225 (Oct. 11, 1913), no. 231 (Oct. 18,
1913), no. 237 (Oct. 25, 1913); ibid., no tr. given,
Vidzemnieku Kalendārs, 1916:3-22 (Latvian); *Faghat*

goosht, tr.: Nozar, no imprint data, 27pp. (Persian).
693. "Keesh, the bear hunter," *Holiday Magazine for Children*,
1,6:163-167 (Jan. 1904); reprinted as "The story of
Keesh," *C. B. Fry's Magazine*, 4:365-368 (Jan. 1906);
Novel Magazine, 7:658-661 (Aug. 1908); *Blackie's New
systematic English readers. Fifth reader*, London,
Blackie & Son, 1915, pp.169-183; Leland B. Jacobs and
Shelton L. Rort, *Ideas in literature*, book 1, Columbus,
Ohio, Merrill Books, c1966, pp.131-138; BSS, BW, JLSB,
LL, SSM. Translations: *Kish*, tr.: M. Kamran, Baku,
Detiunizdat, 1951, 19pp. (Azerbaijani); "Kiša noslepums,"
Dzīve, no. 30:14-16 (1930) (Latvian); "Padavimas apie
Kiša," tr.: N. B., *Skautu aidas*, no. 3:4-6 (1928); ibid.,
tr.: V. Tumēnas, *Švietimo keliai*, no. 5 (1932) (Lithu-
anian); *Eskimosik Kish*, Moscow and Leningrad, Gosizdat.,
1928, 22pp.; 1930, 14pp. (Russian).
694. "Keesh, son of Keesh," *Ainslie's Magazine*, 8:526-532
(Jan. 1902); CF, JLS. Translations: [This story has been
a favorite in the non-Russian languages of the Soviet
Union. The titles have been transliterated from the
Russian alphabet.] *Skazanie o Kishe*, Baku, Azerneshp,
1935, 24pp.; ibid., Minsk, Belgosizdat., 1958, 16pp.
(Dlia mladsh. i sred. vozrasta); ibid., Groznyĭ, Chech-
inggosizdat., 1939, 18pp. (Dlia ml. vozrasta); ibid.,
Alma-Ata, 1937, 17pp.; ibid., tr.: F. Iarkova, Kudymkar,
Komigosizdat, 1938, 16pp. (Dlia mladsh, vozrasta); ibid.,
tr.: A. Lazareva, Tiraspol', Gos. izd. Mold. ASSR, 1938,
16pp. (Dlia ml. vozrasta); ibid., tr.: G. Krinko, Kishinev, "Shkoalacovetiké," 1953, 20pp.; ibid., tr.:
Azamov i Khodzhaev, Tashkent-Samarkand, Detiunizdat
UzSSR, 1940, 16pp. (Dlia ml. vozrasta); ibid., Petrozavodsk, 1936; ibid., tr.: N. Grin, Cheboksary, Chuvashgosizdat, 1937, 11pp.
695. "King of the Greeks," *Youth's Companion*, 79:97-98
(March 2, 1905); Pall Mall Magazine, 35:423-430 (April
1905); TFP.
696. "The king of the Mazy May," *Youth's Companion*, 72:629-
630 (Nov. 30, 1899); *The Captain*, 14:231-235 (Dec. 1905);
Scholars' Own, n.s., 5,52:86-88 (Dec. 1910).
697. "... A Klondyke adventure. A Klondyker tells the story
of an exciting boat-ride through the White Horse Rapids
and the Box Canyon of the Yukon River," *Home Magazine*,
12,6:525-529 (June 1899); reprinted as "Through the
rapids on the way to Klondike" in TA and in *The trail
of ninety-eight*, ed. by Lowell Thomas, Jr., N. Y.,
Duell, Sloan and Pearce, 1962, pp.23-28. Translations:
"Cherez stremninyk Klondaiku," tr.: T. Litvinovoi,
Smena, no. 10:22-23 (1960) (Russian).

698. "Koolau the leper," *Pacific Monthly*, 22:569-578 (Dec.
1909); *Uncle Remus's, the Home Magazine*, 26:5-8 (Jan.
1910); *Observer* (Adelaide), 69:12 (March 16, 1912);
Bulawayo *Chronicle*, 35:8 (Feb. 23, 1912); *The Weekly
Scotsman*, Feb. 17, 1912, p.2; Manchester *Weekly Times*,
Feb. 17, 1912, p.12; HP, SSM; A. Grove Day and Carl
Stroven, *A Hawaiian reader*, New York, Popular Library,
1961, pp.167-182. Translations: 'Vaba mees,' *Vaba Maa*,
March 17-21, 1926; abridged as "Pidalitôbine Koolau,"
tr.: U. Poots, *Noorus*, 1:26-29 (1958) (Estonian);
"Koolau el leproso," *Repertorio americano*, 14:154-158
(1927) reprinted from the Valencia ed. of *La llamada
de la selva*. (Spanish).
699. "Law of life," *McClure*, 16:435-438 (March 1901); BSS,
BSS-EB, CF, CWP, CWOS-1960, JLS, TA. Translations:
"Elu kask," *Nadal, Paevelehe piltidega erileht*, no. 3
(17):5 (1925) (Estonian); "The law of life. Das Gesetz
des Lebens," in *Classic American short stories. Klas-
sische amerikanische Kurzgeschichten* (Munich) Edition
Langewiesche-Brandt [1st ed., 1956; 4th edition, 1961]
pp.34-51. [Bilingual edition with the English on one
page and the German translation by Maria von Schweinitz
on the other]; "Lögmál lífsins," tr.: Steingrímur Matthíasson, *O inn*, 14:30-32 (1918) (Icelandic); "Dzīvības
līkums," *Lidums*, nos. 86-88 (April 13-15, 1915)
(Latvian); *Ghanooné zendegui*, tr.: A. B. Zand, Tehran,
Sepehr Publications, 1957, 8pp. (Persian); "Zakon
zhizni," tr.: G. Alsaliamov, *Sovet édebiiaty*, no. 4:6-8
(1941) (Tatar).
700. 'Lawgivers," *Collier's*, 53:15-16, 28-29 (June 20, 1914).
701. "League of the old men," *Brandur Magazine*, 1:7-11 (Oct.
4, 1902); *California Review*, 2:376-383 (1904); *Grand
Magazine*, 1:86-96 (Aug. 1906); *Golden Book*, 13:56-62
(March 1931); Herman Whitaker, ed., *The Spinner's book
of fiction*, San Francisco, Elder, 1907, pp.141-165; BH,
BSS, CF.
702. "The leopard man's story," *Leslie's Magazine*, 56:408
(Aug. 1903); *Windsor Magazine*, 19:489-491 (March 1904);
JLS, JLSB, MF. Translations: "Leopardide taltsutaja
juttudest," *Tallinna Teataja ja Tallinna Uudiste kirjandusline-teadusline lisa "Kulaline"*, no. 26:201-203
(1913); 'Metsloomad," *Perekonnaleht*, no. 11:82-83 (1914);
"Leopartide taltsutaja jutustus," in J. Aavik, *Katsed
ja näited*, Tartu, 1916, pp.36-41 (Estonian); "Leopardu
dīdītāja stāsts," *Jaunā Dienas Lapa*, nos. 81-83 (April
24-27, 1915); ibid., tr.: V. Davids, *Dzimetenes Vēstnesis*, no. 179 (Aug. 4, 1912) (Latvian).
703. "A lesson in heraldry," *National Magazine*, 11:635-640

(March 1900).

704. "Li Wan, the fair," *Atlantic*, 90:212-221 (Aug. 1902); CF.

705. "Like Argus of the ancient times," *Hearst's Magazine*, 31:176-178, 214-216 (March 1917); RO. Translations: "Vectēvs," *Juanības Tekas*, no. 8:45-50 (1926), no. 9:29-41 (1926), no. 10:22-40 (1926) (Latvian).

706. "A little account with Swithin Hall," *Saturday Evening Post*, 184:12-14, 40-41 (Sept. 2, 1911); *Grand Magazine*, 16:435-445 (Sept. 1912); SS.

707. "Local color," *Ainslie's Magazine*, 12:74-82 (Oct. 1903); JLSB, MF.

708. "Lost face," New York *Herald*, Dec. 13, 1908, art section, p.7; *Lady's realm*, 26:524-532 (1909); *Golden Book*, 16:85-92 (July 1932); BSS, BSS-EB, JLSB, LF, TA. Translations: *Abérou bakhté*, tr.: A. B. Zand, Tehran, Sepehr Publication, 1957, 14pp. (Persian); "Rostro perdido," translated from the French by L.L., *Caras y caretas*, no. 1589:[16pp.] (March 16, 1929) (Spanish).

709. "The lost poacher," *Youth's Companion*, 75:121-122 (March 14, 1901); *C. B. Fry's Magazine*, 4:527-532 (March 1906) CWP, DC, JLS, SSS; L. Thompson, ed., *Youth's Companion*, Boston, Houghton Mifflin, 1954, pp.287-297.

710. "Love of life," *McClure*, 26:141-158 (Dec. 1905); *Blackwoods*, 178:765-780 (Dec. 1905); Los Angeles *Times*, Dec. 1, 1907, iv:11; *Golden Book*, 1:165-174 (Feb. 1925); ACS, BSS, BSS-EB, CWSS, JLSB, LL, LLOS, SDT, SP-1946, SSN, St-K, St-T, TA; S. Graham, ed., *Great American short stories*, London, Benn, 1931, pp.742-764; R. Blankenship, et al., *American literature*, Chicago, Scribners, 1948, pp.223-241; Robert Pearsall and Ursula Spier Erickson, ed., *The Californians: writings of their past and present*, San Francisco, Hesperian House, 1961, 1:452-474; R. L. Ramsay, *Short stories of America*, Boston, Houghton, 1921, pp.231-254; P. Skelton, ed., *Animals all*, New York, Day, 1956, pp.211-235; *Reading prose fiction*, edited by Joseph Satin, Boston, Houghton Mifflin, 1964, pp.377-394; Mark A. Neville and Max J. Herzberg, *Literature in America*, Chicago, Rand McNally, c1958, pp.605-620. Braille edition [U. S.]: Grade 1 1/2, 1 vol. Hand-copied. [n.d.] Translations: "Láska k životu," tr.: Štefan Kýška, in *Dni a noci ameriky*, Spoločnost priatelov Krásnych knih, 1964, pp.103-123 (Czech/Slovak); "L'amour de la vie," tr.: Paul Wenz, *L'Illustration*, supplement for Feb. 10-24, 1912, pp.3-18 (French); *Love of life. Liebe zum Leben* (Munich) Edition Langewiesche-Brandt [1962] 79pp. [Bilingual

edition with the English on one page and the German
translation of Erwin Magnus on the other]; "Zelts un
dzīvība," *Stāsti un Romāni*, no. 47:6-8 (1937); "Ciņa
deļ dzīvības," *Jaunā Dienas Lapa*, no. 19 (Feb. 6, 1915);
ibid., tr.: T. Reinfelde, Darba *Balss*, nos. 144-155
(July 4-17, 1922) (Latvian); *Eshgh be zendēgui*, tr.:
Nozar, Tehran, Ranguin Press, 1951, 30pp. (Persian).
[It has also appeared in the following non-Russian
translations of the Soviet Union:] *Liubov' k zhizni*,
tr.: A. Grigoriana; biographical sketch by A. Roskina,
Erevan, Armgiz., 1938, 40pp. (Armenian); ibid., tr.:
N. Stepanovoǐ, Cheboksary, Chuvashgosizdat, 1940, 48pp.
(Chuvash); ibid., tr.: N. Kanaeva, Iakutsk, Gosizdat,
1948, 29pp. (Iakutsk).

711. "Madness of John Harned," *Everybody's Magazine*, 23:657-
666 (Nov. 1910); *Lady's realm*, 26:570-581 (1909); BH,
NB; F. L. Pattee, ed., *Century readings in the American
short story*, New York, D. Appleton-Century, 1927, pp.
432-440.

712. "Make westing," *Sunset Magazine*, 22:357-360 (April 1909);
ACS, BH, BW, LLOS, SDT, SST, WGL; C. W. Gray, ed., *Deep
waters*, New York, Holt, 1928, pp.71-81; W. McFee, ed.,
World's great tales of the sea, New York, Cleveland,
World, 1944, pp.114-120 and as "Making westing," *Pall
Mall Magazine*, 41:453-458 (April 1908). Translations:
"Hoidku ôhtu poole," *Tallinna Teataja ja Tallinna Uud-
iste kirjandusline-teadusline lisa "Külaline,"* no. 38:
297-302 (1913) (Estonian); "Faire route à l'ouest," tr.:
P. Reneaume, *Revue de Paris*, 24:196-204 (Jan. 1, 1917)
(French).

713. "Man of mine," *Hearst's Magazine*, 31:111, 130-134
(Feb. 1917).

714. "Man with the gash," *McClure*, 15:459-465 (Sept. 1900);
San Francisco *Call*, Dec. 13, 1903, p.8; Los Angeles
Tribune, Sunday magazine section, June 9, 1912, [6];
CWOS-1960, CWP, GHF, JLK, SSM, TA. Translations:
L'uomo della cicatrice, Milan, Sonzogno, 1941, 32pp.
(Italian); "Cilvēks ar rētu," tr.: J. Bite, *Dzīve*, no.
15 (1914) (Latvian).

715. "The marriage of Lit-Lit," *Frank Leslie's Popular
Monthly*, 56:461-468 (Sept. 1903); *Famous Story Magazine*,
3,2:225-229 (Sept. 1926); FM, JLS. Translations: "Lit-
lit ištek ėjimas," tr.: A. Kaliesnykietis, *Rytas*,
March 17, 19, 20, 1928 (Lithuanian).

716. "The master of mystery," *Out West*, 17:330-339 (Sept.
1902); CF; Ellery Queen, ed., *Ellery Queen's 1963
anthology*, New York, Davis Publications, 1962, 4:152-
160. (Russian). Translations: *Charodei*, Gomel, Gomelski,

Rabochi, 1926, 19pp.
717. "Mauki," *Hampton's Magazine*, 23:752-760 (Dec. 1909);
ACS, LLOS, SSM, SST. Translations: "Mauki," *Līdums*,
nos. 151-156 (June 20-25, 1915); ibid., tr.: A. Arājs,
Sarkanais Karogs, nos. 4-8 (Jan. 5-11, 1919) (Latvian).
718. "The men of forty mile: 'Malemute Kid' deals with a
duel," *Overland Monthly*, n.s. 33:401-405 (May 1899);
reprinted in CWP, SW, TFN.
719. "The Mexican," *Saturday Evening Post*, 184-6-8, 27-30
(Aug. 19, 1911); *London Magazine*, 27:631-644 (1912); BH,
BSS, LLOS, MEX, NB, SSM, SSMo, St-K, TA; H. U. Ribalow,
ed., *The world's greatest boxing stories*, New York,
Twayne, 1952, pp.216-239; Robert Pearsall and Ursula
Spier Erickson, eds., *The Californians: writings of
their past and present*, San Francisco, Hesperian House,
1961, 1:475-503. Braille edition (transcribed for The
National Library for the Blind, London, England): 1 vol.
(Grade 1). Also 1 vol. (Grade 2). Each 1948. Translations: *Meksikanets*, tr.: V. G. Shil'dizkov, Cheboksary, Chuvashgosizdat, 1940, 52pp. (Chuvash); *Mexikán*,
tr.: K. Vít, Prague, Kočí, 1925, 36pp.; *Mexičan*, tr.:
S. Kýška, Bratislava, Sport, 1957, 23pp. (Czech/Slovak);
"Mehikaanlane," *Vaba Maa kirjandus ja teadus*, nos. 4-5:
347-350 (1921); "Mehikaanlane," tr.: A. Hint [with re-
marks about the author by the editor's office], *Kehakul-
tuur*, no. 2:52-53, 3:80-81, 5:136-138, 6:164-165 (1950);
Mehhiklane, tr.: P. Jalaja, Tallinn, Pedagoogiline Kir-
jandus, 1941, 40pp. (Estonian); *Das Geheimnis des
Felipe Rivera*, Berlin, Neues Leben, 1950, 1953, 31pp.
(Das neue Abenteuer 8); *Der Mexikaner Felipe Rivera*,
Berlin, Volk und Wissen, 1960, 1961, 31pp.; *Der
Mexikaner Felipe Rivera. Der Schrei des Pferdes*, Leip-
zig, Insel-Verlag, 1951, 1952, 1954, 1960, 69pp. (Insel-
Bucherei 163) (German); "Ha-naar ha-meksikani," in
'Azim veno'azim, ed. and tr. by Sh. Yoram, Tel-Aviv,
Yavneh [1959] pp.208-259 (Hebrew); *Meksikanets*, Syktyv-
kar, Komigosizdat, 1938, 56pp. (Komi); ibid., Nizhni
Novgorod, Nizhegorodskaya Kommuna, 1927, 32pp.; ibid.,
tr.: D. M. Gorfinkel, Moscow and Leningrad, Detizdat,
1937, 47pp.; ibid., *Molodezh' Moldavii* (Kishinev),
Jan. 14, 1956 (Russian); ibid., tr.: A. Kurbanov, Ashkhabad, Turmengosizdat, 1958, 102pp. (Turkoman); ibid.,
tr.: P. Gandziuri, Kiev, Detizdat, 1957, 39pp.
(Ukranian).
720. "Minions of Midas," *Pearson's Magazine*, 11:698-705
(May 1901); *Illustrated London News*, 128:485-486 (April
7, 1906); JLSB, MF. Translations: "Midase lapsed,"
Peterburi Teataja Kirjandusline-teadusline lisa, no. 32:

257-260 (1912) (Estonian).
721. "Moon face," *Argonaut* (San Francisco), no. 1323:36
(July 21, 1902); MF; *Argonaut stories*, San Francisco,
Poyot, Upham & Co., 1906, pp.1-10; JLSB, SDT. Translations: "Kuu nägu," in A. Pranspill, *Ameerika
antoloogia*, Tartu, 1928, pp.187-194 (Estonian);
"Mēneša gīmis," *Jaunā Dienas Lapa*, nos. 74-78 (April
16-21, 1915) (Latvian).
722. "Nam-Bok, the liar," *Ainslie's Magazine*, 10:29-37 (Aug.
1902); reprinted in JLS and as "Nam-Bok, the unveracious," BW, CF, CWP. Translations: "Nam-Bok, valetaja,
Romaan, no. 13:393-398, 14:423-425 (1929) (Estonian);
"Melis," *Jaunā Dienas Lapa*, nos. 39-53 (Feb. 28-March
17, 1916) (Latvian).
723. "Negore, the coward," in LL. Translations: *Negore il
vile*, Milan, Sonzogno, 1937, 1942, 32pp. (Italian);
"Negor el vil," *Revista paraguaya*, año 2, 1:40-42,
2:41-42 (1936) (Spanish).
724. "The night-born," *Everybody's Magazine*, 25:108-117
(July 1911); Canterbury (New Zealand) *Times*, Aug. 16,
1911, pp.10-11; San Francisco *Call*, March 10, 1913,
p.7; NB; *Century readings for a course in American
literature*, New York, Century, 1926, 2:1032-1039.
725. "A night's swim in Yeddo Bay," Oakland High School
Aegis, 10, 9:10-12 (May 27, 1895).
726. "Nose for the king," *Black Cat Magazine*, 11:1-6 (March
1906); Oakland *Tribune*, magazine section, Jan. 14, 1917,
p.2; BH, BW, LLOS, SST, WGL. Translations: "Nina kunin-
gale," *Kodu*, no. 8:151-153 (1922) (Estonian); "Deguns,"
Jauntbas Tekas, no. 12:65-68 (1925); "Deguns priekš
karaļa," *"Unguntiņa,"* 1928:16-22; "Teika par gudro,
kurš maklēja karalim degunu," *Atpūtai*, no. 46 (Nov. 23,
1924) (Latvian).
727. "Nothing that ever came to anything," *Sunset Magazine*,
27:573-574 (Nov. 1911); HD.
728. "Odyssey of the north," *Atlantic Monthly*, 85:85-100
(Jan. 1900); BSS, BSS-EB, CWOS-1960, CWSS, FSST, SW,
TA; separately published as Little Blue Book No. 1022,
ed. by E. Haldeman-Julius, Girard, Kansas, Haldeman-
Julius Co., 1920, 60pp.; Irwin R. Blacker, ed., *The old
West in fiction*, New York, Ivan Obolensky, 1961, pp.
349-373. Translations: *Uusi Odysseus. Kuvaus napaseu-
dulta*, tr.: O[nni] H[amara], Hämeenlinna, Arvi A.
Karisto, 1910, 86pp. (Finnish).
729. "Old Baldy," *Evenings at home*, Sept. 1894, p.218;
Orange Judd Farmer, no. 127:281-282 (Sept. 16, 1899);
American Agriculturist, 64,12:281-283 (Sept. 16, 1899);
New England Homestead, 39:281-283 (Sept. 16, 1899).

730. "On the Makaloa mat," *Cosmopolitan*, 66:16-20, 22-23, 133-135 (March 1919); BSS, OMM.
731. "One more unfortunate," Oakland High School *Aegis*, 10, 18:12-14 (Dec. 18, 1895).
732. "The one thousand dozen," *National Magazine*, 17:703-713 (March 1903); *Windsor Magazine*, 20:175-185 (July 1904); *Sunday Illustrated Magazine of the Commercial Appeal* (Memphis, Tenn.), Oct. 26, 1913, pp.3-5, 13-15; FM, SSM, TA, WFOS.
733. "The passing of Marcus O'Brien," *Reader Magazine*, 11: 135-144 (Jan. 1908); *Illustrated Sporting & Dramatic News*, Christmas no. 1908:19-21; *American Sunday Monthly Magazine*, Feb. 4, 1912, pp.14-15, 19, 25-26; LF, TA.
734. "The pearls of Parlay," *Saturday Evening Post*, 189:9-11, 64-66 (Oct. 14, 1911); *Grand Magazine*, 17:117-131 (Nov. 1912); BSS, BSS-EB, FSSt, SS, TA; Translations: "Parlays Perlen," in *Winde weh'n Schiffe geh'n: die schönsten Seegeschichten*, ausgewählt von Walter G. Armando, Hamburg, Verlag der Freizeit-Bibliothek, 1961, pp.128-156 (German).
735. "A piece of steak," *Saturday Evening Post*, 182:6-8, 36-38 (Nov. 20, 1909); *Windsor Magazine*, 33:345-356 (Feb. 1911); BH, BSS, BSS-EB, FSSt, LLOS, SSM, SST, St-T, St-K, TA, WGL; G. Rice and H. W. H. Powel, eds., *Omnibus of sport*, New York, Harper, 1932, pp.530-549; H. I. Christ and J. Shostak, eds., *Short stories*, New York, Oxford Book Co., 1948, pp.277-295; H. U. Ribalow, ed., *The world's greatest boxing stories*. New York, Twayne, 1952, pp.198-215; *The Saturday Evening Post Treasury*, New York, Simon and Schuster, 1954, pp.102-110; P. Schwed and H. W. Wind, eds., *Great stories of the world of sport*, New York, Simon and Schuster, 1958, 2:129-146. Translations: *Kousek řízku*, tr.: M. Maixner, Prague, Kočí, 1924, 26pp. (Czech/Slovak); "Pēdēja sacīkste," tr.: J. Bite, *Jaunā Avīze*, nos. 2-8 (Jan. 21-Feb. 6, 1915) (Latvian); "Mèsos gabalas," tr.: A. Nekvedavičiūė *Kultūra*, no. 11:634-641 (1931) (Lithuanian); *Yek tekeh gousht*, tr.: Nozar, Tehran, Ranguin Press, 1951, 30pp. (Persian).
736. "Planchette," *Cosmopolitan*, 41:157-165 (June 1906), 259-266 (July 1906), 379-386 (Aug. 1906); MF.
737. "Pluck and pertinacity," *Youth's Companion*, 74:2-3 (Jan. 4, 1900); *C. B. Fry's Magazine*, 5:541-543 (Sept. 1906) as "The man who kept on."
738. "Poppy cargo," *Physical culture*, 66:17-19, 116-122 (July 1931).
739. "The priestly prerogative: sixth of the 'Malemute Kid' stories, *Overland Monthly*, 34:59-65 (July 1899); Los

Angeles *Times*, Dec. 24, 1916, iv;8; SW, TWS.

740. "The princess," *Cosmopolitan*, 65:20-27, 145-149 (June 1918); RO, TA. Translations: "Priznanje" in Raveljen Davorin, *Svet humorja in satire*, Ljubljana, Tiskarna "Slovenskega poročevaica," 1951. (Slovenian [?]).

741. "The prodigal father," *Woman's World*, 28,5;5, 29, 31-33 (May 1912); *Pall Mall Magazine*, 49:711-718 (May 1912); TT. Translations: "Glata i fa irinn," tr.: Axel Thorsteinson, *Sunnudagsbla i*, 2;11-22 (1925) (Icelandic); "Klaidonis tevs," *Jaunības Tekas*, no. 11: 49-61 (1925) (Latvian).

742. "The proper 'girlie'," *Smart Set*, 2:117-119 (Oct.-Nov. 1900).

743. "The proud goat of Aloysius Pankburn," *Saturday Evening Post*, 183:5-7, 33-36 (June 24, 1911); SS. Translations: "Kā izārstējās Aloizigs Penkbergs," *Jaunās Dienas Lapas Pielikums*, no. 177 (Aug. 16, 1913), no. 183 (Aug. 23, 1913), no. 189 (Aug. 30, 1913); "Kā viņš kļuva vesels," *Magazina*, no. 215:16-26, no. 216:17-26 (1936) (Latvian).

744. "Race for number three," *Current Literature*, 52:482-485 (April 1912); *Nash's Magazine*, 5:429-441 (Jan. 1912); SB, TA.

745. "Raid on the oyster pirates," *Youth's Companion*, 79:121-122 (March 16, 1905); *Pall Mall Magazine*, 35:554-560 (May 1905); SDT, TFP; *Children's Digest*, 7,71:74-86 (Oct. 1957); E. Greenlaw, et al., *Literature and life: book one* (rev. ed.), Chicago, Scott, Foresman, 1933, pp.7-15; D. H. Miles and C. M. Keck, eds., *Literature and Life: book one*, Chicago, Scott, Foresman, 1940, pp.19-27; Robert Pearsall and Ursula Spier Erickson, eds., *The Californians: writings of their past and present*, San Francisco, Hesperian House, 1961, pp.438-451.

746. "The red one," *Cosmopolitan*, 65:34-41, 132-138 (Oct. 1918); RO. Translations: "Sarkanā dievība," *Tukuma Balss*, nos. 9-16 (1927) (Latvian); *El idolo rojo*, tr.: D. Lenoir, Buenos Aires, Forjador, 1952, pp.7-57 of volume that also contains a translations of Edgar Allan Poe's "The black cat". [Copyright page gives title as *The red idol*] (Spanish).

747. "The rejuvenation of Major Rathbone," *Conkey's Magazine*, 6:5-6, 29 (Nov. 1899).

748. "A relic of the Pliocene," *Collier's Weekly*, 26:17, 20 (Jan. 12, 1901); FM, ST. Translations: "Pēdējais mamuts," tr.: A. Bite, *Dzīves Pielikums*, no. 36 (1912); "Aizvēsturisko laiku atlkiekas," *Atpūtai*, no. 23 (June 15, 1924) (Latvian).

232   *JACK LONDON: A BIBLIOGRAPHY*

749. "Sakaicho, Hona Asi and Hakadaki," Oakland High School
     Aegis, 10, 7:4-5 (April 19, 1895).
750. "The salt of the earth," *Anglo-American Magazine*, 8:1-
     16 (Aug. 1902).
751. "Samuel," *Bookman*,37:285-296 (May 1913); *Famous Story
     Magazine*, 2,1:98-108 (May 1926); BSS, StSt, TA; E. A.
     Cross, ed., *A book of the short story*, New York,
     American Book Co., 1934, pp.639-654; Anne Freemantle,
     ed., *Mothers*, New York, Day, 1951, pp.317-342.
752. "Scorn of women," *Overland Monthly*, n.s. 37:976-991
     (May 1901); San Francisco *Call*, April 24, 1904, p.7; GF.
753. "The sea-farmer," *Bookman*, 35:51-60 (March 1912); ACS,
     StSt.
754. "The seed of McCoy" *Century*, 77:898-914 (April 1909);
     Saga, 29:29-33, 78-83 (Feb. 1962); LLOS, SST, TA;
     Angus Burrell and B. Cerf, eds., *An Anthology of
     famous American stories*, New York, Modern Library,
     19[?] pp.698-711; A. Jessup, ed., *Representative Amer-
     ican short stories*, Boston, Allyn, 1923, pp.874-894;
     A. Jessup, ed., *Representative modern short stories*,
     New York, Macmillan, 1929, pp.672-702; *The Mast Mag-
     azine*, 3,2:11-13, 37-45 (Feb. 1946); Arthur Kaplan,
     ed., *The wide sea*, New York, Avon Book Division, 1962,
     pp.161-191; E. C. Parnwell, ed., *Stories of the South
     Seas*, New York, Oxford University Press, 1928, pp.266-
     301; C. Stead, ed., *Great stories of the South Sea
     islands*, Toronto, S. J. R. Saunders, 1956, pp.1-32;
     Day, A. Grove and Carl Stroven, *Best South Sea stories*,
     New York, Appleton-Century, 1964, pp.76-106; Bennett,
     George, ed., *Turning point: fourteen great tales of
     daring and decision*, New York, Dell (Laurel Leaf
     Library), 1965, pp.31-62. Translations:"Ujev pôrgu,"
     Odamees, nos. 4-5:109-114, no. 6:141-146 (1925); "Pôlev
     laev," tr.: G. Tammes, *Noorusmaa*, no. 9:267-275, no.
     10:292-296 (1926); *Pôlev laev*, tr.: G. Tammes, Tallinn,
     Eesti Ôpetajate Liit, 1926, 39pp. (Noorusmaa jutukir-
     jastik 2) (Estonian).
755. "Semper idem," *Black Cat*, 6:24-28 (Dec. 1900); ACS,
     LLOS, SST, WGL; Portland *Oregonian*, July 2, 1911, sec.
     6:7; Oakland *Tribune*, magazine section, Jan. 7, 1917,
     p.2; J. M. Cain, ed., *For men only*, Cleveland, World,
     1944, pp.310-314.
756. "Shadow and the flash," *Bookman*, 17:410-417 (June 1903);
     Windsor Magazine, 24:354-362 (Aug. 1906); *Current Lit-
     erature*, 41:585-591 (Nov. 1906); BH, JLSB, MF, SDT.
     Translations: "Vari ja laige," *Postimees*, Jan. 13, 16,
     1917 (Estonian); "Ēna un spožums," tr.: G. Mīlbergs,
     Jaunās Dienas Lapas Pielikums, no. 165 (Aug. 2, 1913),

no. 171 (Aug. 9, 1913) (Latvian).

757. "Sheriff of Kona," *American Magazine*, 68:384-391 (Aug. 1909); *Story-teller*, Jan. 1912, pp.707-712; HP.

758. "Shin-bones" in OMM.

759. "The sickness of Lone Chief," *Out West*, 17:468-475 (Oct. 1902); CF. Translations: "Vienīgā Virsaiša slimība," *Sociāldemokrāts*, nos. 287-290 (Dec. 19-23, 1926) (Latvian).

760. "The siege of the 'Lancashire Queen'," *Youth's Companion*, 79:149-150 (March 30, 1905); *Pall Mall Magazine*, 35:676-683 (June 1905); TFP.

761. "Siwash," *Ainslie's Magazine*, 7:108-115 (March 1901); San Francisco *Call*, June 28, 1903, p.7; Los Angeles *Tribune*, Sunday magazine section, June 2, 1912 [6]; CWP, GF, JLS. Translations:"Sivašiete" *Unguntiņa*, 1933: 47-65 (Latvian); "Sivašaitė," *Rytas*, Sept. 16-17, 19-22, 1927 (Lithuanian).

762. "A son of the sun," *Saturday Evening Post*, 183:18-20, 45 (May 27, 1911); *Grand Magazine*, 15:296-307 (May 1912); SDT, SS; Nella Braddy, *Masterpieces of adventure*..., New York, Doubleday, Page, 1922, pp.102-125.

763. "The son of the wolf: third of the 'Malemute Kid' stories," *Overland Monthly*, n.s. 33:335-343 (April 1899); *Overland Monthly*, n.s. 69:416-424 (May 1917); Los Angeles *Times*, Dec. 10, 1916, iii:20-21; SW, WFOS; T. H. Briggs, et al., *Romance*, Boston, Houghton Mifflin, 1940, pp.31-42; Herman Whitaker, ed., *West winds*..., San Francisco, Paul Elder, 1914, pp.115-133. Translations: Eine Beute der Wölfe, Berlin-Grunewald, Verlag Deutsche Jugendbücherei, 1953, 32pp. (Deutsche Jugendbücherei 78) (German); *Il figlio del lupo*, Milan, Sonzogno, 1937, 32pp. (Italian); *Passare gorg*, tr.: Mohammad Jaafar Mahjoub, Tehran, Sepehr Publications, 1957, 28pp. (Persian); "El hijo del lobo," in *La maldición de los mil besos*, Biblioteca misterio, 1923, [?]pp. (Spanish).

764. "South of the slot," *Saturday Evening Post*, 181:3-4, 36-38 (May 22, 1909); *Labour Leader* (London), Dec. 3, 1914, p.3; Dec. 10, 1914, p.8; Dec. 17, 1914, p.3; Dec. 24, 1914, p.8; ACS, BH, StSt. Translations: "Viņpus 'Spraugia'," tr.: V. Davids, *Brīvais Strēlnieks*, nos. 64-70 (July 1-8, 1917) (Latvian); *Po tu storonu cherty*, Nizhni Novgorod, Nizhegorodskaya Kommuna, 1925, 32pp.; *Po tu storonu "shcheli"*, Moscow, Novaya Moskva, 1924, 44pp.; ibid., Kharkov, Trud, 1923, 35pp. (Russian).

765. "Stalking the pestilence," *Collier's Weekly*, 53:11-12, 28-29 (June 6, 1914).

766. "Story of a typhoon off the coast of Japan," San Fran-
cisco *Call*, Nov. 12, 1893, p.11; reprinted in the San
Francisco *Call*, Oct. 9, 1920, p.1; Charmian London,
Jack London, London, Mills & Boon, 1921, 1:143-148.

767. "The story of Jees Uck," *Smart Set*, 8:57-70 (Sept.
1902); Providence (R.I.) *Tribune*, Sunday magazine,
May 3, 1913, pp.1-3, 12-15; *Famous Story Magazine*,
4,3:420-432 (Jan. 1927); BSS, FM. Translations: "Jees
Uki lugu," in *Kolm jutustust*, Tallinn, 1926, pp.30-58
(Estonian); *Alaskan tyttö*, Porvoo, Werner Söderström oy,
1922, 55pp. (Finnish); "L'histoire de Jiz-Uk," tr.:
Louis Postif, *Les oeuvres libres*, 131:111-142 (1932)
(French); *Historia Jessie Ook*, tr.: S. Kuszelewska-
Matuszewska, Warsaw, Bluszcz, 1923, 39pp. (Polish).

768. "Strength of the strong," *Hampton*, 26:309-318 (March
1911); *Labour Leader* (London), Nov. 5, 1914, p.1;
Nov. 12, 1914, p.3; Nov. 19, 1914, p.3; Nov. 26, 1914,
p.3; *Appeal to reason*, Dec. 11, 1920, p.3; Dec. 18,
1920, p.3; ACS, CWOS, F, SDT, StSt, TA; separately published with illustrations by Dan Sayre Groesbeck,
Chicago, Kerr, c1911, 29pp.; Chicago, Kerr, 1922, 20pp.;
ed. by E. Haldeman-Julius, Girard, Kansas, Haldeman-
Julius, [n.d.,] 30pp. (Little Blue Book no. 148).
Translations: *Silata na silnite*, tr.: Iv. Georgiev,
Sofia, Nova literatura, 1931, 20pp.; ibid., no tr.
given, Sofia, Sl. G. Bonev, 1938, 24pp.; ibid., tr.:
P. Rusev, Sofia, Svetovna misul, 1946, 32pp. (Bulgarian); *La forto de la fortaj*, tr.: Karl Froding, Amsterdam, 1914, 20pp. (Internacia socia revue. Serio da
eldonajoj 18) (Esperanto); *Sila silnego*, Warsaw, Wyd.
Wiezaleznej Partii Chlopskiej, 1926, 37pp. (Polish);
Sila silnykh, Moscow and Leningrad, Gosizdat, 1926,
31pp. (Russian).

769. "Sun-dog trail," *Harper's Magazine*, 112:83-91 (Dec.
1905); *Golden Book*, 4:538-546 (Oct. 1926); JLSB, LL,
SDT; M. L. Becker, ed., *Golden tales of the far West*,
New York, Dodd, 1935, pp.213-230; W. Targ, ed., *American west*, Cleveland, World, 1946, pp.54-66. Translations: "Neīstu sanļu ceļš," tr.: M. Ilgusils, *Talsu
Apriņka Vēstnesis*, nos. 6-20 (1923) (Latvian).

770. "The sunlanders," in CF.

771. "The tears of Ah Kim," *Cosmopolitan*, 65:32-37, 136-138
(July 1918); OMM.

772. "Terrible Solomons," *Hampton*, 24:347-354 (March 1910);
SST; J. L. French, ed., *Great sea stories*, New York,
Tudor Publishing Co., c1943, pp.141-156. Translations:
"Hirmsad Saalomoni saared," *Romaan*, no. 14: 434-440
(1924) (Estonian).

773. "Thanksgiving on Slav Creek," *Harper's Bazaar*, 33:1897-
     1898 (Nov. 24, 1900); *London Opinion & Today*, no. 90:
     326-328 (Dec. 9, 1905. Translations: "Den' Blagodar-
     eniia na Slav-Krik," tr.: I. Maiorova, *Komsomol'skaia
     pravda*, Sept. 27, 1945, p.4. (Russian).
774. "That dead men rise up never," in HD.
775. "That spot," *Sunset Magazine*, 20:371-376 (Feb. 1908);
     BW, DR, JLSB, LF; M. Block, ed., *Favorite dog stories*,
     Cleveland, World, 1950, pp.55-65; E. R. Mirrieless, ed.,
     Twenty-two short stories of America, New York, Heath,
     1937, pp.192-205; H. H. Wagenheim, ed., *Read up on
     life*, New York, Holt, 1952, pp.44-51; H. H. Wagenheim,
     ed., *Exploring life*, New York, Holt, 1956, pp.149-156.
776. "Their alcove," *Woman's Home Companion*, 27:3 (Sept.
     1900).
777. "These bones shall rise again," *Reader*, 2:27-32 (June
     1903); *Revolution*. Translations: "Ces os ressuciteront,"
     tr.: L. Postif, *Mercure de France*, 266:431-437 (March
     1, 1936). (French).
778. "A thousand deaths," *Black Cat Magazine*, 4:33-42
     (May 1899).
779. "To build a fire," *Youth's Companion*, 76:275 (May 29,
     1902).
780. "To build a fire," *Century*, 76:525-534 (Aug. 1908);
     Famous Story Magazine, 5,2:253-261 (March 1927);
     Reader's Digest, 33:128-132 (Nov. 1938); ACS, BH, BSS,
     BSS-EB, CWOS, CWSS, JLSB, LF, SDT, SSM, TA; R. C.
     Andrews, ed., *My favorite stories of the great outdoors*,
     New York, Greystone, 1950, pp.338-352; M. E. Ashmun,
     ed., *Modern short stories*, New York, Macmillan, 1914,
     pp.309-333; Matilda Bailey and Ullin W. Leavell, *A
     world expanding*, New York, American Book Co., 1963,
     pp.84-94; Richard S. Beal and Jacob Korg, *The complete
     reader*, Englewood Cliffs, Prentice-Hall, 1961, pp.154-
     167; J. A. Burrell and B. A. Cerf, eds., *Anthology of
     famous American stories*, New York, Modern Library,
     1953, pp.698-711; J. A. Burrell and B. A. Cerf, eds.,
     Bedside book of famous American stories, New York,
     Random House, 1938, pp.698-711; Elizabeth Collette, et
     al., eds., *Writers in America*, New York, Ginn, 1949,
     pp.288-296; Edmund Fuller and B. Jo Kinnick, *Adventures
     in American literature*, New York, Harcourt, Brace &
     World, c1963, pp.794-804; C. Grayson and Van H. Cart-
     mell, eds., *Golden Argosy*, New York, Dial, 1947, pp.
     380-393; *The Hilton bedside book: a treasury of enter-
     taining reading selected exclusively for the guests of
     the Hilton Hotels*, published by Hilton Hotels Corpor-
     ation, 1960, 5:132-149; Adrian H. Jaffe and Virgil

Scott, eds., *Studies in the short story*, New York, Holt,
Rinehart and Winston, 1960, pp.89-105; B. Kielty, ed.,
Treasury of short stories, New York, Simon and Schuster,
1947, pp.294-305; R. B. Inglis, et al., eds., *Adventures
in American literature*, New York, Harcourt, 1941, pp.
79-89; Rodney A. Kimball, *The short story reader:* re-
vised ed., New York, Odyssey, pp.147-163; Agnes L.
McCarthy and Delmer Rodabaugh, *Prose and poetry of
America*, Syracuse, L. W. Singer, c1963, pp.432-444;
H. W. McGraw, ed., *Prose and poetry of America*, Syra-
cuse, N.Y.; L. W. Singer, 1942, pp.724-740; W. S.
Maugham, ed., *Tellers of tales*, New York, Doubleday,
1939, pp.538-551; G. W. Norvell and Carol Hovious, eds.,
Conquest: book two, Boston, Heath, 1947, pp.355-369;
R. C. Pooley, ed., *All around America*, Chicago, Scott-
Foresman, 1959, pp.369-379; Mary Purcell and Robert C.
Wylder, *The narrative impulse*, New York, Odyssey Press,
1963, pp.1-18; H. C. Schweikert, et al., eds., *Adven-
tures in American literature*, New York, Harcourt, 1930,
pp.159-176; H. Shaw, et al., eds., *Collection of readings for writers*, New York, Harper, 1946, 1949, pp.
399-410; H. Shaw, *Complete course in freshman English*,
New York, Harper, c1959, pp.1025-1036; H. H. Wagenheim,
Ourselves and others, New York, Holt, 1956, pp.336-346;
H. R. Warfel, R. H. Gabriel and S. T. Williams, *The
American mind*, New York, American Book Co., 1937, pp.
1007-1014; H. A. Watts and O. Cargill, ed., *College
reader*, New York, Prentice-Hall, 1948, pp.569-580; Alex
M. Caughran and Lu Harrison Mountain, eds., *High school
reading: book 2*, New York, American Book Co., c1961,
pp.299-313; Gunnar Horn, *A cavalcade of American writing*,
Boston, Allyn & Bacon, 1964, pp.128-145; Barbara Pann-
witt, *The art of short fiction*, Boston, Ginn, 1964, pp.
167-181. It was published as "Never travel alone,"
C. B. Fry's Magazine, 4:441-445 (Feb. 1906). Transla-
tions: "Vuurmaak," *Wereldletterkunde...*, Cape Town,
Kinderkultuurvereniging, 1958, 1:253-269 (Afrikans);
Construire un feu, tr.: P. Gruyer and L. Postif, Paris,
C. Crès, 1929, 73pp.; another ed., Paris, C. Crès, 1929,
v, 45pp. (contains an introduction, "Quelques mots sur
Jack London") (French); "Fare un fuoco," tr.: Giovanni
Marcellini, *Nuova antologia*, 248:32-46 (July 1, 1926)
(Italian); *Dar talashê atesh*, tr.: A. B. Zand, Tehran,
Sepehr Publications, 1957, 19pp.; *Ateshi afrookhtan*,
tr.: Massoud Farzan, Tehran, Afshari Publishing Insti-
tute, n.d., 11pp. (Persian); "Acender um fuego," tr.:
Ruth Leão, *Os norteamericanos antigos e modernos*, Rio,
Leitura, 1945, [?]pp. [Portuguese]; "En las nieves de

Alaska," *Revista de revistas*, no. 283:20 (Sept. 26, 1915); no. 284:17 (Oct. 3, 1915); no. 285:16 (Oct. 10, 1915); "Preparar un fuego," tr.: Nina Maganov, in Cuentos norteamericanos clásicos, introduccion, selección y notas de Tomás Gustavo Escajadillo, (Lima) Instituto latinoamericano de vinculación cultura, 1964, pp.229-24-248 [Page 228 is a biographical sketch of London] (Spanish).

781. "To kill a man," *Saturday Evening Post*, 183:14-15, 40 (Dec. 10, 1910); *London Magazine*, 25:731-738 (1911); NB, St-T, St-K.

782. "To repel boarders," *St. Nicholas*, 29:675-679 (June 1902); DC, SA; Elizabeth O'Daly and Egbert W. Nieman, *Adventures for readers*, book one, New York, Harcourt, 1958, pp.287-293; *Sea stories: retold from St. Nicholas*, New York, Century, 1907, pp.3-16.

783. "To the man on the trail. A Klondike Christmas," *Overland Monthly*, n.s. 84:163-164 (June 1926); published as "To the man on trail," BSS, BSS-EB, CWOS-1960, CWSS, SW, TA, TWS. Translations: "Weihnacht im Norden," in *Unter dem Tannenbaum: die Weihnachtsgeschichten*, ausgewählt von Gisela Fjelrad, Hamburg, Mosaik Verlag, 1961, pp.347-356 (German). See errata following item 812.

784. "Told in the drooling ward," *Bookman*, 39:432-437 (June 1914); ACS, BH, TA, TT.

785. "Too much gold," *Ainslie's Magazine*, 12:109-117 (Dec. 1903); CWP, FM, JLS, SDT.

786. "Trust," *Century*, 75:441-448 (Jan. 1908); *Cassell's Magazine*, Feb. 1908, pp.282-290; *Famous Story Magazine*, 6,1:106-112 (May 1927); BW, JLSB, LF; R. Blankenship and W. H. Nash, eds., *Literature we like*, New York, Scribner, 1939, pp.248-260.

787. "The turning point," *Windsor Magazine*, 26:394-400 (Sept. 1907).

788. "Two gold bricks," *Owl*, 3:45-48 (Sept. 1897); W. McDevitt, *Jack London's first*, pp.12-17.

789. "Under the deck awnings," *Saturday Evening Post*, 183: 18-19 (Nov. 19, 1910); *Bystander*, 32:503-506 (Dec. 6, 1911); NB, St-K, St-T; Day Edgar, ed., *The Saturday Evening Post reader of sea stories*, Garden City, Doubleday, 1962, pp.1-8.

790. "The unexpected," *McClure*, 27:368-382 (Aug. 1906); *Blackwoods*, 164-180 (Aug. 1906); LF, JLSB, LL, SP-1946. Translations: "Negaidīts," *Līduma Pielikums*, nos. 28-30 (July 11, 18, 25, 1914); ibid., tr.: T. Reinfelde, *Darba Balss*, nos. 156-168 (July 18-Aug. 1, 1922) (Latvian); "O inesperado," in *Maravilhas do conto norte-americano*, introdução e notas de Edgard Cavalheiro ... traduçoès

revistas por T. Booker Washington, São Paulo, Editôra
Cultrix, 1957, pp.97-115 [Brief biography of London,
pp.95-96]; "O inesperado," in *Maravilhas do conto norte-
americano*, introdução e notas de Edgard Cavalheiro,
Sao Paulo, Editôra Cultrix, 1958, pp.97-115 [Biograph-
ical sketch of London, pp.95-96] (Portuguese); "Lo
imprevisto," *El Mercurio* (Santiago de Chile), April 18,
1926, Sunday supplement, pp.1, 3 (Spanish).

791. "Unparallelled invasion," *McClure*, 35:308-315 (July
1910); ACS, BH, StSt.

792. "Up the slide," *Youth's Companion*, 80:545 (Oct. 25,
1906); *Pall Mall Magazine*, 38:608-612 (Nov. 1906).

793. "Uri Bram's God," *Sunday Examiner Magazine* of the San
Francisco *Examiner*, June 24, 1900, p.10; reprinted as
"Which makes men remember" in GF; reprinted as "The
dead horse trail," *Ellery Queen's Mystery Magazine*,
43,6:60-66 (June 1964).

794. "War," *Nation* (London), 9:635-636 (July 29, 1911);
Current Literature, 51:452-454 (Oct. 1911); *The Sussex
Patrol*, the journal of the Batt. Royal Sussex Regiment,
no. 16:13-15 (Feb.-July 1918); *Scholastic*, 33:22-23E
(Nov. 5, 1938), NB, TA; F. H. Law, ed., *Modern short
stories*, New York, Century, 1918, pp.141-146; A. Brant
and F. H. Law, eds., *War or peace*, New York, Harper,
1938, pp.79-84; John D. Husband and Frank F. Bright,
From here on, Philadelphia and New York, J. B. Lippin-
cott, c1954, pp.162-167; Glenn McCracken and Charles C.
Walcutt, *Basic reading, book 7*, Philadelphia and New
York, J. B. Lippincott, c1964, pp.62-66.

795. "The water baby," *Cosmopolitan*, 65:80-85, 133 (Sept.
1918); OMM.

796. "The whale tooth," *Sunset*, 24:49-54 (Jan. 1910); ACS,
SST. Translations: "Valaskala kihv," *Odamees*, no. 4:
179-182 (1922); "Valaskala hammas," *Romaan*, no. 15:462-
465 (1923) (Estonian); "Il dente di balena," in Tenato
de Pont-Jest, *Il n. 13 della via Marlot*, Milan, Sonzogno, 1955, [?]pp. (Italian); "Misionars," Laiks,
1919:35-47 (Latvian).

797. "When Alice sold her soul," *Cosmopolitan*, 64:28-33,
105-107 (March 1918); OMM.

798. "When God laughs," *New Smart Set*, 21:39-44 (Jan. 1907);
WGL. Translations: "Kad dievi smejas," tr.: G. Milbergs,
Jaunās Dienas Lapas Pielikums, no. 195 (Sept. 6, 1913),
no. 201 (Sept. 13, 1913); ibid., no tr. given, *Pasaules
Pasts*, no. 33 (Aug. 13, 1933) (Latvian).

799. "When the world was young," *Saturday Evening Post*, 183:
16-17, 45-49 (Sept. 10, 1910); *London Magazine*, 26:679-
689 (1911); NB; J. French, ed., *Best psychic stories*,

New York, Boni & Liveright, 1920, pp.1-23.
800. "Where the trail forks," *Outing*, 37:276-282 (Dec. 1900);
San Francisco *Call*, Oct. 4, 1903, p.8; GF. Translations:
"Où bifurque la piste," tr.: L. Postif, *Annales politiques et littéraires*, 81:687-690 (Dec. 9, 1923)
(French); "Kur celi škiras," tr.: Saša, *Dzīve*, nos.
253-256 (Nov. 1-5, 1912); "Ten, kur skiriasi kiliai,"
tr.: A. Kalesnykietis, *Rytas*, July 6-7, 9-10 (1928);
ibid., no tr. given, *Unguntiņa*, 1932:41-51 (Latvian).
801. "White and yellow," *Youth's Companion*, 79:73-74 (Feb.
16, 1905); *Pall Mall Magazine*, 35:282-289 (1905); ST,
TFP. Translations: "Baltie un dzeltenie," tr.: V.
Dāvids, *Jaunais Vārds*, nos. 122-126 (June 13-17, 1916)
(Latvian).
802. "The white man's way," in JLSB, LL, SSM. Translations:
Valkean niehen tavat, tr.: Rieti Itkohen, Porvoo, Oswus-
kunta Visa, 1913, 24pp. (Finnish); "Kā rīkojās baltie
cilvēki," *Jaunā Dzīve*, no. 3:1-8 (1934); "Kā baltie
ļaudis rīkojās," *Latvija*, nos. 66-69 (April 3-8, 1913)
(Latvian).
803. "The white silence. Another story of the 'Malemute
Kid'," *Overland Monthly*, 33:138-142 (Feb. 1899); Los
Angeles *Times*, Feb. 11, 1917, iii:18; *Golden Book*,
10:51-55 (Oct. 1929); BH, BSS, CWOS-1960, SSM, SW, TA,
TWS; W. J. Dawson and C. W. Dawson, eds., *Great English
short stories*, New York, Harper, 1910, 2:307-320; J. R.
Frahes and Isadore Traschen, *Short fiction: a critical
collection*, Englewood Cliffs, Prentice Hall, 1959, pp.
14-21 [exercises on story, pp.21-24]; Edward Stone,
ed., *What was naturalism?* New York, Appleton-Century-
Crofts, 1959, pp.118-127; excerpt in Ella Sterling
Mighels, *Literary California*, San Francisco, 1918, pp.
344-345; Georgia Gantt Winn, et al., *Flights in friendship*, Syracuse, N. Y., Iroquois, c1953, pp.413-420.
Translations: "Täht," tr.: H. Pöögelmann, *Tapper*, no.
9:263-266 (1917) [fragment] (Estonian); "Le silence
blanc," tr.: P. Reneaume, *Revue de Paris*, 25:556-567
(Jan. 1, 1918) (French); *Il silenzio bianco*, Milan,
Sonzogno, 1937, 32pp. (Italian); "O grande silência
branco," tr.: Edison Carneiro, *Os Mais belos contos
norteamericanos*, Rio, Vecchi, 1945, pp.53-61 (Portuguese); "El gran silencio blanco," *Caras y caretas*,
no. 936, [occupies 4 pages, though all pages unnum-
bered] (Sept. 9, 1916) (Spanish).
804. "Who believes in ghosts!" Oakland High School *Aegis*,
10, 14:[1]-4, (Oct. 21, 1895); [a reproduction of part
of page from *Aegis* containing this story appears in
Oakland *Tribune*, Nov. 28, 1932, p.B3].

805. "Whose business is to live," in DC.
806. "A wicked woman," *New Smart Set*, 20:46-51 (Nov. 1906),
      WGL. Translations: *Podła kobieta*, tr.: M. Kuncewiczowa,
      Warsaw, Zakpady Graficzne Straszewicza, 1923, 15pp.
      (Polish).
807. "The wife of a king," *Overland Monthly*, 34:112-119
      (Aug. 1899); Los Angeles *Times*, Dec. 31, 1916, iiia;2;
      separately printed as Little Blue Book No. 223, ed. by
      E. Haldeman-Julius, Girard, Kansas, Haldeman-Julius
      Co., [n.d.,] 32pp, SW, TFN.
808. "Winged blackmail," *Lever* (Chicago), 1,2:54-57 (Sept.
      1910); NB.
809. "Wisdom of the trail," *Overland Monthly*, n.s. 34:541-
      544 (Dec. 1899); Los Angeles *Times*, Jan. 7, 1917,
      v:12; BSS, CWOS-1960, SSM, SW, TFN.
810. "Wit of Porportuk," *Times Magazine*, 1:11-25 (1909);
      Lady's realm, 25:465-480 (1909); *Sunset*, 24:159-172
      (Feb. 1910); *Famous Story Magazine*, 1,1:9-21 (Feb.
      1926); BSS, BSS-EB, LF. Translations: "L'esprit de
      Porportuk," tr.: Paul Gruyer and Louis Postif, *Les
      oeuvres libres*, 55:123-156 (1926) (French); *Aghlê Por-
      portuck*, tr.: A. B. Zand, Tehran, Sepehr Publications,
      1957, 28pp. (Persian).
811. "Yah! Yah! Yah!" *Columbian Magazine*, 3:439-447 (Dec.
      1910); San Francisco *Examiner*, Feb. 13, 1916, Sunday
      magazine section [13]; *Climax*, 9:31-35, 84-86 (March
      1962); ACS, BH, SSM, SST, TFN. Translations: "Ha-ha-
      haa!" *Odamees*, 1:21-25 (1925) (Estonian); "Yah! Yah!
      Yah!" in Tenato de Pont-Jes, *Il n. 13 della via Marlot*,
      Milan, Sonzogno, 1955; *Jazireh vahshat*, tr.: Mohammad
      Jaafar Mahjoub, Tehran, Sepehr Publications, 1951, 68
      [contains a 28-page biography of London]; ibid., 1957,
      25pp. (Persian).
812. "Yellow handkerchief," *Youth's Companion*, 79:225-226
      (May 11, 1905); *Pall Mall Magazine*, 36:333-339 (Sept.
      1905); BW, TFP.

Errata: Item 783, "To the man on the trail. A Klondike
Christmas," should include the following: *Overland
Monthly*, 33:36-40 (Jan. 1899); *Overland Monthly*, n.s
69:25-29 (Jan. 1917).

CONTRIBUTIONS TO PERIODICALS
ALSO PERIODICAL POEMS AND LETTERS.

813. "Adventures in dream harbor," *Harper's Weekly*, 52:22
(Aug. 8, 1908); reprinted as "The first landfall" in CS.
814. "Adventures with the police," *Cosmopolitan Magazine*,
44:417-423 (March 1908); reprinted as "Bulls," *Contemporary Review*, 95:694-706 (June 1909) and in *The Road*.
Translation: *"Byki,"* Moscow, Novaya Moskva, 1924, 29pp.
(Russian).
815. "Again the literary aspirant," *Critic*, 41:217-220
(Sept. 1902).
816. "Amateur M.D.," *Pacific Monthly*, 24:187-203 (Aug. 1910);
CS.
817. "An amateur navigator," *Pacific Monthly*, 23:493-508
(May 1910); CS.
818. "An Alaskan vacation," *Panama Magazine*, 1:34-40 (May
1911).
819. "Are there any thrills left in life?" *Overland Monthly*,
n.s. 69:432 (May 1917).
820. "Bêche de mer English," *Woman's Home Companion*, 36:4
(April 1909); *Contemporary Review*, 96:359-364 (Sept.
1909); CS; Carl Stroven and A. Grove Day, *The spell of
the Pacific: an anthology of its literature*, New York,
Macmillan, 1949, pp.742-747.
821. "The birth mark," in HD.
822. "Bonin Islands. An incident of the sealing fleet of '93.
I," Oakland High School *Aegis*, 10,1:1-2 (Jan. 18, 1895);
TA.
823. "Bonin Islands. An incident of the sealing fleet of '93.
II," Oakland High School *Aegis*, 10,2:1-2 (Feb. 1, 1895);
TA.
"Bulls" *see* "Adventures with the police."
824. "Class struggle," *Independent*, 55:2603-2610 (Nov. 5,
1903); WC.
825. "Classic of the sea," *Independent*, 71:1297-1299 (Dec.
14, 1911); HD.
"Confession" *see* "My life in the underworld..."
826. "Contradictory teachers," *International Socialist Re-
view*, 3:648-652 (May 1, 1903); WC [Review of W. J.
Ghent's *Our benevolent feudalism* and John Graham Brooks'
The social unrest].
827. "Cruising in the Solomons," *Pacific Monthly*, 23:589-602
(June 1910), 24:35-43 (July 1910); *Uncle Remus's, the
Home Magazine*, 28:9-12 (Nov. 1910); CS.
828. "Daybreak," *National Magazine*, 14:547 (Aug. 1901)
[Poem].

TH. HIGH SCHOOL ÆGIS.

"In virtute summum bonum ponamus."

VOL. X. OAKLAND, CALIFORNIA, JANUARY 18, 1895. No. 1.

THE LAY OF THE STARS.

M. HELEN E. COOPER.

Fleecy clouds of misty vapor covered all the sky with white,
Veiling as with snowy curtains all the twinkling stars' sweet light;
Neither breeze nor sound intruded on the clouded, dusky, calm,
But the faint and gentle murmur of the brooklet's mystic charm.

Then I heard a sound of music, but so sweet and far away
That it seemed the sunbeams' mourning at the closing of the day;
As I listened, soft and plaintive, came a song upon the air,
And I heard the words distinctly, though I knew not whence or where.

"Years agone, as happy sunbeams, free from sorrow, free from care,
Day by day we danced and flitted in the balmy sunlit air.
How we sinned I dare not tell you—no one but ourselves e'er knew;
Neither can I tell how deeply, sadly, we our sin do rue.

"We had tho't to hide our sorrow, we had tho't to hide our shame
In some deep and dark recesses, where no beam of light e'er came;
We were stopped by Higher Powers, we were punished in our flight,
Still we stand all shaking, shivering, and betrayed by our own light.

"Night by night we watch and tremble, lest some stern avenger come,
And we listen for the message, 'Ye may rest, the night is done.
Every morn a golden sunbeam, messenger of gladsome light,
Tells us of the Day's glad coming, and the closing of the Night.

"But we begged one night of pleasure, sought one night our tale to tell,
Craved one night of joyous freedom, as we had before we fell.
It was granted, we have told thee"—lo the stars had stopped their lay,
Came the summons, now unwelcome, "Ye must cease for it is day."

BONIN ISLANDS.

An Incident of the Sealing Fleet of '93.

JACK LONDON, DEC. '97.

I.

How many beautiful, unfrequented spots there are that are practically unknown and unheard of! Unknown and unheard of, not only by that great class, the "stay-at-home" people, but by the wandering sight-seer.

> "Full many a flower is born to blush unseen,
> And waste its fragrance on the desert air."

So it is with these glorious garden spots of nature with which the world abounds—perfect paradises, that the curious traveler has never trod. The ignorant, uncouth inhabitants and the crews of an occasional ship, who do not even pause to realize their beauty, alone see them.

The Bonin Islands, situated between the 25th and 27th degrees of north latitude, and east longitude 140 degrees and 23 minutes, are one of these known, yet unknown spots—known to the navigator and chart-maker and almost entirely unknown to the rest of the world. They were discovered two hundred and fifty years ago, tradition says, by a great junk while beating back to Japan, after having been blown off the coast in a typhoon.

Soon after, the Japanese government took possession and colonized them; but fifty years later they were deserted. During the next two centuries their few inhabitants, abandoned by their mother country and cut off from all intercourse with the outside world, relapsed into a state of semi-barbarism. This beautiful but remote group of islets was forgotten, actually forgotten. The world knew of them no more. During the middle of this century, however, occasional whale ships ran in for water, and bought onions, sweet potatoes and yams from their half-civilized inhabitants, while the crews disported themselves ashore, hunting the wild hogs and deer with which the hills abounded, and catching fish and great green turtles along the reefs and shores.

But soon Japan, having aroused from her lethargy, began her onward march towards the civilization which at the present time causes the whole world to look upon her with astonishment and admiration, and awoke to the fact that the possession of these islands was not so trivial a

829. "Dignity of dollars," *Overland Monthly*, n.s. 36:53-57 (July 1900); *Overland Monthly*, n.s. 50:592-595 (Dec. 1907); *Revolution*.

830. "Economics of the Klondike," *Review of Reviews*, 21:70-74 (Jan. 1900).

831. "Editorial crimes," *Dillettante* (Oakland), March 1901, pp.171-174; *Occident*, 71:182-184 (Jan. 1917).

832. "Eggs without salt" [Joke] *Town Topics* (New York), 42, 9:7 (Aug. 31, 1899).

833. "Finding one's way on the sea," *Harper's Weekly*, 52:9-10 (Aug. 1, 1908); reprinted as "Finding one's way about" in CS.

834. "First aid to rising authors," *Junior Munsey Magazine*, 9:513-517 (Dec. 1900); reprinted as "The material side," *Occident*, 70:139-145 (Dec. 1916); San Francisco *Call*, Dec. 1, 1916, p.5.

835. "First poet," *Century*, 82:251-255 (June 1911); TT.

836. "Getting into print," *Editor*, 17:78-82 (March 1903); *London Opinion*, no. 53:361 (March 25, 1905); *T. P.'s Weekly*, 8,202:364 (Sept. 21, 1906); *Occident*, 71:179-182 (Jan. 1917), James D. Hart, ed., *My first publication: eleven California authors describe their earliest appearances in print*, The Book Club of California, 1961, pp.79-83 [pp.77-78 contain Hart's introduction to this selection]. Translations: "Kak ya nachal pechatatsya," tr.: V. Bykov, *Voprosy literatury*, no. 1:149-152, 168 (Jan. 1963) (Russian).

837. "Gold-hunters of the north," *Atlantic*, 92:42-49 (July 1903); *Revolution*.

838. "He chortled with glee," *Town Topics* (New York), 41, 16:8 (April 20, 1899).

839. "The high seat of abundance," *Woman's Home Companion*, 35:13-14, 70 (Nov. 1908); CS.

840. "Hoboes that pass in the night," *Cosmopolitan Magazine*, 44:190-197 (Dec. 1907); reprinted in *The Road*. Translations: "Piletita sôitjad," Päeveleht, Dec. 29-31, 1925 (selections) (Estonian); *Brodyagi, puteshestvuyushchiye nochyu*, Leningrad, Priboi, 1926, 31pp. (Russian).

841. "Holding her down, more reminiscences of the underworld," *Cosmopolitan Magazine*, 43:142-150 (June 1907); reprinted in *The Road*. Translations: *Zheleznodorozhnyie zaitsy*, Moscow, Novaya Moskva, 1924, 36pp. (Russian). "The house beautiful," *see* "My castle in Spain".

842. "House of the sun," *Pacific Monthly*, 23:1-11 (Jan. 1910); *Mid-Pacific Magazine*, 9:591-596 (June 1915).

843. "Housekeeping in the Klondike," *Harper's Bazaar*, 33:1227-1232 (Sept. 15, 1900).

844.   "How I became a socialist," *Comrade*, 2:122-123 (March
        1903); reprinted in San Francisco *Call*, May 7, 1905,
        p.23: Willard Thorp, et al., eds., *American issues*,
        New York, Lippincott, 1944, 1:723-725. Translations:
        "Ka es paliku par socialistu." Darbs. nos. 136-138
        (June 20-22, 1928) (Latvian).

845.   "How Jack London gets his audiences," *Wilshire's Mag-
        azine*, 13:10-11 (Oct. 1909); first printed in the U. S.
        as "Jack London on the movement and authorship," Oak-
        land *World*, June 5, 1909, p.2 [Reply to Andrew M.
        Anderson's letter in *The Socialist* (Melbourne, Austral-
        ia) entitled "Jack London. An Australian criticism
        with incidental reference to leaders" reprinted in
        Oakland *World*, June 5, 1909, p.2. London's letter is
        undated].

846.   "The human drift," *Forum*, 45:1-14 (Jan. 1911); reprint-
        ed in HD.

847.   "If I were God," *Town Topics* (New York), 41, 19:18
        (May 11, 1899).

848.   "If Japan wakens China," *Sunset Magazine*, 23:597-601
        (Dec. 1909).

849.   "Impossibility of war," *Overland Monthly*, n.s. 35:278-
        282 (March 1900).

850.   "Is civilization useful?" *Ajay Graphic* (San Francisco)
        Issue no. 1, Spring number, 1951, p.4.

851.   "Jack London in a confident mood," ed. by Alison
        Bishop, *Boston Public Library Quarterly*, 3:312-314 (1952)
        [Letter to Fanny K. Hamilton, July 16, 1906].

852.   "Jack London's plea for the square deal," *Overland
        Monthly*, n.s. 69:404 (May 1917) [undated letter].

853.   "Jack London's resignation from the Socialist Party,"
        Overland Monthly, n.s. 69:446 (May 1917) [letter dated
        Honolulu, March 7, 1916].

854.   "The joy of small-boat sailing," *Country Life in Amer-
        ica*, 22:19-23,54-56 (Aug. 1, 1912); reprinted as
        "Small-boat sailing," *Yachting Monthly*, 13:271-276
        (Aug. 1912) HD.

855.   "The joys of the surf-rider," *Pall Mall Magazine*, 42:
        326-331 (Sept. 1908).

856.   "The language of the tribe," *Mid-Pacific Magazine*, 10:
        117-120 (Aug. 1915); *Pan-Pacific*, 2, 2:10 (1938).

857.   "Lepers of Molokai," *Woman's Home Companion*, 35:7-8,
        45 (Jan. 1908); reprinted in *Contemporary Review*, 95:
        288-297 (March 1909); CS.

858.   [Letter dated Aug. 27, 1911 concerning the fictional
        function of the Jew in his works] *American Hebrew*,
        30:609 (Sept. 22, 1911). [The periodical's editor notes
        that "Some remarks upon Mr. London's views will be found

in our editorial columns."]

859. "Letter in reply to an article accusing him of plagiarism," *Independent*, 62:375-376 (Feb. 14, 1907).

860. [Letter to Arthur Stringer dated Aug. 2, 1909] *Canada West* (title later changed to *Canada Monthly*), 7:68-69 (Nov. 1909) [Reply to Arthur Stringer, "The Canada fakers," *Canada West*, 4:1137-1147 (Oct. 1908)].

861. [Letter to the editor of *Architect and Engineer of California*] 25:49 (July 1911).

862. "The lover's liturgy," *The Raven*, 2,1:5 (Feb. 1901); Oakland *Tribune*, Nov. 28, 1932 [Poem].

863. "The march of Kelly's army: the story of an extraordinary migration," *Cosmopolitan Magazine*, 43:643-648 (Oct. 1907).

"The material side," *see* "First aid to rising authors."

864. "A Maui wonderland," *Mid-Pacific Magazine*, 10:241-243 (Sept. 1915).

865. "The message of motion pictures," *Paramount Magazine*, 1,2:1-2 (Feb. 1915).

866. "Mexico's army and ours," *Collier's*, 53:5-7 (May 30, 1914).

867. "Mr. Jack London: knave or fool, or knave and fool?" *Vanity Fair*, 83:102-103 (July 28, 1909). [The article begins with a letter to the editor of *Vanity Fair* from Jack London, headed "Canal Zone, Panama, July 1st, 1909." It replies to Frank Harris's charge that more than half of one of his articles, written in 1901, was taken bodily by London and used in *The iron heel*. The article is Harris's reply to the letter. The original article to which London is replying is Frank Harris, "How Mr. Jack London writes a novel," *Vanity Fair*, 82:454 (April 14, 1909.]

868. "Mr. Jack London again," *Vanity Fair*, 83:519-520 (Oct. 27, 1909) [Comments by Frank Harris, followed by another letter from London to the editor of *Vanity Fair*, dated Aug. 16, 1909, in which he refers to the previous article by Harris and asks for an apology].

869. "My castle in Spain," *House Beautiful*, 21:15-17 (Jan. 1907); reprinted in *The Queen*, Dec. 22, 1906, pp.1116-1117 and as "The house beautiful" in *Revolution*.

870. "My Hawaiian aloha," *Cosmopolitan Magazine*, 61:36-39, 170-174 (Sept. 1916); 61, pt. 2:38-39, 142-144 (Oct. 1916); 61, pt. 2:60-62, 172, 175, 178 (Nov. 1916).

871. "My life in the underworld: a reminiscence and a confession," *Cosmopolitan Magazine*, 43:16-22 (May 1907); reprinted as "Confession," *Cassell's Magazine*, 42:422-429 (March 1909); *The road*. Translations: *Priznanive*, Leningrad, Priboi, 1926, 29pp. (Russian).

872. "The nature man," *Woman's Home Companion*, 35:21-22
      (Sept. 1908); *Cassell's Magazine*, 42:51-58 (Dec. 1908);
      CS.
873. "Navigating four horses north of the bay," *Sunset Mag-
      azine*, 27:233-246 (Sept. 1911); reprinted as "Four
      horses and a sailor" in HD.
874. "The old story " *Bookman*, 23:369-371 (June 1906) [Letter
      of April 10, 1906 concerning the charge of plagiarism
      in *Love of Life*].
875. "On the great war," *Overland Monthly*, n.s. 69:434
      (May 1917).
876. "On the writer's philosophy of life," *Editor*, 10:125-
      129 (Oct. 1899); *Occident*, 70:145-148 (Dec. 1916).
877. "The other animals," *Collier's*, 41:10-11, 25-26 (Sept.
      5, 1908); *Revolution*.
878. "Our adventures in Tampico," *Collier's*, 53:5-7, 24
      (June 27, 1914).
879. "A Pacific traverse," *Pacific Monthly*, 23:163-174 (Feb.
      1910); CS, TA.
880. "The pen, long days in a country penitentiary," *Cosmo-
      politan Magazine*, 43:373-378, 380 (Aug. 1907); re-
      printed in *The road: Years of conscience: the muck-
      rakers: an anthology of reform journalism*, Harvey
      Swados, ed., Cleveland and New York, World Publishing
      Co., 1962, pp.335-343. Translations: *Tyurma*, Moscow,
      Novaya Moskva, 1924, 30pp. (Russian).
881. "Pessimism, optimism and patriotism," Oakland High
      School *Aegis*, 10, 4:5-6 (March 1, 1895).
882. "Phenomena of literary evolution," *Bookman*, 12:148-150
      (Oct. 1900).
883. "Pictures, stray memories of life in the underworld,"
      Cosmopolitan Magazine, 43:513-518 (Sept. 1907); *The
      road*.
884. "Pinched, a prison experience," *Cosmopolitan Magazine*,
      43:263-270 (July 1907); *The tramp*, 1:229-238 (May 1910)
      and *The road*.
885. "Plea for the square deal," *Overland Monthly*, n.s. 69:
      404 ([?]1917).
886. "A problem," *Amateur Bohemian*, 1,3:9-10 (March 1896).
887. "The psychology of the surfboard," *Mid-Pacific Magazine*,
      9:437-441 (May 1915).
888. "The question of a name," *Writer*, 13:177-180 (Dec. 1900).
889. "The question of the maximum," in WC; *Occident*, 71:185-
      188 (Jan. 1917).
890. "Red game of war," *Collier's*, 53:5-7 (May 16, 1914).
891. [Review of Maxim Gorky, *Foma Gordyeeff*] *Impressions*,
      2:85-87 (Nov. 1901).
892. [Review of Frank Norris, *The octopus*] *Impressions*,

2:45-47 (June 1901).

893. "Revolution," *Contemporary Review*, 93:17-31 (Jan. 1908); reprinted in *Revolution*; separately published Chicago, Kerr, [n.d.][1909? date that of publisher's note]. This article was reviewed as "The army of the revolution," *Review of Reviews*, 37, 217:51 (Jan. 1908).

894. "Riding the South Sea surf," *Woman's Home Companion*, 34:9-10 (Oct. 1907).

895. "Rods and gunnels," *Bookman*, 15:541-544 (Aug. 1902); reprinted in *Bookman*, 44:176-179 (Oct. 1916).

896. "Road-kids and gay cats," in *The road*.

897. "Scab," *Atlantic Monthly*, 93:54-63 (Jan. 1904); reprinted in WC; separately published Chicago, Kerr, [n.d.,] 25pp.

898. "Shrinkage of the planet," *Chautauquan*, 31:609-612 (Sept. 1900); *Revolution*; also reprinted in *The Backbone Monthly*, 3,1:28 (Jan. 1912).
"Small-boat sailing" *see* "The joy of small-boat sailing".

899. "Some adventures with the police," *Cosmopolitan Magazine*, 44:417-423 (March 1908).

900. "The somnambulists," *Independent*, 61:1451-1454 (Dec. 20, 1906); Oakland *World*, July 3, 1908, p.1.

901. "A sonnet," *Dilettante*, 7:169 (Feb. 1901) [Poem].

902. "Stalking the pestilence," *Collier's*, 53:11-12, 28-29 (June 6, 1914).

903. "The stampede to thunder mountain: the new Idaho gold camp," *Collier's*, 29:8 (May 3, 1902).

904. "Stone-fishing of Bora Bora," *Pacific Monthly*, 23:335-346 (April 1910); *Badminton Magazine*, 32:421-425 (1911).

905. "The story of an eyewitness," *Collier's*, 35:22-23 (May 5, 1906); TA; reprinted as "Jack London tells of the fire. San Francisco's burning. A lurid tower visible from afar. The deserted heart of San Francisco. The flight before the flames," *Argonaut*, no. 1525:7-8 (June 2, 1906); "San Francisco's rise and recovery," in *The great events* ... edited by Charles F. Horne, N. Y., National Alumni c1926, 20:216-222; "San Francisco is gone!" in L. L. Snyder and R. B. Morris, eds., *Treasury of great reporting*, N. Y., Simon and Schuster, 1949, pp.269-274; McArdle, Kenneth, *A cavalcade of Collier's*, New York, A. S. Barnes, c1959, pp.114-118.

906. "Stranger than fiction," *Critic*, 43:123-125 (Aug. 1903), short précis published as "Jack London on fact and fiction," *T. P.'s Weekly*, 2,41:374 (Aug. 21, 1903).

907. Strunsky, Anna, "Memories of Jack London," *The Bowery News* (N.Y.), 69:8-9. [Undated; early June 1962. Contains excerpts from six letters of Jack London, 1892-

1902.]
908. "Terrible and tragic in fiction," *Critic*, 42;539-543
     (June 1903).
909. "That dead men rise up never," in HD.
910. "Things alive," *Yale monthly magazine*, 1,2;77-79
     (March 1906).
911. "Through the rapids on the way to Klondike," *Home Mag-
     azine*, 12;525-529 (June 1899); *The trail of ninety-
     eight*, ed. by Lowell Thomas, Jr., N. Y., Duell, Sloan
     and Pearce, 1962, pp.23-28. Translations; "Cherez
     stremniny k klondaiku," tr.; T. Litvinovoĭ, *Smena*,
     no. 10:22-23 (1960) [Also includes by the same trans-
     lator "Nastoiashchaia devochka," i.e. "A real girl"]
     (Russian).
912. "To the Chemulpo in a junk," *Overland Monthly*, n.s.
     84:263,271 (Aug. 1926) [Five 1904 letters to Charmian
     London].
913. "The tramp," *Wilshire's Magazine*, 6;70-72 (Feb. 1904),
     6:142-144 (March 1904); separately published as pam-
     phlet, N. Y., *Wilshire's Magazine*, 1904, [24]pp.;
     Chicago, Kerr, 1904 [28]pp.; reprinted in WC.
914. "Tramping with Kelly through Iowa; a Jack London diary,"
     Palimpsest, 7:129-158 (1926) [Followed on pp.159-164
     by commentary signed "J.E.B."].
915. "Trouble makers of Mexico," *Collier's*, 53:13-14, 25
     (June 13, 1914).
916. "Typee," *Pacific Monthly*, 23:267-281 (March 1910);
     Uncle Remus' Home Magazine, 27:10-12 (April 1910); CS.
917. "Two thousand stiffs," *Cosmopolitan Magazine*, 18;643-
     648 (Oct. 1907); *The road*. Translations: *Dve tysyachi
     "stiffov"*, Leningrad, Priboi, 1926, 27pp. (Russian).
918. "Two unpublished letters of Jack London," edited, with
     an introduction by Warren I. Titus, *California Histor-
     ical Society Quarterly*, 39:309-310 (1960) [Letters to
     Winston Churchill, American novelist, dated March 23,
     1913 and April 20, 1913].
919. "Voyage of the Snark," *Cosmopolitan Magazine*, 42;115-
     122 (Dec. 1906).
920. "Wanted: a new law of development," *International
     Socialist Review*, 3:65-78 (Aug. 1, 1902); WC.
921. "What are we to say?" *Journal of Education* (Boston),
     50,3:66 (July 13, 1899).
922. "What communities lose by the competitive system,"
     Cosmopolitan Magazine, 30:59-64 (Nov. 1900); *Appeal
     to reason*, May 11, 1901, p.3, excerpt in *Social Demo-
     cratic Herald*, Dec. 1, 1900. Also separately published
     in London, The Twentieth century press. [1912] 15pp.;
     also London, The Hyndman Literary Committee, 1925, 15pp.

923. "What life means to me," *Cosmopolitan Magazine*, 40:526-530 (March 1906); Upton Sinclair, *The cry for justice*, Philadelphia, Winston, 1915, pp.732-739; Bernard Smith, *The democratic spirit*, N. Y., Knopf, 1941, pp.610-618; S. K. Padover, ed., *Confessions and self-portraits*, N. Y., Day, 1957, pp.303-311; *Papyrus*, 14:7-16 (Jan.-Feb. 1910); San Francisco *Bulletin*, Dec. 2, 1916, part 2:1. It was reprinted separately: Chicago, Kerr, [n.d.,] 21pp.; *What life means to me:* memorial edition, San Francisco, Dec. 3, 1916, no publisher, 23pp.; *What life means to me*. Complimentary copy issued by the First and Last Chance, George Heinold, Prop., Oakland, Calif., [n.d.] Small with white covers; *"What life means to me,"* Girard, Kansas, Haldeman-Julius, c1924 (Little Blue Book No. 30, edited by E. Haldeman-Julius), pp.1-10. Translations: "Kuidas ma elu peale vaatan," *Oras*, no. 5-6:30-33 (1923) (Estonian); "Ciò che la vita significa per me," in Henry Barbusse, *Lettera agli intellecttuali*, Milan, Mastelloni, 1951 (Italian).

924. "Why I voted for equal suffrage," *Independent*, 75:634-635 (Sept. 11, 1913).

925. "With Funston's men," *Collier's*, 53:9-11, 26-27 (May 23, 1914).

926. "The worker and the tramp. A villanelle," *Comrade*, 1,1:14 (Oct. 1901); separately printed by the Jack London Amateur Press Club, undated and unpaged; reprinted in *A book of verses* published by P. C.: A. C., 1910, p.18; *Silhouette*, (Dec. 1916).

CONTRIBUTIONS TO NEWSPAPERS

927. "Direct legislation through the initiative and referendum," Oakland *Times*, May 9, 1896, p.4.
928. "Socialistic views on coin," Oakland *Times*, July 29, 1896, p.4.
929. "Socialistic views ... on the municipal ownership of waterworks," Oakland *Times*, Aug. 12, 1896, p.4, [letter].
930. "Is against the single tax. Jack London disagrees with John McLees, claims it will not regulate present difficulties. He admits, however, that McLees is on the right track and has 'get there' qualities," Oakland *Times*, Aug. 24, 1896, p.1 [letter].
931. "From Dawson to the sea," Buffalo *Express*, June 4, 1899, pp.2-3; reprinted in TA; *Trail of '98*, edited by Lowell Thomas, Jr., N. Y., Duell, Sloan and Pearce, 1962, pp. 178-188. Translations: "Iz Dousona v okean," tr.: V. Bykov, *Vokrug sveta*, no. 8:59-62 (August 1961) (Russian).
932. "Jack London in Boston. Reminiscence by the author of the 'Son of the wolf', Boston *Evening Transcript*, May 26, 1900, p.32.
933. "Letter of acceptance" [as nominee for Mayor of Oakland] Los Angeles *Challenge*, Feb. 27, 1901, p.3 [Letter dated Jan. 29, 1901].
934. "Incarnation of push and go," Los Angeles *Challenge*, Feb. 27, 1901, p.3 [Letter dated Feb. 16, 1901].
935. "Washoe Indians resolve to be white men," San Francisco *Examiner*, Sunday supplement, June 16, 1901, p.3.
936. "Grandly opens the third national Bundes Shooting Fest. Author of 'Son of wolf' describes great invasion. Peaceful conquest by the German sharpshooters. Parade promptness. One of the most picturesque processions this city has seen," San Francisco *Examiner*, July 15, 1901, p.3.
937. "Steady nerve of early rising riflemen. Some of the things that Jack London learned by watching the marksmen at the Shell Mound Butts. Extreme care exercised by the skilful shooters in preparing their trusty weapons and loading them," San Francisco *Examiner*, July 16, 1901, p.3.
938. "California pioneers watch the younger generation pinging the many targets," San Francisco *Examiner*, July 17, 1901, p.9.
939. "Delightful memories suggested and recalled by the visit of Julius Beeker to the Bundesfest Shooting Hall," July 18, 1901, p.2, San Francisco *Examiner*.

940. "How the marksman petrifies for the shot. He may waver and wobble and twist and shiver before he gets his sight, but then he turns to stone. In the modern psychology of marksmanship nerve and brain have superseded quondam supremacy of muscle. Interesting differentiation of method by which champion riflemen appear to arrive at similar results," San Francisco *Examiner*, July 19, 1901, p.9.

941. "How the markers operate in the quiet target pits," San Francisco *Examiner*, July 20, 1901, p.3.

942. "A girl who crossed swords with a burglar," San Francisco *Examiner*, American Magazine supplement, July 21, 1901, pp.1.

943. "Each record broken adds to country's war strength," San Francisco *Examiner*, July 21, 1901, p.27.

944. "Phases of mental condition in the big shoots," San Francisco *Examiner*, July 22, 1901, p.2.

945. "Study of physical traits of men who shoot the best," San Francisco *Examiner*, July 23, 1901, p.3

946. "Lessons of living taught by the visiting riflemen," San Francisco *Examiner*, July 24, 1901, p.3.

947. "Peter de Ville, Alaska's Moon country explorer tells Jack London his story of the luring north," San Francisco *Examiner*, Oct. 14, 1901, pp.1,5.

948. [Review of Edwin Markham, *Lincoln and other poems*] San Francisco *Examiner*, American Magazine supplement, Nov. 10, 1901, p.10.

949. "Gladiators of machine age. Jack London writes entertainingly of his impressions while at the ringside," San Francisco *Examiner*, Nov. 16, 1901, pp.1-2.

950. "Millionaire divides his profits with his workmen to share their happiness," San Francisco *Examiner*, April 18, 1902, p.5.

951. "Simple impressive rite at corner-stone emplacement of Hearst Memorial Mining Building. In hour of elemental stress, Mrs. Hearst lays foundation stone of a temple of work," San Francisco *Examiner*, Nov. 19, 1902, pp.8-9.

952. "What shall be done with this boy? Jack London replies to a vital question," San Francisco *Examiner*, American Magazine section, June 21, 1903, p.3.

953. "How Jack London got in and out of jail in Japan. Story of Japanese official red tape that sounds like comic opera. A vivid glimpse of judicial war-time methods in Mikado's realm. Tale that hangs on innocent snapshots," San Francisco *Examiner*, Feb. 27, 1904, p.2 [Date line: Shimonoseki, Feb. 3, 1904, Photograph of London]. Reprinted as "A camera and a journey," in *In many wars*

edited by George Lynch and Frederick Palmer, Tokyo,
Tokyo Printing Co., [1904?] pp.123-129.

954. "Koreans are fleeing before the Slav advance ... Advancing Russians nearing Japan's army. Muscovites pushing
forward into Korea. Natives in wild panic. Fierce land
battle expected," San Francisco *Examiner*, March 3,
1904, p.1 [Date line: Ping Yang, via Seoul, March 2,
1904. Photograph of London].

955. "Japan's invasion of Korea, as seen by Jack London.
Cavalry weak spot of Japanese. Little brown men now in
field, however, make 'the best infantry in the world'.
Vivid description of army in Korea," San Francisco
Examiner, March 4, 1904, p.1 [Date line: Ping Yang.
March 4, 1904].

956. "Japanese army's equipment excites great admiration.
Troops in Korea highly praised. General Allen, U. S.
attache, regards arrangements to insure soldiers' welfare as unsurpassed," San Francisco *Examiner*, April 3,
1904, p.23 [Date line: Ping Yang. March 5, 1904.
2 photographs taken by London]. Reprinted in TA.

957. "Here are the first pictures direct from the seat of
war in Korea. They were taken by Jack London and give
accurate glimpses of the Japanese army as it appears
at the front," San Francisco *Examiner*, April 4, 1904,
pp.8-9 [8 photographs with captions. No text by London].

958. "Troubles of war correspondent in starting for the
front. Interpreter and canned goods. Jack London also
describes the difficulties he had in obtaining a horse,
the most docile one being blind. "Examiner' man's trip
to Ping Yang," San Francisco *Examiner*, April 4, 1904,
p.3 [Dated: Feb. 26, 1905. Photographs by London]. Reprinted in TA.

959. "Russian warships patrol Pe-Chili gulf. Royal road a
sea of mud. How the Japanese army is advancing into
North Korea. Troops plodding through quagmires. Sidelights on the character and personality of the Koreans.
Typical incidents by way of illustration," San Francisco *Examiner*, April 7, 1904, p.3 [Date line: Ping
Yang, March 3, 1904. 1 photograph].

960. "Koreans have taken to the hills. How the hermit king-
dom behaves in time of war. Jack London draws some
vivid pen pictures of what he is seeing at the front,"
San Francisco *Examiner*, April 17, 1904, p.19 [Date
line: March 12, 1904. Also on this page: "How Jack
London went to the front." 1 photograph].

961. "Footsore, dazed and frozen, the Japanese trudge through
Korea. Dramatic story of the crushing march over the
Pekin Road on the way to the Yalu. By day the path is a

treacherous river of mud and ice and by night a frozen
death trap," San Francisco *Examiner*, April 18, 1904,
p.3 [Date line: Ping Yang, March 7, 1904. Exclusive
photograph]. Reprinted in TA.

962. "Sufferings of the Japanese. Soldiers of the reserves
do field drilling of a strenuous character, and all the
while tortured by sore feet," San Francisco *Examiner*,
April 20, 1904, p.3 [Date line: Sunan, March 13, 1904.
1 photograph].

963. "'Examiner' writer sent back to Seoul. Men sent by
other papers didn't know how to get to firing line,"
San Francisco *Examiner*, April 25, 1904, pp.1-2 [This
issue also contains a front page story by the *Examiner*:
"Jack London the victim of jealous correspondents. Punished for alertness"].

964. "Interpreters and how they cause trouble. War correspondent Jack London gives some idea of the Japanese translator, of his peculiar mental processes and how he does
your thinking for you at the wrong time. A daily report
of progress that furnishes food for thought," San Francisco *Examiner*, April 26, 1904, p.2 [Date line: Poval
Colli, March 8, 1904].

965. "Jack London's graphic story of the Japs driving
Russians across the Yalu River. First pen picture pre-
sented by any war correspondent eyewitness of the re-
markable bravery and skillful tactics of the victorious
Japanese army at Antung," San Francisco *Examiner*,
June 4, 1904, p.1 [Date line: Antung, May 5, 1904].

966. "Few killed nowadays in 'fierce' battles [Headlines of
left column]. Fighting at long range described. Warfare
of ancient times compared with modern days. Savors of
methods of a highwayman. Effort seems to be to force
other side to surrender. Lively shooting causes re-
treats. Avoidance of belligerents to meet in close
quarters. Always dodging from the bullets. [Right column:] Fatalities result of mishaps. Of course some men
fall from shell and shrapnel. Possibilities and not the
facts. Jack London describes how armies engage in con-
tests. Prediction as to future wars. Won't be any kill-
ing at all when arms are more perfect. Soldiers to go on
vacations," San Francisco *Examiner*, June 5, 1904, p.49
[1 photograph].

967. "Japanese swim cold river under fire. Run risk of freez-
ing to death. How the Japanese made sure of their position. Officers want to pick the way. Japanese strategy
that won day at Kieu-Liang-Cheng. Company fought like
Spartans. How Russians were tricked in the crossing of
the Yalu. Slow retreat becomes rout. Every detail of

battle was executed as planned," San Francisco *Examiner*,
June 9, 1904, p.9 [Date line: Antung, May 10, 1904. 1
photograph]. Reprinted in TA.

968.   "Japanese supplies rushed to the front by man and beast,"
San Francisco *Examiner*, June 19, 1904, p.41 [Date line:
Wju, April 21, 1904. 1 photograph].

969.   "Japanese officers consider everything a military
secret. Position of correspondents with the army is an
anomalous one of interloper and honored guest--'Examiner'
correspondent's experience," San Francisco *Examiner*,
June 26, 1904, p.41 [Date line: Antung, June 26, 1904].
Translations: Selections from the Russian-Japanese
correspondence appeared as "Reportazhi iz Korei y
Manchzhuriy (otryvki)," tr.: V. Bykov, *Dalniy Vostok*,
no. 3:161-168 (1962) (Russian).

970.   "The yellow peril," San Francisco *Examiner*, Sept. 25,
1904, p.44; reprinted in *Revolution*.

971.   "Big socialist vote is fraught with meaning. Great
socialist vote explained by Jack London. Mark Hanna's
predition recalled. One of the world's great authorities on socialism analyses campaign made in behalf of
Eugene V. Debs," San Francisco *Examiner*, Nov. 10, 1904,
p.3; F.

972.   "What novelist Jack London thinks of Leroy Scott's
dramatic labor story, 'The walking delegate'. Battle of
the builders and the owners of skyscrapers. Business
world akin to jungle. Author of 'The sea wolf' compares
the twentieth century battle of head and dollars with
the conquests of the middle ages," San Francisco
Examiner, May 28, 1905, p.55.

973.   "Jack London telegraphs to the 'Examiner' about Alexander McLean, the original of the "Sea Wolf," San Francisco *Examiner*, June 15, 1905, p.1 [Text of telegram
of June 14, 1905].

974.   "The author of *The game* writes from personal knowledge
based on experience," New York *Times Book Review*,
Sept. 2, 1905, p.574 [Letter dated Aug. 28, 1905].

975.   "Brain beaten by brute force. Dane's perpetual motion
more effective than Britt's mental superiority, says
Jack London," San Francisco *Examiner*, Sept. 10, 1905,
pp.41,44. Reprinted in *Life, battles and career of
Battling Nelson, lightweight champion of the world*,
by himself, Hagewisch, III., 1909, pp.178-183.

976.   "Jack London reviews 'The Long Day'" San Francisco
Examiner, Oct. 15, 1905, p.48; partially reprinted in
Appeal to reason, Dec. 2, 1905, p.3.

977.   "Jack London sees physical culture boom in holy jumper
stunts. His brand of religion, says noted author and

lecturer, when he chooses," Boston *American*, Dec. 19, 1905, p.3.

978. "Jack London endorses the party press," *Socialist Voice*, June 9, 1906, p.1.

979. "Jack London scores the Idaho-Colorado conspirators," Oakland *Socialist Voice*, June 19, 1906, p.2.

980. [Review of Upton Sinclair, *The jungle*] New York *Evening Journal*, Aug. 8, 1906, p.2; *Wilshire's Magazine*, 10, 8:12 (Aug. 1906); F. [Two versions of same review]; Translations: "Dzhungli", tr.: Vil Bykov, *Nedelya*, July 6, 1963, pp.6-7 (Russian).

981. "Something rotten in Idaho: the tale of the conspiracy against Moyer, Pettibone and Haywood," Chicago *Daily Socialist*, Nov. 4, 1906, p.1; reprinted in F.

982. "Denied admittance to U. S. because he loves liberty," *Socialist Voice*, Jan. 5, 1907, pp.1,4.

983. "London will write for the *Daily World*," *Socialist Voice*, Feb. 2, 1907, p.1.

984. "Jack London misrepresented," *Socialist Voice*, May 25, 1907, p.4 [Reply to letter in Oakland *Tribune* of May 24, 1907 by Col. John P. Irish].

985. "Victor over war and wave; home the Oregon comes again," San Francisco *Examiner*, June 13, 1907, pp.1-2.

986. "Jack London says Johnson made a noise like a lullaby with his fists as he tucked Burns in his little crib in Sleepy Hollow with a laugh," New York *Herald*, second section, Dec. 27, 1908, p.3.

987. "In a modern stadium. The negro's smile. Story of a big fight," *Australian Star* (Sydney), Dec. 28, 1908, p.1.

988. "Jack London's article. First impressions. A candleless hotel. And the garbage men of Phillip-Street," *Australian Star*, Jan. 7, 1909, p.1.

989. "Strike methods. American and Australian. 'The future belongs to labor'," *Australian Star*, Jan. 14, 1909, p.1. Reprinted in Foner as "Strike methods: American and Australian."

990. "Saved--and lost! The Sobraon boys," *Australian Star*, Jan. 28, 1909, p.1.

991. "Running a newspaper. His scheme," *Australian Star*, Feb. 4, 1909, p.1.

992. "The Yankee myth. Americans defy description. A pretty discussion," *Australian Star*, Feb. 11, 1909, p.1.

993. "Jack London will build fine home," Santa Rosa *Press Democrat*, June 3, 1909, p.5 [Letter to Thomas Johnson of Glen Ellen from Panama].

994. "Jack London on the movement and authorship," Oakland *World*, June 5, 1909, p.2 [Reply to Andrew M. Anderson's letter in *The Socialist* (Melbourne, Australia) entitled

"Jack London. An Australian criticism with incidental reference to leaders" reprinted in *World*, June 5, 1909, p.2. London's letter is undated].

995. "Jack London says Honolulu is provincial. Defends himself from the criticism of the Bystander and whacks Hawaii generally," *Pacific Commercial Advertiser* (Honolulu) feature section, Jan. 23, 1910, p.8 [This letter is replied to in the same issue, pp.4-5. The reply is signed by Lorrin A. Thurston].

996. "Letter to editor," *The Workingman's Paper*, June 18, 1910, p.1; H.

997. "Jack London says Reno crowds eagerly await big fight because of 'old red blood of Adam that will not down'. All the men one has met in all the earth he will see in the Nevada city, from 'grizzled fight fans' to 'youngsters' he declares. Novelist declares Nevada got the big combat through a 'foul blow'. 'Mike' Murphy examines Jeffries at his new training camp and is enthusiastic over the big fellow's fighting condition," New York *Herald*, June 24, 1910, p.5 [The bottom of this page contains a brief story: "Jack London will describe the great Jeffries-Johnson fight for the Herald"].

998. "'Jeff a fighter, Johnson a boxer,' says Jack London. 'Mother nature in the white man still red of fang and claw.' Calls him 'mightiest walloper of men'. Negro mastered by the moment and vastly less disciplined than his antagonist. Jeffries more eager to win. Loss would almost break his heart, while Johnson would not be worried much," New York *Herald*, June 25, 1910, pp. 3-4.

999. "Never a man so fit as Jeffries, says Jack London. 'His mighty thighs remind one of the legendary Teutonic warrior.' Muscles all of the right kind. 'Play in matted masses on his back and leap into twisted rolls on his arms.' Fight will not be short. Whoever wins will have to work for it, and combat will be a great one, he says," New York *Herald*, June 26, 1910, pp.3-4; reprinted in TA.

1000. "Fighter with the quality of the 'Abysmal brute' will win the great battle of July 4 at Reno, says Jack London." [Right hand sub-headings:] "Endurance is capacity to assimilate punishment and to keep on administering it. Finds parallel in Britt-Nelson fight. 'Quality of muscle' is the thing that counts, says novelist in commenting on outlook for battle. Will the black fail? Question whether he can make Jeffries put up the 'Fight of his life'." [Left hand sub-headings:] "Man who has ability to hit and keep on hitting endlessly bound to conquer. Thinks Jeffries has the quality to last.

Neither of the big men has ever shown it, but white
man believes he has it in 'reserve power'. Where Johnson excels. Has the faculty of relaxing in most furious
struggle, while his coming opponent is always tense,"
New York *Herald*, June 27, 1910, p.3 [Bottom of page:
"Jack London will report great prize fight for Herald"];
reprinted in TA.

1001. "No 'lucky punch' likely at Reno, says Jack London.
Neither one of the neavyweights is expected to 'blow
up'. Combat may run beyond 30 rounds. Calls Johnson a
'mouth fighter' who will have no chance for repartee
with Jeffries. Negro won't rush battle. Both men are
now well settled in training camps and hard at work,"
New York *Herald*, June 28, 1910, pp.3-4.

1002. "Ape and tiger in U. S. demand fight, says Jack London.
Thrill of combat a passion of race that grew as our
language grew. Must accept it as reality of nature.
Sport of prize fighting a fair one and marks development of humanity. Eventually will cease. Mr. London
says personally he wants to see battle so bad it hurts,"
New York *Herald*, June 29, 1910, pp.3-4; reprinted in TA.

1003. "Jeffries' silence marks a thinker, says Jack London.
His brusqueness not a pose, but is hard on the public.
Has no fear of any stage fright. Author declares the
retiring disposition does not proceed from shyness.
Johnson marked contrast. Will lose his smile and banter-
ing manner as soon as fight is well under way," New
York *Herald*, June 30, 1910, pp.3-4.

1004. "Man never lived who could keep Johnson from landing,
says Jack London, but Jeffries can stand a lot of punishment. White man's quickness will not show to advan-
tage beside the negro's. Johnson will land three blows
to one. But Californian, being left handed, may foil
the famous uppercut. Problem in the clinches. Author
thinks Jeffries may use his crouch and allow the black
pugilist to rest," New York *Herald*, July 1, 1910, p.5.

1005. "Crowning fight of ring's history, says Jack London.
Present generation will never see another combat like
that of next Monday. Jeffries and Johnson alone among
men. There is no third of their type at present in the
human race. Six heavyweights there. Besides these one
time champions, best known figures in sportdom will be
in arena," New York *Herald*, July 2, 1910, pp.3-4.

1006. "Jeffries never wasted energy, says Jack London. Author
analyzcs condition of white fighter from standpoint of
histology. Not only can come back, but is here. Training is now finished and Reno is in a fever of expectan-
cy over to-morrow's combat. 'Mike' Murphy doubtful!

Says Jeffries will shape his whole fight for one deci-
sive blow," New York *Herald*, July 3, 1910, pp.3-4.
1007. "Square fight sure, men prime for it, says Jack London.
Prolonged contest at Reno to-day will mean bent, dented
and maybe broken ribs for 'Jack' Johnson, novelist pro-
phesies. No longer mere brutal game, prize ring offers
valuable lesson in fair dealing. Will Jeffries make
Negro extend himself, and if so, how long will it take
him to do it? Now the all important question. Crowds
surge into the city for contest. By special train and
burro pack visitors have come until Nevada's metropolis
houses greatest throng it has seen in all its busy
history. Fighters spend the day quietly in their camps.
Johnson takes short run in the morning, while Jeffries
lounges on the lawn, entertaining his friends and dodging the curious, who come in steady streams from early
sunrise," New York *Herald*, July 4, 1910, pp.3-4.
1008. "Negro, never in doubt, fear or trouble, played all the
time, says Jack London. Jeffries lost his old time
stamina somewhere outside the ring and did not put up
as strong a battle as did 'Tommy' Burns. 'Golden smile'
shines on adversary, trainers and 20,000 spectators.
'Did you see that, Jim?' he asks of Corbett after landing an especially vicious punch and clinching with his
adversary. Yellow streak question unsettled. Jeffries,
eye closed, loses his defence. First rounds were largely
Johnson. Following ones more Johnson and close all Johnson. Battered and staggering, Californian goes down
three times in last," New York *Herald*, July 5, 1910,
pp.3-4. [All of this series appeared in the first section and had Reno, Nev., date lines; reprinted in TA.
A selection from this series entitled "Jack Johnson vs.
Jim Jeffries," appears in W. C. Heinz, *The fireside
book of boxing*, New York, Simon and Schuster, 1961,
pp.256-260.]
1009. "Author roasts judge - 'I'll get you.'--London. Writer
declares he was bullied in Oakland police court," San
Francisco *Call*, Aug. 2, 1910, p.7 [Contains letter by
London to Police Judge Samuels, dated Glen Ellen, July
29, 1910].
1010. "Jack London files objection," Arkansas City (Kansas)
Daily Traveler, Aug. 30, 1910, p.1 [Concerns double].
1011. "Jack London's protest," Oakland *World*, Dec. 17, 1910,
p.4 [Letter to the Japanese ambassador to the United
States].
1012. "Jack London wants to know," Lima (Ohio) *News*, April 1,
1911, pp.[?] reprinted from the Dayton (Ohio) *Journal*,
March 31, 1911, pp.[?] [Concerns double].

1013. [Advertisement quotes London on *The library of original sources.*] Oakland *World*, Dec. 9, 1911, p.3.
1014. "Jack London approves of no drunkard plan," Bridgeport (Conn.) *Post*, May 23, 1913. [Letter dated May 15, 1913. A Jack London letter also appears in *No drunkard plan*, no imprint data, p.5. The date of this small pamphlet is probably 1913.]
1015. [Letter to Dr. A. H. Purdue] Nashville *Banner*, May 23, 1913, p.4 [Undated].
1016. "Jack London thanks the fire fighters," Santa Rosa *Press Democrat*, Aug. 26, 1913, p.1 [Letter].
1017. "Jack London to his friends," New York *Dramatic Mirror*, Oct. 29, 1913, p.26 [Letter on the *Sea wolf*, Oct. 13, 1913].
1018. "Novelist explains hop riots. Jack London says ruling class is responsible for workers' use of force," San Francisco *Bulletin*, Dec. 12, 1913, p.1.
1019. "Jack London goes to a burlesque show and here is what he has to say about it," San Francisco *Examiner*, March 22, 1914, p.24.
1020. "Jack London pays tribute to Stevenson's *Treasure Island*," Chattanooga *Daily Times*, May 26, 1915, p.6 [Undated letter].
1021. "Molokai ideal for mainland lepers. This is proposition of Jack London. Author says settlement will make islands 'clean' and pays tribute to workers," *Pacific Commercial Advertiser* (Honolulu), June 3, 1915, pp.9-11; reprinted as "Our brothers and sisters, scapegoats in Molokai. Guiltless in our generation, yet deprived by politics at Washington of immunity of benefit of a leprosarium kept idle," Philadelphia *Ledger*, Aug. 6, 1916, section 1, p.10. [This article was refuted in the *Pacific Commercial Advertiser*, June 6, 1915, p.4 by Lorrin A. Thurston, "Hawaii as a national leprosery".]
1022. "Pressure of population and preparedness," *Pittsburgh Press*, April 30, 1916, section 2, p.2.
1023. "Our guiltless scapegoats, the stricken of Molokai," Philadelphia *Public Ledger*, June 21, 1916, p.12.
1024. "What we will lose when the Japs take Hawaii, San Francisco *Examiner*, American Magazine Section, Aug. 20, 1916, p.6.
1025. "Jack has good things to say about Johnny," Oakland *Tribune*, second section, Nov. 23, 1916, p.13 [Contains London letter to Johnny Heinold dated March 24, 1910].
1026. "How London sold his first story for $5," San Francisco *Bulletin*, Nov. 24, 1916, p.8 [Letter written in Nov. 1916 to the editors of *Occident*].
1027. "What Jack London told of himself," Los Angeles *Evening*

Express, Feb. 14, 1917, p.12 [Letter to M. L. Osborne dated March 24, 1900].

1028. "The way of war," San Francisco *Chronicle,* Dec. 16, 1917, p.[24]; reprinted in *Literary California* gathered by Ella Sterling Mighels, San Francisco, Harr Wagner Publishing Co., 1918, pp.202-203. [Charmian London states that this poem was published in *Once a week,* Oct. 27, 1906. The file of this journal in the Library of Congress was examined; we failed to find this poem.]

1029. [Letter to Fred Lockley written shortly before Jack London's death] Oregon *Journal,* Jan. 6, 1923, p.4.

1030. "London explains why he refused to become critic," Oakland *Tribune,* Nov. 28, 1932, p.B3 [Letter dated Feb. 20, 1905. First published in *Ability* (Oakland, Calif.)].

1031. "The last letter by Jack London," San Francisco *Chronicle,* Aug. 1938, p.[?] [Letter dated Nov. 21, 1916].

INTRODUCTIONS AND PREFACES

1032. "Introduction," to *The cry for justice: an anthology
of the literature of social protest,* edited by Upton
Sinclair, Philadelphia, Winston, 1915, pp.3-5; reprinted
in F [For Russian translations of this anthology see
Brown, *A Guide to Soviet Russian Translations...* nos.
1291, 1371-73, 1480].
1033. "Introduction" to H. D. Umbstaetter, *The red hot dollar
and other stories from the Black Cat,* Boston, Page,
1911, pp.v-ix. "Foreword," to Francis A. Cox, *What do
you know about a horse?* London, National Equine Defence
League, 1916, vi-xvi.
1034. "Preface," to Osias L. Schwartz, *General types of
superior men. A philosophico-psychological study of
genius, talent and philistinism in their bearings upon
human society and its struggle for a better social
order* ... Boston, R. G. Badger, 1916, pp.5-6.

SEPARATELY PUBLISHED EPHEMERA

THE TRAMP. 1904

1035. THE TRAMP | BY | JACK LONDON | [reproduction from photo-
graph] | PUBLISHED BY | WILSHIRE'S MAGAZINE | 200
WILLIAM STREET | NEW YORK CITY
    Title enclosed in single-line border. Inside front
cover: printer's mark within decoration. 15 x 8.5 cm.
Text of 22 unnumbered pages. Issued in wrappers, front
cover used as title, rear cover concludes text. Paper
is newsprint pulp, stapled.

1036. Other Editions:
THE TRAMP | BY | JACK LONDON | [Socialist Party Workers
of the World United mark, with "hands across the sea"
motto in center of decoration] | PRICE 5 CENTS, 10
COPIES FOR 20 CENTS. | [printer's mark] | CHICAGO |
CHARLES H. KERR & COMPANY | CO-OPERATIVE
    15 x 9 cm. Front cover used as title, verso,
printer's notice within single-line border, text pp.3-
28, followed by advertisements of 4pp.

THE SCAB. 1904

1037. PRICE 5 CENTS | THE SCAB | BY | JACK LONDON | [REPRINTED
FROM THE ATLANTIC MONTHLY] | [short rule] | POCKET
LIBRARY OF SOCIALISM, NO. 44 | [printer's mark] | PUB-
LISHED BY | CHARLES H. KERR & COMPANY | (CO-OPERATIVE) |
56 FIFTH AVENUE CHICAGO
    15 x 9 cm. Front cover used as title, verso: pub-
lisher's note; text, pp.[3]-25; seven pages of publisher's advertisement including one announcing Walter
Marion Raymond's *Rebels of the new South* as the "Latest
socialistic novel." Issued in white paper wrappers;
front cover, printed in black, used as title.

1038. Other Editions:
THE SCAB | BY | JACK LONDON | REPRINTED FROM THE ATLAN-
TIC MONTHLY | [short rule] | PRICE FIVE CENTS | [short
rule] | [printer's mark] | CHICAGO | CHARLES H. KERR
& COMPANY | CO-OPERATIVE
    14.5 x 8.5 cm. [1909.] Front cover used as title,
verso: blank, text, pp.[3]-25; verso of page 25 advertisement of third edition of Debs, His Life, Writings
and Speeches; Great American Fortunes by Prof. Ira B.
Cross, pp.[1]-3, reprinted from the San Francisco
Bulletin; Special Combination Offer, p.4; advertisement

of Industrial Problems by N. A. Richardson, on inside
of rear cover contains advertisement of The International Socialist Review of thirty-six lines. Issued in
thin paper, printed in black. Front cover used as title.

JACK LONDON. 1905

1039. JACK LONDON | A SKETCH OF | HIS LIFE | AND WORK | [or-
nament] | WITH PORTRAIT | [ornament] | THE MACMILLAN
COMPANY | 66 FIFTH AVENUE, NEW YORK | 1905
    p.[1] Title as above; p.[2] blank; p.[3]-15, text;
p.[16] blank. 16 x 12 cm. Frontispiece portrait on calendared paper tipped in opposite title page. Bound in
blue-gray paper wrappers, stapled. Front wrapper lettered in black same as title page above; inside front
wrapper an advertisement for *The Call of the Wild;* inside back wrapper an advertisement for *Children of the
Frost* and *The Faith of Men;* back wrapper an advertisement for *The Sea-Wolf.*
    There is a copy of this pamphlet in the George H.
Tweney collection, which collates exactly as the one
described above, except it is bound in bright red
wrappers, and instead of the Publisher's name and address at the bottom of the front wrapper, there is
printed a bookseller's name and address. The title page
in this variant is exactly as described above, with the
publisher's name and address as indicated. This leads
authors to suspect that a number of copies were prepar-
ed in this manner, with any desired bookseller's name
on the front wrapper for advertisement purposes. No
other variants in this respect have been noted. Jack
London is known to have personally written the majority
of the text in this sketch of his life, hence the reason for including this pamphlet in ephemera by Jack
London.

RUSKIN CLUB MENU. 1906

1040. [decoration] LONDON NIGHT | IN HONOR OF MR. AND MRS.
JACK LONDON | [club's emblem] | [decoration] RUSKIN
CLUB | OAKLAND, CALIF.
    The inside front cover of this menu contains a quo-
tation from an editorial on Jack London from *The Independent* (New York), March 1, 1906. The program, which
was held at the Piedmont Club House, April 6, 1906, includes as the paper of the evening: "The East--as I saw
it," by Jack London.
    Rear cover contains the conclusion of London's speech

to the students of the University of California, deliv-
ered Friday, March 20, 1905. Following this is a quotation from page 1 of *The people of the abyss.*

WHAT LIFE MEANS TO ME. 1906

1041. WHAT LIFE MEANS TO ME | [heavy rule] | [thin rule] |
BY JACK LONDON |
   Front cover used as title. Inside front cover: Pub-
lished by | The Intercollegiate Socialist Society |
Princeton, N.J. | [printer's mark] Page [3]: (sixteen-
line quotation from *The Independent).* Page [4]: (short
rule) | Appeal to Reason Press | Girard Kansas | (short
rule). Pages [5]-15: Text. Rear wrapper blank.
   13 x 9cm. Issued in white paper wrappers, stapled.

1042. Other Editions:
There is fragmentary evidence in the collection of the
University of Southern California Library at Los Angeles,
that the following *could* be the first edition of this
publication. However, there is no sure way of establish-
ing priority, and the authors of this bibliography are
convinced that the Intercollegiate Socialist Society
edition can be accepted as the true first edition. The
following edition is described to give recognition that
it has been examined and considered.

   WHAT | LIFE MEANS | TO ME | BY JACK LONDON | [Seal of
the Socialist Party] | PRICE FIVE CENTS | SIXTY COPIES
MAILED | FOR $1.00 | [Union label] | CHICAGO | CHARLES
H. KERR & COMPANY | CO-OPERATIVE | [All the foregoing
enclosed within a ruled box, with a star at the corners]
   p.[1] Title as above; p.[2] Copyright page as
follows: JOHN F. HIGGINS | PRINTER AND BINDER | 376-382
MONROE STREET | CHICAGO, ILLINOIS [all enclosed within
a ruled box]; pp.3-21, text; pp.[22-32] advertisements
for socialist publications. Printed on poor quality
pulp newspaper. 15 x 9 cm. Stapled.

   JACK LONDON'S | "WHAT LIFE | MEANS TO ME" | [Title en-
closed in rectangular rules] | MEMORIAL EDITION | SAN
FRANCISCO | December 3, 1916 |"Last of all, my faith
is in the working | class."--Jack London. | [printer's
mark]
   [1] front wrapper as above, [2] blank, [3-4] poem:
George Sterling's Tribute to Jack London, [5]-23, text,
[24] rear wrapper blank. 15 x 8.5 cm. Printed on newsprint, stapled.

What Life Means to Me

BY JACK LONDON

Also published as; LITTLE BLUE BOOK NO. 30, by the
Haldeman-Julius Company, GIRARD, KANSAS. Copyright 1924.
32pp., blue paper wrappers, 13 x 9 cm.

THE APOSTATE. 1906

1043. THE APOSTATE | BY | JACK LONDON | [decoration] |
CHICAGO | CHARLES H. KERR & COMPANY | CO-OPERATIVE
   P.[1], Title, p.[2], [printer's mark], text p.[3]-30,
blank leaf. 17.5 x 12.5 cm. Issued in thin wrappers,
printed in blue-green ink. The front cover reads: Price
10 cents [underlined]. The Apostate | He was reared
from babyhood on the Gospel | of Work, but he renounced
the faith. | Do you blame him? | [portrait of London]
By Jack London
   A variant edition as examined in the George H. Tweney
collection is as follows: the leaf following page 30 of
the text is not blank. It contains: p.[31] advertisement headed: Library of Science for the Workers. P.[32]
is headed by advertisements of *History of the Supreme
Court of the United States* by Gustavus Meyers. The rear
cover contains an advertisement of books by Marx and
Engels. Wrappers are cream-colored paper printed in
blue.

1044. Other Editions:
LITTLE BLUE BOOKS NO. | EDITED BY E. HALDEMAN-JULIUS |
[at right end of above two lines:] 640 | THE APOSTATE |
JACK LONDON | HALDEMAN-JULIUS COMPANY | GIRARD, KANSAS.
   12.5 x 9 cm. P.[1] Title, verso: Printed in the
United States of America; text, pp.[3]-31; p.32: list
of Other Little Blue Books. Issued in light blue wrappers, lettered in black.

"DEAR COMRADES." 1907

1045. "Dear comrades." [Letter by Jack London printed on the
outside cover of Upton Sinclair's *The Jungle: a novel*,
London, William Heinemann, 1907.]

REVOLUTION. 1909

1046. REVOLUTION | BY | JACK LONDON | PRICE FIVE CENTS | 60
COPIES MAILED FOR $1.00; | 100 for $1.50; 1,000 for
$10.00. | [printer's mark] | CHICAGO | CHARLES H. KERR
& COMPANY | CO-OPERATIVE
   15 x 9 cm. Front cover used as title, verso: publisher's note, date October, 1909.; text, pp.3-31; back

cover containing list of 50 books in the Pocket Library of Socialism. Issued in paper wrappers, front cover used as title, back cover contains advertisement. Hundredth thousand edition: 1913.

1047. Other Editions:
REVOLUTION | BY | JACK LONDON | CHICAGO | CHARLES H. KERR & COMPANY | CO-OPERATIVE
19.5 x 13 cm. P.[1], Title, p.[2], verso; [printer's mark]; pp.(3)-4; publisher's note to Hundredth Thousand, Text, pp.5-30; advertisement of *Evolution and Revolution* by Mark Fisher, advertisement of *The physical basis of mind and morals* by M. H. Fitch. Issued in white wrappers, lettered in red. Decoration on front cover in red, signed "E. H. Gonl." Advertisement of *The International Socialist Review* on rear cover. Title of that periodical white on red pennant at top of advertisement. This edition is from new plates. There is a variant of this edition in the George H. Tweney collection. Last page is advertisement for *Ancient Society* by Lewis H. Morgan, otherwise all details as described above.

JACK LONDON | REVOLUTION | BEMYNDIGAD ÖVERSÄTTNING | AV | AXEL AHLSTEDT [Socialist Party. Workers of the World Unite Symbol] COPYRIGHT IN THE UNITED STATES IN THE YEAR 1910, BY THE MACMILLAN COMPANY.
The pagination is 4-39. Page 1, unnumbered, is entitled "Utgivarens not." The essay in translation begins on p.3, also unnumbered. Following p.39, there is a page advertisement. According to the outside back cover, it was printed by Swenson & Madden, Printers, 731 Seventh St., Rockford, Ill. This item does not appear in the London collections of the University of Southern California or in the Huntington Library, nor is it known to the Union Catalog of the Library of Congress. The copy noted here has been lent to the compilers by King Hendricks and is in the Irving Sheperd collection. It is a paper-back.with a blue cover.

THE DREAM OF DEBS. 1909

1048. THE DREAM OF DEBS | A STORY OF INDUSTRIAL REVOLT | BY | JACK LONDON | [decoration] | CHICAGO | CHARLES H. KERR & COMPANY | CO-OPERATIVE
18.5 x 12.5 cm. P.[1], Title, p.[2] printer's mark; text, pp.[3]-32. Issued in white wrappers printed in

blue. Rear cover advertisement of Gustavus Meyers'
History of the Supreme Court of the U. S.

THE IVAN SWIFT BROADSIDE. 1910

1049. ABOUT FAGOTS OF CEDAR | BY IVAN SWIFT | JACK LONDON
SAYS: | INTO THE BOOK I HAVE JUST DIPPED, | AND AM
LOOKING FORWARD TO A SECOND | READING OF IT. IN TOUCH
WITH EVERY | LINE OF IT, I READ IT WITH THE BITE OF |
DELIGHT. IT IS FRESH, KEEN AND STRONG. | ALSO, IT IS
POETRY. THE SAVOR AND | TANG OF THE WILD AND OPEN ARE
IN IT. | IT IS SWEET, AND WHOLESOME, AND CLEAN | AS
MOUNTAIN DEW. AND IT IS STRONG, | ALWAYS STRONG, RUDDY
STRONG WITH | SUN, AND FROST, AND WIND. | WHAT DO YOU
THINK ABOUT IT? | SHEEHAN & CO. SELL IT ALL FOR A
DOLLAR | PHONE YOUR ORDER THIS MORNING
    15.5 x 9 cm. Brown stiff paper, printed in green.
Verso of broadside contains "The pleasure of the hour,"
a poem from *Fagots of Cedar*.

GLEN ELLEN GUEST CARD. 1910

1050. JACK LONDON TELEPHONE | GLEN ELLEN SONOMA, SUBURBAN
245 | SONOMA CO., CALIFORNIA | U. S. A.| WE LIVE IN A
BEAUTIFUL PART OF THE | COUNTRY, ABOUT TWO HOURS FROM
SAN | FRANCISCO BY TWO ROUTES, THE SOUTHERN | PACIFIC
AND THE NORTHWESTERN PACIFIC. | BOTH TRAINS (OR BOATS
CONNECTING WITH | TRAINS), LEAVE SAN FRANCISCO ABOUT
8 A.M. | THE P.M. SOUTHERN PACIFIC TRAIN (BOAT) |
LEAVES SAN FRANCISCO ABOUT 4 O'CLOCK. | THE P.M.
NORTHWESTERN PACIFIC TRAIN CAN | BE CONNECTED WITH AT
16th STREET STATION, | OAKLAND, ALSO. | IF YOU COME
IN THE AFTERNOON IT IS MORE | CONVENIENT FOR US IF YOU
TAKE THE SOUTHERN | PACIFIC ROUTE, AS IT ARRIVES HERE
IN TIME FOR | OUR SUPPER. WE USUALLY ASK OUR GUESTS TO |
DINE ON THE BOAT, IF THEY COME BY THE | NORTHWESTERN
PACIFIC. | WRITE (OR TELEPHONE) IN ADVANCE OF | YOUR
COMING, BECAUSE WE ARE FREQUENTLY | AWAY FROM HOME.
ALSO, IF WE ARE AT HOME, | WORD FROM YOU WILL MAKE IT
SO WE CAN | HAVE A RIG AT THE STATION TO MEET YOU. |
BE SURE [underlined] TO STATE BY WHAT ROUTE, [last two
words underlined] AND BY | WHAT TRAIN, [underlined] YOU
WILL ARRIVE. [Page 2 is blank.] [Page 3, within single-
line border:] OUR LIFE HERE IS SOMETHING AS FOLLOWS:
[followed by 104 words of text.] [printer's decoration
at end.]
    15.5 x 9 cm. P.[1], front cover as above, p.[2]
blank, p.[3] as above, p.[4] blank. One thousand copies

privately printed. Reproduced in *The Book of Jack London*, pp.204-205.

THE STRENGTH OF THE STRONG. 1911

1051. THE STRENGTH OF THE STRONG | BY JACK LONDON | AUTHOR OF "THE CALL OF THE WILD," "WHITE FANG," ETC. | [short rule] | ILLUSTRATIONS BY DAN SAYRE GROESBECK | [short rule] | PARABLES DON'T LIE, BUT LIARS WILL PARABLE.-- LIP-KING | [short rule] | CHICAGO | CHARLES H. KERR & COMPANY | CO-OPERATIVE
  18.5 x 13 cm. P.[1], Title, p.[2], copyright: Copyright 1911 | By Jack London | Reprinted by permission from Hampton Magazine | [printer's mark]; p.[3], illustration by Dan Sayre Groesbeck, signed in the lower right corner, and titled beneath: "Days and nights the eyes of the tribe watched." P.[4], blank; illustration above beginning of text, p.5; text, pp.5-30; advertisement of *Ancient Society* by Lewis H. Morgan, p.[31]; advertisement of *The International Socialist Review*, and *The Appeal to Reason*, p.[32]. Issued in white wrappers, printed in blue. Rear cover contains advertisement of *The Socialist Review*.

1052. Other Editions:
  THE STRENGTH OF THE STRONG | BY JACK LONDON | AUTHOR OF "THE CALL OF THE WILD," "WHITE FANG," ETC. | [short rule] | ILLUSTRATIONS BY DAN SAYRE GROESBECK | [short rule] | PARABLES DON'T LIE, BUT LIARS WILL PARABLE-- LIP-KING | [short rule] | CHICAGO | CHARLES H. KERR & COMPANY | 1912
  19.5 x 13 cm. P.[1], Title-page, p.[2], copyright: Copyright 1911 | By Jack London | Reprinted by permission from Hampton | Magazine | [printer's mark] text, pp.[3]-29; advertisements of 3pp. Issued in white wrappers, printed in sepia. Front cover within double-line border: The Strength | of the Strong | [illustration] | "Days and Nights the Eyes of the Tribe Watched." | Price 10 Cents | [short rule] | By Jack London | Rear Cover: The Strength of | the Strong | [illustration] | By Jack London

  THE STRENGTH OF THE STRONG | BY JACK LONDON | AUTHOR OF "THE CALL OF THE WILD," "WHITE FANG", ETC.| [short rule] | Illustrated by Dan Sayre Groesbeck | [short rule] | CHICAGO | CHARLES H. KERR & COMPANY | CO-OPER- ATIVE
  18 x 12.5 cm. P.[1], Title, p.[2], copyright: Copy-

right 1911 | By Jack London | Reprinted by permission
from Hampton Magazine | [printer's mark] text, pp.[3]-
29; publisher's announcements of 3pp. Last advertisement is for *History of the great American fortunes* by
Gustavus Meyers. Issued in cream-colored wrappers,
printed in blue. Front cover within double-line border:
The Strength | of the Strong | [illustration] | "Days
and Nights the Eyes of the Tribe Watched" | By Jack
London | Beneath border in right corner: Ten Cents |
Rear cover: The Strength of | the Strong | [illustra-
tion] | By Jack London
        There is a variant of the above issue in the George
H. Tweney collection as follows:
THE STRENGTH OF THE STRONG | BY JACK LONDON | AUTHOR OF
"THE CALL OF THE WILD," "WHITE FANG," ETC. | [rule] |
Illustrated by Dan Sayre Groesbeck | [rule] | Parables
don't lie, but liars will parable-- Lip King | [rule] |
Chicago | CHARLES H. KERR & COMPANY | CO-OPERATIVE
        Pagination and all internal details same as above,
except final publisher's advertisement on last page is
for *The Collapse of Capitalism* by Herman Cahn. Issued
in white paper wrappers, printed in light blue. Front
and rear cover details and printing same as above.

TOURNAMENT OF ROSES PROGRAM. 1912

1053. [Program. Tournament of Roses, Pasadena, California,
      Jan. 1, 1912. Contains excerpt from a letter by Jack
      London originally published in the Pasadena *Star*.
      Broadside, Jan. 1, 1912.]

WONDER OF WOMAN. 1912

1054. WONDER OF WOMAN | A "SMOKE BELLEW" STORY | [IN TWO
      PARTS] | JACK LONDON | INTERNATIONAL MAGAZINE CO. |
      NEW YORK
          22 x 15 cm. p.[1-2], Blank leaf, p.[3] title, p.[4]
      copyright of three lines [dated 1912], p.[5], half
      title, p.[6] blank, text, pp.[7]-32, printed in double
      columns. Part two begins near bottom of page 19, text
      ends on page 32. Issued in stiff white paper covers.
      Front cover lettered in blue. Double-ruled in gilt
      above and below. Ribbon design in blue, edged in gilt.

JACK LONDON BY HIMSELF. 1913

1055. JACK LONDON | BY HIMSELF | [portrait bust] | JACK
      LONDON | AUTHOR OF "THE VALLEY OF THE MOON" | PUBLISH-

Jack London

BY HIMSELF

JACK LONDON

Author of "The Valley of the Moon"

PUBLISHERS

THE MACMILLAN COMPANY
64-66 FIFTH AVENUE   NEW YORK

[Item 1055]

ERS | THE MACMILLAN COMPANY | 64-66 FIFTH AVENUE NEW
YORK
  Front cover, within double-line border, used as
title.
  18 x 13.5 cm. Text of eight unnumbered pages. Portrait p.[4]. Running titles in red ink. Text begins on
verso of front cover and ends on inside back cover. The
back cover contains an advertisement of *The Valley of
the Moon*, with a list of twenty-six other works "By
the Same Author." Printed on glossy, off-white wove
paper. Stapled. Reprinted from "In the days of my
youth," *Mainly about people*, a popular weekly of personal portraits and social news. Published in London,
T. P. O'Connor, editor, 15, 376:204-205 (Aug. 26, 1905).
The original manuscript contains 124 words of conclusion which were never printed, although submitted to
several publishers. Charmian London published excerpts
from this conclusion in her *Book of Jack London*.

1056. Other Editions:
  The English edition is 18 x 12 cm. It was published in
  London, Mills & Boon, [n.d.] [1914?], and was printed
  from new plates. There are four reproductions from
  photographs which did not appear in the American issue.
  The interior portrait of the American issue is not contained in the English edition. Rear cover advertises
  The Valley of the Moon, with a list of seven other
  works "By the Same Author." 8 pages, text begins on
  inside front cover. The first issue has the captions
  of the last two photographs reversed.

  Jack London: the author with the sales, London, Mills
  & Boon, Ltd., [n.d.,] [1915?]. Second English edition.
  20 x 15 cm. This contains the autobiographical sketch
  on pages [2], [4], [6], [7], with the addition of eight
  reproductions from photographs which did not appear in
  the first American or first English issues. The interior portrait from the American edition is contained
  on page [6]. It contains excerpts from reviews which
  appeared in English periodicals. Printed on light blue
  paper.

  RESIGNATION FROM THE SOCIALIST PARTY. 1916

1057. THE RESIGNATION OF JACK LONDON | [reproduction of a
  twenty-seven line letter addressed "Dear Comrades:"] |
  JACK LONDON [Broadside, 1916.]
  28 x 21.5 cm. The letter is undated. It was written

The Resignation of Jack London

Dear Comrades:

I am resigning from the Socialist Party, because of its lack of fire and fight, and its loss of emphasis on the class struggle.

I was originally a member of the old, revolutionary, up-on-its-hind legs, fighting Socialist Labor Party. Since then, and to the present time I have been a fighting member of the Socialist Party. My fighting record in the cause is not, even at this late date, already entirely forgotten. Trained in the class struggle, as taught and practised by the Socialist Labor Party, my own highest judgement concurring, I believed that the working class, by fighting, by never fusing, by never making terms with the enemy could emancipate itself. Nay, further, I have always insisted that the working class must emancipate itself. Since the whole trend of socialism in the United States of recent years has been one of peaceableness and compromise, I find that my mind refuses further sanction of my remaining a party member. Hence my resignation.

Please include my comrade wife, Charmian K. London's resignation with mine.

My final word is that liberty, freedom and indeperdence, are royal things that cannot be presented to, nor thrust upon, races or classes. If races and classes cannot rise up and by their own strength of brain and brawn, wrest from the world liberty, freedom and independence, they never in time, can come to these royal possessions--and if such royal things are kindly presented to them by superior individuals, on silver platters, they will know not what to do with them, will fail to make use of them, and will be what they have always been in the past--inferior races and inferior classes.

Yours for the Revolution,

Jack London

in Honolulu, March 7, 1916. Printed on one side only,
of poor quality wove paper with watermark: RAILROAD
BOND | P.C. & P. CO. A few carbon copies of the orig-
inal letter were issued in 1917 by Mrs. Jack London.
The signature is in script-style type.

AN OLD LIE FINALLY NAILED. 1916

1058. AN OLD LIE | FINALLY NAILED | [short-thick rule] | *THE
AUTHORSHIP OF THE LETTER | REPRODUCED ON THE 1st
INSIDE | PAGE HAS BEEN, FOR YEARS, AT- | TRIBUTED TO
JACK LONDON; AND | WIDE-SPREAD PUBLICITY HAS | BEEN
GIVEN TO THE LETTER BY | MANY SO-CALLED SOCIALIST PUB-
LICATIONS AND BY OTHERS WHOSE | PRACTICE IT IS TO
MISREPRESENT | THE ARMY AND NAVY OF THE | UNITED STATES*
[ten small dots] | [short thick rule]
    18 x 10 cm. P.[1], front cover used as title, p.[2],
verso: letter of thirty lines, signed "Jack London.";
p.[3]; letter from Glen Ellen dated August 5, 1916, ad-
dressed to Lieutenant James D. Wilson, Navy Recruiting
Station, Minneapolis, Minn., denying authorship of the
letter reproduced on the first inside page; p.[4];
seventeen line note on the advantages of United States
Naval training. All pages within single-line border.
The first issue of this item is without the stamp
"Navy Recruiting Station, | Minneapolis, Minn." on the
first page.

EIGHT GREAT FACTORS OF LITERARY SUCCESS. [1916]

1059. EIGHT GREAT FACTORS OF LITERARY SUCCESS | "I CONSIDER
THE GREATEST FACTORS OF MY LITERARY SUCCESS TO BE: |
[thirty-six lines] | [facsimile autograph of Jack
London] [Broadside, 1916.]
    21.5 x 15 cm. Printed on white, medium-weight paper,
verso blank.

FOREWORD TO MICHAEL, BROTHER OF JERRY [1918?]

1060. [Issued in four pages:] [Page i:] [four lines] | THE
JACK LONDON CLUB | [three lines] | OUR DUMB ANIMALS |
180 Longwood Avenue | BOSTON, MASS. | FOREWORD |
[twenty-two lines of text] | i [Pages ii, iii: Contin-
uation of text.] [Page iv:] iv Foreword | [twenty-seven
lines of text] | Jack London. | Glen Ellen, Sonoma
County, California, | December 8, 1915. | [short rule]
[six lines of copyright data].
    21 x 14 cm. Printed on off-white wove paper. This

four page reprint is from new plates. It was issued
by the Massachusetts Society for the Prevention of
Cruelty to Animals. Boston, [1918?]. *See* errata at end.

THE SEA SPRITE AND THE SHOOTING STAR. 1932

1061. THE SEA SPRITE AND THE SHOOTING STAR | JACK LONDON
      Leaflet, four pages, unnumbered. P.[1], Title as
above; p.[2-3] text, seventeen six-line verses of
poetry; p.[4] blank. Printed in black, on cream-colored
random embossed paper. 27 x 15 cm. Jack London wanted
to be a poet, and as a youngster in the 1890's, he submitted a lengthy descriptive poem to a metropolitan
daily. There is no record that it was either published,
paid for, or returned. The manuscript was salvaged after
his death, and first privately printed in November,
1932 in the above format. A clue to the date of compo-
sition appears under the heading of page [2] of the
above, with the following line of type enclosed in
parentheses: Jack London, 962 East 16th Street, Oakland,
California, 1899. Subsequent to 1932, it was published
in the following format, but date of publication is not
known: THE SEA SPRITE | AND THE | SHOOTING STAR | [star
ornament in red] | JACK LONDON | Six unnumbered leaves,
printed on rectos only, stapled in stiff, mottled gray
covers, lettered as above. At bottom of back cover
the following is printed in green: A PRESENTATION OF |
JACK LONDON AMATEUR PRESS CLUB | Hand Press Print
[in parentheses] 16 x 12 cm.

JACK LONDON [n.d.]

1062. *"About me are the great natural forces-- | colossal
      menaces . . . The bit | of life that is I will exult |
      over them!"* | JACK LONDON | Who He Is | and | What He
Has Done | [ornament] | THE MACMILLAN COMPANY | 64-66
Fifth Avenue, New York [n.d.]
      P.[1] Title as above; p.[2] blank; p.[3] Illustra-
tion: The Building of the "Snark"; p.[4] blank; pp.5-16,
text, with portraits on p.[9] and p.[14]. Bound in
light mauve paper wrappers, stapled. Front wrapper
lettered in purple: Jack London | his Life and | Liter-
ary Work | [ornament in green] | WITH THE COMPLIMENTS |
OF | THE MACMILLAN COMPANY | NEW YORK [.] The fore-
going is surrounded with an ornamental border printed
in green; inside front wrapper blank; inside back
wrapper a publisher's list of Jack London's books; outside back wrapper contains a portrait of London. Text

pages printed in sepia on calendared paper. There is a
variant copy of this pamphlet in the George H. Tweney
collection. The title page is exactly as described
above, except it is p.[3] in the pagination, with "The
Building of the "Snark" illustration as a frontispiece.
All remaining pagination is as described above. The
pamphlet is bound in light blue-gray wrappers, with
front cover printed in dark blue as follows: Jack
London | his Life and | Literary Work | [ornament] |
WITH THE COMPLIMENTS | OF | HARVARD CO-OPERATIVE |
SOCIETY, INC. | Dane Hall : Cambridge, Mass. This is
surrounded in an ornamental border printed in dark
blue. The remaining wrapper pages are as the issue
above, except the outside back wrapper is blank. Jack
London personally wrote the text for this pamphlet,
although not so stated in the pamphlet.

A SOUVENIR CHAPTER [n.d.]

1063. A | SOUVENIR CHAPTER | OF | A REALLY FINE RED-BLOODED
TALE OF | ADVENTURES IN THE SOUTH SEA ISLANDS | ENTITLED
| A SON OF THE SUN | BY | JACK LONDON | AUTHOR OF
"SOUTH SEA TALES" | Crown 8vo. 6s. | [seven lines] |
[short rule] | MILLS & BOON LTD. 49 RUPERT ST. LONDON,
W.

Front cover used as title. The above enclosed within triple line borders. At the top above the borders
is printed "With Mills & Boon's Compliments." 19 x 12 cm.
Publisher's advertisements, text pp.1-8, advertisements
on inside rear cover, rear cover with Mills & Boon's
List of Novels. Issued in cream colored wrappers.

Errata: A translation of item number 1060 is as follows:
Les clubs Jack London, Paris, Le Club Jack London
[1925?] 32pp. [Consists mainly of extracts from *Michael,*
chien de cirque translated by Paul Gruyer and Louis
Postif.]

SPURIOUS WORKS

1064.   *THE DEFINITION OF A SCAB*

Jack London has been credited with a definition of a scab, which has been reprinted many times over the last thirty years. This definition can be best found in either Philip S. Foner, *Jack London: American rebel* (N. Y., The Citadel Press, c1964, pp.57-58 with further comment on pp.132-133) or George Seldes, *Great quotations* (N. Y., Lyle Stuart, 1962, p.438). This definition also appears in *The Dispatcher*, 4,17:5 (Aug. 23, 1946), an organ of the International Longshoremen's & Warehousemen's Union (San Francisco, Calif.).

As no record of this definition was found to show it was published during London's lifetime, the compilers feel that it is safe to assume that this is a spurious work, especially since neither Foner nor Seldes, the two scholars who have given the most thought to the subject, can show any reason for the attribution. Seldes remembers that he saw the definition used during labor troubles of the first World War. Archie Green remembers the definition from the mid-1940's.

Peter Tamony of San Francisco has "collected notes on the word *scab* over a long period" and was kind enough to send Woodbridge his notes on the subject. He notes that the text of the diatribe as published in the *Labor Herald* (Northern California edition, San Francisco), 10:14:sec. 2:12 (Aug. 30, 1946) under the title of "Portrait of a scab" concludes with "A real man never becomes a strike-breaker." He states that another version concludes with the words: "There is nothing lower than a SCAB."

The strike of agricultural workers around Delano, Calif. in 1965-1966 brought the definition of a scab back into the public eye.

On Oct. 17, 1965 the Rev. Daniel Havens was arrested for reading London's "Definition of a scab" to a group of strikebreakers on the Mid-State Ranch close to Delano, Calif. The following are among the news stories concerning this event:

1065. "Valley strike minister jailed - defining 'scab'," San Francisco *Chronicle*, Oct. 19, 1965, p.37.

1066. Joan London, "Unusual arrest," San Francisco *Chronicle*, Nov. 4, 1965, p.48.

1067. "Cop jugs preacher for 'insulting' scabs with Jack London's famed opinion," *The Dispatcher* (San Francisco), Nov. 12, 1965, p.4.

1068. "Eternal vigilance," *The Dispatcher*, Nov. 12, 1965, p.2.
1069. "Grapes of wrath," *Time*, 86,24:96 (Dec. 10, 1965).
1070. *El malcriado: the voice of the farm worker* presents on
      p.[10] of issue no. 22 [n.d., but probably early Nov.
      1965] an anonymous translation into Spanish of this
      definition under the title, "Definicion de un esquirol."
      The alleged original also appears on the same page un-
      der the title, "Definition of a strike-breaker."
           It is to be noted that the definition as found
      printed contains numerous variants and that there are
      publications that have attributed entirely differently-
      worded definitions to him. For example, "The march of
      labor," *East Bay Labor Journal*, July 19, 1940, p.1
      attributes the following to Jack London as his defin-
      ition of a scab: "A two-legged animal with a corkscrew
      soul, a water-logged brain, and a backbone made of
      jelly and glue." This is but one paragraph of "The def-
      inition of a scab."
           Tony Bubka, who spent numerous hours searching
      California labor newspapers and to whom, along with
      Joan London, we are grateful for many of the preceding
      references, has discovered that in 1936 two labor news-
      papers: *Organized Labor* (San Francisco), Sept. 1936,
      p.4 and the San Francisco *Labor Clarion*, 35:35 (Sept.
      4, 1936) published the definition but preceded the
      definition with the following introductory paragraph:
                A prominent clergyman once gave the foll-
           owing statements as his version of "scabs" or
           strike-breakers, after being compelled to as-
           sociate with them for a short time. The story
           has frequently been reprinted, but it will
           bear repetition: *(Labor Clarion; Organized
           Labor* contains identical text with omission
           of last sentence).
      Bubka has discovered that portions of the *Atlantic
      Monthly* essay, "The scab" were published in the labor
      and socialist press. See, for example, *Organized Labor*,
      June 9, 1917, p.2 and "Jack London noted this fact,"
      Oakland *World*, Jan. 26, 1923, p.3.
           In an attempt to secure additional data on this
      problem, queries were printed in the New York *Times
      Book Review*, July 29, 1962, p.27 and in *American Notes
      and Queries*, 1,3:39-40 (Nov. 1962). A form letter was
      sent to the editors of over a hundred labor newspapers.
      Though such newspapers as *The ACA News*, *Vallejo Labor
      Journal*, *Monterey Bay Labor News*, *Contra Costa County
      Labor Journal* (July 17, 1964) all have published the
      definition, no one could provide information concerning

how Jack London came to be associated with it.

Certain labor unions such as the National Maritime Union have distributed this definition as a reprint or a handbill.

The compilers desire to reiterate that the definition of a scab and London's "The scab" (q.v.) are two entirely separate pieces and that as of now there is no reason to associate Jack London with this definition of a scab. The above evidence shows that during the 1930's this definition was credited to a "prominent clergyman" and that at least as early as 1940 Jack London's name became associated with it.

1071.   *"THE GOOD SOLDIER" CANARD*

For the period 1911 to 1916 a short anti-militarist tract, "The good soldier," was credited to Jack London. He denied its authorship vigorously and it is for this reason that it is here listed as among his doubtful or spurious works. Proof of his authorship is not available. On the whole, his biographers have ignored this episode. Joan London reprints the text and discusses "The good soldier" canard in pp.348-349 of *Jack London and his times*.

The tract was so short that the socialist *Appeal to Reason* published its text on the back of an envelope. This same journal published the tract as its January 1916 leaflet, which it sold at 50 cents per 1,000 copies.

Most of the following citations are found in the Jack London collection in the Huntington Library, San Marino, California.

1072. "Militia after London. Recruits lured away. 'Call of the tame', circular laid to him, attacks the soldiery," San Francisco *Call*, March 2, 1911, p.13.
1073. "Jack London again," Oakland *World*, March 11, 1911, p.1.
1074. "Can't locate Jack London," Oakland *World*, April 8, 1911, p.3.
1075. "Reply to Jack London," Norfolk (Va.) *Landmark*, Sept. 2, 1911, p.6 [Signed: An enlisted man, U. S. S. North Carolina].
1076. "Libel upon military resented by nation," Seattle *Times*, April 18, 1912, p.24.
1077. London, Jack, "The 'good' soldier," *International Socialist Review*, 14:199 (Oct. 1913).
1078. "The good soldier," *Organized labor* (San Francisco), Oct. 18, 1913, p.4.
1079. "Don't be a soldier," London *Daily Express*, Aug. 2, 1915, p.3 [This is an indignant article concerning a

certain anti-recruiting leaflet entitled *The military
ideal* which had been circulated in England at the time.
The words of the leaflet are reprinted, but there is
no mention of the author's name, who is merely referred
to as "a famous American writer".]

1080. "Bar London sentiments from mail. Writer's 'Good
soldier' paragraphs offend Burleson. Envelopes bearing
anti-military writing halted," Oakland *Tribune*, Nov.
19, 1915, p.1 [Reprints tract].

1081. "The war censor arrives in America. United States postal officials deny mails to Jack London's 'The good
soldier'," *American Socialist* (Chicago), Nov. 20, 1915,
p.1 [Reprints tract].

1082. A soldier, "Soldier in United States Army resents the
published statement of Jack London," New York *Herald*,
Nov. 22, 1915, p.[?]. [Clipping found in Huntington
Library London collection. Check of *Herald* failed to
determine page number.]

1083. [Editorial], *Army and Navy Journal*, 53:387 (Nov. 27,
1915).

1084. Snyder, J. E., "Shall we allow militarism in our
schools?" Oakland *World*, Nov. 27, 1915, p.1 [Reprints
tract].

1085. London, Jack, "A spirited denial by ...," *Army and Navy
Journal*, 53:499 (Dec. 18, 1915) [Reply and comment on
editorial of Nov. 27].

1086. "Burleson bars from U. S. mails Jack London's 'A good
soldier'," *Appeal to Reason*, Nov. 27, 1915, p.2.

1087. "Postal czars threaten to shut down Appeal for its
criticism of soldiers," *Appeal to Reason*, Dec. 4, 1915,
p.1. [This is the text of a letter dated Nov. 22, 1915
signed by W. H. Lamar, Solicitor, United States Post
Office Department.]

1088. "Censored by the postmaster general. A good soldier by
Jack London," *Appeal to Reason*, Dec. 4, 1915, p.5
[Reprints tract].

1089. "Help circulate the censored article," *Appeal to Reason*,
Dec. 11, 1915, p.5 ["This leaflet contains an introduction explaining in large type how it was censored.."].

1090. London, Jack, "A good soldier," Oakland *World*, Dec. 18,
1915, p.5.

1091. "Three solar plexus blows at militarism. Read by 'Ruth'
at Hamilton Auditorium entertainment," Oakland *World*,
Dec. 18, 1915, p.5.

1092. "Jack London again disavows diatribe against soldier.
Declares it is not his work but a 'Made in Germany'
sentiment. Anti-militaristic canard was denied repeat-
edly. Country should maintain reasonable preparedness

against attack by foreign foe," *Pacific Commercial
Advertiser*, Jan. 4, 1916, pp.1,7 [Reprints letter to
Army and Navy Journal].

1093. "Mr. Burleson's record," *Appeal to Reason*, Jan. 1, 1916,
p.5 [Reprints editorial from the *Daily Courier News*,
Fargo, N. D., concerning post office censorship of the
Appeal to Reason over publication of "The good soldier"].

1094. "Letters from the Appeal army bring an explanation from
Post Office Department," *Appeal to Reason*, Jan. 15,
1916, p.1.

1095. London, Jack, "A good soldier," *The open letter*,
[4] (March 1916).

1096. "Jack London for U. S. preparedness. Authorship of
'Good soldier' denied. Notorious article declared
canard," Oakland *Tribune*, June 22, 1916.

1097. "London repudiates pacifist pamphlet," San Francisco
Call, June 23, 1916, p.3.

1098. "Preparedness U. S. safeguard says Jack London. Author
denies writing pamphlet, 'A good soldier'; says war
will always be," San Francisco *Examiner*, June 23, 1916.

1099. "Jack London denies rapping soldiers. In personal letter
to naval official he says armies will endure," Minneapolis *News*, Aug. 11, 1916, p.[?]. [Clipping found in
Huntington Library London collection; check of *News*
file failed to determine correct page number.]

1100. "Jack London denies tract authorship. Writer disclaims
anti-enlistment appeal circulated by socialists,"
St. Paul *Pioneer-Press*, Aug. 12, 1916, p.[?].

1101. "Burleson bars from U. S. mails Jack London's 'A good
soldier'. Appeal army will out general P. O. Czar
by distributing millions of copies of censored article
in leaflet form," *Appeal to Reason*, Nov. 27, 1916,
p.1 [Reprints tract].

1102. "The letter Jack London repudiated," New York *Sun*,
July 1, 1918, p.6 [Reprints "The good soldier canard"
and London letter of Aug. 5, 1916 to Lt. J. D. Wilson].

1103. Translations:
"Tubli soldat," *Tapper*, no. 3:8 (1918); *Tööline*, Jan.
18, 1918 (Estonian).

CHRONOLOGICAL LISTING OF MOTION PICTURES BASED ON LONDON'S
WORKS PRODUCED IN THE UNITED STATES

The chief sources for the information given in this section are: *Copyright Office Catalog, The Film Daily Year Book, Motion Picture Herald, Moving Picture World* and the New York *Times.* Data provided by Glenn W. Bunday, Reference Department, University of Southern California Library.

1104. *A piece of steak,* Balboa Amusement Co. 2,000 ft. 1913.
1105. *The sea wolf,* Balboa Amusement Co. 3 reels. 1913.
1106. *The sea wolf,* Bosworth, Inc. Cast: Hobart Bosworth, Viola Barry. 93 prints. 1913.
1107. *To kill a man,* Balboa Amusement Co. 1,000 ft. 1913.
1108. *Burning daylight,* Bosworth, Inc. 5 reels. Released Sept. 14, 1914.
1109. *John Barleycorn,* Bosworth, Inc. Cast: Elmer Clifton, Viola Barry, Matty Roubert. 6 reels. 1914.
1110. *Martin Eden,* Bosworth, Inc. 89 prints. 1914.
1111. *An odyssey of the North,* Bosworth, Inc. 134 prints. 1914.
1112. *Valley of the moon,* Bosworth, Inc. Cast: Jack Conway, Myrtle Stedman. 7 reels. 1914.
1113. *Burning daylight,* Shurtleff, Inc. Dir.: Edward Sloman. Scenario: A. S. LeVino. Cast: Mitchell Lewis, Helen Ferguson, William V. Mong, Alfred Allen, Edward Jobson, Robert Boulder, Gertrude Astor, Edmund E. Carewe, Lew Morrison. 5 parts. 1920.
1114. *The mutiny of the Elsinore,* Shurtleff, Inc. Dir.: Edward Sloman. Adaptation: A. S. LeVino. All star cast. 6 reels. 1920 [Copyright as *The mutiny,* but listed in all film sources under full title].
1115. *The sea wolf,* Paramount-Artcraft. Prod. and dir.: George Melford. Screen play: Will M. Ritchey. Cast: Noah Berry, Mabel Julienne Scott, Tom Forman, Raymond Hatton, Eddie Sutherland, Walter Long, James Gordon, Fred Huntley. 7 reels. 1920.
1116. *The star rover,* Shurtleff, Inc. Dir.: Edward Sloman. Scenario: A. S. LeVino. Cast: Courtenay Foote, Thelma Percy, "Dee" Cannon, Dwight Crittenden, Jack Carlysle, Chance Ward, Marcella Daley. 6 reels. 1920.
1117. *The little fool,* Shurtleff, Inc. Dir.: Philip E. Rosen. Scenario: Mary Parro, Edward Lowe, Jr. Cast: Milton Sills, Ora Carew, Nigel Barrie, Byron Munson, Marjorie Prevost, Helen Howard, Iva Forrester. 6 reels. 1921 [Based on *The little lady of the big house*].
1118. *Mohican's daughter,* P. T. B., Inc. Dir.: S. E. V. Taylor. 5 reels. 1922 [Based on "The story of Jees Uck"].

1119. *The son of the wolf,* R-C. Dir.: Norman Dawn. Scenario:
W. Haywood. Cast: Wheeler Oakman, Edith Roberts, Sam
Allen, Ashley Cooper, Fred Kohler, Thomas Jefferson,
Fred Stanton, Arthur Jasmine, William Eagle Eye.
4,970 ft. 1922 [Based on "The son of the wolf" and
"Wife of a king"].

1120. *Jack London's Tales of the fish patrol,* Universal Film
Mfg. Co. (1) White and yellow. Star: Jack Mulhall;
(2) The channel raiders. Star: Jack Mulhall; (3) Pirates
of the deep; (4) The law of the sea. Ibid. Universal
Pictures Corp. (5) The seige of the Lancashire Queen;
(6) Dangerous waters; (7) Yellow handkerchief; (8)
Wolves of the waterfront. 2 reels each. 1922-1923.

1121. *Call of the wild,* Pathe. Prod.: Hal Roach. Scenario and
direction: Fred Jackman. Photography: Fred Jackman.
Cast: Jack Mulhall, Walter Lang, Sydney d'Albrook,
Frank Butler, Laura Roessing, the dog. 7,000 ft. Released Sept. 23, 1923.

1122. *The abysmal brute,* Universal. Dir.: Hobart Henley.
8 reels. 1923.

1123. *Adventure,* Paramount. Prod. and dir.: Victor Fleming.
Screen play: A. P. Younger and L. G. Rigby. Cast:
Tom Moore, Pauline Starke, Wallace Berry, Raymond
Hatton, Walter McGrail, Duke Kahanamoku, James Spencer,
Noble Johnson. 6,602 ft. 1925.

1124. *White fang,* F. B. D. Dir.: Lawrence Trimble [*Motion
Picture World* gives director as George Berthelon].
Adaptation and scenario: Jane Murtin. Star: Strongheart.
6 reels. 1925.

1125. *The sea wolf,* Producers Distrib. Corp. Presented by
John C. Flinn. Dir.: Ralph W. Ince. Screen play: J.
Grubb Alexander. 7 reels. 1926.

1126. *Morganson's finish,* Tiffany Prod. Dir.: Fred Windermere.
7 reels. 1926.

1127. *The haunted ship,* Tiffany-Stahl. Dir.: Forrest Sheldon.
Adapted by E. Morton Haugh. Cast: Dorothy Sebastian,
Montagu Love, Tom Santschi, Ray Hallor, Pat Harmon,
Alice Lake, Budd Duncan, Blue Washington, Sojin,
William Lowery, Earl Hogan, Jerry Madden. 5 reels. 1927
[Suggested by "The white and the yellow"].

1128. *Burning daylight,* Rowland. Dist.: First National. Dir.:
Charles J. Brabin and Wid Gunning. Cameraman: Sol
Polito. Scenarist: Louis Stevens. Editor: Frank Ware.
Title writers: Dionelle Benthal, Rufus McCash. Star:
Milton Sills. 1928.

1129. *The devil's skipper,* Tiffany-Stahl. Dir.: John G.
Adolfi. Scenarist: John F. Natteford. Adaptation:
Robert Dillon. Cameraman: Ernest Miller. Editor: John

F. Natteford. Title writers: Harry Braxton, Viola
Brothers Shore. Star: Belle Bennett. 6 reels. 1928
[Suggested by "Demetrious Contos"].

1130. *Prowlers of the sea*, Tiffany-Stahl. Supervision: Roy
Fitzroy. Dir.: John G. Adolfi. Scenario: John Francis
Natteford. Titles: Lesley Mason. Editor: Desmond
O'Brien. Stars: Ricardo Cortez, Carmel Myers. 1928
[Suggested by "The Lancashire Queen"].

1131. *Stormy waters*, Tiffany-Stahl. Supervision: Roy Fitzroy.
Dir.: Edgar Lewis. Adaptation and continuity: Harry
Dittmar. Titles: Lesley Mason. Editor: Martin Cohen.
Cast: Eve Southern and Malcolm MacGregor. 6 reels. 1928
[Based on "The yellow handkerchief"].

1132. *Tropical nights*, Tiffany-Stahl. Dir.: Elmer Clifton.
Screen adaptation: Bennett Cohn. Cameramen: John Boyle,
Ernest Miller. Titles: Harry Carr. Editor: Desmond
O'Brien. Star: Malcolm MacGregor. 6 reels. 1928 [Based
on "A raid on the oyster pirates"].

1133. *Smoke Bellew*, First Division. Dir.: Scott Dunlap.
Scenarist: Fred Myton. Editor: Charles Hunt. Cameramen:
J. O. Taylor, Joe Walters. Cast: Conway Tearle, Barbara
Bedford, Mark Hamilton, J. P. Lockney, Al Ethier,
William Scott, Alaska-Jack. 1929.

1134. *The sea wolf*, Fox. Dir.: Alfred Santell. Cameraman:
Glen MacWilliams. Editor: Paul Weatherwax. Scenarist:
Ralph Black. Dialoguer: S. N. Behrman. Sound engineer:
Frank MacKenzie. Cast: Milton Sills, Raymond Hackett,
Jane Keith, Harry Tembrook. 10 reels. Running time:
1 hr. 27 min. Released: Nov. 29, 1930.

1135. *Call of the wild*, United Artists. Prod.: Darryl Zanuck.
Dir.: William Wellman. Screen play: Gene Fowler, Leonard
Praskins. Cameraman: Charles Rocher. Editor: Hanson
Fritch. Music: Alfred Newman. Cast: Clark Gable,
Loretta Young, Jack Oakie, Reginald Owen, Frank Conroy,
Katherine DeMille, Sidney Toler, James Burke, Charles
Stevens, Lalos Encinas, Tommy Jackson, Russ Powell,
Herman Bing, George McQuarrie. 10 reels. 1935.

1136. *Conflict*, Universal. Dir.: David Howard. Prod.: Trem
Carr. Supervision: Paul Malvern. Music dir.: Herman
Heller. Film ed.: Jack Oglivie. Screen play: Charles
Logue, Walter Weems. Cast: John Wayne, Jean Rogers,
Tony Bupp, Eddie Borden, Frank Sheridan, Ward Bond,
Margaret Mann, Harry Wood, Bryant Washburn, Frank Hagney.
1936 [Based on *Abysmal brute*].

1137. *White fang*, 20th Century-Fox. Dir.: David Butler. Prod.:
Darryl F. Zanuck. Music dir.: Arthur Lange. Screen play:
Gene Fowler, Hal Long, S. G. Duncan. Cast: Michael
Whalen, Jean Muir, Slim Sumerville, Charles Winninger,

John Carradine, Jane Darwell, Thomas Beck, Joseph
Herrick, George Ducowat, Marie Chorie, Lightning.
6,720 ft. 1936.

1138. *Romance of the redwoods*, Columbia. Dir.: Charles Vidor.
Screen play: Michael L. Simmons. Music dir.: M. W.
Stoloff. Editor: Byron Robinson. Cast: Charles Bickford,
Jean Parker, Alan Bridges, Gordon Oliver, Anne Shoe-
maker, Lloyd Hughes, Pat O'Malley, Marc Lawrence, Earl
Gunn, Don Beddoe. Running time: 61 min. 7 reels. Re-
leased: March 30, 1939 [Based on "The white silence"].

1139. *Wolf call*, Monogram. Prod.: Paul Malvern. Dir.: George
Waggner. Screenplay: Joseph West. Music dir.: Eddie Kay.
Cast: John Carroll, Novita, Peter George Lynn, Guy
Usher, Holmes Herbert, Polly Ann Young, George Cleve-
land, John Kelly, Wheeler Oakman, John Sheehan, Charlie
Irwin, Grey Shadow (dog). 6 reels. 1939.

1140. *Queen of the Yukon*, Monogram. Assoc. Prod.: Paul Malvern.
Dir.: Phil Rosen. Screen play: Joseph West. Cameraman:
Harry Neumann. Editor: Russell Schoengarth. Cast:
Charles Bickford, Irene Rich, June Carlson, Dave O'Brien,
Melvin Lang, George Cleveland, Guy Usher, Tris Coffin.
Running time: 73 min. Released Aug. 26, 1940.

1141. *The sea wolf*, Warner Brothers. Prod.: Jack L. Warner
and Hal B. Wallis. Assoc. Prod.: Henry Blanks. Dir.:
Michael Curtiz. Screen play: Robert Rossen. Cameraman:
Sol Polito. Editor: George Amy. Cast: Edward G. Robin-
son, Ida Lupino, John Garfield, Alexander Knox, Gene
Lockhart, Barry Fitzgerald, Stanley Ridges, David Bruce,
Francis McDonald, Howard de Silva, Frank Lackteen. Run-
ning time: 100 min. Released March 22, 1941.

1142. *Sign of the wolf*, Monogram. Prod.: Paul Malvern. Dir.:
Howard Bretherton. Screen play: Elizabeth Hopkins,
Edmund Kelso. Mus. dir.: Edward Kay. Photography: Fred
Jackman, Jr. Editor: Jack Ogilvie. Cast: Michael Whalen,
Grace Bradley, Mantan Mareland, Darryl Hickman, Louise
Beavers, Wade Crosby, Tony Paton, Smoky, Shadow. Run-
ning time: 69 min. 7 reels. Released: March 25, 1941
[From "That spot"].

1143. *The adventures of Martin Eden*, Columbia. Prod.: B. P.
Schulberg. Dir.: Sydney Salkow. Screen play: W. L.
River. Editor: Al Clark. Art Dir.: Lionel Banks. Music
dir.: M. W. Stoloff. Cameraman: Franz F. Planer. Cast:
Glenn Ford, Claire Trevor, Evelyn Keyes, Stuart Erwin,
Dickie Moore, Ian MacDonald, Frank Conroy, Rafaele
Ottiano, Pierre Watkin, Regina Wallace, Robert J.
McDonald. Running time: 87 min. Released: Feb. 26, 1942.

1144. *Alaska*, Monogram. Prod.: Lindsley Parsons. Dir.: George
Archainbaud. Screen play: George Wallace Sayre, Harrison

Orkow, Malcolm Stuart Boyland. Art dir.: E. R. Hickson.
Music dir.: Edward Kay. Lyrics and music: Kay and
Cherkose. Dance dir.: Jack Boyle. Cameramen: Mack
Stengler, Archie Stout. Editor: Richard Currier. Cast:
Kent Taylor, Margaret Lindsay, John Carradine, Dean
Jagger, Nils Asther, Iris Adrian, George Cleveland,
Dewey Robinson, Lee "Lasses" White, John Rogers, Jack
Gorton, John Maxwell, Warren Jackson, Dick Scott. Run-
ning time: 76 min. Released: Dec. 22, 1944 [From "The
flush of gold"].

1145. *The fighter,* G-H Production. Released by United
Artists-Gottlieb. Prod.: Alex Gottlieb. Dir.: Herbert
Kline. Screen play: Aben Kandel and H. Kline. Cinema-
tographer: Janes Wong Howe. Editor: Edward Mann. Music
supervisor: Roaul Kraushar. Music composed and played
by Vicente Gómez. Cast: Richard Conte, Vanessa Brown,
Lee J. Cobb, Frank Silvers, Roberta Haynes, Hugh Sanders,
Claire Carleton, Martin Garralaga, Argentina Brunetti,
Rudolfo Hoyos, Jr., Margaret Padilla, Paul Fierro. Run-
ning time: 78 min. 1952 [From "The Mexican"].

1146. *Wolf Larsen,* Allied Artists. Prod.: Lindsley Parsons.
Dir.: Harman Jones. Screen play: Jack DeWitt, Turnley
Walker. Art Dir.: William Ross. Music: Paul Dunlap.
Cinematographer: Floyd Crosby. Editor: John Blunk.
Supervising film editor: Maurice Wright. Cast: Barry
Sullivan, Peter Graves, Gita Hall, Tahyer David, John
Alderson, Rico Alaniz, Robert Gist, Jack Grinnage, Jack
Orrison, Henry Rowland. Running time: 83 min. Released:
Oct. 26, 1958 [*The sea wolf*].

FILM ABOUT JACK LONDON

1147. *Jack London,* United Artists. Prod.: Samuel Bronston.
Dir.: Alfred Santell. Scenario: Ernest Pascal. Music:
Frederic Efrem Rich. Editor: William Ziegler. Art dir.:
Bernard Herzbrun. Cameraman: John W. Boyle. Cast:
Michael O'Shea, Susan Hayward, Osa Massen, Harry Daven-
port, Frank Craven, Virginia Mayo, Ralph Morgan, Louise
Beavers. Running time: 94 min. 1943 [From *The book of
Jack London* by Charmian London].

MOVIE SCENARIO

1148. *White fang.* Screen play by Hal Long and Sam Duncan. Fox
Film Corp. 1936. 134 leaves. Mimeographed. Copy in the
University of Southern California Library [Evidently
used to make 1936, 20th Century Fox version of *White
Fang*].

CZECH/SLOVAK FILM VERSIONS

The following film versions produced in Czechoslovakia are known to the compilers:

1149. *Krádež* reviewed in *Čs. rozhlas a televise*, 22:1 (1958).
1150. *Martin Eden* reviewed in *Květy*, 8:2 (April 1954) by M. Táborská.
1151. *Vik Larsen* [The sea wolf] reviewed in *Lidová kultura*, 49:5 (March 1947) by O. Kříž) and in *Národní osvobození*, June 12, 1947, p.4 by Fr. Kašpar.
1152. *Volání divočiny* [The call of the wild] reviewed in *Obránce vlasti*, 42:7 (April 1956) by F. Swidzinski.
1153. *Železná pata* [Iron heel] reviewed in *Čs. voják*, 13:31 (1954) by Rudolf Kalčík.

ESTONIAN

1154. *Valgekihv*, an Estonian version of White fang, reviewed in *Sirp ja Vasar*, Oct. 12, 1946.

RUSSIAN

In a letter to the senior compiler dated March 30, 1963 Vil Bykov of Moscow State University has provided the following data concerning Russian film versions of London's works:

1155. *Ne dlya deneg rodivshiysya* [based on Martin Eden]. Producer: Nicandr Turkin. Scenario: Vladimir Mayakovsky. Shooting: Levgeny Slavinsky. Star: Vladimir Mayakovsky. Co-star: Margarita Kibalchick. [This movie was shown during the years 1918-1922; it has been lost.]
1156. *Bely klyk* [White fang]. Producer: A. Zgwidi. Shooting: G. Troyansky and V. Asmus. Leading actors: Oleg Zhakov, Lev Sverdlin. 1946.
1157. *Meksicanets* [The Mexican]. Scenario: E. Braginsky. Producer: V. Kapulunovsky. Shooting: S. Poluyanov. Star: Oleg Strizhenov. Co-stars: Boris Andreyev, Mikhail Astrangov, Tartyana Samaylova. 1956.

Jay Leyda, Kino: *a history of the Russian and Soviet film*, London, George Allen, 1960, pp.426,431 presents the following data on two other Soviet movies based on London's works:

1158. *Po zakonu* [By the law, based on "The unexpected"]. Scenario: Victor Shklovsky and Lev Kuleshov. Director: Lev Kileshov. Shooting: Konstantin Kuznetsov. Cast: Alexandra Khokhlova, Sergei Komarov, Vladimir Fogel, Pyotr Galadzhev, Porfiri Podobed. 1926.
1159. *Zhelaznaya pyata* [The iron heel]. Scenario and director:

Vladimir Gardin. Shooting: Alexander Levitsky and
Grigori Giber. Cast: Leonid Leonidov, A. Skakhalov,
N. Znamensky, Olga Preobrazhenskaya. 1919.

Other comments concerning Soviet-made films based
on the works of London are found in Leyda, Kino,
pp.129,158-159,212-213 and 392.

PART TWO
WRITINGS ABOUT JACK LONDON

BOOKS AND PAMPHLETS ABOUT JACK LONDON IN ENGLISH

1160. Asimov, Isaac, *Two out-of-print masterpieces by Jack London:* Extra selection, [The Library of Science,] March, 1963. [This is an unpaged [2-4] review of *Star Rover* and *Before Adam,* which was issued for publicity purposes when these books were chosen as the Dual extra selection of The Library of Science for March, 1963. The review's headline states: "The passing of time supplies the acid test. In half a century, these two books have not lost their fire."]

1161. Bamford, Georgia Loring, *The mystery of Jack London: some of his friends, also a few letters - a reminiscence.* With illustrations and also from photographs. Published by Georgia Loring Bamford, 1428 Castro Street, Oakland, California, 1931, 255pp. Translation into Russian of one of these letters is as follows (from data supplied by Vil Bykov): "Pisma Dzheka Londona," [Letter by Jack London to Frederic Bamford] *Smena,* no. 23:(1956). [This volume contains slightly more than 50 letters, mostly to F. I. Bamford, written between 1902 and 1916.]

1162. Calder-Marshall, Arthur, *Lone wolf: the story of Jack London,* London, Methuen, 1961, 188pp. Also New York, Duell, Sloan and Pearce, c1962, 168pp. [Juvenile biography].

1163. Franchere, Ruth, *Jack London: the pursuit of a dream,* N. Y., Crowell, 1962, 264pp. [Juvenile biography].

1164. Gaer, Joseph, *Jack London. Bibliography and biographical data,* Monograph No. 1 of California Literary Research Project, [n.p.,] 1934, 45pp. (Abstract from the SERA Project 2-F2-132 [3-F2-197] (Mimeographed).

1165. Garst, Shannon, *Jack London, magnet for adventure,* N. Y., Julian Messner, Inc., 1944, 217pp. [Short bibliography of works by and about London, pp.207-212] [Juvenile biography].

1166. ____, *Jack London: la atracción de la aventura,* tr.: Pablo Atanasiu and Nappy d'Antoni, Buenos Aires, Peuser, 1947, 225pp.

1167. Greenwood, Mary S., *Lines to Jack London: a group of verses,* [n.p., n.d.,][3 poems].

1168. Heiney, E. B., *The call of the wild. A tribute in verse,* Huntington, Ind., May 22, 1905, 4pp. [Folder].

1169. Hendricks, King, *Creator and critic: a controversy between Jack London and Philo M. Buck, Jr.,* edited and with an introduction by ... Logan, Utah State University Press, 1961, 45pp. Monograph series, vol. 8, no. 2. [This volume reprints "The American barbarian" by Buck; publishes for the first time the Jack London-Philo Buck correspondence of 1912-1913.]

1170. ____, *Jack London: master craftsman of the short story*, Logan, Utah, The Faculty Association, Utah State University, April 1966, 31pp. (Thirty-Third Faculty Honor Lecture).

1171. J. S., *The call of the wild*, San Francisco, published for members of the Jack London Amateur Press Club, [n.d., no pagination] (London Lore number two).

1172. *Jack London* with comment by Charmian Kittredge London, published for its members by the Book Club of California. The letters of western authors series, Number 12, Dec. 1935. [Reproduces letter by Jack London to Cloudesley Johns from Papete, Tahiti, Feb. 17, 1908. Letter reprinted in Oakland *Tribune*, Jan. 5, 1936].

1173. *Jack London. A sketch of his life and work*. With portrait, N. Y., Macmillan, 1905, 15pp.

1174. Johnson, Martin E., *Through the South Seas with Jack London* with an introduction and postscript by Ralph D. Harrison, N. Y., Dodd, 1913, xi, 369pp.

1175. Lane, Frederick A., *The greatest adventure: a story of Jack London*, Illustrated by Sidney Quinn, N. Y., Aladdin Books, 1954, 192pp. (American heritage series) [Juvenile biography].

1176. Lane, Rose Wilder, *He was a man*, N. Y. and London, Harper, 1925, 380pp. [English title: Gordon Blake] [Fictionalized story based entirely on the life of Jack London]. Partially reprinted in *John O'London's Weekly*, "Jack London's life," 4,103:757 (March 26, 1921); "Jack London in prison," 4,104:798 (April 2, 1921); "Jack London's battle for fame," 5,105:4 (April 9, 1922); "Jack London wins through," 5,106:32 (April 16, 1921); "Jack London married," 5,107:69 (April 23, 1921).

1177. Leonhardy, Alma, et al., *Directed study guides for London's The call of the wild and other stories*, N. Y., Macmillan, 1929, 72pp. [The other stories are: To build a fire. The heathen. The strength of the strong].

1178. Lewis, Sinclair, *Sinclair Lewis on the valley of the moon*, Cambridge, Mass., Harvard Press, 1932, 5pp. [100 copies issued for private distribution by Harvey Taylor.]

1179. [Livingston, Leon Ray,] *From coast to coast with Jack London by A-No. 1 The famous tramp* (pseud.), Erie, Pa., c1917, 136pp. [Paper wrappers].

1180. London, Charmian, *The book of Jack London*, illustrated with photographs, New York, The Century Co., 1921, 2 vols.; published in Great Britain as *Jack London*, London, Mills & Boon, 1921, 2 vols. [These two volumes contain over 250 letters, telegrams and inscriptions

by Jack London to various correspondents, some complete
and some excerpted. The majority are first printings.
Among correspondents included are Ninetta Eames, Cloud-
esly Johns, Charmian Kittredge (later Charmian London),
Lilly Maid, George Sterling, Anna Strunsky, Henry M.
Bland, Lillian Collins, Joseph Conrad, Hugo Erickson,
Ralph Kasper, Hughes Massie and Blanche Partington.]
Translations of three of these letters into Russian are
as follows (from data supplied by Vil Bykov); "Otvet
Dzheka Londona chitatelnitse Lilian Kollinz ot 26
aprelya 1910 goda" [Letter by Jack London to Lillian
Collins, April 26, 1910, from *The book of Jack London*,
2:182-183], *Smena*, no. 10:24 (1960); "Pismo Dzheka
Londona k A. Strunskoi" [Letter by Jack London to Anna
Strunsky, 1901] *Smena*, no. 10:24 (1960); "Pisma Dzheka
Londona," [Letter by Jack London to Cloudesley Johns,
from vol. 1 of The book of Jack London] *Smena*, no. 23:
(1956). Selections from this volume appeared in *Century*
as follows: "The sailor on foot and rod," 101:545-555
(March 1921); "Briton blood and gipsy instinct," 102:
105-111 (May 1921); "Jack London as a boy," 102:287-
293 (June 1921); "Jack London: man and husband," 102:
443-452 (July 1921); "Jack London's last days," 102:
599-606 (Aug. 1921).

1181. ____, *Les aventures de Jack London*, adapté ... par
Alice Bossuet, Paris, Librairie Gallimard, 1927, 249pp.
(Les documents bleus, no. 39) (Partial French trans-
lation).

1182. ____, *Jack London, sein Leben und Werk* ... mit einem
Vorwort von Arthur Holitscher, Berlin, Universitas
[c1928] (Abridged German translation by Karl Hellwig).

1183. ____, *Jack London elete*, tr.: Zsolt Harsanyi, Budapest,
Athenaeum, [n.d.,] 385pp. (Hungarian).

1184. ____, *Džeka Londona dzive un darbs*, tr.: Valdemars
Karkliņš, Riga, Gramatu draugs [1935] 224pp. (Leverojamu
personu dzives romani, no. 27) (Latvian).

1185. ____, *"O moyem muzhe"* [about my husband] with an in-
troductory note by D. Gorbov, *30 Dnei*, no. 9:20-29
(1926) (Russian).

1186. *Doroga* (The road) tr.: S. G. Zaimovski, Moscow and
Leningrad, ZIF, 1927, vol. 1 of *Polnoye sobraniye
sochineni*. [Contains a biographical sketch of London
by Charmian London.]

1187. *Doroga* ... Moscow and Leningrad, ZIF, 1928, vol. 1,
books 1 and 2 of *Polnoye sobraniye sochineni* includes
Zhizn Dzheka Londona (Russian).

1188. ____, *The log of the Snark*, New York, Macmillan, 1915,
ix, 487pp. This volume has been serialized in *Mid-*

Pacific Magazine as follows: "The impossible traverse,"
9:517-523 (June 1915); "The last of the Marquesans,"
10:25-31 (July 1915); "The valley of Typee," 10:121-126
(Aug. 1915); "Through the dangerous archipelago," 10:
221-226 (Sept. 1915); "A visit to the Paris of the
Pacific," 10:355-359 (Oct. 1915); "Stevenson's Samoa,"
10:417-421 (Nov. 1915); "American Samoa," 10:527-534
(Dec. 1915); "Visiting a volcano," 11:127-134 (Feb.
1916); "South Sea cruising," 11:217-224 (March 1916);
"Kora Sea, Fiji Archipelago," 11:317-322 (April 1916);
"Jack London, skipper," 11:417-421 (May 1916); "Tana
and its volcano," 11:517-521 (June 1916); "We reach
the Solomons," 12:133-137 (Aug. 1916); "A Solomon
Island cruise," 12:233-237 (Sept. 1916); "Cruising in
cannibal waters," 12:333-337 (Oct. 1916); "Solomon
Island days," 12:433-437 (Nov. 1916); "Here and there
in the Solomons," 12:533-537 (Dec. 1916); "The first
white face," 13:33-37 (Feb. 1917); "Troubles galore in
the Solomons," 13:133-137 (Feb. 1917); "Taking tall
chances," 13:233-237 (March 1917); "We nearly meet our
fathers," 13:329-333 (April 1917); "Nearing the end of
the log," 13:466-471 (May 1917); "It's all over now,"
13:517-521 (June 1917).

1189. *Voyaging in wild seas; or, A woman among the head hunters (a narrative of the voyage of the Snark in the
years 1907-1908)* [1915?] 256pp. [This volume was reprinted in London by Mills and Boon in several different
versions.]

1190. *A woman among the head hunters* (a narrative of the voyage of the Snark in the years 1908-1909) [n.d.][1915]
255pp.

1191. ____, *Journal de bord du "Snark"*, tr.: Marcel Carret
and Louis Postif, preface by Alain Gerbault, Paris,
Hachette, 1938, 255pp. Avant-propos des traducteurs,
pp.7-10 [On cover: Les meilleurs romans étrangers]
(French).

1192. ____, *Vort Sydhaveseventyr*, tr.: Aslaugh Mikkelsen,
Copenhagen, Martins Forlag, 1917, 511pp. (Danish).

1193. ____, *Snarks Loggbok under Söderhafsfarden* 1907-1909,
tr.: Elin Palmgren, Stockholm, Bohlin, 1917, 387pp.
(Swedish).

1194. ____, *Our Hawaii*, New York, Macmillan, 1917, 345pp.
Printed in Great Britain as *Jack London and Hawaii*,
London, Mills and Boon [1918] 252pp.

1195. ____, *Jack London a Havai*, tr.: I. Schulz, Prague, Koči,
1925, 172pp. (Czech/Slovak).

1196. ____, *Bogen om Jack London*, Autoriseret Oversaettelse
for Norge og Danmark af H. B. J. Cramer, Kobenhavn,

Kristiana, 1922, 2 vols., 412pp. and 393pp.

1197. ____, *Jack London og Havaji*, tr.: Aslaug Mikkelsen, Copenhagen, Martins Forlag, 1920, 2 vols. (Danish).

1198. ____, *Det nya Hawaji*, tr.: Ernst Lundquist, Stockholm, Bohlin, 1923, 164pp. (Swedish).

1199. ____, *Our Hawaii (Islands and Islanders)*, new and revised edition, New York, Macmillan, 1922, xii, 427pp. Printed in Great Britain as *The new Hawaii*, London, Mills & Boon, 1923, 270pp. [This contains the first book printing of "My Hawaiian aloha," three articles by Jack London, pp.1-33.]

1200. London, Joan, *Jack London and his times: an unconventional biography*, N. Y., Doubleday, 1939, 387pp. [Excerpt from pp.313-315 of this volume published as Trotsky, Leon, "Trotsky and *The iron heel*: his observations on the famous novel," *The new international*, 11,3:95 (April 1945).]

1201. ____, *Jack London (primer escritor proletario de América)*, tr.: Miguel Diaz Gonzalez, Buenos Aires, S. Rueda, 1945, 364pp. (Colección El escritor y la sociedad 3).

1202. McDevitt, William, *Jack London as poet and as platform man. Did Jack London commit suicide?* San Francisco, Recorder-Sunset Press, 1947, 32pp. [Rust brown wrappers. Limited to 500 copies]. Contents: "Jack London as poet," pp.5-7 with letter to McDevitt from R. W. Francis concerning his discovery in 1932 of "The sea sprite and the shooting star," which is printed on pp.8-11. "Sonnet," p.11, first published in *Dilettante*, 7,69:8 (Feb. 1901). "Did London quote himself?", p.12, letter to McDevitt of July 31, 1946 from Allen Stanley Lane. "Jack London - soapboxer," pp.13-16. "Jack London on the platform," pp.16-23. "Did Jack London commit suicide?" pp.24-26. "Addendum to genealogy of Jack London," p.27. "Something special for collectors ..." reprints of J. H. Jackson's review of *Jack London's first*, pp.30-31.

1203. ____, *Jack London's first*, San Francisco, Recorder-Sunset Press, 1946, 32pp. [Limited to 500 copies]. Contents: "Jack London's first," pp.3-5. "His travel is cheap," pp.6-11 (reprinted from San Francisco *Chronicle*, Dec. 16, 1894). "Jack London's first story," pp.11-12. "Two gold bricks," pp.12-17. "Jack London - a foreword (written for a forthcoming bibliography)," pp.18-20. "Scripter unearths rare volume: autobiography of Professor Cheney, Jack London's father, found by Wm. McDevitt, LL. M.," pp.20-24. "George Sterling's tribute to Jack London" (poem), p.25; "Was Jack London a journalist?

(what Mrs. Jack says)," pp.26-27; this part of the pamphlet contains a letter to Tuck by London dated Aug. 1906 published in the Oakland *World*. "Addenda. Bibliografic notes. Jack London market values," pp.28-31.

1204. McGimsey, Grover C., *A son of the gods*, Ukiah, Calif., Northern Crown Publishing Co., 1918 [x], [1] 2-25, text, [26], [Paper wrappers]. [This volume was reviewed in the San Francisco *Chronicle*, March 17, 1918, p.22, c.3. The review called it an extended elegy inspired by the life of Jack London. A copy of this obscure pamphlet is in the George H. Tweney collection.]

1205. Morrell, Ed., *Twenty-fifth man: the strange story of Ed Morrell, the hero of Jack London's Star Rover*, Montclair, N. J., New Era Publishing Co., 1924, 390pp.

1206. Mosby, C. V., *A little journey to the home of Jack London*, privately printed and copyrighted by the author, St. Louis, The Front Rank Press, 1917, 18pp. [Paper wrappers].

1207. Norton, Margaret, *Dear Comrades*, Sonoma, The Sonoma Co., 1966, 100pp. [Dramatization of Jack London's life].

1208. O'Connor, Richard, *Jack London: a biography*, Boston, Little, Brown, 1964, x, 430pp.

1209. Payne, Edward Biron, *The soul of Jack London*, edited by Felicia R. Scatcherd; foreword by David Gow; prefatory foreword by Sir Arthur Conan Doyle, London, Rider, 1926, 142pp.

1210. ____, *The soul of Jack London: second edition*, preface by Ninetta Eames Payne, Kingsport, Tenn., Southern Publishers, 1933, 136pp.

1211. Roden, Donald, *London's The Call of the wild also: White Fang*, New York, Monarch Press, c1965, 74pp.

1212. Sanford, Marvin, *California friends say goodbye*, San Francisco, published for members of the Jack London Amateur Press Club, [n.d., no pagination] (London Lore number one).

1213. Stone, Irving, *Sailor on horseback: the biography of Jack London*, Cambridge, Houghton Mifflin, The Riverside Press, 1938, 338pp. [First edition has "1938" printed at bottom of title page; this date is omitted in later editions. It was also published in a special gift edition; inside front cover inserted in a pocket is a facsimile of an autobiographical letter written to Houghton Mifflin by Jack London in connection with the publication of his first book, *The son of the wolf*, 4pp., folio.] This volume was published serially as "Sailor on horseback," *Saturday Evening Post*, 210:5-7, 30, 32-33, 36, 38 (June 25, 1938), 211:16-17, 47, 49-52 (July 2, 1938), 211:16-17, 53-54, 56 (July 9, 1938),

211:20-21, 51-54, 57 (July 16, 1938) 211:16-17, 30-33
(July 30, 1938), 211:14-15, 63-66 (Aug. 6, 1938), 211:
20-21, 61-66 (Aug. 13, 1938), 211:16-17, 48-50, 53-54
(Aug. 27, 1938), 211:16-17, 39-40, 42-45, 48-50 (Sept.
3, 1938). Letters on this volume appeared in the Oakland *Tribune*, Sept. 1, 1938 (Mrs. L. Carter) and Sept.
12, 1938 (D. J. Happ).

1214.   ____, Louisville, Ky., American Printing House for the
Blind, 1939, Braille 2, 3 vols.

1215.   ____, *Sailor on horseback: the biography of Jack London*,
London, Collins, 1938, 327pp.; London, Lane, 1948,
287pp. Reprinted as *Jack London, sailor on horseback:
a biographical novel*, Garden City, N. Y., Doubleday,
1947, 337pp. Condensed in *Reader's Digest*, 50:121-152
(Feb. 1947).

1216.   ____, *Jack London, sailor on horseback: a biographical
novel*, N. Y. Pocket Books, 1960, 314pp. (Giant Cardinal
Edition GC-64).

1217.   ____, *Morjak v sedle*, Erevan, Ajpetrat, 1963, 566pp.
(Armenian).

1218.   ____, *Morjakat na kon (Zivotat na Dzek London)*, tr.:
M. Vasilev, Sofia, NS, OF, 1957, 319pp. (Bulgarian)

1219.   ____, *Námořník na koni*, tr.: St. V. Klíma, Prague,
Toužimský a Moravec, 1941, 301pp.; 2nd ed., 1947, 303pp.

1220.   ____, *Námořník na koni*, tr.: P. Branko, Bratislava,
Pravda, 1948, 484pp.

1221.   ____, *Námořník na koni*, Jarmila Fastrová, Prague, Mladá
fronta, 1963, 320pp. (Czech/Slovak).

1222.   ____, *Somand til Hest. En Jack London-Biografi*, tr.:
Kai Flor, Copenhagen, Martins Forlag, 1939, 399pp.
(Danish).

1223.   ____, *Jack London. Zijn leven en werk*, tr.: A. M. de
Jong, 's Gravenhage, H. P. Leopold, 1939. (Dutch)

1224.   ____, *Merimies hevosen seläsä. Jack Londonin elamakerta*,
tr.: Niilo Wadenström, Riihimäki, Kansankulttuuri, 1946,
340pp. (Finnish)

1225.   ____, *Zur See und im Sattel. Das Leben Jack London*, tr.:
Hans Steinsdorff, Berlin, Universitas, 1948, 332pp.;
Hamburg, Rowohlt, 1955, 257pp.; also published as
Rororo Taschenbuch Ausgabe No. 160. (German)

1226.   ____, *Ha-sapan al Gabey Ha-sus*, tr.: Refael Eliezer,
Merhavya, Sifriyat poslim, 1950, 433pp.

1227.   ____, *Tzak London: Naphtes kavalla st'alogo*, Athens,
Synchrome Gnome, 1962, 464pp. (Greek)

1228.   ____, *Jack London. Zeglarz na koniu*, tr.: Kazimierz
Piotrowski, Warsaw, Panstwowy Instytut Wydawniczy, 1961,
431pp. (Polish)

1229.   ____, *A vida errante de Jack London (marinheiro a cavalo)*, tr.: Genolino Amado and Geraldo Cavalcanti, Rio de Janeiro, J. Olympio, 1941, 350pp. (O romance da vida, 15); 2nd ed., 1946, 327pp. (O romance da vida, 15); 3rd ed., 1952, 309pp. (Portuguese)

1230. ____, *Moryak v sedlye; biografiya Dzheka Londona*, tr.: M. Kan, Moscow, Izdatelstvo TSK VLKSM "Molodaya Gvardiya", 1962, 400pp. [398-400 are advertisements].
(Russian)

1231. ____, *La gran aventura de Jack London*, tr.: Leon Mirlas, Buenos Aires, Editorial Claridad, 1944, 410pp. (Biblioteca de grandes biografías, serie B, vol. 2). (Spanish)

1232. ____, *Sjöman till häst*, tr.: Olof Lagercrantz, Stockholm, Folket i bild, 1958, 339pp. (Swedish)

1233. Tickenor, H. M., *Life of Jack London*, Girard, Kansas, Haldeman-Julius Co., 1923, pp.5-52 (Ten cent pocket series no. 83).

1234. Walcutt, C. C., *Jack London*, Minneapolis, University of Minnesota Press, 1966, 48pp. (University of Minnesota pamphlets on American writers ... no. 57).

PARTS OF BOOKS ABOUT JACK LONDON IN ENGLISH

1235. Adair, Ward, *Vital messages in modern books*, New York, Association Press, 1926, pp.12-22,86-93.
1236. Alexandrova, Vera, *A history of Soviet literature*, translated by Mirra Ginsburg, Garden City, N. Y., Doubleday, 1963, pp.95-96.
1237. Anderson, Carl L., "Swedish criticism before 1920: the reception of Jack London and Upton Sinclair," in *The Swedish acceptance of American literature*, Philadelphia, University of Pennsylvania Press, 1957, pp.33-44.
1238. Ashmun, Margaret, *Modern short-stories*, New York, Macmillan, 1914, pp.333-336.
1239. Atherton, Gertrude, *My San Francisco, a wayward biography*, Indianapolis and New York, Bobbs-Merrill, 1946, pp.96-98,190,284,299.
1240. Austin, Mary, *Earth horizons*, Boston and New York, Houghton Mifflin, 1932, pp.299-304.
1241. Beneditti, Steve, "I knew Jack London," in *An historical background of the city of Benicia*, written and compiled by Capt. Frank B. Fisher, Jr., Fr. Albert Juller and Florence Audraieff [n.p., no publisher,] [1946] p.15.
1242. Blakenship, Russell, *American literature as an expression of the national mind*, New York, Holt, 1931, pp. 566-568.
1243. Blanck, Jacob, *Merle Johnson's American First Editions*, Revised and Enlarged By, New York, R. R. Bowker Co., 1929. Bibliographical check list of Jack London, pp. 318-322. Second Edition, Revised and Enlarged, 1932; Third and Fourth Editions, Revised and Enlarged by Jacob Blanck, 1936 and 1942. Also appeared in a thin paper pocket-sized edition, 1949.
1244. Blodgett, Harold W., "London, Jack," *Collier's Encyclopedia*, New York, Collier & Son, c1957, 12:493-494.
1245. Blotner, Joseph L., *The political novel*, New York, Random House, 1955, Garden City, N. Y., Doubleday, 1955, p.12.
1246. Boas, Ralph Philip and Katherine Burton, *Social backgrounds of American literature*, New York, Little, 1933, pp.195-199.
1247. Bode, Carl, "Rebellion: an American literary tradition," in *Writer's Yearbook*, No. 33 (1962), pp.48-49 mention London.
1248. Boynton, Percy H., *Literature and American life*, New York, Ginn, 1936, pp.653,718,746,754-755,759,892.
1249. Braybrooke, Patrick, "Jack London and the unexpected," in *Peeps at the mighty*, Philadelphia, Lippincott, 1927, pp.113-129.

1250. Bronson, Walter C., *A short history of American liter-ature*, New York, Heath, 1919, pp.310-311.
1251. Brooks, Van Wyck, *Sketches in criticism*, New York, Dutton, 1932, pp.248-252.
1252. ____, "Frank Norris and Jack London," in *Confident years, 1885-1915*, New York, Dutton, 1952, pp.217-237.
1253. Brown, Deming, "Jack London and O. Henry," in *Soviet attitudes toward American writing*, Princeton, Princeton University Press, 1962, pp.219-238.
1254. Brown, Madis, *California's Valley of the Moon. Historic Places and People in the Valley of Sonoma*, Sonoma, Published by the author, 1961, pp.20-21
1255. Burke, William J. and Will D. Howe, *American authors and books, 1640-1940*, New York, Gramercy Publishing Co., 1943, p.436.
1256. Caen, Herb, *Herb Caen's new guide to San Francisco*, Garden City, New York, Doubleday, 1957, pp.197-198.
1257. "The Call of the wild," in *Masterpieces of world liter-ature in digest form*. First series edited by Frank N. Magill, New York, Harpers, c1952, pp.103-105.
1258. Calverton, Victor F., *The liberation of American liter-ature*, New York, Scribner, 1932, pp.419-424,427.
1259. Cantwell, Robert, *Famous American men of letters*, New York, Dodd, 1956, pp.161-170.
1260. Cargill, Oscar, ed., *The social revolt: American liter-ature from 1888 to 1914*, New York, Macmillan, 1933, pp.623-625.
1261. Carnes, Cecil, *Jimmy Hare, news photographer, half a century with a camera*, New York, Macmillan, 1940, pp. 153-155,169,227,230.
1262. Chamberlain, John, *Farewell to reform*, New York, Liver-ight, 1932, pp.186-191.
1263. Chapman, Arnold, *The Spanish American reception of United States fiction 1920-1940*, Berkeley and Los Angeles, University of California Press, 1966, pp.42-56, 205-208 (University of California Publications in Modern Philology vol. 77).
1264. Chislett, William, *Moderns and near moderns*, New York, Grafton Press, 1928, pp.109-111.
1265. Chubb, Edwin W., "Jack London, yarn spinner, in *Stories of authors, British and American*, New York, Macmillan, 1926, pp.374-379.
1266. Commanger, Henry S., *The American mind*, New Haven, Yale University Press, 1950, pp.110-111.
1267. Conrad, Joseph, *Life and letters*, edited by G. Jean Aubry, Garden City, Doubleday Doran, 1927, 2:295.
1268. Cottrell, G. W. and H. N. Fairchild, *Critical guide*, New York, Columbia University Press, 1930, pp.376-377.

1269. Cox, Francis A., *What do you know about a horse?* with
      foreword..., London, Bell and Sons Ltd., 1915. [Preface
      is unsigned. Credited to London by British Museum Cat-
      alog.283533.]
1270. de Casseres, Benjamin, *The superman in America*, Seattle,
      University of Washington Chapbooks, 1929, p.26.
1271. Dickinson, T. H., *The making of American literature*,
      New York, Century, 1932, pp.647-648.
1272. Dickson, Samuel, *Streets of San Francisco*, Palo Alto,
      Stanford University Press, 1955, pp.133-148.
1273. Drinkwater, John ed., *The outline of literature*, New
      York, Putnam, 1923, p.971.
1274. Durham, Philip and Tauno F. Mustanoja, *American fiction
      in Finland*, Helsinki, Société néophilologique de
      Helsinki, 1960, pp.37-41 and other scattered references.
1275. Ellsworth, William W., "Jack London," in *Golden age of
      authors*, London, G. Richards, 1919, pp.97-104; Boston,
      Houghton-Mifflin, 1919, pp.97-102, 109.
1276. Feied, Frederick, *No pie in the sky: the hobo as Amer-
      ican cultural hero in the works of Jack London, John
      Dos Passos and Jack Kerouac*, New York, Citadel, 1964,
      pp.15,18,23-40,41,43,44,45,56,57-58,75,81-85,87,88,89,
      91.
1277. Filler, Louis, *Crusaders for American liberalism*, New
      York, Harcourt, 1939, Yellow Springs, Ohio, Antioch
      Press [c1950] pp.80,124,133,162,164,291,339,374,393.
1278. Freeman, Joseph, *An American testament*, New York,
      Farrar and Rinehart, 1936, pp.113,312-313,375,585,601,
      634,639,665.
1279. French, Warren, *Frank Norris*, New York, Twayne, 1962,
      pp.31,131-132.
1280. Garnett, Edward, *Friday nights*, New York, Knopf, 1922,
      pp.256-260.
1281. Geismar, Maxwell D., "Jack London: the short cut," in
      Rebels and ancestors: the American novel, 1890-1915,
      Boston, Houghton Mifflin, 1953, pp.139-216; N. Y., Hill
      and Wang, 1963.
1282. Ginger, Ray, *Eugene V. Debs: a biography*, New York,
      Collier Books, 1962, pp.198,285,358,447; originally
      published as *The bending cross, a biography of Eugene
      Victor Debs*, Rutgers, N. J., Rutgers University Press,
      1949.
1283. Gerstenberger, Donna and George Hendrick, *The American
      novel 1789-1959, a checklist of twentieth-century crit-
      icism*, Denver, Alan Swallow, 1961, pp.174-176.
1284. Graham, Bessie, *The bookman's manual*, New York, Bowker,
      1921, pp.361-363.
1285. Graham, Stephen, "Jack London," in *The death of yester-*

day, London, E. Benn, 1930, pp.53-61.

1286. Hall, L., "Jack London," *Columbia University course*, New York, Columbia University Press, 1932, p.18.

1287. Haney, John L., *The story of our literature*, New York, Scribner, 1923, p.258.

1288. Harkins, Edward F., "Jack London," in *Little pilgrimages among the men who have written famous books*, Boston, Page, 1902, pp.235-251.

1289. Hart, James D., *The Oxford companion to American literature*, London and New York, Oxford University Press, 1948, pp.429-430.

1290. Hart, Jerome A., *In our second century*, San Francisco, Pioneer Press, 1931, pp.164,168.

1291. Hartwick, Harry, *The foreground of American fiction*, New York, Century, 1934, pp.67-84.

1292. Hatcher, Harlan, *Creating the modern American novel*, New York, Farrar and Rinehart, 1935, pp.17,26-27,46.

1293. Hazard, Lucy L., *The frontier in American literature*, New York, Crowell, 1927, p.269.

1294. Herzberg, Max J., *The readers' encyclopedia of American literature*, New York, Thomas Y. Crowell, 1962, pp.649-650.

1295. Hicks, Granville, *The great tradition*, New York, Macmillan, 1933, pp.188-196.

1296. Higham, John, *Strangers in the land. Patterns of American nativism 1860-1925*, New York, Atheneum, 1963, (Atheneum 32), pp.172-175.

1297. Hinkel, Edgar Joseph, editor and William E. McCann, assistant editor, *Bibliography of California fiction, poetry, drama*. In three volumes. Sponsored by the Alameda County Library, Oakland, California. Produced on a Works Progress Administration Project, Administrative project 165-03-7308, Area serial 0803-1008, Work Project 6463. Oakland, 1938. 1:209-212; 3:70.

1298. ____, editor and William E. McCann, assistant editor, *Biographies of California authors and indexes of California literature*. In two volumes. Published by The Alameda County Library, Oakland, California, as a report of official project no. 65-1-08-2356, conducted under the auspices of the Works Projects Administration, Oakland, 1942. 1:129-131.

1299. ____, editor and William E. McCann, assistant editor, *Criticism of California literature, fiction - poetry - drama:* a digest and bibliography. In three volumes. Published by The Alameda County Library, Oakland, California, as a report of official project no. 665-08-3-85 conducted under the auspices of the Works Projects Administration, Oakland, 1940, 2:502-547. [Each of the

above is mimeographed; out attention has been called
to these volumes by Allan R. Ottley of the California
State Library.]
1300. Holliday, Robert Cortes, "A pal of Jack London," in *Men
and books and cities*, New York, Doran, 1920, pp.232-244.
1301. Irvine, Alexander, *From the bottom up - the life story
of Alexander Irvine*, New York, Doubleday Page & Co.,
1910. [Numerous Jack London references; Irvine was the
Socialist who invited London to speak at Yale University.]
1302. "Jack London," in Eugene T. Maleska and Albert Bura-
nelli, *50 American authors. The educational crossword
puzzle series: volume 1*, New York, Pocket Books, c1963,
pp.101-104. [Crossword puzzle by Kathryn Righter. Also
contains biography and Jack London quiz.]
1303. "Jack London," *National cyclopaedia of American biography*, New York, James T. White, 1906, 13:133-134.
1304. "Jack London," in Dorothy Nyren, ed., *A library of
literary criticism: modern American literature*, New
York, Ungar, 1960, pp.293-296.
1305. "Jack London," in Frank Northern Magill, ed., *Cyclo-
pedia of world authors*, New York, Harper, 1958, pp.
633-635.
1306. "Jack London," *Who was who*, 1916-1928, London, Black,
1929, p.641.
1307. "Jack London," *Who was who in America*, New York,
Marquis, 1942, 1:742.
1308. "Jack London holograph manuscript," *A modern miscellany.
First editions, autograph letters, manuscript material.
Catalogue number four*, Fort Lauderdale, Florida, Roman
Books, Inc. [n.d., probably late 1963] pp.55-56 [Adver-
tisement with brief quotations of a 31-page autograph
manuscript-letter, which is a "review-analysis of the
book *Eternalism* by Orlando Smith, published in 1902"].
1309. Jaher, Frederic Cople, "Jack London: "The stone in the
builders rejected," in *Doubters and dissenters: cata-
clysmic thought in America, 1885-1918*, New York, The
Free Press of Glencoe, 1964, pp.188-216.
1310. James, George Wharton, *Syllabus of a course of lectures
on California literature and its spirit*, Los Angeles,
Arroyo Guild Press, [1909?] pp.33-36; revised edition
of 1916.
1311. Jones, Evan, ed., *Father*, New York, Rinehart, 1960,
pp.73-74.
1312. Kazin, Alfred, "Progressivism: the superman and the
muckrake," in *On native grounds*, New York, Reynal &
Hitchcock, 1942, pp.111-116.
1313. Knight, Grant C., *American literature and culture*, New

York, Long and Smith, 1932, pp.121,378,426,436-439, 446,482.

1314. ___, *The strenuous age in American literature, 1900-1910*, Chapel Hill, University of North Carolina Press, 1954, pp.81-85.

1315. Krupskaya, Nadezhda Konstantinovna, *Memories of Lenin*, tr.: E. Verney, New York, International Publishers, 1930, p.208.

1316. Kunitz, Stanley J., ed., *Authors today and yesterday*, New York, Wilson, 1933, pp.415-418.

1317. Kunitz, Stanley J. and Howard Haycraft, eds., *Twentieth century authors*, New York, Wilson, 1942, pp.843-845.

1318. Leisy, Ernest E., *American literature: an interpretative survey*, New York, Crowell, 1929, pp.208-209.

1319. Lewisohn, Ludwig, *Expression in America*, New York and London, Oxford University Press, 1932, pp.324-325.

1320. Lieberman, Elias, "A glimpse at the frozen north, Alaska -- Jack London, in *The American short story*, Pinewood or Ridgewood, N. J., The editor, 1912, pp. 150-157.

1321. Loggins, Vernon, *I hear America*, New York, Crowell, 1937, pp.253-263.

1322. ___, *Visual outline of American literature*, New York, Longmans, 1933, p.97.

1323. Lynn, Kenneth S., "Jack London: the brain merchant," in *Dream of success: a study of the modern American imagination*, Boston, Little, Brown, 1955, pp.75-118.

1324. Manly, John M. and Edith Rickert, *Contemporary American literature*, New York, Harcourt, 1922, 1929, pp.223-224.

1325. Marble, Annie R., *A study of the modern novel, British and America, since 1890*, New York, Appleton, 1928, pp.246-251.

1326. Markham, Edwin, ed., *Songs and stories*, San Francisco, Powell, 1931, p.16.

1327. ___, *California the wonderful*, New York, Markham, 1923, pp.363-364.

1328. McCabe, Joseph, *A biographical dictionary of modern rationalists*, London, Watts, 1920, pp.455-456.

1329. McCole, C. J., *Lucifer at large*, New York, Longmans, 1937, pp.21-26.

1330. Mencken, Henry L., "Jack London," in *Prejudices* (first series), New York, Knopf, 1919, pp.236-239.

1331. Montgomery, Elizabeth R., *Story behind great books*, New York, McBride, 1946, pp.143-147.

1332. Morris, Lloyd R., "Scepticism of the young," in *Postscript to yesterday*, New York, Random House, 1947, pp. 115-121.

1333. Mott, Frank L., "Great open spaces," in *Golden multi-*

tudes, New York, Macmillan, 1950, pp.233-240.

1334. Mumford, Lewis, *The golden day: a study in American experience and culture*, New York, Boni & Liveright, 1926, pp.125-127.

1335. Noel, Joseph, *Footloose in Arcadia: a personal record of Jack London, George Sterling, Ambrose Bierce*, New York, Carrick & Evans, 1940, pp.15-105,232-241,275-281.

1336. O'Brien, Edward J., *The advance of the American short story*, New York, Dodd, 1923, pp.187-188.

1337. O'Connor, Richard, "Literary Pay dirt," in *High jinks on the Klondike*, New York, Bobbs-Merrill, 1954, pp. 116-139.

1338. Orians, George H., *A short history of American literature*, New York, Crofts, 1940, pp.265,275.

1339. Palmer, Frederick, *With my own eyes*, Indianapolis, Bobbs-Merrill Co., 1933, pp.96,237-239,241-242,293.

1340. Parrington, Vernon L., *Main currents in American thought*, New York, 1930, Harcourt, 3:xiv,198,325,352.

1341. Pattee, Fred L., "The prophet of the last frontier," in *Sidelights on American literature*, New York, Century, 1922, pp.98-160.

1342. ____, *The new American literature*, 1890-1930, New York, Century, 1922, pp.121-143.

1343. ____, *The development of the American short story*, New York, Century, 1923, pp.316,343-344,347-353,356,373.

1344. Perry, Bliss, *The American spirit in literature*, New Haven, Yale University Press, 1921, pp.243-244.

1345. Phelps, William L., *Essays on modern novelists*, New York, Macmillan, 1910, pp.282-284.

1346. Preston, Wheeler, "Jack London," in *American biographies*, New York and London, Harper, 1940, p.628.

1347. Quinn, Arthur Hobson, *American fiction: an historical and critical survey*, New York, D. Appleton-Century Book Co., 1936, pp.541-545,720.

1348. Rankin, Thomas E., *American authorship of the present day*, Ann Arbor, Wahr, 1918, p.23.

1349. Rideout, Walter Bates, "Realism and revolution," in *Radical novel in the United States, 1900-1954*, Cambridge, Harvard University Press, 1956, pp.19-46.

1350. Rives, Hall E. and G. E. Forbush, *John Book*, New York, Beechhurst Press, 1947, pp.291-292.

1351. Roosevelt, Theodore, *Letters*, selected and edited by Elting E. Morison, Cambridge, Harvard University Press, 1952. [See especially vols. 5-6:41,617,1081,1221-1223, 1343.]

1352. Russell, Frank A., "Jack London," in *American pilgrimage*, Toronto, McClelland, 1943, pp.234-252.

1353. St. John, Adela Rogers, *Final verdict*, New York, Double-

day, 1962, pp.81,171,210,272,273,352-364.
1354. Scherman, David E. and Rosemarie Redlick, *America: the land and its writers,* New York, Dodd, 1956, pp.64-65.
1355. ____, *Literary America,* New York, Dodd, 1952, pp.104-105.
1356. Schorer, Mark, *Sinclair Lewis: an American life,* New York, McGraw-Hill, 1961, pp.96,101,104,146-147,157-158, 164-166,169,171-172,175,178,185-187,219,274,356,494, 553 [Letter from London, pp.186-187]; ibid., New York, Crest, 1963.
1357. Shannon, David A., *The Socialist party of America,* New York, The Macmillan Co., 1955, pp.6,34,38,55-57.
1358. Sinclair, Upton, "The press and Jack London," in *The brass check, a study of American journalism,* Pasadena, California, The author [1920] pp.341-345.
1359. ____, *Mammonart,* Pasadena, California, Sinclair, 1925, pp.363-372.
1360. ____, *My lifetime in letters,* Columbia, Missouri, University of Missouri Press, 1960 [London letters found on pp.20-30 dated 1905-1916].
1361. Spiller, Robert E., et al., *Literary history of the United States,* New York, Macmillan, 1948, Vol. 2, pp.1033-1037; Vol. 3, pp.619-622.
1362. Starrett, Vincent, "The Call of the Wild," in *Best loved books of the twentieth century,* New York, Bantam Books, 1965, pp.91-101.
1363. Stone, Irving, "All at sea," in *The Irving Stone reader,* Garden City, N. Y., Doubleday, 1963, pp.96-153 [Selection from *Jack London: sailor on horseback;* p.95 is a brief biography of Jack London].
1364. "Jack London battles against odds," in J. Kenner Agnew and Agnes L. McCarthy, *Prose and poetry for appreciation,* Syracuse and Chicago, L. W. Singer, c1963, pp. 283-301 [Selection from *Sailor on horseback*].
1365. Stovall, Floyd, *American idealism,* Norman, University of Oklahoma Press, 1943, pp.129-134.
1366. Symes, Lillian and Travers Clement, *Rebel America,* New York, Harper, 1934, pp.202,220,233.
1367. Taylor, Walter F., *A history of American letters,* New York, American Book Co., 1936, pp.315-318.
1368. Thorp, Willard, *American writing in the twentieth century,* Cambridge, Harvard University Press, 1960, pp.10, 116,151,161-164.
1369. Trent, William P., et al., *Cambridge history of American literature,* New York, Putnam, 1921, p.336.
1370. Van Doren, Carl, *The American novel,* New York, Macmillan, 1921, pp.225-244.
1371. Van Doren, Carl and Mark Van Doren, *American and*

British literature since 1890, New York, Century, 1925, pp.50-52.

1372. Wagenknecht, Edward C., "Jack London and the cult of primitive sensation," in *Cavalcade of the American novel*, New York, Henry Holt, 1952, pp.222-229.

1373. Walcutt, Charles Child, "Jack London: blond brats and supermen," *American literary naturalism, a divided stream*, Minneapolis, University of Minnesota Press, 1956, pp.87-113.

1374. Walker, Franklin, "Jack London, Martin Eden," in Wallace Stegner, ed., *The American novel from James Fenimore Cooper to William Faulkner*, New York, Basic Books, 1965, pp.133-143.

1375. Warfel, Harry R., et al., eds., *The American mind*, New York, American Book Co., 1947, pp.1005-1007.

1376. West, Ray B., *The short story in America*, Chicago, Regnery, 1952, pp.31-32.

1377. Whicher, George F., ed. "Respectability defied," *The literature of the American people: an historical and critical survey*, New York, Appleton-Century-Crofts, 1951, pp.846-847.

1378. Whipple, Thomas K., "Jack London," *Dictionary of American biography*, New York, Scribner, 1928, 11:372.

1379. ____, "Jack London, wonder boy," in *Study out the land*, Berkeley, University of California Press, 1943, pp.93-104.

1380. Wickersham, James, *A bibliography of Alaskan literature*, Miscellaneous publications of the Alaska agricultural college and school of mines, 1927, Vol. 1, Fairbanks, (College P. O.) Alaska, bibliography of Jack London, pp.231-234.

1381. Williams, Blanche C., "Jack London," in *Our short story writers*, New York, Moffat, 1920, pp.256-277.

1382. Williams, Harold, *Modern English writers*, London, Sidgewick & Jackson, 1918, pp.477-478.

1383. Williamson, Thames, *Far north country*, New York, Duell, Sloan and Pearce, 1944, pp.73-74.

1384. Witham, W. T., *Panorama of American literature*, New York, Stephen Daye Press, 1947, pp.223-226.

1385. Woodward, Robert H., *The history of a sea sprite*, London Lore No. 3, 1960, [4pp.] [The back page is by Edward McNamee and is entitled "Jack London and Chuang Tzu."]

ARTICLES ABOUT JACK LONDON IN ENGLISH

1386. "Advertising for Jack London," New York *Times*, Feb. 10, 1906, p.8.

1387. "After Klondike gold with Jack London," *Literary Digest*, 71:37-41 (Nov. 5, 1921).

1388. Alexander, S., "Jack London's literary lycanthropy," *Reporter*, 16:46-48 (Jan. 24, 1957).

1389. "Alleged spirit messages from Jack London," San Francisco *Chronicle*, Aug. 15, 1926, p.37.

1390. Allen, Louis, "In the wake of Jack London," Oakland *Tribune* magazine section, Jan. 4, 1925, p.3.

1391. ____, "Prince of the oyster pirates," Oakland *Tribune* magazine section, Jan. 11, 1925, p.14.

1392. ____, "When Greek met Greek," Oakland *Tribune* magazine section, Jan. 18, 1925, p.15.

1393. Alexander, Julius Myron, "In memoriam - Jack London," Santa Rosa *Press Democrat*, Nov. 24, 1916, p.1.

1394. Ames, Russell, "Jack London: American rebel," *Our Time*, 7:254-255 (July 1948).

1395. "The anarchist's mistake," Los Angeles *Times*, April 24, 1907, ii:4 [Editorial critical of London].

1396. "Apostle of the primitive," *Current Literature*, 39:673-674 (Dec. 1905).

1397. Arnold, H. H., "My life in the Valley of the Moon," *National Geographic*, 94:689-716 (1948).

1398. "Attempt to place Jack London," *Current Literature*, 42:513-514 (1907)

1399. Austin, Mary, "George Sterling at Carmel," *American Mercury*, 11:68-70 (May 1927).

1400. "Author and his wife go in different ways. 'Jack' London and his better half agree to separate and she retains possession of children," San Francisco *Call*, Aug. 9, 1903, p.33.

1401. "The author of *White Fang*," *Outing*, 48:361 (1906).

1402. "Author 'roasts' judge. 'I'll get you.'--London," San Francisco *Call*, Aug. 2, 1910, p.7.

1403. Baggs, Mae Lacy, "Jack London, a personality of whom the world knew little," Philadelphia *Public Ledger* magazine section, Dec. 3, 1916, p.5.

1404. ____, "The real Jack London as revealed in Hawaii," *Current Opinion*, 62:23 (Jan. 1917).

1405. ____, "The real Jack London in Hawaii," *Overland Monthly*, n.s. 69:405-410 (May, 1917).

1406. "Ban on Jack London's books. Connecticut Library Association withdraws writings of socialist from circulation," *Socialist Voice*, Feb. 17, 1906, p.1.

1407. "Barbarian in Jack London," *Literary Digest*, 45:564

(Oct. 5, 1912).

1408. "Barkeep tells how he gave Jack London his literary start," San Francisco *Bulletin,* April 30, 1921, p.12.

1409. Barry, J. D., "Personal qualities of Jack London," *Overland Monthly,* n.s. 69:431-432 (May, 1917).

1410. Baskett, Sam S., "Jack London's Heart of darkness," *American Quarterly,* 10:66-77 (Spring, 1958).

1411. ____, "Jack London on the Oakland waterfront," *American Literature,* 27:363-371 (Nov. 1955).

1412. ____, "A source for *The iron heel,*" *American Literature,* 27:268-270 (May 1955).

1413. Becker, M. L., "Read this one first," *Scholastic,* 31: 20E (Dec. 11, 1937).

1414. Belton, George R., "The Call of the wild, a plagiarism?" *Reedy's Mirror,* 26:182-183 (March 16, 1917) [Letter dated March 6, 1917. Comment on John L. Hervey's note on London in *Reedy's Mirror*].

1415. Betten, H., "The early haunts of Jack London," *National Motorist,* 8:5-6 (June 1932).

1416. Betten, Henry L., "Writer recalls London as West End school boy," *Times-Star,* March 26, 1953, p.13.

1417. [Biographical data from *Who's Who in America*] California Writers' Club. *Quarterly Bulletin,* 4:11 (Dec. 1916).

1418. "Big jovial Josie Harper is dead. The woman mentioned in Jack London's 'John Barleycorn' passes away," Oakland *Tribune,* May 27, 1913 (0).

1419. Blanck, Joseph, "News from the rare booksellers," *Publishers' Weekly,* 149:3248-3249 (June 22, 1946).

1420. Bland, Henry Meade, "A chat with Charmian London," Oakland *Tribune,* April 13, 1922, p.5.

1421. ____, "From poverty to fame. Jack London's life story recounted by his friend," Oakland *Tribune* magazine section, Sept. 14, 1919, p.3,8.

1422. ____, "Jack London," *Overland Monthly,*n.s. 43:370-375 (May 1904); *Book News Monthly,* 34:292-294 (March 1916).

1423. ____, "Jack London: traveler, novelist and social reformer," *Craftsman,* 9:607-619 (1906); partially reprinted in *Socialist Voice* March 10, 1906, p.1.

1424. ____, "Jack London's literary habits," *Writers Monthly,* 6:3-5 (July 1915).

1425. ____, "John Barleycorn at the plow," *Sunset,* 33:347-349 (1914).

1426. ____, "Where some California writers live," San Francisco *Call* magazine section, Nov. 19, 1911, part 1:5.

1427. "Body of Jack London is cremated, as he directed," San Francisco *Chronicle,* Nov. 25, 1916, p.8. [Article ends with George Sterling poem].

1428. "Books of Jack London banned by Mussolini; defense by

Joan London," San Francisco *Chronicle*, Dec. 29, 1929, p.7, F4.

1429. Borden, Charles, "Jack London," *Paradise of the Pacific*, 53:24-26 (Jan. 1941).

1430. "Born in the working class," Santa Rosa *Press Democrat*, Nov. 23, 1916, p.1.

1431. Bosworth, Hobart, "My Jack London," *Mark Twain Quarterly*, 5:2-5,24 (Fall-Winter 1942-1943).

1432. Bosworth, L. A. M., "Is Jack London a plagiarist?" *Independent*, 62:373-376 (Feb. 14, 1907).

1433. Bowen, E. W., "Jack London's place in American literature," *Reformed Church Review*, 4th series, 24:306-315 (1920).

1434. Boyle, A. M., "Jack London as he lived," *Silhouette*, 1,4:73 (Dec. 1916) [Poem].

1435. Braley, Berton, "Jack London - an appreciation," *Overland Monthly*, n.s. 69:415 (May 1917) [Poem]. Also printed in Oakland *Tribune* second news section, Dec. 3, 1916, p.29; Berton Braley, *Things as they are: ballads*, New York, Doran, 1916, pp.113-114.

1436. ____, "John Barleycorn ... with acknowledgements to Jack London," Birmingham (Ala.) *Ledger*, May 3, 1913, p.4.

1437. Brewster, Herbert, "The literary outlook," Salt Lake *Herald*, March 30, 1902, p.12.

1438. Bridge, J. H., "Millionaires and Grub Street," *Overland Monthly*, n.s. 90:116 (May 1932).

1439. [Brief editorial comment on London's publicizing of poverty in London (England)] *British Californian* (San Francisco), 18,5:1 (Feb. 1906) [On *People of the abyss*].

1440. Brody, A., "Jack London via Moscow," *Nation*, 125:740 (Dec. 28, 1927).

1441. Buchanan, Agnes Foster, "The story of a famous fraternity of writers and artists," *Pacific Monthly*, 17:65-83 (Jan. 1907).

1442. Buck, Philo M., Jr., "The American barbarian," *Methodist Review*, 28:714-724 (1912); reprinted in H.

1443. Burk, Gay, "Three famous personages," *Paradise of the Pacific*, 70:76-79 (Nov. 1958).

1444. Burroughs, John, "Real and sham natural history," *Atlantic Monthly*, 91:298-309 (March 1903).

1445. Burroughs, Jack, "Dead?" San Francisco *Bulletin*, Nov. 24, 1916, p.8 [Verse].

1446. Burton, Howard A., "The human bondage of Martin Eden and the literary bondage of the modern reader," *Annotator*, 4:10-15 (Nov. 1954).

1447. Butler, Clarence E., "From house-boy on Snark to dentistry," *Contact Point* (University of Pacific, School of Dentistry, Stockton, Calif.), 41,2:64 (Nov. 1962) [Article concerning Nakata, the house boy that London picked up in the Pacific and who remained with him until his death].

1448. Bykov, V., "Jack London in the Soviet Union," *Book Club of California Quarterly News Letter*, 24:52-58 (Summer 1959) [See William Hogan, "A Russian student views Jack London," San Francisco *Chronicle*, June 5, 1959, p.31].

1449. Byrnes, William H., "Jack London at district fair," Santa Rosa *Press Democrat*, Sept. 6, 1914, p.6.

1450. Calder-Marshall, Arthur, "The 'Prince of Oyster Bay': Jack London," *Listener*, 62:178-179 (July 30, 1959).

1451. ____, "Yankee super tramp," *Books and Bookmen*, 8,10: 20-22, 24 (July 1963).

1452. "California personalities," San Francisco *Chronicle* Bonanza section, Oct. 17, 1954, pp.2,18.

1453. "California writer passes away suddenly. Medical aid rushed from San Francisco, but without avail," Los Angeles *Times*, Nov. 23, 1916, p.1.

1454. "Can't locate Jack London," Oakland *World*, April 8, 1911, p.3.

1455. "Captain of the Snark killed mate in north. Jack London's sailing master pardoned after receiving a life sentence," San Francisco *Call*, Jan. 30, 1908, p.7.

1456. Carnegie, Dale, "Dale Carnegie's 5-minute biographies. He rode the rods to fame," San Francisco *Chronicle* magazine section, Feb. 6, 1938, part 2, p.2.

1457. Carr, Henry, "The two Jack Londons. Author and artist versus socialist, twaddler and soap-box orator, a brilliant analysis," Los Angeles *Times*, Nov. 26, 1916, part 3, pp.1,3.

1458. Carroll, Lavon B., "Jack London and the American image," *American Book Collector*, 13,5:23-27 (Jan. 1963).

1459. Chamberlain, Arthur H., "Jack London as his wife Charmian knew him," *Current Opinion*, 71:645-648 (Nov. 1921).

1460. "Characteristic American career," *Literary Digest*, 53: 1537-1538 (Dec. 9, 1916).

1461. Cheney, Shelden, "Some California bookplates," *Sunset*, 18:332-336 (Feb. 1907).

1462. Chomet, Otto, "Jack London: works, reviews, and criticism published in German--a bibliography," *Bulletin of Bibliography*, 19:211-215, 239-240 (Jan.-Apr., May-Aug. (1949).

1463. "Jack London's boyhood days recalled. Chum tells of Jack London youth in penned memoirs," Oakland *Tribune*, Aug. 5, 1933, p.13B.

1464. Clark, Robert, "My hunting of the Snark," *Westways*,

39:13 (June 1947).

1465. "Class war," New York *Times*, Feb. 1, 1906, p.8 [Editorial].

1466. Clavinovich, Rose, "Jack London's 'mother mine'," Oakland *Tribune* Sunday magazine section, Oct. 22, 1922, p.5. [Sub-heading: "How Mrs. Edward P. Payne of Berkeley discovered and encouraged author as a boy."]

1467. Colbron, G. I., "The eternal masculine," *Bookman*, 32:157-159 (Oct. 1910).

1468. ____, "Jack London: what he was and what he accomplished," *Bookman*, 44:441-451 (Jan. 1917).

1469. Cole, Vera Heathman, "Jack London: verse," *Overland Monthly*, n.s. 69:160 (Feb. 1917).

1470. Coleman, C. D., "Jinx ship: schooner in 'The sea wolf' saucy lass, now the Hakadate," *Sunset*, 60:35 (Jan. 1928).

1471. Connell, Sarah, "Jack London wooed fame through the *Overland Monthly*," *Overland Monthly*, n.s. 76:65-71 (Oct. 1920).

1472. Connor, Torrey, "The shrine," California Writers' Club. *Monthly Bulletin*, 1:7 (May 1917) [Poem] [Regarding the pilgrimage to Jack London's home].

1473. Coontz, Virginia, "Monument to a dream. Wolf House, tragic ruin of Jack London's lost hopes for sanctuary that would defy the years," Oakland *Tribune* magazine and pictorial section, March 25, 1945, pp.7-8.

1474. Cooper, S., "Primordialism and some recent books," *Bookman*, 30:278-282 (Nov. 1909).

1475. Cordell, Richard, "Quid pro quo," *Annotator*, no. 4:16-19 (Nov. 1954).

1476. "Cosmopolitan editor a guest of Jack London," Santa Rosa *Press Democrat*, Nov. 15, 1916, p.2.

1477. Crossman, R. H. S., "The prohpecies of Jack London," *New Statesman and Nation*, 17:723-724 (June 8, 1940).

1478. *"The Cruise of the Dazzler:* a plea," *The Courier* (Syracuse University Library Associates), 3,4:15 (Dec. 1963).

1479. Cummings, Ridgely, "Jack London lived here," *Argonaut*, 132,3969:8 (Dec. 4, 1953).

1480. C. W. C., [Jack London] California Writers' Club. *Quarterly Bulletin*, 4:6 (Dec. 1916).

1481. ____, "A reminiscence," California Writers' Club. *Monthly Bulletin*, 1:7 (May 1917) [Discussion of an interview by a member of the *Bulletin's* staff with Mayor Davie and the latter's recollection of Jack London].

1482. Dargan, E. Preston, "Jack London in chancery," *New Republic*, 10:7-8, pt.2, (April 21, 1917).

1483. "Daughters to disregard London will," San Francisco *Examiner* news section, Dec. 3, 1916, p.3.

1484. Davis, G. M., "Rebel," *Overland Monthly*, n.s. 90:118 (May 1932) [Verse].

1485. ____, "To Jack London," *Overland Monthly*, n.s. 90:108 (May 1932) [Verse].

1486. "Day at exposition to honor Jack London," San Francisco *Call-Bulletin*, Sept. 20, 1938, p.8.

1487. "Day by day with Jack London," Santa Rosa *Press Democrat*, Nov. 25, 1911, p.7.

1488. "Days of Jack London reviewed," *Pony Express Courier*, 6,10:9 (March 1940).

1489. "Death of Jack London," *Wisconsin Library Bulletin*, 12:422-423 (Dec. 1916).

1490. "Death of Jack London: author - adventurer," *Daily Mail* (London), Nov. 24, 1916, p.7.

1491. "Diaz gets Jack London in the can," Santa Rosa *Press Democrat*, Feb. 19, 1911, p.1.

1492. Dickason, David H., "A note on Jack London and David Starr Jordan," *Indiana Magazine of History*, 38:407-410 (1942).

1493. Dieckmann, Ed, Jr., "From London to Peking in fifty-one years," *American Opinion*, 8,2:79-89 (Feb. 1965).

1494. Dieckmann, E., "House that Jack built," *National Parks Magazine*, 35:4-7 (Nov. 1961).

1495. Doyle, A. C., "Alleged posthumous writings of great authors," *Bookman*, 66:342-349 (1927); *Fortnightly Review*, 128:721-735 (1927).

1496. Duddelson, William, "Legend of Charmian London, her love, her home, her life," Santa Rosa *Press Democrat*, Jan. 17, 1955, p.16.

1497. Dunn, Allen, "The sailing of the Snark," *Sunset*, 19:3-9 (Nov. 1907).

1498. Eames, Ninetta, "A character sketch of Oakland's latest literary genius, Jack London. Ninetta Eames writes entertainingly in the May *Overland Monthly* of his life, stirring experiences, habits of thought and methods of work," Oakland *Enquirer*, May 12, 1900, p.8.

1499. ____, "Haunts of Jack London," *Cosmopolitan*, 40:227-230 (Dec. 1905).

1500. ____, "Jack London," *Overland Monthly*, n.s. 35:417-425 (May 1900).

1501. "Eastern estimates of London's genius," California Writers' Club. *Quarterly Bulletin*, 4:10 (Dec. 1916).

1502. "Editor's note" to "Two sermons by Ninetta Eames Payne," *Pony Express Courier*, 8,4:9 (Sept. 1941).

1503. Edwards, V. W., "The Jack London myth," *News Letter and Wasp*, Nov. 24, 1939, p.7.

1504. Emerson, Edwin, Jr., "When West met East," *Sunset*, 15:515-530 (Oct. 1905).

1505. Estcourt, Zilfa, "London memorial: his effects to be gathered for Library of Congress," San Francisco *Chronicle*, Jan. 26, 1941, p.55.

1506. Farrell, James, "The American novelist and American society - II: Jack London," *Institute in American Studies, July 15 to July 20, 1946*, Minneapolis, Center for continuation study, University of Minnesota, pp. 18-19.

1507. ___, "My favorite forgotten book," *Tomorrow*, 6:63-64 (Nov. 1946) [Short essay on *The iron heel*].

1508. "Fear for the safety of London's party," Santa Rosa *Press Democrat*, Jan. 17, 1908, p.1.

1509. "Fear Jack London is war prisoner," Philadelphia *Press*, Feb. 20, 1911, p.1.

1510. Ferry, Philip, "The Valley of the Moon remembers Jack London," *California Highway Patrolman*, 24,11:10-11 (Jan. 1961).

1511. Fitch, George Hamilton, "Some phases of California literature," *Impressions*, 1:113-114 (Sept. 1900).

1512. "Fitz's hand loses none of its cunning," Santa Rosa *Press Democrat*, Sept. 6, 1910, p.3.

1513. Flowers, B. O., "Jack London at Harvard," *Arena*, 35: 18-19 (Feb. 1906).

1514. Ford, Alexander Hume, "Jack London in Hawaii: rambling reminiscences of the editor," *Mid-Pacific Magazine*, 13:117-127 (Feb. 1917).

1515. Forder, Herbert, "Jack London: a man of a thousand lives," *Pearson's*, 37:230-233 (March 1917).

1516. Fowler, Augusta, "Jack London," *Silhouette*, 1:85 (Dec. 1916).

1517. Francoeur, Jeanne E., "Jack London is dead? There is no death for such as he!" *Everywoman*, 11:14 (Dec. 1916).

1518. French, H., "Cruises of Bay-Pirate Jack," *St. Nicholas*, 44:845-850 (1917).

1519. "Frenchmen condemn Jack London style of writing as in bad taste," Philadelphia *Press*, April 28, 1912, p.15.

1520. Friedland, L. S., "Jack London as Titan, hailed as a mighty prophet in Russia," *Dial*, 62:49-51 (Jan. 25, 1917).

1521. Friedman, Ralph, "Jack London's Valley of the Moon," United *Mainliner* Magazine, 9:[14-16] (July 1965).

1522. Frolich, F., "Bas relief from life," *Overland Monthly*, n.s. 90:98 (May 1932) [Verse].

1523. "From deed to word," *Scholastic*, 49:17 (Jan. 13, 1947).

1524. "From Jack London's latest lecture: Jack London and Thomas Lawson," *Socialist Voice*, April 14, 1906, p.2

[Lecture account].
1525. "From the Valley of the Moon to Valley of Death," Oakland *Enquirer*, Nov. 23, 1916, p.1.
1526. Fuller, Henry Blake, "Frank Norris and Jack London on literary art and the multitude," Chicago *Evening Post*, part 2, Sept. 6, 1902, p.9.
1527. "Gave Jack London glass that cheered. Oakland woman has strange career," Oakland *Tribune*, April 28, 1933 (0).
1528. Garnett, Porter, "Jack London - his relation to literary art," *Pacific Monthly*, 17:446-453 (April 1907).
1529. Ghinsberg, Samuel, "The horses knew the way. A visit with Jack London," San Francisco *Sunday Examiner & Chronicle*, *This World* section, March 6, 1966, pp.33,37. [Contains excerpts from London letters of 1915 to Ghinsberg.]
1530. _____, "Jack London," Oakland *World*, Dec. 22, 1916, p.4.
1531. "Given home to remain single," San Francisco *Chronicle*, Aug. 31, 1904, p.7.
1532. Glancy, Donald R., "Socialist with a valet: Jack London's 'First, last and only' lecture tour," *Quarterly Journal of Speech*, 49:31-39 (Feb. 1963).
1533. Gleeson, Edgar T., "When London was host to baseball scribes. Author's passing recalls visit to his Glen Ellen home when he regaled newspapermen with stories of his travel experiences," San Francisco *Bulletin*, Nov. 23, 1916, p.15.
1534. "Good music for the Jack London Ranch," Santa Rosa *Press Democrat*, Jan. 28, 1916, p.6.
1535. Goodhue, E. S., "Jack London and Martin Eden," *Mid-Pacific Magazine*, 6:359-363 (Oct. 1913).
1536. Gordon, Carl, "Jack London - a little journey: poem," *Era*, 19:63 (May 1917).
1537. Gordon, Dudley C., "Charles F. Lummis and Jack London: an evaluation," *Southern California Quarterly*, 46:83-88 (March 1964).
1538. Gordon, W. D., "Eagle," *Overland Monthly*, n.s. 90:59 (May 1932) [Verse].
1539. Graham, Stephen, "Jack London," *Literary Review*, 4:469-470 (Jan. 26, 1924); reprinted in *English Review*, 38:732-737 (May 1924).
1540. Grant, Oliver Remick, "Writers' Club will hear talk on Jack London," San Francisco *Chronicle*, Sept. 25, 1939, p.10.
1541. Grattan, C. Hartley, "Jack London," *Bookman*, 68:667-671 (Feb. 1929).
1542. "A great treat in store," Oakland *World*, Aug. 31, 1909, p.2.
1543. Greenway, Joe, "Jack London's stupendous chin-wag with

a hobo," *This World* section of the San Francisco Sunday *Chronicle,* Oct. 27, 1963, p.35.

1544. Griswold, Mary Edith, "The sailing of the Snark," *Western World,* 2,1:31-32 (April 1907).

1545. Gurian, J., "The romantic necessity in literary naturalism: Jack London," *Osmania Journal of English Studies,* no. 2:1-11 (1962); reprinted *American Literature,* 38:1,2-120 (1966).

1546. Hamilton, Fannie K., "Jack London," Louisville *Evening Post,* Aug. 1, 1903, 2:[2].

1547. Hamlin, Amy W., "The silent pen--a tribute to Jack London," California Writers' Club. *Monthly Bulletin,* 1,1:1 (April 1917).

1548. Hamlin, Clay, "Forgotten Classics - The Scarlet Plague," *Fadaway* (mimeographed science-fiction fan magazine), 3,2,14:21-23 [n.d.].

1549. Harding, Walter, "Jack London and Thoreau," *Thoreau Society Bulletin,* no. 57:1 (Fall 1956) [Concerning *The night-born*].

1550. Hart, James D., "Californians on Soviet best-seller lists," *Quarterly News Letter* (Book Club of California), 27:61-63 (1962).

1551. Harvey, John L., "Jack London and O. Henry: a parallel," *Reedy's Mirror,* 26:134-136 (March 2, 1917).

1552. Haverland, S., "Jack London's debt to books and libraries," *Pacific Bindery Talk,* 10:135 (1940).

1553. Hawkes, E. G., "Jack London: a brief sketch of his life," *Overland Monthly,* n.s. 90:109-110, 122, 125 (May 1932).

1554. Haydock, J., "Jack London" a bibliography of criticism," *Bulletin of Bibliography,* 23:42-46 (May 1960).

1555. Heinold, Johnny, "Saloonman says friend was determined 'finisher'," Oakland *Tribune,* Nov. 23, 1916, p.13.

1556. "Hero of London stories is dead," San Francisco *Bulletin,* April 21, 1917, p.13 [John C. Stofen identified with Captain Jack of London stories].

1557. Higgins, John C., "Jack London to the waterfront," *Westways,* 26:28-29, 34, 36 (Jan. 1934).

1558. Holden, E. H., "California landmarks: Jack London, Benicia," *Pony Express Courier,* 4,5:7 (Oct. 1937).

1559. "Home again," Oakland *World,* Aug. 7, 1909, p.3.

1560. "Honolulu man reads Jack London ... buys ranch here," Santa Rosa *Press Democrat,* Feb. 11, 1914, p.3.

1561. Hopkins, Ernest J., "Jack London is dead--He who of all men was supremely alive," San Francisco *Bulletin,* Nov. 23, 1916, p.7.

1562. Hopper, James, "Jack London the campus," *California Alumni Fortnightly,* 9:278-279 (Dec. 2, 1916); also

printed in Oakland *Tribune*, Dec. 1, 1916, p.10; California Writers' Club *Quarterly Bulletin*, 4:4-5 (Dec.
1916).

1563. Houck, Chinn B., "Jack London's philosophy of life,"
Overland Monthly, n.s. 84:103-104, 120, 136-137, 141,
147, 149 (April-May 1926).

1564. Howard, Eric, "Men around London," *Esquire*, 13:62,
183-186 (June 1940).

1565. ____, "Jack London. The playboy of American letters,"
San Francisco *Call*, Feb. 1, 1923, 2nd news section,
p.20.

1566. "H. R. Lytle recalls London on march of Coxey's army,"
Sacramento *Bee*, Aug. 2, 1947, p.20.

1567. Hueffer, Oliver Madox, "Jack London: a personal sketch,"
Living Age, 292:124-126 (Jan. 13, 1917); *New Statesman*,
8:206-207 (Dec. 2, 1916).

1568. "I am a sucker but not thief, says London," San Francisco *Examiner*, July 17, 1909, p.1.

1569. "Incineration without prayer," Oakland *Enquirer*, Nov.
25, 1916, p.5.

1570. "The insider tells how Jack London sold the book that
made him famous and replied to magazine editors' requests for stories by returning the manuscripts they
had rejected," San Francisco *Call*, Feb. 14, 1910, p.6.

1571. "Italy bans books of Jack London," San Francisco
Chronicle World Topics Section, Aug. 10, 1929, p.4F.

1572. "Jack London," *Bookbuyer*, 20:277-278 (May 1900).

1573. "Jack London," *Bookman*, 11:200-201 (May 1900); 17:562-
564 (Aug. 1903).

1574. "Jack London," Boston *Transcript*, Feb. 26, 1913, p.22;
Dec. 19, 1917, p.8.

1575. "Jack London," *Current Literature*, 28:283 (June 1900).

1576. "Jack London," Indianapolis *News*, Nov. 23, 1916, p.6.

1577. "Jack London," *Mechanics' Institute Library Bulletin*
(San Francisco) 5,8:3 (Aug. 1901).

1578. "Jack London," Oakland *Enquirer*, Nov. 25, 1916, p.4
[Editorial].

1579. "Jack London," Oakland *Tribune*, Nov. 24, 1916, p.12
[Editorial].

1580. "Jack London," *Outing*, 44:486-487 (July 1904).

1581. "Jack London," *Publishers' Circular*, 85:309 (Sept.
15, 1906).

1582. "Jack London," *Sunset*, 20:500 (March 1908).

1583. "Jack London," Washington *Post*, Nov. 24, 1916, p.6
[Editorial].

1584. "Jack London: a biographical note," *Scholastic*, 33:23
(Nov. 5, 1938).

1585. "Jack London - a foreword," *Book Collecting for love or money*, 4,8:1, 8[n.d.].

1586. "Jack London a member of Oakland local," Oakland *World*, Dec. 1, 1916, p.8.

1587. "Jack London - a rebel against progress," *Observer* (Adelaide), 69,5379:6-7 (April 6, 1912).

1588. "Jack London: a sketch of his life," *Outlook*, 114:742 (Dec. 6, 1916).

1589. "Jack London a suicide? No! says daughter," San Francisco *Chronicle*, Sept. 8, 1938, p.11 [Includes letter from Jack London to Joan London written the day before his death].

1590. "Jack London and Derby Neck," *Socialist Voice*, Feb. 17, 1906, p.1 [Reprints editorial from the Oakland *Enquirer*].

1591. "Jack London and fire fighters save Glen Ellen," Santa Rosa *Press Democrat*, Sept. 23, 1913, p.5.

1592. "Jack London and his work," *Silhouette*, 1:71-72 (Dec. 1916).

1593. "Jack London and Oklahoma," *Historia*, 8:6-7 (Jan. 1, 1920).

1594. "Jack London and wife are going to Japan," Santa Rosa *Press Democrat*, April 8, 1914.

1595. "Jack London and wife have returned home," Santa Rosa *Press Democrat*, June 20, 1914, p.7.

1596. "Jack London as a farmer and the successful running of his estate by his wife and sister," *Touchstone*, 6:416-421 (March 1920).

1597. "Jack London at Berkeley," *Argonaut*, 56,1455:70 (Jan. 30, 1905) ["Dr. Wheeler, Jack London and socialism," *Argonaut*, 56,1456:87 (Feb. 6, 1905) is President Benjamin Wheeler's reply dated Jan. 29, 1905].

1598. "Jack London at sea," *Bookman*, 28:5 (Sept. 1908).

1599. "Jack London at the University of California," California Writers' Club *Quarterly Bulletin*, 4,4:4-5 (Dec. 1916).

1600. "Jack London, author," *Overland Monthly*, 43:349 (April 1904) [photograph of bust of London].

1601. "Jack London bares 'life' via medium," Oakland *Tribune* news section, May 14, 1922, p.B1.

1602. "Jack London bruised in Oakland," Santa Rosa *Press Democrat*, June 22, 1910, p.1.

1603. "The Jack London club ...," *Our Dumb Animals*, 51,6:84 (Nov. 1918).

1604. "Jack London collection. Stanford University," San Francisco *Chronicle*, April 26, 1964, p.19.

1605. "Jack London - death," London *Times*, Nov. 24, 1916, p.6.

1606. "Jack London - death and career," New York *Times*, Nov. 23, 1916, p.13.

1607. "Jack London defendant in court here Tuesday," Santa
      Rosa *Press Democrat*, Dec. 15, 1915, p.5.
1608. "Jack London dies at age of forty," Oakland *World*,
      Nov. 24, 1916, p.1.
1609. "Jack London dies at his home at Glen Ellen," San Fran-
      cisco *Chronicle*, Nov. 23, 1916, p.1,2 [photograph ac-
      companies story].
1610. "Jack London dies in sudden illness," *Morning Oregonian*,
      Nov. 23, 1916, pp.1-5.
1611. "Jack London dies in 'Valley of the Moon'," Santa Rosa
      Press Democrat, Nov. 23, 1916, pp.1,8.
1612. "Jack London dies in western home; ill only one day,"
      Minneapolis *Journal*, Nov. 23, 1916, p.4.
1613. "Jack London fable barn burned. Oakland saloon made
      noted by sea tales destroyed with many relics," San
      Francisco *Call*, Sept. 24, 1928, p.1.
1614. "Jack London, farmer," *Literary Digest*, 46:1195 (May
      24, 1913).
1615. "Jack London, farmer, tells of his ideas of farming,"
      Santa Rosa *Press Democrat*, Nov. 10, 1916, p.6.
1616. "Jack London finds his marriage void," Philadelphia
      Press, Nov. 21, 1905, p.6.
1617. "Jack London finishes his latest novel," Santa Rosa
      Press Democrat, Dec. 30, 1914, p.8.
1618. "Jack London forfeits bail. Brilliant young author of
      Klondike tales was arrested on charge of riding bi-
      cycle without light after dark," Oakland *Herald*, Aug.
      7, 1903, p.[?].
1619. "Jack London found unconscious in bed," Oakland *Tribune*,
      Nov. 22, 1916, p.1.
1620. "Jack London has been entertaining some old friends at
      his ranch," Santa Rosa *Press Democrat*, Dec. 12, 1915,
      p.6.
1621. "Jack London goes on his last cruise," San Francisco
      Examiner, Nov. 25, 1916, p.5.
1622. "Jack London gets his insurance in full," Santa Rosa
      Press Democrat, Sept. 11, 1913, p.5.
1623. "Jack London has bought more fine horses," Santa Rosa
      Press Democrat, March 21, 1914, p.1.
1624. "Jack London has double in desert posing as author,
      imposter is fooling credulous folk in arid region,"
      San Francisco *Call*, Nov. 17, 1908, p.10.
1625. "Jack London has prize bull," Santa Rosa *Press Democrat*,
      Sept. 14, 1916, p.5.
1626. "Jack London: he pictured the life he lived," New York
      Times, Nov. 24, 1916, p.12.
1627. "Jack London, hero, is visitor in Santa Rosa," Santa
      Rosa *Press Democrat*, April 5, 1915, p.7.

1628. "Jack London hired to drive dogs," Oakland *World*, Jan. 18, 1908, p.2.
1629. [Jack London Historical State Park dedicated - story by the "Knave"] Oakland *Tribune*, Oct. 9, 1960, p.C1.
1630. "Jack London home from Hawaii and goes to New York," Santa Rosa *Press Democrat*, Aug. 2, 1916, p.5.
1631. "Jack London, how is this? You're called plagiarist," Los Angeles *Examiner* classified section, May 3, 1909, p.1. [Parallel columns compare *The candid friend and The iron heel*.]
1632. "Jack London - In memoriam," *International Socialist Review*, 17:624 (April 1917).
1633. "Jack London is at home again," Santa Rosa *Press Democrat*, Aug. 1, 1912, p.6.
1634. "Jack London is getting better," Santa Rosa *Press Democrat*, June 19, 1914, p.2.
1635. "Jack London is going to Hawaii," Santa Rosa *Press Democrat*, Nov. 26, 1915, p.7.
1636. "Jack London is hunter's victim," Santa Rosa *Press Democrat*, March 20, 1913, p.1.
1637. "Jack London is sermon theme," San Francisco *Examiner*, Dec. 4, 1916, p.6.
1638. "Jack London is socialist candidate," Santa Rosa *Press Democrat*, March 1, 1914, p.1.
1639. "Jack London is to wed in Iowa," Santa Rosa *Press Democrat*, Nov. 9, 1905, p.5.
1640. "Jack London is vice president of national defense association which aims to regulate drinking of alcoholic beverages," New York *Times*, Dec. 3, 1915, p.1.
1641. "Jack London is visitor at the district fair," Santa Rosa *Press Democrat*, Aug. 10, 1916, p.6.
1642. "Jack London leaves $5 to divorced wife," San Francisco *Examiner*, Dec. 2, 1916, p.1.
1643. "Jack London leaves for Japan as war correspondent for 'The Examiner'," San Francisco *Examiner*, Jan. 7, 1904, p.1 [includes photograph of London].
1644. "Jack London, lecturer," Oakland *Tribune*, Aug. 28, 1953, p.E25.
1645. "Jack London made U. C. men squirm," San Francisco *Examiner*, Nov. 26, 1916, p.4N.
1646. "Jack London may cross border; join insurrectos," Los Angeles *Herald*, Feb. 6, 1911, p.12.
1647. "Jack London Memorial Library will be erected on site near Glen Ellen," Oakland *Tribune* news section, Sept. 26, 1920, p.B1.
1648. "Jack London memorial meeting," Oakland *World*, Dec. 8, 1916, p.1.
1649. "Jack London monument to open," Sacramento *Union*,

July 31, 1960, p.12.

1650. "Jack London narrowly escapes," Oakland *World*, Nov. 28, 1908, p.1.

1651. "Jack London not 'Billy' in 'Valley of the Moon'," Santa Rosa *Press Democrat*, Nov. 11, 1916, p.6.

1652. "Jack London novelist and essayist will be given quiet funeral here," Oakland *Tribune*, 2nd section, Nov. 23, 1916, p.13.

1653. "Jack London of Oakland," Oakland *Tribune*, Nov. 26, 1916, p.33.

1654. "Jack London off to be war correspondent," Santa Rosa *Press Democrat*, April 18, 1914, p.7.

1655. "Jack London now at Glen Ellen," Santa Rosa *Press Democrat*, Jan. 30, 1908, p.8.

1656. "Jack London organized socialist local in Tahiti," Oakland *World*, Aug. 28, 1909, p.1.

1657. "Jack London passes away. Suffers uremic poisoning," San Francisco *Examiner*, Nov. 23, 1916, p.1.

1658. "Jack London - plans for his funeral," New York *Times*, Nov. 24, 1916, p.13.

1659. "Jack London plants eucalyptus forest," San Francisco *Examiner*, April 8, 1914, p.8.

1660. "Jack London plants more eucalyptus trees," Santa Rosa *Press Democrat*, April 8, 1914, p.6.

1661. "Jack London - praise of his work by Russian critics," New York *Times*, April 8, 1917, p.128.

1662. "Jack London receives very warm welcome," Oakland *World*, Aug. 28, 1909, p.1.

1663. "Jack London rides again. Extra! Jack was a love-child, but Double Extra! Irving Stone's serial in *Saturday Evening Post* turns out to be rehash of London's own work, plus sentences and paragraphs in which pronoun is serialist's only contribution. Or might be coincidence, like Old McIntyre's steals from Morley," *Ken*, 2,4:26-27 (Aug. 25, 1938) [Compares *Sailor on horseback* and passages from *John Barleycorn* and "The apostate"].

1664. "Jack London scores San José hostesses," San Francisco *Call*, March 24, 1907, p.24.

1665. "Jack London secures a fine stallion," Santa Rosa *Press Democrat*, March 6, 1913, p.7.

1666. "Jack London, 6 days before death," San Francisco *Bulletin*, Nov. 23, 1916, p.7 [montage of 3 photographs with brief caption].

1667. "Jack London spurns union," Los Angeles *Times*, Sept. 23, 1916, p.3.

1668. "Jack London still alive to his 'forgotten widow'," Alameda *Times-Star*, Jan. 25, 1936, p.2.

1669. "Jack London stricken - abandons world trip at Sydney,"

Philadelphia *Press*, March 31, 1909, p.1.
1670. "Jack London tells why he helped his sister," Santa Rosa *Press Democrat*, Nov. 25, 1915, p.5.
1671. "Jack London--the man," *Brass Tacks*, 8,4:1-3 (Sept. 29, 1915).
1672. "Jack London the socialist--a character study. When and why the author of 'The Call of the Wild' became a convert and propagandist. His literary methods and aims," New York *Times*, Jan. 28, 1906, pt.3, p.6.
1673. "Jack London to exhibit fine cattle at our fair," Santa Rosa *Press Democrat*, June 28, 1913, p.8.
1674. "Jack London to lecture," San Francisco *Call*, Dec. 9, 1906, p.42 [Lecture account].
1675. "Jack London to make exhibit," Santa Rosa *Press Democrat*, June 17, 1916, p.5.
1676. "Jack London to pay that $5,000," Santa Rosa *Press Democrat*, Jan. 28, 1916, p.3.
1677. "Jack London to be the speaker," Santa Rosa *Press Democrat*, Feb. 12, 1913, p.7.
1678. "Jack London to run for governor. Has no idea of success, but hopes to increase the socialist vote," San Francisco *Chronicle*, March 1, 1914, p.35.
1679. "Jack London to sell his own grape juice," San Francisco *Examiner*, July 17, 1914, p.3.
1680. "Jack London to speak at entertainment," Santa Rosa *Press Democrat*, Sept. 4, 1909, p.8.
1681. "Jack London to take the stand," Santa Rosa *Press Democrat*, Nov. 8, 1916, p.2.
1682. "Jack London to undergo operation for appendicitis," New York *Times*, July 8, 1913, p.1.
1683. "Jack London tree in the heart of Oakland," Oakland *World*, Jan. 19, 1917, p.1.
1684. "Jack London undergoes operation at Oakland," Santa Rosa *Press Democrat*, July 9, 1913, p.1.
1685. "Jack London visitor here on Thursday," Santa Rosa *Press Democrat*, May 19, 1905, p.2.
1686. "Jack London whines," *Regeneración* (English edition), July 12, 1913, p.4.
1687. "Jack London will build some good roads," Santa Rosa *Press Democrat*, Feb. 12, 1913, p.2.
1688. "Jack London will build fine home," Santa Rosa *Press Democrat*, June 3, 1909, p.3.
1689. "Jack London will describe opening of Schuetzenfest for 'The Examiner'," San Francisco *Examiner*, July 13, 1901, p.7.
1690. "Jack London will write of the Schuetzenfest," San Francisco *Examiner*, July 14, 1901, p.19.
1691. "Jack London, writer dies at ranch home," Anaconda

Standard, Nov. 23, 1916 (0).

1692. "Jack London's aide a horse all night to be at bier," San Francisco *Call,* Nov. 24, 1916, p.1.

1693. "Jack London's appeal for lepers is heeded," Philadelphia *Public Ledger,* Feb. 11, 1917, p.[?].

1694. "Jack London's books popular in Sweden," San Francisco *Bulletin,* Aug. 1, 1917 (0).

1695. "Jack London's 'Burning daylight' coming to Rose," Santa Rosa *Press Democrat,* April 22, 1915, p.5.

1696. "Jack London's bust will be unveiled in Honolulu under auspices of Pan-Pacific Club of Honolulu," New York *Times,* Aug. 20, 1917, p.6.

1697. "Jack London's call to the land," *Current Opinion,* 46: 212 (March 1914).

1698. "Jack London's castle is to be rebuilt at once," Santa Rosa *Press Democrat,* Aug. 24, 1913, p.9.

1699. "Jack London's correspondents," *Bookman,* 33:567-569 (August 1911).

1700. "Jack London's country home in California destroyed by fire," New York *Times,* Aug. 24, 1913, p.4.

1701. "Jack London's death," *Labor News* (Eureka, Calif.), Dec. 2, 1916, p.2.

1702. "Jack London's death moves poets to song," San Francisco *Bulletin,* Nov. 24, 1916, p.8.

1703. "Jack London's dream house. Writer's brilliant career, tragic life ended at Glen Ellen," *PG and E Progress,* Dec. 1962, p.8.

1704. "Jack London's funeral will be held today," San Francisco *Chronicle,* Nov. 24, 1916, p.3.

1705. "Jack London's home burns," Santa Rosa *Press Democrat,* Aug. 23, 1913, p.8.

1706. "Jack London's horses at the state fair," Santa Rosa *Press Democrat,* Aug. 16, 1916, p.6.

1707. "Jack London's last days in new movies," San Francisco *Bulletin,* Dec. 9, 1916, p.10.

1708. "Jack London's last ride in the 'Valley of the Moon', Santa Rosa *Press Democrat,* Nov. 25, 1916, p.8.

1709. "Jack London's 'Martin Eden' at the Rose today," Santa Rosa *Press Democrat,* April 1, 1915, p.7.

1710. "Jack London's Oakland lecture," *Socialist Voice,* April 7, 1906, p.1 [Lecture account].

1711. "Jack London's one great contribution to American literature," *Current Opinion,* 62:46-47 (Jan. 1917).

1712. "Jack London's place in American literature," *Nation,* 103:502 (Nov. 30, 1916).

1713. "Jack London's politics, creed and personality. Friends and comrades pay tribute to Jack London. Charmian London sends message," Oakland *World,* Dec. 15, 1916, pp.1,8.

1714. "Jack London's ranch is to be a memorial," San Francisco *Examiner*, second main news section, Dec. 3, 1916, p.2N.
1715. "Jack London's resignation from the Socialist party," *Overland Monthly*, n.s. 49:446 (May 1917).
1716. "Jack London's ridiculous vendetta," San Francisco *Call*, Aug. 3, 1910, p.4 [Editorial].
1717. "Jack London's saloon keeper pal under knife," San Francisco *Chronicle*, Aug. 7, 1929 (0).
1718. "Jack London's 'Sea wolf' will be shown in film," Santa Rosa *Press Democrat*, Nov. 22, 1914, p.6.
1719. "Jack London's sister to come into court again," Santa Rosa *Press Democrat*, Jan. 30, 1916, p.6.
1720. "Jack London's Snark reaches Honolulu," San Francisco *Examiner* (Oakland Edition), May 21, 1907, p.1.
1721. "Jack London's spirit sends message. Communication stirs two continents," Oakland *Tribune*, May 13, 1922, p.1,2.
1722. "Jack London's unique country home," *Architect and Engineer of California*, 25:49-51 (July 1911).
1723. "Jack London's widow arrives by plane," San Francisco *Chronicle*, Oct. 14, 1939, p.13.
1724. "Jack London's work," New York *Times*, Dec. 3, 1916, vi:2.
1725. Jackson, Joseph Henry, "A bookman's notebook ... Book-and-author gossip," San Francisco *Chronicle*, April 29, 1937, p.11 [note on exhibit of London first editions at Mills College library].
1726. James, George Wharton, "A study of Jack London in his prime," *Overland Monthly*, n.s. 69:361-399 (May 1917).
1727. Jennings, Ann S., "London's code of the northland," *Alaska Review*, 1,3:43-48 (Fall 1964).
1728. "'John Barleycorn' and Jack London to make a film drama," San Francisco *Bulletin*, Dec. 10, 1913, p.1.
1729. "John Barleycorn's sister Jane of New York only a sporadic type, says Jack London," New York *Evening World*, Jan. 15, 1914, p.3 [Interview with Marguerite Mooers Marshall].
1730. Johnstone, A., "Socialist readers love Jack London best of all," New York *Daily Worker*, Jan. 8, 1956, pp.8,10.
1731. Jones, Idwal, "Days at Glen Ellen," *Westways*, 42:14-15 (Sept. 1950).
1732. ____, "Jack London's ranch," *Westways*, 52:18-19 (Oct. 1960).
1733. Katona, Anna, "American belles lettres in Hungarian translation, 1945-1961," *Hungarian Studies in English* (publications of the English Department of the L. Kossuth University, Debrecen), 1:65-86 (1963).
1734. Kellogg, B. W., "Treasures from the Snark's cruise,"

Overland Monthly, n.s. 90:113-114 (May 1932).

1735. Kelly, S. H., "Martin Eden," *Overland Monthly,* n.s.
90:108 (May 1932) [Verse].

1736. "Kings of bad boys start 'back to soil'. Noted authors
pick nation's worst youths for reform," San Francisco
Examiner, Jan. 11, 1914, p.1 [London named as supporter
of boys' club].

1737. "Kittredge marriage complications," San Francisco *Call,*
Nov. 21, 1905, p.4.

1738. Kronenberger, Louis, "Jack London as legend," *Nation,*
147:420,422 (Oct. 22, 1938).

1739. Kruskopf, A., "Martin Eden of Sonoma," *American Scan-
dinavian Review,* 31:347-348 (1943).

1740. Labor, Earle, "Jack London's symbolic wilderness: four
versions," *Nineteenth-Century Fiction,* 17:149-161
(1962).

1741. Lane, R. W., "Life and Jack London," *Sunset,* 39:17-20
(Oct. 1917), 29-32 (Nov. 1917), 21-23 (Dec. 1917),
40:34-37, 62-64 (Jan. 1918), 30-34, 67-68 (Feb. 1918);
27-30, 64-66 (March 1918), 21-25, 60,62 (April 1918),
28-32, 60,62,64,66,68,70,72 (May 1918).

1742. Langdon, B., Mrs. Jack London's "Log of the Snark,"
Overland Monthly, n.s. 69:447-450 (May 1917).

1743. Lardner, D., "Two schools," *New Yorker,* 20:42 (Feb. 26,
1944).

1744. Larkin, Edgar Lucien, "A recollection of Jack London,"
San Francisco *Examiner,* Dec. 26, 1916, p.16; California
Writers' Club. *Quarterly Bulletin,* 4:7-8 (Dec. 1916).

1745. ____, "Recollections of the late Jack London," *Overland
Monthly,* n.s. 69:433-434 (May 1917).

1746. "Last rites for London; Sterling poem is read," San
Francisco *Bulletin,* Nov. 24, 1916, pp.1,8.

1747. "Last service for London Sunday," San Francisco *Bulletin,* Nov. 25, 1916, p.4.

1748. "Lawsuit losers celebrate at London's ranch," San Francisco *Bulletin,* Nov. 17, 1916, p.1.

1749. Lay, Wilfrid, "John Barleycorn under psychoanalysis,"
Bookman, 45:47-54 (March 1917).

1750. "Legislature provides for acquisition of London home as
state park," California Statutes 1957, ch. 2251 (Senate
Bill 757).

1751. Lewis, Lucien M., "Jack London: poem," *Out West,* n.s.
44:242 (Dec. 1916).

1752. Lewis, O., "London's California," *Book News,* 35:367-369
(June 1917).

1753. Lewis, Sinclair, "The relation of the novel to the
present social unrest," *Bookman,* 40:276-303 (1914).
[This is part two of a symposium, "The passing of cap-

italism."]

1754. "Little pilgrimages among the men and women who have written famous books: No. 6, Jack London," *Literary World* (Boston), 34:337-339 (Dec. 1903).

1755. Little, Richard Henry, "Meester Weelson slightly known in Russia; Yacklunnen American they swear by," San Francisco *Chronicle*, Feb. 9, 1920, p.2.

1756. Lockley, Fred, "Fred Lockley's impressions: Jack London was familiar with nation's jail," Oregon *Journal*, May 24, 1953, p.23A.

1757. ____, "Impressions and observations of the Journal man," *Oregon Journal*, Jan. 4, 1923, section 1:8, Jan. 5, 1923, section 1:8, Jan. 6, 1923, section 1:4.

1758. "London accuses business men," San Francisco *Call*, Dec. 10, 1906, p.3.

1759. "London and Kyne," Oakland *Tribune*, July 22, 1951, p.1C [by "The Knave"].

1760. "London at sea," *Sunset*, 19:400 (Aug. 1907).

1761. "London castle to be rebuilt," Santa Rosa *Press Democrat*, Nov. 16, 1916, p.7.

1762. "London honest and straight as a boy. Johnny Heinold mourns author friend," San Francisco *Chronicle*, Nov. 24, 1916, p.3.

1763. "London income $40,000 yearly from writings," San Francisco *Bulletin*, Nov. 23, 1916, p.7.

1764. "London lauded by socialists. High tribute paid dead writer by speakers at Oakland Memorial building," San Francisco *Examiner*, Dec. 11, 1916, p.7.

1765. "London makes a witty witness," Santa Rosa *Press Democrat*, Dec. 16, 1915, p.3.

1766. "London once newsboy for the *Enquirer*," Oakland *Enquirer*, Nov. 23, 1916, pp.1-2.

1767. "London partner of Santa Rosan," Santa Rosa *Press Democrat*, Nov. 10, 1916, p.8.

1768. "London returns from a duck hunt," Santa Rosa *Press Democrat*, Nov. 12, 1909, p.6.

1769. "London talks to collegians," San Francisco *Call*, Jan. 21, 1905, p.6 [Lecture account].

1770. "London talks to U. C. students," California Writers' Club. *Quarterly Bulletin*, 4:9 (Dec. 1916).

1771. "London to be cremated in Oakland," Oakland *Enquirer*, Nov. 23, 1916, pp.1-2.

1772. "London's body arrives for cremation," Oakland *Enquirer*, Nov. 24, 1916, p.1.

1773. "London's 'Burning daylight' at the Rose today," Santa Rosa *Press Democrat*, April 27, 1915, p.6.

1774. "London's early mentor gives warm praise," San Francisco *Bulletin*, Nov. 23, 1916, p.7.

1775. "London's feast for neighbors," Santa Rosa *Press Democrat*, Nov. 19, 1916, p.5.

1776. "London's first tales written at school," San Francisco *Examiner*, Dec. 3, 1916, p.2E [Reprints "Frisco kid's story," as part of article].

1777. "London's friends pay his memory final tribute," Reno *Gazette*, Nov. 24, 1916.

1778. "London's sealing sea wolf an outcast on the deep," San Francisco *Examiner*, June 15, 1905, pp.1-2.

1779. "London's wild harangue," Santa Rosa *Press Democrat*, Dec. 21, 1905, p.1.

1780. London, Charmian, "As I knew him," *Overland Monthly*, n.s. 85:360-361 (Dec. 1927).

1781. ____, "How Jack London would have ended 'Eyes of Asia'," *Cosmopolitan*, 77:78-79, 124, 126, 128, 130-131 (Oct.-1924).

1782. ____, "My husband - an old contributor," *Overland Monthly*, n.s. 90:106-107, 120 (May 1932).

1783. London, Joan, "Daughter defends Jack London books against Mussolini's ban. Il Duce declared afraid of views on freedom of individual enunciated in works of noted California writer, San Francisco *Chronicle* World Topics Section, Aug. 10, 1929, p.4F.

1784. ____, "Guest editorial," *The Rank and File* (Oakland), 3,1:1,3 (June 1962).

1785. London, John, "Jack London as a collectible author," *Amateur Book Collector*, 5:1-2 (Nov. 1954).

1786. Loughead, Flora Haines, "The call of the tame: an antithesis. The call of the wild: Buck, the St. Bernard, gently born at San Jose, answers the Call of the Wild and becomes leader of the Alaskan wolves. The Call of the Tame. Bones, the Mahlemiut, bred of the wolf in Alaska, answers the Call of the Tame and becomes a household pet at San Jose," San Francisco *Chronicle* Sunday Supplement, Dec. 4, 1904, p.3.

1787. "Love serves at London's bier. Simple rites mark sad hour. Tributes of living paid to dead," Oakland *Tribune*, Nov. 24, 1916, p.1.

1788. Lowf, George N., "Good-by, Jack London," San Francisco *Bulletin*, Nov. 24, 1916, p.8 [Verse].

1789. M. M., "Jack London," *Lone Hand*, Feb. 2, 1909, pp.366-371.

1790. Mackay, Mira, "The blood kin of London. Now there's another Jack London, a husky youngster, son of one of writer's daughters. Two daughters and the baby only descendants of novelist; light is shed on 'Dad' by girls," Oakland *Tribune* magazine section, Jan. 28, 1923, p.3,4.

1791. "Manuscripts of Jack London sold. Original copy purchased by H. E. Huntington," San Francisco *Chronicle*, April 16, 1925, p.7.

1792. "Many view ruins of London's castle," Santa Rosa *Press Democrat*, Aug. 26, 1913, p.2.

1793. "Martin Eden by Jack London. Rose Theatre," Santa Rosa *Press Democrat*, March 31, 1915, p.5.

1794. McConnell, T., "Ghost 'talks'. Conversations are in opposition to author's conception of after life while on earth," Oakland *Post-Enquirer*, April 4, 1922, pp.1-2.

1795. McDevitt, William, "Jack London's father's autobiography," *Hobbies*, 50:121, 128-129 (Feb. 1946).

1796. McDevitt, William, "London's first," San Francisco *Chronicle*, Oct. 23, 1954, p.16 (Letter).

1797. "Many tributes paid to London," Los Angeles *Times*, Nov. 23, 1916, p.1.

1798. Marshall, L. Rudio, "Mrs. Jack London's new viewpoint," *Overland Monthly*, n.s. 69:400-404 (May 1917).

1799. "'Martin Eden' on witness stand," Santa Rosa *Press Democrat*, Nov. 10, 1916, p.7.

1800. Mavity, Nancy Barr, "Jack London rare works discovered," Oakland *Tribune*, Nov. 28, 1932, p.3.

1801. Maynard, Mila Tupper, "Jack London's new word," Oakland *World*, Aug. 21, 1909, p.4.

1802. "Men and women of the outdoor world," *Outing*, 44:486-487 (July 1904).

1803. Metcalfe, Sadie Bowman, "A farewell shot," *Western World*, 2,1:30 (April 1907) [Poem to Jack London].

1804. Michelmore, Peter and Al Stump, "Wild life of the iron wolf," *True Magazine*, 43,299:123-137 (April 1962).

1805. Mighels, Ella Sterling, "The people's safety valve. Already honored in our 'Hall of Fame'," San Francisco *Chronicle*, Jan. 3, 1917, p.18 [Letter].

1806. Mikell, John, "Jack London--a writer for the working man," *People's World* (San Francisco), 11,269:5 (Nov. 18, 1948).

1807. Millard, Bailey, "Hard work made Jack London succeed--'Examiner' published his first story," San Francisco *Examiner*, Nov. 26, 1916, p.4N; reprinted as "Hard work ... succeed," California Writers' Club *Quarterly Bulletin*, 4,4:5-7 (Dec. 1916).

1808. ____, "Jack London, farmer," *Bookman*, 44:151-156 (1916).

1809. ____, "Jack London's promise comes true," Los Angeles *Times Sunday magazine*, May 20, 1934, pp.8,11.

1810. ____, "Jack London's Valley of the Moon ranch. What he is doing in worn-out hillside land," *Orchard and Farm*, 38,10:7-14 (Oct. 1916).

1811. ____, "Valley of the Moon ranch," *Overland Monthly*, n.s.

69:411-415 (May 1917).

1812. Miller, J. C., "Last trail," *Current Opinion*, 62:46-47 (Jan. 1917) [Verse].

1813. Mills, Gordon H., "American first editions at Texas University--VIII. Jack London (1876-1916)," *Library Chronicle*, 4:189-192 (1952).

1814. ____, "Jack London's quest for salvation," *American Quarterly*, 7:3-14 (Spring 1955).

1815. ____, "The symbolic wilderness: James Fenimore Cooper and Jack London," *Nineteenth-Century Fiction*, 13:329-340 (March 1959).

1816. "Moon Valley mourns for Jack London," San Francisco *Examiner*, Nov. 24, 1916, p.5.

1817. Moriarty, Tom, "If Jack London had lived," San Francisco *News Letter*, May 23, 1936, p.15; May 30, 1936, p.10.

1818. ____, "San Francisco sketches," San Francisco *News Letter*, July 23, 1937, p.4 [No. 1 in series is devoted to Jack London].

1819. "Mr. and Mrs. London to leave for Honolulu," Santa Rosa *Press Democrat*, Dec. 15, 1915, p.7.

1820. "Mrs. Jack London buys a big ranch," Santa Rosa *Press Democrat*, July 21, 1910, p.1.

1821. "Mrs. London's aunt lecturer's bride," Santa Rosa *Press Democrat*, Nov. 12, 1910, p.3.

1822. Mumford, Lewis, "Jack London," *New Republic*, 30:145-147 (March 29, 1922).

1823. Murphy, Celeste G., "Jack London's Valley of the Moon," *Overland Monthly*, n.s. 90,4:116-117,120 (May 1932).

1824. ____, "Library collected by Jack London," *Overland Monthly*, n.s. 90,4:111-112,120 (May 1932).

1825. "Nature man," *Letters*, 4,4:3-4 (April 1937), [A. C. Himley requests whereabouts of Ernest Darling whom London discovered on the cruise of the Snark.]

1826. Nethering, Richard, "A tribute to Jack London," Oakland *World*, Dec. 1, 1916, p.3 [Poem].

1827. "No rites for Jack London," San Francisco *Bulletin*, Nov. 23, 1916, p.1,7.

1828. North, Dick, "The influence of Jack London on literature," *Yukon News* (Whitehorse, Yukon), 6,16:12 (April 28, 1965).

1829. "Noted novelist here. Jack London, famous for his stories, en route to the park," Billings (Montana) *Gazette*, June 29, 1906, p.5.

1830. "Novel offer is made to London," Santa Rosa *Press Democrat*, May 3, 1913, p.7.

1831. "Novelist and former champion here," Santa Rosa *Press Democrat*, Sept. 3, 1910, p.3.

1832. "Novelist London said to be engaged now," Santa Rosa *Press Democrat*, June 9, 1905, p.7.
1833. "Novelists and cave-dwellers. Parallel passages in the stories by Stanley Waterloo and Jack London," *Argonaut*, 59,1552:285 (Dec. 8, 1906).
1834. O'Connor, J. E., "Great in mind - Great in heart," Santa Rosa *Press Democrat*, Nov. 25, 1916, p.8.
1835. "On the margin; report of a lecture," Oakland *Herald*, Oct. 31, 1906, p.6 [Lecture account].
1836. "The only man who matters," *Common Sense* (Los Angeles) May 4, 1907, p.3 [A comment on "The anarchist's mistake" (q.v.)].
1837. "Oriental servants grieve for London," San Francisco *Bulletin*, Nov. 25, 1916, p.4.
1838. "Our birthday greetings," *Daily Herald*, no. 622:16 (April 15, 1914) [Brief note from Mrs. London to this London paper].
1839. "Our national honor," New York *Call*, April 16, 1913, p.6.
1840. "Ovation at Harvard to Jack London, socialist," Boston *American*, Dec. 22, 1905, p.6.
1841. "Pacific personalities - a creator of Pacific literature (Jack London," *Mid-Pacific Magazine*, 2:291 (Sept. 1911).
1842. "Pacific personalities - The mate of the Snark (Mrs. Jack London)," *Mid-Pacific Magazine*, 3:289 (March 1912).
1843. "The Pan-Pacific Club of Honolulu," *Mid-Pacific Magazine*, 35:103-104 (Feb. 1928).
1844. Pardee, Mike, "Jack London Park will open soon. Visitors to see writer's collection," Santa Rosa *Press Democrat*, Jan. 31, 1960, pp.1E,4E.
1845. ____, "'Sailor on horseback' was conservationist, farmer," Santa Rosa *Press Democrat (Redwood Empire Magazine)*, March 29, 1953, pp.1,3-4.
1846. Payne, E. B., "The soul of Jack London," *Reason*, 25: 83-84 (May-July 1928).
1847. Pease, Frank, "Impressions of Jack London," *Seven Arts*, 1:522-530 (March 1917).
1848. Peltz, Hamilton, "Mexican policy great blunder," Philadelphia *Enquirer*, June 7, 1914, p.12 [Interview with Jack London].
1849. Perry, Stella George Stern, "A man has just passed by," San Francisco *Bulletin*, Nov. 24, 1916, p.8 [Verse].
1850. Peterson, Clell T., "The Jack London legend," *American Book Collector*, 8,5:13-17 (Jan. 1958).
1851. ____, "Jack London's Alaskan stories," *American Book Collector*, 9,8:15-22 (April 1959).
1852. ____, "Jack London's Sonoma novels," *American Book Collector*, 9,2:15-20 (Oct. 1958).
1853. Pingree, Dorothy, "London park dedicated at impressive

rites," Santa Rosa *Press Democrat*, Sept. 20, 1960, p.5.
1854. "Placing Jack London's books under the ban," *Arena*, 35:435 (April 1906).
1855. "Pledge made to London is kept," San Francisco *Chronicle*, Nov. 23, 1916, p.1.
1856. Prentice, J. H., "Jack London," *Overland Monthly*, n.s. 83:41 (Jan. 1925).
1857. "Preparatory to playing the title role in a screen production of *Martin Eden*, Glenn Ford visits the house of Jack London," Seattle Sunday *Times* rotogravure, Feb. 22, 1942, p.7 [9 illustrations].
1858. "President versus nature .fakir. A wordy war is waged over the accuracy of animal stories," *Argonaut*, 60, 1578:728 (June 8, 1907) [*White Fang* is among novels discussed].
1859. "The quick and the dead," *Independent*, 60:521-523 (March 1, 1906).
1860. "Ranchers laugh at London's pig palace," Santa Rosa *Press Democrat*, Oct. 27, 1915, p.6.
1861. "Real Jack London as revealed in Hawaii," *Current Opinion*, 62:23 (Jan. 1917).
1862. Reimers, Johannes, "Jack London's career affects his writings," Stockton *Evening Mail*, Oct. 15, 1903, p.4.
1863. "Relatives to scatter London's ashes today," San Francisco *Examiner*, Nov. 26, 1916, p.1.
1864. "Reported engagement of Miss Blanche Bates. Rumor says she will marry Jack London, the author," Oakland *Tribune*, Jan. 27, 1905, p.1.
1865. "Reviewers notebook," *Freeman*, 4:407 (Jan. 4, 1922).
1866. Risdon, Hal, "Jack London lived there: eight Oakland houses where author once stayed still stand," Oakland *Tribune* (0).
1867. "The rising tide of revolution. Jack London the Moyer-Haywood outrage," *Socialist Voice*, March 24, 1906, p.1 [Lecture account].
1868. Rogers, Cameron, "Jack London rough and tumble genius of letters," *The Mast Magazine*, 3,2:9 (February 1946).
1869. Romm, Charles, "Jack London, a bibliographical checklist, 1876-1916," *Publishers' Weekly*, 103:1021 (Feb. 4, 1923).
1870. "Roosevelt elects Jack London to Ananias Club," San Francisco *Examiner* (Oakland edition), May 21, 1907, p.1.
1871. R. S. P., "'Jack' or 'John' London," *Argonaut*, 55, 1428:51 (July 25, 1904) [Reply to comment by W. L. Alden, *Argonaut*, 55,1425:9 (July 4, 1904)].
1872. "Ruskin Club has an outing at Glen Ellen," Santa Rosa *Press Democrat*, May 19, 1905, p.7.
1873. Russack, Martin, "Jack London, America's first prole-

Courtesy of the Oakland Public Library

Residence in Oakland, California, 1898-1900.
See Item 1866

tarian writer," *New Masses,* 22:13 (Jan 4, 1929).

1874. Russell, Ernest, "Singular similarity of a story written by Jack London and one printed four years before
a new literary puzzle. Californian writer deals with
the same theme and geographical surroundings as Augus-
tus Bridle and J. K. MacDonald treated - to make the
coincidence stranger both stories were published in the
same magazine. Striking similarity of phrase found in
'Love of life' and 'Lost in the land of the midnight
sun'; both tell of the sufferings of a prospector with
a sprained ankle, deserted in the wilderness and when
at the point of death, saved by chance," New York *World,*
March 25, 1906, editorial section, p.[?]. [Parallel
passages show similarities between two works.]

1875. Rutland, A., "The novel of the open air," *Bookman,* 60:
9-15 (April 1921).

1876. "Says Jack London is plagiarist," San Francisco *Call,*
Oct. 19, 1906, p.15. [Statement made by J. T. Bramhall,
one of the executive officers of the Chicago Press
Club.]

1877. "Scenes in the life of Jack London, who died too young,"
Santa Rosa *Press Democrat,* Dec. 9, 1916, p.2.

1878. "School in memory of Jack London opened," San Francisco
Chronicle, Feb. 14, 1917, p.12.

1879. Scott, Harvey, J., "The Valley of the Moon," *Roycrofter,*
4,5:152 (March 1930).

1880. "'The Seawolf': Thomas Austin Ross, prototype of Wolf
Larsen dies," *Marine Digest,* 36,50:27 (Aug. 1958).

1881. Seelye, John D., "The American tramp: a version of the
picaresque," *American Quarterly,* 14:535-553 (1963).

1882. "Senile Sibley spouts socialism in Congress. Some wild
lying about Jack London,," *Socialist Voice,* Feb. 17,
1906, p.1.

1883. Sheehan, June, "Oakland High proud to claim Jack London," Oakland *Tribune,* April 4, 1943, p.8S.

1884. Shields, Art, "I remember Jack London," *People's World*
(San Francisco), 19,233:10 (Nov. 30, 1956).

1885. Shinn, C. H., "Our boy man novelist," Fresno *Republican,*
May 7, 1916, p.16.

1886. Shivers, Alfred S., "The demoniacs in Jack London,"
American Book Collector, 12,1:11-14 (Sept. 1961).

1887. ____, "Jack London in search of a biographer," *American
Book Collector,* 12,7:25-27 (March 1962).

1888. ____, "Jack London's mate-women," *American Book Collect-
or,* 15,2:17-21 (Oct. 1964).

1889. ____, "The romantic in Jack London: far away frozen
wilderness," *Alaska Review,* 1,1:38-47 (Winter 1963).

1890. Silver, G. V., "Jack London's women," *Overland Monthly,* n.s. 74:24-28 (July 1919).

1891. Sinclair, Upton, "About Jack London," *Masses*, 9:17-20 (Nov.-Dec. 1917).

1892. ____, "The call of the wild. Jack London put an 'If' on the condemned constitution," New York *Times*, Feb. 5, 1906, p.8 [Letter].

1893. ____, "Is this Jack London?" *Occult Review*, 52:394-400 (1930); 53:10-14 (1931).

1894. ____, "The interesting career of Jack London," Oakland *World*, Dec. 1, 1916, p.3.

1895. ____, "London's work 'Bugle call' to the soul," San Francisco *Bulletin*, Nov. 23, 1916, p.7.

1896. ____, "Memories of Jack London," *Labor World* (San Francisco), May 1925, pp.10-11.

1897. ____, "A sad loss to American literature," California Writers' Club. *Quarterly Bulletin*, 4:3-4 (Dec. 1916); Oakland *Tribune*, Nov. 23, 1916, p.13.

1898. [Sketch] *California Alumni Weekly*, 6,26:1 (March 21, 1914).

1899. [Sketch] *Publishers' Circular*, 79:265 (Sept. 19, 1903).

1900. Sloan, Bessie, I., "At Jack London's home, April twenty-second, 1917," California Writers' Club *Monthly Bulletin*, 1:7 (May 1917) [Poem].

1901. "Socialism and its relation to 'scabs'," San Francisco *Call*, Dec. 19, 1904, p.7 [Lecture account].

1902. "Socialists to hold memorial for London," Oakland *Tribune*, Dec. 8, 1916, p.11.

1903. "Society discovers Jack London's socialism," *Appeal to Reason*, April 22, 1905, p.6.

1904. "Special administrators in the estate of Jack London," Santa Rosa *Press Democrat*, Dec. 2, 1916, p.2.

1905. Sprague, Roger, "Contrast as a device: description of coronation day in London," *Saturday Review of Literature*, 6:320 (Oct. 26, 1929).

1906. Stannard, Russell, "The ranch kid," *John O'London's*, 8:774 (March 3, 1923)[Interview with Charmian London].

1907. Stellman. L. J., "Jack London - the man," *Overland Monthly*, n.s. 70:385-387 (Oct. 1917).

1908. ____, "Jack London, super-boy," *Sunset*, 38:42, 81 (Feb. 1917).

1909. Sterling, George, "George Sterling in high tribute to Jack London," San Francisco *Examiner*, Nov. 27, 1916, p.3.

1910. ____, "Jack London's remains consigned to mother earth," Santa Rosa *Press Democrat*, Nov. 28, 1916, p.5.

1911. ____, "To Jack London: poem," *Overland Monthly*, n.s. 69:360 (May 1917); California Writers' Club. *Quarterly Bulletin*, 4:1 (Dec. 1916) as "Farewell, farewell!"; San Francisco *Examiner*, Nov. 25, 1916, p.5

["George Sterling pays high tribute to Jack London"].

1912. "Sterling's tribute to Jack London," California
Writers' Club. *Quarterly Bulletin* 4:7 (Dec. 1916).

1913. Stoy, E., "Personality of Jack London," *Wasp*, 74:1,
14 (Dec. 2, 1916).

1914. Stringer, Arthur, "The Canada of the ink-wells," New
York *Herald* magazine section, Oct. 18, 1908, p.2.
Section entitled: "Jack London's artistic liberties".

1915. Strunsky, Anna, "Memories of Jack London," *The Bowery
News* (N. Y.), no. 69:8-9 [undated: early June 1962.
Contains selections from 6 Jack London letters].

1916. Sutton, Horace, "Jack London's home draws crowds now,"
Nashville *Tennessean*, June 21, 1964, p.2F.

1917. Swankey, Ben, "Jack London--working class rebel," *The
Dispatcher*, 19,1:6-7 (Jan. 13, 1961).

1918. "Text of Jack London's will as written by himself,"
Santa Rosa *Press Democrat*, Dec. 2, 1916, p.3.

1919. "They all wear red to hear Jack London," New York *Times*,
Jan. 20, 1906, p.2.

1920. Thomas, Homer, "If Jack London came back?," Oakland
Tribune, May 28, 1922, magazine section, p.3,11.

1921. ____, "Jack London life novel stirs row. Friends of
Oakland author attack story that scores in East," Oakland *Post Enquirer*, magazine section, March 28, 1925,
p.1 [Comment on Rose Wilder Lane's *He was a man*].

1922. "Tireless romancer," *Current Opinion*, 54:490-491
(June 1913).

1923. Toothaker, Charles R., *"The star rover* and Daniel Foss's
oar," *Papers of the Bibliographical Society of America*,
44:182-185 (1950).

1924. Treadwell, Sophie, "Jack London scores brutality of
capitalist system. 'Am I still a socialist? You bet,'
famous novelist tells Frisco paper," *Appeal to reason*,
March 21, 1914, p.2 [Interview reprinted from San Francisco *Bulletin*].

1925. Tridon, André, "The curse of sociability," *New Review*,
1:916-918 (Nov. 1913) [Discusses reasons why author
thinks that London drank so heavily].

1926. Trimble, A. G., "Jack London, a significant San Fran-
ciscan," *Red Funnel* (New Zealand), Nov. 1, 1908, pp.
407-417.

1927. "The truth will burn," *Socialist Voice*, Dec. 16, 1905,
p.1 [Comment from *Common Sense* on rumor that *Collier's*
will publish "Revolution"].

1928. Tully, Jim, "The baffled greatness of Jack London,"
International Book Review, 1:18 (June 1923).

1929. ____, "The failure of Jack London," *Story World and
Photo-dramatist*, 6,8:11-12, 28 (Feb. 1925).

1930. "Upton Sinclair pays tribute to London," San Francisco *Chronicle,* Nov. 24, 1916, p.3.
1931. "Urge library and school to honor London," San Francisco *Bulletin,* Dec. 12, 1916, p.7.
1932. "Valdon," "Mr. Jack London," *Australian Photographic Journal,* March 20, 1909, pp.70-74.
1933. Valentry, Duana, "The slugger of the seven seas," *Listen,* 13, 3:25 (May-June 1960).
1934. "'Valley of the moon' made in this country," Santa Rosa *Press Democrat,* March 6, 1915, p.6.
1935. Viereck, George S., "The ghost of Jack London," *Liberty,* 8:15-18 (Oct. 10, 1931).
1936. "Virtue and consistency," *Bookman,* 25:228-231 (May 1907).
1937. Walcott, Charles C., "Naturalism and the superman in the novels of Jack London." *Papers of the Michigan Academy of Sciences, Arts & Letters,* 24:89-107 (Part IV, 1938).
1938. Walker, Franklin, "Jack London's use of Sinclair Lewis plots, together with a printing of three of the plots," *Huntington Library Quarterly,* 17:59-74 (Nov. 1953).
1939. Wallace, James, "The *Aegis* published Jack London's first stories. Was student here in 1895. Genius shown in earliest works of great novelist," Weekly *Aegis,* Dec. 8, 1916 (0).
1940. Walling, Anna Strunsky, "The meaning of Jack London," New York *Call Magazine,* Nov. 28, 1920, pp.3-4.
1941. ____, "Memoirs of Jack London," *Masses,* 9:13-17 (July 1917).
1942. Wanhope, Joshua, "In memoriam: Jack London," New York *Call,* Nov. 24, 1916, editorial page.
1943. "Was Martin Eden Jack London?" Oakland *World,* Dec. 1, 1916, p.4.
1944. "We entertain an international visitor. A San Francisco bookstore made famous in Berlin," *Biblio-ana,* 3,1:6-7 (Jan. 1931) [Contains a portion of a letter from a book published by Erich Reiss, Berlin, 1930. The letter discusses some of London's early work].
1945. "We found Jack London's cabin," *Yukon News,* 6,16:8-18 (April 28, 1965).
1946. Weaver, S. Alice, "Among the ruins of the big house: the Jack London ranch," Los Angeles *Times, Illustrated weekly magazine,* April 21, 1917, p.14.
1947. Wells, Bob, "State opens new area of famed London home," Santa Rosa *Press Democrat,* Jan. 5, 1964, pp.1E,6E.
1948. "What manner of man Jack London is," New York *World,* March 25, 1906, editorial section.
1949. Whitaker, Herman, "Retrospection," California Writers' Club. *Monthly Bulletin,* 1:3 (April 1917) [Reminiscences

of twenty-three years of intimate friendship with Jack
London. Presented at the Memorial meeting for Jack London held at Hotel Oakland, March 6, 1917].

1950. Whipple, T. K., "Jack London - wonder boy," *Saturday
Review of Literature*, 18:3-4,16-17 (Sept. 24, 1938).

1951. Wickson, Edward James, "Jack London's legacy," *Pacific
rural press*, 92:2 (Dec. 2, 1916); California Writers'
Club. *Quarterly Bulletin*, 4:8-9 (Dec. 1916).

1952. Williams, P. S., "Jack London, lecturer," *Overland
Monthly*, n.s. 48:247-250 (Oct. 1906).

1953. Wilson, Nell Griffith, "Adventuring" (in memory of Jack
London), *Overland Monthly*, n.s. 90:120 (May 1932)
[Verse]; Oakland *Tribune*, Feb. 26, 1934 (0).

1954. ____, "In memory of Jack London," *Overland Monthly*,
n.s. 90:102 (May 1932).

1955. Wilstach, John, "The man who inspired Jack London,"
Ghost Town News, 4:27 (Oct. 1944) [Concerning Ed
Morrell and *The star rover*].

1956. ____, "Ed Morrell: 'The star rover'," *Famous Fantastic
Mysteries*, 8,6:119-120 (Aug. 1947) [Brief discussion of
London and *The Star rover*].

1957. Wingfield, William, "Jack London's forlorn dream," *The
West*, 5,2:10-13, 49-50 (July, 1966).

1958. Wolfe, Frank E., "Jack London," *Western Comrade*, 4:21
(Dec. 1916).

1959. Woodbridge, Hensley C., "Variants in the American and
English editions of the *War of the classes* by Jack London," *American Book Collector*, 12,3:43-44 (Nov. 1961).

1960. Woodward, Robert H., "Jack London's code of primitiv-
ism," *Folio*, 18:39-44 (May 1953).

1961. ____, "Jack London's lost poem," *Mark Twain Journal*,
12,3:6-7 (Winter 1964-1965) [text of poems given].

1962. Worden, Perry, "Some recollections of Jack London:
chats with the developing author," Los Angeles *Times
illustrated weekly magazine*, Dec. 2, 1916, pp.9,31.

1963. "World expresses sorrow at Jack London's death," Santa
Rosa *Press Democrat*, Nov. 24, 1916, p.8.

1965. "Writer deserts 7-year world cruise," San Francisco
Examiner, Jan. 26, 1908, p.39 [Interview].

1966. "Writer was sought by publishers," Oakland *Tribune*, 2nd
section, Nov. 23, 1916, p.13.

1967. "Writers will honor London," Oakland *Tribune*, Feb. 13,
1931, p.10.

1968. "A young man of promise," Los Angeles *Times illustrated
weekly magazine*, May 20, 1900, p.14.

Errata:
1969. "Jack London's latest lecture," *Socialist Voice*,

March 31, 1906, p.1 [Lecture account].

1969a. "One of Jack London's fine horses that will be shown at the district fair" [Illustration caption], Santa Rosa *Press Democrat*, Aug. 5, 1916, p.6.

FOREIGN WRITINGS ABOUT JACK LONDON

Items in this section are arranged alphabetically by language. Within each language, items are arranged first by books, second by parts of books, and third by periodical articles and newspapers. Each of these sections, where they appear, are separated by spaces.

CZECH/SLOVAK

1970. Boor, Ján, "Jack London," *O západných realistoch*, Bratislava, Slov. spisovatel, 1954, pp.67-88.

1971. "Khunové bratří: Před 30. lety zemřel Jack London," *Lidová kultura*, 40:2 (1946).

1972. Moravec, Jaroslav, "Jack London a něco o sociologii propasti," *Kmen*, 4:535-537 (1920-21).

1973. Peluso, Edmondo, "Vzpomínky na Jacka Londona," *Tvorba*, 10:156,171,188,198,218 (1935).

1974. "Proč vystoupil Jack London z americké sociální demodracie?" *Tvorba*, 4:245 (1929).

1975. Štastný, Al. J., "Jack London 1876-1916 (Literární medailon)," *Literární noviny*, 33:6 (1955).

1976. _____, "Veliký básník Ameriky," *Rudé právo*, Nov. 1, 1956. Veselý, P., "80. výročí Jacka Londona," *Obrana lidu*, Dec. 1, 1956.

DANISH

1977. Ewald, Jesper, *Jack London - En biografi*, Copenhagen, Martin's Forlag, 1917, 62pp. [Portrait of London on outside wrapper, bound in paper wrappers].

1978. Grønlund, H., *Pan hat med Jack London*, Copenhagen, Carl Allers Bogforlag, 1944, 204pp.

1979. Kornerup, Ebbe, *Jack Sømand*, Copenhagen, Martin's Forlag, 1957, 85pp.

1980. Vedde, Sigurd, *Jack London! Introduktion til et Forfatterskab*, Copenhagen, Ejnar Munksgaard, 1943, 140pp.

1981. Schyberg, Frederick, *Moderne amerikansk litteratur 1900-1930*, Copenhagen, Gyldendal, 1930, pp.29-32.

1982. Hansen, H. P. E., "Jack London og Nietzsches Filosofi," *Atlantis. Dansk Maanedsskrift*, 2:49-57 (1924).

1983. Thomsen, Niels Th., "Jack London," *Gads Danske Magasin*, 17:133-138 (1923).

DUTCH

1984. *Boekenschouw*, 10:252-253 (1916-1917)[Obituary].

1985. Houwaard, C., "De laatste dagen van Jack London," *Nu*,

1:434-442 (1928).
1986. Otten, J. F., "Jack London," *Haagsch Maandblad*, 15:53-66 (1931).
1987. Sinclair, Upton, "Jack London," *De Amsterdammer*, March 24, 1917, p.3, March 31, 1917, p.3 [Probably a translation of Sinclair interview at London's death].

ESTONIAN

1988. "Jack London,", in *Armastus elu vastu*, Tallinn, 1950, pp.199-200.
1989. ____, in *Poksija Tom King*, Tartu, 1929, pp.3-4.
1990. ____, in *Raudne kand*, Tallinn, 1955, pp.259-265.
1991. ____, in *Valge-Kihv*, Tallinn, 1923, pp.3-4.
1992. Pärn, A., in J. London, *Elu seadus*, Tartu-Tallinn, 1936, pp.5-6.
1993. Pervik, A., in J. London, *Valgekihv*, Tallinn, 1956, pp.207-209.
1994. Roskin, A. "Jack London," in J. London, *Mehhiklane*, Tallinn, 1941, pp.37-38.
1995. Variste, J., "Jack London," in J. London, *Merehunt*, Tartu, 1936, pp.318-320.

1996. "Ameerika suurim seikleja... 20 aastat Jack Londoni surmast," *Vaba Maa*, Nov. 20, 1936 pp.[?] (America's greatest adventurer... 20 years since the death of Jack London).
1997. Brandis, E., "Jack London. (Tema 75. sünniaastapäevaks)," *Õhtuleht*, Jan. 12, 1951 pp.[?] (Jack London. For his 75th birthday).
1998. Hubel, E., "Jack London," *Tallinna Teataja*, Nov. 15, 1916, pp.[?].
1999. "Jack London," *Sakala*, Nov. 18, 1916, pp.[?].
2000. "Jack London on Hitlerile ohtlik," *Noorte Hääl*, July 20, 1941, pp.[?] (Jack London is dangerous to Hitler).
2001. "Jack Londoni soomlasest seltsimees," *Kunst ja Kirjandus*, no. 38:152 (1936) (Jack London's Finnish comrade).
2002. "Kirjanik, kes elas ise oma romaane," *Postimees*, Nov. 26, 1927, pp.[?] (The writer who lived his own novels).
2003. Kits, M., "Oled sa võlgu Felipe Riverale?" *Noorus*, no. 2:1-4 (1958) [Are you indebted to Felipe Rivera?].
2004. Kutšerjavenko, V., "Jack Londoni kodukohas. Kirjaniku 80. sünniaastapäeva puhul," *Noorte Hääl*, Jan. 12, 1956, pp.[?] (In the birthplace of Jack London. For the writer's 80th birthday).
2005. Mägi, J., "Uue ilma geenius," *Aasta*, 6:53-62 (1917) (The genius of the new world).
2006. Olden, B., "Hulkur jumala armust," *Noorusmaa*, no. 15:

326-329 (1927) (A tramp by the grace of God). [This article and the Estonian translation of "The heathen" are commented upon in *Eesti Kirjandus*, no. 3:149-153 (1930) by A. Vaigla.]

2007. "Püsivuse ja raudse tahtega. 80 aastat Jack Londoni sünnist," *Säde*, Jan. 11, 1956, pp.[?] (By persistency and iron will. 80 years since the birth of Jack London).

2008. "Tema reaamatute kangelaseks on rahbas," *Rahva Hääl*, Jan. 12, 1961, pp.[?] (The hero of his books is the people).

2009. Vesley, A., "Jack London," *Ronk*, no. 2:36-38, no. 3: 62-64 (1925).

FRENCH

2010. Cahen, Jacques-Fernand, *La littérature américaine*, Paris, Presses universitaires de France, 1964, pp.52, 62,65-66.

2011. Lefèvre, Frédéric, "Une heure avec Mme. Jack London," in *Une heure avec* ..., *première série*, Paris, Editions de la Nouvelle revue française, 1924, pp.203-210.

2012. Michaud, Régis, "Jack London, un romancier de l'énergie américaine," in *Mystiques et réalistes anglo-saxons, d'Emerson à Bernard Shaw*, Paris, Libraire Armand Colin, 1918, pp.167-196.

2013. Simon, Jean, *Le roman américain au xxe siècle*, Paris, Boivin, 1950, pp.41-43.

2014. Dutourd, Jean, "Du chien en littérature: Jack London," *Nouvelles littéraires*, March 18, 1965, p.6.

2015. Geismar, Maxwell, "Le drame de Jack London," *Temps modernes*, 9:909-925, 1104-1122, 1301-1334 (1953-1954).

2016. Lefèvre, Frédéric, "Visite à Madame Jack London," *Nouvelles littéraires*, April 21, 1923, pp.1-2.

2017. London, Charmian, "La jeunesse de Jack London," *Revue de Paris*, 34:114-139 (May 1927).

2018. Perrin, E. Sainte-Marie, "Jack London: un romancier californien," *Revue des deux mondes*, 92:171-191 (Sept. 1, 1922).

GERMAN

2019. *Bedeutende Werke der Weltliteratur*. Lehrbrief 8. *Jack London: Martin Eden*, Berlin, Deutscher Verlag d. Wissenschaften, 1956 [?]pp. (Karl-Marx-Universität Leipzig, Fakultät für Journalistik. Lehrbrief f. d. Fernstudium).

2020. Bracher, Hans, *Jack London. Schicksal und Werk eines genialen Abenteurers*, Bern, Schweizerischer Verein Abstinenter Lehrer und Lehrerinnen, 1951, 51pp.

2021. *Jack London*, Mecklenburg, Freie Dt. Jugend, 1947, 20pp. (FDJ. Unser Heimabend. Heft 3).

2022. Jung, Franz, ed., *Jack London: ein Dichter der Arbeiterklasse*, Vienna, *Verlag für Literatur und Politik*, 1924, 143pp. Contents: Vorwort, Die Gesellschaftsschichtung in Amerika. Die soziale Literatur in Amerika. Wie Jack London wurde. Wie Jack London Sozialist wurde. Und was das Leben ihm gab. Jack London ringt sich durch. Jack London. der Liebling des Lesepublikums. Jack London, der Sozialist. Jack London als Kamerad und als Mensch an der Schwelle einer neuen Zeit. Zusammenfassender Ruckblick auf Jack Londons Schriften. Aus den *Menschen des Agrunds:* Daniel Cullen. Der Tag der englischen Königskronung. Eine Nacht und ein Morgen. Aus der *Eisernen Ferse:* Mathematik eines Traums. Aus *Klassenkampf:* Eigenes Vorwort zu Jack Londons sozialistischen Schriften. Aus *Revolution:* Revolution. Aus *The strength of the strong:* Deb's Traum. Bibliografie der Werke von Jack London.

2023. Margolin, Klara, *Jack London's short stories: ihre Form und ihr Gehalt*, Kaunas, Bakas, 1927, 100pp.

2024. Rentmeister, Heinrich, *Jack London. Ein Einzelgänger wider Willen*, Halle, Verlag Sprache und Literatur, 1962, 120pp. (Wege zur Literatur. Monographien, 14).

2025. Rentmeister, Heinz, *Das Weltbild Jack Londons*, Halle, Niemeyer, 1960, 256pp. The main divisions of this work are: Jack London und sein Werk in Spiegel der Kritik. Die sozialen und ideologischen Wurzeln der Weltanschauung Jack London. Das biologistische Weltbild Jack Londons. Jack Londons Flucht in den Individualismus.

2026. Stadlmann, Ingeborg, *Jack London: Weltanschauung, schriftstellerisches Wirken und Romantechnik*, University of Vienna, 1935, 155pp.

2027. Tschörtner, Heinz Dieter, *Zur See und im Sattel. Jack London, 1876-1916*, Halle, Bezirksbibliothek, Abt. Ausleihe und Literaturpropaganda, 1955, 7pp.

2028. Bronner, Augusta, *Amerikanische Literatur-Geschichte*, Vienna, Amandus, 1946, pp.56-57.

2029. Friederich, W. P., *"Götter und Proletarier: Jack London,"* in *Werden und Wachsen der USA in drei Jahrhunderten*, Bern, 10/39, pp.178-192.

2030. Lenmartz, Franz, "Jack London," in *Ausländische Dichter und Schriftsteller unserer Zeit*, Stuttgart, Kröner, 1955, pp.381-385.

2031. Neubauer, Heinz, *Amerikanische Goldgräberliteratur (Bret Harte, Mark Twain, Jack London)*, Ernst-Moritz-Arndt-Universität zu Grefswald, 1936, pp.31-47.

2032. Rakousky, Hans, "Der Sohn des Wolfs," pp.284-285; "In
      den Wäldern des Nordens," pp.285-287; "Wenn die Natur
      ruft," pp.287-288; "Der Seewolf," pp.288-289; "Wolfs-
      blut," pp.289-290; "Die eiserne Ferse," pp.290-291;
      "Abenteurer des Schienenstranges," pp.291-292; "Martin
      Eden," pp.292-294; "Lockruf des Goldes," p.294; "Süds-
      gegeschichten," pp.295-296; "Alaska Kid," p.296; "Kid
      & Co.," p.297; "Das Mondtal," pp.297-298; "Ein Sohn der
      Sonne," pp.298-299; "Meuterei auf der Elsinore," p.300;
      "Jerry der Insulaner," pp.300-301; "Michael, der Bruder
      Jerrys," pp. 302-303 in *Der Romanfuhrer* ... edited by
      Wilhelm Olbrich und Johannes Beer ..., Stuttgart, Anton
      Hiersemann, 1956, vol. 7.
2033. Strasser, Charlot, *Vier neue amerikanische Dichter:
      Jack London, Upton Sinclair, Sinclair Lewis, B. Traven*,
      Zürich, Schweizerischer Verband des Personals der
      öffentlichen Dienste, 1929, 154pp.
2034. Victor, Walter, "Zwischen Himmel und Hölle. Jack London
      - der Roman eines Lebens," in *Das grosse Abenteuer*,
      Zürich, Scheuch, 1937, vol. 1., [?]pp.

2035. "Abenteurer - Künstler - Mensch," *Büchergilde* (Frank-
      fort/Mainz), 1-2:10 (1949).
2036. Arns, Karl, "Jack London," *Der Gral*, 23:814-816 (1929).
2037. "Aus dem Leben Jack Londons," *Der enthaltsame Erzieher*
      (Hamburg), 48:10-13 (1957).
2038. Behl, C. F. W., "Jack London," *Gegenwart* (Berlin) 54:
      10 (1925).
2039. Beierle, Alfred, "Wir ich Jack London erlebte," *Roland
      von Berlin*, no. 28:11 (1949).
2040. Bykov, Wil, "Auf Jack Londons Spuren," *Sowjetliteratur*
      (Moscow), no. 4:152-162 (1960).
2041. Cohn, Alfons F., "Jack London," *Die Glocke*, 10:1213-
      1217 (1924).
2042. Degen, Gert, "Abenteurer von Geblüt," *Germania*, 1936:
      325.
2043. Fedunow, P., "Jack London entlarvt die bürgerliche Ziv-
      ilisation," *Sowjetliteratur*, no. 11:171-180 (1951).
2044. Franzen, E., "Wie erklären sich grosse Bucherfolge?
      (Jack London)," *Frankfurter Zeitung*, April 12, 1931,
      p.6.
2045. Georg, M., "Jack London Selbstbiographie Martin Eden,"
      Badische Presse (Karlsruhe), Jan. 25, 1928, p.15 of the
      Literarische Umschau.
2046. Gross, K., "Die Verwertung der Eidetik als Kunstmittel
      in Jack Londons Roman Martin Eden," *Zeitschrift für
      angewandte Psychologie*, 33:417-438 (1929).
2047. Hermann-Neisse, Max, "Ein Dichter der Arbeiterklasse,"

Die Aktion, 14:471 (1924).

2048. Hoyer, W., "Noch ein Wort über Jack London," *Hefte für Buchereiwesen* (Leipzig), 13:231 (1929).
2049. Hulsenbeck, R., "Jack London - der Dichter Amerikas," *Die literarische Welt,* no. 47:3 (1926).
2050. Huggler, E. H., "Jack London," *Neue Zürcher Zeitung,* Literarische Beilage, no. 72, section 3, pp.[?] (Jan. 15, 1928).
2051. Jensen, Johannes V., "Der soziale Roman in Amerika," *Die neue Rundschau,* 26:680-683 (1915).
2052. Kaemmerling, K., "Jack London," *Welt und Wort* (Wörishofen), 1947:39-43.
2053. Klasing, R., "Ein Shakespeare der Prosa. Jack London und sein Lebensroman," *Schauen und Schaffen* (Leipzig), 54,4:10 (1928).
2054. Köhler, Willi, "Tramp, Seemann und Schriftsteller. Zum 85. Geburtstag von Jack London am 12. Januar," *Neues Deutschland,* Jan. 11, 1961, p.4.
2055. "Jack London," *Der freie Bauer* (Berlin), 2,2:9 (1947).
2056. "Jack London. Ein Sohn der Arbeiterklasse," *Ost und West* (Berlin), 3,4:45-52 (1949).
2057. "Jack London und sein Werk," *München-Augusburger Abendzeitung,* no. 188:4 (July 14, 1929).
2058. "Jack London. Vagabund und Schriftsteller," *Jugend-Telegraf* (Berlin), no. 1:2 (1949).
2059. Lukas, Horst W., "Jack London - ein Ankläger gegen die alte Welt. Zum 77. Geburtstag des grossen realistischen Erzählers," *Junge Welt* (Berlin), Jan. 11, 1953, p.4.
2060. Marcu, Valerio, "Jack London, der Optimist dem Elend," *Berliner Börsencourier,* no. 299 (1925).
2061. Meidinger-Geise, J., "Zwischen Philosophie und Urlust," *Die Erlanger Universität* (Bamberg), 1:274-276 (1947).
2062. Naser, G., "Spannende Abenteuer und bittere Wirklichkeit. Zum 40 Todestag von Jack London," *Der Morgen* (Berlin), no. 275 (Nov. 24, 1956).
2063. Offenburg, Karl, "Jack London, der Mann und das Werk," *Deutsche Republik* (Berlin-Frankfurt), 2:84-88 (1923).
2064. Petry, Walter, "Jack London, sein Leben und sein Werk," *Magdeburger Zeitung,* no. 594 (1926).
2065. Poritzky, J. E., "Jack London oder das Übermass der Anerkennung," *Das literarische Echo* (Stuttgart), 30:84-88 (1927).
2066. Rainalter, E. H., "Drei englische Dichter: London, Conrad, Galsworthy," *Kölnische Volkszeitung: Literarische Beilage,* no. 186 (1929).
2067. Recknagel, Rolf, "An der Schwelle zu unserer Zeit. Zum tragischen Weg Jack Londons," *Nation* (Berlin), 7:490-507 (1959).

2068. ___, "Jack London - Individualist oder Revolutionär?
Mit Literatur-Angaben," *Forum*, no. 5 (Feb. 1, 1962),
Wissenschaftliche Beilage, 8pp.

2069. Reifferscheidt, F. M., "Jack London," *Hochland* (Munich),
25,2:329-332 (1927).

2070. Richter, Helene, "Jack London," *Radio* (Vienna), 3:51
(1927).

2071. Scheffauer, H. G., "Der Schriftsteller Jack London,"
Karl May Jahrbuch, (Radebeul), 12:319-340 (1929).

2072. Schroeder, Karl, "Jack Londons Grenzen," *Arbeiter-
jugend*, 20,1:22-23 (1928).

2073. Schubert, Renate, "Eine Jack-London-Auswahlbiblio-
graphie," *Zeitschrift für Anglistik und Amerikanistik*,
12:94-108,439-444 (1964).

2074. Schulz, F. O. H., "Jack London, Amerikanische Dichter-
profile," *Prager Illustrierte Wochenschau*, 6,4:8 (1944).

2075. ___, "Vagabund von Gottes Gnaden," *Deutsche Zeitung in
den Niederlanden* (Amsterdam), Aug. 14, 1943, p.3.

2076. Schultz-Ewerth, E., "Weihnachten als 'Schiffbrüchiger'
in der Südsee. Mit 'Jack London' auf der 'Snark',"
Schwäbischer Merkur (Stuttgart), Dec. 25, 1931, pp.[?].

2077. "Seine Feder schrieb für den Fortschritt. Zum 80.
Geburtstag Jack Londons," *Der Morgen* (Berlin), 12,10:
Beiblatt (Jan. 12, 1956).

2078. Siemsen, Anna, "Jack London," *Urania* (Jena), 4:80-81
(1927-1928).

2079. Silberberg, Margarete, "Jack London heute," *Der Volks-
bibliothekar* (Berlin), 3:35-39 (1949); also printed in
Börsenblatt für den deutschen Buchhandel (Leipzig),
116,27:221-222 (1949).

2080. Sinclair, Upton, "Jack London," *Das Tagebuch*, 6:601-606
1923).

2081. ___, "Jack London," *Dichtung und Welt. Beil. zur
"Prager Presse"*, no. 45:1-3 (Nov. 8, 1925).

2082. Sora, A. M., "Jack London - Abenteurer und Dichter,"
Selbsthilfe (Stuttgart), 21,8:2 (1947).

2083. Stach, F., "Gehört Jack London in die Schüler - und
Volksbücherei?" *Volksbildung* (Berlin), 63:42-44 (1933).

2084. Stern, Edgar F., "Jack London," *Berliner Börsencourier*,
1916:583.

2085. Stern-Rubarth, Edgar, "Jack London," *Deutsche Rundschau*,
212:75-76 (1927).

2086. Strasser, Charlot, "Jack London und Upton Sinclair,"
Schweizer Heimatskalender, 1927:81-91.

2087. Thiel, R., "Jack London," *Das literarische Echo* (Stuttgart), 31:203-205 (1928).

2088. Thiess, F., "Von Abenteurerromanen [J. Conrad und J.
London]" *Neue Rundschau* (Berlin), 38,2:537-547 (1927).

2089. Tornius, V., "Jack London, der König der Abenteurer," *Universum*, 49,16:595,633 (1933).

2090. Tschörtner, H. D., "Zur See und im Sattel. Jack London 1876-1916," *Hallesches Monatsheft für Heimat und Kultur* (Halle), 3:31-35 (1956).

2091. Untermann, E., "Jack London, wie ich ihn kannte," *Sozialistische Monatshefte*, 69:602-608 (1929).

2092. "Von den Schneefeldern am Yukon bis zur Brandung am Kap Hoorn," Zum 35. Todestag des berühmten Erzählers Jack London am 22. November," *Börsenblatt für den Deutschen Buchhandel* (Leipzig), 3:33 (1951).

2093. "Der Weg des Martin Eden," *Berliner Zeitung*, no. 10:4 (1956).

2094. Weiss, Gertrud, "Jack London und Rudyard Kipling," *Deutsche Woche* (Munich), 6,3:15 (1956).

2095. Zifreund, V., "Jack London," *Bücherei und Bildungspflege*, 11:262-272 (1931).

2096. Weltz, Friedrich, *Vier amerikanische Erzählungszyklen. Jack London: "Tales of the fishpatrol"; Sherwood Anderson: "Winesburg, Ohio"; John Steinbeck: "The pastures of heaven"; Ernest Hemingway: "In our time"*. Dissertation. Munich, 1953.

ICELANDIC

2097. Árnason, Jón P., "Sjór ningi fimmtán ára," *Beztu smásögur eftir Jack London*, Reykjavík, Söguútgáfan Útsyn, 1951, pp.17-24 (A private fifteen years old).

2098. Davíðsson, R. J., "Jack London," Lögberg (Winnipeg, Manitoba), in no. 7, pp.[?] (1921).

2099. Sigurðsson, Steindór, "Um höfund bókarinnar," *Fl kingar* (Reykjavík), 1947:7-9 (On the author).

ITALIAN

2100. Martino, Salvatore, *Jak* (sic) *London. (Spunti per uno studio critico)*, Catanio, Studio ed. moderno, 1934, 51pp.

2101. Romano, Vincenzo, *Jack London*, Firenze, Marzocco-Bemporad, 1952, 31pp.

2102. d'Agostino, Nicola, "Jack London," *Dizionario letterario Bompiani degli autori* ..., Milan, Bompiani, 1957, 2:544.

2103. Balestrieri, Spartaco, "London," *Simpatie. Impressioni critiche*, Milan, Milesi, 1938, pp.57-82.

2104. Cecchi, E., "J. London," *Scrittori inglesi e americani*, Milan, A. Mondadori, 1947, pp.264-269; Il Saggiatore,

1962, 1:381-384. [The 1962 edition is described as "Quarta edizione riveduta e accresciuta."]

2105. "London, Jack," *Dizionario universale della letteratura contemporanea*, Milan, Mondadori, 1961, 3:204-206.

2106. Rossi, M. M., "Jack London," *Verso una nuova teologia*, Bari, L. Macrì, 1946, pp.47-50.

2107. Soffici, A., "Jack London," *Ricordi di vita artistica e letteraria*, Florence, A. Vallecchi, 1942, pp.337-342 (2nd. ed. enlarged).

2108. Chichiavelli, Ezio, "Il senso di Jack London," *Rassegna nazionale*, series 3, 24:20-27 (Jan. 1936).

LATVIAN

2109. Lacis, V., "Džeks Londons," in Dž. London, *Kopoti raksti*, Riga, Kaija, 1936, 1:7-13.

2110. Sudrabkalns, J., "Džeks Londons," *Kopoti raksti*, Riga, 1960, 4:481-484.

2111. Abers, Z., "Džeks Londons," *Signals*, no. 2:18-21 (1928); no. 5: 15-17, no. 8:18-20 (1929).

2112. Briedis, E., "Izcilais amerikanu realists," *Literatura un maksla,"* no. 29, Aug. 18, 1948 (The prominent American realist).

2113. Damburs, E., "Džeks Londons," *Literatura un maksla*, no. 1, Jan. 7, 1951.

2114. Drezinš, E., "Liela dzive," *Radio Vilnis*, no. 21:6-7 (1941) (The great life).

2115. "Džeks Londons miris," *Baltija*, no. 154 (Nov. 25, 1916); *Dzimtenes Vestnesis*, no. 263 (Nov. 28, 1916); *Jauna Dienas Lapa*, in no. 265 (Nov. 26, 1916); *Jaunais Vards*, in no. 264 (Nov. 28, 1916); *Jaunakas Zinas*, in no. 317 (Nov. 26, 1916); *Rigas Zinas*, in no. 317 (Nov. 27, 1916) (Jack London is dead; obituaries). *Tauretajs*, no. 8:54 (1916) (Jack London is dead; obituaries).

2116. "Džeks Londons," *Students*, in no. 5 (Dec. 2, 1936); *Tevijas Sargs*, in no. 15 (April 14, 1939).

2117. Friedenfelds, F., "Džeks Londons miris," *Amerikas Vestnesis*, in no. 1 (Jan. 1, 1917).

2118. Grevinš, V., "Gramtnieks un vikings Džeks Londons," *Brivais Zemnieks*, in no. 18 (Jan. 19, 1941) (Jack London, scholar and Viking).

2119. Lasenberga, R., "Rakstnieks, ko lasa miljoni," *Karogs*, no. 1:122-124 (1956) (The writer read by millions).

2120. Lazda, A., "Džeks Londons," *Padomju Jaunatne*, in no. 10 (Jan. 13, 1951).

2121. Ozolinš, S., "Džeks Londons," *Latvijas Kareivis*, in no. 134 (June 18, 1922); *Prometejs*, no. 1:9-13 (1917).

2122. "Par Džeku Londonu," *Baltija*, in no. 186 (Dec. 21, 1916); *Lidums*, in no. 265 (Nov. 30, 1916) (Concerning Jack London).

2123. Siliņš, K., "Džeks Londons," *Stradnieks*, in nos. 16-19 (Feb. 8-10, 1917).

2124. "Vina gramatu varoni - tauta," *Rigas Balss*, no. 10, pp.[?] (Jan. 12, 1961) (The heroes of his books - people).

LITHUANIAN

2125. B. B. P., "Džeko Londono atsivertimas i socializa. Atpasakotas jo paties," *Naujienos*, in no. 69 (1922) (Jack London's conversion to socialism as told by himself).

2126. Daugirdas, J., "Nenugalima jega. [Meninis filmas 'Meksikietis' pagal Dž. Londono apsakyme. Scenarijaus aut. E. Braginskis. Pastat. V. Kaplonskio]," in *Kauno tiesa*, April 11, 1956 (The unconquerable force) [Artistic film 'The Mexican' using Jack London's short story]. Script by E. Braginskis. Director: V. Kaplanskio].

2127. "Dž. Londonas," in Dž. Londonas, *Martynas Idnas*, Kaunas, 1949, pp.403-406.

2128. "Kaip buvo rašoma knyga," *Jaunimo gretos*, no. 2:3 (1946) (How a book was written).

2129. J. K kis, "Amerikoja yra tokiu galimmu... Pasikalbejimas su musu tautieciu, kuri garsusis Amerikos rasytojas Džekas Londonas ievede placiajan pasaulin," in *Lietuvos zinios*, Oct. 13, 1931 (There are such possibilities in America... a conversation with a fellow patriot, to whom Jack London, the great American writer, has shown the path to the wide world).

2130. Korsakas, K., "Džek London," *Kultura*, no. 11:641-647 (1931).

2131. Puras, K., "Kovotojas prieš socialine neteisybe. Amerikiečiu rasytojo Dž. Londono gimimo 80-sioms metinems 1876-I-12-1916," *Komjaunimo tiesa*, Jan. 13, 1956 (Fighter against social wrongs. American writer's, Jack London, 80th anniversary, Jan. 12, 1876-1916).

2132. V. M., "Jack London," *Laisvoji mintis*, no. 16 (1916).

POLISH

2133. Sobotka, Henryk Andrzej, *Kraj bohaterów Jacka Londona. Stany Zjednoczone Północnej Ameryki w prawdziwym świetle*, Lów, Ksiaznica Atlas, 1929, 494pp.

2134. Sokolicz, Antonina, *Jack London*, Warsaw, Książka, 1925, 32pp.

2135. "Jack London," in Jack London, *Kawał pieczeni i inne opowiadania*, Warsaw, Czytelnik, 1955, pp.167-170.

2136. "O zyciu i twroczości Jacka Londona," in Jack London, *Opowieści z Północy i Południa*, Warsaw, Nasza Ksiegarnia, 1953, pp.v-xix.
2137. Piotrowski, Kazimierz, "Jack London: 1876-1916," in Jack London, *Dzieła wybrane*, Warsaw, Iskry, 1957, 1:5-46.
2138. ____, "Jack London," in Jack London, *Wyga i inne opowiadania*, Warsaw, Iskry, 1955, pp.5-8.
2139. ____, "Kilka słów o autorze," in Jack London, *Nowele*, Warsaw, Iskry, 1954, pp.5-8; also printed in *Nowele*, Warsaw, Iskry, 1956, 1:5-8; *Zew krwi i inne opowaidania*, Warsaw, Iskry, 1955, pp.[?].
2140. Wojtkiewicz, Stanisław Strumph, "O twórczości Jacka Londona," in Jack London, *Zelazna stopa*, Warsaw, Ludowa Spółdz, 1951, pp.[?].

PORTUGUESE
See vols. 1 and 5 of the *Obras completas de Jack London* under Collections, etc.

2141. Silvio, Julio, "Uma novella pleistocena de Jack London," in *Idéas e combates*, Río de Janeiro, Edição da Revista de Lingua Portuguesa, 1927, pp.[?].

2142. Gonçalves, Thomas J., "O revolucionário Jack London," *Leitura*, 5,44:54 (Nov. 1947) [On *The iron heel*].
2143. Pereira, Astrojildo, "Aspectos de Jack London," *Lanterna verde*, 7:18-22 (Aug. 1943) [Notes based on Charmian London's *The book of Jack London*].

RUSSIAN
2144. Bogoslovskii, V. H., *Dzhek London*, Moscow, Izd-vo Prosveshchenie, 1964, 238pp.
2145. ____, K istorii realizma v SShA. Tvorchestvo Dzheka Londona i Eptona Sinklera (1900-1917); avtoreferat dissertatsii na soiskanie uchenoi stepeni doktora filologicheskikh nauk. Moscow, Mosk. oblastnoi pedagog. in-t, 1963, 38pp. [History of realism in the U.S.A. Works of Jack London and Upton Sinclair (1900-1917); author's abstract submitted for the degree of Doctor of Philology].
2146. Bykov, Vil Mateveevich, *Dzhek London*, Moscow, Izdatelstvo Moskovshogo Universiteta, 1964, 253pp.
2147. ____, *Na rodinye Dzheka Londona*, Moscow, Gosudarstevennoye Izdatelstyvo Detskoi Literatury Ministerstva Prosveschcheniya RSFSR. 1962, 85pp.
2148. *Konferentziia chitatelei po knige Dzheka Londona Martin Iden. Metod. materialy*, Moscow, 1959, 12pp.

2149. Chukovskiĭ, K., "Dzhek London," in *Litsa i maski*, SPB. "Shipovnik", 1914, pp.137-151.
2150. "Dzhek London," in *Bolshaya sovetskaya entsiklopediya*, Moscow, 1938, 37:397.
2151. Fedunob, P. G., "Dzhek London (1876-1916)" in Dzhek London, *Sochimeniia*, Moscow, Goslitizdat, 1954, 1:5-38.
2152. Gorbatov, L., "Dzhek London," in Dzhek London, *Liubov' k zhizni*, Stalingrad, 1947, pp.3-6.
2153. Guber, P., "Dzhek London. Biograficheskiĭ ocherk," in Dzhek London, *Sobranie sochinenni*, Moscow and Leningrad, 1926, pp.355-406.
2154. Gruzinskaia, N., "Severnye rasskazy. D. Londona," in *Sbornik studencheskikh nauchnykh rabot po gumanitarnomu tziklu*, Moscow, MOPI [Moskovskiy Oblatsnoy Pedagogicheskiy Institut] 1957, pp.59-79.
2155. Khmel'nitzkaia, T., "Avtobiograficheskiĭ roman Dzheka Londona *Martin Eden*," in Dzhek London, *Martin Iden*, Leningrad, Lenizdat, 1949 (B-chka shkol'nika), pp.367-372.
2156. Khutzshevili, N., "Dzhek London," in Dzhek London, *Rasskazy*, Moscow, Goslitizdat, 1952 (Massovaia seria), pp.3-7.
2157. Kogan, P., "O Dzheke Londone," in Dzhek London, *Polnoye sobraniye sochineni*, Moscow and Leningrad, 1929, 1:19-144.
2158. Kulle, R., "Genial'nyĭ brodiaga (Dzhek London)" in *Etuidy o sovremennoĭ literature zapadno-evropeĭskoĭ i amerikanskoĭ*, Moscow and Leningrad, FIZ, 1930, pp.47-83.
2159. Kuprin, A. I., "Zametka o Dzheke Londone," in *Sochineniia*, Moscow, Goslitizdat, 1953, 3:556-558.
2160. *Lenin o literature*, Moscow, Goslitizdat, 1941, pp.253-254.
2161. Lenobl'. G., "Dzhek London," in D. London, *Smok Bel'iu*, Moscow and Leningrad, Detizdat, 1945, pp.3-8.
2162. Lorie, M., "Dzhek London," in Dzhek London, *Rasskazy*, Moscow and Leningrad, Detgiz, 1948, pp.3-8.
2163. Omilianchuk, P., "Posleslovie," in Dzhek London, *Rasskazy*, Moscow, Goslitizdat, 1956, pp.524-525.
2164. Pranskus, B., "Dzhek London," *Literaturnaya entsiklopediya*, Moscow, 1932, 6:574.
2165. Roskin, A., "Dzhek London," in Dzhek London, *Liubov' k zhizni*, Moscow and Leningrad, Detizdat, 1937, pp.3-5.

2166. Andruson, L., "Dzhek London," *Nov. zh-l dlia vsekh*, no. 7 (1912), pp.75-82.
2167. Anikst, A., "Dzhek London," *Knizhye novosti*, no. 30:22-24 (1936).
2168. Antonova, T., "Severnye rasskazy," *Uchen. zapiski (Mosk.*

*gos. ied. in-t im. Lenina). Kafedra zarubezhnoĭ liter-
atury,* 130:231-242 (1958).

2169. Badanova, I. M., "Gorkiĭ i Dzhek London," *Uchen.
zapiski (Tashk. ped. in-t inostr. iaz),* 4:129-148 (1960).

2170. ____, "Kniga revoliutzionnogo gneva," *Uchenye zapiski
(Tashk. ped. in-t inostr. iazykov),* 1:151-173 (1956)
[On *The iron heel*].

2171. ____, "Protiv mzahkonennogo grabezhe," *Uchenye zapiski
(Tashk. ped. in-t inostr. iaz.),* 4:149-171 (1960) [On
The iron heel].

2172. Bannilov, N., "Kak byli napisany Liudi bezdny (iz in-
storii sozdaniia Dzh. London knigi ocherkov *Liudi
bezdny*), *Ogonek,* no. 5:13 (1956) [On *The people of the
abyss*].

2173. B-ev, Sergeĭ, "Dzhek London," *Knigonosha,* no. 2:10-12
(1926).

2174. "Biografiia Dzheka Londona," *Internatz. lit-ra,* no. 12:
242-243 (1938).

2175. Baratov, B., "Dzhek London. K 75-letiiu so dnia rozhdeniia," *Ogonek,* no. 3:21 (1951).

2176. Bogoslovskiĭ, V. N., "Dzhek London. Ocherk tvorchestva,"
Uchen. zapiski (Mosk. obl. ped. in-t). *Trudy kafedry
zarubezhnoĭ literatury,* 37:3-76 (1956).

2177. ____, "Severnye rasskasy Dzheka Londona," *Uchen. zapin-
ski* (Mosk. obl. ped. in-t) *Trudy kafedry zarubezhnoĭ
literatury,* 78,6:63-117 (1959).

2178. Boroda, M., "Kak rabotal Dzhek London. Ob org-tzii i
kul'ture truda pisatelia," *Na pod' 'eme,* no. 7:153-158
(1931).

2179. Brandis, E., "Dzhek London. K 70-lettiiu so dnie rozhdeniia," *Smena* (Leningrad), no. 10:3 (Jan. 12, 1946).

2180. Bykov, Vil, "Amerikanskie kritiki o Dzheke Londone,"
Voprosy literatury, 9,9:198-206 (Sept. 1965).

2181. ____, "Muzhestvennyĭ talant. (K 40-letiiu so dnia smerti
Dzheka Londona)," *Smena,* no. 23:20 (1956).

2182. ____, "Po sledam Dzheka Londona," *Kosmomol'skaia pravda,*
Sept. 20, 23, 24, 1959, pp.[?].

2183. ____, "Znakomstvo s Dzhekom Londonom prodolzhaersia."
(Glava iz podgotovlennoĭ k pechati knigi o tvorchestve
pisatelia), *Smena,* no. 10:20-21 (1960).

2184. Danilin, Iu., "Dzhek London uchitsia pisatel'stvu," *Na
lit. postu,* no. 23:86-95 (1929).

2185. Dinamov, S., "Zamatki o Dzheke Londone," *30 dnei,* no.
9:53-54 (1933).

2186. Dneprov, V., "V zashchitu realisticheskoĭ éstetiki,"
Zvezda, no. 6:184-196 (1957).

2187. Frimen, Dzhozef, "Dzhek London kak revoluyutsimer," *Na
literaturnom postu,* no. 2:46-51 (1927).

2188. Giiel', O., "Tvorchestvo Dzheka Londona (1876-1916)," *Narodnyĭ uchitel'*, no. 12:116-120 (1926).
2189. Levidova, S., "Dzhek London," *Letopis'*, no. 12:250-253 (1916).
2190. Levit, T., "Dzhek London," *Mol. gvardiia*, no. 1:159-160 (1941).
2191. Morozov, O., "Dzhek London. (K 75-letiiu so dnia rozheniia)", *Komsomoletz Kirgizii*, no. 6:4 (Jan. 14, 1951).
2192. "Dzhek London o samom sebe," *Biullet. lit-ry i zhizni*, no. 13:609-617 (1913).
2193. M-skoĭ, S. V., "Dzhek London," *Sever*, no. 23-26:12-16, no. 27-31:15-16 (1919).
2194. Nemerovskaya, Olga, "Dzhek London. K 65-letiiu so dnia rozheniia," *Krasnoflotetz*, no. 1:51-53 (1941).
2195. ___, "Sudba amerikanskoi novelly," *Literaturnaya uchyoba*, no. 5:79-80 (1935).
2196. Paskhin, N., "Tvorcheskiĭ put' Dzheka Londona," *Chto chitat'*, nos. 7-8:45-48 (1939).
2197. "Pevetz podlinnoĭ zhizni (Dzhek London)," *Biull. lit-ry i zhizni*, nos. 20-21:775-777 (1912).
2198. Sukhoverov, S., "Dzhek London i rabochee dvizhenie. (Obzor tvorchestva 1900-1909 gg.)," *Eniceĭ*, no. 12:254-262 (1953).
2199. ___, "Dzhek London v SSR. (O populiarnosti proizvedeniĭ pisatelia)," *Uchen. zapiski* (Shadrin, ped. in-t), 2:102-143 (1958).
2200. "V. gostiakh u Londona. Iz vospominaniĭ rus. zhurnaliste ob amerikanskom pisatele, 1916," *Krasnoflotetz*, no. 1: 54-56 (1941).
2201. Vaĭnshteĭn, G., "Dzhek London. (K 65-letiiu so dnia rozhdeniia amer. pisatelia)" *Lit. obozrenie*, no. 2:84-85 (1941).

SPANISH

2202. Ordaz, Luis, *Jack London: el rey de los vagabundos*, Buenos Aires, Editorial Abril, 1946, 143pp. (Colección: La marcha de los heroes).

2203. Zardoya, Concha, *Historia de la literatura norteamericana*, Barcelona, Editorial Labor, 1956, pp.217-221.

2204. Greateater, A. [pseudonym?], "Whitechapel, el infernal abismo de Londres, inspiró a Jack London el más admirable y conmovedor de sus libros," *Caras y caretas*, no. 1485 (March 19, 1927) [unpaged].
2205. Lansford, W. Duoglas [sic], "La vida aventurera de Jack London," *Bohemia* (Cuba), no. 31:32-35, 104-105 (1959).
2206. London, Charmian, "Como conocí a Jack London," *Caras*

y caretas, no. 1522 (Dec. 3, 1927) [unpaged].
2207. ___, "Como se enamoraron. Lo confiesa la esposa de Jack London," *Caras y caretas,* no. 1902 (March 16, 1935) [unpaged].
2208. Montenegro, Ernesto, "Horacio Quiroga, pariente literario de Kipling y Jack London," *Nosotros,* 54:134-136 (Sept. 1926) [translated from New York *Times Book Review,* Oct. 25, 1925].
2209. "Muerte de Jack London," *Revista de revistas* (Mexico), no. 350:9 (Jan. 14, 1917) [translated from *The Outlook*].
2210. Núñes, Estuardo, "A propósito de Jack London," *Mercurio peruano,* 17:75 (1928).
2211. Solari Amondarain, Ismael, "Sinclair Lewis y Jack London envueltos en un misterioso "affaire" literario," *El hogar,* año 29, no. 1244:18,25 (Aug. 18, 1933).
2212. Torres Morey, Rafael, "Jack London," *Revista paraguaya,* año 2, no. 1:37-39 (April 1936) [reprinted from *Claridad* of Buenos Aires].
2213. Wenz, Paul, "Los cuellos y el smoking de Jack London," *Caras y caretas,* no. 1581 (Jan. 19, 1929) [unpaged].

SWEDISH

2214. Le Moine, Osborne, *Jack London och hans diktargärning,* Stockholm, Bohlin, 1920, 154pp.

2215. "A., A-A," "Jack London och hans diktargärning," *Svenska Dagbladet,* Aug. 20, 1920, p.6.
2216. "E. H.," "Bland böcker: Jack London," *Dagen,* Sept. 28, 1915, p.3.
2217. Engholm, Stellan, "Jack London," Frihet, no. 2:2-3 (1919).
2218. ___, "Jack London: en overblick," *Folkets Dagblad Politiken,* Aug. 30, 1919, p.7.
2219. ___, "Naturfilosofi," *Frihet,* no. 3:5-6 (1920).
2220. Erikson, Bror, "Jack London och hans diktargärning," *Svenska Morgonbladet,* June 8, 1920, p.7.
2221. ___, "Jack London som dramatiker," *Östögten,* Oct. 20, 1920.
2222. ___, "Litteratur: Jack London," *Östögten,* Sept. 21, 1917.
2223. Gripenberg, Bertel, "En biografi," *Finsk tidskrift,* 99:346-348 (1925).
2224. ___, "Jack London," *Finsk tidskrift,* 82:26-31 (1917).
2225. "J-N., C.," "Litteratur: Jack London," *Social-Demokraten,* June 5, 1914, p.5.
2226. Kämpe, Alfr[ed], "Litterature: En Hawaji-bok av Jack London," *Folkets Dagblad Politiken,* Nov. 11, 1922, p.7.
2227. "L., C.," "Litteratur," *Signalen,* April 22, 1920, p.2.

2228. "Litteratur: Jack London," *Social-Demokraten,* Dec. 5, 1914, p.5.
2229. Magnus-Carlsson, Axel, "Litteratur: Jack London," *Öster-götlands Folkblad,* April 27, 1917.
2230. Mörner, Birger, "Kring Jack London," *Södermanlands Läns Tidning,"* July 1, 1922, p.5.
2231. Nordstrand, G., "Jack Londons sista bok," *Nya Dagligt Allehanda,* Dec. 22, 1922, p.11.
2232. "R-s, O.," "Ny berättelsesamling af Jack London," *Stockholms Dagblad,* Sept. 18, 1915, p.6.
2233. "RBG," "Bokvärlden: Jack London," *Göteborgs Handels-och Sjöfarts-Tidning,* Nov. 19, 1914, p.5.
2234. "S-M, B.," "En bok om Jack London," *Lunds Dagblad,* May 8, 1920, p.4.

THESES AND DISSERTATIONS ABOUT JACK LONDON IN ENGLISH

Undergraduate theses

2235. Lynn, Kenneth S., *Jack London, the brain merchant*, Harvard University, 1954, 55 leaves. Title page bears pseud. Peter Fisher. Bowdoin prize in social studies.
2236. Neary, John A., *The earthly dream: a diagram of Jack London's fiction*, Harvard University, 1959, 44 leaves. Honors thesis.

M. A. theses

2237. Andrew, Loyd D., *Jack London, pioneer naturalist*, Texas Western College of the University of Texas, El Paso, 1956, 127 leaves.
2238. Backus, John E., *Jack London, his works and his philosophy*, Fordham University, New York, 1936, 59 leaves.
2239. Beirne, Thomas F., *A comparative study of the novels of the sea of Jack London*, St. John's University, Brooklyn, 1952, 51 leaves.
2240. Boucher, James J., *The political and economic opinions of Jack London*, University of Kentucky, 1936, 104 leaves.
2241. Bragin, Moses, *The superman in Jack London's works*, Columbia University, New York, 1929, 63 leaves.
2242. Campbell, Harlan Sheldon, *Jack London's principles of writing: a critical appraisal*, Stanford University, Stanford, California, 1950, 90 leaves.
2243. Carroll, Lavon B., *Woman in the novels of Jack London*, Utah State University, Logan, 1963, 122 leaves.
2244. Cost, Charles C., *The Darwinian thought of Jack London*, New York University, New York, 1965, 48 leaves.
2245. Dozier, Mary Dean, *The conflict between individualism and socialism in the life and novels of Jack London*, North Texas State College, Denton, 1948, iii, 126 leaves.
2246. Frauenglass, Ettie, *Jack London as a socialist*, New York University, New York, 1939, 227 leaves.
2247. Freeman, H. A., *Jack London and the problem of poverty*, State University of Iowa, Iowa City, 1932, 92 leaves.
2248. Gleason, Edwin P., *Jack London and socialism*, Columbia University, New York, 1947, 79 leaves.
2249. Green, E. Carl, *Social aspects of some of Jack London's novels*, Utah State University, Logan, 1959, 83 leaves.
2250. Hall, Vivian Halpern, *Jack London: superman and socialist*, University of Colorado, Boulder, 1947, 73 leaves.
2251. Kays, Marjorie, *Jack London's The Valley of the moon: a textual and critical study*, Ohio State University,

Columbus, 1948, 56 leaves.

2252. Kolar, Mildred Marguerite, *Jack London's unstandardized mastery of description and narration,* University of Nebraska, Lincoln, 1927, 166 leaves.

2253. Landis, Joan Selby, *Narrative techniques in Jack London's Alaskan short stories,* Mills College, Oakland, 1956, 181 leaves.

2254. Levitt, Morton P., *The social and economic writings of Jack London,* Columbia University, New York, 1960, 66 leaves.

2255. Masiello, Arthur, *Darwinism in the works of Jack London,* Seton Hall University, South Orange, 1960, 79 leaves.

2256. Nichol, John William, *Local color in the Alaskan stories of Jack London,* Ohio State University, Columbus, 1948, 112 leaves.

2257. Nichols, Thomas W., *The social philosophy of Jack London,* Louisiana State University, Baton Rouge, 1931, 145 leaves.

2258. Peterson, Clell Thompson, *Jack London and the American frontier,* University of Minnesota, Minneapolis, 1951, 144 leaves.

2259. Schmedake, Dorothy May, *Dichotomy in the world of Jack London,* Washington University, St. Louis, 1944, 122 leaves.

2260. Shear, Walter Lewis, *A study of the morality in the novels of three modern American novelists.* State University of Iowa, Iowa City, 1957, 108 leaves.

2261. Shivers, Alfred Samuel, *The characters of Jack London,* University of Florida, Gainesville, 1959, vii, 110 leaves.

2262. Spencer, Arthur Frank, *Jack London: Nietzschean socialist and agrarian,* University of Washington, Seattle, 1935, 54 leaves.

2263. Tudor, Stephen H., *Reversion in Jack London's novels,* State University of Iowa, Iowa City, 1960, 60 leaves.

2264. Winsor, William T., *Nature and naturalism in the works of Jack London,* Columbia University, New York, 1957, 130 leaves.

2265. Young, Thomas Daniel, *The political and social thought of Jack London,* University of Mississippi, Oxford, 1948, 210 leaves.

M. S. thesis

2266. Horton, Arthur L., *Jack London's reputation as a novelist,* Auburn University, Auburn, Ala., 1951, 105 leaves.

Ph. D. dissertations

2267. Baskett, Sam S., *Jack London's fiction: its social milieu*, University of California, Berkeley, 1951, iv, 251 leaves.
2268. Carlson, Roy W., *Jack London's heroes: a study of evolutionary thought*, University of New Mexico, Albuquerque, 1961, 271 leaves.
2269. Edmondson, Elsie, *The writer as hero in important American fiction since Howells (Howells, James, Norris, London, Farrell, Cabell)*, University of Michigan, Ann Arbor, 1954, ii, 269 leaves.
2270. Holland, Robert Belton, *Jack London: his thought and art in relation to his time (1876-1916)*, University of Wisconsin, Madison, 1950, 424 leaves; see also University of Wisonsin, *Summaries of doctoral dissertations*, 12:451-453 (1952).
2271. Labor, Earle Gene, *Jack London's literary artistry; a study of his imagery and symbols in relation to his themes*, University of Wisconsin, Madison, 1961, 365 leaves; see *Dissertation Abstracts*, 21:3098-3099 (1961).
2272. Oppewell, Peter, *The critical reception of American fiction in the Netherlands, 1900-1953*, University of Michigan, Ann Arbor, 1961, 334 leaves; sections on London in both text and bibliography; see *Dissertation Abstracts*, 21:3790 (1961).
2273. Pope, Margaret I., *Jack London: a study in twentieth-century values*, University of Wisconsin, Madison, 1935, iv, 291 leaves.
2274. Price, Starling, *Jack London's America*, University of Minnesota, 1966, [?] leaves.
2275. Rothberg, Abraham, *The house that Jack built: a study of Jack London (1876-1916): the man, his times, and his works*, Columbia University, New York, 1952, 399 leaves; see *Dissertation Abstracts*, 12:438 (1952).
2276. Shivers, Alfred S., *Romanticism in Jack London: a study of romantic qualities in his life and in selected short stories and novels*, Florida State University, Tallahassee, 1962, xi, 142 leaves; *Dissertation Abstracts*, 23: 1709 (1962).
2277. Springer, Anne Marie, "Jack London and Upton Sinclair," in *The American novel in Germany: a study of the critical reception of eight American novelists between the two world wars*, University of Pennsylvania, Philadelphia, 1959, leaves 45-74; published under the same title, Hamburg, Cram. de Gruyter & Co., 1960, 116pp. (Britannica et Americana VII).
2278. Wilcox, Earl J., *Jack London's naturalism*, Vanderbilt

University, 1966, 431 leaves.
2279. Young, Thomas Daniel, *Jack London and the era of social protest*, Vanderbilt University, Nashville, 1950, 283 leaves; see Vanderbilt University, *Abstracts of theses*, 1949-1950, pp.25-26.

REVIEWS OF JACK LONDON BOOKS

ENGLISH

2280. *The abysmal brute:*
ALA *Booklist,* 10:70 (Oct. 1913).
Boston *Transcript,* June 11, 1913, p.4.
Literary Digest, 47:390 (Sept. 6, 1913).
New York *Times,* 18:461 (Sept. 7, 1913).
Outlook, 104:345 (June 14, 1913).
Out West, n.s. 7:233 (April 1914).

2281. *Acorn planter:*
Independent, 86:343 (May 29, 1916).
Nation, 103:151-152 (Aug. 17, 1916).
New York *Times,* 21:320 (Aug. 13, 1916).
Review of Reviews, 53:634 (May 1916).
Springfield *Republican,* May 7, 1916, p.17.

2282. *Adventure:*
ALA *Booklist,* 7:397 (May 1911).
Athenaeum, no. 4351:300 (March 18, 1911).
The Bookman (London), 40:143 (June 1911).
Nation, 92:318 (March 30, 1911).
New York *Times,* 16:185 (April 2, 1911).
Review of Reviews, 43:758 (June 1911).
San Francisco *Call,* April 23, 1911, p.7.
Spectator, 106:569 (April 15, 1911).

2283. *The assassination bureau:*
Best sellers, 23:334 (Dec. 15, 1963) (M. Moriarty).
Chicago Tribune, Dec. 29, 1963, p.4 (Vincent
    Starrett).
Denver (Colo.) *Rocky Mountain News,* Feb. 23, 1964,
    p.20A (Al Shivers).
Inostrannaya literatura, no. 4:284 (1964) [Russian
    review of McGraw-Hill edition].
Library Journal, 89:1472 (March 15, 1964).
New York *Times Book Review,* Dec. 8, 1963, p.49
    (Anthony Boucher).
San Francisco *Chronicle,* Dec. 6, 1963, third section
    of main news, p.39 (William Hogan); same review in
    Syracuse (N. Y.) *Herald-American,* Dec. 29, 1963,
    p.4.
Studies in short fiction, 1,4:303-305 (1964)
    (E. Labor).
Wall Street Journal, Jan. 14, 1964, p.12.

2284. *Before Adam:*

Analog: Science fact and science fiction, 73,2:91
(P. Schuyler Miller).
Appeal to reason, March 6, 1920, p.3.
Athenaeum, no. 4204:633-634 (May 23, 1908).
Atlantic Monthly, 100:125 (July 1907) (Harry J.
Smith).
Bookman, 25:183-184 (April 1907) (Frederic Taber
Cooper).
Bookman, (London) 35:57 (Oct. 1908).
Clarion, no. 860:2 (May 29, 1908).
Country Life, 23:cxl (June 6, 1908).
Independent, 62:620 (March 14, 1907).
Literary Digest, 34:639 (April 30, 1907).
London Opinion, 17:584 (June 27, 1908).
New York *Times,* 12:145 (March 9, 1907).
Outlook, 85:718 (March 23, 1907).
Publishers' Circular, 88:773 (June 13, 1908).
Punch, 134:414 (Jan. 3, 1908).
Review of Reviews, 35:762 (June 1907).
Saturday Review, 105:793-794 (June 20, 1908).

2285. *The Bodley Head Jack London:*
Daily Telegraph and Morning Post. June 21, 1963, p.20
(Anthony Powell).
Country Life, July 4, 1963, p.50 (Paul Scott).
The Listener, 70,1788:27 (July 4, 1963) (David Wright).
Observer, No. 9076:25 (July 14, 1963) (John Davenport).
The Spectator, No. 7045:28 (July 5, 1963) (Mordecai
Richler).

2286. *Burning daylight:*
Athenaeum, no. 4363:653 (June 10, 1911).
Bookman, 32:157 (Oct. 1910) (G. J. Colbron).
Dial, 49:384 (Nov. 16, 1910).
Independent, 69:1091 (Nov. 17, 1910).
Maoriland Worker (New Zealand), 2,42:8 (Dec. 22,
1911) (R. S. Ross).
Nation, 91:443 (Nov. 10, 1910).
New York *Times,* 15:622 (Nov. 5, 1910).
Publishers' Circular 94:844 (June 10, 1911).
Punch, 140:489 (June 21, 1911).
San Francisco *Call,* Dec. 18, 1910, p.7.

2287. *The call of the wild:*
Athenaeum, no. 3957:279 (Aug. 29, 1903).
Atlantic Monthly, 92:695-697 (Nov. 1903).
Bookman, 18:159-160 (Oct. 1903) (A. B. Maurice).
The Bookman (London), 24:220 (Sept. 1903).

Book News Monthly, 22:7-10 (Sept. 1903)(Kate B. Stille).

Books of today and the books of tomorrow, Sept. 1903, p.4.

Boston *Budget*, Aug. 9, 1903 (Anne H. Bradford).

Boston *Saturday Evening Gazette*, Aug. 15, 1903, p.[?].

Brooklyn *Citizen*, Aug. 16, 1903, part 2:20.

Chicago *Inter-Ocean*, Aug. 10, 1903, p.7 (Thomas Dixon, Jr.)

Chicago *Tribune*, Aug. 8, 1903, p.7 (Elia W. Peattie).

Chicago *Unity*, 51:403 (Aug. 20, 1903) (E. P. Powell).

Denver *Times*, Aug. 1, 1903, p.20 (Laura F. Hinsdale).

Detroit *Free Press*, Aug. 8, 1903, p.10.

Detroit *News*, Aug. 1, 1903, p.7.

Edinburgh *Review*, 214:108-110 (1911); also a review of *White fang*.

Gunton's Magazine, 25:364:366 (Oct. 1903).

Literary World (Boston), 34:229 (Sept. 1903).

Memphis *Evening Scimitar*, Aug. 22, 1903, p.12 (Anna B. A. Brown).

New York *American*, Aug. 22, 1903, p.[?].

New York *News*, Aug. 23, 1903, p.[?].

New York *Post*, Sept. 26, 1903, p.[?].

Oakland *Enquirer*, Aug. 24, 1903, p.4.

Philadelphia *Item*, Aug. 8, 1903, p.4. (Sarah Ritter Fitzgerald).

Pittsburgh *Dispatch*, Aug. 9, 1903, p.51 (William J. Groat).

Pittsburgh *Gazette*, Aug. 9, 1903, section 4:4.

Pittsburgh *Post*, Aug. 3, 1903, p.4.

Reader, 2:408-409 (Sept. 1903) (J. Stewart Doubleday).

Review of Reviews, 28:633 (Nov. 1903).

San Francisco *Chronicle*,Aug. 2, 1903, p.32.

San Francisco *Newsletter*, 67:12-13 (Aug. 15, 1903) (W. J. Weymouth).

Saturday Review, 96:678 (Nov. 28, 1903).

Spectator, Aug. 22, 1903, p.[?].

Spectator, July 16, 1965, pp.80-81 (Tony Tanner) [review of reprint].

Stockton *Evening Mail*, Sept. 30, 1903, p.4 (Johannes Reimers).

T. P.'s Weekly, 2:458 (Sept. 11, 1903).

2288. *The children of the frost:*
    Athenaeum, no. 3925:77 (Jan. 17, 1903).
    Bookman, 17:83-84 (March 1903) (C. Hovey).

2289. *The cruise of the Dazzler:*

Punch, 131:288 (Oct. 24, 1906).

2290. *The cruise of the Dazzler and Moonface:*
    Athenaeum, no. 4121:477 (Oct. 20, 1906).
    London Opinion, 11:159 (Nov. 3, 1906).

2291. *The cruise of the Snark:*
    ALA *Booklist,* 8:23 (Sept. 1911).
    Dial, 51:54 (July 16, 1911).
    Independent, 71:100 (July 13, 1911).
    Nation, 93:146 (Aug. 17, 1911).
    New York *Times,* 16:373 (June 11, 1911).
    Outlook, 98:552 (July 8, 1911).
    San Francisco *Call,* July 23, 1911, p.6.

2292. *A daughter of the snows:*
    Athenaeum, no. 4005:140 (July 30, 1904).
    Book Buyer, 25:621-622 (Jan. 1903) (E. Hoyt).
    Books of today and the books of tomorrow, Aug. 1904,
       p.2.
    Publishers' Circular, 81:207 (Jan. 2, 1904).
    Saturday Review, 98:145 (July 30, 1904).
    Wilshire's Magazine, Feb. 1903, pp.84-87.

2293. *Faith of men:*
    Reader, 4:351 (Aug. 1904) (R. M. S.).
    San Francisco *Chronicle,* May 15, 1904, p.8 (George H.
       Fitch).

2294. *The first poet:*
    San Francisco *Examiner,* July 22, 1915, p.6.

2295. *The game:*
    Academy, 68:809 (Aug. 5, 1905).
    Athenaeum, no. 4057:138 (July 29, 1905).
    Atlantic Monthly, 97:49 (Jan. 1906) (Mary Moss).
    Bookman, 22:35 (Sept. 1905).
    Books of today and the books of tomorrow, Aug. 1905,
       p.8.
    Critic, 47:285 (Sept. 1905)
    Independent, 58:1480 (June 29, 1905).
    New York *Times,* 10:394 (June 17, 1905); 10:528
       (Aug. 12, 1905).
    Public Opinion, 39:252 (Aug. 19, 1905).
    Publishers' Circular, 82:896 (June 24, 1905).
    Saturday Review, 100:252 (Aug. 19, 1905).

2296. *The God of his fathers:*

    Athenaeum, no. 3884:435 (April 5, 1902).
    Impressions, 2:59 (Oct. 1901) (Anna Strunsky).
    Nation, 73:15 (July 4, 1901).

2297. *The great interrogation* (play version):
    Current Literature, 39:435-436 (Oct. 1905) ("Jack
      London's first play").
    San Francisco *Chronicle,* Aug. 21, 1905, p.12 ("To
      present play by local authors on stage for first
      time").
    Sunset, 15,6:597-598 (Oct. 1905) [Comment on the Jack
      London play, "The great interrogation", produced
      at Alcazar Theater, San Francisco -- the joint work
      of Jack London and Lee Bascom].

2298. *Hearts of three:*
    Athenaeum, no. 4635:485 (Nov. 1918) (brief notice).
    Freeman, 2:285 (Dec. 1, 1920) (L. B.).
    New York *Times,* Dec. 26, 1920, p.24.
    Outlook, 126:470 (Nov. 10, 1920).
    San Francisco *Chronicle,* May 22, 1921, p.32.

2299. *House of pride:*
    ALA *Booklist,* 8:411 (June 1912).
    Independent, 72:1120 (May 23, 1912).
    New York *Times,* 17:248 (April 21, 1912).
    Review of Reviews, 45:761 (June 1912).
    San Francisco *Call,* May 5, 1912, p.7.

2300. *Human drift:*
    ALA *Booklist,* 13:440 (July 1917).
    Dial, 62:404 (May 3, 1917).
    Independent, 90:4744 (June 9, 1917).
    Nation, 104:583 (May 10, 1917).
    New York *Call,* June 24, 1917, p.15 (D. P. Berenberg).
    New York *Times,* 22:88 (March 11, 1917).
    Oakland *World,* March 23, 1917, p.2 (D. Bobspa).
    Sacramento *Bee,* April 3, 1917, p.13.
    St. Louis *Monthly Bulletin,* 15:151 (May 1917).
    San Francisco *Chronicle,* March 25, 1917, p.32.
    Springfield *Republican,* Dec. 2, 1917, p.19.

2301. *The iron heel:*
    Arena,   39:503-506 (April 1908).
    Athenaeum, no. 4233:757 (Dec. 12, 1908).
    Clarion, no. 890:2 (Dec. 25, 1908).
    Dial, 44:247 (April 16, 1908) (W. M. Payne).
    Independent, 64:865 (April 16, 1908).

Maoriland Worker (New Zealand), 2,11:6 (May 19, 1911)
[Brief comment in column entitled "The moving
finger"].
Nation, 86:264 (March 19, 1908).
Outlook, 89:388 (June 20, 1908) (H. A. Bruce).
Publishers' Circular, 89:838 (Dec. 12, 1908).
Review of Reviews, 37:760 (June 1908).
San Francisco *Call*, April 5, 1908, magazine section,
p.6.
Saturday Review, 107:114 (Jan. 23, 1909).

2302. *Iron heel* (Play):
Oakland *World*, March 28, 1908, p.4; April 4, 1908,
p.4; April 11, 1908, p.4; May 2, 1908, p.4; May 9,
1908, p.4. [With the May 9 review there is a section
of chapter five of the book published.]
"The iron heel last time in Oakland," Oakland *World*,
April 15, 1911, p.2.
"Iron heel staged. Success attained in dramatic ver-
sion of great novel. London's masterpiece arouses
[sic] greatest enthusiasm," Oakland *World*, March
25, 1911, pp.1-2 [Review by Grace V. Silver].
"Iron heel a success," Oakland *World*, March 25, 1911,
p.3 [Austin Lewis].
"Karl Marx players to put on Iron heel," Oakland
World, March 11, 1911, p.2.
Oakland *World*, March 18, 1911, p.1.

2303. *Island tales (i.e. On the Makaloa mat):*
Athenaeum, no. 4713:272 (Aug. 27, 1920); reprinted in
Novels and novelists, London, Constable, 1930,
pp.246-248 (Katherine Mansfield).
John O'London's Weekly, 3:601-602 (Sept. 4, 1920).
Punch, 159:159 (Aug. 25, 1920).

2304. *Jack London: American rebel:*
ALA *Booklist*, 44:199 (Feb. 1, 1948).
Chicago *Sun*, Dec. 11, 1947 (Irving Stone).
London *Daily Worker*, March 3, 1960, p.2 (William
Gallacher, "The story of Jack the rebel") [review
of the Seven Seas Books ed.].
New York *Times*, Jan. 19, 1948, p.24 (Thomas Lask).
New Yorker, 23:145 (Dec. 13, 1947).
San Francisco *Chronicle*, April 11, 1948, p.22.

2305. *The jacket (i.e. The star rover):*
Athenaeum, no. 4579:77 (July 31, 1915).
Bookman (London), 48:178 (Sept. 1915).

Manchester Guardian, Feb. 16, 1917, p.3.
Punch, 149:240 (Sept. 15, 1915).

2306. *Jerry of the islands:*
ALA *Booklist*, 14:60 (Nov. 1917).
Athenaeum, no. 4621:471 (Sept. 1917) [brief notice].
Bookman, 45:536 (July 1917) (H. W. Boynton).
Boston *Transcript*, April 28, 1917, p.6 (E. F. E.).
New York *Call*, Aug. 19, 1917, p.15 (D. P. Berenberg).
New York *Times*, 22:158 (April 22, 1917).
Oakland *World*, May 25, 1917, p.2 (D. Bobspa).
Outlook, 116:116 (May 16, 1917).
Punch, 153:85 (Aug. 1, 1917).
San Francisco *Chronicle*, July 8, 1917, p.22.
Saturday Review, 124:251 (Sept. 29, 1917).
Times Literary Supplement, July 26, 1917, p.356.

2307. *John Barleycorn:*
ALA *Booklist*, 10:70 (Oct. 1913).
Athenaeum, 10:70 (Oct. 1913).
Athenaeum, no. 4527:149 (Aug. 1, 1914).
Bookman, 46:253 (Sept. 1914).
Boston *Transcript*, Aug. 20, 1913, p.18 (E. F. E.).
Chattanooga *News*, May 12, 1913, p.4 (Sam Divine).
Chattanooga *News*, May 9, 1913, p.12 (Frances Fort
    Brown).
Chattanooga *News*, April 19, 1913, p.2 ("Jack London
    in the *Saturday Evening Post*") (Frances Fort Brown).
Current Opinion, 55:269-270 (Oct. 1913).
Day Book (Chicago), 2,180:1 (April 29, 1913) ("John
    Barleycorn" by Berton Braley with acknowledgments
    to Jack London).
Forum, 51:146-154 (Jan. 1914) (C. Vale).
Independent, 76:36 (Oct. 2, 1913).
Los Angeles *Record*, April 30, 1913, p.4 ["Willie
    Wheatoats" by Horatio Budapest (with apologies to
    Jack London)].
Nation, 97:190 (Aug. 28, 1913).
New York *Times*, 18:445 (Aug. 24, 1913) (Joyce Kilmer);
    18:665 (Nov. 30, 1913).
Oakland *World*, Sept. 6, 1913, p.4 (H. H. Caldwell).
Outlook, 104:964 (Aug. 23, 1913).
Overland Monthly, n.s. 62:414 (Oct. 1913).
Portland (Oregon) *Evening Telegram*, April 12, 1913,
    p.6 [Editorial].
Punch, 147:119 (July 29, 1914).
Sacramento *Union*, May 11, 1913, p.14.
San Francisco *Call*, July 28, 1913, p.5.

San Francisco *Evening Post*, June 2, 1913, p.6.

2308. *Kempton-Wace letters:*
    Out West, n.s. 19:219-220 (Aug. 1903).
    World's Work, 6:3701 (July 1903).

2309. *Letters from Jack London:*
    ALA *Booklist*, 62:429 (Jan. 1, 1966).
    American Book Collector, 16,5:2-3 (Jan. 1966) (Alfred
      S. Shivers).
    American Notes and Queries, 4:140-142 (May 1966)
      (Hensley C. Woodbridge).
    Chicago *Tribune*, *Books Today*, Oct. 31, 1965, p.18
      (Vincent Starrett).
    Library Journal, 91:257 (Jan. 15, 1966) (F. Berol-
      zheimer).
    Los Angeles *Herald-Examiner*, Dec. 26, 1965, p.J10
      (Frederick Shroyer).
    Nation, 202:105-107 (Jan. 24, 1966) (Franklin Walker).
    National Observer, Jan. 3, 1966, p.10 (David W.
      Hacker).
    Newsweek, 66,24:106, 108 (Dec. 13, 1965).
    St. Louis *Post-Dispatch*, Dec. 26, 1965, p.4C
      (Reed Hynds).
    San Francisco *Chronicle*, Oct. 27, 1965, p.41
      (William Hogan).
    Saturday Review, 48, 39:38-39 (Sept. 25, 1965) (Earl
      Labor) [This review resulted in letters from Philip
      S. Foner and Roger Daniels published in 48,42:44
      (Oct. 16, 1965) and in Labor's reply in a later
      issue.]
    Western American Literature, 1,1:66,68 (May 1966)
      (George H. Tweney).

2310. *The little lady of the big house:*
    ALA *Booklist*, 12:430 (June 1916).
    Annual Register, 1916, part 2:115.
    Athenaeum, no. 4605:243 (May 1916).
    Atlantic Monthly,118:495 (Oct. 1916) (Wilson Follett).
    Boston *Transcript*, May 6, 1916, p.8.
    Dial, 60:473 (May 11, 1916).
    Independent, 86:305 (May 22, 1916).
    Literary Digest, 52:1461 (May 20, 1916).
    Nation, 102:647-648 (June 15, 1916).
    New York *Times*, 21:129 (April 9, 1916).
    Punch, 150:303 (May 3, 1916).
    Review of Reviews, 53:760 (June 1916).
    Spectator, 116:609 (May 13, 1916).

Springfield *Republican*, April 23, 1916, p.17.
Times Literary Supplement, April 27, 1916, p.202.

2311. *Lost face:*
ALA *Booklist*, 6:303 (April 1910).
Athenaeum, no. 4594:346 (Nov. 13, 1915).
The Bookman (London), 49: supplement, p.89 (Dec. 1915).
Independent, 68:986 (May 5, 1910).
Nation, 90:403 (April 21, 1910).
New York *Times*, 15:183 (April 2, 1910).

2312. *Love of life:*
ALA *Booklist*, 3:202 (Nov. 1907).
Athenaeum, no. 4198:448 (April 11, 1908).
Bookman, 26:419 (Dec. 1907).
Literary Digest, 35:655 (Nov. 2, 1907).
Nation, 85:353 (Oct. 17, 1907).
New York *Times*, 12:584 (Oct. 5, 1907); 12:652 (Oct. 19, 1907).
Outlook, 87:450 (Oct. 26, 1907).
San Francisco *Call*, Dec. 22, 1907, p.6.
Saturday Review, 106:149-150 (Aug. 1, 1908).
Sunset, 20:299 (1908).

2313. *Martin Eden:*
ALA *Booklist*, 6:92 (Nov. 1909).
Athenaeum, no. 4317:93 (July 23, 1910).
Bookman, 30:279 (Nov. 1909) (F. T. Cooper).
Books of today and the books of tomorrow, Aug. 1910, p.1.
Dial, 47:386 (Nov. 16, 1909) (W. M. Payne).
Grizzly Bear, 4:8 (Dec. 1908).
Independent, 67:980 (Oct. 28, 1909).
Labor Action, 10:6 (Aug. 5, 1946) (James T. Farrell).
Manchester Guardian, July 13, 1910, p.5.
Nation, 89:406 (Oct. 28, 1909).
New York *Times*, 14:631 (Oct. 23, 1909); 14:633 (Oct. 23, 1909) (H. W. Boynton).
Outlook, 98:361 (Oct. 16, 1909).
Publishers' Circular, 93:199 (Aug. 13, 1910).
Punch, 139:198 (Sept. 14, 1910).
San Francisco *Call*, Dec. 5, 1909, p.7.

2314. *Michael, brother of Jerry:*
ALA *Booklist*, 14:132 (Jan. 1918).
Boston *Transcript*, Dec. 19, 1917, p.8.
Nation, 105:666-667 (Dec. 13, 1917).

New York *Call*, Dec. 29, 1917, p.14 (D. P. Berenberg).
New York *Times*, 22:490 (Nov. 25, 1917).
Oakland *World*, Dec. 21, 1917, p.2 (D. Bobspa).
Punch, 154:112 (Feb. 20, 1918).
San Francisco *Chronicle*, Jan. 13, 1918, p.2E.

2315. *Moon-face:*
Academy, 71:399 (Oct. 20, 1906).
Athenaeum, no. 4121:477 (Oct. 20, 1906).
Bookman, 24:247 (Nov. 1906).
Catholic World, 84:883 (March 1907).
Independent, 61:698 (Sept. 20, 1906).
Literary Digest, 33:474 (Oct. 6, 1906).
Nation, 83:308 (Oct. 11, 1906).
New York *Times*, 11:296 (Sept. 29, 1906).
Outlook, 84:337 (Oct. 1906).
Punch, 132:18 (Jan. 9, 1907).
Saturday Review of Literature, 103:178 (Feb. 9, 1907).
World today, 11:1222 (Nov. 1906).

2316. *The mutiny of the Elsinore:*
ALA *Booklist*, 11:122 (Nov. 1914).
Athenaeum, no. 4555:140 (Feb. 13, 1915).
Bookman, 40:324-325 (Nov. 1914) (J. Marchand).
The Bookman (London), 47:184 (March 1915).
Boston *Transcript*, Sept. 30, 1914, p.24 (E. F. E.).
Dial, 57:342 (Nov. 1, 1914).
Independent, 80:26 (Oct. 5, 1914); 80:243 (Nov. 16, 1914).
Nation, 99:654 (Dec. 3, 1914) (H. W. Boynton).
New Republic, 1:28 (Dec. 26, 1914).
Outlook, 108:846 (Dec. 9, 1914).
Punch, 148:59 (Jan. 20, 1915).
Review of Reviews, 51:165-166 (Feb. 1915).
San Francisco *Chronicle*, Oct. 4, 1914, p.29.
Springfield *Republican*, Oct. 8, 1914, p.5.

2317. *The night born:*
ALA *Booklist*, 9:344 (April 1913).
Boston *Transcript*, Feb. 26, 1913, p.22.
Current Opinion, 54:490-491 (June 1913).
Nation, 96:443 (May 1, 1913).
New York *Times*, 18:123 (March 9, 1913).
Outlook, 103:863 (April 19, 1913).
Out West, n.s. 6:148 (Sept. 1913).
Overland Monthly, n.s. 61:304 (March 1913).
Publishers' Weekly, 83:1142 (March 22, 1913)
(F. M. Holly).

Punch, 151:132 (Aug. 16, 1916).
San Francisco *Call*, March 10, 1913, p.7.
Springfield *Republican*, April 10, 1913, p.5.

2318. *On the Makaloa mat:*
Nation, 109:693 (Nov. 29, 1919).
New York *Times*, 24:649 (Nov. 16, 1919).
San Francisco *Chronicle*, Jan. 18, 1920, p.26.
New York *Sun*, Nov. 16, 1919, p.16 (N. P. D.).

2319. *People of the abyss:*
Advance, Nov. 26, 1903.
Baptist Commonwealth, 16, 13:17 (Nov. 26, 1903).
Bookman, 18:647-648 (Feb. 1904) (E. C. Marsh).
The Bookman (London), 25:188 (Jan. 1904).
Brooklyn *Eagle*, Nov. 3, 1903, p.2.
Chicago *Evening Post*, Dec. 23, 1903, p.5. (I. K.
    Freeman).
Christian Herald, Nov. 25, 1903, p.[?].
Critic, 44:217-218 (March 1904) (A. Hodder).
Current Literature, 36:413-416 (April 1906).
Daily Express, Nov. 14, 1903, p.[?] (E. Fletcher
    Robinson).
Denver *Republican*, Nov. 15, 1903, p.[?].
Dial, 36:11-12 (Jan. 1, 1904) (T. D. A. Cockerell).
Independent, 55:3063-3064 (Dec. 24, 1903).
Nation, 77:384 (Nov. 12, 1903).
New Statesman, 65:50 (July 13, 1962) (Clancy Sigal).
Out West, n.s. 19:683 (Dec. 1903).
Publishers' Circular, 80:11 (Jan. 2, 1904).
San Francisco *Call*, Nov. 20, 1903, p.7.
San Francisco *Chronicle*, Nov. 29, 1903, p.8.
San Francisco *Examiner*, Nov. 29, 1903, p.8.
Springfield *Republican*, Nov. 8, 1903, p.23.
Week's Survey, Nov. 14, 1903, p.[?] (B. R. N.).

2320. *The red one:*
Boston *Transcript*, Nov. 30, 1918, p.6 (E. F. E.).
Nation, 107:628 (Nov. 23, 1918).
New York *Call*, Nov. 24, 1918, p.6.
New York *Times*, 23:483 (Nov. 10, 1918).
San Francisco *Chronicle*, Nov. 30, 1918, p.7.

2321. *Revolution:*
ALA *Booklist*, 7:22 (Sept. 1910).
Athenaeum, no. 4701:749 (June 4, 1920) (brief notice).
Dial, 49:17 (July 1, 1910).
New York *Times*, 15:302 (May 28, 1910).

San Francisco *Call,* June 5, 1910, p.7.
Survey, 24:830 (Sept. 10, 1910).

2322. *The road:*
Arena, 39:124 (Jan. 1908).
Dial, 44:301 (May 16, 1908) (E. E. Hale, Jr.).
Independent, 64:421 (Feb. 20, 1908).
New York *Times,* 12:861 (Dec. 28, 1907).
San Francisco *Call,* Feb. 9, 1908, p.6.

2323. *Scarlet plague:*
Bookman, 41:566-567 (July 1915) (G. I. Colbron).
Boston *Transcript,* May 15, 1915, p.8 (E. F. E.).
Dial, 59:31 (June 24, 1915).
Nation, 101:17 (July 1, 1915).
New York *Times,* 20:194 (May 23, 1915).
Outlook, 110:285 (June 2, 1915).

2324. *Scorn of women:*
Canadian Monthly, 28:399 (Feb. 1907).
*Nation,*83:495 (Dec. 6, 1906).
New York *Times,* 11:778 (Nov. 24, 1906).
San Francisco *Call,* Dec. 16, 1906, p.13.
Spectator, 99:461 (Oct. 5, 1907).

2325. *The sea wolf:*
Academy (London), 68:14 (Jan. 7, 1905).
Arena, 33:452 (April 1905) (A. O. Rich).
Athenaeum, no. 4024:801 (Dec. 10, 1904).
Bookman, 20:219 (Nov. 1904).
Books of today and the books of tomorrow, Jan. 1905,
  p.5
Dial, 38:16 (Jan. 1, 1905) (W. M. Payne).
Independent, 58:39 (Jan. 5, 1905).
Nation, 79:507 (Dec. 22, 1904).
Outlook, 78:872 (Dec. 3, 1904).
Out West, 21:586 (Dec. 1904).
Publishers' Circular, 82:180 (Feb. 18, 1905).
Reader, 5:378 (Feb. 1905).
Review of Reviews, 31:115 (Jan. 1905).
San Francisco *Call,* Dec. 4, 1911, p.14.
San Francisco *Chronicle,* Nov. 13, 1904, p.8; Jan. 1,
  1905, p.4 (magazine section).

2326. *Smoke and Shorty:*
Athenaeum, no. 4683:158 (Jan. 30, 1920) [brief notice].

2327. *Smoke Bellew:*

Athenaeum, no. 4472:37 (July 12, 1913).
Bookman, 44:220 (Aug. 1913) (E. W.).
Boston *Transcript,* Oct. 23, 1912, p.24 (E. F. E.).
Manchester Guardian, July 16, 1913, p.5.
New York *Times,* 17:612 (Oct. 20, 1912).
Outlook, 102:320 (Oct. 12, 1912).
Out West, 37:214-215 (March-April 1913).
Passenger, 3,73:16 (Sept. 13, 1913).
Punch, 145:79 (July 16, 1913).
San Francisco *Call* magazine section, Oct. 13, 1912,
    p.7.

2328. *Son of the sun:*
    ALA *Booklist,* 9:37 (Sept. 1912).
    Athenaeum, no. 4454:282 (March 8, 1913).
    The Bookman (London), 44:supplement, p.32 (April 1913).
    Independent, 72:1277 (June 6, 1912).
    Manchester Guardian, March 12, 1913, p.7.
    Out West, 4:211 (Aug. 1912).
    Punch, 144:251 (March 26, 1913).
    West Coast, 12:633 (Aug. 1912).

2329. *Son of the wolf:*
    Bookman, 11:200-201 (May 1900).
    Brooklyn *Eagle,* Feb. 14, 1901, p.15.
    Columbus (Ohio) *Press Post,* Sept. 23, 1900, p.4.
    Critic, 37:162-163 (Aug. 1900) (C. A. Pratt).
    National Magazine, 12:50-53 (May 1900) (Maitland
        Leroy Osborne).
    Pacific Monthly, 4:1 (May 1900).
    Town Talk, 8:24 (May 12, 1900).

2330. *South Sea tales:*
    ALA *Booklist,* 8:174 (Dec. 1911).
    Athenaeum, no. 4441:690 (Dec. 7, 1912).
    San Francisco *Call,* Nov. 26, 1911, p.7.

2331. *Star rover:*
    Analog: Science fact and Science Fiction, 73,2:91
        (P. Schuyler Miller).
    Boston *Transcript,* Oct. 15, 1915, p.22 (W. A. M.).
    Dial, 60:30 (Jan. 6, 1916) (E. H. Hale).
    Independent, 84:270 (Nov. 15, 1915).
    Magazine of Fantasy and Science Fiction, 26,1:43
        (Jan. 1964) (Marion Zimmer Bradley).
    Nation, 101:548 (Nov. 4, 1915).
    New York *Times,* 20:389 (Oct. 17, 1915).
    Phoenix, 4,2:33-39 (Jan. 1916) (Michael Monahan).

Review of Reviews, 52:765 (Dec. 1915).
Spectator, 115:280 (Aug. 28, 1915).
Springfield *Republican*, Oct. 31, 1915, p.15.
Wisconsin Library Bulletin, 11:371 (Dec. 1915).

2332. *Strength of the strong:*
  Bookman, 39:679 (Aug. 1914).
  Boston *Transcript*, June 10, 1914, p.4.
  Independent, 78:491 (June 14, 1914).
  Literary Digest, 49:199 (Aug. 1, 1914).
  New York *Times*, June 14, 1914, vi:270.
  Punch, 152:232 (April 4, 1917).
  Springfield *Republican*, July 2, 1914, p.5.
  Strength of the strong [Phamplet]: Oakland *World*,
    Sept. 16, 1911, p.2.

2333. *Sun-dog trail and other stories:*
  ALA *Booklist*, 48:128 (Dec. 1, 1951).
  Chicago Sunday *Tribune*, Aug. 5, 1951, p.5 (V. P. Hass).
  Kirkus, 19:280 (June 1, 1951).
  New York *Times Book Review*, Aug. 19, 1951, p.18
    (Harry Sylvester).

2334. *Tales of adventure:*
  ALA *Booklist*, 53:278 (Feb. 1, 1957).
  San Francisco *Chronicle*, Nov. 27, 1956, p.21 (William
    Hogan).
  Springfield *Republican*, Dec. 30, 1956, p.12B.
  Time, 68:62 (Dec. 24, 1956).

2335. *Tales of the fish patrol:*
  Academy (London), 70:287 (March 24, 1906).
  Athenaeum, no. 4087:229 (Feb. 24, 1906).
  Outlook, 81:579 (Nov. 4, 1905); 81:712 (Nov. 25, 1905).
  Out West, 24:330 (April 1906).
  Public Opinion, 39:763 (Dec. 9, 1905).
  Saturday Review (London), 101:338 (March 17, 1906).
  Spectator, 97:98 (July 21, 1906).

2336. *Theft:*
  Dramatist, 2:156-157 (April 1911).
  San Francisco *Call*, Jan. 1, 1911, p.7.

2337. *Turtles of Tasman:*
  ALA *Booklist*, 13:177 (Jan. 1917).
  Boston *Transcript*, Nov. 8, 1916, p.6 (W. A. M.).
  Dial, 61:353 (Nov. 2, 1916) (E. E. Hale).
  Independent, 88:330 (Nov. 20, 1916).

Los Angeles *Times*, Dec. 3, 1916, III, B7.
Nation, 104:19 (Jan. 4, 1917).
New Republic, 9:55 (Nov. 11, 1916).
New York *Times*, 21:439 (Oct. 22, 1916).
Springfield *Republican*, Oct. 22, 1916, p.13.

2338. *Valley of the moon:*
Athenaeum, no. 4497:11 (Jan. 3, 1914).
Bookman, 45:283 (Feb. 1914).
Boston *Transcript*, Nov. 8, 1913, p.8 (E. F. Edgett).
Current Opinion, 56:212-213 (March 1914).
New York *Sun*, Nov. 8, 1913, p.3.
New York *Times*, 18:607 (Nov. 9, 1913).
Punch, 146:19 (Jan. 7, 1914).

2339. *War of the classes:*
*Annals of the American Academy of Political and
    Social Science*, 29:592 (Sept. 1905).
Athenaeum, no. 4688:320 (March 5, 1920 (brief notice).
Bookman, 22:61-64 (Sept. 1905) (Robert C. Brooks).
Boston *Daily Advertiser*, April 21, 1905, p.8.
Charities, 15:403 (Dec. 23, 1905).
Dial, 40:297 (May 1, 1905).
Independent, 58:1190 (May 1905).
International Socialist Review, 6:184 (1905-1906).
New York *Times*, 10:249 (April 15, 1905); 10:291 (May
    6, 1905).
Outlook, 80:144 (May 13, 1905).
Public Opinion, 38:795 (May 20, 1905).
Reader, 6:595 (Oct. 1905).
Review of Reviews, 32:510 (Oct. 1905).

2340. *When God laughs:*
ALA *Booklist*, 7:348 (April 1911).
Bookman, 33:195 (April 1911) (F. T. Cooper).
Nation, 92:194 (Feb. 23, 1911).
New York *Times*, 16:88 (Feb. 19, 1911).
Review of Reviews, 43:120 (Jan. 1911).

2341. *White Fang:*
Academy (London), 72:274 (March 16, 1907).
Athenaeum, no. 4137:161 (Feb. 9, 1907).
Bookman, 24:599-600 (Feb. 1907) (Grace Isabel
    Colbron).
Books of today and the books of tomorrow, March 1907,
    p.4.
Current Literature, 82:111 (Jan. 1907).
Dial, 41:389 (Dec. 1, 1906) (May Estelle Cook).

Forum, 38:547 (April 1907) (Herbert W. Horwill).
Independent, 61:1055 (Nov. 1, 1906).
Maoriland Worker (New Zealand), 2,21:6 (July 28, 1911)
(R[obert] S[amuel] R[oss]) [3-column review and
synopsis of book with long quotations].
Nation, 83:440-441 (Nov. 22, 1906).
New York *Times*, 11:764 (Nov. 17, 1906); 11:797
(Dec. 1, 1906).
Outlook, 84:710 (Nov. 24, 1906).
Punch, 132:162 (March 6, 1907).
Review of Reviews, 35:128 (Jan. 1907).
Spectator, 97:219 (Feb. 9, 1907).
Times Literary Supplement, 6:46 (Feb. 8, 1907).

CZECH/SLOVAK
2342. *Bílý tesák (White Fang)*:
Růst roč, p.54 (Jan. 1947).
Štepnice, pp.334-336 (1950/1951) (F. V. Kříž).

2343. *Chicagská komuna. Z mého života (Iron heel)*:
Proletkult, 1:177-181 (1922) (A. M. Píša).

2344. *Generální stávka*:
Proletkult, 1:14 (1922) (A. M. Píša).

2345. *Martin Eden*:
Host do domu, 2:85 (1954)(Jan Skácel).
Nový život, 7:101-104 (1954) (Fr. Pilař).
Obránce vlasti, 42:7 (April 1956) (F. Swidzinski).

DUTCH
2346. *Als de natuur roept (The call of the wild)*:
Tijdspiegel, 69, part 1:105 (E. S.).

2347. *Alaska Kid (Smoke Bellew)*:
De Nieuwe Eeuw, 29,1476:11 (Sept. 18, 1948).

2348. *Der Insulaner* [German translation of *Jerry of the
islands*]:
Boekzaal, 3:222 (Aug. 1927).

2349. *Konig Alcohol (John Barleycorn)*:
Boekenschouw, 15:145-146 (1921/1922) (A. Gielen).
Vrij Nederland, 9,8:7 (Oct. 23, 1948).

2350. *Martin Eden*:
Morks Magazijn, 21:187-188 (April 1919).
Nieuwe Rotterdamsche Courant, 68,362:1 (Dec. 31, 1911)

(Augusta de Wit).

2351. *Das Mondtal* [German translation of *Valley of the moon*]:
   Boekzaal, 6:122-123 (April 1930).

2352. *Onder koppensnellers (Adventure[?]):*
   Boekenschouw, 13:146-147 (1919/1920).

2353. *Ein Sohn der Sonne* [German translation of *A son of the
   sun*]:
   Boekzaal, 3:191 (July 1927).

2354. *Strength of the strong:*
   Nieuwe Rotterdamsche Courant, 74,109:1 (part B)
   (April 21, 1917) (Augusta de Wit).

2355. *Terry, De broeder van Jerry (Michael, brother of Jerry):*
   Boekenschouw, 13:177-178 (1919/1920).

2356. *Tusschen de wielen (The road):*
   Getij, 1923:63-64 (Rene Vandeneertwegh).
   "Jack London, vertaald," *Nieuwe Rotterdamsche Courant*,
   80,143:3 (part A) (May 26, 1923) [Review of *Een
   dochter van de sneeuwvelden*, i.e., *Daughter of the
   snows*, and *Verhalen van de Zuidzee*, i.e., *South
   Sea tales*].

ESTONIAN
2357. *Armastus elu vastu (Love of life):*
   Edasi, Jan. 6, 1952 (S. Maaste, "Jack Londoni
   jutustustekogu..." [A collection of Jack London's
   short stories...]).

2358. *Kuningas Alkohol (John Barleycorn):*
   Eesti Naine, no. 11:324 (1933) ("Suure kirjaniku
   elutôeline teos, ..." [The lifelike novel of a
   great writer...]).

2359. *Martin Eden:*
   Eesti Kirjandus, no. 2:80-83 (1929) (J. Schwalbe).
   Rahva Sona, Jan. 20, 1929.

2360. *Morgani miljonid (Burning daylight[?])*
   Päevaleht, March 6, 1926 (Morgani miljonid. *Päevalehe
   uus romaan*") [... The new novel in *Päevaleht*]).

2361. *Poksija Tom King (A piece of steak):*
   Kirjanduslikke Uudiseid, no. 29-30:12 (1929).

Paevaleht, Sept. 12, 1929.

2362. *Raudne kand (The iron heel):*
  Edasi, Jan. 22, 1955 ("Romaan kapitalismi kurite-
  gudest..." [A novel about the crimes of capitalism ...]).
  Rahva Hääl, Oct. 12, 1955 (V. Pomm) ("Oligarhia
  vôimuses ...") [In the power of the oligarchy.]

FINNISH
Philip Durham and Tauno F. Mustanoja, *American fiction in Finland: an essay and bibliography,* Helsinki,
Société néophilogique, 1960, p.38 state that "We have
seen, among many others, 124 reviews of 16 titles, with
67 of these reviews covering *The iron heel, Jerry of
the islands, John Barleycorn, Martin, Eden, The people
of the abyss,* and *Smoke Bellew.*" The following reviews
are all that are listed in this bibliography and as one
of these authors is at work on a study of London in
Finland, no attempt has been made to trace other reviews.

2363. *Elsinoren kapina (The mutiny of the Elsinore):*
  Tampereen Sanomat, May 1, 1926 (J. V.).

2364. *Erämaan ääni (The call of the wild):*
  Aika, 2:161-162 (1908) (F. O. Viitanen; summarized
  in Durham-Mustanoja, p.38).

2365. *Etelämeren auringon alla (The cruise of the Snark):*
  Uusi Aura, Sept. 25, 1924 (J. S-i).
  Uusi Suomi, Oct. 26, 1924.

2366. *Jeri (Jerry of the islands):*
  Metaästya ja Kalastus, no. 12 (1922) (Frjö Ylänne).
  Turun Sanomat, Nov. 28, 1922 (A. K-la).

2367. *Kadotuksen kansa (People of the abyss):*
  Ikka, Dec. 9, 1922 [Durham-Mustanoja note the exis-
  tence of 11 newspaper reviews of this translation].

2368. *Kultaa ja kuntoa (Smoke Bellew):*
  Karjalan Aamulehti, July 3, 1921.

2369. *Martin Eden:*
  Aika, 15:281-282 (1921) (V. A. Koskenniemi) [sum-
  marized in Durham-Mustanoja, pp.39-40].
  Karjata, April 7, 1921 (I. J. J.).

Uusi Suomi, Dec. 21, 1929 (J. F-e.).

2370. *Merisusi (The sea wolf):*
    Aamulehti, Aug. 24, 1915 (U. W. Walakorpi).

2371. *Onnen suosikki (Burning daylight):*
    Aika, 2:313-314 (1908) (V. A. Koskenniemi) [summar-
    ized in Durham-Mustanoja, pp.38-39].

2372. *Pakkopaita (The star rover):*
    Helsingin Sanomat, May 28, 1923 (Aarni Kouta).
    Karjala, July 1, 1923.
    Saarijärven Paavo, July 7, 1923.
    Suomen Sosialidemokraatti, July 2, 1923.

2373. *Rautakorko (The iron heel):*
    Kansas Lehti, Dec. 17, 1921 (T. L.).
    Pohjan Kansa, Nov. 7, 1921.
    Pohjan Kansa, Nov. 18, 1921. [Article attacks pub-
    lisher's note sent out with review copies of the
    translation; for a discussion of these reviews, see
    Durham-Mustanoja, p.40.]

2374. *Tuliliemen tuttavana (John Barleycorn):*
    Aika, 9:223-225 (1915) (Hugo Jalkanen; Durham-Mus-
    tanoja, p.39).
    Kylaväjä, 18:500 (1914); 19:34 (1915). [This journal
    was the principal organ of the Finnish temperance
    movement; it published two opposing views of the
    book; Durham-Mustanoja, p.39.]

2375. *Valkohamma (White Fang):*
    Helsingin Sanomat, Dec. 24, 1918 (T. M.).

FRENCH
2376. *Croc-blanc (White Fang):*
    Nouvelles littéraires, April 28, 1923, p.3 (M. E.).

2377. *Mémoires d'un buveur (John Barleycorn):*
    Revue de France, 11:135-146 (March 1, 1931)
    (L. Pierre-Quint).
    Studium (Chile) 1,3:287-288 (Dec. 1926-Jan. 1927)
    (Jorge Guzman Dinator).

2378. *Le tourbillon (The star rover):*
    Revue de l'enseignement des langues vivantes, 43:466-
    7 (1926) (P. G. D.).

GERMAN
2379. *Abenteuer des Schienenstranges (The road):*
Bücherei und Bildungspflege, 5:250 (1925) (H. J.
Homan).
Deutsche Handelswarte (Nürnberg), 14:475 (1926).
Hefte für Büchereiwesen (Vienna), 10:3 (1925).
Monatsschrift für Kriminalpsychologie (Heidelberg),
19:190 (1928) (V. Hentig).
Zeitschrift für Bücherfreunde (Leipzig), 17:22 (1925).

2380. *Alaska-Kid (Smoke Bellew):*
Die Arbeit (Berlin), no. 4:294-296 (1956) (Alfred
Kraushaar).
Die Literatur (Berlin), 33:651 (1930-1931) (Albert
Ludwig).
Die Literatur (Berlin), 34:580 (1931-1932) (Werner
Schickert).
Neue Literatur (Leipzig), 33:176 (1931) (Kurt Martens).

2381. *An der weissen Grenze (A daughter of the snows):*
Bücherei und Bildung, 5:395 (1953) (Viktor Zifreund).
Bücherei und Bildungspflege, 13:396 (1933) (V.
Zifreund).
Die Literature, 35:635-638 (1932-1933) (Werner
Schickert, "Sieben Romane des Auslandes und was
sie uns angehen").

2382. *Die Austernpiraten (The cruise of the Dazzler):*
Bücherei und Bildungspflege, 12:80 (1932) (R. Koch).

2383. *Drei Sonnen am Himmel (The sun dog trail):*
Gral (München), 29:183 (1934-1935) (G. A. Lutterbeck).
Die Literatur, 37:168-169 (1934-1935) (Werner
Schickert).

2384. *Die eiserne Ferse (The iron heel):*
Bücherei und Bildungspflege (Leipzig), 8:56 (1928)
(W. Schuster).
Deutsche Rundschau (Berlin), 53:72 (July 1927)
(E. Stern-Rubarth).
Gral (München), 22:530 (1927-1928); 28:382 (1933-1934)
(K. Arns).
Hefte für Büchereiwesen (Vienna), 12:106-110 (1928)
(W. Hoyer).
Der Rundfunk (Berlin), 3,3:10 (1948).
Der Scheinwerfer (Essen), 2,2:32 (1928) (K. Westhoven).
Die schöne Literatur (Leipzig), 29:31 (192[?])
(J. Oven).

2385. *Die Fahrt der Snark (The cruise of the Snark)*:
      Gral (München), 26:155 (1931-1932).

2386. *Die glücklichen Inseln* (selections from *On the Makaloa
      mat* and *House of pride*):
      Bücherei und Bildung, 7:13-14 (1955) (Hans Ulrich
         Eberle).
      Bücherwelt (Bonn), 29:70 (1932) (Wippermann).
      Hochschule und Ausland (Berlin), 8,11:41 (1930).
      Der Ring (Berlin), 3:300 (1930).
      Die schöne Literatur (Leipzig), 31:490 (1930)
         (K. Martens).

2387. *Die Goldgräber am Yukon* (adapted from *The son of the
      wolf*):
      Bücherei und Bildungspflege, 12:101 (1932)
         (E. Sielaff).

2388. *Die Goldschlucht (All gold canyon)*:
      Gral, 25:1148 (1930-1931).

2389. *Die Herrin des grossen Hauses (The little lady of the
      big house)*:
      Bücherei und Bildungspflege, 10:228 (1930)
         (W. Schuster).
      Gral, (München), 24:568 (1929-1930).
      Die Literatur, 31:725 (1928-1929) (Werner Schickert).
      Die schöne Literatur, 31:35 (1930) (Käthe Miethe).

2390. *In den Wäldern des Nordens (Children of the frost)*:
      Bücherei und Bildungspflege, 5:[?](1925) (H. J. Homan).
      Gral (München), 29:137 (1934-1935) (G. A. Lutterbeck).
      Hefte für Buchereiwesen (Vienna), 10:3 (1925)
         (Morgenstern).
      Die Literatur, 28:54 (1925) (Albert Ludwig).

2391. *Die Insel Berande (Adventure)*:
      Bücherei und Bildungspflege, 8:56 (1928) (W. Schuster).
      Deutsche Rundschau, 53:72 (1927) (E. Stern-Rubarth)
         [also a review of Die eiserne Ferse].
      Gral, 23:814 (1928-1929) (Karl Arns).

2392. *Jerry der Insulaner (Jerry of the islands)*:
      Bücherei und Bildungspflege, 7:245 (1927)
         (G. Hermann).
      Gral, 22:132 (1927).

2393. *Joe unter Piraten (Cruise of the Dazzler)*:

Bücherei und Bildungspflege, 11:73 (1931)
(G. A. Narciss).

2394. *König Alkohol (John Barleycorn):*
Bios (Hagenau), 2:243-249 (1928) (W. Riese).
Blätter für Volksgesundheitspflege (Velten) 25:180
(1925).
Büchergilde (Frankfurt, Mainz), 11:8 (1949).
Bücherwarte (Berlin), 1:8 (1926) (A Siemsen).
Hefte für Büchereiwesen (Vienna), 11:318 (1925)
(Morgenstern).
Die neue Erziehung. Sozialpädagogische Wochenschrift
(Berlin), 8:512 (1926) (O. Kaufmann).
Die Literatur, 28:54 (1925) (A. Ludwig).
Die Schulreform (Bern), 19:278 (1925) (F. Schwarz).
Sobrietas(Heidhausen), 24,5:20 (1930).
Die sozialistische Erziehung (Vienna), 5:245 (1925)
(A. Jalkotzky).
Zeitschrift für französischen und englischen Unter-
richt (Berlin), 25:177 (1926).

2395. *Lockruf des Goldes (Burning daylight):*
Die literarische Welt (Berlin), 2,30:6 (1926)
(A. Eggebrecht).
Mitteldeutsche Monatshefte (Dresden), 10:109 (1926).

2396. *Love of life:*
Literarisches Echo, 10:278 (1907-1908) (Λ. Ende,
"Amerikanischer Brief").

2397. *Martin Eden:*
Buchbesprechung (Berlin), 7:397-399 (1956) (Johannes
Schellenberger, "Auswegslosigkeit des Individual-
ismus").
Bücherei und Bildungspflege (Leipzig), 8:56 (1928)
(W. Schuster).
Bücherschale (Berlin), 1,2:11-20 (1927) (J. E.
Poritzky).
Eckart (Berlin), 4:132 (1928) (Bartsch).
Germania (Berlin), Nov. 10, 1927 (E. A. Schwarz).
Hefte für Büchereiwesen, 12:106-110 (1928) (W. Hoyer).
Gral, 28:382 (1933-1934), 22:530 (1927-1928) (K. Arns).
Die literarische Welt, 3,41:7 (1927) (F. Gottfurcht).
Neue Züricher Zeitung, Sept. 23, 1927.
Die schöne Literatur, 15:116 (1914) (Arno Schneider);
29:31 (1928) (J. Oven).
Sonntag (Berlin), no. 46:8 (1955) (W. Joho).
Die Weltbünne, 23:52 (1927-1928[?]) (Manfred Georg).

Zeitschrift für Bücherfreunde, n.s. supplement,
20:173 (1928) (Karl Arns).

2398. *Menschen der Tiefe (People of the abyss):*
Berliner Börsencourier, no. 585 (1928).
Goetheanum (Dornach), 8:38 (1929) (Fränkl).
Gral, 23:814 (1928-1929) (Karl Arns).
Die Pause (Vienna), 7,9:32 (1942) (K. Pawek).

2399. *Meuterei auf der Elsinore (Mutiny of the Elsinore):*
Bücherei und Bildungspflege, 13:397 (1937)
(V. Zifreund).

2400. *Michael, der Bruder Jerrys (Michael, brother of Jerry):*
Berliner Börsenzeitung, no. 190 (1928[?])
(H. Herrland).
Bildung und Bücherei, 2:1118 (1950) (Rudolf Jörden).
Bücherei und Bildungspflege, 8:372 (1928)
(G. Hermann).
Gral, 23:814 (1928-1929) (K. Arns).
Neue Freie Presse (Vienna), June 10, 1928
(R. J. Kreutz).

2401. *Das Mondtal (The valley of the moon):*
Englische Studien (Leipzig), 1914:430-432
(A. Schneider).
Gral, 29:479 (1934-1935) (E. A. Lutterbeck).
Die Literatur, 32:724 (1929-1930) (Albert Ludwig).
Der Ring, 2:982 (1929).

2402. *Nur Fleisch (Just Meat):*
Gral, 24:667 (1929-1930) (K. Arns).
Kunst und Kritik (Chemnitz), 1929:237 (M. Mann).

2403. *Der Rote (The red one):*
Bücherei und Bildungspflege, 8:437 (1928)
(W. Schuster).
Gral, 23:814-816 (1928-1929) (Karl Arns).
Die literarische Welt, 4,42:5 (1928) (B. Silber).
Die Literatur, 31:355 (1928-1929) (Albert Ludwig).

2404. *Der Ruhm des Kämpfers (The abysmal brute):*
Das deutsche Wort (Berlin), 12:743 (1936) (P. Partik).
Gral, 31:142 (1936-1937).

2405. *Der Schiffshund der Makamba (Michael, brother of Jerry):*
Bücherei und Bildungspflege, 12:151 (1932)
(E. Sieloff).

Zeitschrift d. Gewerkschaftsbundes der Angestellten
(Berlin), 1931:209.

2406. Der Seewolf (The sea wolf):
Hefte für Büchereiwesen, 12:114 (1928) (W. Hoyer).
Zeitschrift für Bucherfreunde (Leipzig), 18:266
(1926) (E. E. Schwabach).

2407. Der Schrei des Pferdes:
Bücher voll guten Geistes. 30 Jahre Büchergilde
Gutenberg Almanach Frankfurt/M. 1954:162-176.

2408. Siwash (God of his fathers):
Bücherei und Bildungspflege, 9:230 (1929)
(W. Schuster).
Gral, 24:183 (1929-1930).
Kunst und Kritik, 1929:98.
Die Literatur, 31:726 (1928-1929) (Albert Ludwig).

2409. Ein Sohn der Sonne (The son of the sun):
Büchergilde (Frankfurt/Mainz), 5:6:14 (1948).

2410. Der Sohn des Wolfes (The son of the wolf):
Bildung und Bücherei, 8:113 (1956) (Gerhard Goecke).
Bücherei und Bildungspflege, 8:56 (1928)
(W. Schuster).
Deutsche Handelswarte (Leipzig), 16:96 (1928).
Gral, 22:402 (1927-1928) (Ch. Demming).
Zeitschrift für Bücherfreunde, 20:173 (1928)
(Karl Arns).

2411. South Sea tales:
Englische Studien, 47:291-294 (1913-1914)
(Fritz Jung).
Die Schöne Literatur, 15:116 (1914) (Arno Schneider).

2412. Südseegeschichten (South Sea tales):
Der Bibliothekar (Leipzig), 3:288-298 (1957)
(Edwin Orthmann).
Bücherei und Bildungspflege, 5:250 (1925)
(H. J. Homan).
Hefte für Buchereiwesen, 10:3 (1925) (Albert Ludwig).

2413. Die Teufel von Fuatino:
Bücherei und Bildungspflege, 12:151 (1932)
(E. Sieloff).

2414. Valley of the moon:

Englische Studien, 51:430-432 (1917-1918)
(A. Schneider).

2415. *Vor Adam (Before Adam):*
      Bibliothekar, 8:894 (1916[?]).
      Mikrokosmos, 9:106 (1915).

2416. *War of the classes:*
      Documente des Socialismus, 5:441 (1905).

2417. *Wenn die Natur ruft (The call of the wild);*
      Buchbesprechung (Leipzig), no. 12;751-752 (1955)
         (Margarete Schneider).
      Bücherei und Bildungspflege, 7:465 (1927) (two re-
         views by H. J. Homan and Therese Krimmer).
      Literarisches Echo, 10:1461 (1907-1908) (Max
         Meyerfield).
      Neue philologische Rundschau, 1908:88 (herting).
      Zeitschrift des Gewerkschaftsbundes der Angestellten,
         1931:209.

2418. *When God laughs and other stories:*
      Englische Studien, 46:322-324 (1912-1913) (O. Glode).
      Die schöne Literatur, 14:327 (1913) (Karl Seelheim).

2419. *Wolfsblut (White Fang):*
      Baltische Monatshefte (Riga), 1936:180 (Bosse).
      Büchbesprechung, 10:178 (1934) (Margarete Schneider).
      Bücherei und Bildungspflege, 12:238 (1932) (two re-
         views by W. Schuster and R. Koch).
      Gral, 20:733 (1925-1926) (K. Arns).
      Zeitschrift für Anglistik u. Amerikanistik (Berlin)
         1:111-119 (1957) (Dietrich Herrde).

2420. *Das Wort der Männer (The faith of men):*
      Die Literatur, 35:170 (1932-1933) (Werner Schickert).

2421. *Die Zwangsjacke (The star rover or The jacket):*
      Monatsschrift für Kriminalpsychologie (Heidelberg),
         22:256 (1931).

2422. *Zwischen Südsee und Eismeer:*
      Die Räder (Berlin), 13:579 (1932).
      Die Yacht (Berlin), 29,49:20 (1932) (Winter).

ICELANDIC
2423. *Bakkus konungur (John Barleycorn):*
      Eimrei in, 1934:239 (Svainn Sigursson).

Morgunbla i, 20:304 (1933) (G. J.).

2424. *Öbygg irnar kalla (The call of the wild):*
Nyjar kvöldvökur (Akureyri), 1952:103 (Steindór Steindorsson).

ITALIAN
2425. *Martin Eden:*
Italia che scrive, 10:133 (1927) (P. Vita-Finzi).

2426. *La storia di un cane (The call of the wild):*
Italia che scrive, 10:133 (1927) (P. Vita-Finzi).

2427. *Il tallone di ferro (The iron heel):*
Italia che scrive, 10:133 (1927) (P. Vita-Finzi).

LATVIAN
2428. *Kad senču asinis runa (The call of the wild):*
Jaunibas Tekas, no. 3:76-77 (1925) (Jekabs Ligotņu).

2429. *Kopoti raksti (Collected works):*
Domas, no. 9:72 (1924) (A. Upits).
Latvju Gramata, no. 7-8:58-59 (1923) (J. Ziemelnieks).
Latvju Gramata, no. 2:28-29 (1925) (J. Ziemelnieks).

2430. *Pirms Adama laikiem (Before Adam):*
Nakotnes Speks, no. 5:52-53 (1925).

2431. *Zegelejums ar Apzilbinoso (The cruise of the Dazzler):*
Latvju Gramata, no. 7-8:59-60 (1923) (K. O.).

LITHUANIAN
2432. *Vagysto, (Theft, drama review):*
Budzinskas, J. "Vilkiskos sielos. Dž. Londono dramos 'Vagyste' pastatymas Lietuvos TSR Valst. dramos teatre," *Švyturys*, no. 14:17 (1955) [Wolfish souls. The production of Jack London's drama *Theft* by the Lithuanian National Drama Theatre].
Galinis, H., "Vilkišku sielu' pasaulis. Dž. Londono 'Vagyste' Lietuvos TSR Valst; dramos teatre," *Komjaunimo tiesa*, Nov. 11, 1955. [The universe of wolfish souls. Jack London's *Theft* by the Lithuanian National Drama Theatre].

RUSSIAN
2433. *Beloe bezmolvie. Klondaiskie rasskazy (White silence. Klondike Stories):*
Novaia zhizn', no. 1:315-316 (1912) (L. Andruson).

Sovremennyĭ mir, 1911:340-341 (B. Mirov).

2434. *Belyĭ klyk (White fang)*:
      Chto chitat', no. 2:58-60, 93 (1938) (V. Sytin).
      Retzh. Detskaia literatura, no. 16:11-15 (1936).

2435. *Borba klassov (War of the classes)*:
      Zvezda, no. 5:283 (1924).

2436. *Lunaya dolina (Valley of the moon)*:
      Zvezda, no. 5:279 (1924) (L. Vasilevski).

2437. *Serdtsa tryokh (Hearts of three)*:
      Bobrov, Sergei, "Novyie inostrantsi," *Krasnaya nov.*,
      no. 6:252 (1923).
      Pechat i revolyutsivya, no. 6:250 (1923) (K. Loks).

2438. *Smok Bell'iu. Smok i malysh (Smoke Bellew)*:
      Lit. obozrenie, no. 21:47-49 (P. Balashov).

2439. *Za kulisami tsirka (Michael, brother of Jerry)*:
      Pechat i revolyutsiya, no. 4:287 (1925) (Sergei
      Obruchev).

2440. *Zheleznaya pyata (The iron heel)*:
      Pechat i revolyutsiya, no. 5:298 (1923) (I. Rozental).
      Novy mir, no. 5:126-128 (1925) (V. Friche, "Tri
      amerikantia").

      Reviews of anthologies and collected works:
2441. *Polnoe sobranie sochineniĭ*, 1912-1913:
      Rus. bogatstvo, 1913:369-371 (1913).

2442. *Rasskazy*, 1939:
      Detskaia literatura, no. 5:38-42 (1940) (E. Lundberg).

2443. *Sochineniia*, 1955:
      Neva, no. 3:176 (1956) (O. Kushch, "Razmyshleniia nad
      tomom sochineniĭ Dzheka Londona").

2444. *Sobranie sochinenii*:
      Vestnik Evropy, no. 9:391-395 (1912) (E. Kolpon-
      ovskaia).

                         SPANISH
2445. Colmillo blanco *(White fang)*:
      Nosotros, 51:256 (Oct. 1925).
      Studium (Chile), 1,1:93-95 (Aug.-Sept. 1926)

(Jorge Guzmán Dinator).

SWEDISH

2446. *Klasskamp och revolution (War of the classes
       Revolution):*
       Folkets Dagblad Politiken, April 5, 1919, p.4
       (Oscar Lundberg).

2447. *Järnhälen (Iron heel):*
       Verdandisten, June 12, 1913, pp.187-188 ("Jenki").

2448. *Kungen av Klondyke (Burning daylight):*
       Ny Tid, Jan. 3, 1914, p.2 (Martin Koch).
       Social-Demokraten, Dec. 20, 1913, p.6 ("S., O.").

2449. *Martin Eden:*
       [*Nya*] *Argus,* 3:172-174 (1910) (S[igurd] F[rosterus]).

2450. *Skriet från vildmarken (The call of the wild):*
       [*Nya*] *Argus,* 1:7-8 (1908) (Bertel Gripenberg).

TITLE INDEX
It is the purpose of this index to list all English titles
by Jack London. This, then, is essentially an index to part
one of this bibliography. Numbers refer to item numbers, *not*
page numbers.

The abysmal brute, 109, 110,
111, 112, 227, 261, 290,
328, 395, 496, 497, 498,
499, 1122, 1136; *about*
2280, 2404
Account with Swithan Hall,
617
A-cho, 233, 509
The acorn-planter, 136, 137,
582; *about* 2281
Adieu, Jack!, 98
Adventure, 85, 86, 87, 88,
89, 171, 173, 174, 177,
227, 314, 315, 395, 496,
497, 582, 584, 585, 654,
1123; *about* 2282, 2334,
2352, 2391
*An adventure in the upper
sea*, 164, 205, 218, 529,
563, 567, 618
Adventures in dream harbor,
90, 813
Adventures of Captain Grief,
99
Adventures of Martin Eden,
1143
Adventures with the police,
814
Advertisement..., 1013
*Again the literary aspi-
rant*, 815
Alaska, 394, 399, 601, 1144
Alaska Kid, 105, 314, 316,
317; *about* 2032
An Alaskan vacation, 818
All gold canyon, 43, 58,
182, 188, 196, 200, 210,
212, 331, 340, 341, 366,
401, 432, 443, 461, 505,
570, 572, 573, 577, 578,
583, 596, 619, 2388
Aloha oe, 96, 98, 206, 214,

261, 322, 395, 432,
447, 524, 619
Amateur M.D., 89, 90, 816
The amateur navigator,
89, 90, 817
Amateur night, 43, 443,
516, 583, 621
And Frisco Kid comes back,
623
*Ape and tiger in U.S. de-
mand fight*, 1002
The apostate, 22. 58, 82,
185, 186, 189, 191, 196,
200, 206, 209, 261, 262,
263, 274, 277, 278, 308,
320, 341, 362, 395, 401,
403, 432, 438, 455, 456,
459, 460, 519, 540, 548,
561, 562, 563, 567, 568,
569, 571, 572, 574, 577,
578, 579, 597, 599, 624,
1043
*Are there any thrills left
in life?*, 819
Army of the revolution,
893
*The assassination bureau,
ltd.*, 167, 168; *about*
2283
At the rainbow's end, 4, 6,
197, 208, 317, 341, 401,
437, 454, 500, 558, 564,
572, 583, 625
The author of "The game"..,
974
Author roasts Judge, 1009

Bald-face, 164, 218, 529,
556, 626
*The banks of the Sacramen-
to*, 164, 219, 407, 455,
460, 529, 556, 563, 567,

568, 569, 570, 571, 573,
  576, 577, 579, 627
Batard, 3, 12, 22, 26, 200,
  208, 209, 213, 317, 326,
  395, 401, 436, 500, 558,
  572, 578, 583, 628
Bêche de mer English, 89,
  90, 820
Before Adam, 52, 53, 54,
  55, 171, 173, 174, 179,
  227, 394, 496, 497, 500,
  582, 583; about 1160,
  2284, 2415, 2430
Beginning life anew, 129
The beginning of the end,
  129
The benefit of the doubt,
  84, 108, 328, 395, 432,
  444, 461, 525, 532, 549,
  570, 572, 573, 574, 578,
  629
Big socialist vote is
  fraught with meaning, 971
The birth mark, 145, 821
Bloody revenge, 605
The bones of Kahaliki, 162,
  214, 322, 395, 402, 630
Bonin islands, 200, 822,
  823
Born of the wild, 631
The boxers, 290
Brain beaten by brute force,
  975
The brain merchant, 200
Brown wolf, 3, 56, 58, 182,
  197, 208, 261, 266, 342,
  395, 407, 432, 456, 460,
  506, 508, 510, 511, 518,
  526, 542, 556, 561, 570,
  571, 573, 575, 576, 577,
  579, 632
Buck, 22
Buck, the dog that loved
  his master, 21
Buck, the lead dog, 21
Buck wins a wager, 21
Building of the boat, 633
Bulls, 59, 196, 402, 461,

577, 814
Bunches of knuckles, 108,
  328, 444, 525, 528, 534,
  634
Burning daylight, 75, 76,
  77, 78, 79, 171, 172,
  173, 174, 179, 200, 227,
  261, 314, 315, 316, 394,
  395, 496, 497, 498, 499,
  500, 582, 584, 585,
  1108, 1113, 1128; about
  2286, 2360, 2371, 2395,
  2448
By the turtles of Tasman,
  208, 449, 500, 522, 526,
  635

California pioneers watch..,
  938
The call of the wild, 19,
  20, 21, 22, 130, 171,
  172, 173, 174, 176, 179,
  180, 183, 184, 195, 198,
  203, 204, 205, 209, 213,
  227, 261, 310, 364, 394,
  395, 432, 457, 496, 497,
  498, 499, 500, 512, 577,
  582, 583, 584, 585, 589,
  1121, 1135, 1152; about
  1168, 1171, 1177, 1211,
  1257, 1362, 2287, 2346,
  2364, 2417, 2424, 2426,
  2428, 2450
A camera and a journey,
  953
The carter and the carpenter, 24
The channel raiders, 1120
Charley's coup, 40, 217,
  406, 456, 460, 583, 636
Chased by the trail, 637
Cherry, 496, 497
Children of the frost, 7,
  8, 9, 177, 180, 314,
  315, 386, 496, 497, 499,
  582, 583; about 2288,
  2390
The Chinago, 58, 82, 181,

186, 189, 196, 202, 206,
261, 263, 278, 308, 317,
320, 339, 395, 401, 432,
438, 455, 509, 533, 548,
552, 561, 563, 566, 567,
569, 570, 572, 573, 574,
578, 591, 638
*Chris Farrington, able sea-
man,* 164, 205, 219, 529,
540, 556, 563, 567, 568,
569, 570, 639
Chun Ah Chun, 96, 189, 214,
322, 341, 395, 432, 461,
567, 597, 640
Class struggle, 33, 191,
824
Classic of the sea, 145,
825
Coals of fire, 284
Confession, 59, 317, 432,
461, 577, 871
Conflict, 1136
Coronation day, 24
Created he them, 82, 186,
559, 641
*Crowning fight of ring's
history,* 1005
The cruise of the Dazzler,
10, 11, 12, 177, 180,
205, 211, 227, 363, 382,
394, 496, 497, 499, 582,
583; *about* 2289, 2382,
2393, 2431
Cruising in the Solomons,
89, 90, 200, 827
The cruise of the Snark,
89, 90, 91, 92, 173,
177, 227, 394, 395, 432,
496, 497, 499, 582, 909;
about 2291, 2365, 2385
A curious fragment, 82,
181, 186, 206, 262, 402,
516, 533, 578, 642

Dangerous waters, 1120
A daughter of the Aurora,
4, 188, 203, 307, 309,
337, 341, 375, 408, 419,

435, 500, 502, 534, 558,
564, 567, 569, 579, 583,
608, 643
A daughter of the snows,
13, 14, 15, 176, 178,
180, 227, 261, 271, 310,
395, 496, 497, 499, 500,
582, 583, 584, 585; *a-
bout* 2292, 2356, 2381
A day's lodging, 56, 196,
339, 395, 401, 432, 435,
500, 506, 511, 518, 526,
542, 555, 558, 564, 572,
573, 577, 578, 579, 583,
644
Daybreak, 828
Dear comrades, 1045, 1057
The death of Ligoun, 7,
337, 401, 439, 442, 500,
558, 572, 583, 645
The definition of a scab,
1064; *about* 1065, 1066,
1067, 1068, 1069, 1070
*Delightful memories sug-
gested...,* 939
Demetrios Contos, 40, 194,
406, 432, 456, 460, 583,
646, 1129
*Denied admittance to U.S.
because he loves liber-
ty,* 982
The devils of Fuatino, 99,
263, 275, 317, 402, 544,
579, 647
The devil's skipper, 1129
Diable--a dog, 204, 205,
648
The dignity of dollars, 72,
530, 829
*Direct legislation through
the initiative...,* 927
The 'Ditch country', 90
Double-faced man, 270
The dream of Debs, 121,
185, 191, 209, 262, 320,
362, 395, 432, 441, 461,
519, 649, 1048
The dress suit pugilist,

395
Dutch courage, 164, 165, 166, 205, 218, 496, 497, 499, 529, 563, 567, 569, 570, 650

Each record broken adds to country's war strength, 943
The east -- as I saw it, 1040
Economics of the Klondike, 830
Editorial crimes, 831
Eggs without salt, 832
Eight great factors of literary success, 1059
The electrician, 200
The end of the chapter, 651
The end of the story, 142, 208, 323, 338, 368, 395, 405, 448, 497, 500, 512, 525, 575, 579, 652
The enemy of all the world, 121, 262, 317, 441, 527, 653
Engaging a crew, 654
Engraved oarblade, 655
The eternity of forms, 142, 206, 449, 522, 526, 656
Even unto death, 657
"Examiner" writer sent back to Seoul, 963
Explanation of the great socialist vote of 1904, 191
Eyes of Asia, 658

Faith of men, 3, 26, 27, 28, 112, 174, 179, 217, 323, 362, 387, 395, 432, 434, 461, 496, 497, 499, 500, 517, 558, 581, 583, 659; *about* 2293, 2420
The fathers of the sun, 402
The fearless one, 652, 660
Feathers of the sun, 99, 189, 261, 317, 334, 544,

660
Few killed nowadays in "fierce" battles, 966
The fighter, 1145
Fighter with the quality of "Abysmal Brute", 1000
Finding one's way on the sea, 90, 833
Finding one's way about, 89
Finis, 142, 196, 317, 323, 395, 401, 497, 500, 521, 522, 578, 661, 1126
First aid to rising authors, 834
The first landfall, 89, 813
The first poet, 142, 500, 525, 835; *about* 2294
The flush of gold, 70, 200, 261, 323, 395, 515, 528, 541, 582, 662, 1144
A flutter in eggs, 103
Fog, 31
Footsore, dazed and frozen, the Japanese trudge through Korea, 961
For the health of the traveller, 261
For the love of a man, 21, 195
Foreword to Michael, brother of Jerry, 1060
Four horses and a sailor, 145, 873
The Francis Spaight, 82, 181, 186, 189, 263, 320, 339, 395, 533, 538, 591, 663
Frisco Kid's story, 664
From Dawson to the sea, 200, 931
Frying pan alley, 398, 613
Function of the Jew in his works, 858
The fuzziness of Hookla

Heen, 205, 665

Gamblers, 118
The game, 36, 37, 38, 39,
    171, 227, 261, 290, 384,
    394, 447, 496, 497, 498,
    500, 577, 582, 583;
    about 2295
Getting into print, 836
A girl who crossed swords
    with a burglar, 942
Gladiators of machine age,
    949
Glen Ellen guest card, 1050
A glimpse of inferno, 398,
    613
The goat man of Fautino,
    450, 666
A Gobotu night, 99, 218,
    544, 667
God of his fathers, 3, 4, 5,
    6, 9, 175, 177, 314, 382,
    386, 437, 454, 496, 497,
    499, 502, 582, 583, 668;
    about 2296, 2408
Gods of the wild, 669
The gold hunters of the
    North, 72, 205, 530, 837
The golden gleam, 286
The golden poppy, 72, 432,
    461, 499, 513, 530, 557
The golden spark, 426
Goliah, 72, 513, 530, 557,
    670
The good soldier canard,
    1058, 1071; about 1072,
    1073, 1074, 1075, 1076,
    1077, 1078, 1079, 1080,
    1081, 1082, 1083, 1084,
    1085, 1086, 1087, 1088,
    1089, 1090, 1091, 1092,
    1093, 1094, 1095, 1096,
    1097, 1098, 1099, 1100,
    1101, 1102, 1103
Good-by, Jack, 96, 206,
    214, 322, 395, 432, 524,
    538, 539, 597, 671
Grandly opens the third na-

tional Bundes shooting
    fest, 936
Granser and the boys, 129
The great interrogation, 4,
    208, 317, 337, 395, 408,
    432, 435, 461, 502, 534,
    560, 583, 672, 2297
The grilling of Loren El-
    lery, 673
The grit of women, 4, 6,
    196, 208, 278, 309, 338,
    362, 400, 402, 432, 440,
    455, 456, 458, 460, 500,
    559, 575, 576, 577, 578,
    579, 583, 599, 674

The handsome cabin boy,
    675
The hanging of Cultus
    George, 103
The haunted ship, 1127
He chortled with glee, 838
Hearts of three, 157, 158,
    159, 160, 161, 227, 261,
    395, 496, 497, 498, 499;
    about 2298, 2437
The heathen, 84, 93, 95,
    182, 184, 186, 188, 207,
    209, 216, 261, 334, 362,
    371, 395, 397, 403, 404,
    424, 432, 455, 456, 460,
    464, 508, 521, 561, 676;
    about 2006
Here are the first pic-
    tures...of war in Korea,
    957
The high seat of abundance,
    89, 90, 839
The hobo and the fairy,
    142, 182, 261, 449, 510,
    522, 526, 677
The hoboes, 282
Hoboes that pass in the
    night, 59, 317, 330,
    461, 840
Holding her down, 59, 200,
    317, 432, 461, 563, 567,
    569, 841

Home of the north, 408
The house beautiful, 72,
  513, 869
House of Mapuhi, 58, 84, 93,
  186, 188, 189, 194, 208,
  259, 261, 262, 263, 273,
  277, 278, 334, 362, 395,
  397, 401, 432, 456, 460,
  464, 500, 546, 563, 567,
  569, 570, 572, 573, 577,
  578, 579, 678
House of pride, 22, 95, 96,
  97, 98, 174, 177, 196,
  214, 261, 322, 362, 388,
  395, 402, 432, 461, 462,
  496, 497, 499, 524, 539,
  582, 597, 679; *about*
  2299, 2386
House of the sun, 89, 90,
  680, 842
*Housekeeping in the Klon-
  dike,* 843
How I became a socialist,
  33, 185, 191, 261, 432,
  499, 503, 513, 844, 2125
*How I got rid of John
  Barleycorn,* 116
*How Jack London gets his
  audiences,* 845
*How Jack London got in and
  out of jail in Japan,*
  953
*How London sold his first
  story for $5,* 1026
How the markers operate...,
  941
*How the marksmen petrifies
  for the shot,* 940
The human drift, 145, 146,
  384, 846; *about* 2300
*Husky--the wolf-dog of the
  north,* 681
The hussy, 154, 339, 446,
  522, 579, 581, 682
A hyperborean brew, 3, 26,
  262, 317, 395, 432, 436,
  461, 517, 541, 577, 583,
  683

The idolater, 424
If I were God, 847
If Japan wakens China, 848
Impossibility of war, 849
In a far country, 1, 3,
  194, 205, 208, 210, 213,
  220, 261, 277, 307, 362,
  395, 408, 500, 554, 558,
  579, 583, 684
*In a modern stadium...,*987
*In behalf of those who
  travel,* 408
In the cave of the dead,
  685
In the days of my youth,
  1055
*In the forests of the
  north,* 7, 432, 440, 583,
  686; *about* 2032
In the slums of London, 24
*In the time of Prince
  Charley,* 687
In unity there is strength,
  422
In Yeddo Bay, 164, 205,
  219, 529, 688
Incarnation of push and go,
  934
*The inconceivable and mon-
  struous,* 89, 200, 633
The inevitable white man,
  93, 186, 263, 395, 689
*Interpreters and how they
  cause trouble,* 964
*Introductions and prefaces
  by Jack London,* 1032,
  1033, 1034
The iron heel, 62, 63, 64,
  65, 171, 173, 174, 175,
  177, 191, 200, 227, 260,
  261, 314, 432, 496, 497,
  498, 499, 500, 582, 583,
  867, 1153, 1159; *about*
  1200, 2142, 2171, 2302,
  2343, 2362, 2373, 2384,
  2427, 2440, 2447
Is against the single tax,
  930

Is civilization useful, 850
The Ivan Swift broadside,
    1049

*Jack has good things to say
    about Johnny*, 1025
Jack London, 1062
*Jack London, a sketch of his
    life...*, 1039
Jack London about himself,
    497, 499
Jack London: American rebel,
    191
*Jack London approves of no
    drunkard plan*, 1014
Jack London by himself, 134,
    1055, 1056
*Jack London endorses the
    party press*, 978
*Jack London files objec-
    tion*, 1010
*Jack London gets next to
    John D. Barleycorn*, 115
*Jack London goes to a bur-
    lesque show...*, 1019
*Jack London in a confident
    mood*, 851
Jack London in Boston, 932
Jack London letters, 169,
    170, 845, 851, 852, 853,
    858, 859, 860, 861, 867,
    868, 874, 907, 912, 918,
    929, 930, 933, 934, 984,
    993, 994, 995, 996, 1009,
    1010, 1011, 1015, 1016,
    1017, 1020, 1025, 1026,
    1029, 1030, 1031, 1045,
    1057, 1058, 1085, 1092,
    1095, 1099, 1102, 1161,
    1169, 1172, 1180, 1181,
    1182, 1183, 1184, 1185,
    1213, 1308, 1356
Jack London misrepresented,
    984
*Jack London on fact and
    fiction*, 906
*Jack London on the movement
    and authorship*, 845, 994

*Jack London pays tribute to
    Stevenson's "Treasure
    Island"*, 1020
*Jack London reviews "The
    Long Day,"* 976
*Jack London says Honolulu
    is provincial*, 995
Jack London says Johnson..,
    986
*Jack London says Reno
    crowds...*, 997
*Jack London scores Idaho-
    Colorado conspirators*,
    979
*Jack London sees physical
    culture boom in holy
    jumper stunts*, 977
*Jack London telegraphs...
    about Alexander
    McClean...*, 973
*Jack London tells of the
    fire*, 905
*Jack London thanks the fire
    fighters*, 1016
Jack London to his friends,
    1017
*Jack London victim of jeal-
    ous correspondents*, 963
Jack London wants to know,
    1012
*Jack London will build a
    fine home*, 993
Jack London's article...,
    988
*Jack London's graphic
    story of the Japs...*,
    965
*Jack London's plea for a
    square deal*, 852
Jack London's protest,
    1011
*Jack London's resignation
    from the Socialist
    Party*, 853, 1057
*Jack London's sketch of
    "Wolf Larsen"*, 31
The jacket, 134, 177;
    about 2305, 2421

Jan, the unrepentant, 4,
200, 203, 205, 307, 309,
337, 341, 401, 500, 512,
558, 564, 572, 573, 578,
583, 690
Japan's invasion of Korea,
955
*Japanese army's equipment
excites great admiration,*
956
*Japanese officers consider
everything a military
secret,* 969
*Japanese supplies rushed to
the front...,* 968
*Japanese swim cold river
under fire,* 967
Jeff a fighter..., 998
*Jeffries never wasted
energy,* 1006
*Jeffries-Johnson fight,
June 24, 1910-July 5,
1910,* 200, 997, 998,
999, 1000, 1001, 1002,
1003, 1004, 1005, 1006,
1007, 1008
*Jeffries' silence marks a
thinker,* 1003
Jerry of the islands, 147,
148, 149, 150, 174, 178,
227, 314, 315, 316, 317,
364, 432, 462, 496, 497,
499, 582, 585; *about*
2032, 2306, 2348, 2366,
2392
Joe Garland, 95, 334
John Barleycorn, 113, 114,
115, 116, 177, 191, 200,
211, 227, 310, 314, 317,
394, 395, 432, 462, 496,
497, 499, 582, 584, 585,
1109; *about* 2307, 2349,
2358, 2374, 2377, 2394,
2423
John Finkelman, 116
The jokers of New Gibbon,
99, 263, 275, 317, 450,
544, 691

Journey's rule, 408
*The joy of small-boat sail-
ing,* 854
The joys of the surf-rider,
855
Just meat, 82, 182, 186,
189, 261, 263, 320, 395,
438, 567, 597, 692, 2402

The Kanaka surf, 162, 214,
339, 402, 551, 579
Keesh, the bear hunter, 693
Keesh, the son of Keesh, 7,
205, 401, 408, 440, 500,
558, 564, 572, 578, 583,
599, 694
The Kempton-Wace letters,
16, 17, 18, 395, 496,
497, 582, 583; *about*
2308
Kid & Co., 105, 316, 317;
about 2032
King of the Greeks, 40,
345, 406, 583, 695
The king of the Mazy May,
696
Koolau, the leper, 22, 96,
196, 214, 259, 261, 322,
325, 341, 395, 401, 428,
432, 447, 461, 524, 539,
563, 567, 570, 572, 578,
597, 599, 698
*Koreans are fleeing before
the Slav advance,* 954
*Koreans have taken to the
hills,* 960

The language of the tribe,
856
The last battle, 414, 611
*The last letter by Jack
London,* 1031
Law of life, 3, 7, 188, 200,
203, 205, 207, 212, 213,
261, 272, 277, 308, 318,
341, 375, 401, 432, 500,
558, 564, 570, 572, 573,

578, 583, 699
The law of the sea, 1120
Lawgivers, 700
League of the old men, 7,
    22, 58, 188, 209, 261,
    318, 340, 362, 432, 437,
    461, 464, 500, 558, 577,
    579, 583, 701
The leopard man's story,
    43, 205, 317, 395, 448,
    516, 583, 702
The lepers of Molokai, 89,
    90, 857
A lesson in heraldry, 703
Lessons of living taught by
    the visiting firemen,
    946
Letter of acceptance, 933
Letter to Arthur Stringer,
    859
Letter to Dr. A. H. Purdue,
    1015
Letter to editor, 861, 996
Letter to Fred Lockley...,
    1029
Letters by Jack London -
    see Jack London letters
Letters from Jack London,
    169, 170; about 2309
Li Wan, the fair, 7, 340,
    432, 439, 451, 461, 472,
    583, 704
Life's course, 408
Like Argus of the ancient
    times, 154, 325, 340,
    341, 446, 500, 522, 531,
    579, 705
A little account with Swi-
    thin Hall, 99, 317, 402,
    452, 544, 579, 706
The little fool, 1117
The little lady of the big
    house,138, 139, 140, 141,
    174, 178, 227, 261, 317,
    395, 496, 497, 498, 499,
    582, 584, 585, 1117; a-
    bout 2310, 2389
The little man, 103, 570,
    573

Local color, 43, 443, 516,
    577, 578, 583, 707
London explains why he re-
    fused to become critic,
    1030
London sweating den, 24
London will write for the
    "Daily World", 983
London's essays of revolt,
    185
Lost face, 3, 6, 58, 70,
    71, 174, 177, 187, 188,
    200, 207, 371, 387, 395,
    437, 454, 462, 496, 497,
    499, 528, 533, 596, 600,
    708; about 2311
The lost father, 287
The lost poacher, 164, 205,
    219, 529, 591, 709
Love of life, 56, 57, 58,
    173, 174, 175, 187, 188,
    189, 190, 194, 196, 197,
    200, 201, 202, 204, 206,
    207, 213, 215, 253, 257,
    261, 263, 278, 308, 317,
    323, 340, 341, 362, 389,
    390, 395, 396, 401, 407,
    432, 439, 451, 455, 456,
    458, 459, 460, 462, 496,
    497, 499, 500, 514, 558,
    561, 562, 563, 564, 566,
    567, 569, 570, 571, 572,
    573, 574, 575, 576, 577,
    578, 579, 582, 583, 596,
    599, 710; about 2312,
    2357, 2396
The lover's liturgy, 862

The madness of John Harned,
    84, 108, 209, 335, 445,
    500, 532, 711
Make westing, 82, 181, 182,
    186, 189, 197, 206, 209,
    320, 341, 366, 395, 509,
    547, 551, 712
Man never lived who could
    keep Johnson from land-
    ing, 1004
Man of mine, 713

The man on the bank, 103,
268
The man on the other bank,
103
The man on the trail, 435,
464
The man with the gash, 4,
196, 200, 203, 205, 261,
395, 401, 408, 500, 504,
558, 560, 570, 572, 578,
583, 714
The march of Kelly's army,
863
The marriage of Lit-Lit,
26, 205, 317, 337, 395,
432, 440, 461, 541, 560,
583, 715
Martin Eden, 66, 67, 68, 69,
171, 173, 174, 179, 191,
200, 227, 310, 314, 390,
394, 395, 432, 496, 497,
499, 500, 582, 584, 585,
1110, 1143, 1150, 1155;
about 2019, 2032, 2045,
2046, 2093, 2148, 2155,
2313, 2345, 2350, 2359,
2369, 2397, 2425, 2449
The master of mystery, 7,
58, 278, 319, 340, 401,
432, 439, 441, 442, 500,
558, 560, 563, 567, 569,
570, 572, 573, 576, 578,
579, 583, 716
The material side, 834
Mauki, 93, 95, 186, 189,
196, 206, 261, 263, 267,
273, 277, 375, 395, 401,
500, 548, 578, 600, 717
The meat, 103, 268, 512,
570, 573
Memorie, 116
The men of forty mile, 1, 3,
6, 205, 220, 261, 277,
337, 395, 408, 432, 437,
454, 455, 500, 554, 558,
577, 579, 583, 718
Mere hunt, 32
The message of motion pictures, 865
The Mexican, 58, 84, 188,
196, 199, 200, 202, 208,
209, 259, 261, 263, 278,
328, 335, 341, 362, 363,
371, 390, 395, 401, 407,
432, 444, 459, 460, 464,
500, 525, 547, 552, 561,
563, 567, 569, 570, 571,
572, 573, 574, 575, 576,
578, 579, 580, 596, 598,
599, 719, 1145, 1157,
2126
Mexico's army and ours,
866
Michael, brother of Jerry,
151, 152, 153, 174, 178,
261, 310, 314, 395, 462,
496, 499, 582, 584, 585,
1060; about 2032, 2314,
2355, 2400, 2405, 2439
Mike, a tale about an Es-
kimo dog, 416, 606
Millionaire divides his
profits..., 950
Minions of Midas, 43, 317,
583, 720
Mistake of creation, 103,
537, 570
Mohican's daughter, 1118
Molokai ideal for mainland
lepers, 1021
Moon face, 43, 44, 45, 174,
187, 197, 212, 314, 496,
497, 499, 516, 582, 583,
721; about 2315
Morganson's finish, 661,
1126
Mr. Jack London, 867
Mr. Jack London again, 868
Mutiny of the Elsinore,
124, 125, 126, 127, 171,
174, 178, 200, 227, 314,
315, 316, 496, 582, 584,
585, 1114; about 2032,
2316, 2363, 2399
My belated education, 115
My castle in Spain, 869

My definite beginning as a writer, 115
My early reading, 115
My first efforts to write, 115
My Hawaiian aloha, 214, 870, 1199
My life in the underworld, 871

Nam-Bok, the liar, 205, 261, 272, 277, 319, 340, 395, 397, 408, 722
Nam-Bok the unveracious, 189, 215, 432, 439, 451, 560, 577, 579, 583, 722
The nature of man, 89
Navigating four horses north of the bay, 873
Negore, the coward, 56, 58 317, 337, 339, 395, 440, 509, 514, 583, 723
Negro, never in doubt..., 1008
Never a man so fit as Jeffries, 999
The night born, 84, 106, 107, 108, 112, 178, 432, 445, 496, 497, 499, 526, 532, 534, 579, 724; *about* 2317
Night camp, 417, 609
Night in the slums, 24
A night's swim in Yeddo Bay, 725
Nose for the king, 82, 181, 182, 186, 189, 209, 320, 375, 395, 418, 516, 535, 610, 726
Nothing that ever came to anything, 145, 727
Novelist explains hop riots, 1018

An odyssey of the North, 1, 3, 58, 177, 188, 200, 203, 204, 207, 208, 213, 216, 253, 261, 277, 340,

362, 395, 400, 401, 432, 436, 456, 458, 460, 500, 545, 558, 563, 564, 567, 569, 570, 572, 573, 577, 578, 583, 599, 600, 728, 1111
Old Baldy, 729
An old lie finally nailed, 1058
An old soldier's story, 622
The old story, 874
On the banks of the Sacramento-- see The banks of the Sacramento
On the eternity of forms and other stories, 497
On the great war, 875
On the Makaloa mat, 95, 162, 163, 188, 214, 261, 322, 395, 402, 432, 461, 496, 497, 499, 500, 730; *about* 2303, 2318, 2386
On the verge of the world, 269
On the writer's philosophy of life, 499, 876
One more unfortunate, 731
The one thousand dozen, 22, 26, 196, 200, 210, 212, 262, 401, 432, 439, 442, 455, 500, 558, 567, 570, 572, 576, 577, 578, 579, 583, 732
The other animals, 72, 877
Our adventures in Tampico, 878
Our guiltless scapegoats.., 1023

A pacific traverse, 89, 90, 200, 879
The passing of Marcus O'Brien, 3, 70, 200, 395, 436, 456, 457, 460, 523, 528, 533, 534, 733
Pau, 95, 334
The pearls of Parlay, 99, 188, 200, 207, 216, 261,

317, 341, 452, 464, 544, 579, 734

The pen, 59, 317, 563, 567, 880

The people of the abyss, 23, 24, 25, 176, 180, 191, 196, 200, 227, 261, 314, 395, 432, 496, 497, 498, 499, 574, 582, 583, 1040; *about* 2171, 2319, 2367, 2398

Pessimism, optimism, and patriotism, 881

Phases of mental condition in the big shoots, 944

The phenomena of literary evolution, 499, 882

Pictures, 59, 317, 432, 577, 883

A piece of steak, 82, 84, 181, 186, 188, 189, 196, 200, 201, 202, 207, 209, 216, 262, 274, 277, 308, 362, 402, 432, 438, 455, 459, 509, 535, 550, 563, 567, 569, 575, 576, 577, 578, 592, 600, 735, 1104; *about* 2361

Pinched, 59, 196, 199, 317, 402, 423, 456, 460, 572, 574, 577, 578, 615, 884

Pirates of the deep, 1120

Planchette, 43, 45, 443, 583, 736

Plea for the square deal, 852, 885

Pluck and pertinacity, 737

Poems by Jack London, 828, 862, 901, 1028, 1061

Poppy cargo, 738

The priestly prerogative, 1, 221, 261, 276, 277, 395, 408, 434, 554, 583, 739

The princess, 154, 200, 448, 497, 522, 740

A problem, 886

The prodigal father, 142,

449, 497, 522, 543, 741

The proper 'girlie', 742

The proud goat of Aloysius Pankburn, 99, 101, 263, 275, 317, 453, 544, 579, 743

Prowlers of the sea, 1130

The psychology of the surf-board, 887

Queen of the Yukon, 1140

The question of a name, 888

The question of the maximum, 33, 503, 889

The race for number three, 103, 200, 268, 570, 573, 744

Raid on the oyster pirates, 40, 197, 406, 583, 745, 1132

A real girl, 911

Red game of war, 890

The red one, 154, 155, 156, 174, 227, 317, 446, 496, 499, 522, 580, 582, 746; *about* 2320, 2403

The rejuvenation of Major Rathbone, 747

A relic of the Pliocene, 26, 217, 395, 559, 561, 583, 748

Reply to article accusing plagiarism, 859

Resignation from the socialist party, 853, 1057

Return, 427

A review, 33, 503

Review of Edwin Markham, 948

Review of Frank Norris, 892

Review of Maxim Gorky, 891

Review of Upton Sinclair, 980

Revolution, 185, 191, 261, 409, 499, 530, 582, 612, 829, 837, 869, 877, 893

1046, 1047; *about*
2022, 2321, 2446
Revolution and other essays,
72, 73, 74
Riding the South Sea surf,
894
The road, 59, 60, 61, 177,
191, 211, 282, 314, 317,
364, 382, 395, 496, 497,
499, 500, 582, 583, 814,
840, 841, 871, 1186, 1187;
about 2322, 2356, 2379
Road-kids and gay-cats, 59,
317, 896
Rods and gunnels, 895
Romance of the redwoods,
1138
A royal sport, 89, 90, 214
The run across, 200
Running a newspaper, 991
Ruskin Club menu, 1040
Russian-Japanese corres-
pondence Feb. 27, 1904-
June 26, 1904, 200, 953,
954, 955, 956, 957, 958,
959, 960, 961, 962, 963,
964, 965, 966, 967, 968,
969
Russian warships patrol Pe-
Chili gulf, 959

The salt of the earth, 750
Samuel, 121, 156, 188, 200,
261, 401, 527, 572, 578,
580, 751
San Francisco is gone, 905
Saved--and lost!, 990
The scab, 33, 185, 191, 897,
1037, 1070
Scab, definition of, 1064;
about 1065, 1066, 1067,
1068, 1069, 1070
The scarlet plague, 128,
129, 130, 131, 144, 171,
177, 189, 198, 496, 497,
499, 500, 582; *about* 2323
The scorn of women, 4, 50,
51, 307, 317, 408, 439,

558, 560, 567, 569, 579,
582, 583, 752; *about*
2324
The sea farmer, 121, 206,
261, 527, 570, 572, 578,
753
The sea gangsters, 125
The sea sprite and the
shooting star, 1061
The sea wolf, 22, 29, 30,
31, 32, 171, 173, 174,
176, 200, 212, 261, 314,
315, 316, 317, 390, 394,
395, 432, 462, 496, 497,
498, 499, 500, 582, 583,
584, 585, 1105, 1106,
1115, 1125, 1134, 1141,
1146, 1151; *about* 2032,
2325, 2370, 2406
The secret of Manachiki,
607
The seed of McCoy, 84, 93,
186, 189, 200, 261, 263,
277, 318, 395, 432, 456,
460, 754
Semper idem, 82, 181, 186,
189, 206, 227, 228, 234,
267, 274, 555, 755
The shadow and the flash,
43, 197, 209, 317, 449,
543, 583, 756
Sheriff of Kona, 96, 214,
322, 334, 339, 395, 432,
461, 524, 538, 597, 757
Shin-bones, 162, 214, 685,
758
Shorty dreams, 103, 268
Shorty has a dream, 103
The shrinkage of the plan-
et, 72, 513, 530, 898
The sickness of Lone Chief,
7, 272, 277, 339, 432,
461, 500, 531, 558, 583,
759
The seige of the 'Lanca-
shire Queen', 40, 406,
583, 760, 1120
The sign of the wolf, 1142

Silence of dawn, 425
Simple impressive rite at corner-stone emplacement..., 951
Siwash, 4, 6, 205, 307, 309, 314, 317, 400, 440, 461, 504, 583, 761
Small-boat sailing, 145, 854
Smoke and Shorty, 105, 395, 496, 497; *about* 2326
Smoke Bellew, 102, 103, 104, 105, 177, 227, 245, 261, 268, 310, 314, 316, 317, 395, 432, 457, 496, 497, 498, 499, 500, 515, 582, 584, 585, 1133, 2161; *about* 2161, 2327, 2347, 2368, 2380, 2438
Socialistic views on coin, 928
Socialistic views...on the municipal ownership of water works, 929
Some adventures with the police, 899
Something rotten in Idaho, 191, 432, 499, 981
The somnambulists, 72, 900
A son of the sun, 99, 100, 101, 172, 177, 197, 227, 275, 314, 315, 316, 317, 385, 395, 432, 453, 496, 497, 499, 500, 544, 579, 582, 762, 1063; *about* 2032, 2328, 2353, 2409
The son of the wolf, 1, 2, 3, 175, 176, 180, 210, 215, 261, 277, 314, 341, 362, 384, 387, 389, 395, 408, 436, 496, 497, 499, 500, 554, 558, 579, 582, 583, 584, 585, 763, 1119; *about* 1213, 2032, 2329, 2387, 2410
The sonnet, 901
South of the slot, 121, 191, 206, 209, 261, 317, 320, 395, 432, 441, 461, 527, 550, 764
South Sea tales, 84, 93, 94, 95, 171, 173, 174, 177, 231, 314, 315, 316, 317, 388, 394, 496, 497, 499, 500, 582; *about* 2330, 2356, 2412
A souvenir chapter, 1063
Sport, 39
Square fight sure, 1007
Stalking the pestilence, 765, 902
The stampede to Squaw Creek, 103, 268
The stampede to thunder mountain, 903
The star rover, 132, 133, 134, 135, 174, 200, 227, 496, 497, 499, 500, 582, 1116; *about* 1160, 2305, 2331, 2372, 2378, 2421
Steady nerve of early rising firemen, 937
Stone-fishing of Bora Bora, 89, 90, 904
Stormy waters, 1131
Story of a typhoon off the coast of Japan, 200, 766
The story of an eyewitness, 200, 905
The story of Jees Uck, 22, 26, 188, 261, 308, 362, 371, 395, 432, 440, 461, 517, 581, 583, 767, 1118
The story of Keesh, 3, 56, 58, 182, 188, 196, 215, 257, 261, 278, 342, 371, 375, 401, 405, 407, 436, 455, 456, 460, 464, 500, 505, 506, 511, 518, 555, 556, 558, 561, 563, 564, 566, 567, 568, 569, 570, 571, 573, 577, 579, 583, 693
The story of the little man, 103
Stranger than fiction, 906

The strength of the strong,
121, 122, 123, 174, 178,
184, 191, 197, 200, 206,
262, 362, 402, 441, 496,
497, 499, 519, 527, 580,
581, 582, 768, 1051, 1052;
about 2022, 2332, 2354
Strike in San Francisco, 289
Strike methods, 191, 989
String, 614
*Study of physical traits of
men who shoot best,* 945
Sufferings of the Japanese,
962
Sun-dog trail, 56, 197, 215,
265, 326, 345, 390, 395,
435, 500, 506, 511, 518,
558, 579, 583, 769, *about*
2333, 2383
The sunlanders, 7, 339, 340,
560, 583, 770
Surfing at Waikiki, 89, 90,
214
The survival of the fittest,
129

Tales of the fish patrol, 40,
41, 42, 227, 385, 394, 395,
496, 497, 500, 582, 583,
1120; *about* 2096, 2335
The taste of the meat, 103,
268, 570, 573
The tears of Ah Kim, 162,
214, 322, 395, 401, 567,
572, 578, 771
*Terrible and tragic in fic-
tion,* 908
The terrible Savoyard, 281
Terrible Solomons, 84, 93,
186, 261, 334, 395, 402,
432, 461, 500, 772
Thanksgiving on Slav Creek,
773
That dead men rise up never,
145, 200, 774, 909
*That is what is unforget-
table,* 415, 616
That spot, 70, 182, 195,

208, 323, 342, 395, 401,
432, 439, 451, 456, 457,
459, 528, 533, 561, 572,
576, 577, 578, 775, 1142
Theft, 80, 81, 499, 582;
about 2336, 2432
Their alcove, 776
*These bones shall rise a-
gain,* 72, 777
Things alive, 910
A thousand deaths, 778
*Through the rapids on the
way to Klondike,* 200,
697, 911
To build a fire, 58, 70,
184, 188, 196, 197, 204,
206, 207, 209, 213, 215,
261, 320, 338, 341, 342,
362, 395, 401, 408, 434,
528, 572, 578, 579, 592,
596, 600, 779, 780
To kill a man, 84, 108,
201, 202, 262, 317, 432,
438, 445, 456, 460, 532,
570, 573, 575, 579, 781,
1107
To repel boarders, 164,
218, 510, 529, 570, 782
To the Chemulpo in a junk,
912
To the man on trail, 1, 3,
188, 200, 203, 204, 207,
208, 221, 307, 309, 345,
395, 432, 456, 460, 500,
558, 564, 575, 576, 578,
583, 783
Told in the drooling ward,
142, 200, 206, 209, 522,
526, 784
Too much gold, 26, 197,
205, 337, 395, 432, 439,
451, 456, 457, 460, 500,
558, 583, 785
The town-site of Tra-Lee,
103
The tramp, 33, 191, 913,
1035
Tramping with Kelly through

Iowa, 914
Tropical nights, 1132
Trouble makers of Mexico, 915
Troubles of war correspondent..., 958
Trust, 6, 70, 182, 261, 395, 432, 437, 454, 455, 528, 533, 561, 786
The turning point, 641, 787
The turtles of Tasman, 142, 143, 144, 174, 496, 497 499; *about* 2337
Two gold bricks, 788
Two thousand stiffs, 59, 200, 317, 330, 917
Two unpublished letters of Jack London, 918
Typee, 89, 90, 916
Typhoon off the coast of Japan, 164, 219, 320, 395

Under the deck awnings, 108, 201, 202, 345, 432, 438, 444, 525, 528, 532, 578, 579, 789
The unemployed, 285
The unexpected, 6, 56, 190, 215, 342, 396, 401, 432, 437, 454, 461, 500, 514, 526, 536, 558, 572, 573, 578, 583, 790, 1158
The unparalleled invasion, 121, 206, 209, 441, 527, 791
Up the slide, 792
Uri Bram's God, 793

Valley of the moon, 117, 118, 119, 120, 171, 173, 174, 177, 200, 261, 314, 317, 394, 395, 432, 496, 497, 498, 500, 582, 584, 1112; *about* 1178, 2251, 2338, 2351, 2401, 2414, 2436
Victor over war and waver, 985
Voyage of the Snark, 919

The wager on Buck, 21
Waiting the wreck, 269, 280
Wanted: a new law of development, 33, 191, 503, 920
War, 84, 108, 200, 444, 500, 525, 532, 794
War of the classes, 33, 34, 35, 176, 499, 582; *about* 2339, 2416, 2435, 2446
Washoe Indians resolve to be white men, 935
The water baby, 162, 214, 455, 567, 795
The way of the sun shadows, 342
The way of war, 1028
The whale tooth, 93, 186, 206, 261, 334, 395, 401, 500, 572, 796
What are we to say?, 921
What communities lose by the competitive system, 191, 922
What Jack London told of himself, 1027
What life means to me, 72, 185, 191, 192, 261, 308, 432, 461, 513, 530, 923, 1041
What novelist .. thinks of ..labor story, 972
What shall be done with this boy?, 952
What we will lose when the Japs take Hawaii, 1024
When Alice told her soul, 162, 214, 797
When God created them, 261
When God laughs, 82, 83, 84, 172, 174, 177, 186, 255, 261, 385, 388, 402, 447, 496, 497, 499, 500, 798; *about* 2340, 2418

When the world was young,
512, 525, 532, 547, 799
Where the trail forks, 4, 6,
208, 307, 309, 326, 400,
408, 432, 434, 461, 500,
502, 536, 558, 563, 567,
583, 800
Which makes men remember, 4,
6, 208, 307, 309, 339,
395, 434, 500, 504, 512,
558, 583, 793
White and yellow, 40, 217,
406, 583, 801, 1120, 1127
White fang, 46, 47, 48, 49,
130, 171, 173, 174, 178,
179, 198, 210, 213, 227,
260, 261, 310, 394, 395,
432, 496, 497, 498, 499,
500, 564, 582, 583, 584,
585, 1124, 1137, 1148,
1154, 1156; about 1211,
2341, 2342, 2375, 2376,
2419, 2434, 2445
White man's superiority, 410
The white man's way, 6, 56,
58, 196, 215, 342, 390,
402, 435, 437, 454, 500,
512, 514, 545, 558, 567,
569, 583, 602, 802
The white silence, 1, 3, 22,
58, 188, 196, 200, 203,
209, 221, 261, 276, 277,
338, 341, 345, 362, 395,
401, 408, 432, 435, 461,
464, 500, 554, 558, 564,
570, 572, 573, 575, 576,
577, 578, 579, 583, 596,
803, 1138, 2433
Who believes in ghosts!,
804
Why I voted for equal suffrage, 924
Whose business is to live,
164, 529, 805
A wicked woman, 82, 145,
186, 559, 806
The wife of a king, 1, 3,
215, 261, 277, 309, 362,

432, 435, 461, 545, 579,
583, 807, 1119
Winged blackmail, 108, 445,
528, 532, 549, 808
The wisdom of the picture,
261
The wisdom of the trail, 1,
3, 188, 196, 203, 220,
308, 345, 402, 432, 435,
500, 558, 583, 809
The wit of Porportuk, 58,
70, 188, 207, 395, 440,
464, 523, 528, 541, 592,
810
With Funston's men, 925
Wolf call, 1139
Wolf Larsen, 1146
Wolves, 283
Wolves of the waterfront,
1120
A woman's dedication, 408
Wonder of woman, 103, 507,
521, 537, 570, 1054
Wonder tales of fact and
fancy, 129
The worker and the tramp,
926
World's apart, 672

Yah! Yah! Yah!, 93, 95,
186, 196, 206, 209, 261,
263, 277, 279, 395, 402,
432, 546, 811
The Yankee myth, 992
Yellow handkerchief, 40,
182, 406, 583, 812,
1120, 1131
The yellow peril, 72, 345,
970

PERSONAL NAME INDEX
This index attempts to list all translators, book reviewers, authors of books, illustrators of books, parts of books, theses, dissertations, articles as well as editors, authors of prefaces, introductions, and London correspondents. No attempt has been made to index anonymous material and material signed only with initials has been left unindexed. Numbers refer to item numbers, *not* page numbers.

Aava, A., 65
Aavik, J., 702
Abdullaev, F., 599
Abdullin, M., 632
Abers, Z., 2111
Abkinoi, M. E., 498
Abramova, A. M., 496, 497
Adair, Ward, 1235
Ádám, Réz, 22, 364
Adams, A. K., 210
Adamsons, E., 395
Adorján, Sándor, 101
Adrianov, S. A., 61
Agdler, Alf, 585
Agdler, Brita, 585
Agnew, J. Kenner, 1364
d'Agostino, Nicola, 2102
Aleksandresku, Mircja, 49
Aleksandrov, V. A., 69, 95, 522
Alexandrescu, Mircea, 153
Alexandrova, Vera, 1236
Algad, R., 22
Aliff, M. D., 22
Alves, José Parreira, 462
Ambrosini, A., 65
Amsbary, George S., 632
Amza, A. M., 153
Amza, G. M., 49, 105, 127, 150, 153
Anderson, Andrew M., 845, 994
Anderson, Carl L., 1237
Andreev, S., 227, 232, 242
Andreeykowicz, M., 446
Andreĭchin, Iv. St., 135
Andrew, Loyd D., 2237
Andrews, R. C., 780
Andruson, L., 2166, 2433

Andrzeykowicz, M., 135
Anikst, A., 2167
Antonova, T., 2168
Anvelt, L., 58, 278
Arabov, Bl., 228
Arājs, A., 717
Árnason, Jón P., 371, 2097
Arngrímsson, Knút, 116
Arns, Karl, 2384, 2391, 2397, 2398, 2400, 2402, 2403, 2410, 2419, 2036
Asaliamov, G., 699
Asen, G., 260
Ashmun, M. E., 780, 1238
Asimov, Isaac, 1160
Atherton, Gertrude, 1239
Austin, Mary, 1240
Avellano, Arturo, 49
Aylward, W. J., 29
Azov, V. A., 496, 497, 500, 522, 525, 529

Backus, John E., 2238
de Bacque, Maurice, 22
Badanova, I. M., 2169, 2170, 2171
Bailey, Matilda, 780
Bakhmetyvev, I. G., 496
Bakke, Jon, 22
Bakozade, Dzh., 632
Balashov, P., 2438
Balestrieri, Spartaco, 2103
Bamford, Frederic, I., 1161
Bamford, Georgia Loring, 1161
Bănățeanu, I. J., 488
Bandrowski, Jerzy, 105, 457
Bannikova, N. V., 498
Baratov-Umanskiy, B., 208,

2175
Barbera, Manuel, 22, 49
Barbusse, Henri, 923
Barentz-Schönberg, S. J.,
    22, 32, 49, 55, 79, 150,
    153
Barili, P. Ortiz, 150
Baron, Deborah, 638
Barot, Ye. A., 32, 49
Barthel, Max, 25, 88
Bartos, J., 45
Bartos, Zoltán, 12, 22, 32,
    39, 98, 123, 351, 355,
    362, 363
Bartsch, Friedrich, 2397
Bascom, Lee, 2297
Baskett, Sam S., 68, 2267
Bauga, A., 65
Bazán, Armando, 580
Beal, Richard S., 780
Beck, M., 58
Becker, M. L., 769
Bednár, A., 116
Beecroft, John, 21
Behl, C. F. M., 2038
Behrens, Friedrich, 676
Beierle, Alfred, 2039
Beirne, Thomas F., 2239
Belayev, A., 497
Belev, G'oncho, 105, 235
Bém, K., 193
Ben-Dov, H., 55
Beneditti, Steve, 1241
Benke, Fritz, 49, 333
Bennett, George, 754
Benzi, Mario, 15, 32, 69,
    84, 105, 120, 127, 161
Berenberg, D. P., 2300,
    2306, 2314
Berg, A., 6, 32, 55, 58, 65
Berge, Theodor, 161
Bergman, Hanna, 116
Berolzheimer, F., 2309
Berton, Pierre, 21
B-ev, Sergeĭ, 2173
Beurin, Emil, 585
Bezhanovski, Ser. Ant., 84
Bílý, J., 65

Birinski, M. M., 3
Bishop, Alison, 851
Bite, J., 624, 714, 735,
    748
Björnsson, Joh, 69
Blacker, Irwin R., 728
Blagobeshchenskaya, Ye. N.,
    500, 553, 558
Blanck, Joseph, 1243
Blankenship, Russell, 632,
    710, 786, 1242
Bloch, Curt, 628
Block, M., 775
Blodgett, Harold W., 1244
Blotner, Joseph L., 1245
B--m, A. P., 3
Boas, Ralph P., 1246
Bobspa, D., 2300, 2306,
    2314
Bode, Carl, 1247
Boffito, Beatrice, 49, 95
Bogdanovich, T., 153
Bogolovskaya, M., 571
Bogoslovskiĭ, V. N., 2144,
    2145, 2176, 2177
Boheva, Rosina, 105
Boissevain, J. W., 105
Boor, Ján, 69, 1970
Born, Fritz, 22, 65
Boroda, M., 2178
Borudzka, W., 150
Bosch, Cora, 22
Bosquet, Alain, 676
Bossuet, Alice, 79, 1181
Boucher, James J., 2240,
    2283
Boureanul, Eug., 477
del Bourge, Maurice, 21
Bourget, Paul, 22
Boynton, H. W., 1248, 2306,
    2313, 2316
Bracher, Hans, 2020
Braddy, Nella, 762
Bradford, Anne H., 2287
Bradley, Marion Zimmer,
    2331
Bragin, Moses, 2241
Braley, Berton, 2307

Bramson, Paul, 21
Brandis, E., 1997, 2179
Branko, Pavol, 22, 32, 49,
  1220
Brant, A., 794
Braun, Soma, 25
Braybrooke, Patrick, 1249
Brett, George, 170
Brewton, John E., 639
Briedis, E., 2112
Briggs, T. H., 763
Bright, Frank F., 794
Brivlauks, Ž., 628, 659
Broderson, E. K., 120
Brodskaya, L., 496, 497
Broido, Ye., 58, 516
Bronner, Augusta, 22, 2028
Bronson, Walter C., 1250
Brooks, Robert C., 2339
Brooks, Van Wyck, 1251, 1252
Brössler, Franjo, 105
Brown, Anna B. A., 2287
Brown, Beth, 21
Brown, Deming, 1253
Brown, Frances Fort, 2307
Brown, Madis, 1254
Buck, Philo M., Jr., 1169
Buhl, H., 678
Buk, Ivan, 65
Bull, Charles Livingston,
  19, 52
Burdick, Eugene, 207
Burgardta, P., 6
Burian, Z., 12
Burke, William J., 1255
Burrell, J. A., 754, 780
Burris, Mary H., 21
Buzharova, K. Ia., 227
Bykov, Vil, 170, 836, 931,
  969, 980, 1161, 2040,
  2146, 2147, 2180, 2181,
  2182, 2183

Caen, Herb, 1256
Cahen, Jacques-Fernand, 2010
Cain, J. M., 755
Calder-Marshall, Arthur,
  209, 211, 1162

Caldwell, H. H., 2307
Calitri, A., 22
Calverton, Victor F., 1258
Campbell, Harlan Sheldon,
  2242
Canarache, Ana, 65
Canda, Maria Antonietta,
  49
Cantwell, Robert, 1259
Carbone, Olga, 144
Cargill, Oscar, 619, 642,
  780, 1260
Carlson, Roy W., 2268
Carneiro, Edison, 803
Carnes, Cecil, 1261
Carret, Marcel, 1191
Carroll, Lavon B., 2243
Carter, D., 22, 116
Carter, Dienne, 120, 131,
  135
Cartmell, Van H., 780
Casseres, Benjamin de, 1270
Castro, Joaquin R., 69
Caughey, John, 646
Caughey, Laree, 646
Caughran, Alex M., 780
Cecchi, E., 2104
Ceifi, A., 25
Celiński, Roman, 123
Cemal, Behçet, 49
Cemal, Ahmet, 101
Cendree, C., 69
Cerf, Bennett A., 676, 754,
  780
Čermák, J., 65
Cerro, José Novo, 49
Chakalov, G., 65
Chalreu, Silvia Leon, 65
Chamberlain, John, 1262
Chapman, Arnold, 1263
Checkhov, M. P., 496, 497
Ch'en, Fu-an, 3
Chichiavelli, Ezio, 2108
Chislett, William, 1264
Cholakov, Krum, 231
Choudhuri, Abul Hussain, 22
Christ, H. I., 735
Christoforov, G., 260

Chubb, Edwin W., 1265
Chu-ch'ang, Ch'iu, 32
Chukovskiĭ, K., 2149
Chukovski, L., 105
Chukovski, N., 105
Churchill, Winston, 918
Ciatti, Aldo, 32
Čičanovič-Stefoanovič,
    Nevana, 88
Cirker, Blanche, 21
Círulis, J., 120, 394
Clementi, José, 69
Cockerell, T. D. A., 2319
Cohn, Alfons F., 2041
Colbron, Grace Isabel, 2323,
    2341
Colbron, G. J., 2286
Collette, Elizabeth, 780
Commanger, Henry S., 1266
Conrad, Joseph, 1267
Constantinescu, Ion, 495
Cook, May Estelle, 2341
Cooper, Frederic Taber,
    2284, 2313, 2340
Corboda, Maria Angelica
    Lamas de, 49
Cost, Charles C., 2244
Costain, Thomas B., 21
Cottrell, G. W., 1268
Cox, Francis A., 1033, 1269
Cross, T. P., 619, 751
Crothers, Samuel McChord, 21
Cugini, Elsa, 49
Curnain, An t-Athair
    Tadhg O', 49

Dalphin, Maria, 637
Damburs, E., 2113
Damianov, Boris, 261
Dandens, J., 61
Daniels, Roger, 2309
Danilin, Yu., 624, 2184
Danimov, S., 2185
Daryoush, Parviz, 22
Daugirdas, J., 2126
Dauli, G., 22, 65, 69, 79,
    84, 116, 120, 131, 135,
    141, 150, 153, 373

Davenport, John, 2285
Davids, V., 702, 764, 801
Davíõsson, R. J., 2098
Davlet'aev, M., 391
Davydova, N. F., 496, 497
Dawson, C. W., 803
Dawson, W. J., 803
Day, A. Grove, 214, 640,
    678, 698, 754, 820
Debenedetti, Ricardo, 22
Deelen, Martin, 22, 32, 49
Degen, Gert, 2042
Dehesdin, Paul, 55
Dehnęl, T. J., 101, 432
Deikhtenberg, D. Ye., 35,
    98
Dekobra, Maurice, 150
Delchiaro, G., 116, 120
Demiraj, Shaban, 69
Demming, Ch., 2410
Denver, Jim, 21
Dickinson, T. H., 1271
Dickson, Samuel, 1272
Dimitriu, M., 472
Dinator, Jorge Guzán, 2377,
    2445
Dinolov, G., 227
Divine, Sam, 2307
Dixon, Thomas Jr., 2287
Djordjevic, Mihailo S., 22,
    49, 150, 624
Djvavoli na Fuatinu, 101
Dneprov, V., 2186
Dobosi, Pécsi Mária, 49
Doko, Bujar, 49
Dombnaill, Niall o, 22
Dospevska, Neli, 261
Doubleday, J. Stewart, 2287
Doustdar, A., 69
Doyle, Arthur Conan, 1209
Dozier, Mary Dean, 2245
Drangel, M., 3, 6, 15, 22,
    25, 32, 49, 55, 58, 61,
    65, 88, 120, 131, 582,
    584
Drezinš, E., 2114
Drinkwater, John, 1273
Dukelsky, Elena, 49

Dumitrescu, Mircea A., 79, 141
Dumitrescu-Berecht, Marin, 481
Dunn, H. T., 113
Dupuy, Georges, 659
Durham, Philip, 1274
Dutescu, Dan, 32
Dutourd, Jean, 310, 2014
Dzhun'kovskoĭ, 101
Dzintars, M., 101

Eberle, Hans Ulrich, 2386
Edgar, Day, 789
Edgett, E. F., 2338
Edith, Svea, 153
Edlund, Marten, 22, 116
Edmondson, Elsie, 2269
Edžus, Sudrabu, 638, 661
Efremov, G., 22, 95
Eggebrecht, A., 2395
Egorova, I., 365
Ekwall, Ernst, 22
Eiseley, Loren, 54
Ekrem, Celal, 88
Eliezer, Refael, 1226
Ellsworth, William W., 1275
Elson, William H., 21
Engelson, Suzanne, 308
Engholm, Stellan, 2217, 2218, 2219
Eoaunídis, Yiánnis B., 22
Ergin, Mete, 69
Erikson, Bror, 2220, 2221, 2222
Erickson, Ursula Spier, 710, 719, 745
Ermatov, S., 58
Erss, A., 676
Esenova, S. B., 632
Eskeland, A., 6
Espinosa, Maria Isabel, 462
Evans, I. O., 11, 180
Evert, Tadeusz, 79, 432
Ewald, Jesper, 116, 135, 1977
Ewing, K. R. H., 194
Eyles, D. C., 48

Ezerina, Rīga, 402

Fadiman, Clifton, 21
Fairchild, H. N., 1268
Fajmer, Jozefina, 88
Farkas, Ákos, 3, 61, 349, 358
Farrell, James T., 2313
Farzan, Massoud, 431, 780
Favilli, Dora Mangold, 49
Fedunob, P. G., 2151
Fedunova, F. G., 498
Fedunow, P., 2043
Feied, Frederick, 1276
Fenner, P. R., 21
Fergusson, Bernard, 21, 130, 198
Fernández, M., 22
Fernando, Valentin, 120
Filler, Louis, 1277
Fischer, A. O., 99
Fischer, Dr. Walter, 216
Fisher, Leonard Everett, 54, 134
Fitch, George H., 2293
Fitzgerald, Sarah Ritter, 2287
Flor, Kai, 1222
Florin, Sider, 261
Foerster, N., 619
Follain, Madeleine, 69
Follett, Wilson, 2310
Foner, Philip S., 191, 192, 193, 1064, 2309
Fontanelli, Falzone, 22
France, Anatole, 64, 65, 174
Franchere, Ruth, 1163
Franzen, E., 2044
Frateş, Filip, 470
Frates, Lia, 474
Frauenglass, Ettie, 2246
Freeman, H. A., 2247
Freeman, I. K., 1278, 2319
Freemantle, Anne, 751
French, J. L., 772, 799, 1279
Friche, V., 2440

Friedenfelds, F., 2117
Friederich, W. P., 2029
Frimen, Dzhozef, 2187
Frioriksson, Ólafur, 22
Froding, Karl, 768
Frost, J., 55
Frosterus, Sigurd, 2449
Frunze-Kazan', Karachev S., 632
Fu, Yin, 58
Fuat, Memet, 592
Fulda, Emil, 492
Fuller, Edmund, 780
Fulop, Zsigmond, 32
Funtek-Snellman, Gemma, 49

Gabriel, R. H., 780
Gaer, Joseph, 624, 1164
Gaines, N. V. S., 632
Galard, Mme. la comtesse de 22, 310
Gallacher, William, 2304
Gallone, Maria, 168
Gal'perinoi, R. M., 498
Gan, Z., 571
Gandziuri, P., 719
Gannett, Lewis, 31
Gardt, F. D., 524
Garnett, Edward, 1280
Garst, Joseph, 1165, 1166
Gartner, Silvia, 32
Geddes, George, 64
Geismar, Maxwell, 205, 1281, 2015
Gelstein, Isidro, 153
Genov, Todor, 227
Georg, Manfred, 2045, 2397
Georgiev, Angel, 69, 246
Georgiev, Iv., 240, 768
Gerbault, Alain, 1191
Gershenzon, M., 624
Gerstenberger, Donna, 1283
Ghitulescu, A., 22, 486
Giartosio de Courten, Maria L., 92
Gielen, A., 2349
Giiel', O., 2188
Gimelfarb, B., 69

Ginger, Ray, 1282
Giovanni-Milano, Sesto S., 135
Gleason, Edwin P., 2248
Glinczanka, A., 432, 456, 458, 460
Glinka, Zygmunt, 69, 432, 456, 458, 460
Glöde, O., 2418
Goecke, Gerhard, 2410
Golyshevoi, E., 80
Goncalves, Thomas J., 2142
Gonl, E. H., 1047
Goodman, J. A., 21
Goodwin, Philip R., 19
Gorbatov, L., 2152
Gorbov, D., 1185
Gorfinkel, D. M., 32, 69, 150, 563, 565, 567, 569, 624, 639, 719
Gorlin, A. N., 500, 519, 529
Gorvits, N., 112
Gottardi, Silvana, 22
Gottfurcht, F., 2397
Gow, David, 1209
Grafström, Ernst, 3, 12, 15, 22, 42, 49
Graham, Bessie, 1284
Graham, Stephen, 710, 1285
Graher, Olga, 3
Granch, H. C., 79, 105
Grant, Gordon, 128
Grants, Em, 674
Gray, C. W., 712
Grayson, C., 780
Greateater, A., 2204
Green, Archie, 1064
Green, E. Carl, 2249
Greenlaw, E., 745
Greenwood, Mary S., 1167
Grego, Adela, 12, 32, 131, 166
Grenier, Roger, 310
Grēviņa, A., 395
Grevinš, V., 2118
Grieg, Nordahl, 69, 79, 92, 101, 120, 135

Grieg-Müller, John, 88, 112
Grigoriana, A., 710
Grin, N., 694
Grinvald, M. K., 141
Gripenberg, Bertel, 2223, 2224, 2450
Groat, William J., 2287
Groesbeck, Dan Sayre, 768, 1051, 1052
Grønlund, H., 1978
Gross, K., 2046
Grossman, Reuben, 120
Grün, Herbert, 69
Gruyer, Paul, 25, 32, 39, 88, 95, 112, 127, 131, 135, 153, 310, 676, 780, 810, 1060
Gruzinskaia, N., 2154
Guardiola, Antonio, 65, 79, 95, 161
Guber, P. G., 65, 2153
Guicciardi, Laura Ferajorni, 22, 49
Guillermet, Fanny, 15, 88, 116
Guro, Ye. G., 65, 496, 497
Gwis-Adami, Rosalia, 88

Hacker, David W., 2309
Hakánson, Eva, 55
Haldeman-Julius, E., 728, 768, 807
Hale, E. E., Jr., 2322, 2337
Hale, E. H., 2331
Halevi, A., 344
Halkin, Shimeon, 32
Hall, L., 1286
Hall, Vivian Halpern, 2250
Hallén-Frish, Ragnhild, 585
Hamara, Onni, 728
Hamilton, Douglas William, 77
Hamilton, Fannie K., 851
Hanazono, Kanesada, 22
Haney, John L., 1287
Hansen, H. P. E., 1982
Harbitz, Alf, 49
Harkins, Edward F., 1288

Harlow, Henlen J., 21
Harmanci, Mahemet, 58, 593, 595, 596
Harper, George, 117
Harris, Frank, 867, 868
Harrison, Ralph D., 1174
Harsányi, Zsolt, 141, 1183
Hart, James D., 836, 1289
Hart, Jerome A., 1290
Hartwick, Harry, 1291
Hass, V. P., 2333
Határ, Győző, 362
Hatcher, Harlan, 1292
Haycraft, Howard, 1317
Hazard, Lucy L., 1293
Heiney, E. B., 1168
Heinold, Johnny, 1025
Helander, C., 45
Hellwig, Karl, 1182
Hendrick, George, 1283
Hendricks, King, 169, 1169, 1170
Henry, W. G., 63
Hentig, V., 2379
Hermann, G., 2392, 2400
Hermann-Neisse, Max, 2047
Herms, A., 150
Herrde, Dietrich, 2419
Herrland, Hans, 2400
Herzberg, Max J., 710, 1294
Hicks, Granville, 1295
Higham, John, 1296
Himy, Armand, 310
Hinkel, Edgar J., 1297, 1298, 1299
Hinsdale, Laura F., 2287
Hint, A., 58, 278, 719
Hirshberg, Yitshak, 141
Hodder, A., 2319
Hogan, William, 2283, 2309, 2334
Hogeboom, A., 676
Hølaas, Odd, 116
Holeček, Pavel, 9, 49
Holland, Robert Belton, 2270
Holliday, Robert Cortes, 1300

Holly, F. M., 2317
Homan, H. J., 2379, 2390,
    2412, 2417
Honda, Kensho, 49
Hooper, Chas. Edw., 19
Horn, Gunnar, 619, 780
Horne, Ben, 15, 22, 61, 98,
    127, 150, 153
Horne, Charles F., 905
Horton, Arthur L., 2266
Horwill, Herbert W., 2341
Houwaard, C., 1985
Hovey, C., 2288
Hovious, Carol, 780
Howe, Will D., 1255
Hoyer, W., 2048, 2384, 2397,
    2406
Hoyt, E., 2292
Hruša, J., 153
Hubel, E., 1998
Huber, Miriam Blanton, 21
Huggler, E. H., 2050
Hülsenbeck, R., 2049
Huri, Sofi, 22
Husband, John D., 794
Hutt, Henry, 36
Hynds, Reed, 2309
Hynynen, Ville, 69

Iacint, O., 101
Iacobescu, Al., 69
Iarkova, F., 694
Iesanu, I., 471
Ilgusils, M., 768
Imre, Szász, 364
Inglis, R. B., 780
Irish, John P., 984
Irvine, Alexander, 1301
Israki, B., 84
Itkohen, Rieti, 802
Iurdanov, V., 131
Iverson, William J., 21
Iwata, Kinzo, 22
Iz'iurova, I. V., 393

Jacobs, Leland B., 21, 693
Jaffe, Adrian H., 780
Jaher, Frederic Cople, 1309

Jakobsson, Bárður, 32
Jalaja, P., 719
Jalkotzky, A., 2394
James, George Wharton,
    1310
Jankovic, Dusan, 55
Jen, Fong T'u, 137
Jenó, J., 84
Jensen, Johannes V., 2051
Jensen, M. C., 32
Jeřábek, A., 15
Jerndorff-Jensen, P., 161
Jessup, A., 754
Jevtic, Pavle, 131
Jôgi, O., 627
Johansson, Barbro, 585
Johns, Cloudesley, 1172
Johnson, Martin E., 1174
Johnson, Thomas, 993
Joho, W., 2397
Jonason, Olov, 22
Jones, Evan, 1311
Jones, Winifred W., 21
Jong, A. M. de, 1223
Jónsson, Ingólfur, 88
Jörden, Rudolf, 2400
Jost, H., 49
Joubert, S., 3
Jovanovic, Nikola B., 79,
    101
Jovanovski, Meto, 15, 69
Jovčic, R., 15
Judelevičius, D., 42
Jung, Franz, 2022

Kaemmerling, K., 2052
Kaija, V., 32
Kalamaro, Lilian, 12
Kalashnikovoi, E. D., 69,
    498
Kalchev, I., 247
Kalesnykietis, A., 414,
    611, 715, 800
Kalina, Fero, 127
Kalisky, Philip, 638
Kalojanov-Vasilievna,
    Irina, 261
Kalpoki, M., 101

Kamburov-Furen, Svetoslav, 227
Kämpe, Alfred, 2226
Kamran, M., 693
Kan, M., 1230
Kanaeva, N., 710
Känd, A., 272, 273, 276, 277, 279
Kaplan, Arthur, 754
Karaslavov, G., 227
Kare, Aito, 6, 141, 161, 295, 300
Karklinš, Valdemars, 1184
Karnaukhova, A. M., 526, 542
Karski, Gabriel, 432, 438, 456, 460
Kaskan, Selçuk M., 112
Kaufman, N. S., 500, 553, 558
Kaufmann, O., 2394
Kauliņa, E., 69, 395
Kavaleria, Ye., 496
Kavalery, Eugeniy, 496
Kays, Marjorie, 2251
Kazin, Alfred, 1312
Kbakova, B., 81
Keck, C. M., 745
Kelen, Ferenc, 101
Kelmendi, Ramiz, 642
Kertomuksia, Y. M., 144
Kezinaitis, K., 131
Khmel'nitzkaia, T., 2155
Khodzhaev, Azomov i, 694
Khristoforov, Asen G., 49
Khutsishvili, N., 575, 2156
Kielty, B., 780
Kilmer, Joyce, 2307
Kimball, Rodney A., 780
The Kinneys, 66
Kinnick, B. Jo, 780
Kislova, L., 571
Kislovay, K., 574
Kitamura, Kihachi, 49
Kits, M., 2003
Kiuchi, Nobutaka, 69
Klasing, Rudolf, 2053
Klátik, Z., 49

Klechkovski, M. M., 496, 497
Kleist, M. de, 150
Klíma, S., 150, 153
Knight, Grant C., 1313, 1314
Knostantinović, Zora, 105
Knudsen, Mogens, 267
Koch, Martin, 2448
Koch, R., 2382, 2419
Kogan, P. S., 496, 497, 532, 2157
Köhler, Willi, 2054
Kohl, L., 116
Kohn, L. von, 135
Koiudzhieva, T., 105
Kojic, Branko, 32, 116
Kolar, Mildred Marguerite, 2252
Kolmonoveki, A. P., 69
Kolponovskaia, E., 2444
Kopelevic, Yaskov, 69
Kopra, Tauno, 297, 298, 301
Koray, Selma, 105
Korea, Történet, 135
Korg, Jacob, 780
Körmendy, Viktor, 347
Kornerup, Ebbe, 1979
Korpela, Maunu, 112
Korsakas, K., 2130
Koshevich, V., 22, 101, 517
Koskenniemi, V. A., 2369, 2371
Kouta, Aarni, 2372
Koval', V., 65
Kovolenskaya, M. V., 496, 497
Kozer, Karel, 21
Krashik, Lucia, 116
Kraushaar, Alfred, 2380
Kreutz, R. J., 2400
Krimmer, Therese, 2417
Kringen, Olav, 65
Krinko, G., 694
Kristianson, Elof, 65
Kristjánsson, Sverrir, 135

Kristoforov, Asen G., 261
Krivinok, O., 3
Krivtsova, A. F. V., 496,
    497
Kříž, F. V., 2342
Krodere, Z., 88, 395
Kroders, R., 161, 395
Krohn, Helmi, 32, 120
Krompolcienė, T., 79, 120
Krotký, S., 15
Kršić, Nikola, 153
Kršić, Smiljana, 153
Krupskaya, Nadezhda K., 1315
Kudrysvtseva, A. N., 88
Kullé, R., 2158
Kullerkupp, R., 92
Kuncewiczowa, Marja, 477,
    806
Kunitz, Stanley J., 1316,
    1317
Kuosaite, E., 32
Kupiainen, Alpo, 294
Kuprin, A. I., 2159
Kurbanov, A., 598, 719
Kurella, V., 574
Kushch, O., 2443
Kuszelewska-Matuszewska,
    Stainsława, 3, 6, 15, 22,
    32, 61, 69, 88, 98, 127,
    131, 432, 435, 436, 437,
    439, 440, 442, 449, 451,
    454, 456, 460
Kutšerjavenko, V., 2004
Kutukova, A., 49, 509
Kutukova, M. L., 509, 551
Kyška, Štefan, 58, 65, 69,
    710, 719

Labor, Earle Gene, 213,
    2271, 2283, 2309
Lacis, V., 2109
Lagercrantz, Olof, 1232
Lagunova, M. V., 208
Laiviņš, A., 624
Lambrinov, Dimităr, 261
Lami, Adriano, 55, 69, 88
Lami, Annie, 88
Lampert, Rud., 61

Landen, J. H., 65
Landis, Joan Selby, 2253
Lane, Frederick A., 1175
Lane, Rose Wilder, 1176
Langer, J., 49
Lann, Yev., 496, 497
Lansford, W. Douglas, 2205
Lanskaya, L., 496, 497
Lapina, N. V., 81
Lasenberga, R., 2119
Lask, Thomas, 2304
Laughton, Charles, 619
Law, F. H., 794
Lawrence, T. C., 36
Lazar, William, 21, 31
Lazareva, A., 694
Lazda, A., 2120
Lážňovský, B., 22
Le Moine, Osborne, 2214
Leal, Luísa Maria de Eça,
    462
Leão, Ruth, 780
Leavell, Ullin W., 780
Lebedev, J. W., 281
Leclercq, Leo, 92
Leclerq, W. L., 61
Lee, Seung-in, 22
Lefèvre, Frédéric, 2011,
    2016
Lehto, Ilmari, 131, 144,
    304
Leisy, Ernest E., 1318
Lenmartz, Franz, 2030
Lenobl', G., 2161
Lenoir, D., 746
Leó, Vécsey, 92
Leonhard, Altbuch, 490
Leonhardy, Alma, 1177
Lerner, Max, 64
Lesanu, C., 469
Levi, Adele, 12, 15, 95,
    98, 150, 153
Levidova, S., 2189
Levit, T., 2190
Levitt, Morton P., 2254
Lewik, Włodzimierz, 120
Lewis, Austin, 2302
Lewis, Sinclair, 169, 1178

Lewisohn, Ludwig, 1319
Ley, Willie, 54
Lie, Nils, 32
Lieberman, Elias, 1320
Lien, Ank, 600
Ligotņu, Jekabs, 2428
Likhtenbom, Y., 345
Likiardopulo, M., 22, 131, 509, 638
Lima, Campos, 462
Limanovskaya, V., 574
Limanovskoi, V., 498
Lisichenko, M., 105
Litvinovoǐ, T., 697, 911
Livingston, Leon Ray, 1179
Loban, Walter, 676
Lobato, Monteiro, 32, 49
Locatelli, A., 49
Lockley, Fred, 1029
Loggins, Vernon, 1321, 1322
Loks, K., 2437
London, Charmian, 1, 496, 766, 1028, 1147, 1172, 1180, 1181, 1182, 1183, 1184, 1185, 1186, 1188, 1189, 1190, 1191, 1192, 1193, 1194, 1195, 1196, 1197, 1198, 1199, 2017, 2143, 2206, 2207
London, Joan, 1066, 1071, 1200, 1201
London, John, 664
Löns, Lisa, 22
Lori, Ida, 79
Lorie, M. F., 498, 571, 2162
Losannese, Mario, 127
Łosiowa, Natalia, 12
Luchinskya, A. V., 74, 551
Ludvová, M., 105
Ludwig, Albert, 2380, 2390, 2394, 2401, 2403, 2408, 2412
Lufti, G., 588
Lufzhi, G., 587
Lukas, Horst W., 2059
Lundberg, E. G., 65, 2442
Lundberg, Oscar, 2446
Lundquist, Ernst, 12, 18,

42, 45, 101, 105, 108, 112, 135, 150, 153, 582, 584, 1198
Lupaşcu, Paul, 487
Lupsiakova, M., 105
Luszelewska, S., 49
Lutterbeck, G. A., 2383, 2390, 2401
Lvovski, Zin, 22, 32, 49, 55, 65, 79, 81, 101, 105, 112, 496, 497, 501, 502, 507, 512, 520, 521, 535, 543, 546, 547, 548, 559
Lybeck, Bertil, 22
Lybeck, Laveringar, 22
Lynch, George, 953
Lynn, Kenneth S., 1323, 2235

Maaste, S., 2357
Machkarov, Iordan, 79, 227
Maffi, Quirino, 22, 49
Maganov, Nina, 780
Mägi, J., 2005
Magill, Frank Northern, 1305
Magnus, Erwin, 3, 6, 9, 11, 25, 32, 45, 61, 69, 79, 88, 92, 95, 101, 105, 112, 120, 127, 135, 141, 150, 153, 156, 314, 315, 316, 317, 318, 320, 322, 323, 324, 326, 328, 330, 331, 335, 339, 340, 341, 692, 710
Magnus-Carlsson, Axel, 2229
Măgureanu, Marius, 49, 153
Mahjoub, Mohammad Jaafar, 424, 429, 689, 763
Maiorova, I., 773
Mairhofer, Franz, 22
Maixner, M., 735
Mally, E. L., 21
Maltesta, Mario, 127
Man, N., 574
Mandrea, Pavel, 475
Manly, John M., 1324
Mann, M., 2402

Manoliu, Petru, 127
Mansfield, Katherine, 2303
Marble, Annie R., 1325
Marcellini, Giovanni, 15,
    55, 375, 628, 780
Marchand, J., 2316
Marcu, Valerio, 2060
Margolin, Klara, 2023
Markham, Edwin, 674, 1326,
    1327
Marsh, E. C., 2319
Martens, Kurt, 2380, 2386
Martino, Salvatore, 2100
Mascarenhas, Telo de, 462
Masiello, Arthur, 2255
Masiotas, Pr., 606
Mašková, M., 127, 135
Mathiews, F. M., 676
Matthíasson, Steingrímur,
    699
Matveyev, M., 153, 533, 538
Maugham, W. Somerset, 780
Maurice, A. B., 2287
Mayevski, I. A., 65
Mazilu, D., 65, 69
Meidinger-Geise, J., 2061
Meister-Calvino, Paola, 22
Mejurjanu, Marius, 49
Mekuli, Esad, 12
Melnalksnis, S., 395
Mencken, Henry L., 1330
Mendonça, Gustavo de, 668
Meredith, Anthony, 174
Merikallio, Einari, 39
Merkel, E., 196
Meyerfield, Max, 2417
Meysztowicz, Jan, 432
Mezhrabpom, Gart., 523
Michaud, Régis, 2012
Miethe, Käthe, 2389
Mighels, Ella Sterling,
    803, 1028
Mihailov, Panca, 69
Mihailovič, K., 15
Mikaelian, V., 49
Mikhăilov, G., 49, 227
Mikkelsen, Aslaug, 6, 15,
    22, 61, 69, 79, 92, 105,

    120, 127, 150, 1192,
    1197
Mikkelsen, Einar, 92
Milakič, Djordje, 12
Milbergs, G., 624, 692,
    756, 798
Miles, D. H., 745
Milev, Mikala, 261
Milićević, Andreja, 49
Milkhailov, G., 227
Milla, Fernando de la, 153
Miller, P. Schuyler, 2284,
    2331
Minina, V., 638
Minot, J. C., 21
Minou, Ernest, 476
Minozzi, Berto, 22
Mirimanov, G. F., 624
Mirlas, Leon, 1231
Mironova, A., 574, 576
Mirov, B., 2433
Mirrieless, E. R., 775
Mirtič, Milka, 61
Mitchell, Theodore C., 21
Miura, Shin'ichi, 22
Moberg, Olle, 65, 192
Molenaar, Johan de, 168
Moltó, Jaime Puig, 22
Monahan, Michael, 2331
Monahan, P. J., 102
Monteiro, Domingos, 462
Monteiro, Sylvio, 22
Montenegro, Ernestro, 2208
Montgomery, Elizabeth R.,
    1331
Moravec, Jaroslav, 1972
Moriarty, M., 2283
Morozov, O., 2191
Morkúnas, Pr., 32
Mörner, Birger, 2230
Morrell, Ed., 1205
Morris, Lloyd R., 1332
Morris, R. B., 905
Mosby, C. V., 1206
Moss, Mary, 2295
Mott, Frank Luther, 21,
    1333
Moudrá, P., 79

Mountain, Lu Harrison, 780
Movshenson, A. G., 88, 92,
    544
M-skoĭ, S. V., 2193
Müller, Mij Joh, 79
Mullokandov, E., 58
Mumford, Lewis, 1334
Munte, Irene, 95
Murphy, Gardner, 134
Murros, Kaapo, 25, 49, 55
Murtezai, Masar, 642
Muslim, I., 632
Muslimov, G., 632
Musselyuss, R. V., 503
Mustanojo, Tauno F., 1274
Myrdal, Jan, 79

McArdle, Kenneth, 905
McCabe, Joseph, 1328
McCann, William E., 1297,
    1298, 1299
McCarthy, Agnes L., 21,
    780, 1364
McCole, C. J., 1329
McCracken, Glenn, 678, 794
McDevitt, William, 788,
    1202, 1203
McFee, W., 712
McGimsey, Grover C., 1204
McNamee, Edward, 1385
McSpadden, J. W., 21

Nadal, A., 88
Namitokova, Iu., 222
Nanitashvili, B., 312
Narciss, G. A., 2393
Näser, G., 2062
Nash, W. H., 786
Navickas, St., 49
Neary, John A., 2236
Nedal, L., 638
Nedić, Borivoje, 22, 49
Nekovařík, B. Z., 15, 22,
    49, 79
Nekvedavičiue, A., 735
Nekvindová-Nešporová, M.,
    32
Nelidov, Yu. A., 500, 553

Nelimies, Toivo, 84, 302
Nemerovskyaya, Olga, 2194,
    2195
Nenova, M., 112
Neubauer, Heinz, 2031
Neubert, Rudolf, 6
Neville, Mark A., 710
Nezhdanov, D., 116
Nichol, John William, 2256
Nichols, Thomas W., 2257
Nieman, Egbert W., 782
Nister, Der, 22, 61
Noel, Joseph, 1335
Nogan, Efdal, 591
Noian, Eliza, 466
Nondschein, Josef, 65
Nordstrand, G., 2231
Norton, Margaret, 1207
Norvell, G. W., 780
Nosovich, D. P., 18
Novák, J., 32
Novi, Teresa, 95
Núñes, Estuardo, 2210
Nuotio, Tauno, 127
Nutini, Aurelia, 49
Nylen, Einar, 583
Nyren, Dorothy, 1304
Nyuton, F., 123, 519

O'Brien, Edward J., 1336
Obruchev, Sergei, 2439
O'Connor, Richard, 1208,
    1337
O'Daly, Elizabeth, 782
Oesterheld, Elsa, 22
Offenburg, Karl, 2063
Okhrimenko, P., 513
Oksanen, Vilho, 98, 292
Olden, B., 2006
Olmsted, Rosalind A., 676
Omilianchuk, P., 579, 2163
Onegin, V., 116, 150
Oppewell, Peter, 2272
Ordaz, Luis, 2202
Orechkina, V. N., 496
Orians, George H., 1338
Orthmann, Edwin, 2412
Osborne, Maitland Leroy,

2329
Ospanov, S., 392
Otazú, Silvestre, 65
Otten, J. F., 1986
Oven, J., 2384
Owen, Betty, 215
Ozerskoi, T. A., 498
Ozola, V., 395
Ozolinš, S., 2121
Ozon, Hayrullah Ors-Mustafa
    Nihat, 49

Padover, S. K., 923
Pál, Bernát, 69
Palmer, Frederick, 953,
    1339
Palmgren, Elin, 1193
Paltrinieri, Bruno, 22, 49
Palumbo, Aldo, 65
Panova, Ruža, 55
Parisi, M., 79
Parktal, J., 32
Pärn, A., 1992
Parnwell, E. C., 678, 754
Parrington, Vernon L., 1340
Partik, P., 2404
Pas, Ion, 479
Paskhin, N., 2196
Paspaleev, Leonid, 101, 257
Pasquali, Maria Carlesimo,
    28, 58, 61, 84, 380
Pattee, Fred L., 711, 1341,
    1342, 1343
Patterson, Ye, 101
Paulockis, M., 9
Pawek, K., 2398
Payne, Edward Biron, 1209,
    1210
Payne, W. M., 2313, 2325
Pearsall, Robert, 710, 719,
    745
Peattie, Elia W., 2287
Pečaks, P., 394
Pedajas, V., 275
Pegelau, B., 505, 510
Peluso, Edmondo, 1973
Pennwitt, Barbara, 780
Pereira, Astrojildo, 2143

Pereira, Lygia Autran Rod-
    rigues, 463
Perés, Ramón D., 49
Perez, Francisco, 676
Perez, Oreste Vera, 21
Perret, Jacques, 310
Perrin, E. Sainte-Marie,
    2018
Perry, Bliss, 1344
Pervik, A., 1993
Pesic, M. M., 69
Peterka, Robert, 32
Peterson, Clell T., 2258
Petr, V., 420, 614
Petrovic, Ivan, 101
Petrović, Slavka, 101
Petry, Walter, 2064
Peyman, Djavad, 32
Phelps, William L., 1345
Pierre-Quint, L., 2377
Pilař, Fr., 2345
Pimenova, E. K., 3, 32, 55,
    69, 509, 554
Piotrowski, Kazimierz, 116,
    432, 456, 460, 1228,
    2137, 2138, 2139
Piroska, Ferenc, 361
Píša, A. M., 2344
Pluev, A., 372
Plugaru, I., 479
Podvurzachov, D., 15, 88,
    116, 135, 141, 150, 227
Poherecká, Ž., 65, 101, 120
Pollat, M., 624
Polybok, M., 105
Pomm, V., 2362
Pöögelmann, H., 803
Pooley, R. C., 780
Poots, Ü., 698
Pope, Margaret I., 2273
Popescu, C. Sp., 49, 467
Popescu, I. St., 484
Popov, V., 15
Popova, Nadia, 105
Popovic, Jovan, 61
Poritzky, J. E., 2065, 2397
Portsteinsson, Ragnar, 112
Postif, Louis, 9, 12, 15,

25, 32, 39, 55, 65, 88,
92, 95, 98, 105, 112,
120, 127, 131, 135, 141,
153, 161, 307, 310, 624,
643, 676, 767, 777, 780,
800, 810, 1060, 1191
Poulsen, Knud, 35, 45, 153
Powel, H. W. H., 735
Powell, Anthony, 2285
Powell, E. P., 2287
Pranskus, B., 2164
Pranspill, A., 721
Pratt, C. A., 2329
Preston, Wheeler, 1346
Previtali, Oriana, 69
Prezzolini, G., 32
Price, Olive, 21, 2274
Przedpełska-Trzeciakowska,
   Anna, 49, 432
Puras, K., 2131
Purcell, Mary, 780
Purdue, Dr. A. H., 1015
Pusheshnikov, N., 506, 511
Putevodny, F. D., 505, 510

Queen, Ellery, 716
Quinn, Arthur Hobson, 1347

Rachmanovas, U., 202
Radek, Karl, 65
Radina, Bogdana, 32
Radovic, Ognjan, 65
Radulescu-Tilly, Anna, 468
Ragozina, Z. A., 141
Rainalter, E. H., 2066
Rakousky, Hans, 2032
Ramsay, R. L., 710
Rankin, Thomas E., 1348
Rathbone, Charles, 215
Raymond, C. H., 632
Reay, Raphael M., 7
Rebane, L., 22
Recknagel, Rolf, 2067, 2068
Redlick, Rosemarie, 1354,
   1355
Reifferscheidt, F. M., 2069
Reiman, M., 69
Reimers, Johannes, 2287

Rein, Sigmun, 22
Reinfelde, T., 396, 710,
   790
Riese, W., 2394
Reisingrová, M., 69, 92
Reiss-Andersen, Gunnar, 105
Relander, A. I., 3, 306
Reneaume, P., 712, 803
Renner, Lisbeth, 32
Renner, Louis, 32
Rentmeister, Heinrich,
   2024, 2025
Reznik, O., 566
Riabovoi, M., 49, 69
Ribalow, H. U., 719, 735
Rice, G., 735
Rich, A. O., 2325
Richler, Mordecai, 2285
Richter, Helene, 2070
Rickert, Edith, 1324
Rideout, Walter Bates, 1349
Righter, Kathryn, 1302
Riška, K., 49
Rives, Hall E., 1350
Roaati, S., 105
Robinson, E. Fletcher, 2319
Rodabaugh, Delmer, 780
Roden, Donald, 1211
Rogozina, Z. A., 120
Roldanus, W. J. A., 266
Romano, Vincenzo, 12, 2101
Romanowicz, Eleanora, 22,
   432, 458
Roosevelt, Theodore, 1351
Rort, Shelton L., 21, 693
Rosa, Francesco de, 150
Rosenfeld, M., 88
Roskin, A., 1994, 2165
Roskina, A., 710
Ross, Robert Samuel, 2286,
   2341
Rossi, Gastone, 3, 22, 32,
   39, 49, 69, 79, 105,
   120, 131
Rossi, M. M., 2106
Rothberg, Abraham, 2275
Roventa, Ivan, 480, 483
Rozental, I., 2440

Rubinova, R., 22, 49
Rusev, St. E., 135, 768
Russell, Frank A., 1352
Ruzitska, Maria, 120, 352
Rychińskiego, J. B., 450,
    452, 453
Rychliński, Jerzy Bogdan,
    32, 92, 95, 101, 127, 432
Rykova, N., 561
Ryl'skikh, I., 95
Ryndy-Alekseyev, B. K., 500,
    553
Rzakulizade, M., 225

Saastamoinen, J., 105
Sabatini, Rafael, 619
St. John, Adela Rogers, 1353
Saito, Kazue, 69
Sajner, D., 49
Sakai, Toshihiko, 22, 49
Salem, Saeed, 426, 427, 428
Salomen, Louis B., 203
Salten, Felix, 21
Salucci, Arturo, 25, 105,
    116, 135
Samarin, R. M., 499
Samiou, H., 153
Samitca, Madeline, 489
Sandberg, Algot, 69, 79,
    116, 582, 584
Sandrus, Mary Yost, 21
Sanford, Marvin, 1212
Sarić, Viatko, 55, 263
Satin, Joseph, 710
Savchev, Georgi, 88
Saville, George, 65
Saxon, Anders, 22
Scatcherd, Felecia R., 1209
Schaefer, J. W., 619
Scheffauer, H. G., 2071
Schellenberger, Johannes,
    2397
Scherman, David E., 1354,
    1355
Schickert, Werner, 2380,
    2381, 2383, 2389, 2420
Schiefer, Josephina, 482
Schmedake, Dorothy May, 2259

Schneider, Arno, 2397,
    2401, 2414
Schneider, Margarete, 2417,
    2419
Schnöckelborg, Georg, 49
Schöner, Dezsö, 55, 346
Schorer, Mark, 1356
Schuster, W., 2389, 2391
Schyberg, Frederick, 1981
Scott, Paul, 2285
Scott, Virgil, 780
Schramm, S. L., 619
Schroeder, Karl, 2072
Schubert, Renate, 2073
Schultz-Ewerth, E., 2076
Schulz, F. O. H., 2074
Schulz, Ivan, 3, 6, 69, 95,
    98, 101, 105, 112, 150,
    153, 1195
Schuster, W., 2384, 2397,
    2403, 2408, 2410, 2419
Schwabach, E. E., 2406
Schwalbe, J., 2359
Schwarz, E. A., 2397
Schwarz, F., 2394
Schwartz, Osias L., 1034
Schwed, P., 735
Schweikert, H. C., 780
Sebepov, G., 49
Seelheim, Karl, 2418
Segantini, Romana, 49
Seilental, J., 676
Seiler, Richard C., 69, 88
Seizova-Turukove, M., 49,
    127
Seldes, George, 1064
Selles, Sául, 116, 120
Semenovíc, S. Luka, 79
Sesostra, G., 32, 88
Seton, E. T., 21
Seuzova-Iurukova, M., 153
Shaw, H., 780
Shannon, David A., 1357
Shear, Walter Lewis, 2260
Shepard, Irving, 169, 200
Shil'dizkov, V. G., 719
Shima, Sangoro, 95
Shimizu, Sen, 55

Shinozaki, Hikosaburo, 55
Shishmareva, M. A., 496
Shivers, Alfred S., 2261,
    2276, 2283, 2309
Shostak, J., 735
Shroyer, Frederick, 2309
Shteinberg, Ye., 141
Sickle, Jim, 48
Siefers, G., 161
Sieloff, E., 2387, 2405,
    2413
Siemsen, Anna, 2078, 2394
Sieroszewskiego, Wacława,
    22
Sigal, Clancy, 2319
Sigurõsson, Svainn, 2099,
    2423
Sigursson, Steindór, 61
Silber, B., 2403
Silberberg, Margarete,
    2079
Šileika, Pr., 69, 161, 674
Silinš, K., 2123
Sillaots, M., 49
Silva, Rui Guedes da, 22
Silver, Grace V., 2302
Silvera, César Horacio, 153
Silvestri, T., 156
Silvio, Julio, 2141
Šimáčková, B., 69
Simić, Živojin, 69
Simidov, Dimitur, 227
Šimková, B., 3
Simon, Jean, 2013
Simoni, Zef, 22
Sinclair, Upton, 923, 1032,
    1358, 1359, 1360, 1987,
    2080, 2081
Sinding, Holger, 3, 22
Sirven, Claude, 69
Skácel, Jan, 2345
Skaptson, Magnús J., 105
Skelton, P., 710
Skujenicks, E., 394
Skujina, E., 394
Slavu, Mircea, 492
Smaus, A., 116
Smetanich, V. I., 105, 496,

    497, 537
Smetánka, V., 98
Smidth, Tom, 3
Smith, Bernard, 923
Smith, Harry J., 2284
Snajder, Otilija, 153, 264
Snow, William Leonard, 21
Snyder, E. D., 619
Snyder, F. B., 619
Snyder, J. E., 1084
Snyder, L. L., 905
Sobotka, Henryk Andrzej,
    2133
Söderling, Maria, 95
Söderling, Torsten, 95
Soen, Dan, 343
Soffici, A., 2107
Sokolicz, Antonina, 116,
    432, 2134
Solari Amondarain, Ismael,
    2211
Solomon, Petre, 493
Son, Dan, 127
Sora, A. M., 2082
Spencer, Arthur Frank,
    2262
Spiller, Robert E., 1361
Springer, Anne Marie, 2277
Stach, F., 2083
Stadlmann, Ingeborg, 2026
Staněk, J., 3
Stanevich, V. O., 141, 496,
    497
Starrett, Vincent, 1362,
    2283, 2309
Štastný, Al. J., 22, 69,
    1975, 1976
Stawinski, Julian, 432
Stead, C., 754
Steenberg, E. Schack, 22,
    25, 88, 101, 112
Stefánsson, Halldór, 12
Steindórsson, Steindór,
    2424
Stenich, V., 561, 632
Stepanian, B., 627
Stepanovoi, N., 710
Ster, Jac. v.d., 116

Sterling, George, 157
Stern, Edgar P., 2084
Stern-Rubarth, Edgar, 2085,
    2384, 2391
Stille, Kate B., 2287
Stioanov, Liudmil, 25,
    227, 230, 258
Stoevski, Dim, 239
Stoianov, Pacho, 69, 227
Stoianov, Petko, 55
Stoianov, Racho, 95, 120
Stoianov, St., 15, 69
Stojanov, Cvetan, 261
Stojanov, Rico, 261
Stolba, Z., 69
Stone, Edward, 803
Stone, Irving, 1213, 1214,
    1215, 1216, 1217, 1218,
    1219, 1220, 1221, 1222,
    1223, 1224, 1225, 1226,
    1227, 1228, 1229, 1230,
    1231, 1232, 1363, 2304
Stovall, Floyd, 1365
Strasser, Charlot, 2033,
    2086
Stravi, Em, 473
Stropus, R., 84
Stroven, Carl, 640, 678,
    698, 754, 820
Strunsky, Anna, 17, 170,
    907, 2296
Sudrabkalns, J., 2110
Sukhoverov, S., 2198, 2199
Svetlinov, Boris, 32
Svoboda, V., 49
Swados, Harvey, 880
Swanberg, Ella, 61
Swidzinski, F., 150, 2345
Sylvester, Harry, 2333
Symes, Lillian, 1366
Syncenko, O., 49
Szanthmáry-Vlčková, V., 120
Szász, Imre, 55, 61, 153,
    362

Tabakov, Boris, 3
Taddei, Giuseppina, 55, 127
Tainio, T., 291

Tainio-Matti Vuolukka, T.,
    6
Talma, Yrjö, 299
Tammes, G., 754
Tamony, Peter, 1064
Tăng, Căn Huy, 22
Tanner, Tony, 2287
Tarasova, A., 9
Targ, V., 768
Tarnowska, K., 120, 432
Taylor, Jerzy Mariusz, 108,
    444, 445
Taylor, Walter F., 1367
Tedeschi, Alberto, 166
Teodorescu, Paul C., 116
Tersánszky, J. Jenö, 350,
    353, 356, 357, 362
Thiel, R., 2087
Thiess, F., 2088
Thomas, Lowell, Jr., 697,
    911, 931
Thompson, L., 709
Thomsen, Niels Th., 1983
Thorp, Willard, 844, 1368
Thorsch, Eduard, 32, 49,
    65, 69, 79, 120
Thorsteinson, Axel, 368,
    370, 652, 741
Thurston, Lorrin A., 995,
    1021
Tickenor, H. M., 1233
T'ien-hung, Hsu, 262
T'ien-tso, Chiang, 49
Tirzmalietis, L., 668
Titus, Warren I., 918
Tivadar, Szinnai, 65
Todd, Robert, 21
Tolvanen, Aune, 153
Tornius, V., 2089
Torres Morey, Rafael, 2212
Toschi, Gastone, 22
Traschen, Frahes, 803
Traschen, Isadore, 803
Traverso, Aldo, 141
Trent, William P., 1369
Trotzini, V., 65
Tschörtner, Heinz Dieter,
    2027, 2090

Tsederbaum, S., 79
Tsemlin, B., 79
Tsymovich, N. M., 6, 116, 528, 541
Tudeer, Aune, 88
Tudor, Stephen H., 15, 2263
Tulli, Tullio, 15, 135
Tumenas, V., 693
Tutunchan, Zh., 58
Tuura, Kerttu, 79
Tvarožek, E. V., 22, 92
Tweney, George H., 2309
Tyutryumova, R., 504

Ugrinova, Golapka, 55
Ullman, Gudrun, 585
Umbstaetter, H. D., 1033
Untermann, Ernst, 55, 2091
Uotila, Ilmari, 9
Upits, A., 2429
Uray, Fikret, 594, 597
Urvich, A. S., 131
Utkina, N., 496, 497
Utkina, Ye., 496, 497

Vacietis, J., 676
Vadillo, Francisco R., 22
Vaigla, A., 2006
Vaillant-Courtuerier, P., 65
Vaĭnshteĭn, G., 2201
Vaisenberg, L. M., 500, 553, 558
Vajda, Miklos, 362
Valdman, V. S., 570
Vale, C., 2307
Valentini, J., 131
Valera, Fernando, 55, 153
Valinčius, A., 422
Vallvé, Manuel, 69
Van Doren, Carl, 1371
Van Doren, Mark, 1371
Van Zijl, Felix, 105
Vandeneertwegh, Rene, 2356
Varian, George, 40
Varing, L., 676
Variste, J., 32, 1995
Varsamian, A., 69

Vasilev, M., 1218
Vasilev, Orlin, 69, 141, 227
Vasilevski, L., 2436
Vecherov, M., 9
Vécsey, Leó, 135
Vedde, Sigurd, 1980
Velchev, Liuben, 227, 252, 257
Velkov, Pelin, 65, 254
Vengerov, D., 49
Verney, E., 1315
Vershinina, Z. A., 65, 496, 497
Vesley, A., 2009
Victor, Walter, 2034
Viktor, János, 362
Vilde, K., 55
Virgili, A. Rovira, 22
Viscardini, L., 61, 116
Vít, K., 18, 58, 123, 127, 135, 161, 719
Vít, L. F., 58
Vita-Finzi, P., 2425, 2426, 2427
Volzhinoĭ, N., 49
Von Schweinitz, Maria, 699
Vorel, J., 12, 61, 65, 123, 135
Vsevolozhskoi, L., 6
Vukadinovic, Zivojin, 153
Vukićević, Zarija D., 141
Vulchev, Todor, 261

Wagenheim, Harold H., 619, 775, 780
Wagenknecht, Edward C., 1372
Wake, Ritsujiro, 25
Walakorpi, U. W., 2370
Walcutt, Charles C., 678, 794, 1234, 1373
Walker, Franklin, 1374, 2309
Wallenius, Toivo, 12, 116
Warfel, Harry R., 780, 1375
Watkins, D. E., 632
Watts, H. A., 780

Weinberg, M., 65
Weiss, Gertrud, 2094
Wells, H. G., 367
Weltz, Friedrich, 2096
Wenk, Willi, 327
Wenz, Paul, 710, 2213
Wesselink-van Rossum, J. P.,
    3, 15, 39, 58, 84, 123,
    144
West, Ray B., 1376
Westerland, Hans G., 22, 32
Westhoven, K., 2384
Weymouth, W. J., 2287
Whicher, George F., 1377
Whipple, Thomas K., 1378,
    1379
Whitaker, Herman, 701, 763
Wickersham, James, 1380
Wilcox, Earl J., 2278
Williams, Blanche C., 1381
Williams, Harold, 1382
Williams, Mabel, 637
Williams, S. T., 780
Williamson, Thames, 1383
Wilson, James D., 1058
Wilson, Tom, 22, 49
Wind, H. W., 735
Winn, Georgia Gantt, 803
Winsor, William T., 2264
Wit, Augusta de, 2350, 2354
Witham, W. T., 1384
Wojtkiewicz, Stanisław
    Strumph, 2140
Woodbridge, Hensley C., 2309
Woodward, Robert H., 1385
Wright, David, 2285
Wydzga, Adam, 79
Wyeth, N. C., 31
Wylder, Robert C., 780

Ya, B., 496, 497
Yamamoto, Seiki, 22, 25
Yasinski, Ya. I., 150, 153
Ye, D., 61
Yohn, Frederick C., 13
Yoram, Sh., 627, 719
Young, Thomas Daniel, 2265,

2279

Zaiaitzkogo, S., 69
Zaimovski, S. G., 496, 497,
    527, 532, 574, 624, 632,
    638, 1186
Zajaczkowski, J. P., 161
Zamyatim, Yev., 58, 511,
    514
Zand, A. B., 699, 708, 780
    810
Zardoya, Concha, 2203
Zariņš, J., 395
Zariņs, K., 395, 661
Zaslovski, D. O., 35
Zayaitski, S. S., 496, 497
Zdárský, G., 79
Zhechev, Georgi, 22, 39, 61,
    227
Zheji, Gjergj, 223
Zhilkin, I. V., 638
Zhitomirski, Krivtsova, 496
Zhitomirski, V., 496, 497
Zibelis, V., 127
Zielinski, Bronisław, 432,
    456, 460
Ziemelnieks, J., 2429
Zifreund, V., 2095, 2381,
    2399
Ziha, Erika, 49
Zistel, E., 632
Zlatkovic, G., 120
Zolotoe uschel'e, 313
Zoltán, Bartos, 69
Zoltán, Mészáros, 65
Zsolt, Harsányi, 150, 153